Ottemiller's Index to Plays in Collections

an author and title index to plays appearing in collections published between 1900 and 1985

seventh edition
revised and enlarged

by
Billie M. Connor
and
Helene G. Mochedlover

The Scarecrow Press, Inc.
Metuchen, N.J., & London 1988

Library of Congress Cataloging-in-Publication Data

Ottemiller, John H. (John Henry), 1916-1968.
    [Index to plays in collections]
    Ottemiller's index to plays in collections : an author and
title index to plays appearing in collections published between
1900 and 1985. -- 7th ed. / revised and enlarged by Billie M.
Connor and Helene G. Mochedlover.
        p.   cm.
    ISBN 0-8108-2081-1
    1. Drama--Bibliography--Indexes. I. Connor, Billie M.,
1934- . II. Mochedlover, Helen G., 1932- . III. Title.
IV. Title: Index to plays in collections.
Z5781.08   1988
[PN1655]
016.80882--dc19   87-34160

to

John Henry Ottemiller, 1916-1968

and

John Michael Connor, 1908-1978

"The anomalous fact is that the
theater, so called, can flourish
in barbarism, but that any
drama worth speaking of can
develop but in the air of civilization."

--Henry James
(Letter to C. E. Wheeler,
April 9, 1911)

CONTENTS

PREFACE

With the seventh edition Ottemiller's Index to Plays in Collections now includes books published in the English-speaking world from 1900 through 1985.

Anthologies of plays and plays contained in collections of literature are indexed and identified. Since the theatre has become increasingly international in recent years, criteria for inclusion have been expanded to embrace collections published in all English-speaking countries which contain theatrical works originating from all over the world.

Plays indexed are full-length with the following exceptions: 1) the Best Plays... series generally includes excerpts and synopses only; however, it is so important in reflecting the historical panorama of American theatre that it continues to be included in Ottemiller's Index; and 2) when an anthology or collection includes full-length plays together with short plays or excerpts, the latter have been indexed also.

The list of collections analyzed contains a total of 1,350 titles, an increase of 251. A large number of these titles are for series and for multiple-volume sets; therefore, contents represent many hundreds of additional individual volumes. Works of 2,555 different authors are included, and the author index contains 717 additional cross-references for pseudonyms, variant forms or spellings of names, and names of authors of works from which plays were derived. The title index has 6,548 individual entries, over 1,000 more than in the sixth edition.

The following improvements have been made: 1) all errors identified in the sixth edition have been corrected; 2) several collections have been assigned new mnemonics and rearranged to adhere more accurately to alphabetical order;

3) spellings and forms of oriental names have been verified for accuracy and are believed to be correct; and 4) extensive research has been done to determine birth and death dates of playwrights and first performance dates of plays and, although it has not been possible to find all, data are much more complete than in previous editions. In the case of plays when no performance date is known, the date of completion or publication appears in parenthesis. If accuracy of a date is in question it is followed by a question mark.

Every new collection has been located and examined; therefore, contents are believed to be accurate. Should any errors be found by users of the index, the publisher should be notified so that corrections may be made.

Two sad occurrences in recent years have affected this endeavor, the death of John M. Connor, former co-compiler, July 15, 1978, and the disastrous fire at Los Angeles Public Library, April 29, 1986. Tragedies notwithstanding, a seventh edition is complete, at last.

We are exceedingly grateful to many of our friends and colleagues, whose assistance in this undertaking was invaluable. The staff of the Literature and Fiction Department of the Los Angeles Public Library again were of great help, especially M. J. Campbell, Theatre Collection Subject Specialist, whose suggestions and ideas proved most useful. To Violet Kuroki, Renata Martynienko, and Dorothy Wong of the Los Angeles Public Library's Catalog Department, we owe a special thanks. And Patricia Zeidler, Senior Librarian of LAPL's Science, Technology and Patents Department, deserves credit for "holding down the fort" during vacations and leaves prompted by this work. We are grateful to our hosts at the Library of Congress for their kindness and the opportunity to work in clean, well-lighted stacks. We appreciate the great efforts made by our indefatigable typist, Mary Gage, to decipher our manuscript. And to those who have been awaiting this new edition, our sincere thanks for your patience.

Billie M. Connor
Helene G. Mochedlover

Los Angeles
September 17, 1987

INTRODUCTION

Ottemiller's Index was created by John Henry Ottemiller to meet the need for access to plays published in collections or in anthologies of literature. He had completed four editions at the time of his death in 1968. The late Ralph Shaw, then President of Scarecrow Press, encouraged John Michael Connor to take over compilation of the index. Together with his wife, Billie M. Connor, he completed the fifth and sixth editions. Since his death, Helene G. Mochedlover, Department Manager of Los Angeles Public Library's Literature and Fiction Department, has joined Ms. Connor to compile the seventh edition, which covers 1900-1985.

Until this edition, the scope of the Index has been coverage of books published in the United States and England, 1900-1975. For the period 1975-1985, it now includes anthologies and collections published in all of the English-speaking world. The Index is useful for the following purposes: 1) to locate plays not available in separate form or in collections of an individual author; 2) to make available duplicate copies of plays for class assignments, reading groups, amateur theatricals, little theatres, and plays newly popular due to motion pictures, television productions, or renewed interest in a playwright; and 3) to verify and identify authors, dates, titles (English and other languages), partial titles, derivations, and first performance dates. The collections analyzed can be a valuable selection guide for libraries in developing book collections. Only those successive editions of a specific collection or anthology are included which have varying content. Otherwise, only the earliest edition is cited and indexed.

For purposes of inclusion, a play anthology is defined as a collection of plays by three or more authors published in book form. Collections of general literature generally follow the same definition; however, there are exceptions. Plays in languages other than English are included if published in anthologies in any English-speaking country. Standard full-length plays only are included with the exceptions mentioned in the Preface. Generally, collections of children's plays, one-act plays, radio and television plays, holiday and anniversary plays have been excluded. However, such plays are included if they appear in anthologies defined above. Collections containing only the works of one playwright are excluded.

The three parts of this Index are 1) Author Index, 2) List of Collections Analyzed and Key to Symbols, and 3) Title Index. The Author Index is the heart of the book since it identifies all works by each author contained in the collections analyzed and gives the mnemonic symbol for each. One then turns to the second part to get the specific citation for the work represented by each mnemonic symbol. For ease of location, libraries will no doubt annotate the List of Collections Analyzed and Key to Symbols with specific call numbers for those included in the local collection. If only the title of a play is known, the Title Index is used to determine the author; then the Author Index is consulted, and so on.

In addition to the play location function, the Author Index is very useful for a variety of purposes. Included are author's full name and variants thereof; year of birth and death; title of play; the year of first production (or publication if production date cannot be verified or if it was never performed); cross-references from original or variant titles; and references from joint authors and any others with a connection to the play (supposed authors, attributed authors, translators, adapters, composers of musicals, etc.). The translator is given for each play translated into English. Plays of unknown authorship are listed under Anonymous Plays. In the case of dates, if an exact date cannot be determined, an approximate date is given and indicated by a question mark. Authorities vary, but great effort has been made to be as accurate as possible. Plays in a non-English language are entered under the original title with references from translated titles. If translated into English, plays are entered under the English title with references from the original title.

The Title Index contains cross-references from all forms

of the titles including variants and subtitles. The List of
Collections is arranged alphabetically by symbols. A full
bibliographic citation is given for each collection, recent
ones in AACR II format; older ones in the earlier main entry
format. Under each book cited is a contents note of the
plays in the volume, arranged alphabetically by author (or
by title for plays of unknown authorship which are to be
found in the Author Index under Anonymous Plays).
Specific volumes of multiple volume sets or annuals are identified in the Author Index by the appending of a number or
a year after the mnemonic symbol; (e.g., BALLE1, BES77,
etc.).

Suggestions for the improvement of this work are most
welcome and should be forwarded through the publisher.

AARON, JOYCE, and TARLO,
LUNA
   Acrobatics. 1980. WOMA

ABBOTT, GEORGE, 1887- ,
and BISSELL, RICHARD
   The pajama game (lyrics and
   music by Richard Adler
   and Jerry Ross; based on
   the novel, 7-1/2 cents, by
   Richard Bissell.) 1954.
   THEA54

-- and BRIDGERS, ANN PRESTON
   Coquette. 1927. BES27

-- and GLEASON, JAMES
   The fall guy. 1925. BES24

-- See DUNNING, PHILIP; HOLM,
JOHN CECIL; WEIDMAN, JEROME,
jt. auths.

ABE, KOBO (KIMIFUSA), 1924-
   Friends. 1967
     Keene, D., tr. HIBH
     Variant title: Tomodachi
   Omae Nimo Tsumi Ga Aru.
     See You, too, are guilty
   Tomodachi. See Friends
   You, too, are guilty. 1965.
     Takaya, T. T., tr. TAK
     Variant title: Omae Nimo
      Tsumi Ga Aru

A BECKETT, GILBERT ABBOTT,
1811-1856.
   King John, with the Benefit of
   the Act. 1837. NIN2

ABEL, LIONEL, 1910-
   Absalom. 1956. MAH
   The death of Odysseus. 1953.
   PLAA

ABELL, KJELD, 1901-1961

Anna Sophie Hedvig. 1939.
   Larsen, H., tr. SCAN2
Days on a cloud. 1947.
   Roughton, A., and Bredsdorf,
   E., trs. SPR
Dronning gaar igen. See The
   queen on tour
The queen on tour. 1943.
   Pearce, J., tr. CONT
   Variant title: Dronning gaar
   igen

ABLEMAN, PAUL, 1927-
   Green Julia. 1972. BES72

ABSE, DANNIE, 1923-
   House of cowards. 1960. DEAS,
   PLAN23

ABUN, YASUDA. See Yasuda,
Abun

ACEVEDO HERNANDEZ, ANTONIO,
1886-
   Cabrerita. 1927.
     Bailey, W., tr. SSTE

ACHARD, MARCEL, 1889-1974
   Auprès de ma blonde. See
     Behrman, Samuel Nathaniel.
   I know my love (adapted
     from)
   Patate. See Rollo
   Rollo (adapted by Felicity
     Douglas). 1956. PLAN20
     Variant title: Patate

ACHESON, SAM HANNA, 1900-
   We are besieged. 1941. THX

ACKLAND, RODNEY, 1908-
   After October. 1936. FAMI
   Before the party (based on a
     short story by W. Somerset
     Maugham). 1949. PLAN2
   A dead secret. 1957. PLAN16

The diary of a scoundrel.
See Ostrovsky, Alexander.
The diary of a scoundrel
(tr. and adapted by)
The old ladies. 1935. FAMG
Strange orchestra. 1932. FAMC

ADAM DE LA HALLE (Adam Le
Boçus; Adam Le Bossu, pseuds.),
ca. 1250-ca. 1306
Le jeu de la feuillée. 1275?
    Axton, R., and Stevens, J.,
    trs. AXT
    Variant title: The play of
    the greensward
Le jeu de Robin et Marion.
1285?
    Axton, R., and Stevens, J.,
    trs. AXT
    Mandel, O., tr. MARK
    Variant title: The Play of
    Robin and Marion
The play of Robin and Marion.
    See Le jeu de Robin at Marion
The play of the greensward.
    See Le jeu de la feuillée

ADAM LE BOÇUS. See Adam de la
Halle

ADAM LE BOSSU. See Adam de la
Halle

ADAMOV, ARTHUR, 1908-1970
All against all. 1952.
    Gildea, D., tr. WELT
    Variant title: Tous contre
    tous
Professor Toranne. 1953.
    Bermel, A., tr. FOUF,
    TAUJ
Tous contre tous. See All
    against all

ADAMS, LEE, 1924-
Applause (lyrics by).
    See Comden, Betty and
    Green, Adolph. Applause
"It's a bird, it's a plane, it's
    superman" (lyrics by).
    See Newman, David and Ben-
    ton, Robert. "It's a bird,
    it's a plane, it's superman."

ADDISON, JOSEPH, 1672-1719.
Cato. 1713. BELK 3, DOB,
    EIGH, HAN, LIBR, MAND,

MANF, MOR, NET, STM, TAT,
TAU, TUP, TUQ
The drummer. 1716. BELK 11

ADE, GEORGE, 1866-1944
The college widow. 1904. COT
The county chairman. 1903.
    BES99

ADLER, RICHARD, 1921-
The pajama game (lyrics and mu-
    sic by). See Abbott, George
    and Bissell, Richard. The
    pajama game

A. E., pseud. See Russell, George
William

AESCHYLUS, 525-456 B.C.
Agamemnon. 458 B.C.
    Anon. tr. CHR, EVB1
    Blackie, J., tr. BUCK,
        BUCL, BUCM
    Campbell, L., tr. LAP
    Cookson, G., tr. GRDB5
    Hamilton, E., tr. EVC1,
        HAM, KRE, TREB, TREC1,
        TREE1, TREI1
    Lattimore, R., tr. FIFT,
        GREP1, GRER1
    Lucas, F., tr. LUCA, LUCAB,
        LUCAF
    MacNeice, L., tr. ALLK,
        ALLM, DEAP, DEAR, DEAS,
        FIFR, FREG, LIND, MALC,
        MALG1, MALI1, MALN1,
        MALR1, NORG1, NORI,
        SSSI, SWA, VANV1, VON
    Morshead, E., tr. HARC8,
        HOWE, HOWF, LOCM1, MAU,
        OAT1, OAM, OATH, ROBJA,
        THP, WARN1
    Murray, G., tr. CARP, CARPA,
        FEFT, TEN, TRE, TREA2
    Plumptre, E., tr. HIB, HIBA,
        HIBB, HOUS, ROB, THOM,
        THON
    Potter, R., tr. GREE
    Robinson, C., tr. ROBK
    Sylvester, W., tr. COOA
    Thomson, G., tr. AUDE, DIZ,
        FIFV, HAPRL, ROBI, WEAV1
    Vellacourt, P., tr. BENQ,
        SOU, STY
    Verrall, A., tr. GRDG
    Way, A., tr. PLAG
The choephori. See Choephoroe

Choephoroe. 458 B.C.
Arnott, D., tr. CLLC, CLL,
FOR
Cookson, G., tr. GRDB5
Lattimore, R., tr. GREP1,
GRER2
Morshead, E., tr. HARC8,
OAT1
Murray, G., tr. FEFT, TEN
Thomson, G., tr. AUDE,
FIFV, ROBJ
Way, A., tr. PLAG
Variant titles: The choephori;
The libation-bearers; The
mourners
Eumenides. 458 B.C.
Cookson, G., tr. GRDB5
Lattimore, R., tr. GREP1,
GRER3
Morshead, E., tr. HARC8,
OAT1, OAM
Murray, G., tr. FEFT, TEN
Paley, F. GRDG
Plumptre, E., tr. BAT1
Thomson, G., tr. AUDE,
FIFT, FIFV, ROBJ
Way, A., tr. PLAG
Variant titles: The furies:
The gracious ones
The furies. See Eumenides
The gracious ones. See Eumen-
ides
Hepta epi Thebas. See The
seven against Thebes
Hiketides. See The suppliants
The house of Atreus (trilogy:
Agamemnon, Choephoroe, and
Eumenides). See Agamemnon;
Choephoroe; Eumenides; Ores-
teia
The libation-bearers. See Choe-
phoroe
The mourners. See Choephoroe
Oresteia (trilogy: Agamemnon,
Choephoroe, and Eumenides).
458 B.C.
Arranged for the stage by A.
V. Griffin. GRIF
See also Agamemnon; Choepho-
roe; Eumenides
The Persians. 472 B.C.
Anon. tr. WED
Bernadete, S., tr. GREP1
Cookson, G., tr. GRDB5
Potter, R., tr. OAT1
Prometheus bound. 478? B.C.
Anon. tr. ATT3

Blackie, J., tr. BUCK, BUCL,
BUCM, CLF1, SEBO, SEBP
Browning, E., tr. CROS,
DRA1, GREB2, GREE, MAST,
MIK7, PLAB1
Cookson, G., tr. GRDB5
Dolin, E., and Sugg, A., trs.
COOA
Grene, D., tr. GREN, GREP1,
GRER1
Hamilton, E., tr. BURR,
DOWN, FIFT, HAM, HAPRL,
MALI1, NORG1
Havelock, E., tr. BARC
Hilburn, E., tr. TENN
Lucas, F., tr. LUCA, LUCAB,
LUCAF
McLeish, K., tr. MAMB
Mendell, C., tr. CLKW, ROBJ
More, P., tr. MURP, OAT1,
OAM, OATH
Plumptre, E., tr. CROV,
HARC8, SML
Walker, C., tr. BENSB1
Warner, R., tr. LIND
Whitelaw, R., tr. FEET
Variant titles: Prometheus
desmotes; Prometheus vinc-
tus
Prometheus desmotes. See
Prometheus bound
Prometheus vinctus. See
Prometheus bound
Septem contra Thebas. See The
seven against Thebes
The seven against Thebes. 467
B.C.
Cookson, G., tr. GRDB5
Grene, D., tr. GREP1
Variant titles: Hepta epi
Thebas; Septem contra
Thebas
The suppliant maidens. See The
suppliants
The suppliants. 492? B.C.
Bernadete, S., tr. GREP1
Caldwell, R., tr. TENN
Cookson, G., tr. GRDB5
Morshead, E., tr. OAT1
Variant titles: Hiketides;
The suppliant maidens

THE AFANASJEFF FAMILY CIRCUS,
1958-1964? See Afanasjew, Jerzy,
jt. auth.

AFANASJEW, JERZY, 1932-

The World is not such a bad
place... (selections from)
Gerould, D. and Gerould,
E., trs. TWEN

-- and the AFANASJEFF FAMILY
CIRCUS
Good evening, clown (selection
from). 1962.
Gerould, D. and Gerould, E.
trs. TWEN

-- and the BIM-BOM TROUPE
Faust (part of Joy in earnest).
1956.
Gerould, D. and Gerould, E.,
trs. TWEN
Snouts (part of Joy in earnest).
1956.
Gerould, D. and Gerould, E.,
trs. TWEN
Joy in earnest (includes Faust,
Snouts, and The professor by
Mrozek, S.)

AFINOGENYEV, ALEKSANDR NIKO-
LAEVICH, 1904-1941
Distant point. See Far taiga
Far taiga. 1935. Bakshy, A.,
tr. BAKS
Variant titles: Distant point;
Remote
Fear. 1931. Malamuth, C., tr.
LYK
On the eve. 1942. Afinogenova,
E., tr. SEVP
Remote. See Far taiga

AGEE, JAMES, 1909-1955
Abraham Lincoln, the early years.
SHER
The bride comes to yellow sky
(screen play; based on the
story by Stephen Crane).
1971? SUT3
A death in the family. See
Mosel, Tad. All the way home
(based on)

AGENOUX, SOREN
Charles Dickens' Christmas carol.
1966. SMC

AH, CHIA. See Wong, Ou-hung,
jt. auth.

AIKEN, GEORGE L., 1820-1876

Life among the lowly. See
Uncle Tom's cabin
Uncle Tom's cabin; or, Life
among the lowly (based on
the novel by Harriet Beecher
Stowe). 1852. AMEM, BLAI2,
CEY, GARX, GATB1, MONR,
MOSS2

AIKINS, CARROLL
The god of gods. 1919. MAS2

AJIBADE, SEGUN
Rakinyo. AFR

AKALAITIS, JOANNE
Dressed like an egg; taken from
the writings of Colette. 1977.
WOQ4

AKINS, ZOE, 1886-1958
Declassee. 1919. BES19
The old maid. 1935. BES34

AKRITAS, LOUKIS, 1909-1965
Hostages.
Gianos, M., tr. GIA

AKSENOV, VASILII, 1932-
The four temperaments: a comedy
in ten tableaux. (1967?)
Jakim, B., tr. METR

AKSYONOV, VASILY. See
Aksenov, Vasili

ALARCON Y MENDOZA, JUAN RUIZ
DE. See Ruiz de Alarcón y Mendoza,
Juan

ALBEE, EDWARD, 1928-
All over. 1971. GARTL
The American dream. 1961.
BLOND, LEVG, LITC, MANL,
MARO, REIO
A delicate balance. 1966. BES66
The lady from Dubuque. 1980.
BES79
The sandbox. 1960. BARS,
CORB, CUBH, PERT, PERU,
PERV, SATI, SATJ, THOD
Seascape. 1975. BES74
Tiny Alice. 1964. BES64, GAT
Who's afraid of Virginia Woolf?
1962. BES62, FOUX, GARSA,
GATB4, REIL, REIW, REIWE,
TREBJ

The zoo story. 1959. COK,
FAM, GOLH, HAE, HOWP2,
KEN, KERP, LITI, LITJ,
MANC2, MANCB, REIT, SCNT,
SDQ, SHR, WAIW

ALBERTI, RAFAEL, 1902-
Night and war in the Prado
Museum. 1956.
Johnson, L., tr. BENA
Variant title: Noche de
guerra en el Museo del
Prado
Noche de guerra en el Museo
del Prado. See Night and
war in the Prado Museum

ALBERY, JAMES, 1838-1889
Two roses. 1870. ROWE

ALBERY, PETER, 1912-
Anne Boleyn. 1956. PLAN14

ALDRIDGE, IRA, 1807-1867
The Black doctor. 1847. HARY

ALEXANDER, ROBERT
Factwino vs. Armageddonman
(script by). See San Francisco Mime Troupe. Fact-
wino vs. Armageddonman
Home free. 1981. WES 11/12
The hourglass. (1978) CEN

ALFIERI, VITTORIO, 1749-1803
Myrrha. 1788?
Bowring, E., tr. BAT5
Saul. 1784. BIN
Bowring, E., tr. CLF2

ALFRED, WILLIAM, 1922-
Hogan's goat. 1965. BES65,
GAT, GRIH, FAMAH

ALFRIEND, EDWARD M., 1843-?
and WHEELER, ANDREW CARPENTER
The great diamond robbery.
1885. AMP8, CLA

AL-HAKIM, TAWFIG, 1898-
The sultan's dilemma. (1959)
ABL

ALI, AKHUND-ZATH FATH'. See
Fath'Ali, Akhundzadah

ALIANAK, HRANT, 1950-

Mathematics. 1972. BRIP
Western. 1972. BRIP

ALLEN, JAY, 1922-
Forty carats. 1968. BES68

ALLEN, RALPH G., 1934-
Sugar babies. 1979. BES79

ALLEN, WOODY, 1935-
The floating light bulb. 1981.
BES80
Play it again, Sam. 1969.
GARTL

ALPERT, HOLLIS, (Robert Carroll,
pseud.) 1916-
Heat lightning. BRNR

ALSINA, ARTURO, 1897-
La marca de fuego. 1926. ALPE

ALURISTA, pseud. See Urista,
Alberto H.

ALVAREZ QUINTERO, JOAQUIN,
1873-1944. See Alvarez Quintero,
Serafín, jt. auth.

ALVAREZ QUINTERO, SERAFIN,
1871-1938, and ALVAREZ QUINTERO,
JOAQUIN
An autumn morning. See A
bright morning
A bright morning. 1905.
Castillo, C., and Overman, E.,
trs. DIK1
Floyd, L., tr. EDAD, WHF
Variant titles: An autumn
morning; Mañana de sol;
A sunny morning
The centenarian. See A hundred
years old
Doña Clarines. 1909.
Granville-Barker, H., and H.,
trs. CHA, CHAN
A hundred years old. 1909.
Granville-Barker, H., and H.,
trs. PLAP3
Variant titles: The centenarian;
Papá Juan: centenario
Malvaloca. 1912.
Fassett, J., tr. DIE
Mañana de sol. See A bright
morning
Papá Juan: centenario. See A
hundred years old

Pueblo de las mujeres. See
The women's town
A sunny morning. See A bright
morning
The women have their way.
See The women's town
The women's town. 1912.
Turrell, C., tr. TUR
Variant titles: Pueblo de las
mujeres; The women have
their way

ALVARO, CORRADO, 1895-1956
The long night of Medea. 1949.
Friedman, E., tr. PLAC

ALYOSHIN, SAMUEL, 1913-
Alone. 1956.
McLean, H., and Vickery,
W., trs. MAM
Variant title: Odna
Odna. See Alone

AMANO, LYNETTE, 1949-
Ashes. 1972. KUMU

AMES, WINTHROP, 1871-1937
A kiss in Xanadu. 1932? LEV,
LEVE

AMESCUA, ANTONIO MIRA DE.
See Mira de Amescua, Antonio

ANCEY, GEORGES, pseud. See
Curnieu, Georges de

ANDERSON, GARLAND, 1886-1939
Appearances. 1925. HARY

ANDERSON, MAXWELL, 1888-1959
Anne of the thousand days.
1948. BES48, GARW, OHL
The bad seed (based on the novel
by William March). 1954.
BES54, RICI, THEA55
Barefoot in Athens. 1951.
BARS, BES51
Both your houses. 1933.
BES32, CORD, CORE, CORF,
LOOA, LOOB
Candle in the wind. 1941.
BES41
Elizabeth the queen. 1930.
BES30, STEI, THO, TRE,
TREA1, TREBA, TREBJ,
TREC2, TREE3, TREI3,
WATC2, WATI, WHI

The eve of St. Mark. 1942.
BES42
The feast of Ortolans. 1938.
KIN, STAT
A girl from Lorraine. See Joan
of Lorraine
Gypsy. 1929. BES28
High Tor. 1937. BES36, CLH,
CRIT, GAS, GATB2, GAVE,
GOW, GOWA, HAP, MERT
Joan of Lorraine. 1946. BES46
Variant title: A girl from
Lorraine
Journey to Jerusalem. 1940.
GALB
Key Largo. 1940. BES39, ROLF
Mary of Scotland. 1933. BES33,
CLKW, THF
The masque of kings. 1936.
MOSL
Saturday's children. 1927.
BES26, GASB, TUCD
The star-wagon. 1937. BES37
Storm operation. 1944. BES43
Valley Forge. 1934. AMB,
BES34, WARH
The wingless victory. 1936. LOR,
SANM
Winterset. 1935. BES35, BROZ,
CALM, CALN2, CASS, CHAN,
CHAP, COTE, COTH, CRIT,
DAVI, DUR, GAS, GAVE, GRIF,
HAT, HATA, HAVD, HAVE,
HIL, HOLM, MOSH, NELS,
QUIM, QUIN, RAVA, SIXC,
WAIT, WALB

-- and HICKERSON, HAROLD
Gods of the lightning. 1928.
GASB

-- and STALLINGS, LAWRENCE
What price glory? 1924.
BES24, CHA, GASB, MAF,
TRE, TREA1, TREBA, TREC2,
TREE3, TREI3, VANM

-- and WEILL, KURT
Lost in the stars (based on the
novel Cry, the beloved
country by Alan Paton). 1949.
BES49, HEWE, RICM

ANDERSON, ROBERT WOODRUFF,
1917-
I never sang for my father.
1968. BES67, MID

Silent night, lonely night.
1959. GARSA
Tea and sympathy. 1953.
BES53, FAM, GART, GATB4,
NEWV, STS, THEA54
You know I can't hear you
when the water's running.
1967. BES66, GAT

ANDERSON, SHERWOOD, 1876-
1941
Textiles. 193-? ING

ANDREEV, LEONID NIKOLAEVICH,
1871-1919
He who gets slapped. 1915.
Guthrie, J., adapter. HOUG
MacAndrew, A., tr. GARZG,
MABA
Reeve, F. D., tr. REEV2
Zilboorg, G., tr. BES21,
DIE, MOSG, MOSH, THF,
TUCG, TUCM, TUCN,
TUCO, WATI, WATL4
Variant titles: The knock
about; The painted laugh
An incident.
Anon. tr. CHR, ROY
The knock about. See He who
gets slapped
The life of man. 1906.
Meader, C., and Scott, F.,
trs. SML
Seltzer, T., tr. DIK2,
MOSQ
The painted laugh. See He who
gets slapped
Professor Storitsyn. 1912.
Minkoff, I., Noyes, G., and
Kaun, A., trs. NOY

ANDREYEFF, LEONID NIKOLAEVICH.
See Andreev, Leonid Nikolaevich

ANDREYEV, LEONID NIKOLAEVICH.
See Andreev, Leonid Nikolaevich

ANDRIEU DE LA VIGNE. See La
Vigne, Andrieu de

ANDRIEV, LEONID NIKOLAEVICH.
See Andreev, Leonid Nikolaevich

ANGEL, LEONARD, 1945-
Forthcoming wedding. 1972.
BRIQ

ANGEL PEREZ DE SAAVEDRA,
RIVAS. See Rivas, Angel Pérez de
Saavedra

ANNUNZIO, GABRIELE D', 1863-
1938
La città morta. See The dead
city
The daughter of Jorio. 1904.
Porter, C., Isola, P., and
Henry, A., trs. MOSQ
Variant title: La figlia di
Jorio
The dead city. 1898.
Mantellini, G., tr. SAY
Variant title: La città morta
La figlia di Jorio. See The
daughter of Jorio
Francesca da Rimini. 1902.
Symons, A., tr. DIK1,
TUCG, TUCM, WATL3
Gioconda. 1898.
Symons, A., tr. DID, SMI

ANONYMOUS PLAYS
Abraham (Wakefield). 15th
cent. DAVJ, TOWN
Abraham (York). 15th cent.
DAVJ
Abraham and Isaac (Brome).
15th cent. ABRH, ADA,
BARD, BENY, CAWL, CHI,
DAVJ, DAVN, ENGE, FRAN,
FREH, GARZB, GREC1, HOPP,
HUD, KINN, LIE, MAR, MAX,
PAR, PARR, POLL, SCW,
SNYD1, SWIT, TAT, TAU,
TREA2, TREB, TREC1, TREE1,
TREEI1
Variant titles: The Brome
Abraham and Isaac; The
sacrifice of Isaac
Abraham and Isaac (Chester).
See Abraham, Melchisedec and
Isaac
Abraham and Isaac (Dublin). 15th
cent. DAVJ
Abraham and Isaac (N Town).
15th cent. DAVJ
Abraham and Isaac (Northampton.
DAVN
Abraham, Lot, and Melchysedeck.
See Abraham, Melchisedec and
Isaac
Abraham, Melchisedec and Isaac
(Chester). 15th cent. ASH,

ANONYMOUS PLAYS (cont.)
> CHEL, CHES, CHESE, DAVJ,
> ENGE, EVER, KRE, POLL
> Variant titles: Abraham and
> Isaac; Abraham, Lot, and
> Melchysedeck; Abraham,
> Melchizedek and Lot, with
> the sacrifice of Isaac; The
> histories of Lot and Abra-
> ham; Lot and Abraham;
> The sacrifice of Isaac

Abraham, Melchizedek and Lot,
with the sacrifice of Isaac.
See Abraham, Melchisedec and
Isaac

Abstraction. 14th cent.?
> Chamberlin, B., tr. CLF1,
> ORI2

Ad Dominican missam. See For
the Mass of our Lord (from
Limoges)

Ad faciendam similtudinem Dominici sepulcri. See For representing the scene at the Lord's sepulchre (from Fleury)

Ad interfectionem puerorum. See
The slaughter of the innocents
(from Fleury)

Ad repraesentandum conversionem
Beati Pauli Apostoli. See For
representing the conversion of
the Blessed Apostle Paul (from
Fleury)

Ad repraesentandum quomodo Sanctus Nich(o)laus Getron(is)
filium ... liberavit. See For
representing how Saint Nicholas freed the son of Getron
(from Fleury)

Adam. 1150?
> Axton, R., and Stevens, J.,
> trs. AXT
> Barrow, S., and Hulme, W.,
> trs. CROV
> Stone, E., tr. CLF1, KRE
> Variant titles: Le jeu d'Adam;
> Le mystère d'Adam; The
> mystery of Adam; The play
> of Adam

Adam and Eve (Chester). 15th
cent. CHEL

Adam and Eve (Norwich, Text B,
non-cycle mystery play).
12th cent.? FRAN

The adoration (York). 15th
cent. ENGE

The adoration of the kings.

Anon. tr. RAV

The adoration of the kings
(Chester). See The adora-
tion of the magi (Chester)

The adoration of the magi
(Chester). 15th cent. CHES,
CHESE
> Variant title: The adoration
> of the kings

The adoration of the shepherds
(Chester). 15th cent. CHES,
CHESE

Albion, knight. See A moral
play of Albion, knight

All's one, or one of the foure
plaies in one, called A Yorkshire tragedy. See A Yorkshire tragedy

The annunciation (N Town)
15th cent. CAWL

The annunciation (Wakefield).
15th cent. BEVD, LOOM,
TOWN

The annunciation and the
nativity (Chester). 15th
cent. CHEL

Antichrist (Chester). 15th cent.
CHEL, CHES, CHESE

Apius and Virginia (sometimes attributed to Richard Bower).
1563? FARM, HAO
> Variant title: Appius and
> Virginia

The apostles at the tomb (N Town).
15th cent. DAVJ

Appearance to Cleopas and Luke
(N Town). 15th cent. DAVJ

Appearance to Mary Magdalen (N
Town). 15th cent. DAVJ

Appearance to Thomas (N Town).
15th cent. DAVJ

Appius and Virginia. See Apius
and Virginia

Arden of Feversham (sometimes
attributed to Thomas Arden;
Thomas Kyd; William Shakes-
peare). 1586? BAS, BRO,
DPR1, GATG, MAKG, MIN1,
MIO1, MIR, MONV, OLH, OLI1,
SCH
> Variant title: The lamentable
> and true tragedy of Master
> Arden of Feversham in Kent

The ascension (Chester). 15th
cent. CHEL, ENG

Ascension (N Town). 15th cent.
DAVJ

ANONYMOUS PLAYS (cont.)

The ascension of the Lord (Wakefield). 15th cent. TOWN

The Ashmole fragment. DAVN

Assumption (N Town). 15th cent. DAVJ

The assumption and the coronation of the Virgin (York). 15th cent. ENGE

Attowell's jig (Francis' new jig) (sometimes attributed to George Attowell). 1595? BAS, NES
Variant titles: Francis' new jig; Mr. Attowell's jig

Azalea Mountain. 1973. Anon. tr. FIFW

Balaack and Balaam (Chester). 15th cent. CHEL, ENGE
Variant title: Balaam, Balak and the prophets

Balaam, Balak and the prophets. See Balaack and Balaam

Banns (Chester). 15th cent. ENGE

Banns (N Town). 15th cent. ADA, BEVD, SCW

The Battle of Brooklyn (published anonymously by James Rivington). (1776) AMPA, PHI, WORN

Ba-wang bie-ji. See Hegemon king says farewell to his queen

The beauty and good properties of women (commonly called Calisto and Melibaea). 1530? FARO

The Benediktbeuren play. 13th cent.
Robinson, D., and Francke, K., trs. and adapters. ROBM

The betrayal (Wakefield). 15th cent. HEIL

The betrayal of Christ (Chester). 15th cent. CHEL, CHES, CHESE, GARZB

The betraying of Christ (N Town). 15th cent. ADA

The bilker Bilk'd. 1742? HUGH

Bilsen play. See The star

The bird catcher in hell. See Esashi Juo. The bird catcher in hell.

The birth of Jesus (York). 15th cent. ADA, BEVD

The birth of Merlin; or, The child

hath found his father (sometimes attributed to William Rowley; William Shakespeare). 1597? BRO

Birth of the Son (N Town). 15th cent. DAVJ

The blind Chelidonian (Chester). 15th cent. CHEL

The blockheads; or, The affrighted officers (attributed to Mercy Otis Warren). 1776. PHI

The book of Job. See Job

The Brome Abraham and Isaac. See Abraham and Isaac

Brome plays. See Abraham and Isaac

The buffeting (Wakefield). 15th cent. BEVD, ENGE, TOWN

The buggbears. See Jeffere, John (supposed author)

Los buñuelos. NOR

The butterfly dream. 1368? SCX1
Variant title: Hu tieh meng

Buying rouge. 18th cent. Dolby, W., tr. EIG
Variant title: Mai yanzhi

Caesar Augustus (Wakefield). 15th cent. TOWN

Cain and Abel (Chester). 15th cent. CHEL

Cain and Abel. (N Town). 15th cent. CAWL, DAVJ, FRAN

Calisto and Melibaea. See The beauty and good properties of women

The Cambridge prologue. 13th cent? CHEL

Candlemes Day and the Kyllung of þe children of Israelle. See Killing of the children

The castle of perseverance. ca. 1405-25. ADA, BEV, BEVD, FOUN, HOPP, POLL, SCAT

Celestina. See Rojas, Fernando de. Celestina

The chalk circle. 13th cent.? Van Der Meer, E., tr. CLF1, KRE

The Chantilly play. See Bourlet, Katherine. The nativity Chester play of the deluge; The deluge

Chester plays. See Abraham and Isaac; Abraham, Melchisedec

ANONYMOUS PLAYS (cont.)
  and Isaac; Adam and Eve;
  The adoration of the magi;
  The adoration of the shepherds; The annunciation and
  the nativity; Antichrist;
  The ascension; Balaack and
  Balaam; Banns; The betrayal
  of Christ; The blind Chelidonian; Cain and Abel; Christ
  and the doctors; Christ and
  the moneylenders; Christ appears to the disciples; Christ
  at the house of Simon the
  Leper; Christ at the road to
  Emmaus; Christ's ascension;
  Christ's ministry; Christ's
  passion; Christ's resurrection; The creation of man; The
  death of Herod; The deluge;
  Doubting Thomas; The fall of
  Lucifer; The harrowing of
  hell; Judas' plot; The last
  judgment; The last supper;
  The magi's oblation; Moses
  and the law; The nativity;
  The passion; The pentecost;
  The prophets; The prophets
  of antichrist; The purification; The raising of Lazarus;
  The resurrection, harrowing
  of hell, and the last judgment;
  The sacrifice of Isaac; The
  shepherds; Simon the leper;
  The slaying of the innocents;
  The temptation; The three
  kings; The trial and flagella-
  tion; The woman taken in
  adultery
The chicken pie and the choco-
  late cake. 15th cent.
  Mandel, O., tr. MARK
  Variant title: Le pâté et de
  la torte
Chiu keng t'ien. See One missing
  head
Christ and the doctors (Chester).
  15th cent. CHEL
Christ and the moneylenders
  (Chester). 15th cent. CHEL
Christ appears to the disciples
  (Chester). 15th cent. BEVD
Christ at the house of Simon the
  Leper (Chester). 15th cent.
  CHEL
Christ on the road to Emmaus
  (Chester). 15th cent. CHEL

A Christmas mumming: The
  play of Saint [Prince] George.
  15th cent. GARZB
  Variant titles: Christmas
    play of St. George; The
    play of St. George
The Christmas play (from Bene-
  diktbeuern). 12th cent.
  BEVD
  Variant title: Ludus de
    nativitate
Christmas play of St. George
  See A Christmas mumming:
  The play of Saint [Prince]
  George
Christ's appearances to the
  disciples (N Town). 15th cent.
  ENGE
Christ's ascension (Chester).
  15th cent. CHES
Christ's burial and resurrection
  (Digby). 15th cent. DIV,
  LAT
  Variant titles: Christ's
    burial; The prologe of this
    treyte or meditation off the
    buryalle of Christe and
    mowrnying perat
Christ's death and burial (York).
  15th cent. BEVD
Christ's ministry (Chester).
  15th cent. ADA
Christ's passion (Chester). 15th
  cent. CHES
Christ's resurrection (Chester).
  15th cent. CHES
Christ's resurrection (Digby).
  15th cent. LAT
  Variant title: Her begynnes
    his resurrection on Pas(c)he
    Daye at morn
Coliphizacio (Wakefield). 15th
  cent. CAWM
A comedy called Misogonus.
  See Misogonus
Common conditions. 1570? FARM
The conspiracy (Wakefield). 15th
  cent. TOWN
The contract of marriage between
  wit and wisdom. 1579? FARM
  Variant titles: The marriage
    of wit and wisdom; Wit and
    wisdom
The conversion of St. Paul (Dig-
  by). ADA, BEVD, DIV, LAT,
  MARG, SWIT
The Cornish mystery play of the

ANONYMOUS PLAYS (cont.)
Doomsday (N Town). 15th
cent. DAVJ
The double Dutch act (Vaudeville
skit). RAVA
The double Wop act (Vaudeville
skit). RAVA
Doubting Thomas (Chester).
15th cent. CHEL
The dream of Pilate's wife
(York). 15th cent. ENGE
The dream of Vāsavadatta. See
Bhāsa (supposed author)
Duk Moraud. 13th cent. ADA,
DAVN
Variant title: Dux Moraud
The Durham prologue. DAVN
Dux Moraud. See Duk Moraud
An Easter resurrection play.
10th cent. GARZB
Edward III. See The reign of
King Edward the third
The Elche mystery play. See
The mystery play of Elche
Elckerlijk. See Everyman
An enterlude called Lusty Iuuen-
tus; liuely describyng the
frailtie of youth: of nature,
prone to vyce: by grace and
good councell traynable to
vertue. See An enterlude
called Lusty Juventus
An enterlude called Lusty Juven-
tus. 1550? SOME
Variant title: An enterlude
called Lusty Iuuentus;
liuely describyng the frail-
tie of youth: of nature,
prone to vyce: by grace
and good councell traynable
to vertue
Entremés del espejo y burla de
Pablillos. NOR
Everyman. ca. 1495. ABC,
ABRB1, ABRF, ABRH, ABRJ,
ADA, ALLE, ALT, ALTE, ASF,
ASH, BAC, BALL, BARD,
BAT4, BENP, BENY, BEVD,
BIER, BOW, BROJ, BROK,
CALD, CASA, CAWL, CHI,
CLF1, CLK1, COJ, DOWS,
EVE, EVER, FARO, FIF, FREG,
GARZB, GATS, GOOD, GOODE,
GREB1, GREC1, GRIF, HEIL,
HOPP, HOUS, HUD, KER,
KERN, KERO, KON, KRE,
LEV, LEVE, LIE, LOOM,

MABC, MAE, MALI1, MANN,
MOO, PAR, PERS, PERU,
POLL, REIL, REIN, REIWE,
ROB, ROBE, ROHR, RUB,
SCAT, SCNPL, SCNQ, SCW,
SEN, SHAH1, SHAI1, SHAJ1,
SHRO, SML, SNYD1, SSSI,
STA, STY, SWIT, SYM, TAT,
TAU, TAV, THG, TRE, TREA2,
TREB, TREC1, TREE1, TREI1,
WAIW, WEAT1, WELT, WHFM,
WOOD1, WOOE1
Variant titles: Elckerlijk;
The moral play of Everyman;
The summoning of Everyman
The extraction of souls from hell
(Wakefield). See The harrow-
ing of hell
Fair Em. The miller's daughter
of Manchester with the love of
William the conqueror. 1590?
BRO
The faithful harlot.
Hung, J., tr. HUNG
Variant titles: The joyful hall
of jade; Yü t'ang ch'un
The fall of Lucifer (Chester).
15th cent. CHEL, CHES,
CHESE, ENGE
The fall of Lucifer (N Town).
15th cent. ADA, DAVJ, SCW
The fall of man (York). 15th
cent. BEVD, CAWL
The famous victories of Henry the
fifth (sometimes attributed to
Richard Tarlton). 1585? ADA
Variant title: Henry the fifth
La farce de Maître Pathelin.
See La farce de Maître Pierre
Pathelin
La farce de Maître Pierre Pathelin.
1469? SCN, SET
Allen, J., tr. ALLE
Franks, K., tr. SSSI
Holbrook, R., tr. THO
Jagendorf, M., tr. CARA,
CLF1, LOND
Mandel, O., tr. MARK
Pickering, J., tr. PIC
Variant titles: La farce de
Maître Pathelin; The farce
of the worthy Master Pierre
Patelin; The farce of the
worthy master, Pierre Pate-
lin; The farce of the worthy
master, Pierre Patelin, the
lawyer; Master Peter Patelan;

ANONYMOUS PLAYS (cont.)
   Master Pierre Patelin;
   Peter Quill's shenanigans;
   Pierre Patelin
The farce of the worthy Master
   Pierre Patelin. See La farce
   de Maître Pierre Patelin
The farce of the worthy master,
   Pierre Patelin, the lawyer.
   See La farce de Maître
   Pierre Pathelin
The fatal error
   McClatchie, T., tr. BAT21
   Variant title: Kago-Sodo
Feng yi T'ing. See Two men on
   a string
Festa de Elche. See The mystery
   play of Elche
Fifteen strings of cash. 1627?
   SCX2
   Variant title: Shih wu kuan
The final judgment.
   McAfee, B., and Cornyn, J.,
   trs. RAV
The first part of the reign of
   King Richard the second; or,
   Thomas of Woodstock. See
   Woodstock
The first part of the return from
   Parnassus. See The return
   from Parnassus; or, The
   scourge of Simony
The first shepherds' play (Wake-
   field). 15th cent. CAWM,
   ENGE, TOWN
   Variant title: Prima pastorum
The flight into Egypt (Wakefield).
   15th cent. ENGE, TOWN
The flight into Egypt (York).
   15th cent. BEVD
For representing how Saint
   Nicholas freed the son of
   Getron (from Fleury). 12th
   cent. BEVD
   Variant title: Ad repraesen-
   tandum quomodo Sanctus
   Nich[o]laus Getron(is)
   filium... liberavit
For representing the conversion
   of the Blessed Apostle Paul
   (from Fleury). 12th cent.
   BEVD
   Variant title: Ad repraesen-
   tandum conversionem Beati
   Pauli Apostoli
For representing the scene at the
   Lord's sepulchre (from Fleury).
   12th cent.? BEVD

Variant title: Ad faciendam
   similtudinem Dominici sepulcri)
For the Mass of our Lord (from
   Limoges). 11th cent. BEVD
   Variant title: Ad Dominicam
   missam
Forsaken love.
   Duran, L., tr. DUP
The four elements. See The nature
   of the four elements
Francis' new jig. See Attowell's jig
Gammer Gurton's needle. See
   Stevenson, William (supposed
   author)
Le garçon et l'aveugle.
   Axton, R., and Stevens, J.,
   trs. AXT
George a Greene, the pinner of
   Wakefield. See Greene,
   Robert (supposed author)
Godley Queen Hester. 1525?
   FARP
   Variant title: An interlude of
   Godley Queen Hester
Grandee's son takes the wrong
   career. Late 13th or early
   14th cent.
   Dolby, W., tr. EIG
   Variant title: Huan-men zi-
   di cuo li-shen
Grim the collier of Croydon; or,
   The devil and his dame
   (sometimes attributed to John
   Tatham). 1600? FARM
El Hambriento. NOR
Hamlet! The ravin' Prince of
   Denmark!!, or, The Baltic
   swell!!! and the diving
   belle!!! NIN4
The hands in the box.
   Duran, L., tr. DUP
The hanging of Judas (Wakefield).
   15th cent. TOWN
The harrowing of hell (Chester).
   15th cent. ADA, CAWL, CHEL,
   POLL
The harrowing of hell (York).
   15th cent. ENGE
The harrowing of hell; or, The
   extraction of souls from hell
   (Wakefield). 15th cent. BEVD,
   EVER
Harrowing of hell II (N Town).
   15th cent. DAVJ
Hegemon King says farewell to
   his queen. Late 13th or early
   14th cent.
   Dolby, W., tr. EIG

ANONYMOUS PLAYS (cont.)
Variant title: Ba-wang
bie-ji
Hegge plays. See N Town
plays
Henry the fifth. See The
famous victories of Henry
the fifth
Her begynnes his resurrection
on Pas[c]ke Daye at morn.
See Christ's resurrection
(Digby)
Herod (N Town). See The
magi, Herod, and the
slaughter of the innocents
Herod and the magi (N Town).
See The magi, Herod, and
the slaughter of the inno-
cents
Herod and the three kings
(N Town). See The magi,
Herod, and the slaughter
of the innocents
Herod the great (Wakefield).
15th cent. BEVD, CAWL,
TOWN
Herod's killing of the children
(Digby). 15th cent. DIV
He's much to blame. 1798.
INCA4
The Hessian Christmas play.
15th cent.
Robinson, D., tr. and
adapter ROBM
Hickscorner. 1534? FARO
The histories of Lot and
Abraham. See Abraham,
Melchisedec and Isaac
The history of Jacob and
Esau See Jacob and Esau
The holy resurrection. See
La seinte resureccion
The honor of Danzo.
Duran, L., tr. DUP
The horns.
Duran, L., tr. DUP
How the blessed Saint Helen
found the holy cross.
McAfee, B., tr. RAV
Hu tieh meng. See The butter-
fly dream
Huan-men zi-di cuo li-shen. See
Grandee's son takes the wrong
career
Hung luan hsi. See Twice a
bride
Hung teng chi. See The Red

lantern
Identifying footprints in the snow.
(mid-1950's version)
Dolby, W., tr. EIG
Variant title: Ping-xue bian-
zong
Impatient poverty. 1560? FARN
Variant title: An interlude
of impatient poverty
In an oval office (from the Water-
gate Transcripts). 1973. ESA
[I]ncipit ordo ad repraesentandum
Herodum. See The service for
representing Herod (from
Fleury)
Gl'ingannati. See The deceived
An interlude of Godley Queen
Hester. See Godley Queen
Hester
An interlude of impatient poverty.
See Impatient poverty
The interlude of John the evan-
gelist. See John the evangelist
An interlude of wealth and health.
See Wealth and health
The interlude of youth. See
Youth
Irawan Rabi. See Irawan's wedding
Irawan's wedding.
Alkire, S., and Siswoharsojo,
P., trs.; Brandon, J.,
adapter. BQA
Variant title: Irawan Rabi
The iron crown.
Kato, E., tr. KEE
Variant title: Kanawa
Isaac (Wakefield). 15th cent.
TOWN
Item de resurrectione Domini.
See Of the resurrection of the
Lord (from St. Gall)
Jack Juggler (attributed to
Nicholas Udall). 1553?
FAR, THZ
Variant titles: Jacke Jugeler;
A new enterlued for chyldren
to playe named Jacke Juge-
ler: both wytte, very play-
sent, and merye
Jacke Jugeler. See Jack Juggler
Jacob (Wakefield). 15th cent.
TOWN
Jacob and Esau. 1558? FARP
Variant title: The history of
Jacob and Esau
Jesse (N Town). 15th cent. DAVJ
Jesus and the doctors (N Town).

ANONYMOUS PLAYS (cont.)
15th cent. DAVJ
Le jeu d'Adam. See Adam
Job. 400? B.C. BUCL, BUCM,
DAVK, SML, TRE, TREA2
Variant title: The book of
Job
John the Baptist (Wakefield).
15th cent. TOWN
John the Baptist (York). 15th
cent. ENGE
John the evangelist. 1557?
FARN
Variant titles: The interlude
of John the evangelist;
Saint John the evangelist
Joseph (N Town). 15th cent.
ENGE
The joyful hall of jade. See
The faithful harlot
Juan Rana Comilón. NOR
Judas' plot (Chester). 15th
cent. CHEL
The judgment (Wakefield). 15th
cent. TOWN
The judgment (York). See The
judgment day
The judgment day (York). 15th
cent. ADA, CAWL, ENGE,
SCW
Variant title: The judgment
Julius Caesar travestie. (1861)
NIN4
Kaga-Sodo. See The fatal error
Kanawa. See The iron crown
Karna tanding. See The death
of Karna
The kept misteress. 1756.
BEVI
The killing of Abel (Wakefield).
15th cent. ADA, BEVD,
ENGE, TOWN
Killing of the children. 1512.
LAT
Variant title: Candlemes Day
and the kyllung of pe
children of Israelle
King Darius. 1565? FAR
King Edward the third. See
The reign of King Edward the
third
King Herod (Chester). 12th
cent.? FRAN
King Richard III travestie.
(1823) NIN1
Kuruwa Banshō. See Love Letter
from the licensed quarter

The lamentable and true tragedy
of Master Arden of Feversham
in Kent. See Arden of Fever-
sham
The lamentable tragedy of Locrine
(sometimes attributed to
George Peele; William Shake-
speare). 1586? BRO
Variant title: Locrine
The last judgment (Chester).
15th cent. CHEL, CHES,
CHESE
The last judgment (Wakefield).
15th cent. BEVD
The last supper (Chester). 15th
cent. CHEL
Lazarus (Wakefield). 15th cent.
ENGE, TOWN
The legend of the rood (Cornish).
15th cent. HAH
Leicestershire St. George play.
1863. ADA
The life and death of Lord Crom-
well. See Thomas, Lord Crom-
well
The little clay cart. See Shudra-
ka, King (supposed author)
Locrine. See The lamentable
tragedy of Locrine
The London prodigal (sometimes
attributed to William Shake-
speare). 1603? BRO
Longing for worldly pleasures.
1368? SCX2
Variant title: Ssu fan
Lot and Abraham. See Abraham,
Melchisedec and Isaac
Love letter from the licensed
quarter. 1780.
Brandon, J., tr. KAB
Variant title: Kuruwa Bunshō
Ludus Coventriae plays.
See N Town plays
Ludus de nativitate. See The
Christmas play (from Bene-
diktbeuern)
Ludus de passione. See The
passion play (from Benedikt-
beuern)
Ludus super iconia Sancti Nicolai.
15th cent. POLL
The Maastricht play (adapted
from Paachspel). 14th cent.
Robinson, D., tr. and
adapter ROBM
Macro Morals. See The castle of
perseverance; Mankynd; and,

ANONYMOUS PLAYS (cont.)
Mind, will, and understanding
Mactacio Abel (Wakefield). 15th
cent. CAWM, GARZB, ROBE
Variant title: The murder of
Abel
The magi, Herod, and the slaugh-
ter of the innocents (N Town).
15th cent. ADA, DAVJ, MAR
Variant titles: Herod; Herod
and the magi; Herod and
the three kings; The mas-
sacre of the innocents; The
slaughter of the innocents
The magi's oblation (Chester).
15th cent. CHEL, CHES,
CHESE
Variant title: The offerings of
the three kings
Magnus Herodes (Wakefield). 15th
cent. CAWM
Mai yan-zhi. See Buying rouge
Mankind. See Mankynd
Mankynd. ca. 1465-1471. ADA,
BEV, BEVD, FARN, SOME,
THQ
Variant title: Mankind
Manohra.
Bhukkanasut, U., tr. BRA
Man's disobedience and the fall of
man (York). 15th cent.
GARZB
Maria Marten. See Maria Martin;
or, The murder in the red
barn
Maria Martin; or, The murder in
the red barn. 1840. KILG
Variant titles: Maria Marten;
The murder in the red
barn; The red barn
The marriage of wit and science.
1569? FARM
Variant titles: Wit and science;
Wyt and science
The marriage of wit and wisdom.
See The contract of marriage
between wit and wisdom
The martyr'd souldier. BUL1
The martyrdom of Ali.
Pelly, L., tr. BAT3
Variant title: Ta'ziya
Mary Magdalene (Digby). 15th
cent. ADA, BEVD, DIV,
LAT, POLL
Variant title: Saint Mary
Magdalen
Mary Magdalene and the apostles.

See The mystery of Mary Mag-
dalene and the apostles
The masque of flowers. 1614. ETO
The massacre of the innocents.
See The magi, Herod, and the
slaughter of the innocents
Master Peter Patelan. See La
farce de Maître Pierre Pathe-
lin
Master Pierre Matelin. See La
farce de Maître Pierre Pathelin
Matthias (N Town). 15th cent.
DAVJ
The mayde's metamorphosis.
BUL2
Mei lung chen. See The price
of wine
The merchant.
McAfee, B., tr. RAV
The merry devil of Edmonton
(sometimes attributed to
Michael Drayton). 1600? BRO,
GAY2, MAK, OLH, OLI1
The miller's daughter of Manches-
ter with the love of William
the conqueror. See Fair Em
Mind, will, and understanding.
ca. 1460-1463. BEV, LAT
Variant titles: Wisdom; or,
Mind, will, and understand-
ing; Wysdom
Minstrel show. ca. 1850-ca. 1870.
MONR
The miracle of Saint Nicholas and
the school-boys. 15th cent.
LOOM
The miracle of Saint Nicholas and
the virgins. 15th cent. LOOM
Misogonus. 1560? BOND, FARP
Variant title: A comedy called
Misogonus
Mr. Attowell's jib. See Attowell's
jig
A moral play of Albion, knight.
1566? FARP
Variant title: Albion, knight
A morality of wisdom, who is
Christ. (Digby). 15th cent.
DIV
Moses (N Town). 15th cent.
DAVJ
Moses (York). 15th cent. ENGE
Moses and the law (Chester).
15th cent. CHEL
A most pleasant comedie of Muce-
dorus the kings sonne of Valen-
tia and Amadine, the kings

ANONYMOUS PLAYS (cont.)
daughter of Arragon. See
Mucedorus
Mother of Mercy (N Town). 15th
cent.
(Mother of Mercy: Conception;
Parliament of Heaven and An-
nunciation; Joseph; Salutation).
DAVJ
The motley assembly (attributed
to Mercy Otis Warren). 1779.
PHI
Mucedorus (sometimes attributed
to Thomas Lodge; William
Shakespeare). (1598) BAS,
BRO, DPR1, NES, WINN
Variant title: A most pleasant
comedie of Mucedorus the
kings sonne of Valentia
and Amadine, the kings
daughter of Arragon
Mundus et infans. See The world
and the child
The murder in the red barn.
1828. See Maria Martin; or,
The murder in the red barn
The murder of Abel (Wakefield).
See Mactacio Abel (Wakefield).
Le mystère d'Adam. See Adam
Mysterium resurrectionis D. N.
Jhesu Christi. 15th cent.
POLL
The mystery of Adam. See
Adam
The mystery of Mary Magdalene
and the apostles. 15th cent.
EVER
Variant title: Mary Magdalene
and the apostles
The mystery of the delayed
dawn (a Ming Dynasty story).
See One missing head (adapted
from)
The mystery of the redemption
(N Town). 15th cent. LOOM
Variant title: The redemption
The mystery play of Elche. 13th
cent.
Starkie, W., tr. SSTW
Variant title: The Elche
mystery play; Festa de
Elche
N Town plays.
See Abraham and Isaac; The
annunciation; The apostles at
the tomb; Appearance to
Cleopas and Luke; Appearance

to Mary Magdalen; Appearance
to Thomas; Ascension; Assump-
tion; Banns; The betraying
of Christ; Cain and Abel;
Christ's appearances to the
disciples; The creation and
fall of man; The death of
Herod; Doomsday; The fall of
Lucifer; Harrowing of hell II;
Jesse; Jesus and the doctors;
Joseph; The magi, Herod, and
the slaughter of the innocents;
Matthias; Moses; Mother of
Mercy; The Mystery of the redemption; The nativity plays;
Noah; The pageant of the
shearmen and tailors; Passion
I; Passion II; Passion III;
Pentecost; Presentation and
purification; Raising of Lazarus;
Resurrection and appearance
to Mother; The salutation and
conception; The shepherds'
play; Story of the watch;
Three Marys at the tomb; The
trial of Christ; Trial of Joseph
and Mary; The woman taken in
adultery
Variant cycle titles: Coventry
plays; Hegge plays; Ludus
Coventriae plays
The nativity (The Chantilly play).
See Bourlet, Katherine. The
nativity
The nativity (Chester). 15th cent.
CHES
The nativity play (N Town plays).
See The pageant of the shear-
men and tailors
The nativity (Wakefield). See
The second shepherds' play
The nativity (York). See The
York nativity
The nature of the four elements
(sometimes attributed to John
Rastell). 1520. FARO, POLL,
THW
Variant titles: The four ele-
ments; A new interlude and
a mery of the nature of the
four elementis
Nero. 1623? NERO
New custom. 1573? FAR
A new enterlued for chyldren to
playe named Jacke Jugeler:
both wytte, very playsent, and
merye. See Jack Juggler

ANONYMOUS PLAYS (cont.)
A new interlude and a mery of
the nature of the four elemen-
tis. See The nature of the
four elements
The Newcastle play. 15th cent?
DAVN
Variant titles: Noah's ark;
The shipwrights ancient
play, or dirge
Nice wanton. 16th cent. CLKW
Variant title: A pretty inter-
lude called Nice Wanton
Noah (N Town). 15th cent.
DAVJ
Noah (Wakefield). 15th cent.
ADA, BEVD, ENGE, HEIL,
SCW, TOWN
Noah and his sons. See The
deluge (Wakefield)
Noah's ark. See The Newcastle
play
Noah's deluge. See The deluge
(Chester)
Noah's flood. See The deluge
The noble souldier. BUL1
Nonomiya. See The shrine in
the fields
The Norwich Grocers' Play.
Text A and Text B. 15th
cent? DAVN
Variant title: The story of
the creation of Eve, and
the expelling of Adam and
Eve out of paradise
Oberufer plays. See The para-
dise play; The shepherds'
play; The three kings' play
Octavia. See Seneca, Lucius An-
naeus. Octavia
Of the resurrection of the Lord
(from St. Gall). ca. 950.
BEVD
Variant title: Item de resur-
rectione Domini
The offering of the magi (Wake-
field). 15th cent. BEVD,
TOWN
The offerings of the three kings.
See The magi's oblation
Officium pastorum. See The
Shrewsbury fragments
Officium peregrinorum. See The
Shrewbury fragments
Officium resurrectionis. See
The Shrewsbury fragments
One missing head. (Adapted

from: The mystery of the
delayed dawn).
Hung, J., tr. HUNG
Ordo ad peregrinum in secunda
feria pasche ad vesperas.
See The service [for repre-
senting] the pilgrim, at ves-
pers of the second holy day
of Easter
Ordo repraesentationis Adae.
See The service for represent-
ing Adam
Orlando ye brave and ye fayre
Rosalynd; or, "As you lump
it!" NIN4
The Orléans sepulcher. 13th
cent. GARZB
The Oxfordshire St. George play.
18th cent. ADA, CHI, PAR
Paachspel. See The Maastricht
play
The pageant of the shearmen and
the tailors (N Town). 15th
cent. ALLE, ENGE, EVER,
FIF, GARZB
Brown, J., adapter. ROBM
Variant titles: The nativity;
The nativity play; The
shearmen and tailors' play
A pantomime for Easter day.
GARZB
The paradise play (Oberufer).
16th cent.
Harwood, A., tr. HARW
The parliament of Heaven. See
The salutation and conception
Parnassus plays (1598-1601).
See The pilgrimage to Parnas-
sus; The return from Parnas-
sus
The passion (Chester). 15th
cent. CHEL
Passion I (N Town). 15th cent.
(Passion I: Prologues; Council
of Jews I; Entry into Jerusalem;
Maundy I; Council of Jews II;
Maundy II; Betrayal; Maundy
III; Agony at Olivet; Taking of
Jesus). BEVD, DAVJ, ENGE
The passion play (from Benedikt-
beuern). 12th cent. BEVD
Variant title: Ludus de pas-
sione
The passion play of Alsfeld.
Katzin, W., tr. SEVE
Passion II (N Town). 15th cent.
(Passion II: Prologue; Jesus

ANONYMOUS PLAYS (cont.)
before Herod; Before Annas
and Caiphas; Peter's denial;
Before Pilate; Before Herod
II; Dream of Pilate's wife;
Before Pilate II; Way of the
cross; Crucifixion; Harrowing
of Hell I; Centurion; Longeus
and burial; Setting of watch;
Way of the cross). BEVD,
DAVJ
Le pâté et de la torte. See The
chicken pie and the chocolate
cake
The pentecost (Chester). 15th
cent. CHEL
Pentecost (N Town). 15th cent.
DAVJ
Pentecost (York). 15th cent.
ENGE
Pharaoh (Wakefield). 15th cent.
ADA, BEVD, TOWN
Le philosophe dupé de l'amour.
See The philosopher duped by
love
The philosopher duped by love
(sometimes attributed to Fran-
çois Dessandrais-Sebire). 17th
cent.
Chambers, W., tr. BAT7
Variant title: Le philosophe
dupé de l'amour
Phoenix pavilion. See Two men on
a string
Pierre Patelin. See La farce de
Maître Pierre Pathelin
Pilgrimage. See The pilgrimage
to Parnassus
The pilgrimage to Parnassus.
16th cent. LEIS
Variant title: Pilgrimage
The pilgrims (Wakefield). 15th
cent. TOWN
Ping-xue bian-zong. See Identi-
fying footprints in the snow
The play of Adam. See Adam
The play of Daniel (from Beau-
vais). 12th cent. BEVD
Variant title: Daniel Ludus
The play of St. George. See
A Christmas mumming:
The play of Saint [Prince]
George
The play of St. George, version
reconstructed from memory by
Thomas Hardy. 13th cent.?
CLF1

The play of the doctors (Wake-
field). 15th cent. TOWN
The play of the sacrament. 15th
cent. ADA, DAVN
The play of the sacrament
(Croxton). 15th cent. BEVD
Plum dragon town. See The price
of wine
Presentation and purification (N
Town). 15th cent. DAVJ
A pretty interlude called Nice
wanton. See Nice wanton
The price of wine.
Hung, J., tr. BRA, HUNG
Variant titles: Mei lung chen;
Plum dragon town; The
traveling dragon teases a
phoenix; Yu lung hsi feng
The pride of life. 14th cent.
DAVN
Prima pastorum. See The first
shepherds' play
The printer's apprentice.
1648?
Rist, J., tr. (from the Ger-
man of William Blades).
BAT4
Variant title: Depositio cor-
nuti typographici
The procession of the prophets
(Wakefield). 15th cent.
TOWN
Processus noe cum filiis (Wake-
field). 15th cent. CAWM
The prologe of this treyte or
meditation off the buryalle
of Christe and mowrnying
pe rat. See Christ's burial
and resurrection (Digby)
The prophets (Chester). 15th
cent. ADA
The prophets of antichrist
(Chester). 15th cent. CHEL
The Provençal play. 13th cent.
Robinson, D., tr. and adap-
ter. ROBM
The purification (Chester). 15th
cent. CHEL, ENGE
The purification of Mary (Wake-
field). 15th cent. TOWN
The puritan; or, The widow of
Watling street (sometimes attributed to William Shakespeare).
1606? BRO
Variant title: The puritan
widdow
The puritan widdow. See The

ANONYMOUS PLAYS (cont.)
    The puritan; or, The widow
      of Watling street
    The quem quaeritis (trope). 9th
      cent. BARI, CHI, GARZB,
      HUD, PAR, SCW
      Chambers, E., tr. BARH,
        BARIA, BARIC
    Querolus. 15th cent.?
      Duckworth, G., tr. DUC2
    The raigne of King Edward the
      third. See The reign of King
      Edward the third
    The raising of Lazarus (Chester).
      15th cent. CHEL
    Raising of Lazarus (N Town).
      15th cent. DAVJ
    The raising of Lazarus (Wake-
      field). 15th cent. BEVD
    The red barn. See Maria Martin;
      or, The murder in the red barn
    The red detachment of women.
      1969. SNO
      Ebon, M., tr. FIFW
    The Red lantern. 1964.
      Anon. tr. ANDI, FIFW
      Foreign Languages Press,
        Peking, tr., and China
        Peking Opera Troupe, re-
        visers (scenes 1-7 sum-
        marized; 8-11 printed in
        full). TWEH
      Snow, L., tr. SNO
      Wong, O., and Ah, C., adap-
        ters; Yang, H., and Yang,
        G., trs. MESE, WEIP
      Variant title: Hung teng chi
    The redemption (N Town). See
      The mystery of the redemption
    The reign of King Edward the
      third (sometimes attributed to
      Thomas Lodge; Christopher
      Marlowe; William Shakespeare).
      1590? ARMS, BRO, WINN
      Variant titles: Edward III;
        King Edward the third; The
        raigne of King Edward the
        third
    The reincarnation of Rama. Sis-
      Siswoharsojo, P., and Alkire,
      S., trs.; Brandon, J.,
      adapter. BQA
      Variant title: Wahju Purbo
        Sedjati
    Respublica (attributed to Nicholas
      Udall). 1553? FARN, HAO
      (extracts), SCAT

The resurrection (Chester).
  15th cent. CHEL
The resurrection (Wakefield).
  See The resurrection of Christ
  (Wakefield)
Resurrection (York). 15th cent.
  CAWL, SWIT
Resurrection and appearance
  to Mother (N Town). 15th
  cent. DAVJ
The resurrection, harrowing of
  hell, and the last judgment
  (synoptic version of Chester,
  Coventry, and Wakefield plays).
  15th cent. GARZB
The resurrection of Christ (Wake-
  field). 15th cent. ADA,
  BEVD, ENGE, TOWN
  Variant titles: The resurrec-
    tion; The resurrection of
    the Lord
The resurrection of the Lord.
  See The resurrection of Christ
The return from Parnassus; or,
  The scourge of Simony, pt. I
  (1601?). LEIS
  pt. II (1602?) LEIS, SCH, SCI,
    SCJ
  Variant titles: The first part
    of the return from Parnas-
    sus; The second part of the
    return from Parnassus
The Reversby sword play. 1779.
  ADA
The Reynes extracts. 15th cent.?
  DAVN
The Rickinghall (Bury St. Ed-
  munds) fragment. 14th cent.
  DAVN
Rip Van Winkle (as played by
  Joseph Jefferson; adapted by
  Dion Boucicault). 1865. CEY,
  LAW, MASW, NILS, QUIJ,
  QUIK, QUIL, QUIM, QUIN
  --See also Burke, Charles. Rip
  Van Winkle
Robin Hood and the friar. 15th
  cent. ADA, CHI, PAR, SCW
Robin Hood and the knight. 15th
  cent. CHI
Robin Hood and the potter. 15th
  cent. CHI
Robin Hood and the sheriff of
  Nottingham. 15th cent. ADA
The sacrifice of Isaac.
  McAfee, B., and Cornyn, J.,
  trs. RAV

ANONYMOUS PLAYS (cont.)
The sacrifice of Isaac (Brome).
BAIG, BEVD
The sacrifice of Isaac. See
also Abraham and Isaac;
Abraham, Melchisedec and
Isaac
St. George and the dragon.
19th cent. EVER, SCW
St. George plays. See Leicester-
shire St. George play; The Ox-
fordshire St. George play;
The play of St. George, version
reconstructed from memory by
Thomas Hardy; St. George and
the dragon
Saint John the evangelist. See
John the evangelist
Saint Mary Magdalen. See Mary
Magdalene (Digby)
Saint Nicholas and the three
scholars. 12th cent. MAR
Variant title: Tres clerici
Saint Nicholas plays. See The
miracle of Saint Nicholas and
the school-boys; The miracle of
Saint Nicholas and the virgins;
Saint Nicholas and the three
scholars
The salutation and conception (N
Town). 15th cent. ADA,
ENGE, POLL
Variant title: The parliament
of heaven
The salutation of Elizabeth (Wake-
field). 15th cent. BEVD,
TOWN
Schachiapang. SNO
Le savetier calbain. 1500? BRN
The school act (Vaudeville skit).
RAVA
The scourge of Simony. See The
return from Parnassus
The scourging (Wakefield). 15th
cent. BEVD, ENGE, TOWN
The second part of the return
from Parnassus. See The re-
turn from Parnassus; or, The
scourge of Simony
The second play of the shepherds.
See The second shepherds'
play
The second shepherds' pageant.
See The second shepherds'
play
The second shepherds' play
(Wakefield). 15th cent.

ABRB1, ABRF, ABRH, ABRJ,
ADA, ALLK, ALLM, AUB,
BARD, BAUL, BENY, BEVD,
BRIX, BRIY, BRIZ, CALD,
CAWL, CAWM, CHI, CLF1,
CLK1, CLKW, COL1, DAV1,
DOV, ENGE, EVE, EVER,
FRAN, GARZB, HARW, HEA,
HEAL, HEIL, HOPP, HUD,
KER, KRE, LIE, LIED1, LIEE1,
LOOM, MAR, MAX, PAR, POLL,
ROBE, RUB, SCW, SEN, SEVT,
SHAJ1, SPD, SPDB, SPEF1,
SSSI, STA, TAT, TAU, TAV,
TOBI, TOWN, TREB, TREC1,
TREE1, TREI1, WOO1, WOOD1,
WOOE1
Variant titles: The nativity; The
second play of the shepherds;
The second shepherds' pageant;
Secunda pastorum; The shep-
herds; A Wakefield nativity;
The Wakefield second nativity
play
Secunda pastorum. See The
second shepherds' play
La seinte resureccion. 12th cent.
BEVD
Axton, R., and Stevens, J.,
trs. AXT
Variant title: The holy resur-
rection
The service for representing
Adam. 12th cent. BEVD
Variant title: Ordo reprae-
sentationis Adae
The service for representing Herod
(from Fleury). 12th cent.?
BEVD
Variant title: [I]ncipit ordo
ad repraesentandum Herodem
The service [for representing] the
pilgrim, at vespers of the
second holy day of Easter (from
Beauvais). 12th cent. BEVD
Variant title: Ordo ad pere-
grinum in secunda feria
pasche ad vesperas
The shearmen and tailors' pla:.
See The pageant of the shear-
men and the tailors
The shepherds. See The second
shepherds' play
The shepherds (Chester). 15th
cent. CHEL
The shepherds (York). BEVD
The shepherds' play (N Town).

ANONYMOUS PLAYS (cont.)
    boesters are not the greatest
    doers
A thin slice of ham let! (1863)
    NIN4
Thomas, Lord Cromwell. 1592?
    BRO
    Variant titles: The life and
    death of Lord Cromwell;
    The true chronical history
    of the whole life and death
    of Thomas Lord Cromwell
Thomas of India (Wakefield). 15th
    cent. TOWN
Thomas of Woodstock. See Wood-
    stock
The three cuckolds. 16th cent.
    Katz, L., adapter. BENR1
    Variant title: Li tre becchi
The three kings (Chester). 15th
    cent. CHEL
The three kings (York). 15th
    cent. ENGE (introduction to,
    only). FRAN
The three kings' play (Oberufer).
    16th cent. HARW
The three Maries (Cornish). 15th
    cent. EVER
    Variant title: The Cornish
    mystery play of the three
    Maries
Three Marys at the tomb (N Town).
    15th cent. DAVJ
Tom Tyler and his wife. 1550?
    FARP
Totentanz. (tr. by Margaret
    Trinklein from the German text
    of Martin F. Schloss). 15th
    cent. SWIT
    Variant title: The dance of
    death
The Towneley play. 15th cent.
    Burrell, R., adapter. ROBM
Towneley plays. See Wakefield
    plays
Tragedy of Nero. BUL1
The traveling dragon teases a
    phoenix. See The price of
    wine
Li tre becchi. See The three
    cuckolds
Tres clerici. See Saint Nicholas
    and the three scholars
The trial of Atticus before Judge
    Beau, for a rape. 1771?
    AMPA
The trial and flagellation (Ches-

ter). 15th cent. CHEL
The trial of Christ (N Town).
    15th cent. ADA
Trial of Joseph and Mary (N
    Town). 15th cent. DAVJ
Trial of treasure. 1565? FAR
Trope for Easter. ca.923-934.
    BEVD
    Variant title: Trophi in Pasche
Trophi in Pasche. See Trope for
    Easter
The true and honorable historie
    of the life of Sir John Old-
    castle, the good Lord Cobham.
    See Sir John Oldcastle, pt. I
The true chronicle history of the
    whole life and death of Thomas
    Lord Cromwell. See Thomas,
    Lord Cromwell
The tryall of chevalry. BUL2
Twice a bride.
    Hung, J., tr. HUNG
    Variant title: Hung luan hsi
Two men on a string.
    Hung, J., tr. HUNG
    Variant title: Feng yi T'ing;
    Phoenix pavilion
The two noble kinsmen. See
    Fletcher, J., and Shakespeare,
    W.
The Umbrian play. 14th cent.
    Robinson, D., tr. and adapter.
    ROBM
The valley rite.
    Tyler, R., tr. KEE
    Variant title: Tanikō.
The visit to the sepulchre (from
    Aquileia?). BEVD
    Variant title: Visitatio se-
    pulchre
The visit to the sepulchre (from
    The Regularis Concordia of
    St. Ethelwold). 965-975.
    BEVD
    Variant title: Visitatio se-
    pulchri
The visit to the sepulchre (from
    St. Lambrecht). BEVD
The visit to the sepulchre (from
    the Tenth-Century troper of
    Winchester). 978-980. BEVD
Visitatio sepulchre. See The visit
    to the sepulchre (from Aqui-
    leia?)
Visitatio sepulchri. See The visit
    to the sepulchre (from The
    Regularis Concordia of St.

ANONYMOUS PLAYS (cont.)
Ethelwold)
Wahju Purba Sedjati. See The
reincarnation of Rama
Wakefield plays. See Abraham;
The annunciation; The ascension of the Lord; The betrayal;
The buffeting; Caesar Augustus; Coliphizacio; The conspira-
cy; The creation; The cruci-
fixion; The deliverance of souls;
The deluge; The first shep-
herds' play; The flight into
Egypt; The hanging of Judas;
The harrowing of Hell; Herod
the great; Isaac; Jacob; John
the Baptist; The judgment;
The killing of Abel; Lazarus;
Magnus Herodes; Noah; The
offering of the magi; Pharaoh;
The pilgrims; The play of the
doctors; The procession of the
prophets; Processus noe cum
filiis; The purification of Mary;
The resurrection of Christ;
The salutation of Elizabeth;
The scourging; The second
shepherds' play; The talents;
Thomas of India
The Wakefield second nativity play.
See The second shepherds' play
The washtub. 15th cent.
Mandel, O., tr. MAN
Variant title: Le cuvier
Wealth and health. 1557? FARN
Variant title: An interlude of
wealth and health
The wept of the wish-ton-wish
(based on the novel by James
Fenimore Cooper.) 1834.
BAT19
The whisker tweezers. 1717?
See Tsuuchi, Hanjurō; Yasuda,
Abun; and Nakada, Mansuke.
Saint Narukami and the God
Fudō (based on)
The white-haired girl. 1945.
Ebon, M., tr. EIGH
The Widow of Watling Street. See
The puritan
The wisdom of Dr. Dodypoll.
1600. BUL2
Wisdom; or, Mind, will, and under-
standing. See Mind, will, and
understanding
The wise virgins and the foolish
virgins. 1150?

Hughes, B., and G., trs.
CLF1
The wisemen (The Spanish play).
12th cent.
Robinson, D., tr. and
adapter. ROBM
Wit and science. See The mar-
riage of wit and science; Red-
ford, John. The play of wit
and science
Wit and wisdom. See The contract
of marriage between wit and
wisdom
The woman taken in adultery
(Chester). 15th cent. CHEL
The woman taken in adultery (N
Town). 15th cent. BEVD,
CAWL, DAVJ
Woodstock, ca. 1591-ca. 1595.
ARMS
Variant titles: The first part
of the reign of King Richard
the second; or, Thomas of
Woodstock; Thomas of Wood-
stock
The world and the child. 1522?
FARO, SCAT, THQ
Variant title: Mundus et in-
fans
Wysdom. See Mind, will and un-
derstanding
Wyt and science. See The mar-
riage of wit and science; Red-
ford, John. The play of wit
and science
The York crucifixion. See The
crucifixion (York)
The York nativity. 15th cent.
Baird, J., tr. LEV, LEVE,
MAK
Variant title: The nativity
York plays. See The adoration;
The assumption and the corona-
tion of the Virgin; The birth of
Jesus; The creation and the
fall of Lucifer; The creation of
Adam and Eve; The crucifixion;
The death and burial; The
dream of Pilate's wife; The fall
of man; The harrowing of hell;
John the Baptist; The judgment
day; Moses; Pentecost; Resur-
rection; The three kings; The
York nativity
A Yorkshire tragedy (sometimes
attributed to William Shake-
speare). 1605? BRO, OLH,

ANONYMOUS PLAYS (cont.)
OLI1, RUB
Variant title: All's one, or
one of the four plaies in
one, called a York-Shire
tragedy
Youth. 1555? FARP, HAO,
SCAT
Variant title: The interlude
of youth
Yu lung hsi feng. See The price
of wine
Yü t'ang ch'un. See The faithful
harlot

ANOUILH, JEAN, 1910-1987
L'alouette. See The lark
L'amour puni. See The rehear-
sal
Antigone. 1944. GRAF
Anon. tr. FOUA, PATP,
SUT2
Galantière, L., tr. and adapter.
ASF, BES45, BLOC, CASE,
DOT, ELKE, GORDP, JOHO,
MANK, MIJE, SSSU, ULAN,
WATE, WISF
Variant titles: Antigone and
the tyrant; Antigone et le
tyrant
Antigone and the tyrant. See
Antigone
Antigone et le tyrant. See Anti-
gone
Ardèle. 1950.
Hill, L., tr. COTK
Variant titles: Ardèle; ou,
la Marguerite; The cry of
the peacock
Ardèle; ou, la Marguerite. See
Ardèle
Le bal des voleurs. See Thieves'
carnival
Becket; or, The honor of God.
1959.
Hill, L., tr. ALT, ALTE,
BES60, CUBH, GOLH,
MORV, MORX, RICIS
Variant title: Becket; ou,
L'honneur de Dieu
Becket; ou, L'honneur de Dieu.
See Becket; or, The honor of
God
Cecile; or, The school for
fathers. 1953.
Klein, L., and A., trs.
BENS3

Variant title: Cécile; ou,
L'école de pères
Cécile; ou, L'école des pères. See
Cecile; or, The school for fa-
thers
The cry of the peacock. See Ar-
dèle
Le dîner des têtes. See Poor
Bitos
Episode de la vie d'un auteur.
See Episode in the life of an
author
Episode in the life of an author.
1948.
John, M., tr. RICK
Variant title: Episode de la vie
d'un auteur
The ermine. 1932.
John, M., tr. PLAN13
Variant title: L'hermine
Euridice. See Eurydice
Eurydice. 1941.
Black, K., tr. COTKW, COTQ
Variant title: Euridice;
Legend of lovers; Point of
departure
L'hermine. See The ermine
L'invitation au chateau. See
Ring round the moon
The lark. 1955.
Fry, C., tr. BERM, CLL,
WEAN
Hellman, L., adapter. BES55,
GARZH, THEA56, TREBA,
TREBJ, TREI3
Variant title: L'alouette
Legend of lovers. See Eurydice
Léocadia. See Time remembered
Madame de...
Whiting, J., tr. RICJ
Medea. 1948.
Klein, L., and A., trs.
BENT5, SANM
Small, L., tr. PLAN15
Variant title: Médéé
Médéé. See Medea
The orchestra. 1962.
John, M., tr. RICJ
Variant title: L'orchestre
L'orchestre. See The orchestra
Pauvre Bitos. See Poor Bitos
Point of departure. See Eurydice
Poor Bitos. 1956.
Hill, L., tr. BES64
Variant titles: Le dîner des
têtes; Pauvre Bitos
The rehearsal. 1950.

Johnson, P., and Black, K.,
adapters. BES63
Variant titles: L'amour puni;
La répétition; ou, L'amour
puni
La répétition; ou, L'amour puni.
See The rehearsal
Ring round the moon. 1947.
Fry, C., tr. BRZA
Variant title: L'invitation au
chateau
Thieves' carnival. 1932.
Anon. tr. ZIM
Hill, L., tr. BENT3, BLOC
Variant title: Le bal des
voleurs
Time remembered. 1954.
Moyes, P., tr. and adapter.
BES57
Variant title: Léocadia
La valse de toréadors. See
The waltz of the toreadors
The waltz of the toreadors. 1952.
Hill, L., tr. and adapter.
BES56, PLAN8
Variant title: La valse de
toréadors

--and AURENCHE, JEAN
Augustus. See Humulus the
mute
Humulus le muet. See Humulus
the mute
Humulus the mute. 1948.
Benedikt, M., tr. BEN
Hanger, G., tr. TOB
Variant title: Augustus;
Humulus le muet

ANSKI, S. A., pseud. See
Rappoport, Shloyme Zanvl

ANSKY, S. A., pseud. See
Rappoport, Shloyme Zanvl

ANSPACHER, LOUIS KAUFMAN,
1878-1947
The unchastened woman. 1915.
BAK, BES09, DIG

ANTHONY, C. L., pseud. See
Smith, Dorothy Gladys

ANZENGRUBER, LUDWIG, 1839-
1889
The farmer forsworn. 1872.
Busse, A., tr. FRA16

Variant title: Meineidbauer
The fourth commandment.
See Das vierte gebot
Meineidbauer. See The farmer
forsworn
Das vierte gebot. 1877. CAM
Variant title: The fourth
commandment

APOLINAR, DANNY, 1934-
Your own thing (music and lyrics
by). See Driver, Donald.
Your own thing

APOLLINAIRE, GUILLAUME, pseud.
See Kostrowisky, Guillaume Apollinaire de

APPELL, GLENN
Factwino vs. Armageddonman
(music and lyrics by, except
"Blow this mother up" by
Shabaka). See San Francisco
Mime Troupe. Factwino vs.
Armageddonman

APPLEGATE, JAMES EARL
See ADV Adventures in world
literature

APSTEIN, THEODORE, 1918-
Wetback run. (1961) GRIH

ARAGON, LOUIS, 1897-
L'armoire a glace un beau soir.
See The mirror-wardrobe one
fine evening
The mirror-wardrobe one fine
evening. 1923.
Benedikt, M., tr. BEN
Variant title: L'armoire à glace
un beau soir

ARBUZOV, ALEXEI, 1908-
It happened in Irkutsk. 1959?
Prokofieva, R., tr. THY,
WEIM
Tanya. 1939.
Miller, A., tr. CLKX

ARCE, GASPAR NUNEZ DE. See
Núñez de Arce, Gaspar

ARCHER, WILLIAM, 1856-1924
The green goddess. 1921.
BES20, CARP, CEU, LAW,
LOV

ARCHIBALD, WILLIAM, 1924-1970
  The innocents (based on the novel
    The turn of the screw by
    Henry James). 1950. BES49

ARCIPRESTE DE HITA. See Ruiz,
  Juan

ARDEN, JANE
  The party. 1958. PLAN18

ARDEN, JOHN, 1930-
  Death of a cowboy. PLAAB
  Live like pigs. 1958. NEWE3
  Serjeant Musgrave's dance. 1959.
    POP
  Soldier, soldier. 1960. CONB

-- and D'ARCY, MARGRETTA
  The happy haven. 1960.
    NEWE4

ARDEN, THOMAS, d. 1551
  Arden of Feversham (sometimes
    attributed to). See Anonymous
    plays. Arden of Feversham

ARDREY, ROBERT, 1908-1980
  The murderers. See Stone and
    star
  Shadow of heroes. See Stone
    and star
  Stone and star. 1958. BES61
    Variant titles: The murderers;
      Shadow of heroes
  Thunder rock. 1939. FIR

ARENT, ARTHUR, 1904-1972
  One-third of a nation (edited by).
    1938. FEE, NAGE
  Power, a living newspaper. 1937.
    FEF

ARETINO, PIETRO, 1492-1556
  Il Marescalco. See The stable-
    master
  The stablemaster. (1533).
    Bull, G., tr. FIJ
    Variant title: Il Marescalco

ARIOSTO, LUDOVICO, 1474-1533
  I suppositi. See Gascoigne,
    George. Supposes (adapted
    from)
  Lena. (1528).
    Williams, G., tr. FIJ
    Variant title: La Lena

La Lena. See Lena

ARISTOPHANES, 446?-385? B.C.
  The Acharnians. 425 B.C.
    Anon. tr. OAT2
    Casson, L., tr. CASU
    Frere, J., tr. KRE
    Rogers, B., tr. GRDB5
  Aves. See The birds
  The birds. 414 B.C.
    Anon. tr. FIFV, OAT2, WED
    Fitts, D., tr. BARJ, BARK
      FEFL, FIFR
    Frere, J., tr. CROV, HOUS
    Kerr, W., tr. WHFM
    MacGregor, M., tr. CLKW
    McLeish, K., tr. MAMB
    Rogers, B., tr. FEFT,
      GRDB5
    Variant title: Aves
  The clouds. 423 B.C.
    Anon. tr. BAT2, MURP,
      OAT2, PLAG
    Cumberland, R., tr. HOWE,
      HOWF
    Hickie, W., tr. GREE
    Lucas, F., tr. LUCA,
      LUCAB, LUCAF
    Mitchell, T., tr. CLF1
    Rogers, B., tr. BARB, FEFT,
      GRDB5, MIK7, ROBJ,
      WARN1
    Variant title: Nubes
  The council of women. See
    The ecclesiazusae
  The ecclesiazusae. 392 B.C.
    Anon. tr. BAT21, OAT2
    Rogers, B., tr. GRDB5
    Variant title: The council of
      women
  Equites. See The knights
  The frogs. 405 B.C.
    Anon. tr. PLAG
    Fitts, D., tr. SHRO
    Frere, J., tr. BUCK, BUCL,
      BUCM, HIB, HIBA, HIBB,
      LAP, MAU, SEBO, SEBP,
      SMR, TAV, TEN, THOM,
      THON
    Hawthorne, J., tr. MALR1
    McLeish, K., tr. MAMB
    Murray, G., tr. HOWF, OAT2,
      OATH
    Rogers, B., tr. FEFT,
      GRDB5, HARC8, ROB,
      ROBJ, TREB, TREC1,
      TREE1, TREI1

Webb, R., tr. GRDG
Variant title: Ranae
The god of riches. See Plutus
The knights. 424 B.C.
    Anon. tr. OAT2
    Frere, J., tr. DRA1, PLAB1
    Rogers, B., tr. GRDB5
    Variant title: Equites
Lysistrata. 411 B.C.
    Anon. tr. DAVM, GOU1,
      OAT2, PLAG, SCNPL,
      WORP
    Fitts, D., tr. BARL, HEA,
      SAFF, VANV1, WELT
    Murphy, C., tr. ALLK,
      ALLM, BOW, HOLP, JOHN,
      LIND, LOCM1, MALI1,
      NORG1, NORI, OAM,
      ROBI, SCNQ, SOU, SSSI,
      VON, WOM
    Oates, W., and Murphy, C.,
      trs. EVC1, MALN1
    Roby, D., tr. MESS
    Rogers, B., tr. GRDB5
    Seldes, G., tr. TRE, TREA2
    Smolin, D., tr. and adapter.
      PLAH
    Sutherland, D., tr. COTKI,
      COTY, HAPRL, SEVT
    Wilbur, R., tr. WEIS, WEIW
Nubes. See The clouds
Pax. See Peace
Peace. 421 B.C.
    Anon. tr. OAT2
    Reynolds, T., tr. TENN
    Rogers, B., tr. GRDB5
    Variant title: Pax
Plutus, the god of riches.
    388 B.C.
    Anon. tr. OAT2
    Hickie, W., tr. GREE
    Rogers, B., tr. GRDB5
    Sanford, D., tr. TEN
    Variant title: Wealth
Ranae. See The frogs
Thesmophoriazusae. 411 B.C.
    Anon. tr. OAT2
    Rogers, B., tr. GRDB5
    Variant title: The women
      celebrating the Thesmophor-
      ia
Vespae. See The wasps
The wasps. 422 B.C.
    Anon. tr. OAT2
    Rogers, B., tr. GRDB5
    Variant title: Vespae
Wealth. See Plutus

The women celebrating the Thes-
    mophoria. See Thesmophoriazu-
    sae

ARLEN, MICHAEL, 1895-1956
The green hat. 1925. BES25

ARMSTRONG, ANTHONY, pseud.
See Willis, Anthony Armstrong

ARNO, OWEN G.
The other player. BRNB

ARNOLD, MATTHEW, 1822-1888
Empedocles on Etna. 1852. KAU,
    PRAT2
The strayed reveler. 1849.
    PRAT2

AROUT, GABRIEL, 1909-
Beware of the dog (adapted from
    short stories of Chekhov).
    1967.
    Mitchell, Y., tr. PLAN33

ARRABAL, FERNANDO, 1932-
First communion. 1962.
    Benedikt, M., tr. BENA
Picnic on the battlefield. 1959.
    Anon, tr. ANT, HOGI, HOGN,
      OHL
    Hewitt, J., tr. COX, KERO
    Wright, B., tr. BARO
    Variant title: Pique-nique
      en campagne
Pique-nique en campagne. See
    Picnic on the battlefield

ARTAUD, ANTONIN, 1896-1948
Le jet de sang. See The jet of
    blood
The jet of blood. 1925.
    Cohn, R., tr. TREBJ
    Wellwarth, G., tr. BEN
    Variant titles: Le jet de sang;
      The spurt of blood
The spurt of blood. See The jet
    of blood

ASADA, ITCHO. See Namiki,
    Sōsuke, jt. auth.

ASCH, SHOLEM, 1880-1957
God of vengeance.
    Landis, J., tr. LAO, LAOG

ASHBERY, JOHN, 1927-

The heroes. 1953. MAH

ASHTON, WINIFRED (CLEMENCE
DANE, pseud.), d. 1965
A bill of divorcement. 1921.
BES21, COT, MART, MOSO
Granite. 1926. MYB, TUCD
Moonlight is silver. 1934.
SEV
Wild Decembers. 1932. BARV,
SIXH

ASPENSTROM, WERNER, 1918-
The apes shall inherit the
earth. 1959.
Sjöberg, L., and Goodman,
R., trs. GOO
Variant title: Det eviga
Det eviga. See The apes shall
inherit the earth

ATHAS, DAPHNE SPENCER, 1923-
See Campbell, Marion Gurney, jt.
auth.

ATLAS, LEOPOLD LAWRENCE,
1907-
"L." 1928. LEV, LEVE
Wednesday's child. 1934. BES33

ATTOWELL, GEORGE, fl. 1599
Attowell's jig (sometimes attribu-
ted to). See Anonymous plays.
Attowell's jig

AUBIGNY, D', pseud. See Baudouin, Jean Marie Théodore

AUDEN, WYSTAN HUGH, 1907-1973
and ISHERWOOD, CHRISTOPHER
The ascent of F6. 1937. TUCN
The dog beneath the skin.
1935. KOZ, KRE

AUGIER, EMILE, 1820-1889
Le mariage d'Olympe. 1855.
BOR
Clark, B., tr. SSTG
Variant title: Olympe's mar-
riage
Olympe's marriage. See Le mar-
iage d'Olympe

-- and SANDEAU, JULES
Le gendre de M. Poirier. 1854.
BOR, GRA, SEA
Clark, B., tr. CLF2, MAU

Variant titles: M. Poirier's
son-in-law; The son-in-law
of M. Poirier
M. Poirier's son-in-law. See Le
gendre de M. Poirier
The son-in-law of M. Poirier.
See Le gendre de M. Poirier

AULETTA, ROBERT, 1940-
Stops. 1972. BALLE10

AURENCHE, JEAN, 1904- See
Anouilh, Jean, jt. auth.

AURTHUR, ROBERT ALAN, 1922-
A very special baby. 1956.
BES56

AUSTEN, JANE, 1775-1817
Pride and prejudice. See
Jerome, Mrs. Helen (Burton).
Pride and prejudice (based on
the novel by)

AW, ARTHUR
All brand new classical Chinese
theatre. 1978. KUMU

AXELROD, GEORGE, 1923-
The seven year itch. 1952.
GART, GATB4, NEWV, THEA53

AXENFELD, ISRAEL, 1787-1866, and
REZNIK, LIPE
Recruits; or, That's how it was.
1935 (U.S.).
Lifson, D., tr. LIFS

AYALA, ADELARDO LOPEZ DE. See
López de Ayala, Adelardo

AYCKBOURN, ALAN, 1939-
Absurd person singular. 1973.
BEST
Bedroom farce. 1975. BES78
Living together. See The Norman
conquests
The Norman conquests. 1974.
BES75 (Three interlocking
plays, each in two acts: Table
manners; Living together; and
Round and round the garden)
Round and round the garden. See
The Norman conquests
Table manners. See The Norman
conquests

AYME, MARCEL, 1902-1967
Clérambard. 1950.
  Denny, N., tr. FOUF
  Variant title: The Count of
    Clerambard
  The Count of Clerambard. See
    Clérambard

BABE, THOMAS, 1941-
  Kid champion. 1975. WOQ4
  A prayer for my daughter.
    1977. BERS, BES77
  Rebel women. 1976. BES75

BABEL, ISAAC, 1894-1941
  Marya. 1967.
    Glenny, M., tr. GLE
    Glenny, M., and Shukman,
      H., trs. PLAN35
  Sundown. (1928)
    Senelick, L., tr. RV1
    Variant title: Zakat
  Zakat. See Sundown

BABO, JOSEPH MARIUS, 1756-1822
  Dagobert, der franken König.
    See Dagobert, king of the
    Franks
  Dagobert, king of the Franks.
    1779.
    Thompson, B., tr. BAT12
    Variant title: Dagobert, der
      franken König

BACHER, WILLIAM A.
  The snow goose. See Gallico,
    Paul. The snow goose (adapted
    by)

BACON, FRANK, 1864-1922.
  See Smith, Winchell, jt. auth.

BAGNOLD, ENID, 1889-1981
  Call me Jacky. 1968. PLAN34
  The chalk garden. 1955.
    BES55, COTKIT, THEA56
  National velvet. 1946. EMB2

BAHR, HERMANN, 1863-1934
  The concert. 1909.
    Morgan, B., tr. DID
    Variant title: Das konzert
  Das konzert. See The Concert

BAIZLEY, DORIS

Catholic girls. 1979. WES11/12

BAKER, E. IRENE, and DRUMMOND,
ALEXANDER MAGNUS
  A day in the vineyard. DRU

BAKER, ELIZABETH, 1879-
  Chains. 1909. DIG, PLAP1

BALDERSTON, JOHN LLOYD, 1889-
1954
  Berkeley square. 1926. BES29,
    GASB
  --See also Deane, Hamilton, jt.
    auth.

BALDWIN, JAMES, 1924-1987
  The amen corner. 1964. HARY,
    PATR
  Blues for Mister Charlie. 1964.
    GAT, OLIV

-- and HUMPHREY, HUBERT H.
  My childhood. BAYM

BALE, JOHN, 1495-1563
  God's promises. 1538? EVER
    Variant title: A tragedy or
      interlude manifesting the
      chief promises of God unto
      man
  King Johan. See King John
  King John. 1539? ARMS, CRE,
    FOUN, POLL
    Variant title: King Johan;
      Kynge Johan
  Kynge Johan. See King John
  A tragedy or interlude manifesting
    the chief promises of God unto
    man. See God's promises

BALL, ALAN EGERTON, 1944- ,
and BRADBURY, PAUL
  Professor Fuddle's fantastic fairy-
    tale machine. 1974. KAL4

BALL, DAVID
  Assassin. BALLE7
  Woyzeck (adapted by). See
    Büchner, Georg

BALLESTEROS, ANTONIO M.
  The best of all possible worlds.
    1966?
    Salerno, H., and Gross, S.,
      trs. WELL, WELT
  The hero.

Blue, R., tr. WELL

BALZAC, HONORE DE, 1799-1850
Mercadet. 1851. BOR

BANGS, JOHN KENDRICK, 1862-
1922
Katharine: a travesty. 1888.
NIN5

BANKS, JOHN, 1650?-1706
The Albion queens. 1704.
BELK14
Anna Bullen, or Virtue betray'd.
1682. BELK14
Variant titles: Anne Bullen;
Virtue betray'd
Anne Bullen. See Anna Bullen,
or, Virtue betray'd
The Earl of Essex. See The un-
happy favorite
The unhappy favorite, or, The
Earl of Essex. 1682. BELK14
Variant title: The Earl of Es-
sex
Virtue betray'd. See Anna Bullen,
or, Virtue betray'd

BARAKA, IMAMU AMIRI, pseud.
See Jones, LeRoi

BARBA, PRESTON ALBERT, 1883-
Au der lumpa parti. 1933. BUFF
Dié verrechelte rechler (adapted
from the novel by Charles C.
More). 1933. BUFF

BARBER, PHILIP WILLSON, 1903-
I, Elizabeth Otis, being of sound
mind. 1964. BALLE3

BARCA, PEDRO CALDERON DE
LA. See Calderón de la Barca,
Pedro

BARING, MAURICE, 1874-1945
The rehearsal. 1911? WEB

BARKENTIN, MARJORIE
Ulysses in Nighttown (adapted
from the novel Ulysses by
James Joyce). 1958. COTK

BARKER, GEORGE, 1913-
Rococo. WEAN

BARKER, HARLEY GRANVILLE.

See Granville-Barker, Harley Granville

BARKER, JAMES NELSON, 1784-1858
The Indian princess; or, La belle
sauvage. 1808. MOSS1
Superstition. 1824. GARX, HAL,
QUIJ, QUIK, QUIL, QUIM,
QUIN

BARLACH, ERNST, 1870-1938
Squire Blue Boll. 1926?
Ritchie, J., and Garten, H.,
trs. RITS

BARLOW, ANNA MARIE
Mr. Biggs. NEWA1

BARNARD, CHARLES, 1838-1920.
See De Mille, Henry Churchill, jt.
auth.

BARRAS, CHARLES M., 1826-1873
The black crook. 1866. MASW

BARRIE, SIR JAMES MATTHEW,
1860-1937
The admirable Crichton. 1903.
CHAR, CLKW, COTH, DUR,
RED, REDM, SALE, SPER,
TREBA, TREC2, TREE3,
TREI3, WARI
Dear Brutus. 1917. BROW,
COTKR, WATF2, WATI
The little minister. 1897.
BES94
Mary Rose. 1920. BES20
The old lady shows her medals.
1921. INGG, INGH
Shall we join the ladies? 1928.
WORL4
The twelve pound look. 1910.
BOGO, CONP, DAVI, MANK,
WEAT2
A well-remembered voice. 1918.
FULT
What every woman knows. 1908.
CEU, WATF1, WATI, WATO
The will. 1914. MIKL

BARRY, PHILIP, 1896-1949
The animal kingdom. 1932.
BES31, GAS
Foolish notion. 1945. BES44
God bless our home. See The
youngest
Here come the clowns. 1938.

BES38, GARU
Holiday. 1928. BES28,
  KEY, MAF, MERW, MOSK,
  MOSL
Hotel Universe. 1930. LEV,
  LEVE, THF, WATC2,
  WATI, WHI
In a garden. 1925. TUCD,
  TUCM
The joyous season. 1934.
  CATH, DAVI
Paris bound. 1927. BES27,
  GASB, QUIL, QUIM, QUIN
  Variant title: The wedding
The Philadelphia story. 1939.
  BES38, BROZ, GARZ,
  GATB2, WAIT, WAIU
Second threshold (revised by
  Robert E. Sherwood). 1951.
  BES50
Tomorrow and tomorrow. 1931.
  BES30
The wedding. See Paris bound
You and I. 1923. BES22, HAL
The youngest. 1924. BES24
  Variant title: God bless our
  home

BARTHOL, BRUCE
  Factperson (script and songs by).
    See San Francisco Mime
    Troupe. Factperson
  Factwino meets the moral majority
    (songs by). See San Francisco
    Mime Troupe. Factwino meets
    the moral majority
  Factwino vs. Armageddonman
    (music and lyrics by, except
    for "Blow this mother up" by
    Shabaka). See San Francisco
    Mime Troupe. Factwino vs.
    Armageddonman

BART-WILLIAMS, GASTON N.O.,
  1938-
  The drug. PIET

BAR-YOSEF, YOSEF
  Difficult people.
    Bernard, H., Oklans, D.,
    and Silk, D., trs. MOADE

BASS, KINGSLEY B.
  We righteous bombers. 1968.
    TUQT

BASSHE, EMANUEL JO, 1900-1939

Doomsday circus. See The dream
  of the dollar
The dream of the dollar. 1933.
  AME5
  Variant title: Doomsday circus

BATE, HENRY. See Dudley, Sir
Henry Bate

BATEMAN, MRS. SIDNEY FRANCES
  (COWELL), 1823-1881
  Self. 1857. MOSS2

BATES, ESTHER WILLARD, 1884-
  The two thieves. 1925? FED2

BAUDOIN, JEAN MARIE THEODORE
  (D'AUBIGNY, pseud.). See
  Caigniez, Louis Charles, jt. auth.

BAUER, WOLFGANG, 1941-
  Shakespeare the sadist. 1970.
  SHAK

BAUM, L. FRANK (Lyman Frank),
  1856-1919
  The wonderful wizard of Oz.
    See Brown, William F., The
    Wiz (adapted from)

BAUM, VICKI, 1888-1960
  Grand Hotel. 1930.
    Drake, W., tr. BES30, CEW
    Variant title: Menschen im
    hotel
  Menschen im hotel. See Grand
    hotel

BAUS, MANUEL TAMAYO Y. See
  Tamayo y Baus, Manuel

BAX, CLIFFORD, 1886-1962
  The rose without a thorn.
    1932. FAMB, PLAD
  Socrates. 1929. SIXD
  The Venetian. 1930. MYB

BAXTER, JAMES K., 1926-1972
  The wide open cage. 1959. CONZ

BAYARD, J. F. A. See Scribe,
  Augustin Eugène, jt. auth.

BAYON HERRERA, LUIS
  Santos Vega. 1913.
    Fassett, J., tr. BIES

BEACH, LEWIS, 1891-
The clod. 1914. BUR, GASB
The goose hangs high. 1924.
BES23, KEY

BEAUMARCHAIS, PIERRE AUGUSTIN
CARON DE, 1732-1799
The barber of Seville. See Le
barbier de Seville
Le barbier de Seville: ou, La
précaution inutile. 1775.
BOV, BOVE, BRN, STJ1,
ZDA
Bermel, A., tr. BERM, THV
Fowlie, W., tr. FOWL
Myrick, A., tr. MAU
Taylor, W., tr. CLF2
Variant title: The barber of
Seville
Figaro's marriage; or, One mad
day. See Le mariage de Figaro
Le mariage de Figaro. 1784.
BRE, SEA
Barzun, J., tr. BENR4
Variant titles: Figaro's mar-
riage; or, One mad day;
The marriage of Figaro
The marriage of Figaro. See Le
mariage de Figaro

BEAUMONT, FRANCIS, 1584-1616,
and FLETCHER, JOHN
Jovial Crew. See Brome, Richard
A king or no king. 1611. DPR2,
WALL
The knight of the burning pestle.
1610. ANG, BALD, BAS,
BAT14, BENY, BROC, DPR2,
HOW, NEI, OLH, OL12, ORNC,
SCI, SCJ, SPE, WHE, WINE
The maid's tragedy. 1611.
BAS, BROC, CLF1, CLKW,
DUN, MACJ, NEI, OLH, OLI2,
RUB, SCH, SCI, SCJ, SPE
Masque of the inner temple and
Gray's Inn. 1613. ETO
Philaster; or, Love lies ableeding.
1609. BAS, BELK18, BROC,
HARC47, HOW, HUD, LIE, MAX,
NEI, OLH, OLI2, PAR, SCH,
SCI, SCJ, SPE, TAT, TAU,
THA, WAT, WHE, WINE
--See also Fletcher, John, jt.
auth.

BECKETT, SAMUEL, 1906-
Act without words. 1957. ALLJ,

ALLK, ALLM, BROI, HAVH,
HAVHA, REIW, REIWE
Act without words II. 1960. DITA
All that fall. 1957. ALLJ, ALLK,
ALLM, CALD, CLL, CLLC,
SCNO, WEIM, WEIP, WEIS
Les beaux jours. See Happy days
Catastrophe (Programmed with
Ohio impromptu and What
where) 1983. BES83 (synopsis
only)
La dernière bande. See Krapp's
last tape
Embers. 1959. COK
En attendant Godot. See Waiting
for Godot
Endgame. 1957. SSSI
Beckett, S., tr. BLOC,
COTQ
Variant title: Fin de partie
Enough (Short story programmed
with Footfalls and Rockaby.)
1984. BES83 (synopsis only).
Fin de partie. See Endgame
Footfalls (Programmed with Enough
and Rockaby.) 1984. BES83
(synopsis only).
Happy days; ou, Les beaux jours.
1961. GOLD
Variant titles: Les beaux
jours; Ou les beaux jours
Krapp's last tape. 1958.
GOODE, OBG, SCNQ
Variant title: La dernière bande
Ohio impromptu (Programmed with
Catastrophe and What where.)
1981. BES83 (synopsis only).
Ou les beaux jours. See Happy
days.
Rockaby (Programmed with Enough
and Footfalls.) 1981. BES83
(synopsis only).
Waiting for Godot. 1952. BES55
Beckett, S., tr. NIL, SEVD
Variant title: En attendant
Godot
What where (Programmed with Ohio
impromptu and Catastrophe.)
1983. BES83 (synopsis only).

BECKINGTON, CHARLES
Hamlet the Dane, a Burlesque
Burletta. 1847. NIN2

BECQUE, HENRI, 1837-1899
Les corbeaux. 1882. BOR, GRA,
SEA, STJ2

Tilden, F., tr. MOSQ,
TREBA, TREBJ, TREC2,
TREE2, TREI2, WATL1
Variant titles: The crows;
The ravens; The vultures
The crows. See Les corbeaux
The Parisian woman. See La
Parisienne
La Parisienne. 1882.
Barzun, J., tr. BENS1,
BENT1
Vaughn, E., tr. COTKW
Variant titles: The Parisian
woman; The woman of
Paris
The ravens. See Les corbeaux
The vultures. See Les corbeaux
The woman of Paris. See La
Parisienne

BEECHER, CLARE. See Kummer,
Mrs. Clare (Beecher)

BEECHER, HARRIET ELIZABETH.
See Stowe, Mrs. Harriet (Beecher)

BEERBOHM, MAX, 1872-1956
A social success. 1913. BENT6

BEHAN, BRENDAN, 1923-1964
The hostage. 1958. BES60,
POP
The new house. 1958. RICJ
The quare fellow. 1954. SEVD
--See also McMahon, Frank.
Borstal Boy (adapted by)

BEHN, MRS. APHRA (AMIS), 1640-
1689
An alderman's bargain. See The
lucky chance, or, An alder-
man's bargain
The banished cavaliers. See
The rover, or, The banished
cavaliers
The emperor of the moon. 1687.
HUGH
The lucky chance, or An alder-
man's bargain. 1687. FEFO,
JEFF3
Variant title: An alderman's
bargain
The rover, or The banished
cavaliers. 1677. JEFF2
Variant title: The banished
cavaliers

BEHRMAN, SAMUEL NATHANIEL,
1893-1973
Amphitryon 38 (adapted from
Amphitryon 38, by Jean
Giraudoux). 1937. BES37,
CEW, THH
Biography. 1932. BES32, BROZ,
CET, GARU, MIJY, WAIT,
WARH, WARL, WHI
Brief moment. 1931. BES31
The cold wind and the warm.
1958. BES58
End of summer. 1936. BES35,
CLUR, FAMAL, GAS, WATS
I know my love (adapted from
Auprès de ma blonde by
Marcel Achard). 1949. BES49
Jacobowsky and the Colonel
(adapted from the play by
Franz Werfel). 1944. BES43,
GARZH
Jane (from the story by W.
Somerset Maugham). 1952.
BES51
No time for comedy. 1939.
BES38, CER, SIXL
Rain from heaven. 1934.
CHAN, CHAP, THF
The second man. 1927. CARP,
CARPA, GASB, MOSK, MOSL

-- and LOGAN, JOSHUA
Fanny (based on the trilogy
Marius, Fanny and César by
Marcel Pagnol) (music and
lyrics by Harold Rome). 1954.
THEA55

BEITH, JOHN HAY, 1876-1952. See
Hay, Ian, pseud.

BELASCO, DAVID, 1859-1931
La belle Russe. 1881. AMP18
The girl of the golden west.
1905. AMEM, MOSJ, MOSK,
MOSL
The heart of Maryland. 1895.
AMP18, BES94, CLA
Naughty Anthony. 1899. AMP18
The return of Peter Grimm. 1911.
BAK, MIL, MOSS3
The stranglers of Paris. 1881.
AMP18

-- and DE MILLE, HENRY CHURCHILL
The charity ball. 1889. AMP17

Lord Chumley, 1888. AMP17
Men and women. 1890. AMP17
The wife. 1887. AMP17

-- and FYLES, FRANKLIN
The girl I left behind me. 1893.
AMP18

-- and LONG, JOHN LUTHER
The darling of the gods. 1902.
BES99
Madame Butterfly. 1900. QUIJ,
QUIJR, QUIK, QUIL, QUIM,
QUIN, QUIO2

BELL, ROBERT, 1800-1867
Macbeth modernised (attributed
to). (1838) NIN2

BELLIDO, JOSE-MARIA, 1922-
Bread and rice or geometry in
yellow.
Lima, R., tr. WELL
Variant title: El pan y el
arroz o geometría en
amarillo
Football. 1963.
Turner, D., tr. BENA
El pan y el arroz o geometría
en amarillo. See Bread and
rice or geometry in yellow
Train to H... 1968?
Flores, R., tr. WELL
Variant title: Tren a F...
Tren a F... See Train to H...

BELLOW, SAUL, 1915-
The last analysis. 1964.
COTKI, GAT, SSTY
Orange souffle. 1965. RICK,
SANK
The wrecker. 1954? NEWW6

BELLVIS, GUILLEM DE CASTRO
Y. See Castro y Bellvis, Guillem

BENAVENTE, LUIS QUIÑONES DE.
See Quiñones de Benavente, Luis

BENAVENTE Y MARTINEZ, JACIN-
TO, 1866-1954
The bias of the world. See
The bonds of interest
The bonds of interest. 1907.
Underhill, J., tr. DID,
FLOS, MOSQ, WHI
Variant titles: The bias of

the world; Los intereses
creados; Interests created;
Vested interests
Las brujas del domingo. See The
witches' sabbath
His widow's husband. 1908?
Underhill, J., tr. MACN
Variant title: El marido de su
viuda
Los intereses creados. See The
bonds of interest
Interests created. See The bonds
of interest
Los malhechores de bien. 1905.
MARLI2
La malquerida. See The passion
flower
El marido de su viuda. See His
widow's husband
The nest of another. See El
nido ajeno
El nido ajeno. 1895. BRET
Variant title: the nest of
another
No fumadores. See No smoking
No smoking. 1904.
Underhill, J., tr. INGW
Variant title: No fumadores
The passion flower. 1913.
Underhill, J., tr. GARZH,
TUCG, TUCM, TUCN,
TUCO, WATI, WATL3
Variant title: La malquerida
Vested interests. See The bonds
of interest
The witches' sabbath. 1903.
Oliver, W., tr. COTP
Variant title: Las brujas
del domingo

BENEDICTO, JOAQUIN DICENTA Y.
See Dicenta y Benedicto, Joaquín

BENEDIX, RODERICH, 1811-1873
Eigensinn. See Obstinacy
Obstinacy. 1864.
Chambers, W., tr. BAT11
Variant title: Eigensinn

BENELLI, SEM, 1877-1949
L'amore dei tre re. See The
love of the three kings
La cena delle beffe. See The
jest
A Florentine wager. See The
jest
A fool there was. See The

The jest. 1919.
  Sheldon, E., tr. and adapter.
    BES19
  Variant titles: La cena delle
    beffe; A Florentine wager;
    A fool there was; The jes-
    ters' supper; The love
    feast; The love thief; The
    supper of pranks
The jesters' supper. See The
  jest
The love feast. See The jest
The love of the three kings.
  1910.
    Jones, H., tr. DIE
    Variant title: L'amore dei tre
    re
The love thief. See The jest
The supper of pranks. See The
  jest

BENET, STEPHEN VINCENT, 1898-
1943
  The devil and Daniel Webster.
    1939. BART, CARMI, HEIS

BENET I JORNET, JOSEP MARIA,
1940-
  La nau. See The ship
  The ship. 1969.
    Wellwarth, G., tr. WELV
    Variant title: La nau

BENGAL, BEN
  Plant in the sun. 1937? KOZ

BENNETT, ARNOLD, 1867-1931
  Flora. 1933. FIT
  The great adventure. 1913.
    CHU, COT

-- and KNOBLOCK, EDWARD
  Milestones. 1912. CEU, COD,
    DID, MART, MOD, PEN,
    TUCJ, WAGC4

BENNETT, CLARENCE
  A royal slave. 1898? AMP8

BENNETT, MICHAEL, 1943-1987
  A chorus line (conceived by).
    See Kirkwood, James and
    Dante, Nicholas. A chorus
    line

BENNETT, RICHARD R., 1936-
  The mines of sulphur, an

opera (music by). See Cross,
  Beverly. The mines of sulphur, an opera.

BENRIMO, JOSEPH HENRY, 1871-
1942. See Hazleton, George
Cochrane, jt. auth.

BENSON, ROBERT HUGH, 1871-1914
  The upper room. 191-? PRON

BENSON, MRS. SALLY, 1900-1972
  Junior miss (based on the book
    by). See Fields, Joseph and
    Chodorov, Jerome. Junior
    miss

BENTLEY, ERIC RUSSELL, 1916-
  Are you now or have you ever
    been: The investigation of
    show business by the Un-
    American Activities Committee,
    1947-48. (1972) RICK
  Celestina; or, The tragi-comedy
    of Calisto and Melibea. See
    Rojas, Fernando de. Celestina;
    or, The tragi-comedy of Calisto
    and Melibea (adapted by)
  Larry Parks' day in court. See
    Are you now or have you ever
    been... (excerpt)
  Mary Stuart. See Schiller,
    Johann. Mary Stuart (adapted
    by)

BENTON, JAMES GRANT, 1949-
  Twelf nite o wateva! 1974.
    KUMU

BENTON, ROBERT, 1932- See
Newman, David, jt. auth.

BEOLCO, ANGELO (called Ruzzante),
1502-1542
  Bilora, 1527?
    Hughes, B., and G., trs.
      CLF2
  Il reduce. See Ruzzante returns
    from the wars
  Ruzzante returns from the wars.
    1522?
    Ingold, A., and Hoffman, T.,
      trs. BENR1
    Variant title: Il reduce

BERCOVICI, ERIC
  The heart of age. 195-? NEWW4

BERG, GERTRUDE, 1900-1966
Me and Molly. 1948. BES47

BERGER, ADAM L.
It's time for a change. 1982.
YOUP

BERGMAN, HJALMAR, 1883-1931
Herr Sleeman kommer. See
Mr. Sleeman is coming
Mr. Sleeman is coming. 1917
Alexander, H., tr. SCAN1
Variant title: Herr Sleeman
kommer
The swedenhielms. 1925.
Alexander, H., and Jones,
L., trs. SCAN3

BERGMAN, INGMAR, 1918-
The seventh seal. 1956.
Anon. tr. KNO, KNOJ
Malmström, L., and Kushner,
D., trs. ABC
Smiles of a summer night. See
Wheeler, Hugh Callingham.
A little night music (plot and
characters based on the film
by)
Wild strawberries. (1957)
Malmström, L., and Kushner,
D., trs. BARK, BARL

BERKELEY, REGINALD CHEYNE,
1890-1935
The lady with a lamp. 1929.
FAO, PLAD
The white chateau. 1927. MART

BERKEY, RALPH. See Denker,
Henry, jt. auth.

BERKOFF, STEVEN, 1937-
Greek. 1980. WES 15/16

BERMANGE, BARRY, 1933-
No quarter. 1962. NEWE12
Scenes from family life. 1969.
MESS

BERNARD, JEAN-JACQUES, 1888-
1972
Arver's secret. See Le secret
d'Arvers
Glamour. 1924.
Boyd, E., tr. DIK2
Katzin, W., tr. KAT
Variant titles: L'Invitation

au voyage; The years
between
L'invitation au voyage. See
Glamour
Martine. 1922. RHO
Katzin, W., tr. KAT
Le secret d'Arvers. 1926. GRAF
Variant title: Arver's secret
The years between. See Glamour

BERNARD, KENNETH, 1930-
The unknown Chinaman. 1971.
BALLE10

BERNARD, LAWRENCE J.
Lars killed his son. 1935? TOD

BERNARD, PAUL. See Bernard,
Tristan, pseud.

BERNARD, TRISTAN (pseud. of
Paul Bernard), 1866-1947
L'anglais tel qu'on le parle.
1899. SET
Variant titles: English as it
is spoken; French without a
master
English as it is spoken. See
L'anglais tel qu'on le parle
French without a master. See
L'anglais tel qu'on le parle

BERNEY, WILLIAM. 1920-1961
See Richardson, Howard, jt. auth.

BERNHARD, EMIL (pseud. of Emil
Cohn), 1881-
The Marranos. 1935?
Meyer, B., and Arlet, V.,
trs. RUA

BERNSTEIN, HENRY, 1876-1953
Le secret. 1913. HART

BERNSTEIN, LEONARD, 1918-
Candide. See Hellman, Lillian.
Candide (music by)
West side story. See Laurents,
Arthur (music by)
Wonderful town. See Fields,
Joseph and Chodorov, Jerome.
Wonderful town (music by)

BERRIGAN, DANIEL J., S.J., 1921-
The trial of the Catonsville nine.
1971. BES70

BESIER, RUDOLF, 1878-1942
The Barretts of Wimpole
Street. 1930. BES30.
CEU, FAMAN, GATS, GOW,
GOWA, INGH, KNIE, PLAD,
PLAL2, SPER, THO
The virgin goddess. 1906.
MART

BETSUYAKU, MINORU, 1937-
Idō. See The move
The move. 1973.
Takaya, T., tr. TAK
Variant title: Idō

BETTI, UGO, 1892-1953
Corruption in the palace of
justice. 1949.
Reed, H., tr. CONO, COTR,
FREG, KERP
Satin, J., tr. SATI
Variant title: Corruzione
al palazzo di giustizia
Corruzione al palazzo di gius-
tizia. See Corruption in the
palace of justice
Crime on Goat Island. 1950.
Reed, H., tr. COTN
Variant titles: Delitto all'
Isola delle Capre; Island
of Goats
Delitto all' Isola delle Capre.
See Crime on Goat Island
Island of Goats. See Crime on
Goat Island
The queen and the rebels.
1951.
Reed, H., tr. BRZA, COTQ,
REV, ULAN
Variant title: La regina e gli
insorti
Le regine e gli insorti. See The
queen and the rebels

BEYNON, RICHARD
The shifting heart. 1957.
OBSE

BEZE, THEODORE DE, 1519-1605
Abraham sacrifiant. FOUR

BHASA, 4th cent. B.C.-1st cent.
A.D.
The dream of Vāsavadatta (sup-
posed author). 4th cent.
B.C.-1st cent. A.D.
Irwin, V., tr. IRW

Lal, P., tr. LAL
Woolner, A., and Sarup, L.,
trs. ALPJ, WEL
Variant title: The vision of
Vāsavadatta
The vision of Vāsavadatta. See
The dream of Vāsavadatta

BHAVABHUTI, 8th cent.
The later story of Rama. 8th
cent.
Josl, C., tr. WEL
Lal, P., tr. LAL
Variant title: Rama's later
history
Mālati and Mādhara. 8th cent.
Coulson, M., tr. THWI
Rama's later history. See The
later story of Rama

BIBIENA, BERNARDO CARDINAL
DOVIZI DA. See Dovizi da Biblena,
Bernardo Cardinal

BICKERSTAFFE, ISAAC, 1735?-1812?
The hypocrite (altered from the
play by Colley Cibber). 1768.
BELG1
Lionel and Clarissa (adapted from
Colley Cibber's "Nonjuror").
1768. BELG1, BELK21
Variant title: The school for
fathers
Love in a village. 1762. BELK21
Maid of the mill. 1765. BELK21
The padlock. BELC3
The plain dealer (altered from the
play by William Wycherley).
(1766) BELG1
The school for fathers. See
Lionel and Clarissa
The sultan. BELC1
Thomas and Sally. BELC2

BIGGERS, EARL DERR, 1884-1933
Seven keys to Baldpate. See
Cohan, George M. Seven keys
to Baldpate (based on the
novel by)

BILLETDOUX, FRANÇOIS, 1927-
Tchin-Tchin. See Michaels, Sydney. Tchin-Tchin (based on
the play by)

THE BIM-BOM TROUPE, 1953-1960.
See Afanasjew, Jerzy, jt. auth.

BINGHAM, J. See MacBeth, George

BIRD, ROBERT MONTGOMERY, 1806-1854
The broker of Bogota. 1834.
QUIJ, QUIK, QUIL, QUIM, QUIN
Caridorf; or, The avenger. 1827? AMP12
The cowled lover. 1827? AMP12
The gladiator. 1831. HAL, MONR
News of the night; or, A trip to Niagara. 1829. AMP12
'Twas all for the best; or, 'Tis all a notion. 1827? AMP12

BIRMELIN, JOHN, 1873-1950
Der gnopp (based on the play Ein knopf by Julius Rosen). 1935. BUFF
Em Docktor Fogel sei offis schtunn (based on the farce Dr. Kranichs, sprechstunde) 1935? BUFF

BIRMISA, GEORGE, 1924-
Georgie porgie. 1968. SME

BISSELL, RICHARD PIKE, 1913-1977. See Abbott, George, jt. auth.

BIZET, GEORGES, 1838-1875
Carmen. See Brook, Peter; Carrière, Jean Claude; and Cosntant, Marius. La tragédie de Carmen (adapted from the opera by)
Carmencita and the soldier (based on the opera Carmen). See Lipskeroff, Konstantin. Carmencita and the soldier

BJØRNSON, BJØRNSTJERNE, 1832-1910
Between the battles. 1858. Weingarten, J., tr. MACN
Variant title: Mellem slagene
Beyond human might. See Beyond our power
Beyond human power. See Beyond our power
Beyond our power. 1883.
Björkman, E., tr. TUCG
Hollander, L., tr. DIC
Variant titles: Beyond human might; Beyond human power;

Over evne; Pastor song
A gauntlet. 1883.
Edwards, O., tr. BAT17
Variant titles: A glove; En hanske
A glove. See A gauntlet
En hanske. See A gauntlet
Mellem slagene. See Between the battles
Over evne. See Beyond our power
Pastor song. See Beyond our power

BJÖRNSSON, ODDUR, 1932-
Jóólif. See Yolk-life.
Ten variations. (1968)
Tómasdóttir, G., tr. MNOI
Variant title: Tíu tilbrigði
Tíu tilbrigði. See Ten variations
Yolk-life.
Tómasdóttir, G., tr. MNOI
Variant title: Jóólif

BLADES, WILLIAM, 1824-1890
The printer's apprentice (tr. from Latin into German by).
See Anonymous plays. The printer's apprentice

BLAKE, WILLIAM, 1757-1827
The ghost of Abel. (1822) ENGL
King Richard the third. (1769-1778). ENGL

BLANCHARD, EDWARD LITT LEMAN, 1820-1889
Aladdin, or, Harlequin and the wonderful lamp. 1874. BOOA5
Variant title: Harlequin and the wonderful lamp
Harlequin and the wonderful lamp. See Aladdin

BLINN, WILLIAM.
Brian's song. 1971. TOB

BLITZSTEIN, MARC, 1905-1964
Another part of the forest (music by). See Hellman, Lillian. Another part of the forest
The cradle will rock. 1937. KOZ

BLOCK, TONI
You must stay to tea. 1948? RUA

BLOK, ALEKSANDR ALEKSANDRO-
VICH, 1880-1921
The puppet show. 1906.
Reeve, F., tr. REEV2

BOCK, JERRY, 1928-
The apple tree (jt. auth. and
music by). See Harnick,
Sheldon. The apple tree
Fiddler on the roof (music by).
See Stein, Joseph. Fiddler
on the roof
Fiorello! (music by). See
Weidman, Jerome and Abbott,
George. Fiorello!
She loves me (music by). See
Masteroff, Joe. She loves me

BODEL, JEAN. See Bodel, Jehan

BODEL, JEHAN, ca. 1167-ca. 1210
Le jeu de Saint Nicolas.
See The play of Saint Nicho-
las
The play of Saint Nicholas. ca.
1200.
Axton, R., and Stevens, J.,
trs. AXT
Mandel, O., tr. MARK
Variant title: Le jeu de Saint
Nicolas

BOIS ROBERT, FRANÇOIS. See
Bois-Robert, François Le Métel de

BOIS-ROBERT, FRANÇOIS LE
METEL DE, 1592-1662
L'amant ridicule. 1655. LAN

BOKER, GEORGE HENRY, 1823-
1890
The bankrupt. 1855. AMP3
Francesca da Rimini. 1855.
ELLI1, HAL, MADI, MASW,
MONR, MOSS3, QUIJ, QUIK,
QUIL, QUIM, QUIN, QUIO1
Glacus. 1886. AMP3
The world a mask. 1851. AMP3

BOLAND, BRIDGET, 1913-
Cockpit. 1948. PLAN1
Gordon. 1961. PLAN25
The prisoner. 1954. PLAN10
The return. 1953. PLAN9

BOLITHO, WILLIAM, pseud. See
Ryall, William Bolitho

BOLT, CAROL, 1941-
Buffalo jump. 1971. MAJ
Variant title: New year
country
Cyclone Jack (music by Paul
Vigna). 1972. KAL4
New year country. See Buffalo
jump

BOLT, ROBERT, 1924-
A man for all seasons. 1960.
BES61, CEQA, COTKIT,
COTR, FOUX, NEWE6
Vivat! Vivat Regina! 1972.
BES71

BOLTON, GUY REGINALD, 1884-
1961
Anastasia. See Maurette,
Marcelle. Anastasia (adapted
by)
Chicken feed. 1923. BES23
Variant title: Wages for
wives
Don't listen ladies! See Guitry,
Sacha. Don't listen ladies!
(adapted by)
Wages for wives. See Chicken
feed

-- and MIDDLETON, GEORGE
Adam and Eva. 1919. BES19

BOND, CHRISTOPHER, 1945-
Sweeney Todd. See Wheeler, Hugh
Callingham. Sweeney Todd, the
demon barber of Fleet Street
(based on Sweeney Todd: the
demon barber of Fleet Street)

BONNER, MARITA, 1905-
The purple flower. 1928. HARY

BONTEMPS, ARNA, 1903-1973
and CULLEN, COUNTEE
The St. Louis woman. 1946.
PATR

BOOTHE, CLARE, (married name
Clare Boothe Luce), 1903-1987
Kiss the boys good-bye. 1938.
BES38
Margin for error. 1939.
BES39, CER, FIR
The women. 1936. BES36, CET,
FAMK, GAS, SUB

BORCHERT, WOLFGANG, 1921-1947
Draussen von der Tür. See The
outsider
The man outside. See The out-
sider
The outsider. 1947.
Benedikt, M., tr. BENB
Variant titles: Draussen von
der Tür; The man outside

BORETZ, NICK
Shelter area. 1964. BALLE2

BORGEN, JOHAN, 1902-
The house.
Shaw, P., tr. MNON
Variant title: Huset
Huset. See The house

BORSOOK, HENRY
Three weddings of a hunchback.
1924. MAS1

BORUTA, KAZYS, 1905-1965
Baltaragio malūnas. See
Whitehorn's windmill
Whitehorn's windmill (dramatization of novel by E. Ignatavičius and S. Motiejūnas).
(1945)
Sabalis, K., and Abartis, C.,
tr. and adapt. GOLB
Variant title: Baltaragio
malūnas

BOSAKOWSKI, PHILIP A., 1946-
Bierce takes on the railroad.
1972. BALLE11
Chopin in space. 1984. WOQ4

BOSMAN, HERMAN CHARLES,
1905-1951
Street-woman. THI

BOSTON, STEWART
Counsellor extraordinary. 1971.
KAL1

BOTTOMLEY, GORDON, 1874-1948
Gruach. 1923. KRE

BOUCICAULT, DION, 1822-1890
After dark; or, Pardon--for a
price (adapted from a melo-
drama in three acts). 1868.
BAI, MELO
Belle Lamar. 1874. LEV, LEVE

Boursiquot. See The Colleen
Bawn
The Colleen Bawn; or, The brides
of Garryowen. 1860. ROWE
Variant title: Boursiquot
The Corsican brothers. 1852.
BOOA2, BOOM, VIC
Dot (adapted from The cricket
on the hearth, by Charles
Dickens). 1859. AMP1
Flying scud; or, A fourlegged
fortune. 1866. AMP1, CLA
Forbidden fruit. 1876. AMP1
London assurance. 1841. ASG,
BAI, BAT22, BENY, COTKIS,
MAX, MOSN, MOSO
Louis XI. 1855. AMP1
Mercy Dodd; or, Presumptive
evidence. 1869. AMP1
The octoroon; or, Life in
Louisiana. 1859. COY, GARX,
MASW, NILS, QUIJ, QUIK,
QUIL, QUIM, QUIN, SIG
Pardon--for a price. See After
dark
The poor of New York. 1857.
AMEM
Rip Van Winkle (adapted by).
See Anonymous plays. Rip
Van Winkle (as played by
Joseph Jefferson)
Robert Emmet. 1884. AMP1
The Shaughraun. 1874. BOOA2

-- and BYRON, HENRY JAMES
Lost at sea. 1869. KILG

BOURLET, KATHERINE, 15th cent.
The nativity (The Chantilly play).
15th cent.
Sanchez, E., and Robinson,
D., trs. and adapters.
ROBM

BOURSAULT, EDME, 1638-1701
Marie Stuard, reine d'Ecosse.
1683.
Paulson, M., adapter. FALE

BOVASSO, JULIE, 1930-
Schubert's last serenade. 1971.
OWE

BOWEN, JOHN GRIFFITH, 1924-
After the rain. 1967. BES67
The waiting room. 1970. RICK

BOWEN, MARGARET ELIZABETH
Crude and unrefined. 194-?
PROG

BOWEN, RICHARD, fl. 1570
Apius and Virginia (sometimes
attributed to). See Anonymous plays. Apius and Virginia

BOWLES, JANE AUER, 1917-1973
In the summer house. 1953.
BES53

BOWMAN, EDWARD
Salve Regina. 1969. CON2

BOX, MURIEL, 1905-
Angels of war. 1935? FIN

BOX, SYDNEY, 1907-1983
The woman and the walnut tree.
1935? FIN

BOYD, SUSAN
St. Mael and the Maldunkian
penguins. (1977) NEWP

BOYER, CLAUDE, 1618-1698
Le faux Tonaxare. See
Oropastes
Oropaste; ou, Le faux Tonaxare.
See Oropastes
Oropastes. 1662.
Lockert, L., tr. LOCU
Variant titles: Le faux
Tonaxare; Oropaste

BRACCO, ROBERTO, 1862-1943
I fantasmi. See Phantasms
Phantasms. 1906.
St. Cyr, D., tr. TUCG
Variant title: I fantasmi

BRACKENRIDGE, HUGH HENRY,
1748-1816
The battle of Bunkers-hill.
1776? MOSS1, WORN
The death of General Montgomery,
in storming the City of Quebec. 1777. PHI

BRADBURY, PAUL. See Ball, Alan
Egerton, jt. auth.

BRADDON, MARY ELIZABETH, 1837-
1915

Lady Audley's secret. See
Hazlewood, Colin Hazlewood.
Lady Audley's secret (from
the novel by)

BRADDON, RUSSELL, 1921-
Naked island. 1960. PLAN22

BRADFORD, ROARK, 1896-1948
Ol' man Adam and his chillun.
See Connelly, Marc. The
green pastures (based on the
novel by)

BRADLEY, JOHN, 1944-
Irish stew. 1979. THUG

BRAMBLE, MARK, 1950-
See Stewart, Michael, jt. auth.

BRANCH, WILLIAM, 1927-
In splendid error. 1954. HARY,
PATR
A medal for Willie. 1951. KINN

BRAND, MILLEN, 1906-
The outward room. See Kingsley,
Sidney. The world we make
(based on the novel by)

BRANNER, HANS CHRISTIAN, 1903-
1966
The judge. 1951.
Roughton, A., tr. CONT
Variant title: Søskende
Søskende. See The judge
Thermopylae. (1958)
Shaw, P., tr. MNOD

BRECHT, BERTOLT, 1898-1956
Die ausnahme und die regel.
See The exception and the
rule
Baal. 1922.
Bentley, E., and Esslin, M.,
trs. SOK
The Caucasian chalk circle.
1954.
Anon. tr. BLON, CLN, KNIG
Bentley, E., tr. ALLJ, BAUL,
BENSB2, BES62, BLOND,
COTQ, DEAS, DIT, ESS,
FEL, GOU2, HAVH, HAVHA,
JOHO, LITC, MALI2, MIJB,
NIL, REIL, REIO, REIT,
REIWE, SMA
Bentley, E., and Apelman, M.,

trs. COTL, GROV, WEIS, WEIW
Variant title: Der kaukasische Kreidekreis
Dreigroschenoper. See The threepenny opera
The exception and the rule. 1930?
    Bentley, E., tr. NEWD55
    Variant title: Die ausnahme und die regel
Fear and misery of the Third Reich. See The private life of the master race
Furcht und Elend des Dritten Reiches. See The private life of the master race
Galileo. 1947.
    Laughton, C., tr. BENS2, HILP, RAI, TREBJ, TRIA
    Sauerlander, W., and Manheim, R., trs. BEAS
    Variant title: Das Leben des Galilei
The good woman of Setzuan. 1943.
    Bentley, E., tr. ALLM, AUG, BARK, BARL, BLOC, BRIX, BRIY, BRIZ, BUR, DOT, GOLD, REIN, REIP, SHRO, TREBJ, VANV2, WEIM
    Variant title: Der gute mensch von Sezuan
Der gute mensch von Sezuan. See The good woman of Setzuan
Herr Puntila und sein knecht matti. See Puntila and his hired man
Der kaukasische Kreiderkreis. See The Caucasian chalk circle
Das Leben des Galilei. See Galileo
Life of Galileo. See Galileo
Die massnahme. See The measures taken
The measures taken. 1930.
    Bentley, E., tr. BENT6
    Variant title: Die massnahme
Mother Courage. 1941.
    Bentley, E., tr. ANT, BENSB2, BENT2, BES62, BLOC, BONC, CLL, CLLC, COTS, GOLD, HEA, JOHN, KER, KERN, KERO, LITJ, WAIW
    Hays, H., tr. NEWD41
    Manheim, R., tr. NORG, SEVT, WEIP
    Variant titles: Mother

Courage and her children; Mutter Courage und ihre kinder
Mother Courage and her children. See Mother Courage
Mutter Courage und ihre kinder. See Mother Courage
A penny for the poor. See The threepenny opera
The private life of the master race. 1938.
    Bentley, E., tr. KERO, TREBA, TREC2, TREE2, TREI2
    Variant titles: Fear and misery of the Third Reich; Furcht und Elend des Dritten Reiches
Puntila and his hired man. 1940.
    Nellhaus, G., tr. COTKI
    Variant title: Herr Puntila und sein knecht matti
Saint Joan of the stockyards. 1932.
    Jones, F., tr. BENS3, DUK
    Variant title: Die heilige Johanna der schlachthöfe
The seven deadly sins of the lower middle classes. 1933.
    Auden, W., and Kullman, C., trs. GOO
    Variant title: Die sieben todsunden der kleinbürger
Die sieben todsunden der kleinbürger. See The seven deadly sins of the lower middle classes
The threepenny opera (music by Kurt Weill). 1928.
    Bentley, E., tr. ASF
    Vesey, D., and Bentley, E., trs. BENS1, BENT1
    Variant titles: Dreigroschenoper; A penny for the poor
Das verhor des Lukullus. 1939? FEFH2

-- and WEILL, KURT.
He who says yes. (1955)
    Nellhaus, G., tr. PLAAB

-- and HAUPTMANN, ELISABETH.
The threepenny opera (based on The beggar's opera by John Gay; music by Kurt Weill).
    Manheim, R., and Willett, J., trs. BES75, SCNQ, SSSI

BREEN, RICHARD, and SCHNIBBE, HARRY

"Who ride on white horses,"
the story of Edmund Campion.
1940. THEC

BREIT, HARVEY, 1909?-1968
See Schulberg, Budd, jt. auth.

BRENDLE, THOMAS ROYCE, 1889-
Die hoffning. 19-? BUFF
Die mutter. 1934. BUFF

BRETON, ANDRE, 1896-1966, and
SOUPAULT, PHILIPPE
If you please. 1920.
Wellwarth, G., tr. BEN
Variant title: S'il vous
plaît
S'il vous plaît. See If you
please

BRETON DE LOS HERREROS,
MANUEL, 1796-1873
Muérete ¡y verás! 1837. BRET

BREUER, LEE, 1937-
Hajj; the performance. 1983.
WOQ3
A prelude to death in Venice.
1979. NEWQ
The red horse animation. 1970.
THG

BRICUSSE, LESLIE, 1931- , and
NEWLEY, ANTHONY
Stop the world--I want to get
off (book, lyrics and music
by). 1962. BES62

BRIDGERS, ANN PRESTON. See
Abbott, George, jt. auth.

BRIDIE, JAMES, pseud. See
Mavor, Osborne Henry

BRIEUX, EUGENE, 1858-1932
The aim of the law. See La
robe rouge
False gods. 1909.
Fagan, J., tr. TUCG
Variant title: La foi
La foi. See False gods
The letter of the law. See La
robe rouge
The red robe. See La robe
rouge
La robe rouge. 1900. GRA
Reed, F., tr. DIC, DIK2, WHI

Variant titles: The aim of the
law; The letter of the law;
The red robe
The three daughters of M. Dupont.
See Les trois filles de M. Du-
pont
Les trois filles de M. Dupont.
1897. BER, BOR
Variant title: The three
daughters of M. Dupont

BRIGADERE, ANNA, 1861-1933
Maija and Paija. (1921)
Raudsepa, I., tr. GOLB
Variant title: Maija un Paija
Maija un Paija. See Maija and
Paija

BRIGHOUSE, HAROLD, 1882-1958
Hobson's choice. 1916. MART,
TUCD

BRITTON, KENNETH PHILLIPS and
HARGRAVE, ROY
Houseparty. 1928? LEV, LEVE

BROCH, HERMANN, 1886-1951
The atonement. 1934.
Wellwarth, G., and Rotherman,
H., trs. WELG

BROME, RICHARD, 1590-1652
The antipodes. 1638. GAY3,
KNOW
A jovial crew. 1641.
BELK21, LAWS, OLH, OL12
A mad couple well matched. 1653?
KNOW, WALL

BRONTË, CHARLOTTE, 1816-1855
Jane Eyre. See Jerome, Mrs.
Helen (Burton). Jane Eyre
(based on the novel by)

BROOK, PETER, 1925- , CARRI-
ERE, JEAN CLAUDE, and CONSTANT,
MARIUS
La tragédie de Carmen; a full-
length musical in one act;
(adapted from the opera Carmen; music by Georges Bizet).
1982. BES83

BROOKE, HENRY, 1703?-1783
The deliverer of his country.
See Gustavus Vasa, or, The
deliverer of his country

Gustavus Vasa, or, The deliverer
of his country. (1739) BELK18
Variant title: The deliverer
of his country

BROOKS, HARRY, 1876-
See Malleson, Miles, jt. auth.

BROPHY, BRIGID, 1929-
The waste disposal unit. 1964.
RICJ

BROUGH, ROBERT BARNABAS,
1828-1860. See Brough, William,
jt. auth.

BROUGH, WILLIAM, 1826-1870
The field of the cloth of gold.
1868. BOOA5
Perdita; or, The royal Milkmaid.
1856. NIN3

-- and BROUGH, ROBERT BARNA-
BAS
The enchanted isle; or "Raising
the wind" on the most ap-
proved principles. 1848.
BOOA5
Variant title: "Raising the
wind" on the most approved
principles
"Raising the wind" on the most
approved principles. See The
enchanted isle; or, "Raising
the wind" on the most approved
principles

-- and HALLIDAY, ANDREW
The area belle. 1864. BOOA4

BROUGHAM, JOHN, 1810-1880
The duke's motto; or, I am here!
1862. AMP14
Much ado about a merchant of
Venice. 1869. NIN5
Po-ca-hon-tas. See Pocahontas;
or, The gentle savage
Pocahontas; or, The gentle
savage. 1855. AMPA, BAT20,
MONR
Variant title: Po-ca-hon-tas

BROWER, BROCK, 1931-
A little to the left. 1959. PAJ

BROWN, AL
Back to back. 1981. WES9

BROWN, CHARLES, fl. 1814.
See Keats, John, jt. auth.

BROWN, DAVID PAUL, 1795-1875
Sertorius; or, The Roman patriot.
1830. MOSS2

BROWN, JOHN, 1715-1766
Barbarossa. (1755) BELK10

BROWN, LENNOX JOHN, 1934-
Devil Mas'. 1974. CARR

BROWN, WILLIAM F., 1928-
The Wiz (adapted from The
Wonderful Wizard of Oz by
L. Frank Baum; music and
lyrics by Charlie Smalls).
1975. GREAA

BROWN, WILLIAM WELLS, 1814-1884
The escape; or, A leap to freedom. 1858. HARY, RAVA

BROWNE, FELICITY
The family dance. 1976. PLAN46

BROWNE, MAURICE, 1881-1955
See Nichols, Robert Malise Boyer,
jt. auth.

BROWNE, PORTER EMERSON, 1879-
1934
The bad man. 1920. BES20

BROWNE, ROBERT F. GORE. See
Gore-Browne, Robert F.

BROWNE, THEODORE, 1910-
Natural man. 1937. HARY

BROWNE, WYNYARD, 1911-1964
The holly and the ivy. 1950.
PLAN3

BROWNING, ROBERT, 1812-1889
A blot in the 'scutcheon. 1843.
ASH, GRE, HARC18, MOSN,
MOSO, TAT
In a balcony. 1884. GREC2
King Victor and King Charles.
KAU
Pippa passes. 1841. BAI

BRUCE, RICHARD, 1905-
Sahdji, an African ballet. 1927.
LOC

BRUNDAGE, JOHN HERBERT,
1926- See Herbert, John (pseud.
of)

BRUNO, GIORDANO, 1548-1600
Il candelaio. See The candle
bearer
The candle bearer. 16th cent.
Hale, J., tr. BENSA
Variant title: Il candelaio

BRUNSON, BEVERLY
A bastard of the blood. 19-?
NEWW10

BRUST, ALFRED, 1891-1934
Die Wölff. See The wolves
The wolves. 1922.
Ritchie, J., and Garten, H.,
trs. RITS
Variant title: Die Wölff

BRYDEN, BILL, 1942-
Willie Rough. 1973. PLAN43

BRYKS, RACHMIL, 1912-1974
A cat in the ghetto. See
Wincelberg, Shimon. Resort
76 (based on)

BUCHANAN, GEORGE, 1506-1582
Jephté; ou, Le voeu. 1552?
FOUR

BUCHNER, GEORG, 1813-1837
Danton's death. 1836.
Holmstrom, J., tr. BENT5
Lustig, T., tr. LUST
Spender, S., and Rees, G.,
trs. BENS1, TREB,
TREC1, TREE1, TREI1
Variant title: Dantons tod
Dantons tod. See Danton's death
Leonce and Lena. 1911.
Bentley, E., tr. BENS3,
ESS
Woyzeck. 1879.
Ball, D., adapter. 1913.
(First performance of adap-
tation, 1972; music by Susan
Hesse Keller). MIMN
Hoffman, T., tr. BENT1,
SEVT
Mueller, C., tr. COTKIR,
COTL, COTQ, NORG
Sorell, W., tr. ASF
Schnitzler, H., and Ulman, S.,

trs. NEWD50
Wellwarth, G., tr. WELT
Variant title: Wozzeck
Wozzeck. See Woyzeck

BUCK, PEARL S. 1892-1973
Will this earth hold? INGA

BUCKHURST, LORD. See Sackville,
Thomas

BUCKINGHAM, GEORGE VILLIERS,
1628-1687.
The rehearsal. 1671. BELK15,
FAL, LEV, LEVE, MAND,
MANF, MOSE1, NET, REST,
STM

BUCKSTONE, JOHN BALDWIN, 1802-
1879
Luke the labourer; or, The lost
son. 1828. BAI, KILG, MOR

BUECHNER, GEORG. See Büchner,
Georg

BUENAVENTURA, ENRIQUE, 1925-
In the right hand of God the
father. 1960.
Oliver, W., tr. OLIW

BUERO VALLEJO, ANTONIO, 1916-
The concert at Saint Ovide.
1962.
Anderson, F., tr. HOLT
Variant title: El concierto
de San Ovidio
El concierto de San Ovidio. See
The concert at Saint Ovide
The dream weaver. 1952.
Oliver W., tr. COTP
Variant title: La tejedora
de sueños
Irene, o el tesoro. 1954.
MARLI2
La tejedora de sueños. See The
dream weaver

BULGAKOV, MIKHAIL ALFANASE-
VICH, 1891-1940
Days of the Turbins. 1926.
Daglish, R., tr. CLKX
Lyons, E., tr. LYK
Reeve, F., tr. REEV2
Variant title: Last of the
Turbins
Dead souls (based on the novel by

Nikolai Vasilevich Gogol).
1980.
    Cole, T., tr. and adapter.
    NEWQ
Ivan Vasilievich. (1935-36)
    Senelick, L., tr. RVI
    Variant title: Ivan Vasil'-
        evich
Last of the Turbins. See
    Days of the Turbins

BULKLEY, A. M.
    The crown of light. 1934.
    SEVE

BULLINS, ED, 1935-
    The corner. 1972. KINH
    Dialect determinism. 1965. OWE
    Electronic nigger. 1968.
        HOGI, NEWA3, STS
    The fabulous Miss Marie. 1971.
        NEWL
    Gentleman caller. 1970. BLA,
        OLIV
    Goin' a Buffalo. 1966. HARY
    How do you do. 1969. JON
    In the wine time. 1968. PATR,
        SCNPL
    Jo Anne! 1981. WES9
    A son, come home. 1968.
        BAIC, BAIE, BAIG, CLLC,
        CLN, KEN, LITC, LITI
    The taking of Miss Janie. 1975.
        BES74, FAMAD

BULLOCK, MICHAEL, 1918-
    Not to Hong Kong. 1972(?)
        ALI

BULWER-LYTTON, EDWARD GEORGE
EARLE LYTTON, 1803-1873
    The conspiracy. See Richelieu
    The lady of Lyons; or, Love and
        pride. 1838. ASG, STA,
        TAT, TAU
        Variant title: Love and pride
    Love and pride. See The lady of
        Lyons
    Money. 1840. BAT16, BOOA3,
        ROWE
    Richelieu; or, The conspiracy.
        1839. BAI, BOOA1, CROS,
        DUR, MAX, MOSN, MOSO
        Variant title: The conspiracy

BUNCE, OLIVER BELL, 1828-1890
    Love in '76. 1857. MOSS3

BURGESS, JOHN, and MAROWITZ,
CHARLES
    The Chicago conspiracy (based
        on a script by Jonathan Cross).
        1972. MARR

BURK, JOHN DALY, 1775?-1808
    Bunker-Hill; or, The death of
        General Warren. 1797. MONR
        Variant title: The death of
            General Warren
    The death of General Warren. See
        Bunker-Hill

BURKE, CHARLES ST. THOMAS,
1822-1854
    Rip Van Winkle. 1850. BAT19,
        MOSS3
        See also Anonymous plays.
        Rip Van Winkle (as played by
        Joseph Jefferson)

BURKE, INEZ M.
    Two races. RIR

BURNAND, FRANCIS COWLEY,
1836-1917
    Antony and Cleopatra; or, History
        and her-story in a modern nilo-
        metre. 1866. NIN4
    The rise and fall of Richard III;
        or, A new front to an old
        Dicky. 1868. NIN4

BURNEY, CHARLES, 1726-1814
    Cunning man. 1766. BELC2

BURNHAM, BARBARA, 1900-
    Children in uniform (tr. and
        adapted by). See Winsloe,
        Christa. Children in uniform

BURNS, ALAN, 1929- , and
MAROWITZ, CHARLES
    Palach. 1970. MARR

BURRILL, MARY BURRILL
    They that sit in darkness. 1919.
        HARY

BURROWS, ABE. See Burrows,
Abram S.

BURROWS, ABRAM S., 1910-1985
    Cactus flower. 1965. BES65,
        MOST

-- WEINSTOCK, JACK, and GIL-
BERT, WILLIE
How to succeed in business
without really trying (based
on the book by Shepherd
Mead) (music by Frank
Loesser). 1961. BES61
--See also Swerling, Jo, jt. auth.

BURTON, HELEN. See Jerome,
Mrs. Helen (Burton)

BUSH, JOSEF, 1933-
French gray. 1966. NEWA2

BUSH, THOMAS
Santiago; a drama in five acts.
1866. WAGN1

BUTLER, RACHEL BARTON, d.
1920
Mamma's affair. 1920. BES19

BUZO, ALEXANDER, 1944-
The front room boys. 1969.
FOUAC

BY, WILLIAM
Richard III travestie. (1816)
NIN1

BYRNE, MRS. DOLLY. See Varesi,
Gilda, jt. auth.

BYRNE, JOHN, 1940-
The loveliest night of the year.
1976. DEC
Variant title: Threads
Threads. See The loveliest night
of the year

BYRNE, MURIEL ST. CLARE, 1895-
See Sayers, Dorothy Leigh, jt. auth.

BYRNE, SEAMUS, 1904-1968
Design for a headstone. 1950.
HOGE

BYRON, GEORGE GORDON, 1788-
1824
Cain. 1821. BARG, ENGL,
KOH2
Harlequin Friday and the King
of the Caribee Islands. See
Robinson Crusoe
Heaven and earth. 1821?
KOH2

Manfred. 1817. ABRJ, BERN,
ENGL, GREB2, HAPT2, HARC18,
KAU, SML
Robinson Crusoe, or Harlequin
Friday and the King of the
Caribee Islands. 1860.
BOOA5
Variant title: Harlequin
Friday and the King of the
Caribee Islands
Sardanapalus. (1821) ENGL
--See also Boucicault, Dion, jt.
auth.

CABANA, AUGUSTIN MORETO Y.
See Moreto y Cavaña, Augustin

CAIGNIEZ, LOUIS CHARLES, 1762-
1842, and BAUDOUIN, JEAN MARIE
THEODORE (d'Aubigny, pseud.)
La pie voleuse; ou, La servante
de Palaiseau. See Payne,
John Howard. Trial without
jury (adapted from)

CALDERON DE LA BARCA, PEDRO,
1600-1681
El alcalde de Zalamea. See The
mayor of Zalamea
Amar después de la muerte.
See Love after death
Beishazzar's feast. 1632.
MacCarthy, D., tr. BAT4
Variant title: La cena de
Baltasar
La cena de Baltasar. See
Belshazzar's feast
The constant prince. 1629?
MacCarthy, D., tr. CLF2,
STA
Variant title: El principe con-
stante
El gran teatro del mundo. See
The great theater of the world
Elvira. See No siempre lo peor
es cierto
The great theater of the world.
1642.
Singleton, M., tr. FLOR
Variant title: El gran teatro
del mundo
Guárdate del agua mansa. See
Keep your own secret
Keep your own secret. 1649.
Fitzgerald, E., tr. ROB

Variant title: Guárdate del
 agua mansa
Life a dream. See La vida es
 sueño
Life is a dream. See La vida es
 sueño
Love after death. 1651?
 Campbell, R., tr. BENR3
 Variant title: Amar después
 de la muerte
El mágico prodigioso. See The
 wonder-working magician
The mayor of Zalamea. 1651.
 Starkie, W., tr. SSTW
 Variant title: El alcalde de
 Zalamea
El médico y su honra. 1635.
 MACU
No siempre lo peor es cierto.
 1648? HILL
 Variant titles: Elvira; The
 worst not always true
El postrer duelo de España. See
 Payne, John Howard. The last
 duel in Spain (adapted from)
El príncipe constante. See The
 constant prince
Such stuff as dreams are made
 of. See La vida es sueño
La vida es sueño. 1635. ALP,
 MARLI1
 Campbell, R., tr. BENR3,
 BENSB1, MALI1, MALN1,
 NORG1, NORI
 Fitzgerald, E., tr. DRA1,
 HARC26, PLAB1
 Huberman, E., and E., trs.
 FLOS, HOUE, TREB
 MacCarthy, D., tr. ALPF,
 MAU, TAV
 Variant titles: Life a dream;
 Life is a dream; Such stuff
 as dreams are made of
The wonder-working magician.
 1637?
 Shelley, P., tr. BENR3
 Variant title: El mágico pro-
 digioso
The worst not always true. See
 No siempre lo peor es cierto

CALDWELL, BEN, 1937-
 All white caste. (1971) KINH
 The devil and Otis Redding.
 See The king of soul
 The first militant minister. See
 Prayer meeting

The king of soul; or, The devil
 and Otis Redding. (1969)
 RAVA
Prayer meeting; or, The first
 militant minister. (1969)
 BLA, JON

CALDWELL, ERSKINE, 1903-1987
See Kirkland, Jack, jt. auth.

CAMERON, KENNETH, 1931-
 The hundred and first. 1963?
 NEWA1
 Papp. 1969? SCV

CAMPBELL, BARTLEY, 1843-1888
 Fairfax. 1879. AMP19
 The galley slave. 1879. AMP19
 My partner. 1879. AMP19,
 CLA
 The Virginian. 1873. AMP19
 The white slave. 1882. AMP19

CAMPBELL, MARION GURNEY and
ATHAS, DAPHNE SPENCER
 Sit on the earth. 19-? OBSE

CAMERON, RONALD, 1944-
 Masque (an adaptation of James
 Reaney's play "One-man
 masque"). 1972. KAL4

CAMPBELL, ALISTAIR, 1926-
 When the bough breaks. 1969.
 CON2

CAMPBELL, PADDY, 1944-
 Hoarse muse. 1974. WIM

CAMPBELL, WILLIAM EDWARD
MARCH. See March, William (pseud.)

CAMPION, THOMAS, 1567-1620
 Lords' masque. 1613. ETO

CAMPISTRON, JEAN GALBERT
DE, 1656-1723
 Andronic. See Andronicus
 Andronicus. 1685.
 Lockert, L., tr. LOCR
 Variant title: Andronic
 Tiridate. 1691.
 Lockert, L., tr. LOCU

CAMPTON, DAVID, 1924-
 Incident. 1965. PLAAB
 Soldier from the wars returning.

1963. PLAJ1

Then... 1960. THOD

CAMUS, ALBERT, 1913-1960
Caligula. 1945.
    Anon. tr. FOUA
    Gilbert, S., tr. BLOC,
      KNIH, MORW, MORXB,
      RAI, TAUJ
    O'Brien, J., tr. and adapter.
      BES59
Le malentendu. 1944. PUCC

CANALE, RAYMOND
The jingo ring. 1971. BRIN

CANDIDUS, CAROLI, ESQ.
The female consistory of Brock-
    ville (a melodrama in three
    acts). (1856) WAGN1

ČAPEK, JOSEF, 1887-1927.
See Čapek, Karel, jt. auth.

ČAPEK, KAREL, 1890-1939
R. U. R. (Rossum's universal
    robots). 1923.
    Anon. tr. BART, BROZ,
      STAU
    Selver, P., tr. BES22,
      BROF, BROG, BRR3,
      CALN1, COTH, DIE,
      DIK1, HAV, HAVD, HAVE,
      HORN, HUDT, MAD, NAGE,
      PROX, TREBA, TREI2,
      TUCG, TUCM, TUCN,
      TUCO, WATI, WATL4,
      WATO
    Selver, P., and Playfair, N.,
      trs. CEW, CONG, COTKJ,
      TREC2, TREE2

-- and ČAPEK, JOSEF
Adam stvoritel. See Adam the
    creator
Adam the creator. 1927.
    Round, D., tr. MOSG, MOSH
    Variant title: Adam stvoritel
And so ad infinitum. 1921.
    Davis, O., tr. and adapter.
      GARZH
    Selver, P., tr. CHA, CHAN,
      CLKW, INTE, SSTF
    Variant titles: The insect
      comedy; The insect play;
      The life of the insects; The
      world we live in; Ze zivota

honyzu
The insect comedy. See And
    so ad infinitum
The insect play. See And so
    ad infinitum
The life of the insects. See
    And so ad infinitum
The world we live in. See And
    so ad infinitum
Ze zivota honyzu. See And so
    ad infinitum

CAPOTE, TRUMAN, 1924-1984
The grass harp. 1953. WISF

CARBALLIDO, EMILIO, 1925-
The day the lions got loose. See
    The day they let the lions loose
The day they let the lions loose.
    1963.
    Oliver, W., tr. OLIW
    Variant titles: The day the
      lions got loose; El día que
      se soltaron los leones
El día que se soltaron los leones.
    See The day they let the
    lions loose
I also speak of the rose. See
    I too speak of roses
I too speak of roses. 1966.
    Oliver, W., tr. WOOG
    Variant titles: I also speak
      of the rose; Yo también hablo
      de la rosa
Yo también hablo de la rosa. See
    I too speak of roses

CAREY, HENRY, 1687?-1743
Chrononhotonthologos. 1734.
    BELC2
The contrivances. 1715. BELC4

CARMINES, AL, 1936-
Promenade (music by). See
    Fornés, María Irene.
    Promenade

CARRETTE, LOUIS, 1913-
See Marceau, Félicien, pseud.

CARRIÈRE, JEAN CLAUDE
La tragédie de Carmen. See
    Brook, Peter, jt. auth.

CARROLL, PAUL VINCENT, 1900-
1968
Shadow and substance. 1937.

BES37, CALM, CEW, DUR,
FIG, MOSH
The strings, my Lord, are
false. 1943? NEWR1
The white steed. 1939. BES38

CARROLL, ROBERT, pseud. See
Alpert, Hollis

CARTER, STEVE, 1929-
Nevis mountain dew. 1978.
BES78

CARTER-HARRISON, PAUL. See
Harrison, Paul Carter

CARY, FALKLAND, L., 1897- .
See King, Philip, jt. auth.

CASALE, MICHAEL, 1949-
Cold. GUTR

CASALIS, JEANNE DE. See
De Casalis, Jeanne

CASELLA, ALBERTO, 1891-
Death takes a holiday. 1929.
Ferris, W., tr. and adapter.
BES29
Variant title: La morte in
vacanze
La morte in vacanze. See
Death takes a holiday

CASEY, WARREN, 1935-
Grease. See Jacobs, Jim, jt.
auth.

CASINO, JESUS. See Sicam,
Gerônimo [D.], jt. auth.

CASONA, ALEJANDRO, pseud.
See Rodríguez Alvarez, Alejandro

CASTRO Y BELLVIS, GUILLEM DE,
1569-1631
Exploits of the Cid. See Las
mocedades del Cid
Las mocedades del Cid. 1621.
ALP, MACU
Anon. tr. BENR4
Variant title: Exploits of the
Cid; The youthful adven-
tures of El Cid
The youthful adventures of El
Cid. See Las mocedades del
Cid

CASULE, KOLE, 1921-
Darkness. 1962.
Čašule, I., tr. MIG

CAVAN, ROMILLY, 1914?-1975
All my own work. 1958. OBSE

CAVANA, AUGUSTIN MORETO Y.
See Moreto y Cavaña, Augustín

CAVERHILL, ALAN, 1910-
See Melville, Alan, pseud.

CAYZER, CHARLES WILLIAM,
1869-?
David and Bathshua. 1911?
KOH2

CENTLIVRE, SUSANNA, 1667-1723
A bold stroke for a wife.
1718. BELK6
The busy body. See The busy
body
The busy body. 1709. BELK8
The wonder. 1714. BELK4,
FEFO
The wonder! A woman keeps a
secret. See The wonder

CERVANTES SAAVEDRA, MIGUEL DE,
1547-1616
The cave of Salamanca. 1615?
Honig, E., tr. TREB
Jagendorf, M., tr. CLF2
Variant title: La cueva de
Salamanca
La cueva de Salamanca. NOR
--See also The cave of
Salamanca.
Los dos habladores (atribuído a).
NOR
Entremés de refranes (atribuído a).
NOR
Entremés del retablo de las mara-
villas. MACU
La guarda cuidadosa. See The
vigilant sentinel
The jealous old man. 1611.
Starkie, W., tr. SSTW
Variant title: El viejo celoso
La Numance. See La Numancia
La Numancia. 1585. ALP
Campbell, R., tr. BENR3
Variant titles: La Numance;
The siege of Numantia
Pedro de Urdemalas. See Pedro,
the artful dodger

Pedro, the artful dodger. 1615.
Starkie, W., tr. SSTW
Variant title: Pedro de
Urdemalas
The siege of Numantia. See
La Numancia
El viejo celoso. See The jealous
old man
The vigilant sentinel. 158-?
Flores, A., and Liss, J., trs.
FLOS
Variant title: La guarda
cuidadosa

CÉSAIRE, AIMÉ, 1913-
A season in the Congo. (1968)
CARR

CHAMBERS, CHARLES HADDON,
1860-1921
The tyranny of tears. 1899.
BOOA3

CHAMBERS, JANE, 1937-1983
A late snow. 1974. HOF

CHANCEL, LA GRANGE. See
La Grange-Chancel

CHANDEZON, LEOPOLD (Léopold,
pseud.) and CUVELIER DE TYRE,
JEAN GUILLAUME ANTOINE
Mazeppa; ou, Le cheval Tartare.
See Payne, John Howard.
Mazeppa; or, The wild horse
of Tartary (adapted from)

CHANG, PAO-HUA. See Chao,
Chung, jt. auth.

CHAO, CHUNG; CHANG, PAO-
HUA; and CHUNG, YI-PING
Yesterday. (1961)
Shapiro, S., tr. MESE

CHAPIN, HAROLD, 1886-1915
Augustus in search of a father.
1910. WEB
The new morality. 1920. MART

CHAPMAN, GEORGE, 1559?-1634
Bussy D'Ambois. 1604. BAS,
BROC, DPR2, HAPRA1,
HAPRB1, MAKJ, NEI, NES,
ORNT, RYL, SPE
The revenge of Bussy D'Ambois.
1610? WALL

The widow's tears. 1612. DPR2

-- JONSON, BEN, and MARSTON,
JOHN
Eastward ho! 1605. BROC,
GAY2, OLI1, RUB, SCH, SCI,
SCJ, SPE, WALL
Variant title: Eastward hoe
Eastward hoe. See Eastward ho!

CHAPMAN, JOHN, 1927-
Simple spymen. 1958. PLAJ2

CHAPMAN, ROBERT HARRIS, 1919-
See Coxe, Louis O., jt. auth.

CHARLES, MARTIE
Black cycle. KINH
Job security. 1970. HARY

CHARNIN, MARTIN, 1934-
Annie (lyrics by). See Meehan,
Thomas. Annie, a musical in
two acts

CHASE, MARY COYLE, 1912-
Bernardine. 1952. BES52,
THEA53
Harvey. 1944. BES44, COLT,
CORB, GARU, GATB3, MIJY,
MOST
Mr. Thing. See Mrs. McThing
Mrs. McThing. 1952. BES51
Variant title: Mr. Thing

CHAUSEE, PIERRE CLAUDE
NIVELLE DE LA. See La Chaussée,
Pierre Claude Nivelle de

CHAYEFSKY, PADDY, 1923-1981
[given name: SIDNEY]
The dybbuk from Woodhaven.
See The tenth man
Gideon. 1961. BES61, GARSA
The latent heterosexual. 1966.
SANK
Marty. 1953? BLAH, BLOC,
DAVM, DOD, HEIS, MANK,
PLAU, SHER, STS
The passion of Josef D. 1964.
BES63
The tenth man. 1959. BES59,
CEQ, CES
Variant title: The dybbuk
from Woodhaven

CHEKHOV, ANTON PAVLOVICH,

Fen, E., tr. CAPU, CLKY,
   GOLH, HOGF, REIN,
   REIP, SANE, SIXB, WEIP
Garnett, C., tr. BAIC,
   BAIE, BAIG, BLOND, BLOO,
   DOWS, LEG
Guerney, B., tr. GUE
MacAndrew, A., tr. GARZG,
   MABA
Magarshack, D., tr. BENSB2
Young, S., tr. FREG,
   REIL, SCNR
Uncle Vanya. 1897.
   Anon. tr. CLN, MESS, SILK,
      SILN, SILO, SILQ
   Corrigan, R., tr. COTO,
      COTQ, COTY
   Covan, J., tr. MOS
   Fell, M., tr. BARB, BENQ,
      HARB, MIL, SATI, SATJ,
      WATA, WATI, WATL2
   Garnett, C., tr. WEIS, WEIW
   Garrett, C., tr. HAPO
   Hampton, C., tr. PLAN39
   Magarshack, D., tr. MAP
   Young, S., tr. CLM
   Variant title: The wood de-
      mon
A wedding; a joke in one act
   1890.
   Bentley, E., tr. ALL, FEFL
   Roberts, C., tr. ROE
   Variant titles: A joke in one
      act; Svadba; The wedding
The wedding. See A wedding
The wood demon. See Uncle
   Vanya

CH'EN, PAI-CHEN, 1908-
   Luan-shih nan-nü. See Men
      and women in wild times
   Men and women in wild times.
      (1939)
      Gunn, E., tr. TWEH (Acts I
         and III only)
      Variant title: Luan-shih
         nan-nü

CHEN-CHIN HSIUNG. See Hsiung,
Cheng-chin

CHENG, TEH-HUI (CHENG, KUANG-
TSU, pseud.)
   The soul of Ch'ien-nu leaves her
      body.
      Liu, J., tr. LIU

CHETHAM-STRODE, WARREN, 1897-
   Background. 1950. PLAN4
   Sometimes even now. 1933.
      FAMD

CHI, CHUN-HSIANG
   The orphan of Chao.
      Liu, J., tr. LIU

CHIA, AH. See Ah, Chia

CHIARELLI, LUIGI, 1884-1947
   La maschera ed il volto. See
      The mask and the face
   The mask and the face. 1916.
      Vic Beamish, N., tr. INTE
      Variant title: La maschera ed
         il volto

CHI-HUANG, LI. See Li, Chi-
huang

CHI-YUAN, MA. See Ma, Chih-
yuan

CHIKAMATSU (SUGIMORI NOBU-
MORI). See Chikamatsu, Monzaemon

CHIKAMATSU, MONZAEMON (pseud.
of Sugimori Nobumori), 1653-1725
   The courier for Hades. See The
      courier for hell
   The courier for hell. 1711.
      Keene, D., tr. ANDF, ANDI
      Variant titles: The courier
         for Hades; Meido No
         Hikyaku
   Fair ladies at a game of poem-
      cards. 1705.
      Miyamora, A., and Nichols,
         R., trs. CLF1
   Meido No Hikyaku. See The
      courier for hell
   Yūgiri and the Straits of Naruto.
      See Anonymous Plays.
      Love letter from a licensed
      quarter (based on the first
      act of)

CHILDRESS, ALICE, 1920-
   Trouble in mind. 1955. PATR
   Wedding band: a love/hate story
      in black and white. 1972.
      NEWVM
   Wine in the wilderness. 1969.
      HARY, SUB

CHILTON, NOLA
Naïm (adapted from the novel,
The lover, by A. B.
Yehoshua). (1978?)
Auerbach, J., tr. MOADE

CHINA PEKING OPERA TROUPE
The red lantern. See Anony-
mous Plays. The red lan-
tern (revised collectively by)
--See also Wong, Ou-hung, and
Ah, Chia

CHLUMBERG, HANS, 1897-1930
The miracle at Verdun. 1931.
Crankshaw, E., tr. FAMC
Leigh, J., tr. CHA, CHAN
Variant title: Wunder um
Verdun
Wunder um Verdun. See The
miracle at Verdun

CHODOROV, EDWARD, 1904-
Decision. 1944. BES43
Kind lady (adapted from a story
by Hugh Walpole). 1935.
CART, FREE
Oh, men! oh, women! 1953.
THEA54

CHODOROV, JEROME, 1911-
See Fields, Joseph, jt. auth.

CHORELL, WALENTIN, 1912-
The sisters. 1955.
Morduch, T., tr. FIL
Variant title: Systrarna
Systrarna. See The sisters

CHOU, SHU-JEN. See Lu, Hsun,
pseud.

CHOU, WEI-PO; TUNG, YANG-
SHENG; and YEH, HSIAO-NAN
The artillery commander's
son. 1979.
Dubinsky, S., and Gunn, E.,
trs. TWEH
Variant title: P'ao-ping szu-
ling ti erh-tzu
P'ao-ping szu-ling ti erh-tzu.
See The artillery commander's
son

CHRISTIE, AGATHA (MILLER)
1891-1976
Witness for the prosecution.

1953. BES54, FAMO, RICI,
THEA55

CHRISTIE, CAMPBELL, 1893-1963
See Christie, Dorothy, jt. auth.

CHRISTIE, DOROTHY, 1896- ,
and CHRISTIE, CAMPBELL
Carrington, V. C. 1953. FAMO
His excellency. 1950. PLAN4

CHUNG, YI-PING, See Chao, Chung,
jt. auth.

CHUN-HSIANG, CHI. See Chi,
Chün-hsiang

CHURCH, MRS. VIRGINIA WOODSON
(FRAME), 1880-
What men live by. 1924?
CHU, LAW, SRYG

CHURCHILL, CARYL, 1938-
The ants. 1962. NEWE12
Cloud 9. 1979. BES80
Vinegar Tom. 1976. PLABE1

CIBBER, COLLEY, 1671-1757
The careless husband. 1704.
BELK8, JEFF4, MOSE1, NET
The double gallant. 1707.
BELK13
Flora. BELC4
Hob; or, The country wake (some-
times attributed to). See
Dogget, Thomas. Hob; or,
The country wake
The hypocrite. See Bickerstaffe,
I. The hypocrite (altered by)
The lady's last stake. 1707.
BELK19
Love makes a man. 1700. BELG2
Love's last shift; or, The fool in
fashion. 1696. BELK17,
JEFF3, MAND, MANF, TUQ
Non-juror. See Bickerstaffe, I.
Lionel and Clarissa (adapted
by)
The provoked husband; or, A
journey to London (from an
unfinished play by John Van-
brugh). 1727? BAT15,
TICK
The refusal. 1721. BELK11
She wou'd and she wou'd not.
1702. BELK6
Ximena. 1718. BELK14

CIBBER, THEOPHILUS, 1703-1758.
See Jevons, Thomas, jt. auth.

CIZMAR, PAULA
Candy and Shelley go to the
desert. 1983. WOMB

CLARK, BRIAN, 1932-
Whose life is it anyway? 1978.
BES78, BEST

CLARK, JOHN PEPPER, 1935-
Song of a goat. (1964). LITT

CLARK, MRS. MABEL MARGARET
(COWIE). See Storm, Lesley,
pseud.

CLARKE, WILLIAM KENDALL, 1911?-
1981
The ghost patrol (based on a
story by Sinclair Lewis).
195-? INGB

CLAUDEL, PAUL, 1868-1955
L'annonce faite à Marie. 1912.
HART, RHO
Sill, L., tr. DIK1, HAV,
TREBA, TREBJ, TREI3,
TUCG
Variant title: The tidings
brought to Mary
L'histoire de Tobie et de Sara.
See Tobias and Sara
The satin slipper; or, The
worst is not the worst. 1919?
O'Connor, J., tr. HIBB
Variant title: Le soulier de
satin; ou, Le père n'est
pas toujours sûr
The tidings brought to Mary.
See L'annonce faite à Marie
Tobias and Sara. 1942?
Fiske, A., tr. HAYE
Variant title: L'histoire de
Tobie et de Sara

CLAUSEN, SVEN, 1893-1961
The bird of contention. 1933?
Thornton, P., and A., trs.
CONT
Variant title: Kivflugen
Kivflugen. See The bird of con-
tention

CLEMENS, SAMUEL LANGHORNE,
1835-1910

The king and the duke. See
Fergusson, Francis. The
king and the duke (based on
the novel Huckleberry Finn by)

CLEMENTS, COLIN CAMPBELL,
1894-1948
Columbine. 1922? SHAY
The siege. 1922? SHAY
--See Ryerson, Florence, jt.
auth.

CLINCH, CHARLES POWELL, 1797-
1880
The spy, a tale of the neutral
ground. 1822. AMP14

CLOUGH, DAVID, 1952-
In Kanada. 1982. PLACI

COBB, JAMES, 1756-1818
Ramah Droog. INCA6
The wife of two husbands. INCA6

COBURN, D. L., 1938-
The gin game. 1976. BES77

COCTEAU, JEAN, 1891-1963
Antigone. See Sophocles.
Antigone (adapted by)
The Eiffel Tower wedding party.
See Les mariés de la Tour
Eiffel
The infernal machine. See La
machine infernale
Intimate relations. 1938.
Frank, C., tr. BENS3
Variant titles: Les parents
terribles; The storm within
La machine infernale. 1934.
PUCC
Anon. tr. BOYN, SANO
Wildman, C., tr. BENS1, BOY,
INTE, LOCL, LOCLA,
LOCLB, TUCN, TUCO
Variant title: The infernal
machine
Les mariés de la Tour Eiffel.
1921.
Benedikt, M., tr. BEN
Fitts, D., tr. MIJE, NEWD37
Variant titles: The Eiffel
Tower wedding party; The
wedding on the Eiffel Tower
Les parents terrible. See Intimate
relations
Orphée. 1926.

Wildman, C., tr. BLOC
The storm within. See Intimate
relations
The wedding on the Eiffel
Tower. See Les mariés de
la Tour Eiffel

COFFEE, LENORE (MRS. W. J.
COWEN), 1900?- , and COWEN,
WILLIAM JOYCE
Family portrait. 1939. BES38,
PLAN1

COFFEY, CHARLES, 1700?-1745.
See Jevon, Thomas, jt. auth.

COHAN, GEORGE MICHAEL, 1878-
1942
Pigeons and people. 1933.
BES32, WAGC3
Seven keys to Baldpate (based
on the novel by Earl Derr
Biggers). 1913. BESO9,
CART, CONG

COHEN, BENNETT
Tequila. 1980. WES8

COHN, EMIL, 1881-1948
See Bernhard, Emil, pseud.

COKAIN, SIR ASTON, 1608-1684
Trappolin suppos'd a prince.
See Tate, Nahum. A duke
or no duke (adapted from)

COKAYNE, SIR ASTON. See
Cokain, Sir Aston

COLE, TOM
Dead souls. See Bulgakov,
Mikhail Alfanasevich

COLERIDGE, SAMUEL TAYLOR,
1820-1894
Remorse. 1813. ENGL, KAU

COLETTE, SIDONIE GABRIELLE,
1873-1954
Gigi. See Loos, Anita. Gigi
(from the novel by)
--See also Akalaitis, J.
Dressed like an egg (based
on the writings of)

COLLEY, PETER
The Donnellys. 1974. WIM

COLLINGS, PIERRE. See Gibney,
Sheridan, jt. auth.

COLLINS, ARTHUR, 1863-1932.
See Wood, J. Hickory, jt. auth.

COLLINS, KATHLEEN
The brothers. 1982. WOMB
In the midnight hour. 1980.
WOMA

COLLINS, MARGARET, 1909-
Love is a daisy. COLI
3 filosofers in a fire-tower.
COLI

COLLINSON, LAURENCE, 1925-
Thinking straight. 1975. HOM

COLMAN, GEORGE, 1732-1794
Bonduca (altered from Beaumont
and Fletcher). 1778. BELG3
Comus (altered from the masque
by John Milton). (1772)
BELC4
The deuce is in him. 1762.
BELC1
The English merchant. 1767.
INCA9
The jealous wife. 1761. BELG3,
NET, NIC
The musical lady. 1762. BELC2
Polly Honeycombe. 1760.
BELC3, BEVI

-- and GARRICK, DAVID
The clandestine marriage. 1766.
BAT15, HAN, MAND, MANF,
MOR, MOSE2, TWE

COLMAN, GEORGE, the younger,
1762-1836
The iron chest. 1796. BOO
John Bull. 1803. BOOA3, BOOM
Who wants a guinea? 1805.
INCA3

COLTON, JOHN, 1889-1946, and
RANDOLPH, CLEMENCE
Rain (based on the story, Miss
Thompson, by W. Somerset
Maugham). 1922. BES22,
GARU, GATB1, TUCD

COLUM, PADRIAC, 1881-1972
The land. 1905. CAP
Thomas Muskerry. 1910. MOSN

COMDEN, BETTY, 1919-   , and
GREEN, ADOLPH
   Applause (music by Charles
      Strouse; lyrics by Lee
      Adams). 1970. BES69,
      RICM
   Wonderful town (lyrics by).
      See Fields, Joseph and
      Chodorov, Jerome. Won-
      derful town

COMPANY THEATRE ENSEMBLE.
See Opper, Don Keith (script by)

CONDON, FRANK
See Sossi, Ron, jt. auth.

CONE, THOMAS, 1947-
   Cabistique. 1974. BRIQ

CONGREVE, WILLIAM, 1670-1729
   The double dealer. 1693.
      BELK13
   Love for love. 1695. ABRJ,
      AUB, BELK8, BENY, CARP,
      CARPA, FIS, JEFF3, KRM,
      MIL, SALR, STM, TWE
   The mourning bride. 1697.
      BELK3
   The old batchelor. 1693.
      BELK2
   The way of the world. 1700.
      ABRF, ABRH, ALLK, ARB1,
      ASH, BARG, BELK11, BENY,
      BLON, BLOND, BROJ, BROK,
      COL1, COTKIR, DEAP, DEAR,
      FAL, FOUB, GAY4, GOS,
      GOSA, GREB1, GREC1,
      HAVHA, JEFF4, KER, KRM,
      KRON, LIE, MAND, MANF,
      MANH, MAX, MEN, MOR,
      MORR, MOSE1, NET, RES,
      REST, ROET, RUB, SHAI1,
      SMO, SPD, SPDB, SPEF1,
      STM, TAT, TAU, TRE,
      TREA2, TREB, TREC1,
      TREE1, TREI1, TUP, TUQ,
      TWE, WALJ, WILS, WOOE,
      WRIR

CONN, STEWART, 1936-
   Play donkey. 1977. DEC

CONKLE, ELLSWORTH PROUTY,
1899-
   Minnie Field. 1928. GASB
   Prologue to glory. 1938.

BES37, FEE, SWI

CONNELLY, MARCUS COOK, 1890-
   The green pastures (based on
      the novel, Ol' man Adam and
      his chillun, by Roark Brad-
      ford). 1930. BES29, CET,
      CHA, CHAN, CHAP, CONN,
      CORD, CORE, CORF, COTE,
      DUR, FUL, GAS, GATB1,
      GRD, KNIC, KNID, KNIE,
      LOOA, LOOB, LOOC, LOOD,
      LOOE, MADG, MOSK, MOSL,
      PROI, SIM, SIXD, TRE,
      TREA1, TREBA, TREC2,
      TREE3, TREI3, WATE
   The wisdom tooth. 1926. BES25
   --See also Elser, Frank Ball;
      Kaufman, George S., jt. auths.

CONRAD, JOSEPH, 1857-1924
   One day more. 1905. BENT3

CONRAD, ROBERT TAYLOR, 1810-
1858
   Jack Cade, the captain of the
      commons. 1835. MOSS2

CONSTANT, MARIUS
   La tragédie de Carmen. See
      Brook, Peter, jt. auth.

CONWAY, HIRAM J.
   The battle of Stillwater; or, The
      maniac. 1840. AMP14

COOK, MICHAEL, 1933-
   Colour the flesh the colour of
      dust. 1972. KAL1
   The head, guts and soundbone
      dance. 1973. MAJ

COOKE, BRITTON, d.1923
   The translation of John Snaith.
      1923. MAS1

COOPER, GILES, 1918-1966
   Everything in the garden.
      1962. NEWE7
   Happy family. 1966. NEWE11
   The object. 1964. NEWE12
   Out of the crocodile. 1963.
      PLAN27
   Unman, Wittering, and Zigo. 1950.
      ENG

COOPER, JAMES FENIMORE, 1789-

1851
  The wept of the wish-ton-wish
  (based on the novel by).
  See Anonymous plays. The
  wept of the wish-ton-wish

COOPER, JOAN "CALIFORNIA"
  Lovers. (1979) CEN

COOPER, SUSAN, 1935- , and
CRONYN, HUME
  Foxfire; a play with songs in
  two acts (music and col-
  laboration for lyrics by
  Jonathan Holtzman). 1980.
  BES82

COPEAU, JACQUES, 1879-1949
  The little poor man. 1925?
    Thurman, B., tr. HAYE
    Variant title: Le petit
    pauvre
  Le petit pauvre. See The
  little poor man

COPPEE, FRANÇOIS EDOUARD
JOACHIM, 1842-1908
  Le luthier de Crêmone. See
    The violin maker of Cremona
  The violin maker of Cremona.
    1877.
    Jerome J., tr. BEAC
    Lord, I., tr. COOK1
    Variant title: Le luthier
    de Crêmone

COPPEL, ALEC, 1909?-1972
  I killed the count. 1937. SIXP

CORLETT, WILLIAM, 1938-
  Tinker's curse. 1968. PLAN34

CORMACK, BARTLETT, 1898-1942
  The racket. 1927. BES27

CORMON, EUGENE, 1811-1903.
See D'Ennery, Adolphe, jt. auth.

CORNEAU, PERRY BOYER
  Masks. 1922? LAW

CORNEILLE, PIERRE, 1606-1684
  Le cid. 1636. LYO, SCN, SER,
    SERD, STJ1
    Anonymous tr. GAUB
    Cooper, F., tr. CLF2, CROV,
    GREA, MAU, SMN, TAV

Fowlie, W., tr. FOWL,
  TREB
Schevill, J., tr. HOUE
Schevill, J., Goldsby, R.,
  and A., trs. BENR4
  Variant title: The cid
The cid. See Le cid
Cinna; or, The mercy of Augustus.
  1639.
  Landis, P., tr. KRE
Horace. 1639. SER
The liar. See Le menteur
Le menteur. 1642. LYO
  Variant title: The liar
Polyeucte. 1640. LYO, SER
  Constable, T., tr. HARC26,
  LOGG, STA

CORNEILLE, THOMAS, 1625-1709
  Ariadne. 1672.
    Lockert, L., tr. LOCU
    Variant title: Ariane
  Ariane. See Ariadne
  Le comte d'Essex. See The earl
    of Essex
  The earl of Essex. 1678.
    Lockert, L., tr. LOCR
    Variant title: Le comte
    d'Essex
  Laodice. 1668.
    Lockert, L., tr. LOCR
  Maximian. 1662.
    Lockert, L., tr. LOCU
  Timocrate. See Timocrates
  Timocrates. 1656.
    Lockert, L., tr. LOCU
    Variant title: Timocrate

CORNISH, ROGER
  Open twenty-four hours. 1968.
    HAVL, WELT

CORWIN, NORMAN LEWIS, 1910-
  Ann Rutledge. 1942? LOVR
  El capitan and the corporal.
    1942? NAGE
  Good heavens. 1941. BRS,
    LOOD
  My client Curley. 1942. WATS
  The odyssey of Runyon Jones.
    1942? PROD
  Radio primer. 1942. WATS
  They fly through the air.
    1939? PROC
  We hold these truths. 1941.
    BROZ

COTTER, JOSEPH S., SR.,
1861-1949
    Caleb the degenerate. 1903.
      HARY

COULTER, JOHN, 1888-1980
    The house in the quiet glen.
      1937. WAGN3
    Riel. 1950. MAJ, PENJ

COURTELINE, GEORGES (pseud.
of Georges Moinaux), 1860-1929
    Les boulingrin. See These
      cornfields
    These cornfields. 1898.
      Bentley, E., tr. BENSC
      Variant title: Les boulingrin

-- and LEVY, JULES
    La commissionaire est bon en-
      fant. See The commissioner
      has a big heart
    The commissioner. See The
      commissioner has a big
      heart
    The commissioner has a big
      heart. 1899.
      Bermel, A., tr. FOUF, THV
      Variant titles: The commis-
        sioner; La commissionaire
        est bon enfant

COWARD, NOEL PIERCE, 1899-
1973
    Blithe spirit. 1941. BES41,
      FULT, KRM, TREBA, TREC2,
      TREE3, TREI3, WALB, WARI
    Brief encounter. 1946. GREAB
    Cavalcade. 1931. CEU, VOAD
    Come into the garden Maud.
      1966. RICJ
    Conversation piece. 1934. SEV
    Design for living. 1932.
      BES32, SIXH
    Easy virtue. 1925. MOSO
    Fumed oak. 1936. ANDE,
      COOP
    Hay fever. 1925. MOD, MYB
    Noel Coward in two keys. 1974.
      BES73
    Point Valaine. 1934. SIXP
    Private lives. 1930. CHA, CHAN,
      CHAR, COLT, COTKIT, FOUX,
      LONO, PLAL2
    A song at twilight. 1966. RICK
    The vortex. 1924. TUCD,
      TUCM

Ways and means. 1935. WATE
The young idea. 1923. MART

COWEN, MRS. LENORE (COFFEE).
See Coffee, Lenore

COWEN, RON, 1944-
    Summertree. 1967. HOLP

COWEN, WILLIAM JOYCE. See
Coffee, Lenore, jt. auth.

COWIE, MABEL MARGARET, 1903-
1975. See Storm, Lesley, pseud.

COWLEY, ABRAHAM, 1618-1677
    Cutter of Coleman-street.
      1661. GAY4

COWLEY, MRS. HANNAH (PARK-
HOUSE), 1743-1809
    Albina, Countess Raimond. 1779.
      BELG14
    The belle's stratagem. 1780.
      BAT15
    Which is the man? INCA10

COXE, LOUIS O., 1918- , and
CHAPMAN, ROBERT HARRIS
    Billy Budd (based on the novel
      by Herman Melville). 1949.
      BES50, COTX, DAVI, GARW,
      HAVG, SSST, SSSU
      Variant title: Uniform of
        flesh
    Uniform of flesh. See Billy Budd

COYLE, MC CARTHY
    The root. 1973. BALLE12

COYNE, JOSEPH STIRLING, 1803-
1868
    How to settle accounts with your
      laundress. 1847. BOOA4,
      BOOM

CRABBE, KERRY LEE
    The last romantic. 1975.
      PLAN45

CRANE, STEPHEN, 1871-1900
    The bride comes to yellow sky.
      See Agee, James. The bride
      comes to yellow sky (based on)

CRAVEN, FRANK, 1880-1945
    The first year. 1920. BES20

CREBILLON, PROSPER JOLYOT DE,
1674-1762
Rhadamiste et Zénobie. 1711.
BRE
Lockert, L., tr. LOCR
Variant title: Rhadamistus
and Zenobia
Rhadamistus and Zenobia. See
Rhadamiste et Zénobie

CREGAN, DAVID, 1931-
Transcending. 1966. CONB

CREIGHTON, ANTHONY, 1920-
See Osborne, John, jt. auth.

CRISP, JACK H.
A wife in the land. 1968. WIM

CRISP, SAMUEL, d.1783
Virginia. 1754? BELK18

CRISTOFER, MICHAEL, 1946-
The shadow box. 1975. BES76

CROCKER, CHARLES TEMPLETON
The land of happiness. 1917.
BOH3

CROMMELYNCK, FERNAND, 1885-
1970
Le sculpteur de masques. See
The sculptor of masks
The sculptor of masks. 1911.
ANTM
Dormoy-Savage, N., tr.
ANTM
Variant title: Le sculpteur
de masques

CRONYN, HUME, 1911-
Foxfire; a play with songs in two
acts. See Cooper, Susan, jt.
auth.

CROPPER, MARGARET
Two sides of the door. 1925.
FED2

CROSS, BEVERLEY, 1931-
The mines of sulphur, an opera
(music by Richard R. Bennett).
1965. PLAN30

CROSS, JONATHAN
The Chicago conspiracy.
See Burgess, John, and

Marowitz, Charles. The Chicago conspiracy (based on a
script by)

CROTHERS, RACHEL, 1871-1958
As husbands go. 1931. BES30,
CHA
Expressing Willie. 1924. COT
He and she. 1911. QUIJ, QUIJR,
QUIK, QUIL, QUIM, QUIN
Variant title: The Herfords
The Herfords. See He and she
Let us be gay. 1929. BES28
A man's world. 1909. PLAAD
Mary the third. 1923. BES22,
DIG, TUCD, TUCJ, TUCM
Nice people. 1921. BES20, MOSJ,
MOSK, MOSL, QUI
Susan and God. 1937. BES37
When ladies meet. 1932. BES32

CROUSE, RUSSEL, 1893-1966.
See Lindsay, Howard, jt. auth.

CROWLEY, MART, 1935-
The boys in the band. 1968.
BES67, FAMAH, GARTL,
RICIS

CROWNE, JOHN, 1640?-1712
The destruction of Jerusalem, pt.
2. 1677. DOA
Sir Courtly Nice; or, It cannot
be. 1685. JEFF2, SUM

CRUZ CANO Y OLMEDILLA, RAMON
(FRANCISCO) DE LA, 1731-1794
Las tertulias de Madrid. NOR

CULBERTSON, ERNEST HOWARD
Rackey. 1919. LOC

CULLEN, COUNTEE PORTER, 1903-
1946. See Bontemps, Arna, jt. auth.

CUMALI, NECATI, 1921-
Dry summer. 1967.
Özdoğru, N., tr. HALM
Variant title: Susuz Yaz
Susuz Yaz. See Dry summer

CUMBERLAND, RICHARD, 1732-
1811
Battle of Hastings. 1778. BELG6
The box-lobby challenge. 1794.
INCA5
The brothers. 1769. BELG5

The carmelite. 1784. BELG5,
INCA5
The choleric man. 1774. BELG6
False impressions. 1797. INCA5
The fashionable lover. 1772.
BELG6, MOSE2
The imposters. 1789. INCA6
The mysterious husband. 1783.
INCA5
The natural son. 1784. BELG6,
INCA5
The West Indian. 1771. BELG5,
BENY, HAN, MAND, MANF,
MIL, MOR, NET

CUMMINGS, EDWARD ESTLIN, 1894-
1962
him. 1928. BENS2, DUK

CUNEY-HARE, MAUD, 1874-1936
Antar of Araby. (1929) RIR

CUREL, FRANÇOIS DE, 1854-1928
L'envers d'une sainte. 1892.
BOR
Variant title: The other side
of a saint
The fossils. 1892.
Clark, B., tr. CLD, WATI,
WATL1
The lion's share. See Le repas
du lion
The other side of a saint. See
L'envers d'une sainte
Le repas du lion. 1897. RHO
Variant title: The lion's
share

CURNIEU, GEORGES DE (Georges
Ancey, pseud.), 1860-1917
The dupe. 1891.
Clark, B., tr. CLD

CURRIE, CARLETON H.
Whither goest thou? 1926. FED2

CURZON, SARAH ANNE, 1833-1898
Laura Secord, the heroine of
1812. (1876) WAGN2
The sweet girl graduate; a
comedy in four acts. (1882)
WAGN2

CUSHING, ELIZA LANESFORD,
1794-1886
The fatal ring; a drama. (1840)
WAGN2

CUSTIS, GEORGE WASHINGTON
PARKE, 1781-1857
Pocahontas; or, The settlers
of Virginia. 1830. QUIJ,
QUIK, QUIL, QUIM, QUIN

CUVELIER DE TRYE, JEAN GUIL-
LAUME ANTOINE, 1766-1824. See
Chandezon, Léopold, jt. auth.

DA BIBIENA, BERNARDO CARDINAL
DOVIZI. See Dovizi da Bibiena,
Bernardo Cardinal

DAGERMAN, STIG, 1923-1954
The condemned. 1947.
Alexander, H., and Jones, L.,
trs. SCAN3
Variant title: Den dödsdömde
Den dödsdömde. See The con-
demned

DALY, AUGUSTIN, 1838-1899
The big bonanza (adapted from
Ultimo, by Gustav von Moser).
1875. AMP20
Divorce. 1871. AMP20
Horizon. 1871. HAL
Man and wife. 1870. AMP20
Needles and pins (adapted from
Starke mitteln, by Julius Rosen).
1880. AMP20
Pique. 1875. AMP20
Under the gaslight. 1867. AMEM,
BOOB

DAMEL, CARLOS S. See Darthes,
Juan Fernando, jt. auth.

DAMCHENKO, VLADIMIR IVANOVICH
NEMIROVICH. See Nemfrovich-
Danchenko, Vladímir Ivanovích

DANCOURT, FLORENT CARTON,
1661-1725
Les bourgeoises de qualité. See
Woman's craze for titles
Le chevalier à la mode. 1687.
BRE
Woman's craze for titles. 1700.
Chambers, W., tr. BAT8
Variant title: Les bourgeoises
de qualité

DANE, CLEMENCE, pseud. See

Ashton, Winifred

DANIEL, SAMUEL, 1562-1619
The vision of the twelve goddesses. 1604. ETO, PAR

DANJURO I, 1660-1704
The God Fudō. 1697. See
Tsuuchi, Hanjurō; Yasuda,
Abun; and Nakada, Mansuke.
Saint Narukami and the God
Fudō
Narukami. 1684.
Irwin, V., tr. IRW
Variant title: Saint Narukami
Saint Narukami. See Narukami;
See also Tsuuchi, Hanjurō;
Yasuda, Abun; and Nakada,
Mansuke. Saint Narukami
and the God Fudō

DANJURO, ICHIKAWA. See Danjūrō
I

D'ANNUNZIO, GABRIELE. See Annunzio, Gabriele d'

DANTE, NICHOLAS, 1941- . See
Kirkwood, James, jt. auth.

DARKE, NICK, 1948-
High water. 1980. PLACI

DA PONTE, LORENZO. See Ponte,
Lorenzo Da

D'ARCY, MARGRETTA. See Arden,
John, jt. auth.

DARION, JOSEPH, 1917-
Man of La Mancha (lyrics by).
See Wasserman, Dale. Man
of La Mancha

DARTHES, JUAN FERNANDO CAMILO,
and DAMEL, CARLOS S.
La hermana Josefina. See The
quack doctor
The quack doctor. 1938.
Jones, W., tr. JONA
Variant title: La hermana
Josefina

DAS, K. , 1929-
Lela Mayang. 1968. NEWDE

DAUMAL, RENE, 1908-1944

En gggarrrde! 1924.
Benedikt, M., tr. BEN

D'AVENANT, SIR WILLIAM, 1606-
1668
Love and honor. 1934. WALL
Salmacida spolia. 1640. ETO
The siege of Rhodes, pt. I.
1661. MAND, MANF
The wits. 1635. KNOW

-- and DRYDEN, JOHN
The tempest; or, The enchanted
island. 1667. SUMB

DAVENANT, WILLIAM. See D'Avenant, Sir William

DAVENPORT, ROBERT, 1600?-
1651?
The city night-cap. 1624? BUL4
A crowne for a conquerour.
1623? BUL4
King John and Matilda. 1655?
ARMS, BUL4
A new trick to cheat the divell.
1639? BUL4
A survey of the sciences. BUL4
Too late to call backe yesterday.
1623? BUL4

DAVIDSON, ROBERT, 1808-1876
Elijah. 1860? KOH2

DAVIES, HUBERT HENRY, 1865-1917
The mollusc. 1907. DIG, ROWC

DAVIES, MARY CAROLYN
The slave with two faces. 1918?
PEN

DAVIES, ROBERTSON, 1913-
At my heart's core. 1950. MAJ
Hope deferred. 1948. WAGN3

DAVIN, NICHOLAS FLOOD, 1943-1901
Advantages of coalition. See The
fair grit
The fair grit; or, The advantages
of coalition, a farce. (1876)
WAGN1
Variant title: The advantages
of coalition

DAVIOT, GORDON, pseud. See
MacKintosh, Elizabeth

DAVIS, ANDRE
Four men. 1938? OBSE

DAVIS, BILL C., 1951-
Mass appeal. 1979. BES81

DAVIS, BOB
Renaissance radar: a performance landscape (music by). See Finneran, Alan. Renaissance radar: a performance landscape

DAVIS, DONALD, 1907- . See Davis, Owen, jt. auth.

DAVIS, MRS. IRVING KAYE.
See Shelley, Elsa (Mrs. Irving Kaye Davis)

DAVIS, OSSIE, 1917-
Curtain call, Mr. Aldridge, sir. (1963). REAG
Purlie victorious. 1961. ALLK, BRAS, DIZ, FAD, OLIV, PATR, TUGT

DAVIS, OWEN, 1874-1956
And so ad infinitum. See Capek, Karel and Capek, Josef. And so ad infinitum (adapted by)
The detour. 1921. MOSJ, MOSK, MOSL
Icebound. 1923. BES22, CORD, CORE, CORF, DIG, HAL
Mr. and Mrs. North (based on the novel, The Norths meet murder, by Frances and Richard Lockridge). 1941. BES40

-- and DAVIS, DONALD
Ethan Frome (based on the novel by Edith Wharton). 1936. BES35, GATB2, GARU

DAY, CLARENCE, 1874-1935
Life with father. See Lindsay, Howard and Crouse, Russel. Life with father (based on the book by)
Life with mother. See Lindsay, Howard and Crouse, Russel. Life with mother (based on the book by)

DAY, JOHN, 1574-1640?
Humour out of breath. 1608? NER
The parliament of bees. 1641? NER

DAYTON, KATHARINE, d.1945, and KAUFMAN, GEORGE S.
First lady. 1935. BES35

DE AMESCUA, ANTONIO MIRA. See Mira de Amescua, Antonio

DEAN, ALEXANDER, 1893-1939
Just neighborly. 1921. LAW

DEAN, PHILIP H.
The owl killer. (1972). KINH

DE ANDA, PETER, 1940-
Ladies in waiting. 1971. BES70, KINH

DEANE, HAMILTON, 1891-1958, and BALDERSTON, JOHN
Dracula. 1927. RICI

DEBERHAM, ARTHUR HENRY, 1881-
Good will toward men. 1934. SEVE
The prince of peace. 1934. SEVE

DE CASALIS, JEANNE, 1897-1966. See Sherriff, Robert Cedric, jt. auth.

DECOUR, CHARLES HERBERT and THEODORE, ANNE
Le coq de village. See Smith, Richard Penn (adapted from). The last man

DE CUREL, FRANÇOIS. See Curel, François de

DE CURNIEU, GEORGES. See Curnieu, Georges de

DEEVY, TERESA, 1894-1963
Kati Roche. 1936. FAMI

DE FILIPPO, EDUARDO. See Filippo, Eduardo de

DE GHELDERODE, MICHEL. See Ghelderode, Michel de

DEKKER, THOMAS, 1507?-1641?
The gentle craft. See The shoe-
makers' holiday
A pleasant comedy of a gentle
craft. See The shoemakers'
holiday
The pleasant comedy of Old
Fortunatus. 1599. SCH,
SCI
The roaring girl. 1610. DPR2
The shoemakers' holiday; or,
The gentle craft. 1599.
BALD, BAS, BENY, BLOO,
BROC, CLKW, COF, DPR1,
DUN, FOUD, GATG, GAY3,
GREC1, HARC47, HAY, HOW,
LAWR, MACL, MAK, MONV,
NEI, NES, ORNC, PAR,
RUB, SCI, SCJ, SCW, SHAJ1,
SPD, SPE, SPEF1, TAT, TAU,
TAV, WHE, WINE, WOO1,
WRIH
Variant titles: The gentle
craft; A pleasant comedy
of gentle craft
---See Ford, John, jt. auth.

-- and MIDDLETON, THOMAS
The honest whore, pt. I.
1604. BAS, NEI, NES, SPE,
WALL
The honest whore, pt. II. 1605.
NEI, OLH, OLI1, SPE

DE KOCK, CHARLES PAUL. See
Kock, Charles Paul de

DE KRUIF, PAUL HENRY, 1890-
1971. See Howard, Sidney Coe,
jt. auth.

DE LA BARCA, PEDRO CALDERON.
See Calderón de la Barca, Pedro

DELACOUR, ALFRED CHARLEMAGNE
LARTIGNE, known as, 1817-1883.
See Labiche, Eugène Marin, jt. auth.

DELAFIELD, E. M., pseud. See
De La Pasture, Edmée Elizabeth
Monica

DELANEY, SHELAGH, 1939-
A taste of honey. 1958.
BES60, POP, SEVC

DE LA PASTURE, EDMEE ELIZABETH

MONICA (E. M. Delafield, pseud.),
1890-1943
To see ourselves. 1930. FAMAN,
PLAD

DE LA TAILLE, JEAN. See Taille,
Jean de La

DELAVIGNE, CASIMIR. See
Delavigne, Jean François Casimir

DELAVIGNE, JEAN FRANÇOIS
CASIMIR, 1793-1843
Marino Faliero. 1829. BOR

DELBO, CHARLOTTE, 1913-
Who will carry the word? 1974.
Haft, C., tr. THL

DELDERFIELD, RONALD FREDERICK,
1912-1972
Peace comes to Peckham. 1947.
EMB3
Worm's eye view. 1945. EMB1

DEL GRANDE, LOUIS
So who's Goldberg. 1973. BRIP

DELL, FLOYD, 1887-1969, and
MITCHELL, THOMAS
Little accident. 1928. BES28

DELL, JEFFREY, 1899-
Payment deferred (based on the
novel by Cecil Forester).
1934? CART

THE DELL'ARTE PLAYERS
Intrigue at Ah-pah. 1979.
WES8

DEL VALLE-INCLAN, RAMON MARIA.
See Valle-Inclán, Ramón María del

DE MAUPASSANT, GUY. See
Maupassant, Guy de

DE MILLE, HENRY CHURCHILL,
1850-1893, and BARNARD, CHARLES
The main line; or, Rawson's Y.
1886. AMP17
--See Belasco, David, jt. auth.

DE MILLE, WILLIAM CHURCHILL,
1878-1955
The Warrens of Virginia. 1907.
AMP16

DE MONTHERLANT, HENRY.
See Montherlant, Henry Marie
Joseph Millon de

DENISON, MERRILL, 1893-1975
    Balm. 1923. MAS1
    Brothers in arms. 1921. MAS1
    Mash hay. 1974. KAL3
    The weather breeder. 1924.
      MAS1, WAGN3

DENKER, HENRY, 1912-
    A far country. 1961. BES60

-- and BERKEY, RALPH
    Breaking point. See Time limit!
    Time limit! 1956. THEA56
      Variant title: Breaking point

D'ENNERY, ADOLPHE, 1811-1899,
and CORMON, EUGENE
    Les deux orphelines. See The
      two orphans
    In the hands of heaven. See
      the two orphans
    Orphans of the storm. See The
      two orphans
    The two orphans; or, In the
      hands of heaven. 1874.
      Jackson, N. Hart, tr. and
        adapter. CEY, MELO
      Variant titles: Les deux
        orphelines; In the hands
        of heaven; Orphans of the
        storm

DENNEY, REUEL, 1913-
    September lemonade. 1955?
      NEWW7

DENNIS, NIGEL FORBES, 1912-
    August for the people. 1961.
      RHE
    Cards of identity. 1956. WELT

DESNOS, ROBERT, 1900-1945
    La Place de l'Etoile. (1944)
      Benedikt, M., tr. BEN

DESSANDRAIS-SEBIRE, FRANÇOIS
    The philosopher duped by love
      (sometimes attributed to).
      See Anonymous plays. The
      philosopher duped by love

DESTOUCHES, PHILLIPPE NERI-
CAULT, 1680-1754

The conceited count. See Le
    glorieux
Le glorieux. 1732. BRE
    Aldington, R., tr. ALD
    Variant title: The conceited
      count

DEVAL, JACQUES, 1894?-1972
    Tovarich. 1936.
      Sherwood, R., tr. and adapted.
        BES36, CEW

DE VISE, JEAN DONNEAU. See
Donneau de Visé, Jean

DEWHURST, KEITH, 1931-
    Lark rise (from the book by Flora
      Thompson). 1978. PLAN48
    Rafferty's chant. 1967. PLAN33

DEY, JAMES PAUL, 1930-
    Passacaglia. 1965. NEWA2

DIAMANT-BERGER, MAURICE (André
Gillois, pseud.)
    Paddle your own canoe. See
      Regnier, Max. A. M. (based
      on)

DIAZ, JORGE, 1930-
    El lugar donde mueren los
      mamíferos. See The place
      where the mammals die
    The mammals' graveyard.
      See The place where the mam-
      mals die
    The place where the mammals die.
      1963.
      Nelson, N., tr. WOOG
      Variant titles: El lugar donde
        mueren los mamíferos; The
        mammals' graveyard

DIBDIN, CHARLES, 1745-1814
    The deserter. 1782. BELC4

DIBDIN, THOMAS JOHN PITT, 1771-
1841
    Fire, water, earth and air. See
      Harlequin in his element
    Harlequin Harper; or A jump
      from Japan. 1813. BOOA5
      Variant title: A jump from
        Japan
    A jump from Japan. See Harle-
      quin Harper
    Harlequin in his element, or Fire,

water, earth and air. 1807.
BOOA5
Variant title: Fire, water,
earth and air
The school for prejudice. 1801.
INCA4

DICENTA Y BENEDICTO, JOAQUIN,
1860-1917
Juan José. 1895.
Skidmore, M., tr. TUR

DICKENS, CHARLES, 1812-1870
A Christmas carol. See Shay,
Frank. A Christmas carol
(adapted from the story by)
The cricket on the hearth.
See Smith, Albert Richard.
The cricket on the hearth
(adapted from the story by)
Dot. See Boucicault, Dion. Dot
(adapted from The cricket on
the hearth)
Nicholas Nickleby. See Edgar,
David. The life & adventures
of Nicholas Nickleby; a play
in two parts with five acts
(based on)
Pickwick Papers. See Young,
Stanley. Mr. Pickwick (based
on)

DIDEROT, DENIS, 1713-1784
The father. See Le père de
famille
Jacques le fataliste et son
maître. See Kundera, Milan.
Jacques and his master
(adapted from)
Le père de famille. 1761. BRE
Variant title: The father

DIEB, RON, 1932-
The mating of Alice May. [1972]
PIC

DIFUSCO, JOHN, 1947-
Tracers. 1980. BES84

DIGHTON, JOHN, 1909-
The happiest days of your life.
1948. PLAN1
Who goes there! 1951. PLAN6

DIKE, FATIMA
The sacrifice of Kreli. 1976.
THI

DILMEN, GÜNGÖR (KALYONCU),
1930-
The ears of Midas. 1959.
Graham, C., tr. HALM
Variant title: Midasin Kulak-
lari
Midasin Kulaklari. See The ears
of Midas

DINNER, WILLIAM, and MORUM,
WILLIAM
The late Edwina Black. 1949.
PLAN2

DIZENZO, CHARLES JOHN, 1938-
The drapes come. 1965. OFF
An evening for Merlin Finch.
1968. OFF

DOBIE, LAURENCE, and SLOMAN,
ROBERT
The tinker. 1960. PLAN24

DODD, LEE WILSON, 1879-1933
The changelings. 1923. BES23

DODSLEY, ROBERT, 1703-1764
Cleone. 1758. BELG15
The miller of Mansfield. 1737.
BELC3
The toy shop. 1735. BELC3

DODSON, OWEN, 1914-
Bayou legend. 1946. TUQT
Divine comedy. 1938. HARY

DOGGET, THOMAS, d.1721
Flora; or, Hob in the well. See
Hob; or, The country wake
Hob; or, The country wake
(sometimes attributed to Colley
Cibber). 1711. HUGH
Variant titles: Flora; or,
Hob in the well; The opera
of Flora; or, Hob in the
well
The opera of Flora; or, Hob in
the well. See Hob; or, The
country wake

DOHERTY, BRIAN
Father Malachy's miracle (adapted
from the novel by Bruce
Marshall). 1945. EMBI

DOLAN, HARRY
Losers weepers. (1967). DOD

DONAHUE, JOHN CLARK
The cookie jar. 1972. MIMN

DONLEAVY, JAMES PATRICK,
1926-
The interview. THOD

DONNAY, MAURICE CHARLES,
1859-1945
Les amants. See The lovers
L'autre danger. See The
other danger
The lovers. 1895.
Clark, B., tr. MOSQ
Steeves, H., tr. STE
Variant title: Les amants
The other danger. 1902.
David, C., tr. THR
Variant title: L'autre danger

DONNEAU DE VISE, JEAN, 1638?-
1710?
Le gentilhomme guespin.
1670? LAN

DORALL, EDWARD, 1936-
A tiger is loose in our community.
1967. NEWDE

DORSET, THOMAS SACKVILLE, 1st
earl of. See Sackville, Thomas

DORST, TANKRED, 1925-
The curve. 1960.
Rosenberg, J., tr. COTT
Variant title: Die Kurve
Freedom for Clemens. 1960.
Wellwarth, G., tr. BENB
Variant titles: Freedom for
Clement; Freiheit für Clemens
Freedom for Clement. See Free-
dom for Clemens
Freiheit für Clemens. See Free-
dom for Clemens
Die Kurve. See The curve

DOSTOEVSKII, FEDOR MIKHAILO-
VICH, 1821-1881
The brothers Karamazoff
(based on the novel by). See
Nemirovich-Danchenko, Vladi-
mir. The brothers Karamazoff

DOSTOIEVSKY, FEDOR. See
Dostoevskii, Fedor Mikhailovich

DOUGLAS, FELICITY, 1910-

Rollo. See Achard, Marcel.
Rollo (adapted by)

DOUGLAS, GEORGIA. See Johnson,
Mrs. Georgia (Douglas)

DOUGLAS, JAMES, 1929-
The ice goddess. 1964. HOGE

DOVIZI DA BIBIENA, BERNARDO
CARDINAL, 1470-1520
La Calandria. See The follies
of Calandro
The follies of Calandro. Early
16th cent.
Evans, O., tr. BENSA
Variant title: La Calandria

DOWLING, JENNETTE and LETTON,
FRANCIS
Before the throne. See The
young Elizabeth
Princess Elizabeth. See The
young Elizabeth
The young Elizabeth. 1951.
PLAN7
Variant titles: Before the
throne; Princess Elizabeth

DOWLING, MAURICE MATHEW
GEORGE, 1793?-?
Othello travestie. 1834. NIN2
Romeo and Juliet, as the law
directs. 1837. NIN2

DOWN, OLIPHANT, 1885-1917
The maker of dreams. 1912.
BEAC12

DOWSON, ERNEST CHRISTOPHER,
1867-1900
The pierrot of the minute. 1902.
BENP, SECK

DOYLE, SIR ARTHUR CONAN, 1859-
1930
Sherlock Holmes. See Gillette,
William Hooker. Sherlock
Holmes (based on the stories
by)

DRAGUN, OSVALDO, 1929-
And they told us we were im-
mortal. 1963.
Green, A., tr. WOOG
Variant title: Y nos dijeron
que éramos inmortales

Y nos dijeron que éramos inmortales. See And they told
us we were immortal

DRAKE, WILLIAM A., 1899-1965
Grand hotel (tr. and adapted
by). See Baum, Vicki.
Grand hotel

DRANSFIELD, JANE, 1875-1975
The lost pleiad. 1910. SHAY

DRAYTON, MICHAEL, 1563-1631
The merry devil of Edmonton
(sometimes attributed to).
See Anonymous plays. The
merry devil of Edmonton
Sir John Oldcastle, pt. I
(sometimes attributed to).
See Anonymous plays.
Sir John Oldcastle, pt. I

DRAYTON, RONALD
Notes from a strange God.
(1968) JON

DRINKWATER, JOHN, 1882-1937
Abraham Lincoln. 1918.
BES19, DID, PLAP1, SWI
Cophetua. 1911. PEN
Oliver Cromwell. 1923. DIG

DRIVER, DONALD, 1922-
Your own thing (suggested by
Twelfth night by William
Shakespeare; music and
lyrics by Hal Hester and
Danny Apolinar). 1968.
BES67, GREAA

DRIVER, JOHN, 1947- , and HAD-
DOW, JEFFREY, 1947-
Chekhov in Yalta (music composed
by Catherine MacDonald).
1981. BES80, WES11/12

DRUMMOND, ALEXANDER MAGNUS,
1884-1956
The lake guns of Seneca and
Cayuga. DRU
--See also Baker, E. Irene, jt.
auth.

DRUTEN, JOHN VAN. See Van Druten, John

DRYDEN, JOHN, 1631-1700

All for love; or, The world well
lost. 1677. BAUG, BELK5,
BENY, CLK1, COTX, DOB,
FREG, GOS, GOSA, HARC18,
KET, LIE, LIED1, LIEE1,
MACL, MAND, MANF, MARG,
MAX, MIL, MOO, MOR, NET,
RES, REST, RET, SHAH1,
SHAJ1, SMN, SNYD1, STM,
TUP, TUQ, TWE, WILS,
WOOE1, WRIR
Almanzor and Almahide; or, The
conquest of Granada by the
Spaniards. 1670. MOR, NET,
TAT, TAU, TUP, TUQ
Variant titles: The conquest
of Granada; The conquest
of Granada by the Spaniards,
pt. I
Amphitryon. 1690. BELK11
Aureng-zebe. 1675. DOA, MEN,
STM, TICK
The conquest of Granada. See
Almanzor and Almahide
The conquest of Granada by The
Spaniards, pt. I. See Alman-
zor and Almahide
Don Sebastian, King of Portugal.
(1690). BELK12
The feigned innocence. See Sir
Martin Mar-all
The kind keeper; or, Mr. Limber-
ham. 1677-78. JEFF2
Variant title: Mr. Limberham
Marriage a la mode. 1572. DAVR
Mr. Limberham. See The kind
keeper
Secular masque. 1700. ABRA,
ABRE, ABRF, ABRH, ABRJ,
HAPT1
Sir Martin Mar-all; or, The
feigned innocence. 1667.
JEFF1
Variant title: The feigned
innocence
The Spanish fryar; or, The
double discovery. 1679.
BELK13, GAY4, MOSE1
The tempest. See D'Avenant,
William, jt. auth.

-- and HOWARD, SIR ROBERT
The Indian queen. 1663.
BENY, MAND, MANF

-- and LEE, NATHANIEL
Oedipus. 1679. BELK12

DUBERMAN, MARTIN B., 1930-
In white America. 1963. LAM,
GAT

DUBIN, AL, 1891-1945
42nd Street (music and lyrics
by). See Stewart, Michael.
42nd Street

DUBOIS, WILLIAM EDWARD
BURGHARDT, 1868-1963
Haiti. 1938. FEE

DUCANGE, VICTOR HENRY JOSEPH
BRAHAIN, 1783-1833.
See Goubaux, Prosper Parfait, jt.
auth.

DUDLEY, SIR HENRY BATE, 1745-
1824
The rival candidates. 1775.
BELC4

DUERRENMATT, FRIEDRICH, 1921-
Abendstunde im Spätherbst.
See Incident at twilight
Der besuch der alten dame.
See The visit
Incident at twilight. 1959.
Wellwarth, G., tr. BENB,
WELT
Variant title: Abendstunde im
Spätherbst
The old lady's visit. See The
visit
The physicists. 1962.
Kirkup, J., tr. BES64,
HAVHA
Variant title: Die Physiker
Die Physiker. See The physicists
Time and again. See The visit
Trapps. See Yaffe, James.
The deadly game (adapted
from)
The visit. 1956.
Bowles, P., tr. COTQ, NIL
Valency, M., tr. and adapter.
BAUL, BES57, BLOC, BOW,
CALD, CASF, GOOD,
GOODE, KNIG, KNIH
Variant titles: Der besuch der
alten dame; La visite de la
vieille dame; The old lady's
visit; Time and again
La visite de la vieille dame. See
The visit

DUFFET, THOMAS, fl. 1678
The mock-tempest; or, The enchanted castle. 1674. SUMB

DUFFIELD, BRAINERD
The lottery (from the story by
Shirley Jackson). 1953? LOVR

DUFFY, MAUREEN, 1933-
Rites. 1969. PLABE2, SUB

DUKES, ASHLEY, 1885-1959
The man with a load of mischief.
1925. MART, PLAP3
The mask of virtue (tr. and
adapted by). See Sternheim,
Carl. The mask of virtue
Such men are dangerous (adapted
from The patriot, by Alfred
Neumann). 1928. FAO

DUMAS, ALEXANDRE, père, 1802-
1870
Antony. 1831. BOR, COM
The Count of Monte Cristo.
See Fechter, Charles Albert.
Monte Cristo (based on the
novel, The Count of Monte
Cristo, by)
Henry III et sa cour. 1829.
BOR, GRA

DUMAS, ALEXANDRE, fils, 1824-
1895
Camilla; or, The fate of a coquette.
See La dame aux camélias
Camille. See La dame aux camélias
La dame aux camélias. 1852. BOR,
GRA
Ashley, L., tr. ASF
Reynolds, E., and Playfair, N.,
trs. SSTG
Variant titles: Camilla; or, The
fate of a coquette; Camille;
The lady of the camelias;
The queen of the camelias
Le demi-monde. See The outer
edge of society
The ideas of Madame Aubray. See
Les idées de Madame Aubray
Les idées de Madame Aubray. 1867.
BOR
Variant title: The ideas of
Madame Aubray
The lady of the camelias. See
La dame aux camélias

The outer edge of society.
1855.
Clark, B., tr. MAU
Harper, H., tr. CLF2
Variant title: Le demimonde
The queen of the camelias. See
La dame aux camélias

DUNBAR-NELSON, ALICE, 1875-
1935
Mine eyes have seen. 1918.
HARY

DUNCAN, RONALD FREDERICK,
1914-1982
The death of Satan. 1954. LOR,
SATA
The gift. 1968. RICK

DUNCAN, THELMA M., 1902-
The death dance. 1923. LOC
Sacrifice. (1930). RIR

DUNLAP, WILLIAM, 1766-1839
André. 1798. COY, HAL,
MOSS1, QUIJ, QUIK, QUIL,
QUIM, QUIN
Darby's return. 1789. AMPA
False shame; or, The American
orphan in Germany (adapted
from Falsche scham, by
August Kotzebue). 1799.
AMP2
The glory of Columbia: Her
yeomancy! 1803. MONR
Thirty years; or, The gambler's
fate (adapted from Trente ans,
by Prosper Goubaux and Vic-
tor Ducange). 1828. AMP2
A trip to Niagara; or, Travellers
in America. 1828. MONR

DUNN, THEO M.
Maada and Ulka. SHAT

DUNNING, PHILIP HART, 1891-1968,
and ABBOTT, GEORGE
Broadway. 1926. BES26, CART,
GASB

DUNSANY, EDWARD JOHN MORETON,
1878-1957
The glittering gate. 1909.
WATF1, WATI
The gods of the mountain. 1911.
MOSN, MOSO
If. 1921. HAU

King Argimenes and the unknown
warrior. 1911. DID
The lost silk hat. 1921. CHU,
PROM, PRON, SCWI
A night at an inn. 1916.
BEAC11, BLAG, BLAH,
COOK3, GARZAP, GATS, HUD,
PEN, PROB
The queen's enemies. 1916. AND

DURANG, CHRISTOPHER, 1949-
Marriage of Bette and Boo. 1985.
BES84

DURAS, MARGUERITE, 1914-
Department of forestry. See The
rivers and forests
Les eaux at forêts. See The
rivers and forests
The rivers and forests. 1965.
Brae, B., tr. MIJE
Variant titles: Department of
forestry; Les eaux et forêts

D'URFEY, THOMAS, 1653-1723
Madam Fickle; or, The witty false
one. 1677. JEFF2

DURRENMATT, FRIEDRICH. See
Duerrenmatt, Friedrich

DU RYER, PIERRE, 1606-1658
Esther. 1642?
Lockert, L., tr. LOCU
Saul. 1640.
Lockert, L., tr. LOCR
Scaevola. 1644?
Lockert, L., tr. LOCR

D'USSEAU, ARNAUD, 1916- . See
Gow, James Ellis, jt. auth.

DUVAL, ALEXANDRE VINCENT,
1767-1842
La jeunesse de Henri V. See
Payne, John Howard.
Charles the second (adapted
from
Shakespeare amoureux; ou, La
pièce â l'étude. See Smith,
Richard Penn. Shakespeare in
love (adapted from)

DYER, CHARLES, 1926-
Rattle of a simple man. 1961.
BES62, PLAN26
Staircase. 1966. BES67

E., A., pseud. See Russell, George William

EBB, FRED, 1932-
    Cabaret (lyrics by). See Master-
        off, Joe. Cabaret

-- and FOSSE, BOB
    Chicago (music by John Kander,
        lyrics by Fred Ebb; based on
        the play by Maurine Dallas
        Watkins). 1975. BES75

EBERHART, RICHARD, 1904-
    The visionary forms. 1952.
        NEWW3

ECHEGARAY Y EIZAGUIRRE, JOSE,
1832-1916
    La esposa del vengador. See
        The street singer
    El gran Galeoto. 1891. BRET
        Bontecou, E., tr. CLDM,
            DIK2
        Lynch, H., tr. FLOS
        Nirdlinger, C., tr. and adapter.
            MOSQ
        Variant titles: The great Galeo-
            to; Slander; The world and
            his wife
    The great Galeoto. See El gran
        Galeoto
    Slander. See El gran Galeoto
    The street singer. 1874.
        Underhill, J., tr. MACN
        Variant title: La esposa del
            vengador
    The world and his wife. See El
        gran Galeoto

EDGAR, DAVID, 1948-
    The life & adventures of Nicholas
        Nickleby; a play in two parts
        with five acts (adapted from
        the novel by Charles Dickens).
        1980. BES81

EDMONDS, RANDOLPH, 1900-
    Bad man. 1934. HARY
    Earth and stars. 1946. TUQT

EDWARD, H. F. V., 1898-1973
    Job hunters. 1931. HARY

EDWARDS, GUS, 1939-
    Three fallen angels. (1979) CEN

EDWARDS, RICHARD, 1523?-1566
    Damon and Pithias. 1564? ADA

EDWARDS, SHERMAN, 1919-
    1776 (music and lyrics by).
        See Stone, Peter H. 1776

EGAN, MICHAEL, 1895-1956
    The dominant sex. 1934. FAMG
    To love and to cherish. 1938.
        FAML

EICHELBAUM, SAMUEL, 1894-1967
    Divorcio nupcial. 1941. ALPE

EISELE, ROBERT H., 1948-
    Animals are passing from our
        lives. 1973. WES3

EISENSTEIN, MARK
    The fighter. 1958. GARZAL

EISENSTEIN, SERGEI, 1898-1948
    Ivan the terrible: the screenplay,
        part one. 1944.
        Montagu, I., and Marshall, H.,
            trs. WEIP

EIZAGUIRRE, JOSE ECHEGARAY Y.
See Echegaray y Eizaguirre, José

ELDER, LONNE, III, 1931-
    Ceremonies in dark old men. 1969.
        GARTL, HAVHA, PATR
    Charades on East Fourth Street.
        1967. KINH

ELIOT, THOMAS STEARNS, 1888-
1965
    Cats (words by). See Lloyd Web-
        ber, Andrew. Cats (based on
        the book, Old Possum's book
        of practical cats, by T. S.
        Eliot)
    The cocktail party. 1949. BES49,
        FEL
    The confidential clerk. 1954.
        BES53, THEA54
    The family reunion. 1939. BRZ
    Murder in the cathedral. 1935.
        BALL, BROH, BROI, COK,
        CONP, COTQ, CUBH, DEAP,
        DEAR, HAVG, LEVJ, MALI2,
        TAUJ, TUCO, WARI, WATA
    Old Possum's book of practical cats.
        See Lloyd Webber, Andrew.

Cats (based on)
Sweeney Agonistes. 1926. BENS1

ELLIOTT, SUMNER LOCKE. See
Locke-Elliott, Sumner

ELSER, FRANK BALL, 1885-1935,
and CONNELLY, MARCUS COOK
The farmer takes a wife. See
Low bridge
Low bridge. 1934. BES34, LEV
Variant title: The farmer
takes a wife

EMERY, GILBERT, pseud. See
Pottle, Emery Bemsley

EMIG, EVELYN (MELLON), 1895-
The china pig. 1920? SHAY

ENAMAI NO SAYEMON. See Enami
Sayemon

ENAMI SAYEMON, fl.1400
The cormorant fisher. 15th
cent.
Waley, A., tr. TAV

ENGLAND, BARRY, 1934-
Conduct unbecoming. 1970.
BES70

ENNERY, ADOLPHE D'. See
D'Ennery, Adolphe

ENRICO, ROBERT, 1931-
On Owl Creek. 1961. HAVL

EPSTEIN, MARTIN
Autobiography of a pearl diver.
1979. WES5
Mysteries of the bridal night.
1982. PLACE

ERCKMANN-CHATRIAN (pseud. of
Erckmann, Emile, 1822-1899, and
Chatrain, Alexandre, 1826-1890, col-
laborators)
The Polish Jew. See Lewis,
Leopold David. The bells
(adapted from Le julf polonais
by)

ERVINE, ST. JOHN GREER, 1883-
1971
The first Mrs. Fraser. 1929.
BES29

Jane Clegg. 1913. BES19, PALP1
John Ferguson. 1915. BESO9,
CHA, CHAN, CHAR, DUR,
THF, TUCD, TUCM, TUCN,
TUCO
Mixed marriage. 1911. DID

ESASHI JUO
The bird catcher in hell.
Waley, A., tr. INGW, TAV

ESSON, LOUIS, 1879-1943
The drovers. (1919) FIO

ESTABROOK, HOWARD, 1894-
The human comedy (screen play
based on the book by William
Saroyan). 1943. NAGE

ESTRIN, MARC
An American playground sampler.
(1970). NEWA3

ETHEREGE, SIR GEORGE, 1635?-
1691
The man of mode; or, Sir
Fopling Flutter. 1675.
CLKW, FIS, GOSA, JEFF1,
KRM, LID, MAND, MANF,
MANH, MOR, MOSE1, NET,
REIL, REIWE, RES, REST,
SALR, SSSI, STM, TUQ,
WILS
She would if she could. 1668.
DAVR, JEFF1

ETIENNE, CHARLES GUILLAUME,
1777-1845
Les deux gendres. See Payne,
John Howard. The two sons-
in-law (adapted from)

EUBA, FEMI, 1935?-
Abiko. PIET

EURIPIDES, 480?-406? B.C.
Alcestis. 438 B.C.
Aldington, R., tr. ALLI,
LIND, LOCK, OAT1, OATH
Browning, R., tr. MAST
Coleridge, E., tr. GRDB5
Fitts, D., and Fitzgerald, R.,
trs. FEL, FIFR, FIFT
Lattimore, R., tr. GREP3,
GRER3, WEAN
Murray, G., tr. CLKW
Potter, R., tr. CLF1

Way, A., tr. GREE, HOWE,
HOWF, THOM, THON
Andromache. 431? B.C.
Coleridge, E., tr. GRDB5,
OAT1
Johnson, V., tr. FIFV
LeRue, J., tr. COOA
Lind, L., tr. LIND
Nims, J., tr. GREP3
The bacchae. 405 B.C.
Anon. tr. ALLK
Arrowsmith, W., tr. GREP4,
GRER3, TREB
Birkhead, H., tr. LIND
Boer, C., tr. COOA
Cavender, K., tr. COTX,
SSSI
Coleridge, E., tr. GRDB5
Curry, N., tr. BENSB1
Doria, C., tr. TENN
Kerr, A., tr. DOWS
Lucas, F., tr. LUCA, LUCAB,
LUCAF
Milman, H., tr. ROBJ, VON
Murray, G., tr. HARC8,
OAM, OAT2
Vellacott, M., tr. BAIC
Vellacott, P., tr. ALLJ,
ALLM, BAIE, BAIG, SANE,
WEIS, WELT
Volanakis, M., tr. HAPRL
Variant title: The bacchantes
--See also Ferguson, Ian. Ritual
2378 (based on)
The bacchantes. See The bacchae
The children of Heracles. See
The Heracleidae
The cyclops. 5th cent. B.C.
Arrowsmith, W., tr. GREP3
Coleridge, E., tr. GRDB5,
OAT2
Economou, G., tr. TENN
Green, R., tr. RUSV
Shelley, P., tr. PLAG
Smith, G., tr. BAT1
Electra. 413? B.C.
Coleridge, E., tr. GRDB5,
OAT2
Murray, G., tr. FEFT, TEN,
TRE, TREA2
Vellacott, P., tr. FOR
Vermeule, E., tr. GREP4,
GRER2
Way, A., tr. WEAV1
Hecuba. 425? B.C.
Arrowsmith, W., tr. GREP3
Coleridge, E., tr. GRDB5,

OAT1
Helen. 412 B.C.
Coleridge, E., tr. GRDB5,
OAT2
Lattimore, R., tr. GREP3
The Heracleidae. 431? B.C.
Coleridge, E., tr. GRDB5,
OAT1
Gladstone, R., tr. GREP3
Variant title: The children of
Heracles
Heracles. 420? B.C.
Arrowsmith, W., tr. GREP3
Coleridge, E., tr. GRDB5,
OAT
Variant titles: Heracles mad;
The madness of Heracles
Heracles mad. See Heracles
Hiketides. See The suppliants
Hippolytus. 428 B.C.
Coleridge, E., tr. GRDB5,
OAT1, THP, WARN1
Grene, G., tr. FIFT, GREN,
GREP3, GRER1
Hadas, M., and McLean, J.,
trs. GRDG
Lucas, F., tr. BARC, LUCA,
LUCAB, LUCAF
Murray, G., tr. FEFT,
HARC8, MIL, MURP, OAM
Vellacott, P., tr. GOLH,
SANL
Warner, R., tr. NORG1,
NORI, VANV1
Way, A., tr. ATT2, HOUS,
ROBI
Ion. 5th cent. B.C.
Coleridge, E., tr. GRDB5
Doolittle, H., tr. KRE
Potter, R., tr. OAT1
Willetts, R., tr. GREP4
Iphigenia among the Tauri. See
Iphigenia in Tauris
Iphigenia at Aulis. 405 B.C.
Coleridge, E., tr. GRDB5
Potter, R., tr. CROS, ROB
Stawell, F., tr. OAT2
Walker, C., tr. GREP4
Way, A., tr. BUCK, BUCL,
BUCM
Variant title: Iphigenia in
Aulis
Iphigenia in Aulis. See Iphigenia
at Aulis
Iphigenia in Tauris. 420? B.C.
Anon. tr. WED
Bynner, W., tr. GREP3,

GRER2
Coleridge, E., tr. GRDB5
Murray, G., tr. FEFT, TEN
Potter, R., tr. OAT1, PLAG
Variant title: Iphigenia among
   the Tauri
The madness of Heracles. See
Heracles
Medea. 431 B.C.
   Anon. tr. EVB1, SSTF
   Agard, W., tr. MALR1
   Coleridge, E., tr. EDAD,
      GRDB5, LOCM1, OAT1,
      OATH
   Hadas, M., and McLean, J.,
      trs. GRDG, SSTF
   Jeffers, R., tr. and adapter.
      GARW, GATB3, KIN, LOR,
      SANM
   McLeish, K., tr. MAMB
   Murray, G., tr. FEFT, MAU,
      ROET, SEBO, SEBP, SMP,
      TEN
   Prokosh, F., tr. FIFT, FREG,
      GOOD, GOODE, TAUJ
   Robinson, C., tr. ROBK
   Taylor, J., tr. TAV
   Trevelyan, R., tr. ROBI
   Vellacott, P., tr. HAPRL,
      SANM
   Warner, R., tr. FOT, GREP3,
      MALC, MALG1, MALI1,
      MALN1, NORG1, NORI, WOM
   Way, A., tr. ATT2, BUCL,
      BUCM, GREE, HOWE, HOWF,
      LAP, PROW, ROBJA
   Wodhull, M., tr. DRA1, EVA1,
      EVC1, HIB, HIBB, MIK7,
      PLAB1
Orestes. 408 B.C.
   Arrowsmith, W., tr. GREP4
   Coleridge, E., tr. GRDB5,
      OAT2
   Kirn, H., tr. TAUJ
The Phoenician Maidens. See The
Phoenissae
The Phoenician women. See The
Phoenissae
The Phoenissae. 413? B.C.
   Coleridge, E., tr. GRDB5,
      OAT2
   Wyckoff, E., tr. GREP4
   Variant titles: The Phoenician
      maidens; The Phoenician
      women
Rhesus. 5th cent. B.C.
   Coleridge, E., tr. GRDB5

Lattimore, R., tr. GREP4
Murray, G., tr. OAT2
The suppliants. 424 B.C.
   Coleridge, E., tr. GRDB5,
      OAT1
   Jones, F., tr. GREP4
   Lind, L., tr. LIND
   Variant titles: Hiketides;
      The suppliant women
The suppliant women. See The
suppliants
Troades. See The Trojan women
The Trojan women. 415 B.C.
   Coleridge, E., tr. GRDB5
   Doria, C., tr. COOA
   Hadas, M., and McLean, J.,
      trs. GRDG
   Hamilton, E., tr. CLL, HAM,
      MALI1, SCNR
   Lattimore, R., tr. FIFT,
      GREP3, GRER2, TREB,
      TREC1, TREE1, TREI1
   Murray, G., tr. CARP,
      CARPA, OAT1, STA
   Potter, R., tr. ROBJA
   Raubitschek, I., and A., trs.
      (assisted by A. McCabe)
      ROBJ
   Variant title: Troades

EVELING, STANLEY, 1925-
Mister. 1970. DEC

EVREINOV, NIKOLAI NIKOLAEVICH,
1879-1953
   The back stage of the soul. See
      The theatre of the soul
   The beautiful despot. 1906.
      Roberts, C., tr. ROE
   Behind the curtain of the soul.
      See The theatre of the soul
   Chetvyortaya stena. See The
      fourth wall
   The fourth wall. (1915)
      Senelick, L., tr. RVI
      Variant title: Chetvyortaya
         stena
   A merry death, a harlequinade.
      1914.
      Collins, M., tr. COLI
      Roberts, C., tr. ROE
   Styopic and Manya.
      Collins, M., tr. COLI
   The theatre of the soul. 1912.
      Potapenko, M., and St. John,
         C., trs. DIE, HIB, HIBA
      Variant titles: The back stage

of the soul; Behind the
curtain of the soul

EWING, THOMAS, 1862-1942
Jonathan. 1902? KOH2

EXTON, CLIVE, 1930-
Have you any dirty washing,
mother dear. 1969. PLAN37

EYEN, TOM, 1940-
Grand tenement and November 22.
1967. SME
The white whore and the bit
player. 1964. NEWA2

FAGAN, JAMES BERNARD, 1873-1933
The improper duchess. 1931.
FAMAN, PLAD

FAIRCHILD, WILLIAM, 1918-
The sound of murder. 1959.
PLAN20

FALKLAND, SAMUEL. See Heijermans, Herman (pseud. of)

FARABOUGH, LAURA
Surface tension. 1981. WES11/12

FARIGOULE, LOUIS HENRI JEAN.
See Romains, Jules

FARJEON, ELEANOR, 1881-1965
The plane-tree. 1950. OULD

-- and FARJEON, HERBERT
The two bouquets. 1936. FAMJ

FARJEON, HERBERT, 1887-1945.
See Farjeon, Eleanor, jt. auth.

FARMILOE, DOROTHY A., 1920-
What do you save from a burning
building? ALI

FARQUHAR, GEORGE, 1678-1707
The beaux' stratagem. 1707.
BAT22, BELK2, BLOO, CLF1,
CLK1, GOS, GOSA, HUD,
JEFF4, MAND, MANF, MAX,
MOR, MOSE2, NET, RES,
REST, SIG, STM, TAY, TICK,
TUP, TUQ, TWE, UHL,WEAT1,
WILS, WRIR

The constant couple; or, A trip
to the Jubilee. 1699. BELK15,
JEFF4
Variant title: A trip to the
Jubilee
The inconstant. 1702. BELK13
The recruiting officer. 1706.
BELK4, FIS, GAY4, JEFF4,
RUB
Sir Harry Wildair. 1701. BELK15
A trip to the jubilee. See The
constant couple; or, A trip to
the jubilee
The twin rivals. 1702. BELK17

FASSBINDER, RAINER WERNER, 1946-
1982
Bremen coffee. 1971.
Vivis, A., tr. SOUT
Variant title: Bremer Freibeit
Bremer Freibeit. See Bremen
coffee

FATH'ALI, AKHUND-ZADAH, 1812-
1878
The alchemist. 186-?
Le Strange, G., tr. BAT3
The magistrates. 186-?
Wilson, E., tr. TUQH

FATH ALI, MIRZA. See Fath'-Ali,
Akhund-zadah

FAUCHOIS, RENE, 1882-1962
The late Christopher Bean.
1933.
Howard, S., tr. and adapter.
BES32, GATS, GARZH,
SPES, WARH
Williams, E., tr. and adapter.
FAMD
Variant titles: Muse of all
work; Prenez garde à la
peinture
Muse of all work. See The late
Christopher Bean
Prenez garde à la peinture. See
The late Christopher Bean

FAULKNER, WILLIAM, 1897-1962.
See Ford, Ruth, jt. auth.

FECHTER, CHARLES ALBERT, 1824-
1879
Monte Cristo (based on the novel,
The Count of Monte Cristo, by
Alexandre Dumas, père). 1883.

AMP16, CLA, GARX, SAFM

FEELY, TERENCE, 1928-
Don't let summer come. 1964.
PLAN29

FEIFFER, JULES, 1929-
Crawling Arnold. 1961. RICJ
Knock knock. 1976. BES75
Little murders. 1966. GARTL,
LIEF, LIEG
The White House murder case.
1970. BES69, GROV

FELDSHUH, DAVID
The Bremen Town Musicians.
See Fables here and then
The centipede. See Fables here
and then
Fables here and then (music by
Roberta Carlson). 1971.
(Made up of: The wise man;
The centipede; How the snake
lost his voice; Gassir the hero;
The silver bell; The shirt
collar; The suicide; The fisher-
man and the sea king's daugh-
ter; The gas company; The
Indians and death; The Bremen
Town Musicians). MIMN
The fisherman and the sea king's
daughter. See Fables here
and then
The gas company. See Fables
here and then
Gassir the hero. See Fables here
and then
How the snake lost his voice. See
Fables here and then
The Indians and death. See
Fables here and then
The shirt collar. See Fables here
and then
The silver bell. See Fables here
and then
The suicide. See Fables here and
then
The wise man. See Fables here
and then

FELTHAUS-WEBER, MARY
The world tipped over and laying
on its side. 1966. BALLE4

FENTON, ELIJAH, 1683-1730
Mariamne. 1723. BELK14

FERBER, EDNA, 1887-1968.
See Kaufman, George S., jt. auth.

FERDINAND, VAL, 1947-
Blk love song #1. 1969. HARY

FERGUSON, IAN, 1937-
Ritual 2378 (a modern rendering
of The Bacchae by Euripides).
1972. CONZI

FERGUSSON, FRANCIS, 1904-
The king and the duke (based on
Huckleberry Finn, by Samuel
Clemens). 1939? BENS2

FERLINGHETTI, LAWRENCE, 1919-
Our little trip. FREH

FERNANDEZ DE MORATIN, LEANDRO.
See Moratín, Leandro Fernández de

FERRIS, WALTER, 1882-
Death takes a holiday (tr. and
adapted by). See Casella,
Alberto. Death takes a holiday

FETH-ALI, AKHOUD ZAIDE MIRZA.
See Fath'Ali, Akhundzadah

FEYDEAU, GEORGES LEON JULES
MARIE, 1862-1921
Breakfast in bed. See Keep an
eye on Amélie!
Get out of my hair.
Davies, F., tr. LAB
Keep an eye on Amélie! 1908.
Duffield, B., tr. BENSC
Variant titles: Breakfast in
bed; Occupe-toi d'Amélie;
Oh, Amelia
Occupe-toi d'Amélie. See Keep
an eye on Amélie!
Oh, Amelia. See Keep an eye
on Amélie!

FIELD, CHARLES KELLOGG, 1873-
The cave man. 1910. BOH2
The man in the forest. 1902.
BOH1
The owl and cave. 1906. BOH1

FIELD, EDWARD SALISBURY, 1876-
1936
Wedding bells. 1919. BES19

FIELD, JOSEPH M., 1810-1856

Job and his children. 1852.
AMP14

FIELD, NATHANIEL, 1587-1633
Amends for ladies. 1611. NER
Woman is a weathercock. 1609.
NER

FIELD, RACHEL, 1894-1942
The patchwork quilt. 193-?
COOK2

FIELDING, HENRY (H. Scriblerus
Secundus, pseud.), 1707-1754
The historical register for year
1736. 1737. BEVI
The intriguing chambermaid.
1781. BELC3
The lottery. 1732. BELC2
The miser. See Molière, Jean
Baptiste Poquilin. The miser
(tr. and adapted by)
The mock doctor. 1732.
(adapted from Molière's Le
médecin malgré lui). BELC1
The tragedy of tragedies; or,
The life and death of Tom
Thumb the great. 1731.
EIGH, HAN, KEN, LITI, NET,
STM, TAT, TAU, TAY, TUP,
TUQ
The virgin unmasked. BELC2

FIELDS, JOSEPH, 1895-1966
The doughgirls. 1942. BES42

-- and CHODOROV, JEROME
Junior miss (based on the book by
Mrs. Sally Benson). 1941.
BES41, GOW, GOWA
My sister Eileen (based on the
stories by Ruth McKenney).
1940. BES40
The ponder heart (adapted from
the story by Eudora Welty).
1956. BES55, THEA56
Wonderful town (based on the
play My sister Eileen; music by
Leonard Bernstein; lyrics by
Betty Comden and Adolph
Green). 1953. BES52, RICM,
THEA53

FIERSTEIN, HARVEY, 1954-
La cage aux folles (based on the
French play by the same title
by Jean Poiret; music and

lyrics by Jerry Herman).
1983. BES83
Fugue in a nursery. See Torch
song trilogy
The international stud. See
Torch song trilogy
Torch song trilogy. 1981. (A
program of three one-act plays:
The international stud. 1976;
Fugue in a nursery. 1979; and
Widows and children first.
(1979)
Widows and children first. See
Torch song trilogy

FIGUEROA, JOHN, 1912-
Everybody's a Jew. RAVA

FILIPPO, EDUARDO DE, 1900-
Filumena Marturano. 1946.
Bentley, E., tr. BENSA, COTN
Variant title: A mother's a
mother
A mother's a mother. See Filumena
Marturano

FINK, EDITH ROMIG
Nooschens duhn viel. See
Noshions duhn
Noshions duhn. 1950? BUFF
Variant title: Nooschens duhn
viel

FINLEY, IAN HAMILTON, 1925-
The estate hunters. NEWE14
Walking through seaweed. 1962.
NEWE14

FINNERAN, ALAN
Renaissance radar: a performance
landscape (music by Bob Davis).
1982. WES13/14

FISCHER, LECK, 1904-1956
The mystery tour. 1949.
Pearce, J., tr. CONT
Variant title: Selskabsrejsen
Selskabsrejsen. See The mystery
tour

FITCH, CLYDE, 1865-1909
Barbara Frietchie. 1899. BES99
Beau Brummell. 1890. COH
Captain Jinks of the horse
marines. 1901. BENT4
The city. 1909. MONR, MOSJ,
MOSK, MOSL

The climbers. 1901. BES99, COT
The girl with the green eyes. 1902. QUIL, QUIM, QUIN, SHA2
Her great match. 1905. QUIJ, QUIJR, QUIK
The moth and the flame. 1898. MOSS3
Nathan Hale. 1898. COOK2, PROF, PROG, PROH, SCWE
A trip abroad. See Labiche, Eugène Marin and Martin, Edouard. Le voyage de Monsieur Perrichon
The truth. 1907. DIC, GARX, STA

FITCH, WILLIAM CLYDE. See Fitch, Clyde

FITZ-BALL, EDWARD, 1792-1873
The devil's elixir. 1829. HOUR
The flying Dutchman; or, The phantom ship: a nautical drama. 1827. HOUR
Variant title: The phantom ship: a nautical drama
The phantom ship: a nautical drama. See The flying Dutchman

FITZMAURICE, GEORGE, 1877-1963
The dandy dolls. 1945. CAP

FLAVIN, MARTIN, 1883-1967
Amaco. 1933. TOD
The criminal code. 1929. BES29

FLEMING, Mrs. DOROTHY (SAYERS). See Sayers, Dorothy

FLETCHER, JOHN, 1579-1625
Babylon has fallen. 1983. PLACI
The chances. 1616. BELK15, RUB
Buckingham, Duke of, adapter. PLAN25
An equal match. See Rule a wife and have a wife
The faithful shepherdess. 1609. BAS, GRE, NEI, SCI, SCJ
The island princess; or, The generous Portugal. 1621. BROC
Rule a wife and have a wife. 1624.

BELK4, GAY3, SCH, SCI
Variant title: An equal match
The wild-goose chase. 1609? BENY, DPR2, NEI, SPE, TAT, TAU, WALL
--See also Beaumont, Francis, jt. auth.

-- MASSINGER, PHILIP [and BEAUMONT, FRANCIS]
Beggars' bush. 1609. BROC

-- and SHAKESPEARE, WILLIAM
The two noble kinsmen. 1613. BRO, PAR, THA

FLETCHER, LUCILLE
Sorry, wrong number. 1948. HEIS, WHF

FONTAINE, ROBERT, 1912-
The happy time. See Taylor, Samuel. The happy time (based on the novel by)

FONVIZIN, DINIS IVANOVICH, 1744-1792
The choice of a tutor. 1792. Roberts, C., tr. ROE
The infant. Cooper, J., tr. COOPA
The minor. 1782. Reeve, F., tr. REEV1
The young hopeful. 1782. Patrick, G., and Noyes, G., trs. NOY

FOOTE, HORTON, 1916-
The dancers (television play). 1954. WAGC2

FOOTE, SAMUEL, 1720-1777
The author. (1757). BELC3
The commissary. 1765. BELC4, BEVI
The Englishman in Paris. 1753. BELC3
The Englishman return'd from Paris. (1756) BELC3
The knights. 1747? BELC1
The liar. See The lyar
The lyar. 1762. BELC2
Variant title: The liar
The mayor of Garratt. 1763. BELC2, MOR
The minor. 1760. BELG15
The orators. 1762. BELC4

The patron. 1764. BELC4
Taste. 1752. BELC1

FORBES, JAMES, 1871-1938
The famous Mrs. Fair. 1919.
BES19, MOSJ, MOSK, MOSL

FORBES, KATHRYN, 1909-1966
Mama's bank account. See
Van Druten, John. I re-
member mama (based on the
book by)

FORD, FRANK B., 1932-
Waterman. 1976. GUTR

FORD, HARRIET, 1868-1949
Youth must be served. 1926?
TOD

FORD, JOHN, 1586-1640?
The broken heart. 1629?
BALD, BAS, BROC, HAPRA2,
HAPRB2, NEI, OLH, OLI2,
ORNT, SCI, SCJ, SPE, WINE
The chronicle history of Perkin
Warbeck. 1633? ARMS, BAS,
DPR2, LAWT, SCH
Variant title: Perkin Warbeck
Perkin Warbeck. See The chron-
icle history of Perkin Warbeck
'Tis a pity she's a whore. 1633.
BENY, DPR2, DUN, HUST,
MAKJ, PAR, RUB, RYL, WALL

-- DEKKER, THOMAS and ROWLEY,
WILLIAM
The witch of Edmonton. 1623?
BAS, LAWS

FORD, RUTH, 1920- , and FAULK-
NER, WILLIAM
Requiem for a nun (adapted from
the novel by William Faulkner).
1956? BES58

FOREMAN, FARRELL J.
Daddy's seashore blues. (1979)
CEN

FOREMAN, RICHARD, 1937-
Pandering to the masses: a misrepresentation. 1975. THG

FOREST, LOUIS, 1872-1933
Par un jour de pluie. 192-? SET

FORESTER, CECIL SCOTT, 1899-
1966
Payment deferred. See Dell,
Jeffrey. Payment deferred
(based on the novel by)

FORNÉS, MARÍA IRENE, 1930-
The Danube. 1982. PLACE
Dr. Kheal. 1968. SMC
Fefu and her friends. 1977.
WOQ1
Promenade (music by Al Car-
mines). 1965. GREAA
The successful life of 3. 1965.
BALLE2, ORZ
Tango palace. 1961. BALLE2

FORSSELL, LARS, 1928-
Galenpannan. See The madcap
The madcap. (1964)
Carlson, H., tr. MNOS
Variant title: Galenpannan
Söndags promenaden. See The
Sunday promenade
The Sunday promenade. (1963)
Carlson, H., tr. COTT
Variant title: Söndags
promenaden

FORSYTH, JAMES, 1913-
Héloise. 1931. COTK

FORTUNE, MRS. JAN ISABELLE,
1892-
The cavalier from France. 194-?
PROG

FOSSE, BOB, 1927-1987. See Ebb,
Fred, jt. auth.

FOSSE, ROBERT LOUIS. See
Fosse, Bob

FOSTER, PAUL, 1931-
Balls. 1964. ORZ
Tom Paine. 1967. GARTL

FOX, ELLEN, 1954-
Ladies in waiting. 1981. PLACI

FOX, STEPHEN
Never come Monday. See Knight,
Eric. Never come Monday
(adapted by)

FRAME, VIRGINIA. See Church,
Mrs. Virginia Woodson (Frame)

FRANCE, ANATOLE, 1844-1924
La comédie de celui qui épousa
une femme muette. 1913.
SET
Jackson, W., and E., trs.
SMR
Page, C., tr. LEV, LEVE
Variant title: The man who
married a dumb wife
The man who married a dumb
wife. See La comédie de celui
qui épousa une femme muette

FRANCIS, ANN
The song of songs which is
Solomon's. 1781? KOH2

FRANCIS, WILLIAM, 1922-
Portrait of a queen. 1965.
PLAN30

FRANK, ANNE, 1929-1945
Diary of a young girl. See
Goodrich, Frances and Hackett,
Albert. The diary of Anne
Frank (based on the book by)

FRANK, MAUDE MORRISON, 1870-
A mistake at the manor. 1915?
WEB

FRANK, MIGUEL
El hombre del siglo. See The
man of the century
The man of the century. 1958.
Jones, W., tr. JONA
Variant title: El hombre del
siglo

FRANK, WALDO DAVID, 1889-1967
New Year's eve. 1928? AME2

FRANCKLIN, THOMAS, 1721-1784
Earl of Warwick. 1766. BELG16
Matilda. 1775. INCA8

FRANKEN, MRS. ROSE D. (Lewin),
1898-
Another language. 1932.
BES31
Claudia. 1940. BES40, CALN1
Outrageous fortune. 1943.
BES43
Soldier's wife. 1944. BES44

FRANKLIN, THOMAS. See Francklin,
Thomas

FRATTI, MARIO, 1927-
The academy. (1962)
Rosenthal, R., tr. COTN,
RICJ
Variant title: L'accademia
L'accademia. See The academy
The bridge. 1969.
Anon. tr. DIZ
Variant title: Il ponte
The cage. (1961)
Carra, M., and Warner, L.,
trs. COTS
Variant title: La gabbia
La gabbia. See The cage
Nine (adapted from the Italian by).
See Kopit, Arthur Lee. Nine
Il ponte. See The bridge
The return. (1960)
Corrigan, R., and Fratti,
M., trs. COTN
Variant title: Il ritorno
Il ritorno. See The return
The suicide. (1959)
Carra, M., and Warner, L.,
trs. COTS
Variant title: Il suicidio
Il suicidio. See Fratti, M. The
suicide

FRAYN, MICHAEL, 1933-
Noises off. 1982. BES83

FREDERICKS, CLAUDE, 1923-
A summer ghost. 1961. NEWA1

FREED, Donald, 1932- , and STONE,
ARNOLD M.
Secret honor: The last testament
of Richard M. Nixon; a political
myth. 1983. NEWQA

FREEMAN, BRIAN
Factwino meets the moral majority
(script by). See San Francisco
Mime Troupe. Factwino meets
the moral majority

FREEMAN, CAROL, 1941-
The suicide. (1968). JON

FREEMAN, DAVID, 1941-
Jesse and the bandit queen.
1975. BES75

FREEMAN, DAVID E., 1945-
Creeps. 1971. BES73, PENG

FRENCH, DAVID, 1939-
Of the fields, lately. 1973.
MAJ, PENG

FREYTAG, GUSTAV, 1816-1895
The journalists. 1853?
Henderson, E., tr. FRA12
Variant title: Die journalisten
Die journalisten. See The jour-
nalists

FRIDELL, FOLKE, 1904-
Denandresbröd. See One man's
bread
One man's bread. (1961)
Austin, P., tr. MNOS
Variant title: Denandresbröd

FRIEDMAN, BRUCE JAY, 1930-
Scuba duba. 1967. BES67,
GARTL
Steambath. 1970. BES70

FRIEL, BRIAN, 1929-
Lovers. 1968. BES68
Philadelphia, here I come!
BES65, RICIS
Translations. 1980. BES80

FRINGS, KETTI (HARTLEY), 1916-
1981
Look homeward, angel (based on
the novel by Thomas Wolfe).
1957. BES57, GARSA, GATB4,
WATA

FRISBY, TERENCE
Thre's a girl in my soup.
1966. PLAN32

FRISCH, MAX, 1911-
Andorra. 1961.
Bullock, M., tr. BES62
Biedermann and the firebugs.
1958.
Gorelik, M., tr. and adapter.
BLOC, BLOND, JOHO,
KNIG, KNO, RICJ, STY
Variant titles: Biedermann
und die brandstifter; The
fire raisers; The firebugs
Biedermann und die brandstifter.
See Biedermann and the fire-
bugs
The Chinese wall. 1946.
Rosenberg, J., tr. COTQ
Variant title: Die chinesische

Mauer
Die chinesische Mauer. See The
Chinese wall
The fire raisers. See Biedermann
and the firebugs
The firebugs. See Biedermann
and the firebugs
The great fury of Philip Hotz.
1958.
Benedikt, M., tr. BENB
Variant titles: The great rage
of Philip Hotz; Die grosse
Wut des Philipp Hotz; Philip
Hotz's fury
The great rage of Philip Hotz.
See The great fury of Philip
Hotz
Die grosse Wut des Philipp Hotz.
See The great fury of Philip
Hotz
Philip Hotz's fury. See The
great fury of Philip Hotz

FROST, REX, 1914-
Small hotel. 1955. PLAN13

FROST, ROBERT, 1875-1963
A masque of reason. 1945. KNID

FRUET, WILLIAM, 1933-
Wedding in white. 1970. KAL2,
PENG

FRY, CHRISTOPHER, 1907-
The boy with a cart. 1938. POOL
The dark is light enough. 1954.
BES54
Duel of angels. See Giraudoux,
Jean. Duel of angels (adapted
by)
A phoenix too frequent. 1946.
BAC, BLAH, BRZ, FEFL, WARI,
WARL
A sleep of prisoners. 1951.
COTQ
Tiger at the gates. See Giraudoux,
Jean. Tiger at the gates (tr.
and adapted by)
Venus observed. 1950. BES51,
HAVG, WATE

FU, TO. See Sha, Seh, jt. auth.

FUGARD, ATHOL, 1932-
The blood knot. 1960. NEWE13,
WELT
Boesman and Lena. 1970. BES70

A lesson from aloes. 1980.
BES80
"Master Harold" ... and the
boys. 1982. BES81
Orestes. 1971. THI

-- KANI, JOHN; AND NTSHONA,
WINSTON
The island. 1974. BES74

FULDA, LUDWIG, 1862-1939
Beneath four eyes. See Tête
à-tête
By ourselves. See Tête-à-tête
Tête-à-tête 1886.
Townsend, E., tr. FRA17
Variant titles: Beneath four
eyes; By ourselves; Unter
vier augen
Unter vier augen. See Tête-à-
tête

FULLER, CHARLES, 1939-
A soldier's play. 1981. BES81
Zooman and the sign. 1980.
BES80

FULLER, WILLIAM HENRY
H.M.S. Parliament; or, The lady
who loved a government clerk.
1880. WAGN1

FULWELL, ULPIAN, 1530?-1585?
Like will to like; an enterlude
intituled Like wil to like quod
the Deuel to the Colier....
1568. HAO, SOME

FUNT, JULIAN, 1907?-1980
Child of Grace. See The magic
and the loss
The magic and the loss. 1954.
BES53
Variant title: Child of Grace

FURTH, GEORGE, 1932-
Company (music and lyrics by
Stephen Sondheim). 1970.
BES69, RICO

FYLES, FRANKLIN, 1847-1911.
See Belasco, David, jt. auth.

GAGLIANO, FRANK, 1931-
Father Uxbridge wants to marry.

1967. LAH

GAINES, FREDERICK
The new Chautauqua. 1968.
BALLE5

GAINES, J. E.
What if it had never turned up
heads. 1972. NEWL

GAINES-SHELTON, RUTH, 1873-
The church fight. 1925. HARY

GALANTIERE, LEWIS, 1893-
Antigone. See Anouilh, Jean.
Antigone (adapted by)

GALBRAITH, ROBERT. See Thury,
Fred, jt. auth.

GALCZYŃSKI, KONSTANTY ILDE-
FONS, 1905-1953
The atrocious uncle. 1946.
Gerould, D. and Gerould, E.,
trs. TWEN
A bloody drama in three acts
with vinegar taken from life
in the upper reaches of aca-
demic high society entitled
"Pickled alive". 1947.
Gerould, D., and Gerould, E.,
trs. TWEN
Variant title: Pickled alive
The burial of a war criminal.
1946.
Gerould, D., and Gerould, E.,
trs. TWEN
Crushed by the credenza. See
The drama of a deceived hus-
band; or, Crushed by the
credenza
The drama of a deceived husband;
or, Crushed by the credenza.
1949.
Gerould, D., and Gerould, E.,
trs. TWEN
Variant title: Crushed by the
credenza
The end of the world. 1947.
Gerould, D., and Gerould, E.,
trs. TWEN
Family happiness; or, Watch out
for expletives (a meteorological
drama). 1947.
Gerould, D., and Gerould, E.,
trs. TWEN
Variant title: Watch out for

expletives

The flood that failed in winter.
1947.
Gerould, D., and Gerould, E.,
trs. TWEN

The frightful effects of an illegal
operation. See In the clutches
of caffeine; or, The frightful
effects of an illegal operation

Greedy Eve. 1946.
Gerould, D., and Gerould, E.,
trs. TWEN

The green goose.
Gerould, D., and Gerould, E.,
trs. TWEN
Variant titles: (Twenty-two
short plays from The Little
Theatre of the Green Goose:
A Salvation Army concert;
the drama of a deceived husband; or, Crushed by the
credenza; The atrocious
uncle; A bloody drama in
three acts with vinegar
taken from life in the upper
reaches of high society
entitled "Pickled alive"; The
peculiar waiter; The burial
of a war criminal; Judith
and Holofernes (Act III of
an opera called); When Orpheus played; The flood
that failed in winter; In the
clutches of caffeine; or,
The frightful effects of an
illegal operation; Miracle in
the desert; The poet is in
bad form (a ballet called);
Hamlet and the waitress (a
play about the life of the
intellectual elite entitled);
He couldn't wait it out (a
Polish drama of the so-called
"ponderous" variety en-
titled); The tragic end of
mythology (Its author
wielding a terrible pen);
Principles of the relay cure;
or, The so-called "Transfer
therapy"; The seven sleeping brothers; Greedy Eve;
Rain; Lord Hamilton's night;
Family happiness; or, Watch
out for expletives (a meteorological drama); The end of
the world

Hamlet and the waitress (a play

about the life of the intellectual
elite entitled). 1948.
Gerould, D., and Gerould, E.,
trs. TWEN

He couldn't wait it out (a Polish
drama of the so-called "ponderous" variety entitled). 1947.
Gerould, D., and Gerould, E.,
trs. TWEN

In the clutches of caffeine; or,
The frightful effects of an illegal operation. 1946.
Gerould, D., and Gerould, E.,
trs. TWEN
Variant title: The frightful
effects of an illegal operation

Judith and Holofernes (Act III
of an opera called). 1947.
Gerould, D., and Gerould, E.,
trs. TWEN

Lord Hamilton's night. 1947.
Gerould, D., and Gerould, E.,
trs. TWEN

Miracle in the desert. 1947.
Gerould, D., and Gerould, E.,
trs. TWEN

The peculiar waiter. 1946.
Gerould, D., and Gerould, E.,
trs. TWEN

Pickled alive. See A bloody
drama in three acts with vinegar taken from life in the upper
reaches of academic high society
entitled "Pickled alive"

The poet is in bad form (a ballet
called). 1950.
Gerould, D., and Gerould, E.,
trs. TWEN

Principles of the relay cure; or,
The so-called "Transfer thera-
py". 1947.
Gerould, D., and Gerould, E.,
trs. TWEN
Variant title: The so-called
"Transfer therapy"

Rain. 1949.
Gerould, D., and Gerould, E.,
trs. TWEN

A Salvation Army concert. 1946.
Gerould, D., and Gerould, E.,
trs. TWEN

The seven sleeping brothers.
1946.
Gerould, D., and Gerould, E.,
trs. TWEN

The so-called "Transfer therapy".

See Principles of the relay
cure; or, The so-called
"Transfer therapy"
The tragic end of mythology
(Its author wielding a ter-
rible pen). 1949.
Gerould, D., and Gerould,
E., trs. TWEN
Watch out for expletives. See
Family happiness; or, Watch
out for expletives (a meteor-
ological drama)
When Orpheus played. 1949.
Gerould, D., and Gerould, E.,
trs. TWEN

GALDOS, BENITO PEREZ
See Pérez Galdós, Benito

GALE, ZONA, 1874-1938
Miss Lulu Bett. 1920. CORD,
CORE, CORF, PLAAD

GALLARATI-SCOTTI, TOMMASO,
1878-1966
Cosi sia. See Thy will be done
Thy will be done. 1923.
Petri, V., tr.
Variant title: Cosi sia

GALLICO, PAUL, 1897-1976
The snow goose (adapted for
radio by William A. Bacher
and Malcolm Meacham).
195-? INGA, INGB

GALLOWAY, TERRY
Heart of a dog. 1983. WOMB

GALSWORTHY, JOHN, 1867-1933
Escape. 1926. BES27, TRE,
TREA1, TREBA, TREC2,
TREE3, TREI3
Justice. 1910. BROW, HAU,
HAVD, HAVE, ROWC, WATF1,
WATI, WATO, WATR
Loyalties. 1922. ANDE, BES22,
BROX, CEU, COTKIT,
COTKR, LEWI, PEN, SNYD2,
SPER, WARI, WATF2, WATI
The pigeon. 1912. HARB
The silver box. 1906. CHAR,
CLKW, COTH, CROS, MOSN,
MOSO, SALE, STAT, TOD
The skin game. 1920. BES20
Strife. 1909. DIC, DUR, INGE,
INGG, MACB, MACC, MACE,

MACF, MART, STET, WATS,
WHI, WHK, WOO2

GAMBARO, GRISELDA, 1928-
The camp. 1967.
Oliver, W., tr. OLIW

GAMEL, FRED, 1944-
Wasted. 1984. BES83

GARCIA GUTIERREZ, ANTONIO,
1813-1884
Juan Lorenzo. 1865. BRET
El trovador. 1835. TRES

GARCIA LORCA, FEDERICO, 1899-
1936
Amor de don Perlimplín. See the
love of don Perlimplín and
Belisa in the garden
El amor de don Perlimplín con
Belisa en su jardín. See The
love of don Perlimplín and
Belisa in the garden
Bitter oleander. See Blood wed-
ding
Blood wedding. 1933.
Neiman, G., tr. NEW39
O'Connell, R., and
Graham-Luján, J., trs.
ALT, ALTE, BIER, BLOC,
CLL, FLOX, FOUX, KERP,
LOCLB, PERS, PERT, PERU,
TREBA, TREBJ, TREC2,
TREE2, TREI2, WATA, WEIP
Variant titles: Bitter oleander;
Bodas de sangre
Bodas de sangre. See Blood
wedding
La casa de Bernarda Alba. See
The house of Bernarda Alba
The house of Bernarda Alba.
1945. PARV
Anon. tr. CLN
Graham-Luján, J., and
O'Connell, R., tr. ALLI,
ALLJ, ALLK, CLM, CLO,
DOT, ENC, HOGF, SEN,
SSSI, WEIM
Variant title: La casa de
Bernarda Alba
In the frame of don Cristobal.
193-?
Honig, E., tr. NEWD44
The king of Harlem.
Morison, W., tr. VANV2
Lament for Ignacio Sánchez Mejías.

Spender, S., and Gill, J.,
  trs. VANV2
  Variant titles: Lament for
    the death of a bullfighter;
    Llanto por Ignacio Sánchez
    Mejías
Lament for the death of a bull-
    fighter. See Lament for
    Ignacio Sánchez Mejías
Llanto por Ignacio Sánchez
    Mejías. See Lament for
    Ignacio Sánchez Mejías
The love of don Perlimplín and
    Belisa in the garden. 1931.
  O'Connell, R., and Graham-
    Luján, J., trs. BENS1,
    CLLC, COTP
  Variant titles: Amor de don
    Perlimplín; El amor de don
    Perlimplín con Belisa en su
    jardín
The shoemaker's prodigious wife.
    1930.
  O'Connell, R., and Graham-
    Luján, J., trs. BENA
  Variant title: La zapatera
    prodigiosa
The tragi-comedy of Don Cristobita
    and Doña Rosita. 1937.
  Oliver, W., tr. NEWW8
Yerma. 1934.
  Graham-Luján, J., and
    O'Connell, R., trs. COTQ,
    FREG, ULAN
La zapatera prodigiosa. 1930.
    MARLI2
  --See also The shoemaker's
    prodigious wife

GARCIA VILLA, JOSE. See Villa,
José García

GARD, ROBERT E., 1910-
  Let's get on with the marrin'.
    DRU
  Mixing up the rent. DRU
  Raisin' the devil. DRU

GARDEL, JULIO SANCHEZ. See
Sánchez Gardel, Julio

GARDINER, WREY
  The last refuge. 1943? NEWR1

GARDNER, MRS. DOROTHY (Butts)
  Eastward in Eden. 1947. BES47

GARDNER, HERB, 1934-
  A thousand clowns. 1962.
    BES61, ESA, GARSA, HOLP

GARNEAU, MICHEL, 1939-
  Four to four. 1973.
    Bedard, C., and Turnbull, K.,
      trs. KAL5
    Variant title: Quatre à quatre
  Quatre à quatre. See Four to
    four

GARNER, HUGH, 1913-
  The magnet. See Three women:
    Some are so lucky; The mag-
    net; A trip for Mrs. Taylor
  Some are so lucky. See Three
    women: Some are so lucky;
    The magnet; A trip for Mrs.
    Taylor
  A trip for Mrs. Taylor. See
    Three women: Some are so
    lucky; The magnet; A trip for
    Mrs. Taylor
  Three women: Some are so lucky;
    The magnet; A trip for Mrs.
    Taylor. 1966. KAL2
    Variant titles: Some are so
      lucky; The magnet; A trip
      for Mrs. Taylor

GARNETT, PORTER, 1871-1950
  The green knight. 1911. BOH2

GARNIER, ROBERT, ca. 1545-1590
  The Hebrew women. [1583]
    Zoltak, M., tr. FOUAF
    Variant titles: Les juifves;
      Les juives
  Les juifves. See The Hebrew
    women
  Les juives. See The Hebrew
    women

GARRETT, JIMMY
  We own the night. 1968. JON

GARRICK, DAVID, 1717-1779
  Bon ton. 1775. BELC4
  Bucks, have at ye all. BELC4
  Catharine and Petruchio (alter-
    nate of Shakespeare's Taming
    of the Shrew). 1756. BELC3
  Cymon (altered from). 1767.
    BELC3, BELG7
  The guardian. 1759. BELC1

High life below stairs. BELC1
Lethe. 1740. BELC1
The lying valet. 1741. BELC2,
NET
Miss in her teens. 1747. BELC1,
BEVI
Neck or nothing. 1766. BELC2
--See also Colman, George, jt.
auth.

GARSON, JULIET
So what are we gonna do now?
1982. YOUP

GARZA, ROBERTO JESUS, 1934-
No nos venceremos. CONR

GASCOIGNE, GEORGE, 1525?-1577
Supposes (adapted from I suppositi, by Ludovico Ariosto).
1566. ADA, BAS, BOA, BON,
DPR1, NES, ORNC

-- and KINWELMERSH, FRANCIS
Jocasta. 1566. CUN

GASCOYGNE, GEORGE. See
Gascoigne, George

GASS, KEN, 1945-
Hurray for Johnny Canuck.
1974. FIFVE

GASSNER, JOHN, 1903-1967
Les précieuses ridicules.
See Molière, Jean Baptiste
Poquelin. Les précieuses
ridicules (tr. and adapted
by)
Then and now (adapted from
The marriage proposal and
The harmful effects of smok-
ing, by Anton Chekhov).
19-? GATS

GAY, DELPHINE. See Girardin,
Delphine (Gay) de

GAY, JOHN, 1685-1732
Achilles. 1733. BELK9
The beggar's opera. 1728.
ASH, BARB, BELK9, CASA,
CLKJ, EIGH, FEL, HAN, KER,
KRO, MAL, MAND, MANF,
MOR, MOSE2, NET, SIG,
SMR, STJM, STM, TAY,
TREB, TUP, TUQ, TWE,

UHL, WILE
--See also Brecht, Bertolt, and
Hauptmann, Elisabeth. The
threepenny opera (based on)
Polly (second part of Beggar's
opera, suppressed 1728).
BELK9

GAY SWEATSHOP
Care and control. 1977.
Wandor, Michelene, scripted
by. STR

GAZUL, CLARA, pseud. See
Mérimée, Prosper

GAZZO, MICHAEL VINCENTE, 1923-
A hatful of rain. 1956. FAM,
GART, THEA56

GEAR, BRIAN
The sky is green. 1963. PLAN27

GEDDES, VIRGIL, 1897-
The stable and the grove. 1933.
AME4

GEIJI, NAMIKI. See Namiki, Sōsuke,
jt. auth.

GELBART, LARRY, 1928-
Sly fox (based on Ben Jonson's
Volpone). 1976. BES76
--See also Shevelove, Burt, jt.
auth.

GELBER, JACK, 1932-
The connection. 1959. OBG,
SEVD

GÉLINAS, GRATIEN, 1909-
Bousille et les justes. See
Bousille and the just
Bousille and the just. 1961.
Johnstone, K., and Milville-
Dechêne J., trs. MAJ
Variant titles: Bousille et
les justes; The innocent
and the just
The innocent and the just. See
Bousille and the just

GEMS, PAM, 1925-
Aunt Mary; scenes from provincial
life. 1982. PLABE3
Dead fish. See Dusa, Fish, Stas
and Vi

Dusa, Fish, Stas and Vi. 1976.
  PLABE1
  Variant title: Dead fish

GENET, JEAN, 1910-1986
  Le balcon. See The balcony
  The balcony. 1960.
    Frechtman, B., tr. NIL,
      SEVD
    Variant title: Le balcon
  The blacks: a clown show. 1961.
    Frechtman, B., tr. GROV,
      OBG
    Variant title: Les nègres
  Les bonnes. See The maids
  Deathwatch. 1949.
    Frechtman, B., tr. COTQ
    Variant title: Haute surveil-
      lance
  Haute surveillance. See Death-
    watch
  The maids. 1947.
    Frechtman, B., tr. TREBA,
      TREI3
    Variant title: Les bonnes
  Les nègres. See The blacks: a
    clown show
  The screens. 1971.
    Volanakis, M., tr. BES71

GENSHICHI, TSUUCHI. See
Tsuuchi, Genshichi

GEORGE, ERNEST, pseud. See
Wise, Ernst George

GEORGE, GRACE, 1883-
  The next (tr. and adapted by).
    See Geraldy, Paul. The nest

GERALDY, PAUL, 1885-
  The nest. 1922.
    George, G., tr. and adapter.
      BES21
    Variant titles: Les noces
      d'argent; Silver weddings
  Les noces d'argent. See The nest
  Silver weddings. See The nest

GERSHE, LEONARD
  Butterflies are free. 1969.
    BES69

GERSHWIN, GEORGE, 1899-1937
  Of thee I sing (music by).
    See Kaufman, George S.
    and Ryskind, Morris. Of

thee I sing
  Porgy and Bess (music by).
    See Heyward, DuBose. Porgy
    and Bess

GERSHWIN, IRA, 1896-1983
  Lady in the dark (lyrics by).
    See Hart, Moss. Lady in the
    dark
  Porgy and Bess (lyrics by).
    See Heyward, DuBose. Porgy
    and Bess
  --See also Kaufman, George S.,
    jt. auth.

GERSTENBERG, ALICE, 1885-1972
  Ever young. 1920? SHAY
  Overtones. 1915. HUD, SUB
  A patroness. 1917? SHAY

GESNER, CLARK, 1942-
  You're a good man, Charlie
    Brown (book, music and lyrics
    by). 1967. BES66

GHELDERODE, MICHEL DE, 1898-
1962
  Christophe Colomb. 1927. PRO
    Hauger, G., tr. COTKW
    Valency, M., tr. CASE
    Variant title: Christopher
      Columbus
  Christopher Columbus. See
    Christophe Colomb
  The chronicles of hell. 1949.
    Hauger, G., tr. DUK, REIT
    Variant title: Fastes d'enfer
  Escurial. 1929.
    Abel, L., tr. BENT5
    Gherman, I., tr. ANTM
  Fastes d'enfer. See Chronicles
    of hell
  La pie sur le gibet. See The
    magpie on the gallows
  The magpie on the gallows.
    (1935)
    Dormoy-Savage, N., tr. ANTM
    Variant title: La pie sur le
      gibet
  Pantagleize. 1930.
    Haugher, G., tr. COTR

GIACOSA, GIUSEPPE, 1847-1908
  As the leaves fall. See Like falling
    leaves
  Come le foglie. See Like falling
    leaves

Like falling leaves. 1900.
　　Updegraff, E., and A., trs.
　　MOSQ
　　Variant titles: As the leaves
　　fall; Come le foglie

GIBBS, WOLCOTT, 1902-1958
　　Season in the sun. 1950. BES50

GIBNEY, SHERIDAN, 1903- , and
COLLINS, PIERRE
　　The story of Louis Pasteur.
　　195-? STAT, STAU

GIBSON, PAULINE, 1908- . See
Gilsdorf, Frederic, jt. auth.

GIBSON, WILFRID WILSON, 1878-
1962
　　The family's pride. 1914. RICH

GIBSON, WILLIAM, 1914-
　　The miracle worker. 1960.
　　CARMI, SUT1, WHFA
　　Two for the seesaw. 1958.
　　GARSA, GATB4

GIDE, ANDRE PAUL GUILLAUME,
1869-1951
　　The immoralist. See Goetz, Ruth
　　and Goetz, Augustus. The im-
　　moralist (based on the novel
　　by)
　　Oedipus.
　　Russell, J., tr. SANO

GIELGUD, VAL HENRY, 1900-1981
　　Away from it all. 1946. EMB3
　　Chinese white. 1928. FIT

GIL Y ZARATE, ANTONIO, 1793-
1861
　　Guzmán el Bueno. 185-? BRET

GILBERT, MICHAEL FRANCIS,
1912-
　　The bargain. 1961. PLAN23
　　A clean kill. 1959. PLAN21

GILBERT, STUART REID, 1948-
　　A glass darkly. 1972. ALI

GILBERT, WILLIAM SCHWENCK,
1836-1911, [and SULLIVAN, SIR
ARTHUR SEYMOUR, composer]
　　Dan'l Druce. 1876. KILG
　　Engaged. 1877. BAI, BOOA3,

BOOM
H.M.S. Pinafore; or, The lass
　　that loved a sailor. 1878.
　　ASG, COOP, MOSN, MOSO
--See also Moss, Alfred Charles.
　　H.M.S. Pinafore; oder, Das
　　maedle und ihr sailor kerl
　　(based on)
Iolanthe; or, The peer and the
　　peri. 1882. BOWY, HUD,
　　LAW
The mikado; or, The town of
　　Titipu. 1885. MIJ2, PROD
Patience; or, Bunthorne's bride.
　　1881. COTKIS, SMR
Pygmalion and Galatea. 1871.
　　MART, MAX
Rosencrantz and Guildenstern.
　　1891. NIN4
Ruddigore; or, The witch's curse.
　　1887. SIG
Sweethearts. 1874. BAT16,
　　COT, WEB
Tom Cobb. 1875. BOOA4
Trial by jury. 1875. REIWE

GILBERT, WILLIE, 1916- . See
Burrows, Abram S., and Weinstock,
Jack, jt. auths.

GILBERT-LECOMTE, ROGER, 1907-
1943
　　L'odyssée d'Ulysse le palmipède.
　　See The odyssey of Ulysses the
　　palmiped
　　The odyssey of Ulysses the palmi-
　　ped. 1924.
　　Wellwarth, G., tr. BEN
　　Variant title: L'odyssée
　　d'Ulysse le palmipède

GILLETTE, WILLIAM HOOKER, 1855-
1937
　　Secret service. 1896.
　　BES94, GARX, QUIJ, QUIJR,
　　QUIK, QUIL, QUIM, QUIN
　　Sherlock Holmes (based on the
　　stories by Sir Arthur Conan
　　Doyle). 1899. CART, PLAN44

GILLAT, SIDNEY, 1908- . See
Launder, Frank, jt. auth.

GILLIATT, PENELOPE, 1932- .
　　Property. 1979. WOMA

GILLMAN, JONATHAN

The marriage test. 1968.
BALLE6

GILLOIS, ANDRE, pseud. See
Diamond-Berger, Maurice

GILROY, FRANK D., 1925- .
The subject was roses. 1964.
BES64, GAT, RICT

GILSDORF, FREDERICH, 1903- ,
and GIBSON, PAULINE
The ghost of Benjamin Sweet.
1956? WAGC1

GINSBURY, NORMAN, 1903-
The advertisement. 1968. SUB
The first gentleman. 1935. FIR
John Gabriel Borkman. See
Ibsen, Henrik. John Gabriel
Borkman (adapted by)
The safety match (based on a
short story by Anton
Pavlovich Chekhov). RICK
Viceroy Sarah. 1934. FAMG

GIRARDIN, DELPHINE (Gay) de
("Mme. Emile de Girardin"), 1804-
1855
La joie fait peur. 1854. BENZ
Variant titles: Sunshine
follows rain; Sunshine
through the clouds
Sunshine follows rain. See La
joie fait peur
Sunshine through the clouds.
See La joie fait peur

"GIRARDIN, MME. EMILE DE."
See Girardin, Delphine (Gay) de

GIRAUDOUX, JEAN, 1882-1944
Amphitryon 38. See Behrman,
Samuel Nathaniel. Amphitryon
38 (adapted from)
The Apollo of Bellac. 1942.
Valency, M., adapter.
COX, GATS, MIJE
Variant titles: L'Apollon de
Bellac; L'Apollon de
Marsac
L'Apollon de Bellac. See The
Apollo of Bellac
L'Apollon de Marsac. See The
Apollo of Bellac
Cantique des cantiques. See
Song of songs

Duel of angels. 1953.
Fry, C., tr. and adapter.
BES59
Variant title: Pour Lucrece
Electra. 1937.
Smith, W., tr. BENS2,
BENT1, BLOC, COTKW,
COTQ, FOR, LOR
Variant title: Electre
Electre. See Electra
The enchanted (adapted by
Maurice Valency). 1950.
BES49
Variant title: Intermezzo
La folle de Chaillot. See The
madwoman of Chaillot
La guerre de Troie n'aura pas
lieu. See Tiger at the gates
Intermezzo. See The enchanted
Judith. 1931.
Savacool, J., tr. BENT3
The madwoman of Chaillot
(adapted by Maurice Valency).
1948. ALLI, ALLK, BES48,
BLOC, BROX, COTKI, FOUA,
GARZH, GRIF, HAVG, PERV,
SCAR, TREBJ, WATE
Variant title: La folle de
Chaillot
Ondine. 1954? (from the novel
Undine by Baron de la Motte
Fouque; adapted by Maurice
Valency). CLM, CLN, GARZH,
THEA54, WEIM
Pour Lucrece. See Duel of angels
Siegfried. 1928. GRAF
Sodom and Gomorrah. 1943.
Anon. tr. SANK
Briffault, H., tr. ULAN
Valency, M., tr. ALLJ, BROY,
JOHN, TREBA, TREI3
Song of songs. 1938?
Briffault, H., tr. ULAN
Raikes, J., tr. BERM
Variant title: Cantique des
cantiques
Tiger at the gates. 1955.
CLOU, PUCC
Fry, C., tr. BES55, CLL,
DOT, DOWS, GARZH, KERO,
ROET, SATJ, SCNR,
THEA56, WAIU
Variant title: La guerre de
Troie n'aura pas lieu

GLASPELL, SUSAN, 1882-1948
Alison's house. 1930.

BES30, CORD, CORE, CORF,
SIXD
Trifles. 1916. ACE, BEAC11,
CARM, FREI, GASB, HUD,
MOAD, PEN, PLAAD, PROD,
PROF, PROG, STAT, STAU,
STAV, WOM

GLEASON, JAMES, 1885-1959. See
Abbott, George, jt. auth.

GLEBOV, ANATOLE GLEBOVITCH,
1899-
Inga. 1928.
Malamuth, C., tr. LYK

GLOVER, HALCOTT, 1877-1949
The king's jewry. 1928. TUCD

GLOVER, RICHARD, 1712-1785
Boadicia. 1753. BELK20
Medea. (1761) BELG15

GODFREY, THOMAS, 1736-1763
The prince of Parthia. 1767?
MOSS1, QUIJ, QUIK, QUIL,
QUIM, QUIN

GODLOVITCH, CHARLES Z., 1921-
Timewatch. SHAT

GOERING, REINHARD, 1887-1936
Naval encounter. 1917.
Ritchie, J., and Stowell, J.,
trs. RITV
Variant titles: Sea flight;
Seeschlacht
Sea flight. See Naval encounter
Seeschlacht. See Naval en-
counter

GOETHE, JOHANN WOLFGANG VON,
1749-1832
Egmont. 1791.
Hamburger, M., tr. BENR2
Lamport, F., tr. LAMP
Lustig, T., tr. LUST
Swanwick, A., tr. CLF3,
HARC19
Faust, pt. I. 1829. EVB2
Anon. tr. DRA2, PLAB2
MacIntyre, C., tr. TREB,
TREC1, TREE1, TREI1,
VANV2
MacNeice, L., tr. MALC,
MALG2, MALI2, MALN2
Priest, G., tr. EVC2,

GRDB47, HOUK
Raphael, A., jr. GOUZ
Swanwick, A., tr. BUCK,
BUCL, BUCM, CROV,
ESS, EVA2, FRA1, HARC19,
ROB, THOM, THON, WEAV2
Taylor, B., tr. HIB, HIBA,
HIBB, LOCM2, TRE, TREA2,
VON, WORP
Faust, pt. II. 1829.
MacNeice, L., tr. MACJ,
MACL2
Priest, G., tr. GRDB47
Swanwick, A., tr. BUCM,
FRA1
Goetz von Berlichinger. 1774.
Scott, W., tr. MAU
Iphigenia in Tauris. 1802.
Swanwick, A., tr. BAT11,
FRA1
Variant titles: Iphigenia of
Tauris; Iphigenie auf
Tauris
Iphigenia of Tauris. See
Iphigenia in Tauris
Iphigenie auf Tauris. See
Iphigenia in Tauris
Stella. 1776.
Thompson, B., tr. BAT12
Torquato Tasso. 1807.
Swanwick, A., tr. KRE

GOETZ, AUGUSTUS, d.1957. See
Goetz, Ruth Goodman, jt. auth.

GOETZ, RUTH GOODMAN, 1912-
and GOETZ, AUGUSTUS
The doctor's daughter. See The
heiress
The heiress (based on the novel,
Washington Square, by Henry
James, Jr.). 1947. BES47
Variant titles: The doctor's
daughter; Washington
Square
The immoralist (based on the novel
by André Gide). 1954.
BES53
Washington Square. See The
heiress

GOGGAN, JOHN PATRICK. See
Patrick, John, pseud.

GOGOL', NIKOLAI VASIL'EVICH,
1809-1852
Dead souls. See Bulgakov,

Mikhail Alfanasevich. Dead
souls (based on the novel by)
Gamblers. 1833.
Bentley, E., tr. BENT3
The government inspector. See
The inspector
The inspector. 1836.
Anon. tr. COUR
Cooper, J., tr. COOPA
Davies, T., tr. BAT18
Guerney, B., tr. GUE, HOUG
MacAndrew, A., tr. GARZE,
MAB
Magarshack, D., tr. MAP
Reeve, F., tr. REEV1
Saffron, R., tr. SAFF
Seymour, J., and Noyes, G.,
trs. NOY, TREB, TREC1,
TREE1, TREI1
Sykes, A., tr. CLKW, COUS
Variant titles: The government
inspector; The inspector
general; Revisor
The inspector general. See The
inspector
The marriage. 1842.
Bentley, E., tr. BENT4
Revisor. See The inspector

GOHEI, NAMIKI, III. See Namiki,
Gohei III

GOLD, MICHAEL, 1894-1967
Hoboken blues; or, The black
Rip Van Winkle. 1927?
AME1

GOLDBERG, DICK, 1947-
Family business. 1978. BES77

GOLDEMBERG, ROSE LEIMAN
Letters home (based on Sylvia
Plath's Letters home, selected
and edited by Aurelia Schober
Plath). 1979. PLABE2,
WOMA

GOLDING, WILLIAM GERALD, 1911-
The brass butterfly. 1958.
BARG

GOLDMAN, JAMES, 1927-
Follies (music and lyrics by
Stephen Sondheim). 1971.
BES70
The lion in winter. 1966.
BES65, GAT

GOLDONI, CARLO, 1707-1793
Accomplished maid (attributed to).
BELK21
Un curioso accidente. 1757. BIN
Zimmern, H., tr. CROV
Variant titles: A curious mis-
hap; A curious misunder-
standing
A curious mishap. See Un cu-
rioso accidente
A curious misunderstanding. See
Un curioso accidente
The fan. 1763.
Fuller, H., tr. CLF2
Variant title: Il ventaglio
La locandiera. See The mistress
of the inn
Mirandolina. See The mistress of
the inn
The mistress of the inn. 1753.
Gregory, I., tr. BENR1
Lohmann, H., tr. LEG
Pierson, M., tr. MAU, MOSA
Variant titles: La locandiera;
Mirandolina
L'osteria della posta. See The
post-inn
The post-inn. 1761.
Chambers, W., tr. BAT5
Variant title: L'osteria della
posta
The servant of two masters.
1743?
Dent, E., tr. BENR1, SMA
Lopworth, P., tr. PLAN36
Variant title: Il servitore di
due padroni
Il servitore di due padroni.
See The servant of two masters
Il ventaglio. See The fan

GOLDSMITH, CLIFFORD, 1900-1971
What a life. 1938. BES37

GOLDSMITH, OLIVER, 1728-1774
The good-natured man. 1768.
BELG1, STM
She stoops to conquer; or, The
mistakes of a night. 1773.
BARG, BARU, BEAC11, BELG8,
BENN, BENY, CLF1, CLKY,
COL1, DAI, DEM, DOWS,
DRA1, DUH, EIGH, FOUB,
GOU2, HARC18, HUD, JAFF,
KEY, KRM, MAND, MANF,
MAX, MOO, MOR, MORR,
MOSE2, NET, PLAB1, POOL,

PROM, RUB, SHAH1, SMO,
SRY, SRYG, STA, STM, TAT,
TAU, TAY, TUP, TUQ, TWE,
UHL, WILE

GOLL, IWAN, 1891-1950
The eternal bourgeois. See
Methusalem
Der ewige Bürger. See
Methusalem
The immortal one. (1920).
Sokel, W., and J., trs.
SOK
Methusalem; oder, Der ewige
Bürger. See Methusalem; or,
The eternal bourgeois
Methusalem; or, The eternal
bourgeois. 1922.
Ritchie, J., and Garten, H.,
trs. RITS
Wensinger, A., and Atkinson,
C., tr. PLAC

GOLL, YVAN. See Goll, Iwan

GOMES, ALFREDO DIAS, 1922-
O pagador de promesas. See
Payment as pledged
Payment as pledged. 1960.
Fernández, O., tr. WOOG
Variant title: O pagador de
promesas

GONDINET, EDMOND, 1829?-1888
See Labiche, Eugène Marin, jt.
auth.

GONNE, FRANCIS
In the city of David. 1934.
SEVE

GOODHART, WILLIAM
Generation. 1965. BES65

GOODMAN, KENNETH SAWYER,
1883-1918
Dust of the road. 1912? FED1

-- and HECHT, BEN
The hand of Siva. 192-? STAT,
STAU

GOODMAN, PAUL, 1911-
The tower of Babel. 1940.
NEWD40

GOODRICH, FRANCES, 1891-1984,

and HACKETT, ALBERT
The diary of Anne Frank (based
on the book by Anne Frank).
1955. BES55, CARM, CARME,
GARU, GATB4, RICT,
THEA56, WHFA

GOOLD, MARSHALL NEWTON, 1881-
1935
The quest divine. 1925? FED2
St. Claudia. 1924? FED2
The shepherds. 192-? FED2

GORDON, GEORGE, 1788-1824. See
Byron, George Gordon

GORDON, ROBERT
And. 1974. WES2
The tunes of Chicken Little.
1972. BALLE13

GORDON, RUTH (Mrs. GARSON
KANIN), 1896-1985
Over 21. 1943. BES43
Years ago. 1946. BES46,
WAGC1, WAGE

GORDONE, CHARLES, 1925-
The breakout. KINH
No place to be somebody. 1969.
BES68, OLIV, PATR, WEIP

GORE-BROWNE, ROBERT F., 1893- .
See Harwood, Harold Marsh, jt. auth.

GORKI, MAXIM (pseud. of Aleksíeĭ
Maksimovich Píeskov), 1868-1936
At the bottom. See The lower
depths
Dans les fonds. See The lower
depths
Down and out. See The lower
depths
From the depths. See The lower
depths
In the depths. See The lower
depths
The lower depths. 1902.
Anon. tr. SMA
Bakshy, A., tr. BLOC, FOUM
Burke, H., tr. COTO, COTQ
Chambers, W., tr. BAT18
Covan, J., tr. CEW, DIK2,
HAV, HOUG, MOS, TRE,
TREA1, TREBA, TREBJ,
TREC2, TREE2, TREI2,
TUCN, TUCO, WHI

Guerney, B., tr. GUE
Hopkins, E., tr. DID, MOSG,
    MOSH, SMP, TUCG, WATI,
    WATL3
MacAndrew, W., tr. GARZG,
    MABA
Magarshack, D., tr. MAP
Noyes, G., and Kaun, A.,
    trs. NOY
Reeve, F., tr. REEV2
Variant titles: At the bottom;
    Dans les fonds; Down and
    out; From the depths; In
    the depths; A night shelter;
    Night's lodging; Submerged
A night shelter. See The lower
    depths
Night's lodging. See The lower
    depths
Submerged. See The lower depths
Yegor Bulichov and others. 1932.
    CLKX
    Bakshy, A., tr. HOGF
    Wixley, A., tr. FOUS

GORKY, MAXIM. See Gorki, Maxim

GORLING, LARS, 1931-1966
The sandwiching. (1962)
    Austin, P., tr. MNOS
    Variant title: Trängningen
Trängningen. See The sandwich-
    ing

GOSS, CLAY, 1946-
Mars: Monument to the last
    black eunuch. 1972. CARR
On being hit. 1970. NEWL

GOTANDA, PHILIP KAN, 1949-
The dream of Kitamura. 1982.
    WES15/16

GOUBAUX, PROSPER PARFAIT,
1795-1859, and DUCANGE VICTOR
HENRY JOSEPH BRAHAIN
Trente ans; ou, La vie d'un
    joueur. See Dunlap, William.
    Thirty years; or, The gamb-
    ler's fate (adapted from)

GOULDING, EDMUND, 1891-1959.
See Selwyn, Edgar, jt. auth.

GOW, JAMES ELLIS, 1907-1952 and
D'USSEAU, ARNAUD
Deep are the roots. 1945. BES45

Tomorrow the world. 1942.
    BES42, GARZ

GOW, ROGER, 1899- , and GREEN-
WOOD, WALTER
Love on the dole. 1934. PLAL

GOW, RONALD, 1897-
Ann Veronica (adapted from the
    novel by H. G. Wells). 1949.
    PLAN2
The Edwardians (adapted from
    the novel by Victoria Mary
    Sackville-West). 1959.
    PLAN20
Variant title: Weekend in May
Weekend in May. See The Ed-
    wardians

GOWER, DOUGLAS
Daddies. 1977. WES1

GOZZI, CARLO, conte, 1722-1806
The king stag. 1762?
    Wildman, C., tr. BENR1
Turandot. 1761.
    Levy, J., tr. BENSA

GRABBE, CHRISTIAN DIETRICH,
1801-1836
Don Juan and Faust. (1829)
    Edwards, E., tr. MARL
    Variant title: Don Juan und
    Faust
Don Juan und Faust. See Don
    Juan and Faust
Jest, satire, irony, and deeper
    significance. 1827?
    Edwards, M., tr. BENS2

GRAINGER, TOM, 1921-
The helper. 1972. BRIQ

GRANGE, CHANCEL LA. See La
Grange-Chancel

GRANT, DAVID
The king cat. FRO

GRANT, DIANE
What glorious times they had
    Nellie McClung. 1974. WIM

GRANVILLE-BARKER, HARLEY
GRANVILLE, 1877-1946
Deburau (tr. and adapted by).
    See Guitry, Sacha. Deburau

The Madras house. 1910.
DIC, MOSN, MOSO, WEAL
The voysey inheritance. 1905.
DIG, PLAP1, ROWC
Waste. 1909. TUCD
--See Houseman, Laurence, jt.
auth.

GRASS, GUNTHER, 1927-
Beritten hin und zurück. See
Rocking back and forth
Die bösen Köche. See The
wicked cooks
Rocking back and forth. 1960.
Benedikt, M., and
Goradza, J., trs. BENB
Variant title: Beritten hin
und zurück
The wicked cooks. 1961.
Rosenberg, J., tr. COTS
Variant title: Die bösen
Köche

GRAVES, RUSSELL, 1922-
The battle of the carnival and
Lent. 1967. PAJ

GRAVES, WARREN G., 1933-
The proper perspective. SHAT

GRAY, SIMON, 1936-
Butley. 1972. BES72
Otherwise engaged. 1975.
BES76, BEST
Quartermaine's terms; a play in
two acts. 1981. BES82

GRAY, STEPHEN, 1941-
'n Aandjie by die Vernes. See
An evening at the Vernes
An evening at the Vernes (based
on the writings of Jules
Verne). 1975. CONZI
Variant title: 'n Aandjie by
die Vernes (first per-
formed as an Afrikaans
adaptation by Louis van
Rooyen and Johann Papen-
dorf)

GREANIAS, GEORGE, 1948-
Wilson. 1973. BAALE12

GREAVES, DONALD, 1943-
The marriage. (1971) KINH

GRECCO, STEPHEN

The Orientals. BALLE7

GREEN, ADOLPH, 1915-
See Comden, Betty, jt. auth.

GREEN, ERMA, 1894-
See Green, Paul, jt. auth.

GREEN, JANET, 1913-
Murder mistaken. 1952.

GREEN, JULIEN, 1900-
South. 1953.
Anon. tr. PLAN12
Variant title: Sud
Sud. See South

GREEN, PAUL, 1894-1981
The field god. 1927. HAL,
TUCD, TUCM, TUCN
The house of Connelly. 1931.
BES31, GARU
Hymn to the rising sun. 1936.
KOZ
In Abraham's bosom. 1927.
BES26, CORD, CORE, CORF,
DIE, LOC, MOAD, TOD, WHI
Johnny Johnson (music by Kurt
Weill). 1937. AND, ANDE,
BES36, GAS
The Lord's will. 1925. LEV,
LEVE
The man who died at twelve
o'clock. 1925. CHU
The no'count boy. 1924. LOC
Potter's field. See Roll sweet
chariot
Roll sweet chariot. 1934. CLKW
Variant title: Potter's field
Supper for the dead. 1926?
AME1
Tread the green grass. 1928.
AME3
Unto such glory. 1926? FLAN,
HUDS2
White dresses. 1920. GASB, LOC
--See Wright, Richard, jt. auth.

-- and GREEN, ERMA
Fixin's: the tragedy of a tenant
farm woman. 1934. RAVA
Variant title: The renewal
The renewal. See Fixin's: the
tragedy of a tenant farm woman

GREENBERG, DANIEL. See Levine,
Mark L., jt. auth.

GREENE, GRAHAM, 1904-
　The complaisant lover.　1959.
　　BES61
　The living room.　1952.　BES54
　The potting shed.　1957.
　　BES56

GREENE, PATTERSON, 1899-1968
　Papa is all.　1942.　GALB

GREENE, ROBERT, 1558-1592
　Friar Bacon and Friar Bungay.
　　See The honorable history of
　　Friar Bacon and Friar Bungay
　George a Greene, The pinner of
　　Wakefield (supposed author).
　　1588?　ADA, BAS, NES,
　　SCH
　　　Variant title: A pleasant con-
　　　　ceited comedy of [George a
　　　　Greene] the pinner of
　　　　Wakefield
　The honorable history of Friar
　　Bacon and Friar Bungay.
　　1589?　ASH, BAS, BENY,
　　BROC, DPR1, GATG, GAY1,
　　HEIL, HOW, MAK, MIN2, MIO2,
　　NEI, NES, OLH, OLI1, ORNC,
　　PAR, SCI, SCJ, SCW, SPE,
　　TICO
　　　Variant title: Friar Bacon
　　　　and Friar Bungay
　James the fourth.　1591?　MIN2,
　　MIO2
　A pleasant conceited comedy of
　　[George a Greene] the pinner
　　of Wakefield.　See George a
　　Greene, the pinner of Wake-
　　field
　--See also Lodge, Thomas, jt.
　　auth.

GREENLAND, BILL
　We three, you and I.　1970.
　　BRIN

GREENWOOD, WALTER, 1903-1974
See Gow, Roger, jt. auth.

GREGORY, ISABELLA AUGUSTA
(PERSSE), Lady, 1859-1932
　The Canavans.　1906.　BARF
　The dragon.　1917.　WEB
　Hyacinth Halvey.　1906.　CAP,
　　MIL, WATF1, WATI, WATT2
　The rising of the moon.　1907.
　　BEAC12, DIC, PROB, SHAR,

SSTA
　Spreading the news.　1904.
　　BEAC8, FIG, PEN, PROC,
　　WATS
　The workhouse ward.　1908.
　　COD, KEN, LITI, LITJ, MOSN,
　　MOSO, TOD, TREBA, TREC2,
　　TREE2, TREI3

GRESSET, JEAN BAPTISTE LOUIS,
1709-1777
　Le méchant.　1747.　BRE

GRIBOIEDOV, ALEXANDR SERGIEE-
VICH, 1795-1829
　Chatsky; or, The misery of having
　　a mind.　1823.
　　Cooper, J., tr.　COOPA
　Intelligence comes to grief.　See
　　Wit works woe
　The misery of having a mind.
　　See Chatsky
　The misfortune of being clever.
　　See Wit works woe
　The trouble with reason.　1824?
　　Reeve, F., tr.　REEV1
　Wit works woe.　1831.
　　Pares, B., tr.　NOY
　　　Variant titles: Intelligence
　　　　comes to grief; the misfor-
　　　　tune of being clever; Woe
　　　　from wit
　Woe from wit.　See Wit works woe

GRIBOYEDOV, ALEXSANDER.　See
Gribofedov, Alexandr Sergîevich

GRIEG, NORDAHL, 1902-1943
　The defeat: a play about the
　　Paris Commune.　1936.
　　Watkins, J., tr.　SCAN2
　　Variant title: Nederlaget
　Nederlaget.　See The defeat
　Our power and our glory.
　　Gathorne-Hardy, G., tr.　FIL

GRIFFIN, ALICE VENEZKY, 1921-
　Oresteia.　See Aeschylus.
　　Oresteia (arranged for the
　　stage by)

GRIFFIN, G. W. H.
　Hamlet the dainty.　(1870?)　NIN5
　Othello.　(1870?)　NIN5
　Shylock.　(1870?)　NIN5

GRIFFITH, ELIZABETH, 1720?-1793

School for rakes. 1769. BELG2

bissness

GRIFFITH, HUBERT FREELING
1896-1953
Youth at the helm (tr. and
adapted by). See Vulpius,
Paul. Youth at the helm

GRIFFITHS, ELIZABETH. See
GRIFFITH, ELIZABETH

GRIFFITHS, TREVOR, 1935-
Comedians. 1975. BES76

GRILLPARZER, FRANZ, 1791-1872
The fortunes and death uf King
Ottokar. See König Ottokars
glück und ende
The Jewess of Toledo. 1873.
Danton, G., and A., trs.
FRA6
Variant title: Die jüdin von
Toledo
Die jüdin von Toledo. See The
Jewess of Toledo
King Ottakar, his rise and fall.
See König Ottokars glück und
ende
König Ottokars glück und ende.
1825. CAM
Burkhard, A., tr. ANTH
Variant titles: The fortunes
and death of King Ottokar;
King Ottokar, his rise and
fall
Medea. 1821.
Lamport, F., tr. LAMP
Miller, T., tr. FRA6
Sappho. 1818. CAM
Frothingham, E., tr. SMN
Der traum ein leben. 1834.
FEFH1

GRIMKE, ANGELINA WELD, 1880-
1958
Rachel. 1916. HARY

GROVER, LEONARD, d.1926
Our boarding house. 1877.
AMP4

GRUMBINE, EZRA LIGHT, 1845-1880
Die inschurens bissness. See
Die insurance business
Die insurance business. 1880?
BUFF
Variant title: Die inschurens

GRUNDY, SYDNEY, 1848-1914
A pair of spectacles (adapted from
Les petits oiseaux by Eugène
Labiche and Delacour). 1890.
ROWE

GUARE, JOHN, 1938-
Cop-out. 1968. OFF
The house of blue leaves. 1971.
BES70, GARTL
Muzeeka. 1967. LAH, OFF

-- and SHAPIRO, MEL
Two gentlemen of Verona (music
by Galt MacDermot; lyrics by
John Guare). 1971. GREAA

GUARINI, GIOVANNI BATTISTA,
1538-1612
The faithful shepherd. 1595.
Fanshawe, R., tr. FIJ
Variant title: Il pastor fido

GUERDON, DAVID
The laundry. 1962.
Richardson, H., tr. COTT

GUERRERO, WILFRIDO MARIA,
1917-
Forever. 1947. EDAD

GUIMERA, ANGEL, 1847-1924
Daniela. 1902.
Underhill, J., tr. CLDM
Variant titles: La pecadora;
The sinner
La pecadora. See Daniela
The sinner. See Daniela

GUINN, DOROTHY C.
Out of the dark. RIR

GUINNESS, ALEC, 1914- , and
STRACHAN, ALAN
Yahoo. 1976. PLAN46

GUINON, ALBERT, 1863-1923, and
MARNIERE, JEANNE MARIE FRAN-
ÇOISE
Le joug. See The yoke
The yoke. 1902.
Anon. tr. BAT21
Variant title: Le joug

GUITRY, SACHA, 1885-1957

Deburau. 1920.
  Granville-Barker, H., tr.
  and adapter. BES20
Don't listen, ladies! (adapted
  by Stephen Powys and Guy
  Bolton). 1948. PLAN1
Pasteur. 1919.
  Brown, I., tr. DID

GUNNER, FRANCES
  The light of the women. RIR

GURNEY, A. R., Jr., 1930-
  The dining room. 1982. BES81
  The golden fleece. 1968.
  BAYM

GURNEY, RICHARD
  Romeo and Juliet travesty.
  (1812) NIN1

GUTHRIE, J.
  He who gets slapped. See
  Andreev, Leonid Nikolaevich.
  He who gets slapped (adapted
  by)

GUTHRIE, TYRONE, 1900-1971
  Top of the ladder. 1950.
  PLAN3

GUTIERREZ, ANTONIO GARCIA.
See García Gutiérrez, Antonio

GUTWILLIG, STEPHEN
  In the way. 1982. YOUP

GUTZKOW, KARL FERDINAND,
1811-1878
  Pigtail and sword. See Sword
  and queue
  Sword and queue. 1843.
  Colbron, G., tr. FRA7
  Variant titles: Pigtail and
  sword; Zopf und schwert
  Zopf und schwert. See Sword
  and queue

HAAVIKKO, PAAVO, 1931-
  The superintendent. 1968.
  Binham, P., tr. MNOF

HACKETT, ALBERT, 1900-
See Goodrich, Frances, jt. auth.

HACKETT, WALTER, 1876-1944.
See Megrue, Roi Cooper, jt. auth.

HADDOW, JEFFREY, 1947-
See Driver, John, jt. auth.

HADLER, WILLIAM
  Flite cage. 1969. SME

HAGAN, JAMES, 1887?-1947
  One Sunday afternoon. 1933.
  BES32

HAILEY, ARTHUR, 1920-
  Flight into danger. 1956. BRNB
  Shadow of suspicion. GREG

HAILEY, OLIVER, 1932-
  Hey you, light man! 1961. GASY
  Who's happy now? 1967. LAH

HAINES, JOHN THOMAS, 1799?-
1843
  My Poll and my partner Joe.
  1835. BOOB
  The ocean of life. 1836. KILG

HAINES, WILLIAM WISTER, 1908-
  Command decision. 1947.
  BES47, CLH, MIJY, QUIN,
  TUCN

HALBE, MAX, 1865-1944
  Mother earth. 1897.
  Grummann, P., tr. FRA20
  Variant title: Mutter erde
  Mutter erde. See Mother earth

HALE, JOHN, 1926-
  The black swan winter. 1969.
  PLAN37
  Spithead. 1969. PLAN38

HALL, CAROL, 1936?-
  The best little whorehouse in
  Texas; a musical in two acts
  (music and lyrics by). See
  King, Larry L. and Masterson,
  Peter. The best little whore-
  house in Texas

HALL, HOLWORTHY, 1887-1936, and
MIDDLEMASS, ROBERT M.
  The valiant. 1921. BEAC10

HALL, WILLIS, 1929-

The long and the short and the tall. 1959. NEWE3
--See Waterhouse, Keith, jt. auth.

HALLDÓRSSON, ERLINGUR E., 1930-
Mink. (1965)
Boucher, A., tr. MNOI
Variant title: Minkarnir
Minkarnir. See Mink

HALLE, ADAM DE LA. See Adam de la Halle

HALLIDAY, ANDREW, 1830-1877
Romeo and Juliet travestie; or, The cup of cold poison. 1859. NIN3

-- See also BROUGH, WILLIAM, jt. auth.

HALPER, LEIVICK (H. Leivick, pseud.), 1888-1962
The golem. 1920.
Landis, J., tr. LAO, LAOG
Heroic years. See Hirsh Lekert
Hirsh Lekert; or, Heroic years. 1928.
Lifson, D., tr. LIFS
Variant title: Heroic years

HALPERN, LEIVICK. See Halper, Leivick

HAMBLIN, LOUISA (MEDINA), d.1838
Nick of the woods. 1838. VIC

HAMILTON, PATRICK, 1904-1962
Angel street. 1941. BES41, CART, MOST, RICI, SAFM
Variant title: Gaslight
Gaslight. See Angel street

HAMLIN, MARY P.
The rock. 1921? FED1

HAMLISCH, MARVIN, 1943-
A chorus line (music by). See Kirkwood, James and Dante, Nicholas. A chorus line

HAMMERSTEIN II, OSCAR, 1895-1960
Allegro (music by Richard

Rodgers). 1947. BES47
The king and I (music by Richard Rodgers). 1951. CORB
Oklahoma! (based on Green grown the lilacs by Lynn Riggs; music by Richard Rodgers). 1943. BES42, CEY

-- and LOGAN, JOSHUA
South Pacific (based on Tales of the South Pacific by James A. Michener; music by Richard Rodgers). 1949. QUIN

HAMPTON, CHRISTOPHER, 1946-
The philanthropist. 1971. BES70

HAN-CH'ING, KUAN. See Kuan, Han-ch'ing

HANDKE, PETER, 1942-
Das Mündel will Vormund sein.
See My foot my tutor
My foot my tutor. 1969.
Roloff, M., tr. SHAK
Variant title: Das Mündel will Vormund sein

HANEMON, TSUUCHI. See Tsuuchi, Hanemon

HANJURŌ, TSUUCHI. See Tsuuchi, Hanjurō

HANKIN, ST. JOHN EMILE CLAVERING, 1869-1909
The Cassilis engagement. 1907. DIG, MOSN, MOSO, ROWC
The last of the De Mullins. 1908. CHA, CHAN, CHAR
The return of the prodigal. 1905. MART, WEAL

HANLEY, JAMES, 1901-1985
Say nothing. 1962. PLAN27

HANLEY, WILLIAM, 1931-
Slow dance on the killing ground. 1964. BES64, GAT

HANSBERRY, LORRAINE, 1930-1965
The drinking gourd. 1960. HARY
A raisin in the sun. 1959. ALS, ANT, BARO, BES58, BRIZ, CASA, CEQ, CEQA, CES, DIP, DIT, DITA, FORD (act 1 only),

FOT, GRIH, HAPO, HEIS,
KIN, LAV, MONA, OLIV,
PATR, PERU, PERV, PLAU,
SCNP, SILKI, SYM, WHFM
The sign in Sidney Brustein's
window. 1964. GAT, THT

HANSHEW, THOMAS W., 1857-1914
The forty-niners. 1879. BAT20

HAN TIEN. See Tien, Han

HAO-KU, LI. See Li, Hao-ku

HARBURG, EDGAR Y., 1896-1981,
and SAIDY, FRED
Finian's rainbow. 1947. HUDE

HARDT, ERNST, 1876-1947
Tantris the fool. See Tristram
the jester
Tristram the jester. 1907.
Heard, J., tr. FRA20
Variant title: Tantris the
fool

HARDY, ALEXANDRE, 1575?-1631?
Mariamne. 1605-1615?
Lockert, L., tr. LOCU

HARDY, THOMAS, 1840-1928
The day after the fair. See
Harvey, Frank. The day
after the fair (based on a
story by)
The play of St. George (reconstructed from memory by).
See Anonymous plays. The
play of St. George

HARE, DAVID, 1947-
Plenty; a play in two acts.
1978. BES82

HARGRAVE, ROY, 1908- . See
Britton, Kenneth Phillips, jt. auth.

HARLAN, WALTER, 1867-1931
The Nüremberg egg. 1913.
Katzin, W., tr. KAT
Variant title: Das Nürn-
burgisch ei
Das Nürnburgisch ei. See
The Nüremberg egg

HARNICK, SHELDON, 1924-
The apple tree (jt. auth. and

music by Jerry Bock). 1966.
BES66
Fiddler on the roof (lyrics by).
See Stein, Joseph. Fiddler
on the roof
Fiorello! (lyrics by). See
Weidman, Jerome and Abbott,
George. Fiorello!
She loves me (lyrics by). See
Masteroff, Joe. She loves me

HARNWELL, MRS. ANNA JANE (WIL-
COX), 1872- , and MEAKER, MRS.
ISABELLE (JACKSON)
The alabaster box. 1940. FED2

HARRIGAN, EDWARD, 1845-1911
The Mulligan guard ball. 1879.
MONR

HARRIS, TOM, 1930-
Always with love. 1967. NEWA3

HARRISON, JOHN, 1937-
Knight in four acts. PLAN38
Unaccompanied cello. 1970.
PLAN40

HARRISON, PAUL CARTER, 1936-
The great MacDaddy. 1973.
CARR

HARSHA, SON OF HIRA, 12th cen-
tury
Naganada. 12th century.
Boyd, P., tr. WEL
The necklace. See Retnavali
Ratnavali. See Retnavali
Retnavali; or, The necklace.
12th century.
Lal, P., tr. LAL
Wilson, H., tr. BAT3
Variant titles: The neck-
lace; Ratnavali

HART, MOSS, 1904-1961
Christopher Blake. 1946. BES46
The climate of Eden (based on the
novel Shadows move among them
by Edgar Mittelhölzer). 1952.
BES52, THEA53
Lady in the dark (music by Kurt
Weill; lyrics by Ira Gershwin).
1941. BES40, RICM
Light up the sky. 1948. BES48
Winged victory (music by David
Rose). 1943. BES43

--See Kaufman, George S., jt.
auth.

HARTOG, JAN DE, 1914-
The fourposter. 1951. BES51,
GART, GATB4, RICT
Skipper next to God. 1945.
BES47, EMB2

HARTSON, HALL, 1739?-1773
The countess of Salisbury
(adapted from the romance
Longsword, earl of Salisbury,
attributed to Thomas Leland
and John Leland). 1765.
BELG11

HARTZENBUSCH, JUAN EUGENIO,
1806-1880
Los amantes de Teruel. 1837.
BRET
Variant title: The lovers of
Teruel
The lovers of Teruel. See Los
amantes de Teruel

HARVEY, FRANK, 1912-
The day after the fair (based on
a story by Thomas Hardy).
1972. PLAN43

HARWOOD, HAROLD MARSH, 1874-
1959
Old folks at home. 1933. FAMF

-- and GORE-BROWN, ROBERT F.
Cynara. 1930. BES31

HARWOOD, RONALD, 1934-
The dresser, 1980. BES81

HASENCLEVER, WALTER, 1890-1940
Antigone. 1917.
Ritchie, J., and Stowell, J.,
trs. RITV
Humanity. 1918.
Sokel, W., and J., trs. SOK
Variant title: Die Menschen
Die Menschen. See Humanity

-- and TUCHOLSKY, KARL
Christopher Columbus. 1932.
Spalter, M. and Wellwarth, G.,
trs. WELG

HASHIMOTO, SHINOBU. See Kurosawa, Akira, jt. auth.

HASTINGS, BASIL MACDONALD,
1881-1928
The new sin. 1912. PLAP2

HASTINGS, CHARLOTTE
Bonaventure. 1949. PLAN3
Variant titles: Mary Bonaven-
ture; Sister Cecilia
Mary Bonaventure. See Bonaven-
ture
Sister Cecilia. See Bonaventure
Uncertain joy. 1953. PLAN12

HASTINGS, HUGH, 1917-
Seagulls over Sorrento. 1950.
PLAN4

HASTINGS, MICHAEL, 1938-
Yes, and after. 1957. NEWE4

HATCH, JAMES V., 1928-
See Jackson, C. Bernard, jt. auth.

HATHWAY, RICHARD, fl.1602
Sir John Oldcastle, pt. I (some-
times attributed to). See
Anonymous plays. Sir John
Oldcastle, pt. I

HAUPTMAN, WILLIAM
Domino courts. 1975. WOQ1

HAUPTMANN, CARL FERDINAND
MAXIMILIAN, 1858-1921
Kreig, ein Te Deum. See War,
A Te Deum
War, a Te Deum. 1913?
Ritchie, J., and Stowell, J.,
trs. RITV
Variant title: Kreig, ein Te
Deum

HAUPTMANN, ELISABETH. See
Brecht, Bertolt, jt. auth.

HAUPTMANN, GERHART, 1862-1946
The assumption of Hannele. See
Hannele
The beaver coat. 1893.
Lewisohn, L., tr. STE,
WATI, WATL1
Variant title: Der biberpelz,
eine diebs komödie
Der biberpelz, eine diebs komödie.
See The beaver coat
The coming of peace. See Das
friedensfest

Einsame menschen. 1891. CAM
    Variant title: Lonely lives
The festival of peace. See Das
    friedensfest
Das friedensfest. 1890. STI1
    Variant titles: The coming
      of peace; The festival of
      peace; The reconciliation
Hannele. 1893.
    Archer, W., tr. BAT12
    Frenz, H., and Waggoner, M.,
      trs. ULAN
    Meltzer, C., tr. HAV, HUD,
      INTE
    Variant titles: The assumption
      of Hannele; Hannele's as-
      sumption; Hanneles himmel-
      fahrt; The journey to heaven
      of Hannele
Hannele's assumption. See Hannele
Hanneles himmelfahrt. See Hannele
The journey to heaven of Hannele.
    See Hannele
Lonely lives. See Einsame
    menschen
Michael Kramer. 1900. FEFH2
    Lewisohn, L., tr. FRA18
The rats. 1911.
    Lewisohn, L., tr. TUCG,
      TUCM, TUCN, TUCO
    Variant title: Die ratten
Die ratten. See The rats
The reconciliation. See Das frie-
    densfest
The sunken bell. 1896.
    Meltzer, C., tr. BUCK,
      BUCL, BUCM, FRA18,
      MACN, MOSQ, WHK
    Variant title: Die versunkene
      glocke
Die versunkene glocke. See The
    sunken bell
The weavers. 1892.
    Frenz, H., and Waggoner, M.,
      trs. BLOC, HOUP
    Huebsch, B., tr. THON
    Morison, M., tr. CEW, DIC,
      DIK1, FRA18, SMP, TRE,
      TREA1, TREBA, TREBJ,
      TREC2, TREE2, TREI2,
      WHI
    Mueller, C., tr. COTL, COTQ
    Variant title: Die weber
Die weber. See The weavers
Der weisse heiland. See The white
    saviour
The white saviour. 1920.

    Muir, W., and E., trs. KRE
    Variant titles: Der weisse
      heiland; The white redeemer

HAUTEROCHE, NOEL LEBRETON,
1617-1707
    Crispin médecin. See Ravenscroft,
      Edward and Motteux, P. A.
      The sham doctor (based on)

HAVARD, WILLIAM, 1710-1778
    King Charles I. (1737) BELK12
    Variant title: Charles I

HAVEL, VACLAV, 1936-
    The memorandum. 1965.
      Backwell, V., tr. THOR
    Protest. 1977?
      Blackwell, V., tr. and adapter.
      DBG

HAVRVOLD, FINN, 1905-
    The injustice. (1955)
      Brown, J., tr. MNON
      Variant title: Uretten
    Uretten. See The injustice

HAWKES, JACQUETTA (HOPKINS),
1910- . See Priestley, John
Boynton, jt. auth.

HAWKES, JOHN, 1925-
    The wax museum. 1966. PLAC

HAWKESWORTH, JOHN, 1715?-1773
    Edgar and Emmeline. 1761. BELC4

HAWTHORNE, RUTH (WARREN).
See Kennedy, Mary, jt. auth.

HAY, IAN (pseud. of John Hay
Beith), 1876-1952
    "Let my people go!" 1948. EMB3

HAY, JULIUS, 1900-1975
    The horse. 1964.
      Hap, P., tr. THOR

HAYDEN, JOHN
    Lost horizons. 1935. BES34

HAYES, ALFRED, 1911-
    Act of love. See The girl on the
      Via Flaminia
    The girl on the Via Flaminia. 1954.
      BES53, COTK
    Variant title: Act of love

HAYES, JOSEPH, 1918-
The desperate hours. 1955.
BES54, BIER, THEA55

HAZELTON, GEORGE COCHRANE,
JR., 1868-1921
Mistress Nell. 1900. AMP16

-- and BENRIMO, JOSEPH HENRY
The yellow jacket. 1912. DID

HAZELWOOD, COLIN HAZELWOOD,
1820-1875
Lady Audley's secret (from the
novel by Mary Elizabeth Braddon). 1863. ROWE

HEALEY, FRANCES
The copper pot. 1919? WEB

HEBBEL, CHRISTIAN FRIEDRICH,
1813-1863
Agnes Bernauer. 1852. CAM
Pattee, L., tr. SMK
Herodes und Mariamne. 1849.
CAM
Maria Magdalena. See Maria
Magdalene
Maria Magdalene. 1844. CAM
Fairley, B., tr. BUCK,
BUCL, BUCM, FEFH1,
TREA2, TREB, TREC1,
TREE1, TREI1
Green, P., tr. CLKW, GRIF
Mueller, C., tr. COTL, COTQ
Thomas, P., tr. FRA9, SMI
Variant title: Maria Magda-
lena
Siegfried's death. 1862.
Royce, K., tr. FRA9

HECHT, BEN, 1893-1964.
See also Goodman, Kenneth S., jt.
auth.

-- and MacARTHUR, CHARLES
The front page. 1928.
BES28, CET, GASB, GATB1

HEGGEN, THOMAS, 1918-1949, and
LOGAN, JOSHUA
Mister Roberts. 1948. BES47,
CEQA, COLT, GARW, GATB3,
HATA, RICT, SIXC

HEIBERG, GUNNAR EDWARD RODE,
1857-1929

Kjaerlighedens tragedie. See
The tragedy of love
The tragedy of love. 1904.
Björkman, E., tr. DID
Variant title: Kjaerlighedens
tragedie

HEIDE, ROBERT, 1939-
At war with the Mongols. 1970.
Moon. 1967. SMC

HEIJERMANS, HERMAN (Samuel Falk-
land, pseud.), 1864-1924
The good hope. 1900?
Saunders, L., and Heijermans-
Houwink, C., trs. GARZH
Variant title: Op hoop van
zegen
Op hoop van zegen. See The good
hope

HELLER, JOSEPH, 1923-
We bombed in New Haven. 1967.
FAMAH

HELLMAN, LILLIAN, 1905-1984
Another part of the forest (music
by Marc Blitzstein). 1946.
BES46, WATE
The autumn garden. 1951. BES50,
CLM, FAM, GARW
Candide (based on Candide by
Voltaire; music by Leonard
Bernstein; lyrics by Richard
Wilbur, John Latouche and
Dorothy Parker). 1956. BES56
The children's hour. 1934.
BES34, FIP, GAS, GATB2,
PLAN5, SUB
The lark. See Anouilh, Jean.
The lark (tr. and adapted by)
The little foxes. 1939. BARS,
BES38, BLOO, CET, CORB,
COTE, COTH, COTQ, DOT,
HARB, HAVE, HILP, LITL,
LITN, MIJY, SIXC, SIXL,
TREBA, TREBJ, TREC2,
TREE3, TREI3
Variant title: Regina
Regina. See The little foxes
The searching wind. 1944. BES43
Toys in the attic. 1960. BES59,
CEQ, CES
Watch on the Rhine. 1941. BES40,
CALN2, CALP, CALQ, CASS,
CRIT, CUBE, GARZ, GAVE,
HAVD, NAGE

HEMRO.
Poor ostrich. 1948? RUA

HENLEY, BETH, 1952-
Crimes of the heart. 1979.
BERS, BES80
The Miss Firecracker contest;
a play in two acts. 1981.
BES83

HENSEL, KAREN; JOHNS, PATTI;
KENT, ALANA; MEREDITH, SYL-
VIA; SHAW, ELIZABETH LLOYD;
and TOFFENETTI, LAURA
Going to see the elephant.
(Original writing and struc-
ture, Hensel and Kent;
character development and
dialogue, Johns, Meredith,
Shaw, Toffenetti; concept,
Johns). 1982. WES15/16

HENSHAW, JAMES ENE, 1924-
The jewels of the shrine.
1952? HOGN, LITT

HERBERT, FREDERICK HUGH, 1897-
1958
Kiss and tell. 1943. BES42
The moon is blue. 1951. GARW

HERBERT, JOHN (pseud. of John
Herbert Brundage), 1926-
Fortune and men's eyes. 1967.
MAJ, MARR, PENG

HERMAN, HENRY, 1832-1894. See
Jones, Henry Arthur, jt. auth.

HERMAN, JERRY, 1932-
La cage aux folles (music and
lyrics by). See Fierstein,
Harvey. La cage aux folles
Hello, Dolly! (music and lyrics
by). See Stewart, Michael.
Hello, Dolly!

L'HERMITE, FRANÇOIS TRISTAN.
See Tristan l'Hermite, François

HERNANDEZ, ANTONIO ACEVEDO.
See Acevedo Hernández, Antonio

HERNANDEZ, LOUISA JOSEFINA,
1928-
Mullato's orgy. 1966?
Oliver, W., tr. OLIW

HERNDON, VENABLE, 1927-
Until the monkey comes. 1966.
NEWA2

HERNE, JAMES A., 1839-1901
Drifting apart. 1888. AMP7
Variant title: The fisherman's
child
The fisherman's child. See
drifting apart
Margaret Fleming. 1890. COY,
MASW, NILS, QUIL, QUIM,
QUIN
The minute men of 1774-1775.
1886. AMP7
The Reverend Griffith Davenport,
Act. IV. 1899. AMP7
Shore acres. 1892. DOWM,
MONR
Within an inch of his life. 1879.
AMP7

HERRERA, LUIS BAYON. See
Bayón Herrera, Luis

HERREROS, MANUEL BRETON DE
LOS. See Bretón de los Herreros,
Manuel

HERSEY, JOHN, 1914-
A bell for Adano. See Osborn,
Paul. A bell for Adano (based
on the novel by)

HERSHADEVA, SRI. See Harsha,
son of Hira

HERVERA, LUIS BAYON. See
Bayón Herrera, Luis

HERVIEU, PAUL ERNEST, 1857-1915
Connais-toi. See Know thyself
La course du flambeau. 1901.
BER
Variant titles: The passing of
the torch; The torch race;
The trail of the torch
Know thyself. 1909.
Cerf, B., tr. DIC
Variant title: Connais-toi
The passing of the torch. See
La course du flambeau
The torch race. See La course du
flambeau
The trail of the torch. See La
course du flambeau

HESTER, HAL, 1933–
Your own thing (music and
lyrics by). See Driver,
Donald. Your own thing

HEVI, JACOB
Amavi. AFR

HEYWARD, MRS. DOROTHY
HARTZELL (KUHNS), 1890-1961,
and HEYWARD, DuBOSE
Porgy. 1927. BES27, GASB,
GATB1, MAF, MIJY, THF

HEYWARD, DuBOSE, 1885-1940
Porgy and Bess (based on Porgy,
by Mrs. Dorothy Hartzell
(Kuhns) Heyward and DuBose
Heyward; lyrics by DuBose
Heyward and Ira Gershwin;
music by George Gershwin).
1935. RICO
--See also Heyward, Mrs. Dorothy
Hartzell (Kuhns), jt. auth.

HEYWOOD, JOHN, 1497?-1580?
The four pp. 1569? ADA, BOA,
DPRL, GARZB, HOPP, PARR,
TAV, TICO
Variant titles: The four p's;
The playe called The foure
pp
The four p's. See The four pp
Gentleness and nobility. c.1525.
THW
Variant title: Of gentylnes and
nobylyte a dyaloge
Johan Johan. See John, Tyb and
Sir John
Johan Johan, the husbande. See
John, Tyb and Sir John
Johan, Tyb his wife, and Sir Jhan
the preest. See John, Tyb and
Sir John
John, Tyb and Sir John. 1533.
ADA, BEVD, CRE, GAY1,
HOPP, LOOM, PAR, RUB
Variant titles: Johan Johan;
Johan Johan, the husbande;
Johan, Tyb his wife and Sir
Jhan the preest; John, Tyb
and the curate; A merry
play; A mery play betweene
Johan Johan, the husbande,
Tyb his wyfe, and Syr Jhan,
the preest; A mery play be-
tweene Johan Johan, Tyb,

his wyfe and Syr Jhan, the
preest; A mery play betwene
Johan Johan the husbande,
Tib his wife, and Sir Johan
the preest
John, Tyb and the curate. See
John, Tyb and Sir John
A merry play. See John, Tyb
and Sir John
A mery play betweene Johan Johan,
the husbande, Tyb his wyfe,
and Syr Jhan, the preest. See
John, Tyb and Sir John
A mery play betweene Johan Johan,
Tyb, his wyfe and Syr Jhan,
the preest. See John, Tyb and
Sir John
A mery play betwene Johan Johan
the husbande, Tib his wife, and
Sir Johan the preest. See John,
Tyb and Sir John
A mery play betwene Johan Johan,
the husbande, Tyb his wyfe,
and Syr Jhan, the preest. See
John, Tyb and Sir John
A mery playe betwene the pardoner
and the frere, the curate and
neybour Pratte. See The par-
doner and the friar
Of gentylnes and nobylyte a dya-
loge. See Gentleness and no-
bility
The pardoner and the friar. 1521?
LOOM, POLL
Variant title: A mery playe
betwene the pardoner and
the frere, the curate and
neybour Pratte
A play of love; A newe and a mery
enterlude concernyng pleasure
and payne in love, made by
Iohn Heywood. (1533) SOME
The play of the weather; a new
and a very mery enterlude of
all maner wethers. See The
play of the wether
The play of the wether. 1525-1533.
ADA, BEVD, HAO, GAY1, PARR
The playe called the foure pp. See
The four pp

HEYWOOD, THOMAS, 1574?-1641
The fair maid of the west. 1631.
MARG
A woman killed with kindness.
1603. ASH, BAS, BROC, CLF1,
DPR1, DUN, GATG, LAWR,

MAKG, MAX, NEI, NES, OLH,
OLI1, PAR, RYL, SCH, SCI,
SCJ, SMI, SPE, TAT, TAU,
WALL

HIBBERD, JACK, 1940-
White with wire wheels. 1967.
FOUAC
Who? 1968. FOUAC

HICKERSON, HAROLD. See Anderson, Maxwell, jt. auth.

HIERHOLZER, ALEXANDER
Grace and George and God.
1970. BALLE7

HILARIUS, 12th century
Ludus super iconia Sancti
Nicolai. See The statue of
Saint Nicholas
The miracle of Saint Nicholas
and the image. 12th cent.
LOOM
The raising of Lazarus. 12th
century. BEVD
Variant title: Suscitatio
Lazari
The statue of Saint Nicholas.
12th cent. MAR
Variant title: Ludus super
iconia Sancti Nicolai
Suscitatio Lazari. See The
raising of Lazarus

HILDESHEIMER, WOLFGANG, 1916-
Nachtstück. See Nightpiece
Nightpiece. 1962.
Hildesheimer, W., tr. BENB
Variant title: Nachtstück

HILL, AARON, 1685-1750
Alzira. 1736. BELK10
Merope. 1749. BELK10
Zara. 1736. BELK1

HILL, ABRAHAM, 1911-
Walk hard. 1944. HARY

HILL, ERROL, 1921-
Man better man. 1960. GASY
Strictly matrimony. 1959. KINH

HILL, FREDERIC STANHOPE, 1805-
1851
The six degrees of crime. 1834.
SATI

HILL, GARY LEON
Food from trash. 1983. NEWQA

HILL, LUCIENNE
Paddle your own canoe. See
Regnier, Max Albert Marie.
Paddle your own canoe (tr.
and adapted by)
The waltz of the toreadors. See
Anouilh, Jean. The waltz of
the toreadors (tr. and adapted
by)

HILTON, ARTHUR CLEMENT, 1851-
1877
Hamlet; or, Not such a fool as he
looks. (1882) NIN4

HINES, LEONARD JOHN
Simon. 1934. SEVE

HIRSHBEIN, PERETZ, 1880-1948
Farvorfen vinkel. 1918.
Lifson, D., tr. LIFS
Green fields. 1917.
Landis, J., tr. LAO, LAOG

HITE, BARBARA
Birdwatchers. COLI
Sandcastle. COLI

HIVNOR, ROBERT, 1916-
The assault upon Charles Sumner.
1966. PLAC
The ticklish acrobat. 1954. PLAA

HIYOSHI, SA-AMI YASUKIYO, 1383?-
1458
Benkei on the bridge. 15th cent.
Waley, A., tr. ANDF
Variant title: Hashi-Benki
Hashi-Benki. See Benkei on the
bridge

HO, CHING-CHIH, and TING, YI
The white-haired girl. 1945.
Anon. tr. FIFW
Yang, H., and Yang, G.,
trs. MESE

HOADLY, BENJAMIN, 1706-1757
The suspicious husband. 1747.
BELK4, MOR

HOARE, PRINCE, 1755-1834
No song no supper (music by
Stephen Storace). 1790. HUGH

HOBBES, DWIGHT
You can't always sometimes never
tell. (1977) CEN

HOCHHUTH, ROLF, 1931-
The deputy. 1963.
Winston, R., and C., trs.
BES63
Variant titles: The representa-
tive; Der Stellvertreter
The representative. See The depu-
ty
Der Stellvertreter. See The depu-
ty

HOCHWÄLDER, FRITZ, 1911-1986
Das heilige experiment. See The
strong are lonely
Die Hïmbeere Pflücker. See The
raspberry picker
The holy experiment. See The
strong are lonely
Der öffentliche ankläger. See
The public prosecutor
The public prosecutor. 1947.
Black, K., tr. PLAN16
Variant title: Der öffentliche
ankläger
The raspberry picker. 1965.
Bullock, M., tr. ANTH
Variant title: Die Hïmbeere
Pflücker
The strong are lonely. 1942.
LeGallienne, E., tr. PLAN14
Wellwarth, G., tr. WELT
Variant titles: Das heilige
experiment; The holy experi-
ment

HODGE, MERTON, 1904-1958
As it was in the beginning. See
The wind and the rain
Grief goes over. 1935. FAMH
The island. 1937. SIXP
The wind and the rain. 1933.
FAME
Variant title: As it was in the
beginning

HODSON, JAMES LANSDALE, 1891-
1956
Harvest in the north. 1939.
FAML
Red night. 1936. FAMI

HOFFE, MONCKTON, 1880-1951
Many waters. 1926. FAO, PLAD

HOFFMAN, BYRD
The king of Spain. 1969. NEWA3

HOFFMAN, WILLIAM M., 1939-
A quick nut bread to make your
mouth water. 1970. OWE
As is. 1985. BES84
Thank you, Miss Victoria. 1965.
NEWA3
X
X
X X
X. 1969. SME

-- and HOLLAND, ANTHONY
Cornbury: The queen's govern-
nor. 1976. HOF

HOFMANNSTAHL, HUGO HOFMANN
VON, 1874-1929
Death and the fool. See Der tor
und der tod
The death of Titian. 1892.
Heard, J., tr. FRA17
Variant title: Der tod des
Tizian
Electra. 1904.
Mueller, C., tr. ANTH,
COTKJ, COTQ
Symons, A., tr. DIE
Die hochzeit der Sobeide. See
The marriage of Sobeide
The marriage of Sobeide. 1899.
Morgan, B., tr. FRA20
Variant title: Die hochzeit
der Sobeide
Das Salzburger grosse weltheater.
1920. FEFH2
Der tod des Tizian. See The
death of Titian
Der tor und der tod. 1893.
STI1
Hamburger, M., tr. BLOC
Heard, J., tr. FRA17
Variant title: Death and the
fool

HOGAN, R., and MOLIN, S. E.
The silent woman. See Jonson,
Ben. The silent woman
(adapted by)

HOIJER, BJORN-ERIK, 1907-
Isak Juntti had many sons.
(1954)
Austin, P., tr. MNOS
Variant title: Isak Juntti hade

många söner

HOLBERG, LUDWIG, 1684-1754
Erasmus Montanus. See Rasmus
Montanus
Jeppe of the hill. 1722.
Campbell, O., tr. SPR
Jagendorf, M., tr. CLF2
Variant title: Jeppe paa
bjerget
Jeppe paa bjerget. See Jeppe of
the hill
The loquacious barber. 1723.
Chambers, W., tr. BAT17
Variant title: Mester Gert
Westphaler eller den meget
talende barbeer
Mester Gert Westphaler eller den
meget talende barbeer. See
The loquacious barber
Rasmus Montanus. 1747.
Campbell, O., and Schenck,
F., trs. MAU
Variant title: Erasmus Mon-
tanus

HOLCROFT, THOMAS, 1745-1809
Duplicity. 1781. INCA4
The school for arrogance. 1791.
INCA4
Seduction. 1787. INCA4
A tale of mystery. 1802.
ACE, BAI, HOUR, KILG

HOLDEN, JOAN
Factperson (script by). See
San Francisco Mime Troupe.
Factperson
Factwino meets the moral majority
(script by). See San Francisco
Mime Troupe. Factwino meets
the moral majority
Factwino vs. Armageddonman
(script by). See San Francisco
Mime Troupe. Factwino vs.
Armageddonman

HOLLAND, ANTHONY, 1933- .
See Hoffman, William M., jt. auth.

HOLLINGSWORTH, MARGARET
Ever loving. 1980. PENG
Operators. 1974. BRIQ

HOLLINGSWORTH, MICHAEL
Strawberry fields. 1972. BRIN

HOLM, JOHN CECIL, 1906-1981, and
ABBOTT, GEORGE
Three men on a horse. 1935. GAS

HOLMAN, JOSEPH GEORGE, 1764-1817
The votary of wealth. 1799.
INCA3

HOLME, CONSTANCE, 1881?-1955
"I want!" 1933. FIT

HOLT, BRIAN
Noah's ark. 1963. FRO

HOLTZMAN, JONATHAN, 1953-
Foxfire; a play with songs in two
acts (music and collaboration
for lyrics by). See Cooper,
Susan and Cronyn, Hume. Foxfire...

HOME, JOHN, 1722-1808
Douglas. 1756. BAT14, BELK20,
BOO, MAND, MANF, MOR,
MOSE2, NET, STM

HOME, WILLIAM DOUGLAS, 1912-
The jockey club stakes. 1970.
PLAN40
Lloyd George knew my father.
1972. PLAN42
The queen's highland servant.
1968. PLAN35
The secretary bird. 1963.
PLAN36
The thistle and the rose. 1949.
PLAN4

HOOLE, JOHN, 1727-1803
Cyrus. 1768. BELG9
Timanthes. 1770. BELG9

HOPKINS, ARTHUR MELANCTHON,
1878-1950
Moonshine. 1921. PROF, PROG,
PROH, PROI, TOD
--See Watters, George Manker,
jt. auth.

HOPKINS, JOHN, 1931-
Find your way home. 1974. BES73

HOPKINSON, FRANCIS, 1737-1791
A dialogue and ode. 1762. MONR
Variant title: An exercise con-
taining a dialogue and ode

on the accession of His
present gracious Majesty
George III
An exercise containing a dialogue
and ode on the accession of
His present gracious Majesty
George III. See A dialogue
and ode

HOPWOOD, AVERY, 1862-1928. See
Rinehart, Mary Roberts, jt. auth.

HORACE. See Horatius Flaccus,
Quintus

HORATIUS FLACCUS, QUINTUS,
65-8 B.C.
Ars poetica.
DeWitt, N., tr. COTU
The bore; a dramatic version of
Horace (Satires I,9)
Ullman, B., tr. HOWK

HORNE, KENNETH, 1900-
Trial and error. 1953. PLAN9

HOROVITZ, ISRAEL, 1939-
The Indian wants the Bronx.
1968. FAMAH, LAN, OBG,
OFF1
It's called the sugar plum. 1967.
OFF1, RICK
Morning. 1968. GARTL
The widow's blind date. 1980.
WES13/14

HOROWITZ, DAN
Cherli ka cherli.
Alkalaya, K., and Gut, H.,
trs. MOADE

HORSFIELD, DEBBIE
Red devils. 1983. PLABE3

HOUGHTON, STANLEY, 1881-1913
Fanny Hawthorne. See Hindle
wakes
Hindle wakes. 1912. DIG,
PLAP1, ROWC, TUCD
Variant title: Fanny Haw-
thorne

HOUSMAN, LAURENCE, 1865-1959
A good lesson! (from Victoria
Regina). 1934. COOP
Victoria Regina. 1935. BES35,
CEU

-- and GRANVILLE-BARKER,
HARLEY GRANVILLE
Prunella; or, Love in a Dutch
garden. 1906. PLAP2

HOUSTON, DIANNE, 1954-
The fishermen. 1980. CEN

HOWARD, BRONSON CROCKER,
1842-1908
The banker's daughter. 1873.
AMP10, CLA
Baron Rudolph. 1881. AMP10
The Henrietta. 1887. HAL
Hurricanes. 1878. AMP10
Old love letters. 1878. AMP10
One of our girls. 1885. AMP10
Shenandoah. 1888. COY,
MASW, MONR, MOSS3, QUIJ,
QUIJR, QUIK, QUIL, QUIM,
QUIN
--See Young, Sir Charles
Lawrence, jt. auth.

HOWARD, SIR ROBERT, 1626-1698
The committee. 1662. BELK2
--See also Dryden, John, jt. auth.

HOWARD, SIDNEY COE, 1891-1939
Alien corn. 1933. BES32, FAMD
Dodsworth (based on the novel by
Sinclair Lewis). 1934. BES33,
HAT
The late Christopher Bean (tr.
and adapted by). See Fauchois,
René. The late Christopher
Bean
Lucky Sam McCarver. 1925.
MOAD, MOSK, MOSL
Madam, will you walk. 1939.
THEA54
Ned McCobb's daughter. 1926.
MIL
Pi-Pa-Ki. See Lute song
The silver cord. 1926. BES26,
BROW, BROX, CHAN, CHAP,
COTE, DIE, FUL, JORG, MOSG,
MOSH, QUIL, QUIM, QUIN,
THF, TUCD, TUCM, TUCN,
TUCO, WATC1, WATI, WATO,
WHI
They knew what they wanted.
1924. BES24, CET, CORD,
CORE, CORF, GASB, MAD,
MAF, MERW
--See also Loesser, Frank. The
most happy fella (based on

the play by)

-- and De KRUIF, PAUL HENRY
Yellow jack. 1934. GARU,
MERV, NAGE, SCWI

-- and IRWIN, WILLIAM HENRY
Lute song (adapted from the
Chinese classic Pi-Pa-Ki by
Kao-Tong-Kia or Tse-Tching).
1946. BES45
Variant title: Pi-Pa-Ki

HOWARTH, DONALD, 1931-
A lily in little India. 1965.
NEWE9
Three months gone. 1970.
PLAN39

HOWE, MRS. JULIA (WARD), 1819-
1910
Hippolytus. 1911. AMP16
Leonora; or, The world's own.
1857. QUIJ, QUIK

HOWE, TINA, 1937-
Birth and after birth. 1974.
NEWVM
Painting churches. 1983.
BES83

HOWELLS, WILLIAM DEAN, 1837-
1920
A letter of introduction. 1892.
MONR
The mouse trap. 1889? GARX
The unexpected guests. 1893?
QUIO2

HOYT, CHARLES HALE, 1860-1900
A bunch of keys; or, The hotel.
1883. AMP9
A midnight bell. 1889. AMP9
A milk white flag. 1894. AMP9
A temperance town. 1893.
AMP9, MONR
A Texas steer; or, "Money makes
the mare go." 1890. MOSJ,
MOSK, MOSL
A trip to Chinatown; or, Idyl of
San Francisco. 1891. AMP9,
CLA

HROSWITHA. See Hrotsvit, of Gandersheim

HROTSVIT, OF GANDERSHEIM,

935?-1000?
Dulcitius. 10th cent.
Butler, M., tr. GARZB
Taylor, J., tr. TAV
Paphnutius. 10th cent.
Butler, M., tr. GARZB, TREB

HROTSVITHA. See Hrotsvit, of
Gandersheim

HSIA, YEN (SHEN, TUAN-HSIEN),
1900-
Shanghai wu-yen hsia. See
Under Shanghai eaves
Under Shanghai eaves. (1937)
Hayden, G., tr. TWEH
Variant title: Shanghai wu-
yen hsia

HSIUNG, CHEN-CHIN
The thrice promised bride. WEB

HSUN, LU. See Lu, Hsun, pseud.

HU, SHIH, 1891-1962
Chung-shen ta shih. See The
greatest event in life
The greatest event in life. (1919)
Gunn, E., tr. TWEH
Variant title: Chung-shen ta
shih

HUBERT, CAM, 1938-
The twin sinks of Allan Sammy.
1973. FIFVE

HUGHES, HATCHER, 1881?-1945
Hell-bent fer heaven. 1924.
BES23, CORD, CORE, CORF,
COT, MAD, TUCJ

HUGHES, JAMES LANGSTON. See
Hughes, Langston

HUGHES, JOHN, 1677-1720
Siege of Damascus. 1720. BELK1

HUGHES, LANGSTON, 1902-1967
Don't you want to be free? 1937.
HARY
Emperor of Haiti. 1938. TUQR
Limitations of life. 1938. HARY
Little ham. 1935. HARY
Mother and child. 1973. KINH,
PERV, SCNQ
Mulatto. 1963. BRAS, THT
Simply heaven. 1957. PATR

Soul gone home. 1937. RAVA

HUGHES, RICHARD ARTHUR
WARREN, 1900-1976
A high wind in Jamaica. See
Osborn, Paul. The innocent
voyage (based on the novel
by)
The sister's tragedy. 1922.
MORT, SUTL

HUGHES, THOMAS, fl.1587
The misfortunes of Arthur.
1588. CUN

HUGO, VICTOR MARIE, 1802-1885
Hernani. 1830. BOR, COM,
GRA, SEA
Asher, L., tr. BERM,
HOUK, TREB
Crosland, Mrs. N., tr.
CARP, CLF2, MAU
Ruy Blas. 1838. COM, GRA,
SCN, STJ2
Crosland, Mrs. N., tr.
GREA

HULL, THOMAS, 1728-1808
Henry II; or, The fall of
Rosamond. 1773. INCA9
Variant title: The fall of
Rosamond

HUMPHREY, HUBERT H., 1911-
1978. See Baldwin, James, jt.
auth.

HUNG, SHEN, 1893-1955
Chao Yen-wang. See Yama chao
Yama chao. (1922)
Brown, C., tr. TWEH
Variant title: Chao Yen-
wang
HUNKINS, LEE, 1930-
Revival. (1980) CEN

HUNTER, G. K.
Androboros. AMPA

HUNTER, NORMAN C., 1908-1971
A day by the sea. 1953. FAMO
Waters of the moon. 1951.
FAOS

HURLBUT, WILLIAM JAMES, 1883-
The bride of the lamb. 1926.
BES25

HUSSON, ALBERT, 1912-
La cuisine des anges. See
Spewack, Bella and Spewack,
Samuel. My 3 angels (adapted
from)

HUSTON, JOHN, 1906-1987. See
Koch, Howard, jt. auth.

HUTCHINS, MRS. MAUDE (PHELPS),
1889?-
Aunt Julia's Caesar. 195-? SPC
The case of Astrolabe. 1944?
NEWD44
A play about Joseph Smith, jr.
1944? NEWD44
The wandering Jew. 1951?
NEWD51

HUTCHINSON, ALFRED, 1924-
The rain-killers. LITT

HUTTON, JOSEPH, 1787-1828
Fashionable follies. 1809. MOSS2

HWANG, DAVID HENRY, 1957-
The dance and the railroad.
1981? BES81
FOB. 1979. NEWQ

HYDE, DOUGLAS, 1860-1949
The twisting of the rope. 1901.
CAP

HYMAN, MAC, 1923-
No time for sergeants. See
Levin, Ira. No time for
sergeants (adapted from the
novel by)

IBBITSON, JOHN
Catalyst. 1974. KAL4

IBSEN, HENRIK, 1828-1906
Bygmester solness. See The
master builder
The child wife. See A doll's
house
A doll's house. 1879.
Anon. tr. SCNPL, SILO
Archer, W., tr. CLF2, COJ,
DRA2, EDAD, FOUX,
HOUS, HUD, KNIC, KNID,
MAU, MAD, PLAB2, PROW,
THOM, THON, WATI,

WATL1, WHT
Fjelde, R., tr. LITJ, LITN
LeGallienne, E., tr. AUG,
DITA
McFarlane, J., tr. ANT
Meyer, M., tr. BARI, BARIA,
KEN, LITI, SCNP, SCNQ,
SSSI
Reinert, E., tr. BARIC,
REIW, REIWE
Watts, P., tr. SEVT
Variant titles: The child
wife; Et dukkehjem; Nora
Et dukkehjem. See A doll's
house
An enemy of society. See An
enemy of the people
An enemy of the people. 1882.
Anon. tr. BUCK, BUCL,
BUCM, CARLG, DEAR,
EVB2, GATS, HARB, JOHO,
KNIE, KNIG, KON, LAM,
MCA, MESS, OHL, PERS,
PERT, PERV, ROGE,
SAND, ZIM
Archer, W., tr. CASA
Farquhorson, R., tr. BONB,
BONC
Goodman, R., tr. GOODE
Le Gallienne, E., tr. PATM
Mark-Aveling, E., tr.
FREH, HOLM, MOSA,
WALJ, WHK
Miller, A., adapter. BUR,
HAVH, HAVHA, HOUP,
MERV
Meyer, M., tr. CASE
Sharp, R., tr. ABC, BONA,
COD, DOV, DUR, EVA2,
FOT, GOLK, INGW, STA,
THO
Variant titles: An enemy of
society; En folkefiende
En folkefiende. See An enemy of
the people
Fruen fra havet. See The lady
from the sea
Gengangere. See Ghosts
Ghosts. 1881.
Anon. tr. DOWN, KNIH,
MABC, SILK, SILM, SILN
Archer, W., tr. ALT, ALTE,
BARC, BAT17, BOY, CROW,
DEAS, FEL, FREG, GLO,
KERP, LITC, MIL, ROB,
SAY, SEBO, SEBP, SHR,

SMP, STE, TREBA, TREBJ,
TREC2, TREE2, TREI2
Le Gallienne, E., tr.
BENU, BLOC, LEVI
Meyer, M., tr. BARO, BOW,
CLL, CLLC, COTKIR
Sharp, F., tr. ADV, SILKI,
WEIS, WEIW, WHFM
Variant title: Gengangere
Hedda Gabler. 1890.
Anon. tr. BLON, BROI, HAVL,
LOCL, LOR
Ellis-Fermor, U., tr. GOLH,
SIN, SOM, SOMA, TAUJ
Goodman, R., tr. GOO
Gosse, E., tr. GPA
Gosse, E., and Archer, W., trs.
ALLI, ALLJ, ALLK, ALLM,
BLAG, BLOND, BLOO, BROF,
BROG, BROH, CARP, CARPA,
CLKW, COOP, FOUK, FOUM,
GLO, GOU2, GRIF, HAE,
HAV, HAVD, HAVE, KERN,
KERO, SMI, TRE, TREA1,
TREBA, TREBJ, TREC2,
TREE2, TREI2, WALB, WATA,
WATI, WATL2, WATR
Le Gallienne, E., tr. LOCLA,
LOCLB
Legallienne, J., and Leysac, P.,
trs. LEG
Meyer, M., tr. CLKY, NORG2,
VANV2
Paulson, A., tr. WAIW
Reinert, O., tr. ALS, BARJ,
BARK, BARL, BAUL, COTQ,
HEA, KNO, KNOJ, REIO,
SILP
John Gabriel Borkman. 1897.
Archer, W., tr. ULAN
Ginsbury, N., adapter. PLAN23
Kongsemnerna. See The preten-
ders
The lady from the sea. 1888.
Archer, W., tr. SAY
Fjelde, R., tr. WOM
Variant title: Fruen fra havet
Lille Eyolf. See Little Eyolf
Little Eyolf. 1894.
Archer, W., tr. LID
Variant title: Lille Eyolf
The master builder. 1892.
Amble, K., tr. COTX
Anon. tr. BONB, BRIT, CROS,
GUTH, GUTL, HIB, HIBA,
HIBB, SIXB

Archer, W., tr. DOWS,
VON
Fjelde, R., tr. SPR
Gosse, E., and Archer, W.,
trs. WARL, WORP
McFarlane, J., tr. SANE
Paulson, A., tr. WEIP
Perone, E., tr. CALD
Variant titles: Bygmester
solness; Solness, the
master builder
Nora. See A doll's house
Peer Gynt. 1876.
Ginsbury, N., tr. BLOC
Pillars of society. 1877.
Le Gallienne, E., tr. MADB
Variant title: Samfundets
støtter
The pretenders. 1864.
Archer, W., tr. SMK
Variant title: Kongsemnerna
Rosmersholm. 1886.
Anon. tr. BROJ, BROK,
LOCM2
Archer, W., tr. BENQ,
TUCN, TUCO
Jellicoe, A., tr. CUBH,
FOUM
Le Gallienne, E., tr. JOHN,
ROET
McFarlane, J., tr. CLKJ
Meyer, M., tr. BENSB2
Samfundets støtter. See Pillars
of society
Solness, the master builder.
See The master builder
Vildanden. See The wild duck
The wild duck. 1885.
Anon. tr. CEW, CLN, SSST,
SSSU
Archer, F., tr. ASF, BIER,
DLM, CUBE, CUBG, DEAP,
GOLD, LEV, LEVE, MALC,
MALG2, MALI2, MALN2,
MOSQ, SPR, WEAN, WEAV2,
WHI
Archer, W., tr. BRIX, BRIY,
BRIZ
Christiani, D., tr. BAIG
Ellis-Fermor, U., tr. LEVJ
Faber, M., tr. WEIM
Fjelde, R., tr. CLKY, TRI,
TRIA
LeGallienne, E., tr. DOT,
VOLI
McFarlane, J., tr. CAPU,
SEN

Meyer, M., tr. AUB, BENSB2,
SEN
Reinert, O., tr. COTQ, DIT,
REIL, REIN, REIP, REIT
Sharp, R., tr. BARR
Variant title: Vildanden

ICHIKAWA DANJURO. See Danjuro
I

IDRIS, YUSUF, 1927-
The farfoors. (1964) ABL

IDZUMO TAKEDA. See Takeda, Izumo

IFFLAND, AUGUST WILHELM, 1759-
1814
Conscience. 1800?
Thompson, B., tr. BAT11
Variant title: Das gewissen
Das gewissen. See Conscience

IGNATAVIČIUS, E., and MOTIEJŪNAS,
S.
Whitehorn's windmill. See Boruta,
Kazys. Whitehorn's windmill
(dramatization of the novel by)

IJIMERE, OBOTUNDE, 1930-
Born with the fire on his head.
THTN

ILF, ILYA ARNOLDOVICH, 1897-
1937, and PETROV, EVGENY
The power of love. (1933).
Senelick, L., tr. RVI
Variant title: Silnoe chuvstvo
Silnoe chuvstvo. See The power
of love

ILYENKOV, VASSILY PAVLOVICH,
1897-
Campo dei fiori. See The square
of flowers
The square of flowers. 1944.
Bakshy, A., tr. BAKS
Variant title: Campo dei fiori

INCHBALD, MRS. ELIZABETH (SIMP-
SON), 1753-1821
Adventures of a shawl. See
Appearance is against them
Appearance is against them.
1785. HUGH
Variant titles: Adventure of
a shawl; Mistake upon mis-
take; or, Appearance is

against them
Everyone has his fault. 1793.
    NIC
I'll tell you what. 1785. INCA7
Mistake upon mistake; or, Ap-
    pearance is against them.
    See Appearance is against
    them
Next door neighbors. INCA7
The wise man of the East.
    INCA7

INGE, WILLIAM, 1913-1973
The boy in the basement.
    (1950) CAL
Bus stop. 1955. BES54, GART,
    HOGF, THEA55
Come back, little Sheba. 1950.
    BES49, CEQA, CUBG, GARW,
    GATB4, NEWV, STS, WATA
The dark at the top of the
    stairs. 1957. BES57, CES,
    GARSA, HUDE
    Variant title: Farther off
        from heaven
The disposal. 1972. RICJ
Farther off from heaven. See
    The dark at the top of the
    stairs
Margaret's bed. RICK
Picnic. 1953. BES52, GART,
    GAVE, THEA53

INGHAM, ROBERT E., 1934-
Custer, or whoever heard of
    Fred Benteen? 1977. BES79
A simple life. 1964. GARZAL

INNAURATO, ALBERT, 1948-
Gemini. 1976. FAMAD

INOUYE, BESSIE TOISHIGAWA.
See Inouye, Lisa Toishigawa

INOUYE, LISA TOISHIGAWA
Reunion. 1947. KUMU

GL'INTRONATI DI SIENA (16th cen-
tury literary society)
The deceived. (1538)
    Penman, B., tr. FIJ
    Variant title: Gl'Ingannati
Gl'Ingannati. See The deceived

IOBST, CLARENCE F., 1894-
Die Calline browierts. 1930.
    BUFF

Es Heller's Chrischtdag (based on
    the story Es wasch Heller's
    Chrischtdag's zug by Charles
    C. More). 1931. BUFF
IONESCO, EUGENE, 1912-
The bald prima donna. See The
    bald soprano
The bald soprano. 1950.
    Allen, D., tr. AUG, BLOC,
        NEWW9, ULAN, WEIM
    Variant title: The bald prima
        donna; La cantatrice chauve
La cantatrice chauve. See The
    bald soprano
The chairs. See Les chaises
Les chaises. 1952. PRO
    Allen, D., tr. ALT, ALTE,
        COTQ, JOHN, KERP,
        TREBA, TREI3
    Anon. tr. SILP
    Variant title: The chairs
The gap. 1966.
    Lamont, R., tr. ACE, BARI,
        BARIA, BARIC, BARK,
        BARL, DITA, HOLP, LITL,
        SEVI, SILKI
    Variant title: La lacune
L'impromptu de l'alma. See Im-
    provisation
Improvisation; or, The shepherd's
    chameleon
    Watson, D., tr. COTKW,
        SCNO
    Variant title: L'impromptu de
        l'alma; The shepherd's
        chameleon
Jack; or, The submission. 1955.
    Allen, D. M., tr. WEIP
    Variant title: Jacques, ou
        La soumission
Jacques, ou La soumission. See
    Jack; or, The submission
La jeune fille a marier. See Maid
    to marry
La lacune. See The gap
The leader. 1953.
    Prouse, D., tr. HAVHA,
        HAVN, RAI
    Variant title: Le maître
La leçon. See The lesson
The lesson. 1951.
    Allen, D., tr. REIN, REIP
    Variant title: La leçon
Maid to marry. 1953.
    Calder, J., tr. LID
    Variant title: La jeune fille
        a marier

Le maître. See The leader
The new tenant. 1955.
  Watson, D., tr. BRIY,
  BRIZ, COTY, THOD
  Variant title: Le nouveau
    locataire
Le nouveau locataire. See The
  new tenant
The painting. 1954.
  Watson, D., tr. DIP
  Wellwarth, G., tr. BEN
  Variant titles: The picture;
  Le tableau
The picture. See The painting
Rhinoceros. 1959.
  Prouse, D., tr. BES60, GROV,
  NIL, SEVD
  Variant title: Les rhinocéros
Les rhinocéros. See Rhinoceros
The shepherd's chameleon. See
  Improvisation
Le tableau. See The painting

IRELAND, WILLIAM HENRY, 1777-
1835
Vortigern. 1796. BAT22

IRVING, WASHINGTON, 1783-1859
Rip Van Winkle. See Rauch,
  Edward H. Rip Van Winkle
  (based on the book by)
--See Payne, John Howard, jt.
  auth.

IRWIN, WILL. See Irwin, William
Henry

IRWIN, WILLIAM HENRY, 1873-1948
The Hamadryads. 1804. BOH1
--See Howard, Sidney, jt. auth.

ISHERWOOD, CHRISTOPHER, 1904-
1986
The Berlin stories. See Van
  Druten, John. I am a camera
  (adapted from the stories by).
  See also Masteroff, Joe.
  Cabaret (adapted from the
  stories by Isherwood and the
  play by van Druten)
--See also Auden, Wystan Hugh,
  jt. auth.

ITALLIE, JEAN-CLAUDE VAN.
See Van Itallie, Jean-Claude

ITCHO, ASADA. See Asada, Itcho

IZUMO TAKEDA. See Takeda, Izumo

JACK, DONALD L., 1924-
Exit muttering. 1962. KAL1

JACKER, CORINNE L., 1933-
Bits and pieces. 1973. NEWVM

JACKMAN, ISAAC, 1752?-1831
All the world's a stage. 1777.
  BELC4

JACKMAN, MARVIN E.
Flowers for the trashman. JON

JACKSON, C. BERNARD, 1927- ,
and HATCH, JAMES V.
Fly blackbird. 1960. HARY,
  REAG

JACKSON, CHERRY
In the Master's house there are
  many mansions. (1979) CEN

JACKSON, ELAINE
Toe jam. (1971) KINH

JACKSON, ISABELLE. See Meaker,
Mrs. Isabelle (Jackson)

JACKSON N. HART
The two orphans. See D'Ennery,
  Adolphe Phillippe and Corman,
  Eugène. The two orphans
  (adapted by)

JACKSON, SHIRLEY, 1919-1965
The lottery. See Duffield,
  Brainerd. The lottery (from
  a story by)

JACOBS, JIM, 1942- , and CASEY,
WARREN
Grease. 1972. GREAA

JACOBS, WILLIAM WYMARK, 1863-
1943
A love passage. 1897? PEN

JAKOBSSON, JÖKULL, 1933-
The seaway to Baghdad. (1965)
  Boucher, A., tr. MNOI
  Variant title: Sjóleidin til
  Bagdad
Sjóleidin til Bagdad. See The
  Seaway to Baghdad

JAMES, DAN, 1911-
Winter soldiers. 1942. BES42

JAMES, HENRY, 1843-1916
The American. 1891. HOGF
The turn of the screw. See
Archibald, William. The in-
nocents (based on the novel
by)
Washington Square. See
Goetz, Ruth Goodman and
Goetz, Augustus. The heiress
(based on the novel by)

JAMES, LENNIE
Trial and error. (1984) PLACI

JAMESON, STORM (née Margaret
Storm Jameson), 1897-
William the defeated. 194-?
OULD

JÄRNER, VÄINÖ VILHELM, 1910-
Eva Maria. (1965?)
Connolly, D., tr. MNOF

JARRY, ALFRED, 1873-1907
King Ubu. 1896.
Bagley, D., tr. TREBJ
Benedict, M., and Wellwarth,
G., trs. BEN, WELT
Gans, M., and Ashley, L.,
trs. ASF
Variant titles: Ubu Roi;
Ubu the king
Ubu Roi. See King Ubu
Ubu the King. See King Ubu

JASUDOWICZ, DENNIS
Blood money. 1965? NEWA1

JEANS, RONALD, 1887-1973
Count your blessings. 1951.
PLAN5
Young wives' tale. 1949.
PLAN3

JEFFERE, JOHN
The buggbears (supposed author).
1561? BOND

JEFFERS, ROBINSON, 1887-1962
The Cretan woman. 1951. BENS3,
SANL
Medea. See Euripides.
Medea (tr. and adapted by)

JEFFERSON, JOSEPH, 1829-1905

Rip Van Winkle. See Anonymous
plays. Rip Van Winkle (as
played by); see also Burke,
Charles. Rip Van Winkle

JELLICOE, ANNE, 1927-
The knack. 1961. AUB, COTKIR,
COTKIT
The sport of my mad mother.
(1957) OBSE

JEN, TEH-YAO
Magic aster. (1963)
White, W., tr. MESE

JENKIN, LEN
Dark ride. 1981. WOQ2

JENKINS, RAY, 1935-
The whole truth. PLAAB

JENKINS, RAYMOND LEONARD.
See Jenkins, Ray

JENNINGS, GERTRUDE E., 1877-
1958
Family affairs. 1934. FAMF

JENNINGS, TALBOT, 1905?-
No more frontier. 1929. TOD

JEPHSON, ROBERT, 1736-1803
Braganza. 1775. INCA6
The law of Lombardy. 1779.
INCA6

JEROME, MRS. HELEN (BURTON),
1883-
Charlotte Corday. 1939. FIP
Jane Eyre (based on the novel by
Charlotte Brontë). 1936.
FOUP, THH
Pride and prejudice (based on the
novel by Jane Austen). 1935.
BES35, FOUP, THH, VOAD

JERROLD, DOUGLAS WILLIAM, 1803-
1857
All in the downs. See Black ey'd
Susan
Black ey'd Susan; or, All in the
downs. 1829. ASG, BOOA1,
MOSN, MOSO, ROWE
Variant title: All in the
downs
Fifteen years of a drunkard's life.
1828. KILG

Mr. Paul Pry. 1826. BOOA4
The rent-day. 1832. BAI

JESSOP, GEORGE HENRY, 1850?-
1915
Sam'l of Posen; or, The commer-
cial drummer. 1881. AMP4

JEVON, THOMAS, 1652-1688
Devil of a wife. See The devil
to pay; or, The wives metamorphos'd (adapted from)

-- and COFFEY, CHARLES: MOTTLEY,
JOHN: CIBBER, THEOPHILUS
The devil to pay; or, The wives
metamorphos'd (adapted from
Devil of a wife by Thomas
Jevon). 1731. BELC2, HUGH
Variant title: The wives meta-
morphos'd
The wives metamorphos'd. See
The devil to pay; or, The
wives metamorphos'd

JIHEI II, TSUUCHI. See Tsuuchi,
Jihei II

JISUKE II, SAKURADA. See
Sakurada, Jisuke II

JOAQUIN, NICK, 1917-
A portrait of the artist as
Filipino. 1952. EDAD

JOB, THOMAS, 1900-1947
Uncle Harry. 1942. BES41

JODELLE, ETIENNE, 1532-1573
Didon se sacrifiant. 1560?
FOUR
Eugene. 1552?
Stabler, A. P., tr. FOUAF
Variant title: L'Eugene
L'Eugene. See Eugene

JOHN, ERROL, 1925?-
Moon on a rainbow shawl. 1957.
OBSE

JOHNS, PATTI. See Hensel, Karen,
jt. auth.

JOHNSON, BRYAN STANLEY, 1933-
1973
You're human like the rest of
them. 1967. NEWE14

JOHNSON, CHARLES, 1679-1748
The cobler of Preston. 1716.
HUGH
Country lasses; or, The custom
of the manor. 1715. BELK19
Variant title: The custom of
the manor
The custom of the manor. See
Country lasses; or, The custom
of the manor

JOHNSON, ELIZABETH
A bad play for an old lady.
1964. BALLE1

JOHNSON, MRS. GEORGIA (DOUGLAS),
1886-1966
Plumes. 1927? LOC
A Sunday morning in the south.
1925? HARY

JOHNSON, PAMELA HANSFORD,
1912-1981
The duchess at sunset. 1948.
OULD

JOHNSON, PHILIP, 1900-
Lovers' leap. 1934. FAMG

JOHNSON, SAMUEL, 1709-1784
Irene. 1749. BELG8, BOO

JOHNSTON, DENIS, 1901-1984
The moon in the Yellow river.
1931. BRZE
The old lady says "No!" 1929.
CAN

JONES, EDITH NEWBOLD. See
Wharton, Mrs. Edith Newbold (Jones)

JONES, HENRY, 1721-1770
The Earl of Essex. 1753. BELK3

JONES, HENRY ARTHUR, 1851-1929
The case of rebellious Susan.
1894. BES94
The dancing girl. 1891. MARG
Dolly reforming herself. 1908.
CHA, CHAN, CHAR
The goal. 1898. HUD, PEN
Judah. 1894. RUB
The liars. 1897. DUR, MART,
MAX, ROWC, SALE
The masqueraders. 1894. BAI,
MOSN, MOSO
Michael and his lost angel. 1896.

ASG, BOWY, DIC
Mrs. Dane's defence. 1900.
BOOA2, BOOM, COT

-- and HERMAN, HENRY
The silver king. 1882. BAI

JONES, JACK, 1895-1970
Rhondda roundabout. 1939.
SIXL

JONES, JEFFREY M.
Night coil. 1979. WOQ4

JONES, JOSEPH STEVENS, 1809-
1877
The people's lawyer. See
Solon Shingle
Solon Shingle. 1839. BAT20,
MOSS2
Variant title: The people's
lawyer
The usurper; or, Americans in
Tripoli. 1841? AMP14

JONES, LEROI (IMAMU AMIRI
BARAKA, pseud.), 1934-
Ba-ra-ka. OWE
Bloodrites. (1971) KINH
Dutchman. 1964. ALLM, BARK,
BARL, DOV, HOLP, HOWP2,
KNO, KNOJ, MANC2, OLIV,
PATR, REIL, REIW, REIWE,
SCNT, SSSI, TREBJ
Great goodness of life: a coon
show. (1967). BLA, CARR,
RAVA, RICJ
Junkies are full of (SHHH...).
KINH
Madheart. 1967. JON
The slave. 1964. HARY, SEVT,
TAUJ, THT
The toilet. 1964. ALLK, BES64,
CAL, GAT, GROV

JONES, PAUL, d.1966
Birthday honours. 1953. PLAN9

JONES, PETER, 1920-   , and
JOWETT, JOHN
The party spirit. 1954. PLAN11

JONES, PRESTON, 1936-1979
The last meeting of the Knights
of the White Magnolia (part of:
A Texas trilogy; a repertory
of three plays). 1973. BES76,
PLAN47
The oldest living graduate (part
of: A Texas trilogy; a repertory of three plays). 1974.
BES76
A Texas trilogy; a repertory of
three plays. Made up of:
The last meeting of the Knights
of the White Magnolia; Lu Ann
Hampton Laverty Oberlander;
and, The oldest living graduate. See The last meeting of
the Knights of the White Magnolia, and The odlest living
graduate.

JONES, TOM, 1928-
Celebration (music by Harvey
Schmidt). 1969. BES68
The fantasticks. 1960. GAT

JONSON, BEN, 1572-1637
The alchemist. 1610. ASH, BAS,
BELG16, BELK17, BENY, BROC,
CASE, DEAS, DPR2, GAY2,
GRE, HARC47, HOW, KRM, LIE,
LIEE1, NEI, OLH, OLI2, ORNC,
REIO, ROET, SPE, TAT, TAU,
THA
The alchymist. See The alchemist
Bartholomew Fair. 1614. DPR2,
OLH, OLI2, SPE
The devil is an ass. 1616. SALF
Epicoene; or, The silent woman.
1609. BALD, BROC, CLKW,
DPR2, GAY2, RUB, STA
Hogan, R., and Molin, S.,
adapters. HOGF
Every man in his humour. 1598.
ANG, BAS, BAT14, BELK2,
BROC, CLF1, CLK1, GATG,
GAY2, HAPRA1, HAPRB1, MAX,
NEI, ORNC, PAR, SCI, SCJ,
SCW, SPE, WAT
Fortunate isles, and their union.
1624. ETO
The gipsies metamorphosed. 1621.
BROC
Golden age restored. 1616. ETO
The hue and cry after cupid.
1608. BAS, SCH, SCI, SCJ
Lovers made men. 1617. ETO
Masque at Lord Haddington's mar-
riage. 1608. ETO
Masque of Augurs. 1622. ETO
The masque of blackness. 1605. WINE
Masque of Queens. 1609. ETO

Neptune's triumph for the return of Albion. 1624. ETO
News from the New World discovered in the Moon. 1621. ETO
Oberon, the fairy prince. 1611. ETO, PAR
Pan's anniversary; or, The shepherd's Holyday. 1625. ETO
    Variant title: The Shepherd's Holyday
Pleasure reconciled to virtue. 1619. ABRH, ABRJ
The sad shepherd; or, A tale of Robin Hood. 1641? BAS, SCH
Sejanus, his fall. 1603. BAS, NEI, PAR
The Shepherd's Holyday. See Pan's anniversary
The silent woman. See Epicoene
The vision of delight. 1617. ABRA, ABRB1, ABRE, TREB
Volpone; or, The fox. 1606.
    ABRJ, ALLI, ALLJ, ALLK, ALLM, BAC, BARD, BAS, BELK19, BENSB1, BROC, COTKI, DEAO, DEAP, DEAR, DPR2, DUN, FOS, FOUD, HUD, HUST, KRE, KRM, LIED1, MORR, NEI, OLH, OLI1, PAR, PARR, SCH, SCI, SCJ, SEN, SPE, SSSI, SUL, TRE, TREA2, TREB, TREC1, TREE1, TREI1, WAIW, WALL, WINE, WRIH
--See also Gelbart, Larry. Sly Fox (adapted by)
--See also Zweig, Stefan. Volpone (adapted by)
--See Chapman, George, jt. auth.

JOSELOVITZ, ERNEST A., 1942-
The inheritance. 1973. BALLE13

JOSEPH, ALLEN
Anniversary on weedy hill. (1970) BALLE8

JOSEPHSON, RAGNAR, 1891-1966
Kanske en diktare. See Perhaps a poet
Perhaps a poet. 1932.
    Lundbergh, H., tr. SCAN1
    Variant title: Kanske en diktare

JOUDRY, PATRICIA, 1921-

Teach me how to cry; a drama in three acts. 1953. WAGN2

JOWETT, JOHN. See Jones, Peter, jt. auth.

JOYCE, JAMES, 1882-1941. See Barkentin, Marjorie
Ulysses in Nighttown (based on the novel by)
--See Leonard, Hugh.
    Stephen D (based on Portrait of the artist as a young man, and Stephen Hero)

JULLIEN, JEAN, 1854-1919
The serenade. 1887.
    Clark, B., tr. CLD

JUO, ESASHI. See Esashi Jūō

JUPP, KENNETH, 1939-
The socialites. 1961? SATA

KABAHAR, PIO A.
Babaye ug lalake. See Woman and man
Miss Dolying. 1920? RAP
Woman and man. RAP
    Variant title: Babaye ug lalake

KABWE KASOMA, GODFREY PETER
Black mamba two. AFR

KAFKA, FRANZ, 1883-1924
The guardian of the tomb. 1916?
    Ritchie, J., and Garten, H., trs. RITS

KAISER, GEORGE, 1878-1945
Alkibiades saved. 1920?
    Morgan, B., tr. SOK
    Variant title: Der gerettete Alkibiades
Der brand im opernhaus. See The fire in the opera house
The conflagration of the opera house. See The fire in the opera house
The coral. 1917.
    Katzin, W., tr. DIK2, TUCG, TUCM, TUCN, TUCO
    Variant title: Die koralle
The fire in the opera house. 1916.

Katzin, W., tr. KAT
Variant titles: Der brand
im opernhaus; The con-
flagration of the opera
house
Das Floss der Medusa. See
The raft of the Medusa
From morn to midnight. 1916.
Dukes, A., tr. BLOC, DIE,
GARZH, MOSG, MOSH,
ROET
Weisstein, U., tr. BRIX,
BRIY, BRIZ
Variant title: Von morgens
bis mitternachts
Gas I. 1918.
Scheffauer, H., tr. TUCG,
TUCM, TUCN, TUCO
Gas II. 1920. FEFH2
Katzin, W., tr. TUCG,
TUCM, TUCN, TUCO
Der gerettete Alkibiades. See
Alkibiades saved
Die koralle. See The coral
Der Protagonist. See The pro-
tagonist
The protagonist. 1922.
Ritchie, J., and Garten, H.,
trs. RITS
Variant title: Der Protagonist
The raft of the Medusa. 1943.
Wellwarth, G., tr. BENB,
ENG
Variant title: Das Floss der
Medusa
Von morgens bis mitternachts.
See From morn to midnight

KALCHEIM, LEE H., 1938-
...and the boy who came to leave.
1965. BALLE2

KALIDASA. 4th century
Abhijnanashakuntala. See
Shakuntalā
The fatal ring. See Shakuntalā
The hero and the nymph. See
Vikramorvacie
Sakoontalā. See Shakuntalā
Shakuntalā. 4th cent.
Coulson, M., tr. THWI
Edgren, A., tr. WEL
Jones, W., tr. TAV
Lal, P., tr. LAL
Monier-Williams, M., tr. ANDF,
BUCK, BUCL, BUCM,
CLF1, EDAD, ORI3, TRE,

TREA2, TREB, TREC1,
TREE1, TREI1, YOHA
Ryder, A., tr. ANDI, WARN1
Variant titles: Abhijnana-
shakuntala; The fatal ring;
Sakoontala; Shakuntala and
the ring of recognition;
Shakuntala recognized by
a ring-token
Shakuntala and the ring of recog-
nition. See Shakuntalā
Shakuntala recognized by a ring-
token. See Shakuntalā
Urvashi won by valour. See
Vikramorvacie
Vikramorvacie; or, The hero and
the nymph. 4th cent.
Aurobindo, S., tr. WEL
Variant titles: The hero and
the nymph; Urvashi won by
valour; Vikramorvashiya
Vikramorvashiya. See Vikramor-
vacie

KAMARCK, EDWARD
Chenango crone. DRU

KAN'AMI, KANZE KIYOTSUGU. See
Kwanze, Kiyotsugu Kan'ami

KAN-AMI KIYOTSUGU. See Kwanze,
Kiyotsugu Kan'ami

KANDER, JOHN, 1927-
Cabaret (music by). See
Masteroff, Joe. Cabaret
Chicago (music by). See Ebb,
Fred and Fosse, Bob. Chicago

K'ANG, CHIN-CHIH, fl.1279
Li K'uei carries thorns (attributed
to).
Crump, J., tr. BIR1, CRU
Variant title: Li K'uei fu ching
Li K'uei fu ching. See Li K'uei
carries thorns

KANI, JOHN. See Fugard, Athol,
jt. auth.

KANIN, FAY (MITCHELL)
(Michael Kanin), 1917-
Goodbye, my fancy. 1948. BES48
Variant title: Most likely to
succeed
Most likely to succeed. See Good-
bye, my fancy

KANIN, GARSON, 1912-
Born yesterday. 1946. BES45,
COLT, GARZ, GATB3

KANIN, MRS. GARSON. See
Gordon, Ruth

KANIN, MICHAEL. See Kanin, Fay
(Mitchell)

KANZE KIYOTSUGU KAN'AMI. See
Kwanze, Kiyotsugu

KANZE, KOJIRŌ NOBUMITSU. See
Kwanze, Kojiro Nobumitsu

KANZE MOTOKIYO. See Seami,
Motokiyo

KANZE MOTOKIYO ZEAMI. See
Seami, Motokiyo

KAO, MING, fl.1345
Pi-Pa-Ki. See Howard, Sidney
and Irwin, William Henry.
Lute song (adapted from)

KAO, TONG-KIA. See Kao, Ming

KARDISH, LAURENCE, 1945-
Brussels sprouts. 1972. BRIN

KATAEV, VALENTIN PETROVICH,
1897-
Squaring the circle. 1928.
Malamuth, C., and Lyons, E.,
trs. HAV, HAVE, LYK

KATAYEV, VALENTIN PETROVICH.
See Kataev, Valentin Petrovich

KATES, CHARLES R., 1948-
The travels of Heikiki. 1976.
KUMU

KATZ, L.
The three cuckolds. See Anonymous plays. The three
cuckolds (converted by)

KATZ, LEON, 1919-
Swellfoot's tears. GUTR

KAUFMAN, GEORGE S., 1889-1961
The butter and egg man. 1925.
BES25, LEV, LEVE
--See Dayton, Katharine;

Lardner, Ring; Marquand,
John P.; Teichmann, Howard,
jt. auths.

-- and CONNELLY, MARCUS COOK
Beggar on horseback. 1923.
BES23, CARP, CARPA, CHAN,
CHAP, COT, GASB, WARH,
WATC1, WATI
Dulcy. 1921. BES21, COH,
CONG, MOSJ, MOSK, MOSL
Merton of the movies (based on
the novel by Harry L. Wilson).
1922. BEAC12, BESS22, PEN
To the ladies! 1922. QUI, TUCD

-- and FERBER, EDNA
Dinner at eight. 1932. BES32,
SIXH
Minich. 1924. BES24
The royal family. 1927. BES27
Stage door. 1936. BES36, CLH,
GAS

-- and HART, MOSS
The American way. 1939. BES38,
PROC
George Washington slept here.
1940. BES40
The man who came to dinner.
1939. BES39, CET, COLT,
DAVK, GARZ, GATB2, SIXC
Merrily we roll along. 1934.
BES34
Once in a lifetime. 1930. BES30,
FAMB
You can't take it with you. 1936.
BES36, CLH, CORE, CORF,
GATB2, GAS, LAM, LOOC,
LOOD, LOOE, LOOF, MERS,
SPES

-- RYSKIND, MORRIE, and GERSH-
WIN, IRA.
Of thee I sing (music by George
Gershwin). 1931. BES31,
CORD, CORE, CORF, DUR,
FAMD, HIL, RICO, ROLF, TRE,
VAN

-- and TEICHMANN, HOWARD
The solid gold cadillac. 1953.
GART

KAWATAKE, MOKUAMI, 1816-1893
Aoto Zōshi Hana no Nishikie.
See Benten the thief

Benten the thief. 1862.
Uyehara, Y., tr. (English
version by Earle Ernst). ERN
Variant title: Aoto Zōshi
Hana no Nishikie; or,
Shiranami Gonin Otoko
Shiranami Gonin Otoko. See
Benten the thief

KAY, KWESI, 1940?-
Laughter and hubbub in the
house. PIET

KAZAN, NICHOLAS
Safe house. 1977. WES3

KEANE, JOHN B., 1928-
Many young men of twenty.
1961. HOGE
Sharon's grave. 1960. HOGE

KEATS, JOHN, 1795-1821
King Stephen. (1820) ENGL

-- and BROWN, CHARLES.
Otho the Great. 1950. ENGL,
KAU

KEEFE, BARRIE, 1945-
Gimme shelter. Three plays:
Gem, Gotcha, and Getaway.
1975. BES78

KELLER, SUSAN HESSE
Woyzeck (music by). See
Büchner, Georg. Woyzeck
(adapted by David Ball)

KELLY, GEORGE EDWARD, 1887-
1974
Behold the bridegroom. 1927.
BES27
Craig's wife. 1925. BES25,
CORD, CORE, CORF, GASB,
HARB, MERW, MOSG, MOSH
Daisy Mayme. 1926. BES26
The fatal weakness. 1946.
BES46
Finders-keepers. 1916? WAGC3
Variant title: The lesson
The lesson. See Finders-keepers
Poor Aubrey. 1925. GASB,
PROH, SCWG, THO
The show-off. 1924. BES23,
KRM, MOAD, MOSJ, MOSK,
MOSL

KELLY, HUGH, 1739-1777
False delicacy. 1768. BELG10,
MAND, MANF
School for wives. 1773. BELG10,
INCA9
A word to the wise. 1770.
BELG10

KEMP, DAVID
King Grumbletum and the magic
pie (1974). KAL4

KEMP, R.
The satire of the three estates.
See Lindsay, Sir David.
The satire of the three es-
tates (modernized by)

KENNAWAY, JAMES PEBLES EWING,
1928-
Country dance. 1967. PLAN33

KENNEDY, ADRIENNE, 1931-
A beast story (part of Cities in
Bezique). 1965. CARR
Cities in Bezique: The owl
answers, and A beast story.
(1969). CARR
Funnyhouse of a negro. 1964.
BRAS, OLIV
A movie star has to star in black
and white. 1976. WOQ3
The owl answers. 1965. ASF,
HARY, NEWA2
The owl answers (part of Cities
in Bezique). 1965. CARR
A rat's mass. 1966. SME
Sun. (1972) OWE

-- LENNON, JOHN, and SPINETTI,
VICTOR
The Lennon play: in his own
write. (1972). RICK

KENNEDY, MARGARET, 1896-1967
Escape me never! 1933. SEV

KENNEDY, MARY AND HAWTHORNE,
RUTH (WARREN)
Mrs. Partridge presents. 1925.
BES24

KENNEY, JAMES, 1780-1849
Raising the wind. 1803. BOOA4

KENRICK, WILLIAM, 1725?-1779

KIPPHARDT, HEINAR, 1922-
In der Sache J. Robert Oppen-
heimer. See In the matter
of J. Robert Oppenheimer
In the matter of J. Robert Op-
penheimer. 1964.
Speirs, R., tr. BES68
Variant title: In der Sache
J. Robert Oppenheimer

KIRKLAND, JACK, 1904-1969, and
CALDWELL, ERSKINE
Tobacco road. 1933. CEY, GAS,
GATB1, MOST

KIRKWOOD, JAMES, 1930- , and
DANTE, NICHOLAS
A chorus line (music by Marvin
Hamlisch; lyrics by Edward
Kleban; conceived by Michael
Bennett). 1975. BES74

KIRSHON, VLADIMIR MIKHAILOVICH,
1902-1938
Bread. 1931.
Volochora, S., tr. LYK

KITZBERG, AUGUST, 1855-1927
Libahunt. See The werewolf
The werewolf. (1912)
Lepasaar, M., tr. GOLB
Variant title: Libahunt

KIYOTSUGU, KWANAMI. See
Kwanze, Kiyotsugu Kan'ami

KLEB, WILLIAM, 1939-
Honeymoon in Haiti. 1965.
GARZAL

KLEBAN, EDWARD, 1939-
A chorus line (lyrics by).
See Kirkwood, James and
Dante, Nicholas. A chorus
line

KLEIST, HEINRICH BERNT WIL-
HELM VON, 1777-1811
The broken jug. See Der
zerbrochene krug
Kaethchen of Heilbronn; or,
The test of fire. 1810.
Pierce, F., tr. PIE
Variant title: Das Käthchen
von Heilbronn; oder, Die
feuerprobe

Das Käthchen von Heilbronn;
oder, Die Feuerprobe.
See Kaethchen of Heilbronn; or,
The test of fire
Penthesilae. 1876.
Lamport, F., tr. LAMP
Trevelyan, H., tr. BENR2
Prince Frederick of Homburg.
See Prinz Friedrich von Hom-
burg
The Prince of Homburg. See
Prinz Friedrich von Homburg
Prinz Friedrich von Homburg.
1821. CAM
Anon. tr. PLAN36
Esselin, M., tr. ESS
Hagedorn, H., tr. FRA4, SMK
Kirkup, J., tr. BENR2,
WEIS
Lustig, T., tr. LUST
Scheurer, L., tr. BENSB1
Variant titles: Prince Frederick
of Homburg; The Prince of
Homburg
Der zerbrochene krug. 1808.
CAM
Wilson, L., tr. ALL
Variant title: The broken jug

KLIEWER, WARREN, 1931-
A lean and hungry priest.
1973. BALLE12

KLIMA, IVAN, 1931-
Games. (1973)
Drabek, J., tr. DBG

KNIGHT, ERIC MOWBRAY, 1897-
1943
Never come Monday (adapted by
Stephen Fox). 1939? PROC

KNIGHT, VICK, 1908-
Cartwheel. 194-? PROC

KNOBLOCK, EDWARD, 1874-1945.
See Bennett, Arnold, jt. auth.

KNOTT, FREDERICK, 1919-
Dial "M" for murder. 1952.
BES52, FAOS, FICI, THEA53

KNOWLES, JAMES SHERIDAN, 1784-
1862
The love-chase. 1937. MARG
Virginius. 1820. BOOA1, MOSN,

MOSO

KNOX, FLORENCE CLAY
For distinguished service.
1918. SHAY

KOBER, ARTHUR, 1900-1975
"Having wonderful time."
1937. CET
Wish you were here (based on
"Having wonderful time;"
music and lyrics by Harold
Rome). 1953. THEA53

KOBRIN, LEON, 1872-1946
Boila. See Yankel Boyla
Boile. See Yankel Boyla
Boxle. See Yankel Boyla
Boxleh. See Yankel Boyla
Children of nature. See
Yankel Boyla
Dorf's Yung. See Yankel Boyla
Yankel Boyla. 1912.
Lifson, D., tr. LIFS
Variant titles: Boila; Boile,
Boxle; Boxleh; Children of
nature; Dorf's Yung

KOCH, HOWARD, 1902- , and
HUSTON, JOHN
In time to come. 1940.
AMB, BES41

KOCH, KENNETH, 1925-
The academic murders. 1966.
GLI

KOCHERGA, IVAN, 1885-
Masters of time. 1934.
Wixley, A., tr. FOUS
Variant title: Watchmaker
and the hen
Watchmaker and the hen.
See Masters of time

KOCK, CHARLES PAUL DE, 1794-
1871
A happy day. 184-?
Chambers, W., tr. BAT9
Variant title: Une journée
de bonheur
Un journée de bonheur. See
A happy day

KOEBNICK, SARAH MONSON
Fair beckoning one. 1967.
BALLE5

KOESTLER, ARTHUR, 1905-1983
Darkness at noon. See Kingsley,
Sidney. Darkness at noon
(based on the novel by)

KOHOUT, PAVEL, 1928-
Fire in the basement. 1974.
Stenberg, P., and Goetz-
Stankiewicz, M., trs. DBG

KOKOSCHKA, OSKAR, 1886-1980
Hiob. See Job
Job. 1917.
Benedikt, M., tr. WELG
Sokol, W., and J., trs.
SOK
Variant title: Hiob
Mörder, Haffnung der Frauen.
See Murderer hope of woman-
kind
Murderer hope of womankind.
1907.
Hamburger, M., tr. SOK
Ritchie, J., and Garten, H.,
trs. RITS
Variant titles: Mörder, Haff-
nung der Frauen; Murderer
the women's hope
Murderer the women's hope. See
Murderer hope of womankind

KOMPARU-ZENCHIKU, 1405-1468
The queen mother of the West
(attributed to). 15th cent.
Sesar, C., tr. KEE
Variant title: Seiōbo
Seiōbo. See The queen mother of
the West
Yōkihi. 15th cent.
Sesar, C., tr. KEE

KONDOLEON, HARRY
The brides. 1980. WOQ2
Variant title: Disrobing the
bride
Disrobing the bride. See The
brides

KONGO, YAGORO, 16th cent.?
The bird-scaring boat (attributed
to). 16th cent.?
Tyler, R., tr. KEE
Variant title: Torioibune
Torioibune. See The bird-scaring
boat

KOPIT, ARTHUR LEE, 1937-

The hero. 1970. KEN, LITI
Indians. 1969. BES69, GARTL
Nine (music and lyrics by Maury
Yeston; adaptation from the
Italian by Mario Fratti).
1979. BES81
Oh dad, poor dad, mamma's hung
you in the closet and I'm feelin'
so sad. 1960. BES61, CASA,
FREH, GARSA, GATB4, OFF,
SMA, WHFM
Wings. 1978. BERS, BES78

KOPS, BERNARD, 1926-
Enter Solly Gold. 1961?
COTKR, SATA
The hamlet of Stepney Green.
1958. NEWE1

KORNEICHUK, ALEKSANDR
EVDOKONOVICH, 1905-1972
The front. 1942.
Anon. tr. FOUT
Kotem, B., and Voynow, Z.,
trs. SEVP
Guerillas of the Ukrainian
Steppes. 1942.
Anon. tr. FOUT
Variant title: Partisans on
the steppes of the Ukraine;
Partizany v stepakh
Ukrainy
Partisans on the steppes of the
Ukraine. See Guerillas on the
Ukrainian Steppes
Partizany v stepakh Ukrainy.
See Guerillas on the steppes
of the Ukraine
Platon Krechet. 1935?
Prokofieva, R., tr. THY

KORNEICHUK, ALEXANDER
EVDOKONOVICH. See Korneichuk,
Aleksandr Evdokonovich

KORR, DAVID
Encore. 1970. BALLE9

KOSACH, LARISA PETROVNA
(Lesya Ukrainka, pseud.)
The Babylonian captivity. 19th
cent.
Volska, S., tr. ROE

KOSTROWISKY, GUILLAUME
APOLLINAIRE DE (GUILLAUME
APOLLINAIRE, pseud.), 1880-1918

The breasts of Tiresias. 1917.
Simpson, L., tr. BEN
Variant title: Les mamelles
de Tirésias
Les mamelles de Tirésias. See
The breasts of Tiresias

KOSTROWITZKI, WILHELM. See
Kostrowisky, Guillaume Apollinaire de

KOTZEBUE, AUGUST FRIEDRICH
FERDINAND VON, 1761-1819
Der egoist und kritikus. See
Egotist and pseudo-critic Herr
Gottlieb Merks
Egotist and pseudo-critic Herr
Gottlieb Merks. 179-?
Chambers, W., tr. BAT11
Variant title: Der egoist und
kritikus
Falsche scham. See Dunlap,
William. False shame (adapted
from)
Das kind der liebe. See Lovers'
vows
Lovers' vows; or, The natural
son. 1798?
Thompson, B., tr. BAT21
Variant title: Das kind der
liebe
Menschenhass und reue. See The
stranger
Pharoah's daughter. 179-?
Beebe, B., tr. WEB
Variant title: Die tochter
Pharaonis
The stranger. 1789.
Thompson, B., tr. MAND,
MANF
Variant title: Menschenhass
une reue
Die tochter Pharaonis. See
Pharaoh's daughter

KOUTOUKAS, H. M., 1947-
Kill, kaleidoscope, kill. See
Tidy passions
Tidy passions; or, Kill, kaleidos-
cope, kill. 1972. SME
Variant title: Kill, kaleidos-
cope, kill

KOZAK, PRIMOŽ, 1929-
An affair. 1961.
Anderson, E., and Salamun, T.,
trs. MIG

KOZLENKO, WILLIAM, 1908-
This earth is ours. 1937?
KOZ

KRAL, BRIAN
One to grow on. 1980. WES15/16

KRAMM, JOSEPH, 1907-
The shrike. 1952. BES51

KRANES, DAVID
Drive-in. BALLE7

KRASIŃSKI, ZYGMUNT, 1812-1859
Nieboska komedia. See The
un-divine comedy
The un-divine comedy. 1902.
Segel, H., tr. POB
Variant title: Nieboska
komedia

KRASNA, NORMAN, 1909-1984
Dear Ruth. 1944. BES44
John loves Mary. 1947. BES46

KRAUS, JOANNA HALPERT, 1937-
The ice wolf: a tale of the Eskimos. 1973. NEWVM

KRAUS, KARL, 1874-1936
The last days of mankind,
(excerpt). 1919-1922.
Spalter, M., tr. WELG
Variant title: Die letzten tage
der menschheit
Die letzten tage der menschheit.
See The last days of mankind

KREYMBORG, ALFRED, 1883-1966
The dead are free. 1935. AME5
Hole in the wall. 192-? KRE
Lima beans. 1925? LEV, LEVE
Manikin and Minikin. 1918. SHAY
Rocking chairs. 1921? SHAY

KROG, HELGE, 1889-1962
Konkylien. See The sounding
shell
The sounding shell. 1929.
Campbell, R., tr. SCAN2
Variant title: Konkylien

KROETZ, FRANZ XAVER, 1946-
Mensch Meier: a play of every-
day life. 1978.
Downey, R., tr. NEWQA
Stallerhof. 1972.

Hehn, K., tr. SHAK

KRYLOV, IVAN ANDREEVICH, 1768-
1844
The milliner's shop. (1806)
Senelick, L., tr. RVI
Variant title: Modnaya Lavka
Modnaya Lavka. See The Milliner's
shop

KUAN, HAN-CH'ING, 1210?-1298?
The butterfly dream. MANM
The injustice done to Tou Ngo.
Liu, J., tr. LIU
Snow in midsummer. 13th cent.
Yang, H., and Yang, G., trs.
MESE
Variant title: Tou Ngo
Tou Ngo. See Snow in midsummer

KUHNS, DOROTHY HARTZELL. See
Heyward, Mrs. Dorothy Hartzell
(Kuhns)

KUMMER, MRS. CLARE (BEECHER),
1888-1958
Good gracious Annabelle. 1916.
BESO9
Her master's voice. 1933. BES33

KUNDERA, MILAN, 1929-
Jacques and his master; an homage
to Diderot in three acts. 1982.
Heim, M., tr. DBG
Variant title: Jacques et son
maître; Jacques le fataliste
et son maître
Jacques et son maître. See
Jacques and his master; an
homage to Diderot in three acts
Jacques le fataliste et son maître.
See Jacques and his master;
an homage to Diderot in three
acts

KURNITZ, HARRY, 1909-1968
Reclining figure. 1954. THEA55

KUROSAWA, AKIRA, 1910- ,
HASHIMOTO, SHINOBU, AND OGUNI,
HIDEO
Ikiru (screenplay). 1952.
Richie, D., tr. HIBH
Variant title: To live
To live. See Ikiru

KVARES, DONALD

Mushrooms. 1967. SMC

KWANAMI KIYOTSUGU. See Kwanze,
Kiyotsugu

KWANZE, KIYOTSUGU, 1333-1384
Kayoi Komachi. See Komachi
and the hundred nights
Komachi and the hundred nights.
14th cent.
Kato, E., tr. KEE
Variant title: Kayoi Komachi
Matsukase. 14th cent.
Tyler, R., tr. KEE
Motomezuka. See The sought-
for grave
Sotoba Komachi. 14th cent.
Waley, A., tr. TRE, TREB,
TREC1, TREE1, TREI1
The sought-for grave. 14th
cent.
Jackman, B., tr. KEE
Variant title: Motomezuka

KWANZE KOJIRŌ NOBUMITSU.
See Kwanze, Kijirō Nobumitsu

KWANZE, KOJIRŌ NOBUMITSU,
1434-1516
Dōjōji (attributed to)
Keene, D., tr. KEE
The maple viewing (attributed
to)
Weatherby, M., tr. ERN
Variant title: Momijigari
Momijigari. See The maple
viewing
The priest and the willow.
Beichman, J., tr. KEE
Variant title: Yugyō Yanagi
Yugyō Yanagi. See The priest
and the willow

KYD, THOMAS, 1558-1594
Arden of Feversham (sometimes
attributed to). See Anony-
mous plays. Arden of
Feversham
Hieronimo is mad again. See
The Spanish tragedy; or,
Hieronimo is mad again
The Spanish tragedy; or,
Hieronimo is mad again.
1589? BAS, BROC, DPR1,
GATG, HEIL, HOW, HUST,
MAKG, MAX, MINI, MIO1,
MIR, NEI, NES, OLH, OLI1,

ORNT, PAR, RUB, SCI, SCJ,
SCW, SPE, TICO
Variant title: Hieronimo is
mad again

LABICHE, EUGENE MARIN, 1815-
1888, and DELACOUR, ALFRED
CHARLEMAGNE LARTIGNE
La cagnotte. See Pots of money
Célimare. 1863.
Hoffman, L., and T., and
Bentley, E., trs. BENSB
Variant title: Célimare le
bien-aimé
Célimare le bien-aimé. See
Célimare
Les petits oiseaux. See Grundy,
Sydney. A pair of spectacles
(adapted from)
Pots of money. 1864.
Bermel, A., tr. BERM, THV
Variant title: La cagnotte

-- and GONDINET, EDMOND
The happiest of the three.
Davies, F., tr. LAB

-- and LEVEAUX, ALPHONSE
La grammaire. 1867. BENZ,
STOC

-- and MARTIN, EDOUARD
Bluffers. See La poudre aux
yeux
Cousin Billy. See Le voyage de
Monsieur Perrichon
Dust in the eyes. See La poudre
aux yeux
Perrichon's voyage. See Le
voyage de Monsieur Perrichon
La poudre aux yeux. 1861. SCN
Variant titles: Bluffers; Dust
in the eyes
The 37 sons of M. Montaudoin.
See Les trente-sept sous de
M. Montaudoin
Les trente-sept sous de M.
Montaudoin. 1862. BRN
Variant title: The 37 sous of
M. Montaudoin
A trip abroad. See Le voyage de
Monsieur Perrichon
Le voyage de Monsieur Perrichon.
1860. MANA
Ward, R., tr. BENSC

Variant titles: Cousin Billy;
Perrichon's voyage; A trip
abroad

-- and MICHEL, MARC ANTOINE
AMEDEE
Haste to the wedding. See
An Italian straw hat
An Italian straw hat. 1851.
Hoffman, L., and T., trs.
BENT3, COTKIR
Variant titles: Haste to the
wedding; The wedding
march
The wedding march. See An
Italian straw hat
--See also Legouve, Ernest, jt.
auth.

LA CHAUSEE, PIERRE CLAUDE
NIVELLE DE, 1692-1754
Fashionable prejudice. See Le
préjugé à la mode
Le préjugé à la mode. 1735.
BRE
Variant title: Fashionable
prejudice

LAPIDO, DURO
Moremi.
Beier, U., tr. THTN

LA FARGE, W. E. R.
Escape by balloon. 1972.
BALLE10

LA FOSSE, ANTOINE DE, sieur
d'Aubigny, 1653-1708
Manlius Capitolinus. 1698.
Lockert, L., tr. LOCR

LAGERKVIST, PAR, 1891-1974
The difficult hour, I-III.
1918
Buckman, T., tr. SPR
Variant title: Den svåra
stunden, I-III
Låt människan leva. See Let
man live
Let man live. 1949.
Alexander, H., and Jones,
L., trs. SCAN3
Gustafsson, W., tr. FIL
Variant titles: Låt människan
leva; The man who lived
his life over
The man without a soul. 1936.

Kökeritz, H., tr. SCAN1
Variant title: Mannen utan
själ
Mannen utan själ. See The man
without a soul
Den svåra stunden, I-III. See
The difficult hour, I-III

LA GRANGE-CHANCEL, 1677-1758
Ino and Melicertes. 1713.
Lockert, L., tr. LOCU
Variant title: Ino et Mélicerte
Ino et Mélicerte. See Ino and
Melicertes

LAMB, MYRNA, 1931-
But what have you done for me
lately? See Scyklon Z: But
what have you done for me
lately?; or, Pure polemic
I lost a pair of gloves yesterday.
NEWVM
Pure polemic. See Scyklon Z:
But what have you done for
me lately?; or, Pure polemic
Scyklon Z: But what have you
done for me lately? or, Pure
polemic. 1969. BAYM, RAVA
Variant titles: Pure polemic;
But what have you done for
me lately

LANDON, JOSEPH, 1951?-
Blessing. 1973. BALLE13

LANDOVSKÝ, PAVEL, 1936-
The detour
Osers, E., tr. and Soule, D.,
adapter. DBG

LANDSBERGIS, ALGIRDAS, 1924-
Five posts in a market place.
(1958)
Landsbergis, A., tr. and
adapter. CONF
Variant title: Penki stulpai
turgaus aikštėje
Penki stulpai turgaus aikštėje.
See Five posts in a market-
place

LANGLEY, NOEL, 1911- . See
Morley, Robert, jt. auth.

LAO, SHEH (pseud. of Sha, Ch'ing-
ch'ien), 1898-1966
Dragon beard ditch. (1950)

Liao, H., tr. MESE

LAPINE, JAMES, 1949-
Sunday in the park with George
(music and lyrics by
Stephen Sondheim). 1984.
BES83
Table settings. 1979. BES79

LARDNER, RING WILMER, 1885-
1933
Thompson's vacation. (1934)
CARL, CARLE

-- and KAUFMAN, GEORGE S.
June moon. 1929. BES29

LARIVEY, PIERRE DE, 1540-1619
The spirits. (1579)
Seigneuret, J. C., tr.
FOUAF
Variant title: Les esprits

LARSON, NANCY, 1950-
Imitations. 1978. WES5

LASZLO, CARL
The Chinese icebox. 1956.
Wellwarth, G., tr. BENB
Variant title: Der Chinesische
Kühlschrank
Der Chinesische Kühlschrank.
See The Chinese icebox
Essen wir Haare. See Let's
eat hair!
Let's eat hair! 1956.
Wellwarth, G., tr. BENB
Variant title: Essen wir
Haare

LASZLO, MIKLOS, 1904-1973
She loves me. See Masteroff,
Joe. She loves me (based
on a play by)

LA TAILLE, JEAN DE. See
Taille, Jean de La

LA TEMPA, SUSAN
The life of the party. (1979)
NEWP
Sunset Beach. 1982. PLACE

LATOUCHE, JOHN TREVILLE,
1917-1956
Candide. See Hellman, Lillian.
Candide (lyrics by)

The golden apple (music by
Jerome Moross). 1954.
BES53, THEA54

LAUCKNER, ROLF T., 1887-1954
Cry in the street. 1922.
Edwards, M., and Reich, V.,
trs. SOK
Variant title: Schrei aus
der Strasse
Schrei aus der Strasse. See
Cry in the street

LAUNDER, FRANK, 1907- , and
GILLIAT, SIDNEY
The body was well nourished.
See Meet a body
Meet a body. 1940. PLAN10
Variant title: The body was
well nourished

LAURENTS, ARTHUR, 1918-
A clearing in the woods. 1957.
BES56
Gypsy (music by Jule Styne,
lyrics by Stephen Sondheim).
1959. RICO
Home of the brave. 1945.
BES45, GARZ, HEWE
The time of the cuckoo. 1952.
BES52, THEA53
West side story (music by Leonard
Bernstein; lyrics by Stephen
Sondheim). 1957. RICO

LAVEDAN, HENRI LEON EMILE,
1859-1940
The prince d'Aurec. 1892.
Clark, B., tr. THR

LAVERY, EMMET, 1902-
The magnificent Yankee. 1946.
BES45, MERT, SPES

-- and MURPHY, GRACE
Kamiano, the story of Damien.
1938. THEC

LA VIGNE, ANDRIEU DE, d.ca.1515
The miracle of the blind man and
the cripple. 15th cent. LOOM

LAVIGNE, LOUIS-DOMINIQUE, 1949-
Are you afraid of thieves? 1977?
Beissel, H., tr. KAL5
Variant title: As-tu peur des
voleurs?

As-tu peur des voleurs? See
Are you afraid of thieves?

LAW, WARNER
Indomitable blacksmith. 195-?
LOVR

LAWLER, RAY, 1922-
Summer of the 17th doll. 1955.
BES57

LAWRENCE, JEROME, 1915- , and
LEE, ROBERT E.
First Monday in October. 1978.
BES78
Inherit the wind. 1955.
AMB, BES54, GART, PLAU,
REA, SHER, THEA55

LAWSON, JOHN HOWARD, 1894-1977
Processional. 1925. IFKO,
WATC1, WATI
Roger Bloomer. 1923. FULT
Success story. 1932. LOO

LAXNESS, HALLDOR, 1902-
Dúfnaveizlan. See The pigeon
banquet
The pigeon banquet. 1966.
Boucher, A., tr. MNOI
Variant title: Dúfnaveizlan

LAYA, JEAN LOUIS, 1761-1833
L'ami des lois. 1793. BRE

LAZARUS, JOHN, 1947-
Babel rap. 1972. FIFVE

LEACOCK, JOHN
The fall of British tyranny;
or, American liberty triumphant. 1776. MOSS1, PHI

LEAMON, DOROTHY
Barabas. 20th cent. FED2

LEAVITT, JOHN McDOWELL, 1824-
190-?
The Jewish captives. 1876?
KOH2

LEBOVIĆ, DJORDJE, 1928-
Hallelujah. 1960.
Koljevic, N., tr. MIG

LECOCQ, ALEXANDRE CHARLES,
1832-1918

The daughter of Madame Angot.
1872.
Seldes, G., and G., trs. PLAH
Variant title: La fille de
Madame Angot
La fille de Madame Angot. See
The daughter of Madame Angot

LEE, JAMES HENRY, 1923-
Career. 1956. COTK

LEE, JEANNIE
On the corner of Cherry and
elsewhere. COLI

LEE, JOO FOR, 1929-
The happening in the bungalow.
1970. NEWDE

LEE, LANCE, 1942-
Fox, hound and huntress.
1971. BALLE10

LEE, NATHANIEL, 1653?-1692
Alexander the great; or, The
rival queens (an adaptation
of The rival queens). See
The rival queens
The death of Alexander the Great.
See The rival queens; or, The
death of Alexander the Great
Lucius Junius Brutus; father of
his country. 1680. BELG11,
RET
The rival queens; or, The death
of Alexander the great. 1677.
BELK7, MAND, MANF
Variant titles: Alexander the
Great; The death of Alexan-
der the Great
Sophonisba. 1675. DOA
Theodosius; or, The force of love.
(1680) BELK7
--See also Dryden, J., jt. auth.

LEE, ROBERT E., 1918- . See
Lawrence, Jerome, jt. auth.

LEE, SOPHIA, 1750-1824
The chapter of accidents. 1780.
BELG11, INCA9

LEEDS, CHARLIE
The love song of rotten John
Calabrese. (1970) ALI

LEGOUVE, ERNEST, 1807-1903, and

LABICHE, EUGENE MARIN
La cigale chez les fourmis.
188-? BOVE
Variant title: The grass-
hopper at the home of the
ants
The grasshopper at the home of
the ants. See La cigale chez
les fourmis

LEICHMAN, SEYMOUR, 1933-
Freddie the pigeon. BALLE7

LEIGH, MIKE, 1943?-
Abigail's party. 1977. PLAN47

LEIGH, MITCH, 1928-
Man of La Mancha (music by).
See Wasserman, Dale. Man of
La Mancha

LEIWIK, H. See Halper, Leivick

LELAND, JOHN, 1506?-1552. See
Leland, Thomas, jt. auth.

LELAND, THOMAS, 1722-1785, and
LELAND, JOHN
Longsword, earl of Salisbury
(romance attributed to). See
Hartson, H. The countess of
Salisbury (adapted from)

LEMAITRE, JULES, 1853-1914
Forgiveness. See The pardon
Le pardon. See The pardon
The pardon. 1895.
Clark, B., tr. THR
Variant titles: Forgiveness;
Le pardon

LENNON, JOHN, 1940-1980
See Kennedy, Adrienne, jt. auth.

LENNOX, GILBERT
Close quarters. See Somin,
W. O. Close quarters (tr.
and adapted by)

LENORMAND, HENRI RENE, 1882-
1938
The coward. 1925.
Orna, D., tr. CHA, CHAN
Variant title: La lâche
Crêpuscle du théâtre. See
In Theatre street
The devourer of dreams. See

The dream doctor
The dream doctor. 1922. Orna,
D., tr. MOSG, MOSH
Variant title: The devourer
of dreams; Le mangeur de
rêves
L'homme et ses fantômes 1924.
RHO
Variant title: Man and his
phantoms
In Theatre street. 1936.
Dukes, A., tr. FAMK
Variant title: Crêpuscle du
théâtre
Le lâche. See The coward
Man and his phantoms. See
L'homme et ses fantômes
Le mangeur de rêves. See The
dream doctor
Simoom. See Le simoun
Le simoun. 1920. HART
Variant title: Simoom
Le temps est un songe. See
Time is a dream
Time is a dream. 1919.
Katzin, W., tr. DIE, HAV
Variant title: Le temps est
un songe

LEONARD, HUGH, 1926-
"Da". 1973. BES77, BEST,
PLAN44
A life. 1979. BES80
The Patrick Pearse motel. 1971.
PLAN41
The poker session. 1964. PLAN28
Stephen D (based on James Joyce's
Portrait of the artist as a
young man, and Stephen Hero).
1962. ENG

LEONOV, LEONID MAXIMOVICH,
1899-
Invasion. 1943.
Anon. tr. FOUT
Miller, A., tr. CLKX
The orchards of Polovchansk.
1938.
Robbins, J., tr. SEVP

LEOPOLD, pseud. See Chandezon,
Léopold

LERNER, ALAN JAY, 1918-
Brigadoon (music by Frederick
Loewe). 1947. BES46, RICO
Camelot (based on The once and

future king, by Terence Hanbury White; music by Frederick Loewe). 1960. RICM
My fair lady (adapted from Bernard Shaw's Pygmalion; music by Frederick Loewe). 1956. BES55

LE SAGE, ALAIN RENE, 1668-1747
Crispin, rival de son maître.
See Crispin, rival of his master
Crispin, rival of his master. 1707.
Chambers, w., tr. BAT8
Variant title: Crispin, rival de son maître
The financier. See Turcaret
Turcaret. 1709. BRE, ZDA
Aldington, R., tr. ALD
Merwin, W., tr. BENR4
Variant titles: The financier; Turcaret; or, The financier
Turcaret; or, The financier.
See Turcaret

LESHOAI, BENJAMIN LETHOLOA
Lines draw monsters (Act I).
(1965) CONZI

LESSING, DORIS MAE, 1919-
Each his own wilderness. 1958.
NEWE1
Play with a tiger. 1962. SUB, PLAJ1

LESSING, GOTTHOLD EPHRAIM, 1729-1781
Emilia Galotti. 1772.
Lamport, F., tr. LAMP
Lewes, C., tr. ESS
Minna von Barnhelm; or, The soldier's fortune. 1767.
Bell, E., tr. BAT10, CROV, GREA, HARC26, MAU
Miss Sara Sampson. 1753.
Bell, E., tr. CLF2
Nathan der weise. See Nathan the wise
Nathan the wise. 1783.
Frothingham, E., tr. KOH2
Lustig, T., tr. LUST
Variant title: Nathan der weise

LETHBRIDGE, NEMONE
The Portsmouth defence. 1966.

PLAN32

LETTON, FRANCIS, 1912- . See Dowling, Jennette, jt. auth.

LEVEAUX, ALPHONSE, b.1810.
See Labiche, Eugène Marin, jt. auth.

LEVIN, IRA, 1929-
Deathtrap. 1978. BES77
No time for sergeants (adapted from the novel by Mac Hyman).
1955. BES55, GART, THEA56

LEVINE, MARK L., 1943- , McNAMEE, GEORGE C., and GREENBERG, DANIEL
The tales of Hoffman - a series of excerpts from the "Chicago conspiracy" trial. RAVA

LEVINSON, ALFRED
Socrates wounded. 1959? NEWA1

LEVITT, SAUL, 1911-
The Andersonville trial. 1959.
AMB, BES59, CEQ

LEVY, BENN WOLF, 1900-1973
Clutterbuck. 1949. BES49
The devil passes. 1932. BES31
The member for Gaza. 1966.
PLAN32
Mrs. Moonlight. 1928. FAO
Springtime for Henry. 1931.
LEV, LEVE

LEVY, JULES. See Courteline, Georges, jt. auth.

LEWIN, JOHN
Five easy payments. 1966.
BALLE3

LEWIN, ROSE D. See Franken, Mrs. Rose D. (Lewin)

LEWIS, LEOPOLD DAVID, 1828-1890
The bells (adapted from Le juif Polonais by Erckmann-Chatrian).
1871. ASG, BOOB, COTKIS, ROWE
Variant title: The Polish Jew
The Polish Jew. See The bells

LEWIS, MATTHEW GREGORY "MONK", 1775-1818

The castle spectre. 1797.
HOUR

LEWIS, SAUNDERS, 1893-
King's daughter. See Siwan
Siwan. 1954.
  Humphreys, E., tr. PLAN21
  Variant title: King's daughter

LEWIS, SINCLAIR, 1885-1951
Dodsworth. See Howard, Sidney.
  Dodsworth (based on the novel
  by)
The ghost patrol. See Clarke,
  William Kendall. The ghost
  patrol (based on the story
  by)

LI, CHI-HUANG. See Sha, Seh,
jt. auth.

LI, CHIEN-WU, 1906-
Ch'ing-ch'un. See Springtime
Springtime. (1944)
  Pollard, D., tr. TWEH
  Variant title: Ch'ing-ch'un

LI, HAO-KU, 13th cent.
Chang boils the sea. 13th cent.
  Liu, J., tr. LIU

LI SHOUCHENG. See Li, Shou-
ch'eng

LI, SHOU-CH'ENG. See Sha,
Yeh-Hsin, jt. auth.

LI, SYAU-CHWUN
The wild boar forest. (1960)
  Mitchell, J. and Chang, D.,
  trs. MIT

LIANG, CHENYU, 1520-c.1580
"Secret liaison with Chancellor
  Bo Pi". See Washing silk
Wan-sha ji. See Washing silk
Washing silk (Act VII).
  Dolby, W., tr. EIG
  Variant titles: "Secret
  liaison with Chancellor Bo
  Pi"; Wan-sha ji

LIBMAN, CARL
Follow the leader. 1968. ALI

LIEBERMAN, EDITH, d.1975
See Lieberman, Harold, jt. auth.

LIEBERMAN, HAROLD, and LIEBER-
MAN, EDITH
Throne of straw. 1973. THL

LILLO, GEORGE, 1693-1739
The fatal curiosity. 1736. BELG9
The London merchant; or, The
  history of George Barnwell.
  1731. BELK5, BENY, BOO,
  BROJ, BROK, EIGH, HAN,
  MAND, MANF, MOR, NET,
  SIG, SMI, STM, TAU, TREB,
  TUQ, WILE

LINARES RIVAS, MANUEL, 1867-1938
The claws. 1914.
  Turrell, C., tr. TUR
  Variant title: La garra
La garra. See The claws

LINDSAY, SIR DAVID, 1490-1555
Ane satire of the thrie estaitis.
  See The satire of the three
  estates
The satire of the three estates.
  1540. FOUN
  Kemp, R., modernizer. ROET
  Variant title: Ane satire of
  the thrie estaitis

LINDSAY, HOWARD, 1889-1968, and
CROUSE, RUSSEL
Life with father (based on the
  book by Clarence Day). 1939.
  BES39, CASS, CET, CEY,
  COLT, COOP, GARZ, GATB2,
  LOVR, MERS, MOST, SPER,
  STRB
Life with mother (based on the
  book by Clarence Day). 1948.
  BES48
Remains to be seen. 1951. BES51
State of the union. 1945. BES45,
  GARW, GATB3

LINFANTE, MICHELE
Pizza. 1980. WES6

LIPSCOMB, WILLIAM PERCY, 1887-
1958, and MINNEY, RUBEIGH J.
Clive of India. 1934. FAME

LIPSKEROFF, KONSTANTIN, 1899-
Carmencita and the soldier (based
  on the opera Carmen by
  Georges Bizet; libretto by
  Prosper Mérimée.) 1923.

Seldes, G., and G., trs.
PLAH

LITT, JENNIFER, A.
Epiphany. 1982. YOUP

LIU, TANGQING, Late 13th or
early 14th cent.
"The battling doctors". See
Cai Shun shares the mulberries.
Cai Shun fen-shen. See
Cai Shun shares the mulberries.
Cai Shun shares the mulberries.
(attributed to.)
Late 13th or early 14th cent.
Dolby, W., tr. EIG (ex-
cerpt)
Variant titles: "The battling
doctors"; Cai Shun fen-
shen

LIVING NEWSPAPER. See Staff of
the Living Newspaper

LIVINGS, HENRY, 1929-
The gamecock (part of Pongo
Plays 1-6). 1969. PLAAB
Nil carborundum. 1962. NEWE6
Stop it, whoever you are. 1961.
NEWE5
There's no room for you here for
a start. 1963. CONB

LIVINGSTON, MYRTLE SMITH,
1901-
The unborn children. 1901.
HARY

LIVINGSTONE, DOUGLAS JAMES,
1932-
A rhino for the boardroom, a
radio play. 1974. CONZI
The sea my winding sheet.
1964. THI

LLOYD, HORACE AMELIUS
Rummio and Judy; or, Oh, this
love! This love! This love!
(1841) NIN2

LLOYD WEBBER, ANDREW, 1948-
Cats; a musical in two acts
(based on Old Possum's book
of practical cats by Thomas
Stearns Eliot; music by Andrew
Lloyd Webber; additional lyrics
by Trevor Nunn). 1980.

BES82
Jesus Christ superstar (music by).
See Rice, Tim. Jesus Christ
superstar, a rock opera

LOCHER, JENS, 1889-1952
Tea for three. 1943.
Anon. trs. (revised by Fur-
bank, P., and Bredsdorff,
E.) CONT
Variant title: Tre maa man
vaere
Tre maa man vaere. See Tea for
three

LOCKE-ELLIOTT, SUMNER
Rusty bugles. 1948. HANG

LOCKRIDGE, FRANCES (MRS.
RICHARD LOCKRIDGE), d.1963, and
LOCKRIDGE, RICHARD
The Norths meet murder. See
Davis, Owen. Mr. and Mrs.
North (based on the novel by)

LOCKRIDGE, RICHARD, 1898- .
See Lockridge, Frances, jt. auth.

LODGE, THOMAS, 1558?-1625
Mucedorus (sometimes attributed
to). See Anonymous plays.
Mucedorus
The reign of King Edward the
third (sometimes attributed to).
See Anonymous plays. The
reign of King Edward the third

-- and GREENE, ROBERT.
A looking glass for London and
England. 1592. DPR1

LOESSER, FRANK, 1910-1969
Guys and dolls. See Swerling,
Jo, and Burrows, Abe.
Guys and dolls (music and
lyrics by)
How to succeed in business without
really trying. See Burrows,
Abram S. How to succeed in
business without really trying
(music and lyrics by)
The most happy fella (based on
Sidney Howard's play They
knew what they wanted). 1956.
THEA56

LOEWE, FREDERICK, 1901-

Brigadoon (music by). See
Lerner, Alan Jay. Brigadoon
Camelot (music by). See
Lerner, Alan Jay. Camelot
My fair lady (music by). See
Lerner, Alan Jay. My fair
lady

LOGAN, JOSHUA, 1908-
The wisteria trees (based on the
Cherry orchard by Anton
Chekhov). 1950. BES49
--See also Behrman, Samuel
Nathaniel; Hammerstein II,
Oscar; Heggen, Thomas;
Kober, Arthur, jt. auths.

LONERGAN, KENNETH
The Rennings children. 1982.
YOUP

LONG, JOHN LUTHER, 1861-1927.
See Belasco, David, jt. auth.

LONGFELLOW, HENRY WADSWORTH,
1807-1882
The Spanish student. 1843?
BAT19

LONGFORD, CHRISTINE
Mr. Jiggins of Jigginstown.
1933. CAN

LONGFORD, EDWARD ARTHUR
HENRY, 1902-1961
Yahoo. 1933. CAN

LONSDALE, FREDERICK, 1881-1954
Aren't we all? 1923. SEV
Half a loaf. See Let them eat
cake
The last of Mrs. Cheyney.
1925. BES25
Let them eat cake. 1959.
PLAN19
Variant titles: Half a loaf;
Once is enough
Once is enough. See Let them
eat cake

LOOS, ANITA, 1893-
Gigi (from the novel by Colette).
1951. BES51

LOPE DE RUEDA. See Rueda, Lope
de

LOPE DE VEGA. See Vega Carpio,
Lope Félix de

LOPEZ, SABATINO, 1867-1951
Il passero. See The sparrow
The sparrow. 1918.
Goldberg, I., tr. GOL
Variant title: Il passero

LOPEZ DE AYALA, ADELARDO,
1828-1879
Consuelo. 1878. BRET

LOPEZ MOZO, JERONIMO
The testament. (1968)
Wellwarth, M., tr. WELK
Variant title: El testamento
El testamento. See The testament

LOPEZ RUBIO, JOSE, 1903-
The blindfold. (1954)
Holt, M., tr. HOLT
Variant title: La venda en
los ojos
La venda en los ojos. See The
blindfold

LORCA, FEDERICO GARCIA. See
García Lorca, Federico

LOS HERREROS, MANUEL BRETON
DE. See Bretón de los Herreros,
Manuel

LOW, SAMUEL, b.1765
The politician out-witted. 1789.
MOSS1

LOWELL, ROBERT, 1917-1977
Beneto Cereno. 1964. ABC,
BROTA, BUR, DOV, FAMAH,
GAT, REV, RICJ, TREBJ,
VON
Variant title: Old glory:
Beneto Cereno
My kinsman, Major Molineux.
1964. ALS, CASE, DOD,
SCNR
Old glory: Beneto Cereno.
See Beneto Cereno

LA HSUN ACADEMY OF ART AND
LITERATURE
The white-haired girl. See Ho,
Ching-chih, and Ting, Yi. The
white-haired girl (written by)

LU, HSUN (pseud. of Cho
Shu-Jen), 1881-1936
The passer-by (1925)
Yang, H., and Yang, G.,
trs. MESE

LUCE, CLARE BOOTHE. See
Boothe, Clare

LUCKHAM, CLAIRE
Trafford Tanzi. 1980. PLABE2

LUDLAM, CHARLES, 1943-
Bluebeard. 1970. SME

LUDWIG, OTTO, 1813-1865
Der erbförster. 1850. CAM
Remy, A., tr. FRA9
Variant title: The heredi-
tary forester
The hereditary forester. See
Der erbförster

LUKE, PETER, 1919-
Hadrian VII. 1967. BES68,
PLAN33, RICIS

LUM, DARRELL H. Y.
Oranges are lucky. 1976.
KUMU

LUPTON, THOMAS, fl. 1588
All for money. 1577. SCAT

LUTS, OSKAR, 1887-1953
Sootuluke. See The will-o'-
the-wisp
The spirit of Lake Ülemiste.
1916.
Kukk, H., tr. GOLB
Variant title: Ülemiste
vanake
Ülemiste vanake. See The
spirit of Lake Ülemiste
The will-o'-the-wisp. 1919.
Kukk, H., tr. GOLB
Variant title: Sootuluke

LYLY, JOHN, 1554?-1606
Alexander and Campaspe. See
Campaspe
Campaspe. 1584. ADA, GAY1,
MAK, OLH, OLI1
Variant title: Alexander and
Campaspe
Endimion. See Endymion, the
man in the moon

Endymion, the man in the moon.
1588. BAS, BROC, MIN2,
MIO2, NEI, NES, ORNC,
PAR, SCH, SCI, SCJ, SCW,
SPE
Variant title: Endimion
Gallathea. 1588. DPR1
Midas. 1589. WINN
Mother Bombie. 1589? TAT, TAU

LYNCH, HAL
Three miles to Poley. 1971.
BALLE10

LYNCH, MICHAEL
Sylvester the Cat vs. Galloping
Billy Bronco. 1979. WES6

LYNDON, BARRE, 1896-1972
The amazing Dr. Clitterhouse.
1936. FOUP, THH
The man in Half moon street.
1939. SIXL
They came by night. 1937. FIP

LYNNE, JAMES BROOM, 1920-
The trigon. 1963. NEWE8

LYTTON, EDWARD GEORGE BULWER.
See Bulwer-Lytton, Edward George
Earle Lytton

MA, CHIH-YUAN, fl. 1251
Autumn in Han Palace. See
Autumn in the Palace of Han
Autumn in the Palace of Han.
13th cent.
Liu, J., tr. BIR1, LIU
Variant titles: Autumn in Han
Palace; Han Kung Ch'in
Han Kung Ch'in. See Autumn in
the Palace of Han

MA, YUNG. See Sha, Seh, jt. auth.

MacARTHUR, CHARLES, 1895-
1956. See Hecht, Ben, jt. auth.

MACAULEY, PAULINE
The creeper. 1964. PLAN29
Monica. RICJ

MacBETH, GEORGE, 1932- , and
BINGHAM, J.
The doomsday show. 1964. NEWE14

McCARTHY, JUSTIN HUNTLEY,
1861-1936
  If I were king. 1901. BES99
    Variant title: The vagabond
      king
  The vagabond king. See If I
    were king

McCAULEY, CLARICE VALLETTE
  The conflict. 1920. SHAY
  The seeker. 1919. FED1

McCLENAGHAN, TOM
  Submariners. 1980. GAW

McCLOSKEY, JAMES J., 1825-1913
  Across the continent; or, Scenes
    from New York life and the
    Pacific railroad. 1870. AMP4,
    MONR

McCLURE, MICHAEL, 1932-
  Goethe: Ein Fragment. 1978.
    WES2

McCOO, EDWARD J.
  Ethiopia at the bar of justice.
    RIR

McCRACKEN, MRS. ESTHER
(ARMSTRONG), 1902-
  Quiet wedding. 1938. SIXL

McCULLERS, MRS. CARSON
(SMITH), 1917-1967
  The member of the wedding.
    1950. BES49, GARW, GATB3,
    GAVE, HEWE, MIJY, PATM,
    PATP, STS

McCUTCHEON, GEORGE BARR,
1866-1928
  The double doctor: a farce.
    INDI

McDANIEL, CHARLES A.
  The ends of justice. 1968.
    BRNB

MacDERMOT, GALT, 1928-
  Hair (music by). See Ragni,
    Gerome and Rado, James.
    Hair
  Two gentlemen of Verona (music
    by). See Guare, John and
    Shapiro, Mel. Two gentlemen
    of Verona

MacDONAGH, DONAGH, 1912-
  Happy as Larry. 1947. BRZ,
    NEWW6
  Step-in-the-hollow. 1957.
    BRZE

MacDONALD, CATHERINE, 1940-
  Chekhov in Yalta (music by).
    See Driver, John and Haddow,
    Jeffrey. Chekhov in Yalta

McDONALD, CATHERINE, and MASON,
WILTON
  Spring for sure. 1950. PAJ

MacDONALD, ROBERT DAVID
  Chinchilla. 1977. DEC

MacDOUGALL, ROGER, 1910-
  The gentle gunman. 1950. PLAN5
  To Dorothy, a son. 1950. PLAN4

McENROE, ROBERT EDWARD, 1916-
  Oliver Erwenter. See The silver
    whistle
  The silver whistle. 1948. BES48
    Variant title: Oliver Erwenter

McEVOY, CHARLES, 1879-1929
  The likes of her. 1923. MART

McGEEHAN, MRS. SOPHIE (TREAD-
WELL). See Treadwell, Sophie

McGOUGH, ROGER, 1937-
  The puny little life show. 1970.
    MARR

McGUIRE, WILLIAM ANTHONY, 1885-
1940
  Six cylinder love. 1921. BES21

McHARDY, AIMEE. See Stuart, Mrs.
Aimée (McHardy)

MACHIAVELLI, NICCOLO, 1469-1527
  La mandragola. See Mandragola
  Mandragola. 1520.
    Hale, J., tr. BARB
    May, F., and Bentley, E., trs.
      BENR1
    Penman, B., tr. FIJ
    Young, S., tr. HAYD
    Variant titles: La mandragola;
      The mandrake
  The mandrake. See Mandra-
    gola

MACIAS, YSIDRO R.
    Martir Montezuma. CONR
    The ultimate pendejada. CONR

McINTYRE, DENNIS, 1942-
    Split second. 1984. BES84

McILWRAITH, BILL
    The anniversary. 1966. PLAN31

McILWRAITH, JEAN NEWTON, 1859-
1938
    Ptarmigan, or a Canadian Carni-
        val. 1895. WAGN

MACK, CAROL K., 1941-
    Territorial rites. 1982. WOMB

MACKAY, CONSTANCE D'ARCY,
d.1966
    Benjamin Franklin, journeyman.
        1912? LAW
    Counsel retained. 1915? PEN
    The prince of court painters.
        1915? WEB

MACKAY, MRS. ISABEL (MAC-
PHERSON) ECCLESTONE, 1875-1928
    The second life. 1921. MAS1

MACKAY, LOUIS ALEXANDER,
1901-
    The freedom of Jean Guichet.
        1925. MAS2

MacKAYE, PERCY WALLACE, 1875-
1956
    Napoleon crossing the Rockies.
        1924. CHU
    The pilgrim and the book.
        1920. FED1
    Sam Average. 1911. BEAC11
    The scarecrow. 1909. DIC,
        FLAN, GARX, GATS, MOSJ,
        MOSK, MOSL, QUIJ, QUIJR,
        QUIK, QUIL, QUIM, QUIN

MacKAYE, STEELE, 1842-1894
    Adrift from her father's love.
        See Hazel Kirke
    An arrant knave. 1889. AMP11
    Hazel Kirke. 1880. QUIJ,
        QUIJR, QUIK, QUIL, QUIM,
        QUIN
    Hazel Kirke; or, Adrift from
        her father's love (adapted
        into a melodrama in three

acts). MELO
    In spite of all. 1885. AMP11
    Paul Kauvar; or, Anarchy. 1890.
        MOSS3
    Rose Michel. 1875. AMP11
    Won at last. 1877. AMP11

McKENNEY, RUTH, 1911-1972
    My sister Eileen (based on the
        stories by). See Fields,
        Joseph and Chodorov, Jerome.
        My sister Eileen
    Wonderful town. See Fields,
        Joseph and Chodorov, Jerome.
        Wonderful town (based on the
        stories My sister Eileen by)

MacKENZIE, RONALD, 1903-1932
    The Maitlands. 1934. FAMF
    Musical chairs. 1931. FAMB,
        PLAD

MACKEY, WILLIAM W.
    Requiem for Brother X. KINH

MACKIE, PHILIP, 1918-
    The big killing. 1962. PLAN25
    The whole truth. 1955. PLAN13

McKILLOP, MENZIES, 1929-
    The future pit. 1972. GUTR

McKINNEY, JACK
    The well. 1960. HANG

MacKINTOSH, ELIZABETH (Gordon
Daviot, pseud.), 1897-1952
    The laughing woman. 1934.
        FAME
    The pen of my aunt. 1954.
        BRNB, CARME
    Queen of Scots. 1934. FAMF
    Richard of Bordeaux. 1933.
        FAMD, PLAL1

MACKLIN, CHARLES, 1697?-1797
    Man of the world. 1781. BELG4
    A will and no will. 1746. BEVI

MacLEISH, ARCHIBALD, 1892-1982
    Air raid. 1938. MACE
    The fall of the city. 1937.
        BROZ, BRR3, GAS, KERN,
        KRE, LOOB, LOOC, LOOD,
        LOOE, NELS, VOAD, WAIT
    J.B. 1958. BES58, COTX,
        GARSA, HILP, SCNP

The music crept by me upon
the waters. 1953? SUL
The Trojan horse. 1952.
WHF

McLELLAN, C. M. S. (Hugh
Morton, pseud.), 1865-1916
Leah Kleschna. 1904. BES99

MacLENNAN, DON, 1929-
An enquiry into the voyage of
the Santiago. 1974. CONZI

MacMAHON, BRYAN, 1909-
Song of the anvil. 1916. HOGE

McMAHON, FRANK
Borstal Boy. See Brendan
Behan's Borstal Boy
Brendan Behan's Borstal Boy.
1967. RICT
Variant title: Borstal Boy

McMASTER, BETH, 1935-
Put on the spot. 1975. WIM
When everybody cares. (1976)
WIM
Which witch is which? (1974)
KAL4

MacMILLAN, DOUGALD, 1897-
Off Nags head; or, The bell
buoy. 1922? LAW

MacMILLAN, HECTOR
The rising. 1973. DEC

MACMILLAN, MARY LOUISE,
1870-1936
The pioneers. 1917? LAW

MacNALLY, LEONARD, 1752-1820
Fashionable levities. 1785.
INCA10

McNALLY, TERRENCE, 1930-
And things that go bump in
the night. 1964. BALLE1
Bad habits. 1974. BES73, OBG
Botticelli. 1969. BEAS, BOYN,
OFF
Next. 1969. BES68
Noon. 1968. GARTL
The ritz. 1975. BERS, BES74
Sweet eros. 1968. OFF
Tour. 1968. GLI
Where has Tommy Flowers gone?

1971. BES71

McNAMARA, JOHN, 1962-
Present tense. 1982. YOUP

McNAMEE, GEORGE C. See Levine,
Mark L., jt. auth.

MACNEICE, LOUIS, 1907-1963
The dark tower. 1946. ANDE,
BENS2

MacOWAN, NORMAN, 1877-1961
Glorious morning. 1938. FAML

MACPHERSON, ISABEL. See Mackay,
Mrs. Isabel (Macpherson) Ecclestone

MACRAE, ARTHUR, 1908-1962
Both ends meet. 1954. PLAN10

MACREADY, WILLIAM, d.1829
The bank note. 1795. INCA9

McTAGGART, JAMES, 1928-1974
Candide (television script translated and adapted from Candide
by Voltaire). 1973. CLKY

MAETERLINCK, MAURICE, 1862-1949
Les avengles. See The blind
The blind. 1891.
Amoia, A., tr. ANTM
The death of Tintagiles. 1899.
Sutro, A., tr. BAT21, SHAY
Variant title: La mort de
Tintagiles
Home. See Interior
L'intérieur. See Interior
Interior. 1894.
Archer, W., tr. MACN, MIL
Variant titles: Home;
L'intérieur
The intruder. 1891.
Anon. tr. PATM, TREBA,
TREBJ, TREI2
Block, H., tr. BLOC
Hovey, R., tr. BENP, CARP,
CARPA, HUD, TREC2,
TREE2
Knapp, B. L., tr. ANTM
Variant title: L'intruse
L'intruse. See The intruder
Monna Vanna. 1903.
Sutro, A., tr. MOSQ
La mort de Tintagiles. See The
death of Tintagiles

Pelléas and Mélisande. See
Pelléas et Mélisande
Pelléas et Mélisande. 1893.
RHO
Amoia, A., tr. ANTM
Hovey, R., tr. AUG, DIC,
DIK1, HAV, SMN, TUCG,
TUCM, TUCN, TUCO,
WATI, WATL2, WATR,
WHI
Variant title: Pelléas and
Mélisande

MAGGI, CARLOS, 1922-
The library. 1959.
Oliver, W., tr. OLIW

MAGNUSON, JIM
African Medea. 1968. NEWA4

MAIRET, JEAN DE, 1604-1686
Sophonisba. 1634.
Lockert, L., tr. LOCR

MALJEAN, JEAN RAYMOND
A message from cougar. 1967.
NEWA2

MALLESON, MILES, 1888-1969
La malade imaginaire. See
Molière, Jean Baptiste
Poquelin. Le malade
imaginaire (tr. and
adapted by)
The misanthrope. See Molière,
Jean Baptiste Poquelin. Le
misanthrope (tr. and adapted
by)
The miser. See Molière, Jean
Baptiste Poquelin. The
miser (tr. and adapted by)
The prodigious snob. See
Molière, Jean Baptiste
Poquelin. Le bourgeois
gentilhomme (tr. and adapted
by)
School for wives. See Molière,
Jean Baptiste Poquelin.
L'école des femmes (tr. and
adapted by)
Sganarelle. See Molière, Jean
Baptiste Poquelin. Sganarelle
(tr. and adapted by)
Tartuffe. See Molière, Jean
Baptiste Poquelin. Tartuffe

(tr. and adapted by)
-- and BROOKS, HARRY
Six men of Dorset. 1938. FAML

MALLET, DAVID, 1705-1765
Elvira. 1763. BELK20
Eurydice. 1731. BELK16

MALTZ, ALBERT, 1908-1985
Private Hicks. 1936. KOZ

MAMET, DAVID, 1947-
American buffalo. 1975. BERS,
BES76, NIL, OBG
Glengarry Glen Ross; a play in
two acts. 1984. BES83
A life in the theater; a play in
one act and 26 scenes. 1977.
BES77

MANCO, SILVERIO
Juan Moreira. 1886.
Fassett, J., tr. BIE

MANHOFF, BILL
The owl and the pussycat. 1964.
GAT

MANKIEWICZ, HERMAN J., 1897-
1953, and WELLES, ORSON
Citizen Kane: The shooting
script. 1941. SCNQ

MANKOWITZ, WOLF, 1924-
It should happen to a dog. THOD

MANLEY, MARY DELARIVIER, 1663?-
1724
The royal mischief. 1696. FEFO

MANN, EMILY, 1952-
Still life. 1980. NEWQ

MANN, HEINRICH, 1871-1950
Madame Legros. 1914.
Katzin, W., tr. KAT

MANNER, EEVA-LIISA, 1921-
Snow in May. (1966)
Binham, P., tr. MNOF

MANNERS, JOHN HARTLEY, 1870-
1928
Peg o' my heart. 1912. CEY

MANNING, MARY
Youth's the season...? 1931.
CAN

MANSUKE, NAKADA. See Nakada,
Mansuke

MARASCO, ROBERT, 1936-
Child's play. 1970. BES69,
RICI

MARCEAU, FELICIEN (pseud. of
Louis Carrette), 1913-
The egg. 1957?
Schlitt, R., tr. and adapter
BES61
Variant title: L'oeuf
L'oeuf. See The egg

MARCEL, GABRIEL, 1887-1973
Ariadne. 1936?
Heywood, R., tr. ULAN
Variant title: Le chemin
de Crête
Le chemin de Crête. See
Ariadne

MARCH, WILLIAM (pseud. of
William Edward March Campbell),
1894-1954
The bad seed. See Anderson,
Maxwell. The bad seed
(based on the novel by)

MARCHAND, SHOSHANA
Half fare. 1982. YOUP

MARC-MICHEL (pseud. of Marc
Antoine Amédee Michel), 1812-
1868. See Labiche, Eugène, jt.
auth.

MARCUS, FRANK, 1928-
Beauty and the beast. 1975.
PLAN46
Formation dancers. 1964.
PLAN28
The killing of Sister George.
1965. BES66, HOF, PLAN31,
RICIS
Mrs. Mouse are you within?
1968. PLAN35
Notes on a love affair. 1972.
PLAN42
The window. RICJ

MARINKOVIC, RANKO, 1913-

Gloria. 1955.
Mladinov, D., and Reeder, R.,
trs. MIG

MARIVAUX, PIERRE CARLET DE
CHAMBLAIN DE, 1688-1763
The false confessions. 1737.
Merwin, W., tr. BENR4
Variant title: Les fausses
confidences
Les fausses confidences. See
The false confessions
The game of love and chance.
See Le jeu de l'amour et du
hazard
Le jeu de l'amour et du hazard.
1730. BRE, SEA, STJ1,
ZDA
Aldington, R., tr. ALD
Fowlie, W., tr. FOWL
Variant title: The game of
love and chance

MARKS, MRS. L. S. See Peabody,
Josephine Preston

MARLOWE, CHRISTOPHER, 1564-
1593
Doctor Faustus. See The tragical
history of Doctor Faustus
Edward II. See The troublesome
reign and lamentable death of
Edward the second
Faustus. See The tragical history
of Doctor Faustus
The Jew of Malta. 1589? BROC,
DPR1, NEI, PAR, SPE, THA
The reign of King Edward the
third (sometimes attributed to).
See Anonymous plays. The
reign of King Edward the third
Tamburlaine the great. 1587?
BROC, HOW, HUST, SCW
Tamburlaine the great, pt. I.
1587? BALD, BAS, DPR1,
KRE, NEI, RYL, SCI, SCJ,
SPE, TICO
The tragical history of Doctor
Faustus. 1588? ABRB1,
ABRF, ABRH, ABRJ, ASF,
BALL, BARD, BAS, BAUG,
BENY, BROC, BROK, CLF1,
CLK1, COF, COJ, COL1, CONO,
COTX, DEAN, DEAO, DOWN,
DPR1, DUN, FOUD, FREG,
GATG, GREB1, GREC1, GRIF,
HARC19, HAY, HEIL, HOW,

HUD, KER, LIE, LIED1,
LIEE1, LOCK, LOCL, MABC,
MADB, MALI1, MALN1,
MANN, MIL, MONV, MOO,
NEI, NES, NORI, OLH, OLI1,
ORNT, PAR, RUB, SCH, SCI,
SCJ, SCW, SHAH1, SHAHI1,
SHAJ1, SMI, SNYD1, SPD,
SPDB, SPE, SPEF1, STA,
SWA, TOBI, TREB, TREC1,
TREE1, TREI1, WAT, WEAT1,
WINE, WOO1, WOOD1, WOOE1,
WRIH
    Variant titles: Doctor Faustus;
    The tragical history of the
    life and death of Doctor
    Faustus See The tragical
    history of Doctor Faustus
The troublesome reign and
lamentable death of Edward
the second. 1592? ASH,
BAS, BROC, CLKW, CLKY,
DPR1, GATG, GRE, HARC46,
MAX, NEI, OLH, OLI1, PAR,
RUB, SCH, SCI, SCJ, SPE,
SSSI, TAT, TAU
    Variant title: Edward II

MARNI, JEANNE, pseud. See
Marnière, Jeanne Marie Françoise

MARNIERE, JEANNE MARIE
FRANÇOIS (Jeanne Marni, pseud.),
1854-1910. See Guinon, Albert, jt.
auth.

MAROWITZ, CHARLES, 1934-
An Othello. 1972. MARR
--See Burgess, John, jt. auth.
--See Burns, Alan, jt. auth.

MARQUAND, JOHN PHILLIPS,
1894-1960, and KAUFMAN, GEORGE
S.
The late George Apley. 1944.
BES44, COTE, COTH
Point of no return. See Osborn,
Paul. Point of no return
(adapted from the novel by)

MARQUES, RENE, 1919-
La carreta. See The oxcart
The fanlights. 1958.
Wiezell, R., tr. WOOG
Variant title: Los soles
truncos
The oxcart. 1953.

Los soles truncos. See The fan-
lights
Pilditch, C., tr. GRIH
Variant title: La carreta

MARQUINA, EDUARDO, 1879-1946
Cuando florezcan las rosales.
See When the roses bloom
again
When the roses bloom again. 1913.
Turrell, C., tr. TUR
Variant title: Cuando florezcan
las rosales

MARQUIS, DON. See Marquis, Donald
Robert Perry

MARQUIS, DONALD ROBERT PERRY,
1878-1937
The old soak. 1922. BES22

MARSHAK, SAMUEL YAKOVLEVICH,
1887-1964
Twelve months. 1943?
Bakshy, A., tr. BAKS

MARSHALL, BRUCE, 1899-
Father Malachy's miracle. See
Doherty, Brian. Father
Malachy's miracle (based on
the novel by)

MARSTON, JOHN, 1576-1634
The Dutch courtesan. 1603.
DPR2, SALF, WALL
The malcontent. 1604. BAS
BROC, GOM, HAPRA1,
HAPRB1, LAWR, NEI, NES,
SPE

MARSTON, JOHN WESTLAND, 1819-
1890
The patrician's daughter. 1842.
BAI

MARTELL, LEON
Hoss drawin'. 1982. PLACE,
WES13/14

MARTENS, ANNE COULTER
Blue beads. 1938? LOVR

MARTIN, EDOUARD, 1828-1866.
See Labiche, Eugène Marin, jt. auth.

MARTIN, JANE
Clear glass marbles. WOQ3

Rodeo. WOQ3

MARTIN, SHARON STOCKARD,
1948-
The moving violation. 1979?
CEN

MARTINEZ, JACINTO BENAVENTE
Y. See Benavente y Martínez,
Jacinto

MARTINEZ SIERRA, GREGORIO,
1881-1947, and MARTINEZ SIERRA,
MARIA
Canción de cuna. See The
cradle song
The cradle song. 1911.
Underhill, J., tr. BES26,
CEW, COTP, HAV
Variant title: Canción de
cuna
The kingdom of God. 1916.
Granville-Barker, H., and
H., trs. BES28
Variant title: El reino de
Dios
A lily among thorns. 1911.
Granville-Barker, H., and
H., trs. DIE
Variant title: Lirio entre
espinas
Lirio entre espinas. See A lily
among thorns
Los pastores. See The two
shepherds
El reino de Dios. See The
kingdom of God
The two shepherds. 1913.
Granville-Barker, H., and
H., trs. LEV, LEVE
Variant title: Los pastores

MARTINEZ SIERRA, MARIA,
1880-1947. See Martínez Sierra,
Gregorio, jt. auth.

MARTYN, EDWARD, 1859-1923
Maeve. 1900. CAP

MARY, V. V.
A dialogue between a southern
delegate, and his spouse, on
his return from the grand
Continental Congress (at-
tributed to). See Anonymous
plays. A dialogue, between a
southern delegate, and his

spouse, on his return from
the grand Continental Congress

MASEFIELD, JOHN, 1878-1967
The tragedy of Pompey the great.
1910. MOSN, PLAP2

MASON, BRUCE, 1921-
Hongi. 1968. CONZ

MASON, CLIFFORD, 1932-
Gabriel. KINH
The verandah. (1976) CEN

MASON, HARRY SILVERNALE, 1881-
At the gate beautiful. 1925?
FED2

MASON, WILLIAM, 1724-1797
Caractacus. (1759) BELG12
Elfrida. (1752) BELG12

MASON, WILTON. See McDonald,
Catherine, jt. auth.

MASSEY, EDWARD, 1893-1942
Plots and playwrights. 1917?
BAK

MASSINGER, PHILIP, 1583-1640
The bondman. 1623. RUB
The city madam. 1632. PLAN28
The maid of honor. 1621? BAS
A new way to pay old debts.
1632. ANG, BAS, BAT13,
BROC, DPR2, DUN, GAY3,
HARC47, HOW, KRE, LAWR,
MAX, NEI, OLH, OLI2, ORNC,
PAR, RUB, SALF, SCH, SCI,
SCJ, SMO, SPE, TAV, WALL,
WHE
The Roman actor. 1626. DPR2,
MAKJ
--See Fletcher, John, jt. auth.

MASTEROFF, JOE, 1919-
Cabaret (music by John Kander,
lyrics by Fred Ebb; based on
the play "I am a camera" by
John van Druten and stories
by Christopher Isherwood).
1967. BES66, RICM
She loves me (based on a play by
Miklos Laszlo; music by Jerry
Bock, lyrics by Sheldon Harnick). 1963. BES62

MASTERSON, PETER, 1934-
　　The best little whorehouse in
　　　　Texas. See King, Larry L.,
　　　　jt. auth.

MASTROSIMONE, WILLIAM, 1947-
　　Extremities; a play in two acts.
　　　　1982. BES82

MATHEUS, JOHN, 1887-
　　'Cruiter. 1926. LOC, HARY

MATHEW, RAY, 1929-
　　We find the bunyip. 1955.
　　　　HANG

MATHEWS, CHARLES J., 1803-1878
　　Patter versus clatter. 1838.
　　　　BOOA4

MATHEWS, JOHN
　　Ti Yette. RIR

MATILLA, LUIS
　　Post mortem. (1970)
　　　　Wellwarth, M., tr. WELK

MATTHEWS, TEDE
　　Factwino meets the moral
　　　　majority (script by).
　　　　See San Francisco Mime
　　　　Troupe. Factwino meets
　　　　the moral majority

MATURIN, CHARLES ROBERT,
1780-1824
　　Bertram; or, The castle of
　　　　St. Aldobrand. 1816. BAI

MAUGHAM, ROBIN, 1916-
　　Enemy. 1969. PLAN39

MAUGHAM, WILLIAM SOMERSET,
1874-1965
　　Before the party. See Ackland,
　　　　Rodney. Before the party
　　　　(based on a short story by)
　　The breadwinner. 1930.
　　　　CHA, CHAN, CHAR
　　The circle. 1921. BES21, BROH,
　　　　CEU, CLM, COT, COTH, DIG,
　　　　DUR, FOUX, HAVE, KRM,
　　　　MAD, MART, MOSG, MOSH,
　　　　MYB, TREBA, TREBJ, TREC2,
　　　　TREE2, TREI3, TUCD, TUCM,
　　　　WALB, WATF2, WATI, WATO,
　　　　WEE

The colonel's lady. See Sherriff,
　　　　Robert Cedric. The colonel's
　　　　lady (based on the story by)
The constant wife. 1927.
　　　　BES26, HAU, LOR, WARI,
　　　　WARL
For services rendered. 1932.
　　　　MOD
Jane. See Behrman, Samuel
　　　　Nathaniel. Jane (based on the
　　　　story by)
The letter. 1927. RICI, SAFM
Loaves and fishes. 1911. WEAL
Miss Thompson. See Colton, John
　　　　and Randolph, Clemence. Rain
　　　　(based on the story by)
Our betters. 1917. DID, MOSO,
　　　　SALE, SMO, WHI
Sheppey. 1933. SIXH

MAUPASSANT, GUY DE, 1850-1893
　　The household peace. 1893.
　　　　Chambers, W., tr. BAT9
　　　　Variant title: La paix du
　　　　ménage
　　La paix du ménage. See The
　　　　household peace

MAURETTE, MARCELLE
　　Anastasia. 1953?
　　　　Bolton, G., adapter. PLAN9,
　　　　THEA55

MAUREY, MAX, 1868-1947
　　Rosalie. 1900. SET

MAURIAC, FRANÇOIS, 1885-1970
　　Asmodée. 1938.
　　　　Thurman, B., tr. HAYE

MAVOR, OSBORNE HENRY (JAMES
BRIDIE, pseud.), 1888-1951
　　Tobias and the angel. 1930.
　　　　PLAL1

MAY, ELAINE, 1932-
　　Adaptation. 1969. BES68

MAY, VAL, 1927-
　　Sixty thousand nights (script
　　　　and research by George
　　　　Rowell, music by Julian Slade,
　　　　lyrics by Julian Slade and
　　　　George Rowell). 1966.
　　　　PLAN31

MAYAKOVSKY, VLADIMIR

VLADIMIROVICH, 1894-1930
The bathhouse. 1929?
  MacAndrew, A., tr.
    GARZG, HABA
The bedbug. 1929.
  Hayward, M., tr. COTO,
    GLE, RUSV
  Reeve, F., tr. REEV2
Mystery-bouffe. (Second
  variant). 1921.
  Noyes, G., and Kaun, A.,
    trs. NOY
  Rottenberg, D., tr. CLKX

MAYER, EDWIN JUSTUS, 1897-1960
Children of darkness. 1930.
  GARU, KRM
The firebrand. 1924. BES24

MAYER, TIMOTHY S., 1944-
See Stone, Peter H., jt. auth.

MAYNE, RUTHERFORD, pseud.
See Waddell, Samuel

MAYOR, BEATRICE, 1886-1971
The pleasure garden. 1924.
  PLAP3

MEACHAM, MALCOLM
The snow goose. See Gallico,
  Paul. The snow goose
  (adapted by)

MEAD, SHEPHERD, 1914-
How to succeed in business
  without really trying. See
  Burrows, Abram S. How
  to succeed in business without really trying (based on
  the book by)

MEAKER, MRS. ISABELLA
(JACKSON), 1874- . See
Harnwell, Mrs. Anna Jane (Wilcox),
jt. auth.

MEDNICK, MURRAY, 1939-
The coyote cycle. See Coyote I:
  Pointing; Coyote V: Listening
  to old Nana; Coyote IV: Other
  side camp; Coyote III: Planet
  of the spider people; Coyote
  II: The shadow ripens
Coyote I: Pointing. 1978. WES7
Coyote V: Listening to old Nana.
  1982. PLACE, WES13/14

Coyote IV: Other side camp.
  1981. WES9
Coyote III: Planet of the spider
  people. 1980. WES7
Coyote II: The shadow ripens.
  1979. WES7
Listening to old Nana. See
  Coyote V: Listening to old
  Nana
Other side camp. See Coyote IV:
  Other side camp
Planet of the spider people.
  See Coyote III: Planet of the
  spider people
Pointing. See Coyote I: Pointing
The shadow ripens. See Coyote II:
  The shadow ripens
Taxes. 1976. WOQ3
Willie the germ. 1968. SME

MEDOFF, MARK, 1940-
Children of a lesser God. 1979.
  BES79
The Kramer. 1973. BALLE13
The wager. 1974. BES74
When you comin' back, Red Ryder?
  1973. BES73

MEDWALL, HENRY, fl. 1486-1500?
Fulgens and Lucrece. See Fulgens
  and Lucres
Fulgens and Lucres. 1497?
  BOA, CRE, HAO (extracts)
  Variant title: Fulgens and
  Lucrece
Nature. 1495? FARN

MEE, CHARLES L., JR., 1938-
Constantiniple Smith. 1961.
  NEWA1
The investigation of the murder
  in El Salvador. 1984. WOQ4

MEEHAN, THOMAS, 1929-
Annie; a musical in two acts.
  (music by Charles Strouse;
  lyrics by Martin Charnin).
  1977. BES76

MEGGED, AHARON, 1920-
The first sin. (1962)
  Eingad, S., and Arad, M., trs.
    MOADE

MEGRUE, ROI COOPER, 1883-1927
Under cover. 1914. CART

-- and HACKETT, WALTER
    It pays to advertise. 1914.
      MOSJ, MOSK, MOSL

MEI, LANFANG, 1894-1961.
  See Anonymous Plays.
      Hegemon King says farewell
      to his queen (Peking opera:
      version by)

MELDON, MAURICE
    Purple path to the poppy field.
    1953. NEWW5

MELFI, LEONARD, 1935-
    Birdbath. 1967. RICJ
    Cinque. 1972. OWE
    Night. 1968. GARTL

MELL, MAX, 1882-1971
    The apostle play. 1934.
      White, M., tr. SEVE

MELLON, EVELYN EMIG. See
Emig, Evelyn

MELVILLE, ALAN (pseud. of
Alan Caverhill), 1910-
    Castle in the air. 1949. PLAN3
    Dear Charles. 1952. PLAN8
    Simon and Laura. 1954. PLAN11

MELVILLE, HERMAN, 1819-1891
    Billy Budd. See Coxe, Louis O.,
    and Chapman, Robert.
    Billy Budd (based on the
    novel by)

MENANDER, OF ATHENS, 342?-
292? B.C.
    The arbitration. 4th cent. B.C.
      Allinson, F., tr. HOWE,
      HOWF
      Casson, L., tr. CASU
      Post, L., tr. OAM, OAT2
      Variant title: Epitrepontes
    Dyskolos. See The grouch
    Epitrepontes. See The arbitra-
    tion
    The girl from Samos. 4th cent.
    B.C.
      Casson, L., tr. CASU
      Post, L., tr. OAT2
      Variant titles: Samia; The
      woman of Samos
    The grouch. 317 B.C.
      Casson, L., tr. CASU

    Variant title: Dyskolos
    The perikeiromene. See The
    shearing of Glycera
    Samia. See The girl from Samos
    The shearing of Glycera. 4th
    cent. B.C.
      Casson, L., tr. CASU
      Post, L., tr. OAT2
      Variant titles: The perikei-
      romene; She who was shorn
    She who was shorn. See The
    shearing of Glycera
    The woman of Samos. See The
    girl from Samos

MENDEZ, MOSES, d.1758
    The chaplet. (1749) BELC1

MENDOZA, JUAN RUIZ DE ALARCON.
See Ruiz de Alarcón y Mendoza, Juan

MENG, HAN-CH'ING, fl.1279
    The Mo-ho-lo doll (attributed to).
      Crump, J., tr. CRU

MENOTTI, GIAN- CARLO, 1911-
    The saint of Bleecker Street.
    1954. THEA55

MERCER, DAVID, 1928-
    The governor's lady. 1965. RICJ

MERCIER, MARY
    Johnny no-trump. 1967. SSTY

MERCIER, SERGE, 1944-
    Encore un peu. See A little bit
    left
    A little bit left. 1975.
      Van Meer, A., tr. KAL5
      Variant title: Encore un peu

MEREDITH, SYLVIA. See Hensel,
Karen, jt. auth.

MERI, VEIJO, 1928-
    Private Jokinen's marriage leave.
      Pitkin, J., tr. MNOF

MERIMEE, PROSPER (Clara Gazul,
pseud.), 1803-1870
    Carmencita and the soldier
    (based on the opera Carmen,
    by Georges Bizet). See
    Lipskeroff, Konstantin. Car-
    mencita and the soldier

Inez Mendo; or, The triumph of prejudice. 1825. BAT21

MERRIAM, EVE, 1916- , WAGNER, PAULA, and HOFFSISS, JACK
Out of our fathers' house. 1975. NEWVM

MERRILL, JAMES, 1926-
The bait. 1953. MAH
The immortal husband. 1955. PLAA

MERRITT, CATHARINE NINA, 1859-1926
When George the Third was King; an historical drama in three acts. (1897) WAGN

MESSAGER, CHARLES. See Vildrac, Charles, pseud.

METASTASIO, PIETRO ANTONIO DOMENICO BUONAVENTURA (pseud. of Pietro Trepassi), 1698-1782
Achilles in Scyros. 1800? Hoole, J., tr. JOH
Attilo Rigolo. 1740. BIN
The dream of Scipio. 1800? Hoole, J., tr. BAT5
Variant title: Il sogno di Scipione
Il sogno di Scipione. See The dream of Scipio

MEYERS, PATRICK, 1947-
K2; a play in one act. 1982. BES82

MICHAELS, SIDNEY, 1927-
Dylan. 1964. BES63
Tchin-Tchin (based on the play, Chin-Chin, by François Billet-doux). 1962. BES62

MICHEL, MARC ANTOINE AMEDEE. See Labiche, Eugène, jt. auth.

MICHENER, JAMES, 1907-
Tales of the South Pacific. See Hammerstein II, Oscar and Logan, Joshua. South Pacific (adapted from)

MICK, HETTIE LOUISE
The maid who wouldn't be proper.

1921? LAW

MICKIEWICZ, ADAM, 1798-1855
Dziady. See Forefathers' eve, Part III
Forefathers' eve, Part III. 1901. Segel, H., tr. (revised earlier translations edited by Noyes, G.) POB

MIDDLEMASS, ROBERT M., 1885-1949. See Hall, Holworthy, jt. auth.

MIDDLETON, GEORGE, 1880-1967. See Bolton, Guy Reginald, jt. auth.

MIDDLETON, THOMAS, 1580-1627
A chaste maid in Cheapside. 1612? DPR2, WALL
A game at chess. 1624. BROC
A mad world, my masters. (1608) SALF
Michaelmas term. 1606? SCI, SCJ
A trick to catch the old one. 1608. BAS, LAWS, NEI, SPE
Women beware women. 1622. GOM, LAWT, OLH, OLI2
--See also Dekker, Thomas, jt. auth.

-- and ROWLEY, WILLIAM
The changeling. 1622. BAS, BROC, GOM, HAPRA2, HAPRB2, HUST, LAWR, NEI, OLH, OLI2, ORNT, SALG, SCH, SCI, SCJ, SPE, TAT, TAU, TAUJ, WINE
A fair quarrel. 1617? OLH, OLI2
The Spanish gipsie. 1623. GAY3

MIHURA, MIGUEL, 1905-
Three top hats. 1932. Wellwarth, G., tr. BENA
Variant title: Tres sombreros de copa
Tres sombreros de copa. See Three top hats

MILLAR, RONALD, 1919-
Abelard and Heloise. 1970. PLAN39
The affair. 1961. PLAJ2
Waiting for Gillian. 1954. PLAN10

MILLAY, EDNA ST. VINCENT, 1892-1950

Aria da capo. 1919. CHU,
GASB, KRE
The king's henchman. 1927.
TUCD
The lamp and the bell. 1921.
SHAY

MILLER, ALLAN
The fox. 1981. WES13/14

MILLER, ARTHUR, 1915-
After the fall. 1964. BES63
All my sons. 1947. BARO,
BES46, BROH, CLKJ, GARW,
GAVE, HATA, HEWE, MABC,
MADB, SILO, SIXB, STS,
WEAN
The creation of the world and
other business. 1972.
BES72
The crucible. 1953. AMB,
BAUL, BES52, COOP, DOT,
FOT, GART, GATB4, GATT,
GOLK, GUTH, GUTL, LOR,
MIJY, MORV, MORW, MORX,
MORXB, MORXD, SUL, TAUJ,
TREA53, WATA
Variant title: Those familiar
spirits
Death of a salesman. 1949.
ALLK, ALLM, ANT, AUG,
BARIC, BARK, BARL, BENU,
BES48, BIER, BLOC, BRIX,
BRIY, BRIZ, BROX, BROY,
CALQ, CEQA, COTX, DITA,
FOUM, FOUX, GARW, GATB3,
GAVE, HAE, HAVL, HEA,
HEAL, HUNT, KEN, LITI,
MANK, MANL, NEWV, PERS,
PERT, PERU, PERV, REIW,
REIWE, SSSI, STEI, STJM,
STJN, TREBA, TREBJ, TREC2,
TREE3, TREI3, TUCO, WARH,
WARN, WATE, WISE, WISF
An enemy of the people. See
Ibsen, Henrik. An enemy of
the people (adapted by)
Incident at Vichy. 1964. BES64,
MARO
The man who had all the luck.
1943. CROZ1
A memory of two Mondays. 1955.
ACE, LIEF, SSTF
The price. 1968. BES67, GARTL
Pussycat and the expert plumber
who was a man. 194-? PROX
Those familiar spirits. See The

crucible
A view from the bridge. 1956.
BAIC, BES55, BRIT, CLLC,
CLM, CLN, COTKIR, COTQ,
CUBH, DIT, DOWS, GART,
HILP, HOGI, HOGN, MOL,
REIN, THEA56, ULAN, WORM

MILLER, CINCINNATUS HEINE, 1841?-
1913. See Miller, Joaquin, pseud.

MILLER, DANIEL, 1843-1909?
En gespräch zwischer zweb demokrate über politiks. 18-? BUFF
Noch eppes vom Peter seim handwerk. BUFF
Der Peter soil en handwerk lernen.
18-? BUFF

MILLER, JAMES, 1706-1744
Mahomet. 1744. BELK7

MILLER, JASON, 1939-
Lou Gehrig did not die of cancer.
RICK
That championship season. 1972.
BERS, BES71

MILLER, JOAQUIN (pseud. of Cincinnatus Hiner (or Heine) Miller),
1841?-1913
The Danites in the Sierras. 1877.
HAL, RAVA

MILLER, MAY
Graven images. 1929. RIR
Riding the goat. RIR

MILLER, SIGMUND STEPHEN, 1917-
One bright day. 1956. PLAN14

MILLER, SUSAN, 1944-
Confessions of a female disorder.
1973. HOF
Cross country. 1975. WES1

MILLS, HUGH
The little glass clock. 1954.
PLAN11
The house by the lake. 1956.
PLAN14

MILMAN, HENRY HART, 1791-1868
Belshazzar. 1822? KOH2
The fall of Jerusalem. 1820.
KOH2

MILNE, ALAN ALEXANDER, 1882-
1956
    The boy comes home. 1918.
      SRY, SRYG
    The Dover road. 1922.
      BES21, DIE, MOD, WATT2
    The great Broxopp. 1923. CHU
    The ivory door. 1927. TUCJ
    Michael and Mary. 1929. BES29
    Mr. Pim passes by. 1919. CALM,
      CEU, MAD, THF, WATF2, WATI
    Success. 1923. COT, MYB
    The truth about Blayds. 1921.
      MOSG, MOSH, TUCD, TUCM
    The ugly duckling. (1941)
      BART

MILNER, HENRY M.
    The demon of Switzerland. See
      Frankenstein; or, The man and
      the monster
    Frankenstein; or, The demon of
      Switzerland. See Frankenstein;
      or, The man and the monster
    Frankenstein; or, The man and
      the monster. 1823. HOUR
      Variant titles: Frankenstein;
        or, The demon of Switzer-
        land; The demon of Switzer-
        land; The man and the
        monster
    The man and the monster. See
      Frankenstein; or, The Man and
      the monster
    Mazeppa. 1831. VIC

MILNER, ROGER, 1925-
    How's the world treating you?
      1965. PLAN30

MILNER, RONALD, 1938-
    The warning--a theme for Linda.
      1969. BLA
    Who's got his own. 1966. KINH

MILTON, JOHN, 1608-1674
    Comus. 1634. CLK1, HARC4,
      OLH, OLI2, PAR, RICH
    Comus. See also Colman, G.
      (altered by). BELK9
    Samson Agonistes. 1670? BARD,
      BELG12, FREG, GREB1,
      GREC1, GREAB, HAPT2,
      HARC4, KOH2, SML

MINNEY, RUBEIGH J., 1895- .
See Lipscomb, William Percy, jt. auth.

MIRA DE AMESCUA, ANTONIO,
1570?-1644
    El esclavo del demonio. 1612.
      ALP

MIRBEAU, OCTAVE, 1850-1917
    Les affaires sont les affaires.
      1903. BER
      Variant title: Business is
        business
    Business is business. See Les
      affaires sont les affaires
    The epidemic. 1898?
      Barzun, J., tr. BENS2
      Variant title: L'epidêmie
    L'epidêmie. See The epidemic

MIRZA FATH-ALI. See Fath'-Alī,
Akhund-zadah

MIRZA FETH-ALI AKHOUD ZAIDE.
See Fath'Alī, Akhundzadah

MISHIMA, YUKIO, 1925-1970
    Yoroboshi. See Yoroboshi:
      the blind young man
    Yoroboshi: the blind young
      man. 1965.
      Takaya, T. T., tr. TAK
      Variant title: Yoroboshi

"MR. PUNCH," pseud.
    A dramatic sequel to Hamlet;
      or, The new wing at Elsinor.
      19th cent. BAT22
    A dramatic sequel to The lady
      of Lyons; or, In the Lyons
      den. 19th cent. BAT22
    Omar and oh my! 19th cent.
      BAT21

"MR. S. MR. OF ART," pseud.
See Stevenson, William

MITCHELL, JULIAN, 1935-
    A family and a fortune. 1975.
      PLAN45
    A heritage and its history. 1965.
      PLAN30

MITCHELL, KEN, 1940-
    Heroes. 1975. FIFVE

MITCHELL, LANGDON ELWYN, 1862-
1935
    Becky Sharp. 1899. AMP16
    The New York idea. 1906.

BENT4, BLAI2, GARX,
HAL, MONR, MOSS3,
QUIJ, QUIJR, QUIK,
QUIM, QUIN, WATC1

MITCHELL, LOFTEN, 1919-
A land beyond the river. 1957.
REAG
Star of the morning. 1964.
HARY, KINH
Tell Pharaoh. 1967. REAG

MITCHELL, THOMAS. See Dell,
Floyd, jt. auth.

MITCHELL, WILLIAM ORMOND,
1914-
The devil's instrument. 1972.
KAL2

MITCHELL, YVONNE, 1925-
Here choose I. See The same
sky
The same sky. 1951. PLAN6
Variant title: Here choose
I

MITSON, RONALD
Beyond the bourn; or, The
night time stood still. 1966?
FRO
Variant title: The night time
stood still
The night time stood still. See
Beyond the bourn

MITTELHOLZER, EDGAR A., 1909-
1965
Shadows move among them. See
Hart, Moss. The climate of
Eden (based on the novel by)

MIYAMASU, 16th century?
Eboshi-ori. See The hatmaker
The hatmaker. 16th cent.?
Waley, A., tr. ANDF
Variant title: Eboshi-ori

MIYOSHI, SHORAKU, 1606?-1722?
See Takeda, Izumo, jt. auth.

MOELLER, PHILIP, 1880-1958
Helena's husband. 1915.
BEAC12
Madame Sand. 1917. HAL,
TUCD

MOINAUX, GEORGES, 1861-1929.
See Courteline, George (pseud. of)

MOLETTE, BARBARA. See Molette,
Carlton, jt. auth.

MOLETTE, CARLTON, 1939- , and
MOLETTE, BARBARA
Noah's ark. 1974. CEN

MOLIERE, JEAN BAPTISTE POQUE-
LIN, 1622-1673
The affected young ladies. See
Les précieuses ridicules
L'amour médecin. See Love is
the best doctor
L'avare. See The miser
Le bourgeois gentilhomme. 1670.
SCN
Anon. tr. GAUB
Baker, H., and Miller, J.,
trs. CLF2, MALC, MALG2
Bishop, M., tr. BAUL
Malleson, M., tr. and adapter.
PLAN6
Porter, M., tr. LOCLA
Taylor, H., tr. SAFF
Wood, J., tr. WELT
Variant titles: The bourgeois
gentleman; The cit turned
gentleman; The prodigious
snob; The would-be gentle-
man
The bourgeois gentleman. See
Le bourgeois gentilhomme
The cit turned gentleman.
See Le bourgeois gentilhomme
The doctor in spite of himself.
1666.
Anon. tr. COPB, INGW,
KNIE, SHAR
Clark, B., tr. LEV, LEVE
Van Laun, H., tr. SATI,
WEAV2
Wall, C., tr. SMR
Variant titles: Le médecin
malgré lui; The physician
in spite of himself
Doctor's delight. See Le
malade imaginaire
Dom Juan, ou les festin de
Pierre. See Don Juan
Don John; or, The libertine.
See Don Juan
Don Juan. 1665.
Calder, J., tr. LID

BES26, COTKJ, GARZH
Variant title: The play in
the castle
Still life. 1937.
Anon. tr. CHR
Variant title: Csendélet
The swan. 1914.
Baker, M., tr. BES23
Glazer, B., tr. CHA, CHAN

MONCRIEFF, WILLIAM THOMAS, 1794-
1857
Giovanni in London; or, The
libertine reclaimed. 1828.
MARL
Variant title: The libertine
reclaimed
The libertine reclaimed. See
Giovanni in London

MONKHOUSE, ALLAN NOBLE,
1858-1936
The conquering hero. 1924.
HAU
First blood. 1926. MOSO
The grand cham's diamond.
1924. BEAC10, COOK2,
PROB
Variant title: The grand
cham's necklace
The grand cham's necklace.
See The grand cham's
diamond
Mary Broome. 1911. PLAP2

MONROE, MICHAEL
Politesse: a piece for tape
and landscape. 1982. PLACE

MONSON, WILLIAM N.
The nihilist. 1971. BALLE8

MONTANO, SEVERINO
Sabina. 195-? EDAD

MONTCHRESTIEN, ANTOINE DE,
c.1575-1621
L'Ecossaire. See La Reine
d'Ecosse
The Queen of Scots. See La
Reine d'Ecosse
La Reine d'Ecosse. (1601)
FALE
Bourque, J. H., tr. FOUAF
Variant titles: L'ecossaise;
The Queen of Scots

MONTCHRÉTIEN, ANTOINE DE. See
Montchrestien, Antoine de

MONTELLANO, BERNARDO ORTIZ DE.
See Ortiz de Montellano, Bernardo

MONTENOY, CHARLES PALISSOT DE.
See Palissot de Montenoy, Charles

MONTGOMERY, ROBERT, 1946-
Subject to fits. 1971. GARTL

MONTHERLANT, HENRY MARIE JO-
SEPH MILLON DE, 1896-1972
Le cardinal d'Espagne. See The
cardinal of Spain
The cardinal of Spain. 1969.
Griffin, J., tr. PLAN37
Variant title: Le cardinal
d'Espagne
Le maître de Santiago. See The
master of Santiago
The master of Santiago. 1947.
Griffin, J., tr. ULAN
Variant title: La maître de
Santiago
Port-Royal. 1954.
Griffin, J., tr. HAYE
The queen after death. See
La reine morte
La reine morte. 1942. PUCC
Griffin, J., tr. COTKW
Variant title: The queen after
death

MONZAEMON CHIKAMATSU. See
Chikamatsu, Monzaemon

MOOCK, ARMANDO. See Moock
Bousquet, Armando

MOOCK BOUSQUET, ARMANDO,
1894-1942
La serpeinte. 1920. ALPE

MOODY, WILLIAM VAUGHN, 1869-
1910
The death of Eve. 1912? KRE
The faith healer. 1909. QUIJ,
QUIJR, QUIK, QUIL, QUIN
The great divide. 1906. BES99,
DIC, DOWN, GARX, MONR
Variant title: A Sabine woman
A Sabine woman. See The great
divide

MOORE, EDWARD, 1712-1757

The foundling. 1748. BELK13
The gamester. 1753. BELK12,
BOO

MOORE, EDWARD J., 1935-
The sea horse. 1974. BES73

MOORE, ELVIE A., 1942-
Angela is happening. 1971.
RAVA

MOORE, HONOR, 1945-
Mourning pictures. 1974.
NEWVM

MOORE, MAVOR, 1919-
Inside out. See The pile, the
store, inside out
The pile. See The pile, the
store, inside out
The pile, the store, inside out
(three short plays).
(1971-73) KAL2
Variant titles: The pile; The
store; Inside out
The store. See The pile; the
store; inside out

MORAL, JOSE ZORILLA Y. See
Zorrilla y Moral, José

MORATIN, LEANDRO FERNANDEZ
DE, 1760-1828
The girls' acquiescence. See
El sí de las niñas
El sí de las niñas. 1805.
BRET, MARLI1
Davis, W., tr. FLOS
Variant titles: The girls'
acquiescence; When a
girl says yes
When a girl says yes. See
El sí de las niñas

MORE, CHARLES C., 1851-1940
Die verrechelte rechler. See
Barba, Preston Albert.
Die verrechelte rechler
(adapted from the novel by)
Es wasch Heller's Chrischtdag's
zug. See Iobst, Clarence F.
Es Heller's Chrischtdag (based
on the story by)

MORE, HANNAH, 1745-1833
Belshazzar. 1782? KOH2
Daniel. 1782? KOH2
David and Goliath. 1782?

KOH2
Moses in the bulrushes. 1782?
KOH2
Percy. 1780. INCA7

MORETO Y CABANA, AGUSTIN.
See Moreto y Cavana, Agustín

MORETO Y CAVANA, AGUSTIN,
1618-1669
El desdén con el desdén. 1654.
ALP
Variant titles: Donna Diana;
Love's victory; or, The
school for pride
Donna Diana. See El desdén con
el desdén
Love's victory; or, The school for
pride. See El desdén con el
desdén

MORGAN, DIANA, 1913-
A house in the square. 1940.
FIR

MORLEY, CHRISTOPHER DARLING-
TON, 1890-1957
Good theatre. 1926? CHU
Really, my dear... 1928? WEE
Rehearsal. 1922? SHAY
Thursday evening. 1922? PEN
Wagon-lits. 1928? WEE

MORLEY, ROBERT, 1908- , and
LANGLEY, NOEL
Edward, my son. 1948. BES48

MOROSS, JEROME, 1913-
The golden apple. See Latouche,
John. The golden apple (mu-
sic by)

MORRIS, MRS. ELIZABETH (WOOD-
BRIDGE), 1870-
The crusade of the children.
1923? FED1

MORRIS, LLOYD, 1893-1954. See
Van Druten, John, jt. auth.

MORRIS, ROBERT J., 1945-
Paradise tours. 1976.

MORSELLI, ERCOLE LUIGI, 1882-
1921
Acqua sul fuoco. See Water upon
fire

Il domatore Gastone. See Gastone
the animal tamer
Gastone the animal tamer. 1923.
Goldberg, I., tr. GOL
Variant title: Il domatore
Gastone
Water upon fire. 1920.
Goldberg, I., tr. GOL
Variant title: Aqua sul fuoco

MORTIMER, JOHN CLIFFORD,
1923-
Bermondsey. 1970. RICK
David and broccoli. 1960. CONB
The dock brief. 1957. LONG,
PLAN17
What shall we tell Caroline?
1958. PLAN17

MORTIMER, LILLIAN, d.1946
No mother to guide her. 1905.
AMP8

MORTON, HUGH, pseud. See
McClellan, C. M. S.

MORTON, JOHN MADDISON, 1811-
1891
Box and Cox. 1847. BOOA4,
BOOM, THO

MORTON, THOMAS, 1764?-1838
Secrets worth knowing. 1798.
INCA3
Speed the plough. 1800. MOR,
NIC
Zorinski. 1795. INCA3

MORUM, WILLIAM. See Dinner,
William, jt. auth.

MOSEL, TAD, 1922-
All the way home (based on A
death in the family by
James Agee). 1960. BES60,
GARSA

MOSER, GUSTAV VON, 1825-1903
Ultimo. See Daly, Augustin.
The big bonanza (adapted
from)

MOSS, ALFRED CHARLES and
NEWHARD, ELWOOD L.
H.M.S. Pinafore; oder, Das
maedle und ihr sailor kerl
(based on the opera by W. S.

Gilbert and Sir A. S. Sullivan).
1882. BUFF

MOSS, HOWARD, 1922-
No strings attached. 1944?
NEWD44

MOTOKIYO, SEAMI. See Seami,
Motokiyo

MOTOYASU, ZEMBO. See Zembō,
Motoyasu

MOTTE FOUQUE, HENRI AUGUSTE,
BARON DE LA, 1698-1774
Undine. See Giraudoux, Jean.
Ondine. (from the novel by)

MOTTEUX, PETER ANTHONY, 1663-
1718. See Ravenscroft, Edward,
jt. auth.

MOTTLEY, JOHN, 1692-1750. See
Jevon, Thomas, jt. auth.

MOWATT, MRS. ANNA CORA
(OGDEN) RITCHIE. See Ritchie,
Mrs. Anna Cora (Ogden) Mowatt

MOYES, PATRICIA, 1923-
Time remembered. See Anouilh,
Jean. Time remembered (tr.
and adapted by)

MOZART, WOLFGANG AMADEUS,
1756-1791
Eine Kleine Nachtmusik. See
Wheeler, Hugh. A little night
music (title from)

MROZEK, SŁAWOMIR, 1930-
Joy in earnest. See Afanasjeu,
J., and the Bim-Bom Troupe.
Faust; Afanasjew, J., and the
Bim-Bom Troupe. Snouts;
and Mrożek, S., The professor
The police. 1958.
Bethell, N., tr. SCNP
Variant title: Policja
Policja. See The police
The professor (part of Joy in
earnest). 1956.
Gerould, D., and Gerould, E.,
trs. TWEN
Tango. 1965.
Bethell, N., and Stoppard, T.,
trs. THOR

Manheim, R., and
Dzieduscycka, T., trs.
GROV, NIL

MUELLER, LAVONNE
Killings on the last line. 1979.
WOMA
Little victories. 1983. WOMB

MUKERJI, DHAN GOPEL, 1890-
1946
The judgment of Indra. (1920)
PATM, PATP

MULLER, ROMEO
The great git-away. 1966.
BALLE3

MULVAY, TIMOTHY J.
Letter to Tuffy. 194-? PROI

MUNDAY, ANTHONY, 1553-1633
Sir John Oldcastle, pt. I
(sometimes attributed to).
See Anonymous plays. Sir
John Oldcastle, pt. I
Sir Thomas More (sometimes at-
tributed to). See Anonymous
plays. Sir Thomas More

MUNFORD, ROBERT (COLONEL),
1730?-1784
The candidates; or, The humours
of a Virginia election.
(1798) MONR
Variant title: The humours
of a Virginia election
The humours of a Virginia election. See The candidates
The patriots. 1778. PHI

MUNK, KAY, 1898-1944
Egelykke. 1939.
Jones, L., tr. MODS
Herod the king. 1933.
Keigwin, R., tr. CONT
Variant title: En idealist
En idealist. See Herod the king
Niels Ebbesen. 1942.
Larsen, H., tr. SCAN2

MUNRO, CHARLES KIRKPATRICK,
1889-1973
At Mrs. Beam's. 1923.
MART, MOSO, PLAP3
The rumour. 1922. MYB

MURDOCH, FRANK HITCHCOCK,
1843-1872
Davy Crockett; or, Be sure you're
right, then go ahead. 1872.
AMP4, CLA

MURDOCH, IRIS, 1919- , and
PRIESTLEY, JOHN BOYNTON
A severed head. 1963. PLAJ2

MURPHY, ARTHUR, 1727-1805
All in the wrong. 1761. MOR
The apprentice. (1756) BELC1
The citizen. 1761. BELC3
Grecian daughter. 1772. BELG13
The old maid. 1761. BELC2
The orphan of China. 1759.
BELG14
School for guardians. 1767.
BELG14
Three weeks after marriage; or,
what we must all come to.
1764. BELC4
The upholsterer. 1758. BELC1,
BEVI
The way to keep him. 1760.
BELG13, BEVI, NIC
Zenobia. 1768. BELG13

MURPHY, GRACE. See Lavery,
Emmet, jt. auth.

MURPHY, PETER
Bluffing. 1982. YOUP

MURRAY, ROBERT BRUCE
The good lieutenant. (1965)
GARZAL

MURRAY, THOMAS C., 1873-1959
Birthright. 1910. CAP

MURRAY, WILLIAM H., 1790-1852
Diamond cut diamond. 1838.
BOOA4

MURRELL, JOHN, 1945-
Memoir. 1977. PLAN48

MUSINGA, VICTOR ELEAME
The tragedy of Mr. No-Balance.
1966. AFR

MUSSET, ALFRED DE, 1810-1857
Camille and Perdican.
Meyer, P., tr. WEAN

Les caprices de Marianne. 1851.
BOR
Variant title: The follies of
Marianne
The chandelier. 1847.
Chambers, W., tr. BAT9
A door should be either open or
shut. 1848.
Barzun, J., tr. BENS3
Variant title: Il faut qu'-une
porte soit ouverte ou fer-
mée
Fantasio. 1834.
Baring, M., tr. BENS1,
BENT2, CLOU
The follies of Marianne. See
Les caprices de Marianne
Il faut qu'une porte soit ouverte
ou fermée. See A door should
be either open or shut
Lorenzaccio. 1896.
Bruce, R., tr. BENT6
No trifling with love. See On
ne badine pas avec l'amour
On ne badine pas avec l'amour.
1861. COM, GRA
Pellissier, R., tr. TREB,
TREC1, TREE1, TREI1
Variant title: No trifling with
love

MUTWA, CREDO V.
uNosilemela. 1973. SOUT

MYGATT, TRACY DICKINSON
The sword of the Samurai.
1925? FED2

MYRTLE, FREDERICK S.
Gold. 1916. BOH3

NABBES, THOMAS, 1605-1946
Covent Garden. 1632-3? BUL3
Hannibal and Scipio. 1635.
BUL3
Tottenham Court. 1633. BUL3

NAGLE, URBAN, BROTHER, 1905-
1965
Savonarola, the flame of
Florence. 1941. THEC

NAHARRO, BARTHOLOME TORRES
DE. See Torres de Naharro,
Bartholomé de

NAJAC, EMILE DE, 1828-1889.
See Sardou, Victorien, jt. auth.

NAKADA, MANSUKE. See Tsuuchi,
Hanjurō, jt. auth.

NAMBOKU IV, TSURUYA. See
Tsuruya, Namboku IV

NAMIKI, GEIJI. See Namiki, Sōsuke,
jt. auth.

NAMIKI, GOHEI III, 1789-1855
Kanjinchō. See The subscription
list
The subscription list. 1840.
Scott, A., tr. ANDF, ASF
Variant titles: Kanjinchō;
The subscription scroll
The subscription scroll. See
The subscription list

NAMIKI, SENRYŪ, pseud. See
Namiki, Sōsuke

NAMIKI, SHŌZŌ I. See Namiki,
Sōsuke, jt. auth.

NAMIKI, SOSUKE (Namiki Senryu,
pseud.), 1695-1751; NAMIKI,
SHOZO I; NAMIKI, GEIJI; and
ASADA, ITCHO
Chronicle of the Battle of Ichino-
tani. 1751.
Brandon, J., tr. KAB
Variant title: Ichinotani
Futaba Gunki
Ichinotani Futaba Gunki. See
Chronicle of the Battle of
Ichinotani
--See also Takeda, Izumo, jt.
auth.

NASH, N. RICHARD, 1916-
The rainmaker. 1954. CORB

NASH, OGDEN, 1902-1971. See
Perelman, S. J., jt. auth.

NASHE, THOMAS, 1567-1601
Summer's last will and testament.
(1600) DPR1

NEILSON, KEITH
The end of the world; or, Fragments from a work in progress.
1968. BALLE6

Variant title: Fragments
From a work in progress
Fragments from a work in
progress. See The end of
the world

NELSON, RICHARD
Vienna Notes. 1978. WOQ1

NEMEROV, HOWARD, 1920-
Cain. FAD

NEMIROVICH-DANCHENKO,
VLADIMIR IVANOVICH, 1848-1936
The brothers Karamazoff (based
on the novel by Fedor
Dostoevskii). 1922?
Covan, J., tr. MOSA
Love and death, featuring
"Aleko," by Rachmaninoff
(based on the story by
Aleksandr Pushkin). 1891.
Seldes, G. and G., trs.
PLAH

NESTROY, JOHANN, 1802-1862
The talisman. 1840.
Knight, M., and Fabry, J.,
tr. and adapter. ANTH
Variant title: Der talisman
Der talisman. See The talisman

NEUMANN, ALFRED, 1895-1952
The patriot. See Dukes, Ashley.
Such men are dangerous
(adapted from)

NEVEUX, GEORGES, 1900-
Juliett ou la cié des songes.
(1930) PRO

NEWBOUND, BERNARD SLADE.
See Slade, Bernard

NEWHARD, ELWOOD L. See Moss,
Alfred Charles, jt. auth.

NEWLEY, ANTHONY, 1931- . See
Bricusse, Leslie, jt. auth.

NEWMAN, DAVID, 1937- , and
BENTON, ROBERT
"It's a bird, it's a plane, it's
superman" (music by Charles
Strouse, lyrics by Lee Adams).
1966. BES65

NEWSPAPER, STAFF OF THE LIVING.
See Staff of the Living Newspaper

NICCODEMI, DARIO, 1877-1934
The poet.
Rietty, R., tr. ALL
Variant title: Il poeta
Il poeta. See The poet

NICHOLS, ANNE, 1891-1966
Abie's Irish rose. 1922. CEY,
MOST

NICHOLS, DUDLEY, 1895-1960
The informer. See O'Flaherty,
Liam. The informer (adapted
by)

NICHOLS, PETER, 1927-
A day in the death of Joe Egg.
1968. BES67, DITA
The National Health. 1969. BES74

NICHOLS, ROBERT MALISE BOYER,
1893-1944, and BROWNE, MAURICE
Wings over Europe. 1928.
BES28, CHU, MACF, MOSG,
MOSH

NICOL, ERIC PATRICK, 1919-
The clam made a face. 1967.
KAL4

NIGGLI, JOSEFINA, 1910-
Singing valley. 1936. PAJ
The ring of General Macías.
BRNB
This bull ate nutmeg. 1937?
GALB

NIRDLINGER, CHARLES FREDERIC,
1863-1940
The world and his life. See
Echegaray y Eizaguirre, José.
The great Galeoto (tr. and
adapted by)

NIVELLE DE LA CHAUSEE, PIERRE
CLAUDE. See La Chausée, Pierre
Claude Nivelle de

NIVOIX, PAUL, 1889-1958. See
Pagnol, Marcel, jt. auth.

NKOSI, LEWIS, 1936-
The rhythm of violence. (1964)

GREJ, LITT, WELT

NO SAYEMON, ENAMAI. See Enami
Sayemon

NOAH, MORDECAI MANUEL, 1785-
1851
She would be a soldier; or, The
plains of Chippewa. 1819.
MONR, MOSS1

NOBUMITSU, KANZE KOJIRO. See
Kwanze, Kojiro Nobumitsu

NOBUMORI, SUGIMORI. See Chikamatsu, Monzaemon

NODA, KŌGŌ. See Ozu, Yasujirō,
jt. auth.

NOLTE, CHARLES M., 1926-
Do not pass go. 1965. MIMN

NORMAN, MARSHA (WILLIAMS),
1947-
Getting out. 1977. BES77,
BES78
'night, Mother. 1981. BES82

NORTON, THOMAS, 1532-1584.
See Sackville, Thomas, jt. auth.

NTSHONA, WINSTON. See Fugard,
Athol, jt. auth.

NŪ, CH'I-CHIEH
A girl setting out for trial.
Scott, A., tr. SCX3

NUGENT, ELLIOTT, 1900-1965.
See Thurber, James, jt. auth.

NUNEZ DE ARCE, GASPAR, 1834-
1903
The face of wood. See El haz
de leña
El haz de leña. 1872. BRET
Variant title: The face of
wood

NUNN, TREVOR, 1940-
Cats (additional lyrics by).
See Lloyd Webber, Andrew.
Cats

OBEY, ANDRE, 1892-1975
Noah. 1931.
Wilmurt, A., tr. and adapter.
GARZH
Venus and Adonis. 1932?
Becker, W., tr. BENS2

OBRENOVIĆ, ALEKSANDAR, 1928-
The bird. 1958. (Part of his
Variations).
Drndić, D., tr. MIG

O'BRIEN, EDNA, 1932-
A cheap bunch of nice flowers.
1962. PLAN26

O'BRIEN, JUSTIN, 1906-1968
Caligula. See Camus, Albert.
Caligula (adapted by)

O'BRIEN, LIAM, 1913-
The remarkable Mr. Pennypacker.
1953. THEA54

O'CASEY, SEAN, 1884-1964
Bedtime story. 1951. BRIU
Cock-a-doodle dandy. 1949.
BENT5, BLOC, CLKWI, COTM
The end of the beginning. 1939.
FREI, STAV, SUT4
Hall of healing. THOD
Juno and the paycock. ALLI,
ALLJ, ALLK, ALLM, BARR,
BLOC, CAP, CLM, CLN, COT,
CUBE, CUBG, DIE, DUR, FIG,
HAVG, KRM, SNYD2, WARI,
WARL, WATF2, WATI, WHI
Nannie's night out. 1924. RICJ
The plough and the stars. 1926.
BES27, BARU, COTQ, HOGF,
REV, TREBA, TREBJ, TREC2,
TREE3, TREI3, TUCN, TUCO,
WORP
Purple dust. 1953. BARF, COTK,
ULAN, WATA
Red roses for me. 1943. MORT,
SIXB
The shadow of a gunman. 1923.
MERC
The silver tassie. 1929. COTM

O'CONNELL, LOUISE
Donalds O'Rourk. DRU

O'CONNOR, FRANK. See O'Donovan,
Michael (pseud. of)

O'CONOR, JOSEPH, 1916-
The iron harp. 1955. BES56,
BRZE

ODETS, CLIFFORD, 1906-1963
Awake and sing. 1935. BES34,
BLOC, CER, CLOR, COK,
ENC, FAMAL, FAMI, GARU,
GATB2, GRIF, GROS, HAT,
MOSL, TREA1
The big knife. 1954. FAMO
The country girl. 1950.
BES50, CLM, CLN
Variant title: A winter
journey
The flowering peach. 1954.
BES54
Golden boy. 1937. BES37,
FAML, GATB2, GAS, MERT,
MOSH, TREBA, TREBJ,
TREC2, TREE3, TREI3
Rocket to the moon. 1938.
BES38
Till the day I die. 1935. FAMJ
Waiting for Lefty. 1935.
BROE, CASS, CET, DUR,
GREG, HIL, KOZ, SUTL,
WARH
A winter journey. See The
country girl

O'DONOVAN, JOHN, 1921-
Copperfaced Jack. 1963. HOGE

O'DONOVAN, MICHAEL (Frank
O'Connor, pseud.), 1903-1966
In the train. 1937. BARF

OFFENBACH, JACQUES, 1819-1880
La périchole. 1868.
Seldes, G., and G., trs.
PLAM
Variant title: Singing birds
Singing birds. See La périchole

O'FLAHERTY, LIAM, 1897-1984
The informer (adapted by Dudley
Nichols). 1935. HAU, HAVD

OFLAZOĞLU, A. TURAN, 1932-
Deli Ibrahim. See Ibrahim the
mad
Ibrahim the mad. 1967.
Nemet-Nejat, M., tr. HALM
Variant title: Deli Ibrahim

OGDEN, ANNA CORA. See Ritchie,

Mrs. Anna Cora (Ogden) Mowatt

OGUNI, HIDEO. See Kurosawa,
Akira, jt. auth.

OGUNYEMI, WALE, 1939-
The scheme. THTN

O'HARA, FRANK, 1926-1966
The general returns from one
place to another. 1964. ORZ
Try! Try! 1953. MAH

O'HARA, KANE, 1722-1782
The golden pippin. 1773. BELC3
Midas. 1762. BELC2

OHNET, GEORGES, 1848-1918
The forge master. See The iron
manufacturer
The iron manufacturer. 1883.
Leslie, G., tr. BAT9
Variant titles: The forge
master; The iron master;
Le maître de forges
The iron master. See The iron
manufacturer
Le maître de forges. See The
iron manufacturer

OKAMURA, SHIKO, 1881-1925
The Zen substitute. 1963.
Brandon, J., and Niwa, T.,
trs. BRA

O'KEEFE, JOHN, 1747-1833
Lie of a day. 1796. INCA10

O'KEEFE, JOHN
All night long. WOQ2
Bercilak's dream. 1982. PLACE
Chamber piece. 1972. BALLE11

OKONKWO, R.
The game of love. OBI

OLDENBURG, CLAES, 1929-
Fotodeath. 1961. HILP

OLESHA, YURI, 1899-1960
The conspiracy of feelings. 1929.
Gerould, D. C., and Gerould,
E. S., trs. DUK
Variant title: Zagovor chyvstv
A list of assets. 1931?
MacAndrew, A., tr. GARZG,
MABA

Marco millions. 1928. CHA,
HUB, HUDS2, HUDT
A moon for the misbegotten.
1947. BES56, GART, LOR,
SSSI, TREBJ
The moon of the Caribbees.
1918. LEV, LEVE, LOO,
MAF
Mourning becomes Electra.
1931. BES31, WARH
The rope. 1919. ELLI2
Strange interlude. 1928.
BES27, CORD, CORE, CORF,
THF
A touch of the poet. 1957.
BES58, COX, FOT, GARSA
Where the cross is made. 1918.
BENP, COD, ING, INGA,
PROW, SCWE, TOD

OPEN THEATER
The mutation show. 1970.
OPE
Nighwalk. 1973. OPE

OPPENHEIMER, JOEL, 1930-
The great American desert.
1961. ORZ

OPPER, DON KEITH, and the
COMPANY THEATRE ENSEMBLE
Children of the kingdom (script
by Don Keith Opper). 1970.
BALLE9

ORRERY, ROGER BOYLE, 1st
earl of, 1621-1679
The tragedy of Mustapha, the
son of Solyman the magnificent.
1665. DOA

ORTIZ DE MONTELLANO, BERNARDO,
1899-
Salome's head. 1944?
Mallan, L., tr. NEWD44

ORTON, JOE, 1933-1967
Entertaining Mr. Sloane. 1964.
CALD, HOF, NEWE8
Loot. 1966. NEWE13
What the butler saw. 1970.
BES69

OSBORN, PAUL, 1901-
A bell for Adano (based on the
novel by John Hersey). 1944.
BES44

The innocent voyage (based on
the novel A high wind in
Jamaica by Richard Hughes).
1943. BES43
Morning's at seven. 1939.
BES39, GARU, KRM
On borrowed time (based on the
novel by Lawrence E. Watkin).
1938. BES37, GARU, GATB2,
GOW, GOWA
Point of no return (adapted from
the novel by John P. Mar-
quand). 1950. BES51, WAGC3

OSBORNE, JOHN, 1929-
The entertainer. 1957.
BES44, TAUJ
Inadmissable evidence. 1964.
BES65, COTT
Look back in anger. 1956.
BES57, BLOC, CEQA, COK,
HAVHA
Luther. 1961. BES63, DIT,
RICT
A subject of scandal and concern.
1960. BARU, RICJ

-- and CREIGHTON, ANTHONY
Epitaph for George Dillon. 1958.
BES58, NEWE2, TREBJ

OSBORNE, MARIAN
The point of view. 1923. MAS1

OSGOOD, PHILLIPS ENDECOTT,
1882-1956
A sinner beloved. 192-? FED1

OSTROVSKII, ALEKSANDR NIKOLAE-
VICH, 1823-1886
The diary of a scoundrel. 1868.
Ackland, R., tr. BENT2
Kasherman, P., tr. MOSA
Variant titles: Enough stupidity
in every wise man; Even a
wise man stumbles
A domestic picture. 18-?
Voynich, E., tr. COUR
Easy money. 1870?
Magarshack, D., tr. BENS2
Variant title: Fairy gold
Enough stupidity in every wise
man. See The diary of a
scoundrel
Even a wise man stumbles. See
The diary of a scoundrel
Fairy gold. See Easy money

The poor bride. 1852.
Seymour, J., and Noyes,
G., trs. NOY
The storm. See The thunder-
storm
Thunder. See The thunder-
storm
The thunderstorm. 1880.
Cooper, J., tr. COOPA
MacAndrew, A., tr.
GARZE, MAB, TREB
Magarshack, D., tr. MAP
Reeve, F., tr. REEV1
Whyte, F., and Noyes, G.,
trs. CLF2
Variant titles: The storm;
Thunder

OSTROVSKY, ALEKSANDER. See
Ostrovskiĭ, Aleksandr Nikolaevich

OTIS, MERCY. See Warren, Mrs.
Mercy (Otis)

OTWAY, THOMAS, 1652-1685
The orphan. 1680. BELK5
Venice preserv'd; or, A
plot discover'd. 1682.
BELK1, DOB, GOS, GOSA,
MAND, MANF, MAX, MEN,
MOR, MOSE1, NET, RES,
REST, RET, RUB, STM,
TAT, TAU, TICK, TUP,
TUQ, TWE, WILS

OULESS, E. U.
Our pageant. 1926? THU

OULTON, BRIAN, 1908-
Mr. Sydney Smith coming up-
stairs. 1972. PLAN42

OU-YANG, YÜ-CHIEN, 1889-1962
P'an Chin-lien. (1928)
Swatek, C., tr. TWEH

OVERMYER, ERIC
Native speech. 1983. WOQ3

OWA
The Soledad tedrad, Part II:
Transitions for a mime poem.
(1975) CEN

OWEN, ALUN DAVIES, 1926-
Male of the species. 1969.
RICK

Progress to the park. 1961.
NEWE5

OWENS, ROCHELLE, 1936-
Chucky's lunch. WOQ2
Futz. 1967. NEWA2
He wants shih. (1972) OWE

OXENFORD, JOHN, 1812-1877
East Lynne. 1866. KILG

OYAM O, pseud. See Gordon,
Charles F.

OYAMO, 1943-
His first step. 1972. NEWL

OYONO, FERDINAND L., 1929-
Houseboy. PIET

OZU, YASUJIRO, 1903-1963,
and NODA, KOGO
Tokyo story. 1953.
Richie, D., and Klestadt, E.,
trs. HIBH
Variant title: Tōkyō monogatari
Tōkyō monogatari. See Tokyo
story

PAGE, LOUISE
Tissue. 1978. PLABE1

PAGNOL, MARCEL, 1899-1974
Marius, Fanny and César. See
Behrman, Samuel Nathaniel
and Logan, Joshua. Fanny
(based on the trilogy by)

-- and NIVOIX, PAUL
Les marchands de gloire. 1925.
GRAF

PAILLERON, EDOUARD JULES HENRI,
1834-1899
The art of being bored. See Le
mond où l'on s'ennuie
The cult of boredom. See Le
monde où l'on s'ennuie
Le monde où l'on s'ennuie. 1881.
BOR, BOV
Variant titles: The art of
being bored; The cult of
boredom; This bored world;
The world of boredom

This bored world. See Le
monde où l'on s'ennuie
The world of boredom. See
Le monde où l'on s'ennuie

PAKINGTON, MARY AGUSTA,
1878-
The queen of hearts. 1926?
THU

PALARCA, JULIA
Other tomorrows. 195-?
EDAD

PALISSOT DE MONTENOY,
CHARLES, 1730-1814
Les philosophes. 1760. BRE

PALMER, T. A., 1838-1905
East Lynne. 1874. ASG

PARKER, DOROTHY (ROTHS-
CHILD), 1893-1967
Candide. See Hellman,
Lillian. Candide (lyrics by)

PARKER, LOUIS NAPOLEON,
1852-1944
Disraeli. 1911. BES09
A minuet. 1915. CAR

PARKHOUSE, HANNAH. See Cowley, Mrs. Hannah (Parkhouse)

PASSEUR, STEVE, 1899-1966
L'acheteuse. See A measure
of cruelty
A measure of cruelty. 1930.
Mitchell, Y., tr. PLAN29
Variant title: L'acheteuse

PATON, ALAN, 1903-
Cry, the beloved country.
See Anderson, Maxwell and
Weill, Kurt. Lost in the
stars (based on the novel
by)

PATRICK, JOHN (pseud. of John
Patrick Goggan), 1907-
The hasty heart. 1945. BES44,
GARZ
The story of Mary Surratt.
1947. BES46
Variant title: This gentle
ghost
The teahouse of the August moon

(based on the novel by Vern
Sneider). 1953. BES53,
BES53, CORB, GARU, GATB4,
GAVE, RICT, THEA54
This gentle ghost. See The story
of Mary Surratt

PATRICK, ROBERT, 1937-
Fred and Harold. 1975. HOM
The golden circle. 1969. NEWA3
The haunted host. 1974. HOM
Judas. 1978. WES5
One person. 1975. HOM
T-shirts. 1978. HOF

PATTERSON, CHARLES, 1941-
Black ice. (1968) JON

PAUL, MRS. CLIFFORD
The fugitive king. 1926? THU

PAULDING, JAMES KIRKE, 1778-
1860
The bucktails; or, Americans
in England. 1947. HAL

PAWLEY, THOMAS, 1917-
The tumult and the shouting.
1969. HARY

PAYNE, JOHN HOWARD, 1791-1852
The black man; or, The spleen.
181-? AMP6
The boarding schools; or, Life
among the little folks. 1841?
AMP5
Brutus; or, The fall of Tarquin.
1818. GRE, MOSS
The Italian bride. 1832? AMP6
The last duel in Spain (adapted
from El postrer duelo de Es-
paña, by Calderón de la
Barca). 1822? AMP6
Mazeppa; or, The wild horse of
Tartary (adapted from Mazeppa,
by Léopold Chandezon and
Jean Cuvilier de Trye). 1825?
AMP5
Mount Savage (adapted from Le
mont sauvage, by René
Pixérécourt). 1822. AMP5
Romulus, the shepherd king.
1839? AMP6
The Spanish husband; or, First
and last love. 1830. AMP5
Thérèse, the orphan of Geneva.
1821. BAT19

Trial without jury; or, The
magpie and the maid (adapted from La pie voleuse,
by Louis Caigniez and Jean
Marie Théodore Baudoin).
1815? AMP5
The two sons-in-law (adapted
from Les deux gendres, by
Charles Etienne). 1824?
AMP5
Woman's revenge. 1832. AMP6

-- and IRVING, WASHINGTON
Charles the second; or, The
merry monarch (adapted
from the book, La jeunesse
de Henri V, by Alexandre
Duval). 1824. GARX, QUIJ,
QUIK, QUIL, QUIM, QUIN,
TAFT

PEABODY, JOSEPHINE PRESTON
(MRS. L. S. MARKS), 1874-1922
The piper. 1910. BRIK, DID,
MOSJ, MOSK, MOSL

PEACOCK, MRS. BARBARA (BURN-
HAM). See Burnham, Barbara

PEACOCK, JOHN
Children of the wolf. 1971.
PLAN40

PEACOCK, THOMAS LOVE, 1785-
1866
Nightmare abbey. See Sharp,
Anthony. Nightmare abbey
(adapted from the frolic by)

PEARSE, PADRIAC, 1880-1916
The singer. 1915. CAP

PECHANTRE, 1638?-1709
Geta. 1687.
Lockert, L., tr. LOCU

PECHANTRES. See Péchantré

PEDROLO, MANUEL DE, 1918-
Cruma. (1957)
Wellwarth, G., tr. WELV
Full circle. (1958)
Steel, B., tr. WELV
Variant title: Situació bis
The room. (1959)
Webster, J., tr. WELV
Variant title: Tècnica de

cambra
Situació bis. See Full circle
Tècnica de cambra. See The
room

PEELE, GEORGE, 1558?-1597?
The arraignment of Paris.
1584? BAS, BROC, NES
David and Bethsabe. 1593.
DPR1, MIN1, MIO1
The lamentable tragedy of Locrine
(sometimes attributed to).
See Anonymous plays. The
lamentable tragedy of Locrine
The old wife's tale. See The
old wives' tale
The old wives' tale. 1593?
BAS, BROC, GAY1, MAK,
MIN2, MIO2, NEI, NES, OLH,
OLI1, PAR, PARR, RUB, SCI,
SCJ, SCW, THWO
Variant title: The old wife's
tale

PELUSO, EMANUEL
Good day. 1965. OFF
Little fears. 1967? OFF
Moby tick. 1970. NEWA4

PERELMAN, SIDNEY JOSEPH, 1904-
1979
The beauty part. 1962. SSTY

-- and NASH, OGDEN
One touch of Venus (music by
Kurt Weill; lyrics by Ogden
Nash). 1943. RICO

PEREZ DE SAAVEDRA RIVAS,
ANGEL. See Rivas, Angel Pérez de
Saavedra

PEREZ GALDOS, BENITO, 1845-1920
La de San Quintín. 1894. BRET
Hayden, P., tr. CLDM
Variant title: The duchess of
San Quentin
The duchess of San Quentin. See
La de San Quintín
Electra. 1901.
Anon. tr. BUCK
Turrell, C., tr. TUCG, TUR
Variant title: The nun and
the barbarian
The nun and the barbarian. See
Electra

PERR, HARVEY
Afternoon tea. GUTR

PERTWEE, MICHAEL, 1916-
See Pertwee, Roland, jt. auth.

PERTWEE, ROLAND, 1885-1963
Heat wave. 1929. FIT

-- and PERTWEE, MICHAEL
The paragon. 1948. PLAN1

PERYALIS, NOTIS
Masks of angels. 195-?
Finer, L., tr. COTR

PESHKEV, ALEXEI MAXIMOVITCH.
See Pieskov, Aleksieĭ Maksimovich

PETCH, STEVE, 1952-
The general. 1972. BRIP

PETERS, PAUL
Nat Turner. 1940. CROZ1

PETERSON, LEONARD, 1917-
Billy Bishop and the Red
Baron. (1974) KAL4

PETERSON, LOUIS STAMFORD,
1922-
Take a giant step. 1953.
BES53, FORD, HARY,
PATR, TUQT

PETROV, EVGENY. See Ilf,
Ilya Arnoldovich, jt. auth.

PEZZULO, TED, 1936-1979
Skaters. 1978. WES4

PHILLIPS, AMBROSE, 1675-1749
Distressed mother. 1712.
BELK1

PHILLIPS, DAVID GRAHAM, 1867-
1911
The worth of a woman. 1908.
INDI

PHILLIPS, LOUIS, 1942-
The last of the Marx Brothers'
writers. 1977. WES2

PHILLIPS, STEPHEN, 1868-1915
Paolo and Francesca. 1902.
DIG, SMN

PHILLIPS, WATTS, 1825-1874
Lost in London. 1867? BOOB

PHILON, FREDERIC
He would be a soldier. 1786.
INCA8

PICARD, LOUIS BENOIT, 1769-1828
The rebound. See Les ricochets
Les ricochets. 1807. BOR
Variant title: The rebound

PICASSO, PABLO, 1881-1974
Le désir attrapé par la queue.
See Desire trapped by the tail
Desire trapped by the tail. 195-?
Briffault, H., tr. NEWW2
Variant title: Le désir attrapé
par la que

PICCIOTO, HENRY
Factwino meets the moral majority
(script by). See San Francisco
Mime Troupe. Factwino meets
the moral majority
Factwino vs. Armageddonman
(script by). See San Francisco
Mime Troupe. Factwino vs.
Armageddonman

PIELMEIER, JOHN, 1949-
Agnes of God. 1979. BES81

PIESHKOV, ALEXEI. See Pieskov,
Aleksieĭ Maksimovich

PIESKOV, ALEKSIEI MAKSIMOVICH,
1868-1926. See Gorki, Maxim, pseud.

PIETRO TREPASSI. See Metastasio,
Pietro Antonio Domenico Buonaventura,
pseud.

PIFER, DRURY
An evening in our century. 1981.
WES10

PIKERYNG, JOHN, fl.1560
Horestes. (1530-67). THZ
Variant title: A newe enterlude of vice conteyning the
history of Horestes with the
cruell rengment of his
fathers death upon his one
naturall mother
A newe enterlude of vice conteyning the history of Horestes

with the cruell rengment
of his fathers death upon
his one naturall mother.
See Horestes

PILLOT, EUGENE
My lady dreams. 1922? SHAY
Two crooks and a lady. 1917.
COOK3

PILLOT, JOSEPH EUGENE. See
Pillot, Eugene

PINERO, SIR ARTHUR WING,
1865-1934
The gay Lord Quex. 1899.
MOSN, MOSO, SMO
Iris. 1901. COT
The magistrate. 1885. BENS3,
BOOA4, BOOM, PLAN38,
SMR
Mid-channel. 1909. HAU,
SMI, WATF1, WATI, WEAL,
WHI
The notorious Mrs. Ebbsmith.
1895. BAI
The second Mrs. Tanqueray.
1893. ASG, BENY, BOOA2,
BOWY, CEU, CLK2, COF,
COTKIS, DIC, DUR, FULT,
HUD, MAX, ROWC, SALE,
STE, TAU, WATT2
The thunder-bolt. 1908. CHA,
CHAN, CHAR, TUCD, TUCM,
TUCN, TUCO
Trelawny of the "Wells". 1898.
BES94, CLKY, MART
--See also Woods, Aubrey...
Trelawny (based on)

PIÑERO, MIGUEL, 1946-
Short eyes. 1974. BES73

PINGET, ROBERT, 1919-
Architruc. 1961.
Benedikt, M., tr. BEN
La manivelle. See The old
tune
The old tune. 1962
Beckett, S., tr. GOO
Variant title: La manivelle

PINNER, DAVID, 1940-
Dickon. 1966. NEWE10
The drums of snow. NEWE13,
PLAN42

PINSKI, DAVID, 1872-1959
King David and his wives. 1923.
Landis, J., tr. LAO, LAOG

PINTER, HAROLD, 1930-
Betrayal. 1979. BES79
The birthday party. 1958.
NIL, SEVD
The black and white. 1959.
THOD
The caretaker. 1960. BES61,
POP
The collection. 1962. BES62
The dumbwaiter. 1960. ABRJ,
CLLC, COK, HEA, LITJ,
NEWE3, REIW, REIWE, SOU
The homecoming. 1965. BES66,
SSSI
Last to go. 1959. THOD
A night out. 1960. CONB, MAE
Request stop. 1959. PLAAB
A slight ache. 1961. AUB,
SCNPL, SDQ, TREBJ
Trouble in the works. 1959.
GLI

PIRANDELLO, LUIGI, 1867-1936
And that's the truth. See Right
you are! If you think so
As you desire me. 1931.
Alba, M., tr. GARZH
Putnam, S., tr. HAV
Variant title: Come tu mi
vuoi
Bellavita.
Murray, W., tr. RICJ
Ciascuno a suo modo. See
Each in his own way
Come tu mi vuoi. See As you
desire me
Cosi è se vi pare! See Right you
are! If you think so
Each in his own way. 1924.
Livingston, A., tr. CHA,
CHAN, DUK, SEVT
Variant title: Ciascuno a suo
modo
The emperor. See Henry IV
Enrico IV. See Henry IV
La giara. See The jar
Henry IV. 1922.
Bentley, E., tr. BENSA,
COTQ
Caputi, A., tr. CAPU
Storer, E., tr. BARJ, BARK,
BLOC, DOT, DOV, FREG,

JOHN, MALN2, NORG2,
SANE, ULAN, WATA, WATI,
WATL4, WEIP, WELT
Variant titles: The emperor;
Enrico IV; The living mask;
The mock emperor
The jar. 1917.
Anon. tr. CHR
Livingston, A., tr. HIBB
May, F., tr. ALL
Variant title: La giara
The living mask. See Henry IV
Lumie di Sicilia. See Sicilian
limes
The man with the flower in his
mouth. (1928)
Bentley, E., tr. HOGN
The mock emperor. See Henry IV
Naked. 1922.
Livingston, A., tr. CLKW,
DIE
Variant title: Vestire
gl'ignudi
Our lord of the ships. 1925.
Anon. tr. MACN
Variant title: La sagra del
signore della nave
Il placere dell'onestà. See The
pleasure of honesty
The pleasure of honesty. 1917.
Murray, W., tr. COTN
Variant title: Il placere dell'
onestà
Questa sera si recita a soggetto.
See Tonight we improvise
Right you are! If you think so.
1918.
Bentley, E., tr. BENSB2
Livingston, A., tr. ALT,
ALTE, MOSG, MOSH
Variant titles: And that's
the truth; Così è se vi
pare !; It is so (if you
think so)
La sagra del signore della nave.
See Our lord of the ships
Sei personaggi in cerca d'autore.
See Six characters in search
of an author
Sicilian limes. 1910.
Goldberg, I., tr. GOL
Variant title: Lumie di
Sicilia
Six characters in search of an
author. 1921.
Anon. tr. ALLK, ALLM,
MANL

Bentley, E., tr. BENSB2
May, F., tr. SSSI, STY
Mayer, P., tr. COTN, COTQ
Storer, E., tr. ASF, AUG,
BAIC, BAIE, BAIG, BARL,
BARR, CEW, DEAS, DIK2,
DIP, DIT, DITA, DOWS,
GOLD, HAVL, HEA, KEN,
KERP, KINN, LITI, REIO,
REIP, REIT, REIW, REIWE,
SEN, TRE, TREA1, TREBA,
TREBJ, TREC2, TREE2,
TREI2, TRI, TRIA, VON,
WAIW, WEIM, WEIS, WEIW,
WHFM, WHI
Variant title: Sei personaggi
in cerca d'autore
Such is life. (1925)
Duplaix, L., tr. VANV2
Variant title: La vita che ti
diedi
Tonight we improvise. 1930.
Abba, M., tr. WEAN
Variant title: Questa sera
si recita a soggetto
Vestire gl'ignudi. See Naked
La vita che ti diedi. See Such is
life

PISEMSKII, ALEKSIEI FEOFILAKTO-
VICH, 1820-1881
A bitter fate. 1859.
Kagan, A., and Noyes, G.,
trs. NOY
Variant titles: Cruel fate;
A hard fate
Cruel fate. See A bitter fate
A hard fate. See A bitter fate

PITCHER, OLIVER, 1924-
The one. (1971) KINH

PITT, GEORGE DIBDIN, 1799-1855
The fiend of Fleet Street. See
The string of pearls (Sweeney
Todd)
The string of pearls (Sweeney
Todd). 1847. KILG
Variant titles: The fiend of
Fleet Street; Sweeney Todd,
the barber of Fleet Street
Sweeney Todd, the barber of
Fleet Street. See The string
of pearls (Sweeney Todd)

PIX, MARY, 1666-1720?
The innocent mistress. 1697. FEFO

PIXERECOURT, RENE CHARLES
GUILBERT DE, 1773-1844
Coelina; ou, L'enfant du mys-
tère. 1800. BOR
Le mont sauvage; ou, Le soli-
taire. See Payne, John
Howard. Mount Savage
(adapted from)

PIXLEY, FRANK, 1865-1919
Apollo. 1915. BOH3

PLANCHE, JAMES ROBINSON,
1796-1880
The bride of the isles. See
The vampire
Fortunio and his seven gifted
servants. 1843. BOOA5
The island of jewels. 1849.
BOOA5
The vampire. 1820. HOUR,
KILG
Variant title: The bride
of the isles

PLAUTUS, TITUS MACCIUS,
254?-184? B.C.
Amphitryon. 188? B.C.
Allison, R., tr. DUC1,
POR
Anon. tr. BAT21
Carrier, C., tr. BOVI
Cassoon, L., tr. ALTE
Sugden, E., tr. LOCM1
Variant title: Jupiter in
disguise
Asinaria. See The comedy of
asses
Aulularia. 194? B.C.
Alison, R., tr. DUC1
Bennett, C., tr. CLKW
Nixon, P., tr. ASF
Riley, H., tr. BUCM
Rogers, H., tr. SEBO
Sugden, E., tr. STA
Variant titles: The crock of
gold; the pot of gold
The braggart captain. See
Miles gloriosus
The braggart soldier. See
Miles gloriosus
The braggart warrior. See
Miles gloriosus
The captives. 254?-184? B.C.
Anon. tr. CROV
Alison, R., tr. DUC1
Lieberman, S., tr. LIDE

Riley, H., tr. MIK8
Sugden, E., tr. CLF1, HOUS,
MAU, ROB, THOM, THON
Variant titles: Captivi;
Prisoners of war
Captivi. See The captives
The Carthaginian. 2d cent. B.C.
Burroway, J., tr. BOVI
Duckworth, G., tr. DUC1
Variant title: The poenulus
Casina. 185? B.C.
Duckworth, G., tr. DUC1
The casket. 2d cent. B.C.
Duckworth, G., tr. DUC1
Variant title: Cistellaria
The churl. See Truculentus
Cistellaria. See The casket
The comedy of asses. 2d cent.
B.C.
Sugden, E., tr. DUC1
Variant title: Asinaria
The crock of gold. See Aulularia
Curculio. 194? B.C.
Duckworth, G., tr. DUC1
Variant title: The weevil
Epidicus. 2d cent. B.C.
Duckworth, G., tr. DUC1
The girl from Persia. 2d cent.
B.C.
Murphy, C., tr. DUC1
Variant title: The Persa
The haunted house. 2d cent.
B.C.
Anon. tr. MALR2
Bassett, E., Jarcho, L.,
and Murphy, C., trs.
Bovie, P., tr. BOVI
Casson, L., tr. CASU
Copley, F., tr. ROM
Downer, S., tr. DOWS
Mitchell, L., tr. DUC1, GRIF
Nixon, P., tr. MIL
Variant titles: The little ghost;
Mostellaria
Jupiter in disguise. See Amphi-
tryon
The little ghost. See The haunted
house
The Menaechmi. 2d cent. B.C.
Anon. tr. HOWJ, TREA2,
TREB, TREC1, TREE1,
TREI1
Bovie, P., tr. COTKIR, COTU
Copley, F., tr. ROM
Hyde, R., and Weist, E., trs.
BRIX, BRIY, BRIZ, BROJ,
BROK, DUC1, EDAD, GUI,

GUIN, HAPV
Lieberman, S., tr.   LIDE
Nixon, P., tr.   HUD
Riley, H., tr.   CROS, MIK8,
   SEBP
Taylor, J., tr.   TAV
Thornton, B., and Warner, R.,
   trs.   SMR
Variant titles: Menaechmi
   twins; The twin brothers;
   The twin Menaechmi
Menaechmi twins.   See Menaech-
   mi
Mercator.   See The merchant
The merchant.   2d cent. B.C.
   Murphy, C., tr.   DUC1
   Wilmurt, A., tr.   COTU
   Variant title: Mercator
Miles gloriosus.   205? B.C.
   Anon. tr.   PAR
   Duckworth, G., tr.   DUC1,
      ROET
   Riley, H., tr.   MIK8
   Suskin, A., tr.   HOWK
   Variant titles: The braggart
      captain; The braggart sol-
      dier; The braggart warrior
Mostellaria.   See The haunted
   house
The Persa.   See The girl from
   Persia
The poenulus.   See The Cartha-
   ginian
The pot of gold.   See Aulularia
Prisoners of war.   See The cap-
   tives
Pseudolus.   2d cent. B.C.
   Murphy, C., tr.   DUC1
   Variant title: The trickster
--See also Shevelove, B.   A funny
   thing happened on the way to
   the Forum (based on)
The rope.   2d cent. B.C.
   Casson, L., tr.   CASU
   Chase, C., tr.   DUC1,
      GUI, GUIN, HAPV
   Copley, F., tr.   ROM
   Lieberman, S., tr.   LIDE
   MacCary, W., tr.   TENN
   Variant titles: The rudens;
      The slipknot
The rudens.   See The rope
The slipknot.   See The rope
Stichus.   200 B.C.
   Workman, J., tr.   DUC2
The three penny day.   2d cent.
   B.C.

Duckworth, G., tr.   DUC2
   Variant titles: The three
      pieces of money; Trinummus
The three pieces of money.   See
   The three penny day
The trickster.   See Pseudolus
Trinummus.   See The three penny
   day
Truculentus.   2d cent. B.C.
   Duckworth, G., tr.   DUC2
   Variant title: The churl
The twin brothers.   See The
   Menaechmi
The twin Menaechmi.   See The
   Menaechmi
The two bacchides.   189? B.C.
   Sugden, E., tr.   DUC1
The weevil.   See Curculio

PLIEKŠĀNS, JANIS
See Rainis, Jānis (pseud.)

PLUTA, LEONARD
Little guy Napoleon.   1966.   ALI

POCOCK, ISAAC, 1782-1835
The miller and his men.
   1813.   BOOA1, BOOB, BOOM

POGODIN, NIKOLAI FEDEROVICH,
1900-1962 (pseud. of Stukalov, N.F.)
Aristocrats.   1935.
   Wixley, A., and Carr, R., trs.
      FOUS
   Variant title: Aristokraty
Aristokraty.   See Aristocrats
The chimes of the Kremlin.   1941.
   Bakshy, A., tr.   BAKS
   Shoett, A., tr.   CLKX, THY
   Variant titles: Kremlin chimes;
      Kremlevskie kuranty
Kremlin chimes.   See The chimes
   of the Kremlin
Kremlevskie kuranty.   See The
   chimes of the Kremlin
Temp.   See Tempo
Tempo.   1930.
   Talmadg, I., tr.   LYK
   Variant title: Temp

POIRET, JEAN, 1926-
La cage aux folles.   See Fierstein,
   Harvey.   La cage aux folles
   (adaptation of)

POLLOCK, CHANNING, 1880-1946
The enemy.   1925.   BES25

The fool. 1922. BES22

POLLOCK, RICHARD
Zoo in Silesia. 1945. EMB1

POLLOCK, SHARON, 1936-
Blood relations. 1980. PENG,
PLABE3
Variant title: My name is
Lisbeth
Generations. 1980. MAJ
My name is Lisbeth. See Blood
relations

POMERANCE, BERNARD, 1940-
The elephant man. 1977. BERS,
BES78, BEST

PONTE, LORENZO DA, 1749-1838
Don Giovanni. See The punished
libertine
The punished libertine; or, Don
Giovanni. 1787.
Schizzano, A., and Mandel, O.,
trs. MARL

POOLE, JOHN, 1786?-1872
Hamlet travestie. 1811. NIN1
Ye comedie of errours. (Late
1850's?) NIN5

POPPLE, WILLIAM, 1701-1764?
Cure for jealousy. See The
double deceit
The double deceit. 1735.
PLAN26
Variant title: Cure for
jealousy

POPPLEWELL, JACK, 1911-
Dead on nine. 1955. PLAN13
Dear delinquent. 1957. PLAN16

POPPLEWELL, OLIVE M.
This bondage. 1935. FIN

PORTER, COLE, 1891-1964
Kiss me Kate (music and lyrics
by). See Spewack, Mrs. Bella
(Cohen) and Spewack, Samuel.
Kiss me Kate
Leave it to me! (music and lyrics
by). See Spewack, Mrs. Bella
(Cohen) and Spewack, Samuel.
Leave it to me!

PORTER, HAL, 1911-

The tower. 1963. THOP

PORTER, HENRY, fl.1589-1599
The pleasant history of the two
angry women of Abington.
1598? GAY1, NER, OLH, OLI1
Variant title: The two angry
women of Abington
The two angry women of Abington.
See The pleasant history of
the two angry women of Abington

PORTER, J. PAUL
St. George. 1978. WES3

PORTILLO, ESTELA, 1936-
The day of the swallows. (1971)
CONR, ORT, ROMA

PORTILLO TRAMBLEY, ESTELA
See Portillo, Estela

PORTO-RICHE, GEORGES DE, 1849-
1930
Amoureuse. 1891. RHO
Crawford, J., tr. DID
Variant titles: Cupid's rival;
The impassioned wife; A
loving wife; The tyranny
of love
La chance de Françoise. See
Françoise' luck
Cupid's rival. See Amoureuse
Françoise' luck. 1888.
Clark, B., tr. CLD
Variant title: La chance de
Françoise
The impassioned wife. See
Amoureuse
A loving wife. See Amoureuse
The tyranny of love. See
Amoureuse

POTTER, PAUL M., 1853-1921
Trilby. 1895. KILG

POTTLE, EMERY BEMSLEY (GILBERT
EMERY, pseud.), 1875-
The hero. 1921. BES21, QUI,
TUCD
Tarnish. 1923. BES23

POWELL, ARNOLD
The death of everymom. SHRO
The strangler. 1966. BALLE4

POWYS, STEPHEN, 1907- (Mrs. GUY
BOLTON) (née Virginia de Lanty).
See Guitry, Sacha. Don't listen,
ladies! (Adapted by)

PRAGA, MARCO, 1862-1929
The closed door. 1913.
MacDonald, A., tr. SAY
Variant title: La porta chiusa
La porta chiusa. See The closed
door

PRATT, WILLIAM W.
Ten nights in a bar-room.
1858. BOOB

PRESS, TONI, 1949-
Mash note to an old codger.
(1977) NEWP

PRESTON, JOHN
The brave Irishman (sometimes
attributed). See Sheridan,
Thomas. The brave Irishman

PRESTON, THOMAS, 1537-1598
Cambises, King of Persia. 1569.
ADA, BAS, CRE, DPR1,
MIO1, MIR, NES
Variant titles: Cambyses;
The life of Cambises, King
of Persia
Cambyses. See Cambises, King
of Persia
The life of Cambises, King of
Percia. See Cambises, King
of Persia

PREVELAKIS, PANDELIS, 1909-
The last tournament. 1966.
Gianos, M., tr. GIA

PREVERT, JACQUES, 1900-1977
La famille tuyare de poile;
ou, Une famille bien unie.
See A united family
A united family. 1955?
Allen, J., tr. BENSC
Variant title: La famille tuyare
de poile; ou, Une famille
bien unie

PRIEDE, GUNĀRS, 1928-
The blue one.
Sedriks, A., tr. CONF
Variant title: Zilā
Zilā. See The blue one

PRIESTLEY, JOHN BOYNTON, 1894-
1984
Cornelius. 1935. SIXP
Dangerous corner. 1932. CEU,
RICI, SIXH
An inspector calls. 1945. BES47,
FOUX, HUDE
Laburnum grove. 1933. SEV
They came to the city. 1943.
BARV

-- and HAWKES, JACQUETTA
Dragon's mouth. 1952. COTK,
FAOS
--See Murdoch, Iris, jt. auth.

PRITCHARD, BARRY
Captain Fantastic meets the ecto-
morph. 1965. SCAR
The day Roosevelt died. 1980.
WES10
Visions of sugar plums. 1966.
BALLE4

THE PROVISIONAL THEATRE, 1972-
Inching through the Everglades.
1978. WES10

PRUTKOV, KOZ'MA (pseud. of
Aleksiei Konstantinovich Tolstoi;
Aleksandr Mikhailovich Zhemchuzhnikov; Aleksei Mikhailovich Zhemchuzhnikov; and Vladimir Mikhailovich
Zhemchuzhnikov)
The headstrong Turk, or, Is it
nice to be a grandson? (1863)
Senelick, L., tr. RVI
Variant title: Oprometchiviy
turka: ili Plilichno li byt
vnukom?
Oprometchiviy Turka: ili Plilichno
li byt vnukom? See The headstrong Turk, or, Is it nice to
be a grandson?

PRYCE, RICHARD, 1864-1942
Frolic wind. 1935. FAMG

PUCCIONI, MADELINE
Laundromat. 1975. NEWP
Two o'clock feeding. 1978. WES4

PULMAN, JACK, 1928?-1979
The happy apple. 1967. PLAN34

"PUNCH." See "Mr. Punch,"
pseud.

PURSCELL, PHYLLIS
Separate ceremonies. 1979.
WOMA

PUSHKIN, ALEKSANDR SERGIE-
EVICH, 1799-1837
Boris Godunov. 1870.
Reeve, F., tr. REEV1
Love and death featuring
"Aleko," by Rachmaninoff
(based on the story by).
See Nemirovich-Danchenko,
Vladimir Ivanovich. Love
and death
The stone guest. 1847.
MacAndrew, A., tr. MAB,
GARZE

QUILES, EDUARDO
El asalariado. See The employee
The bridal chamber. (1972)
Wellwarth, M., tr. WELK
Variant title: El tálamo
The employee. (1969)
Wellwarth, M., tr. WELK
Variant title: El asalariado
El frigorífico. See The refrigera-
tor
The refrigerator. (1972)
Wellwarth, M., tr. WELK
Variant title: El frigorífico
El tálamo. See The bridal chamber

QUINAULT, PHILIPPE, 1635-1688
Astrate. See Astrates
Astrates. 1664-1665.
Lockert, L., tr. LOCU
Variant title: Astrate

QUIÑONES DE BENAVENTE, LUIS,
1589?-1651
The doctor and the patient. See
El doctor y el enfermo.
El doctor y el enfermo. (1644)
NOR
Variant title: The doctor
and the patient

QUINTANA, EDUARDO DE ZAMACOIS
Y. See Zamacois, Eduardo

QUINTERO, JOAQUIN ALVAREZ.
See Alvarez Quintero, Joaquín

QUINTERO, SERAFIN ALVAREZ.

See Alvarez Quintero, Serafín

RABE, DAVID (WILLIAM), 1940-
The basic training of Pavlo
Hummel. 1971. FAMAD, OBG
Hurly burly. 1984. BES84
Sticks and bones. 1971. BES71,
BRIY, BRIZ, GARTL, RICT
Streamers. 1976. BES75, BEST,
BRIZ

RABINDRANATH TAGORE. See
Tagore, Rabindranath

RACHMANINOFF, SERGEI, 1873-
1943
Aleko. See Nemirovich-Danchenko,
Vladimir Ivanovich. Love and
death featuring "Aleko," by
Rachmaninoff

RACINE, JEAN BAPTISTE, 1639-1699
Andromache. See Andromaque
Andromaque. 1667. LYO, SCN,
SER, SERD, STJ1
Abel, L., tr. BERM
Boswell, R., tr. CLKW
Variant title: Andromache
Athaliah. 1691.
Anon. tr. GAUB, HOUS
Boswell, R., tr. BUCK, BUCL,
BUCM, GREA, KOH2, KRE
Muir, K., tr. ENC
Bérénice. 1670.
Boswell, R., tr. CLF2
Masefield, J., tr. STA
Esther. 1689. SER
Phaedra. See Phèdre
Phèdre. 1677. LYO, SER
Anon. tr. GAUB, EVB2, WORM
Arnott, P., tr. REIWE
Boswell, R., tr. CARP,
CARPA, DRA1, HARC26,
LOCM2, LOGG, MALC,
MALG2, MAU, MIL, PLAB1,
ROB, SEBO, SEBP, SMP
Cairncross, J., tr. ALLM
Fowlie, W., tr. DOV, FOWL
Goddard, W., tr. CALD, WEIS
Henderson, R., tr. EVA2,
EVC2, HIB, HIBB, THOM,
THON, TRE, TREA2, TREB,
TREC1, TREE1, TREI1,
WALJ
Lockert, L., tr. WEAV2

Lowell, R., tr. ALLK, AUB,
BENR4, BENSB1, BOW,
COTX, FREG, HOUE,
MALI2, MALN2, NORG2,
SANL, VANV2
Muir, K., tr. GOUZ, ROET
Variant titles: Phaedra;
Phèdre and Hippolyte
Phèdre and Hippolyte. See
Phèdre
Les plaideurs. 1668.
Browne, I., tr. BAT7
Variant title: The suitors
The suitors. See Les plaideurs

RADIGUET, RAYMOND, 1903-1923
Les pélican. See The pelicans
The pelicans. 1921.
Benedikt, M., tr. BEN
Variant title: Les pèlican

RADO, JAMES, 1939-
Hair. See Ragni, Gerome, jt.
auth.

RAGNI, GEROME, 1942- , and
RADO, JAMES
Hair (music by Galt MacDermot).
1967. GREAA

RAINIS, JĀNIS (pseud. of Jānis
Pliekšāns), 1865-1929
The golden steed. (1910)
Barbina-Stahnke, A., tr.
GOLB
Variant title: Zelta zirgs
Zelta zirgs. See The golden
steed

RAISIN, JACQUES, 1653?-1702
Merlin gascon. 1690. LAN

RAMSAY, ALLAN, 1686-1758
The gentle shepherd. 1725.
BELK9

RANDALL, BOB, 1937-
6 rms riv vu. 1972. BES72

RANDOLPH, CLEMENCE. See
Colton, John, jt. auth.

RAPHAELSON, SAMSON, 1896-
1983
Accent on youth. 1934. BES34,
FAMH
Jason. 1942. BES41

Skylark. 1939. BES39

RAPPOPORT, SHLOYME ZANVL
(A. S. ANSKY, pseud.), 1863-1920
Between two worlds. See The
dybbuk
The dybbuk. 1920.
Alsberg, H., and Katzin, W.,
trs. BES25, CEW, DIE,
GARZH
Landis, J., tr. LAO, LAOG
Variant title: Between two
worlds

RAPPOPORT, SOLOMON. See
Rappoport, Shloyme Zanvl

RASTELL, JOHN, 1475?-1536
The nature of the four elements
(sometimes attributed to).
See Anonymous plays. The
nature of the four elements

RATCLIFFE, HELEN
Railroad women. 1978. NEWP

RATTIGAN, SIR TERENCE MERVYN.
See RATTIGAN, TERENCE

RATTIGAN, TERENCE, 1911-1977
After the dance. 1939. SIXL
The Browning version. 1949.
HAMI
The deep blue sea. 1952. FAOS
French without tears. 1936.
FIP, PLAL2, THH
Love in idleness. See O mistress
mine
O mistress mine. 1946. BES45
Variant title: Love in idleness
Ross, 1960. PLAJ1
Separate tables. 1954. BES56
(2 one-act plays: Table by
the window: Table number
seven)
Table number seven (part of
Separate tables). 1956.
BENPB
The Winslow boy. 1946.
BES47, BOGO, LOND, RED,
REDM, SPER, WAGC2

RAUCH, EDWARD H. (PIT
SCHWEFFELBRENNER, pseud.),
1826-1902
Rip Van Winkle; oder, Die
shpooks fun Blowa Barrick

(based on the book by
Washington Irving). 18-?
BUFF

RAVEL, AVIVA, 1928-
Black dreams. (1973) SHAT
Dispossessed. 1977. MAJ
Soft voices. See Two short
plays: The twisted loaf;
Soft voices
The twisted loaf. See Two
short plays: The twisted
loaf; Soft voices
Two short plays: The twisted
loaf; Soft voices. 1966. KAL 3
Variant titles: Soft voices;
The twisted loaf

RAVENSCROFT, EDWARD, fl.
1671-1697
The London cuckolds. 1681.
JEFF2, SUM

-- and MOTTEUX, PETER ANTHONY
The anatomist; or, The sham
doctor ... with the loves of
Mars and Venus (based upon
Crispin médecin, by Hautroche).
1696. BELC1, HUGH

RAYFIEL, DAVID, 1923-
P.S. 193. 1962. BES62

RAYNAL, PAUL, 1890-1971
The tomb beneath the Arc de
triomphe. See Le tombeau
sous l'Arc de triomphe
Le tombeau sous l'Arc de
triomphe. 1924. RHO
Variant title: The tomb
beneath the Arc de tri-
omphe; The unknown war-
rior
The unknown warrior. See Le
tombeau sous l'Arc de triomphe

READE, CHARLES, 1814-1884. See
Taylor, Tom, jt. auth.

REANEY, JAMES CRERAR, 1926-
The Canadian brothers; or, The
prophecy fulfilled. 1983. MAJ
Handcuffs (part three of The
Donnellys). 1975. PENG
--See also Cameron, Ronald.
Masque (adapted from One-

man masque)

RECKORD, BARRY, 1928-
Skyvers. 1963. NEWE9

RED LADDER THEATRE
Strike while the iron is hot.
1974. STR
Variant title: A woman's work
is never done; or, Strike
while the iron is hot
A woman's work is never done.
See Strike while the iron is
hot

REDDING, JOSEPH DEIGHN, 1859-
1932
The attonement of Pan. 1912.
BOH2

REDFORD, JOHN, 1486?-1547
The play of wit and science.
1541? ADA, BEVD, FARN,
HAO, SCAT
Variant titles: Wit and
science; Wyt and science
Wit and science. See The play
of wit and science
Wyt and science. See The play
of wit and science
--See also Anonymous Plays.
The marriage of wit and
science

REED, JOSEPH, 1723-1787
The register-office. 1761. BELC3

REED, MARK WHITE, 1890?-1969
Yes, my darling daughter. 1937.
BES36, GAS

REELY, MARY KATHERINE, 1881-
1959
Flittermouse. 1927. GALB

REGNARD, JEAN FRANÇOIS, 1655-
1709
Le légataire universel. 1708.
BRE
Aldington, R., tr. ALD
Variant title: The residuary
légatee
The residuary légatee. See
Le légataire universel

REGNAULT, CHARLES, fl.1640
Marie Stuard, reyne d'Écosse.

1639.
Paulson, M. (rendered into
modern French by). FALE

REGNIER, MAX ALBERT MARIE,
1908-
The headshrinkers. See Paddle
your own canoe
Paddle your own canoe (based on
the scenario by André Gillois).
1957?
Hill, L., tr. and adapter.
PLAN17
Variant title: The head-
shrinkers

REID, ARTHUR
People in love. 1937. FAMK

REID, BEN
The fourth room. 1944? NEWD44

REID, LESLIE
Trespassers. 1923. MAS2

REIZENSTEIN, ELMER. See
Rice, Elmer L.

RELLAN, MIGUEL ANGEL
The blind warrior. (1967)
Wellwarth, M., tr. WELK
Variant title: El guerrero
ciego
El guerrero ciego. See The
blind warrior

REXROTH, KENNETH, 1905-
Iphigenia at Aulis. 1944?
NEWD44
Phaedra. 1944? NEWD44

REYNOLDS, FREDERICK, 1764-
1841
The delinquent. 1805. INCA2
The dramatist; or, Stop him
who can! 1789. MOR, NIC
Folly as it flies. (1802) INCA2
Fortune's fool. 1796. INCA2
The fugitive. INCA8
How to grow rich. (1793) INCA1
Laugh when you can. 1798.
INCA2
Life. 1800. INCA1
Notoriety. 1792. INCA1
The rage. 1794. INCA1
Speculation. 1795. INCA2
Werter. (1786) INCA3

The will. INCA1

REZNIK, LIPE, 1890-1943?
See Axenfeld, Israel, jt. auth.

RHODES, CRYSTAL
The trip. (1979) CEN

RIBMAN, RONALD, 1932-
Buck. 1983. NEWQA
Fingernails blue as flowers.
1971. SCV

RICARDO DE LA VEGA. See Vega,
Ricardo de la

RICE, ELMER L. (formerly Elmer
Reizenstein), 1892-1967
The adding machine. 1923.
DAV1, DIG, DUR, GARU, HAT,
HATA, JORG, MOSJ, MOSK,
MOSL, RAVA, SCNN, SMA,
SSSF, THF
Counsellor-at-law. 1931. FAMC
Dream girl. 1945. BES45,
GARZ, GATB3
Flight to the west. 1940.
BES40
Judgment day. 1934. FAMK
The left bank. 1931. BES31
On trial. 1914. BES09, CART
See Naples and die. 1929.
FAMB
Street scene. 1929. BES28,
CER, CHA, CHAN, CHAP,
CLH, CORD, CORE, CORF,
COTE, COTH, FULT, GASB,
GATB1, GRIF, MAF, MERU,
SIXD, WATC2, WATI, WATO
We, the people. 1933. BES32

RICE, GEORGE EDWARD, 1822-
1861
Hamlet, Prince of Denmark.
(1852) NIN5

RICE, TIM, 1944-
Jesus Christ superstar, a rock
opera (music by Andrew Lloyd
Webber). 1971. GREAA

RICHARDS, IVOR ARMSTRONG,
1893-1979
A leak in the universe. 1954.
PLAA

RICHARDS, STANELY, 1918-1980

District of Columbia. 1945.
HARY

RICHARDSON, HOWARD, 1917- ,
and BERNEY, WILLIAM
  Barbara Allen. See Dark of the
  moon
  Dark of the moon. 1945. PLAN2
  Variant title: Barbara Allen

RICHARDSON, JACK CARTER,
1935-
  Gallows humor. 1961. DOD,
  MARO, WELT
  The prodigal. 1960. FOR
  Xmas in Las Vegas. 1965.
  SSTY

RICHARDSON, WILLIS, 1889-
  The black horseman. 1931. RIR
  The broken banjo. 1925. LOC
  The chip woman's fortune. 1923.
  TUQT
  The flight of the natives. 1927.
  HARY, LOC
  The house of sham. (1929) RIR
  The idle head. 1927. HARY
  The king's dilemma. (1929)
  RIR

RICHE, GEORGES DE PORTO. See
Porto-Riche, Georges de

RICHMAN, ARTHUR, 1886-1944
  Ambush. 1921. BES21

RICHMOND, SAMUEL S.
  Career for Ralph. 1949? LOVR

RICKERT, VAN DUSEN, JR.
  The bishop's candlesticks.
  1945? GALB

RIFBJERG, KLAUS, 1931-
  Developments. (1963)
  Shaw, P., tr. MNOD
  Variant title: Udviklinger
  Udviklinger. See Developments

RIGGS, LYNN, 1899-1954
  Green grow the lilacs. 1931.
  BES30, CLH, GARU, LEV,
  LEVE, SIM
  --See also Hammerstein II, Oscar.
  Oklahoma! (based on)
  Knives from Syria. 1927. BENP,
  TOD

Roadside. 1930. TUCN, TUCO

RINEHART, MRS. MARY (ROBERTS),
1876-1958, and HOPWOOD, AVERY
  The bat. 1920. CART, CEY
  Variant title: The circular
  staircase
  The circular staircase. See The
  bat

RINGWOOD, GWEN PHARIS, 1910-
1984
  Drum song. 1982. MAJ
  Garage sale. 1981. PENG
  Pasque flower; a play of the
  Canadian prairie. 1939.
  WAGN2
  The rainmaker. 1945. WAGN3

RITCHIE, MRS. ANNA CORA (OGDEN
Mowatt, 1819-1870
  Fashion; or, Life in New York.
  1845. COY, GARX, HAL,
  MASW, MONR, MOSS2, NILS,
  PLAAD, QUIJ, QUIK, QUIL,
  QUIM, QUIN

RIVAROLA MATTO, JOSE MARIA,
1917-
  The fate of Chipí González.
  1954.
  Jones, W., tr. JONA
  Variant title: El fin de Chipí
  Gonzáles
  El fin de Chipí Gonzáles. See
  The fate of Chipí González

RIVAS, ANGEL PEREZ DE SAAVEDRA,
1791-1865
  Don Alvaro; ó la fuerza del sino.
  1835. BRET, PATT, TRES
  Variant title: Don Alvaro;
  or, The force of destiny;
  La forza del destino
  Don Alvaro; or, The force of
  destiny. See Don Alvaro ó la
  fuerza del sino
  La forza del destino. See Don
  Alvaro

RIVAS, MANUEL LINARES. See
Linares Rivas, Manuel

RIVERS, LOUIS, 1922-
  More bread and the circus.
  (1976) CEN

RIVERS, SUSAN, 1954-
Maud Gonne says no to the poet.
1978. WES3

RIVES, AMELIE. See Troubetskoy,
Amélie (Rives) Chanler

RIVINGTON, JAMES, 1724-1802
"The Battle of Brooklyn."
See Anonymous Plays. The
Battle of Brooklyn

ROBERT, FRANÇOIS LE METEL DE
BOIS. See Bois-Robert, François Le
Mêtel de

ROBERTS, CYRIL, 1892-
Tails up. 1935? GALB

ROBERTS, SHEILA, 1942-
Weekend (Scene I only). CONZI

ROBERTS, TED
Lindsay's boy (TV play). 1974.
FIO

ROBERTSON, LOUIS ALEXANDER,
1856-1910
Montezuma. 1903. BOH1

ROBERTSON, THOMAS WILLIAM,
1829-1871
Caste. 1867. ASG, BAI,
BOWY, COD, COT, DUR,
MART, MAX, MOSN, MOSO,
ROWE, TAU
Society. 1865. BAT16, RUB

ROBINSON, BETSY JULIA, 1951-
The Shanglers. 1979. NEWP

ROBINSON, JOHN
Wolves. 1978. WES2

ROBINSON, LENNOX, 1886-1958
The bighouse. 1926. CAP
Church street. 1934. CAN
The far-off hills. 1928. CHA,
CHAN, CHAR
The whiteheaded boy. 1916.
MYB, PLAP3

RODGERS, RICHARD, 1902-
Allegro (music by). See
Hammerstein II, Oscar.
Allegro
The king and I (music by).

See Hammerstein II, Oscar.
The king and I
Oklahoma! (music by). See
Hammerstein II, Oscar. Okla-
homa!
South Pacific (music by). See
Hammerstein II, Oscar. South
Pacific

RODRIGUEZ, BUENAVENTURA,
d.1941
Bomba Nyor! 1925? RAP
Variant title: Bombs away!
Bombs away! See Bomba Nyor!

RODRIGUEZ ALVAREZ, ALEJANDRO
(ALEJANDRO CASONA, pseud.),
1903-1965
La barca sin pescador. See The
boat without the fisherman
The boat without the fisherman.
1945
Damar, R., tr. HOLT
Variant title: La barca
sin pescador
Prohibido suicidarse en prima-
vera. See Suicide prohibited
in springtime
Suicide prohibited in springtime.
1937.
Horvath, A., tr. BENA
Variant title: Prohibido
suicidarse en primavera

ROEMER, MICHAEL, 1928- , and
YOUNG, ROBERT
Nothing but a man. 1963. MESS

ROGERS, JOHN WILLIAM, JR., 1894-
1965
Judge Lynch. 1924. LOC, PROG
Where the dear antelope play.
1941. THX

ROGERS, ROBERT, 1731-1795
Ponteach; or, The savages of
America. 1766? MOSS1

ROGERS, SAMUEL SHEPARD. See
Shepard, Sam

ROJAS, FERNANDO DE, 1465?-1541
Calisto and Melebea (a commodye
in englysh in maner of an
enterlude). See Celestina
Celestina; or, The tragi-comedy
of Calisto and Melibea (attributed

to). (1499)
Anon. adapter. THW
Mabbe, J., tr. and Bentley,
    E., adapter. BENR3
Variant titles: Calisto and
    Melebea (a new commodye
    in englysh in maner of an
    enterlude); La Celestina;
    Comedia de Calisto y
    Melibea; Tragicomedia de
    Calixto y Melibea
La Celestina. See Celestina
Comedia de Calisto y Melibea.
    See Celestina
Tragicomedia de Calixto y
    Melibea. See Celestina

ROJAS, RICARDO, 1882-1957
Ollántay. 1938. ALPE

ROJAS ZORRILLA, FRANCISCO DE,
1607-1648
Del rey abajo, ninguno. 1650.
    ALP
    Goldberg, I., tr. ALPF
    Variant title: None beneath
        the king
None beneath the king. See
    del rey abajo, ninguno

ROKK, VSEVOLOD
Engineer Sergeyev. 1941.
    Moss, H., tr. SEVP

ROMAINS, JULES (formerly Louis
Henri Jean Farigoule), 1885-1972
Cromedeyre-le-vieil. 1920. RHO
Dr. Knock. 1923.
    Granville-Barker, H., tr.
        BENS3

ROMAN, MIKHAIL
The new arrival. (1965) ABL

ROME, HAROLD JACOB, 1908-
Fanny. See Behrman, Samuel
    Nathaniel and Logan, Joshua.
    Fanny (music and lyrics by)
Wish you were here. See Kober,
    Arthur and Logan, Joshua.
    Wish you were here (music
    and lyrics by)

ROMERIL, JOHN
Chicago, Chicago. See The man
    from Chicago
The man from Chicago. 1969.

FOUAC

RONDER, JACK, 1924-
This year, next year. 1960.
    PLAN22
    Variant title: Wedding day
Wedding day. See This year,
    next year

RONILD, PETER, 1928-
Boxing for one person. See
    Boxing for one
Boxing for one. (1964)
    Shaw, P., tr. MNOD
    Variant titles: Boxing for
        one person; Boxning for en
        person
Boxning for en person. See
    Boxing for one

ROPES, BRADFORD
42nd Street. See Stewart,
    Michael. 42nd Street (from
    the novel by)

ROSE, DAVID, 1910-
Winged victory (music by). See
    Hart, Moss. Winged victory

ROSE, REGINALD, 1920-
Dino. (1957) GRIH
Thunder on Sycamore Street.
    BRNB
Twelve angry men. CARL,
    CARLE

ROSEN, JULIUS, 1833-1892
Ein knopf. See Birmelin, John.
    Der gnopp (based on the play
    by)
Starke mitteln. See Daly,
    Augustin. Needles and pins
    (adapted from)

ROSEN, SHELDON, 1943-
The box. 1974. BRIQ
Love mouse. See Two plays:
    Love mouse; Meyer's room
Meyer's room. See Two plays:
    Love mouse; Meyer's room
Two plays: Love mouse; Meyer's
    room. 1971. KAL1
    Variant titles: Love mouse;
        Meyer's room

ROSENBERG, JAMES L., 1921-
The death and life of Sneaky

Fitch. NEWA1

ROSENBERG, JEROLD. See
Ross, Jerry (pseud.)

ROSENTHAL, ANDREW, 1917-
Third person. 1951. PLAN7

ROSS, GEORGE, 1907- , and
SINGER, CAMPBELL
Any other business. 1957.
PLAN18
Difference of opinion. 1965.
PLAN27
Guilty party. 1960. PLAN24
Variant title: Refer to
drawer
Refer to drawer. See Guilty
party
The sacking of Norman Banks.
1969. PLAN37

ROSS, JERRY (pseud. of JEROLD
ROSENBERG), 1926-1955
The pajama game. See Abbott,
George and Bissell, Richard.
The pajama game (lyrics and
music by)

ROSSO DI SAN SECONDO, PIER-
MARIA, 1889-1958
La scale. See The stairs
The stairs. 1925.
Katzin, W., tr. KAT
Variant title: La scala

ROSTAND, EDMOND, 1868-1918
Cyrano de Bergerac. 1897.
BOR, GRA, SEA
Anon. tr. LAM, WISD, ZIM
Dole, H., tr. SMN, STRB
Hall, G., tr. COTH, DID,
DIK2, HAV, HUDS2,
MACC, MACE, MACF,
MOSQ, TUCG, TUCM,
TUCN, TUCO, WATI,
WATL2, WATO, WATR,
WHI, WHK
Henderson, D., tr. HUD
Hooker, B., tr. BLOO,
CARPA, CEW, GATT,
GOLK, HILP, KNIC,
TREBA, TREBJ, TREC2,
TREE2, TREI2, WALJ,
WISE
Kingsbury, H., tr. BLOD1,
COJ, HOUK, KON, LEV,

LEVE, SHRO, TREA1
Thomas, G., and Guillemard,
M., trs. MIL
Whitehall, H., tr. WORP
Wolfe, H., tr. BENU, FOUM
La dernière nuit de Don Juan.
See The last night of Don
Juan
Don Juan's last night. See The
last night of Don Juan
The fantasticks. See The ro-
mancers
The last night of Don Juan.
1922.
Bagley, D., tr. MARL
Riggs, T., tr. KRE
Variant titles: La dernière
nuit de Don Juan; Don
Juan; Don Juan's last night
The romancers. 1894.
Anon. tr. COOK2
Clark, B., tr. BERM, PATM
Hendee, M., tr. COD
Variant titles: The fantasticks;
The romantics; Les roman-
esques
Les romanesques. See The ro-
mancers
The romantics. See The ro-
mancers

ROSTEN, NORMAN, 1914-
Mister Johnson. 1955. THEA56

ROSWITHA VON GANDERSHEIM.
See Hrotsvit, of Gandersheim

ROSZKOWSKI, DAVID
Canvas. 1972. BALLE11

ROSTROU, JEAN DE, 1609-1650
Chosroes. 1648.
Lockert, L., tr. LCOR
Variant title: Cosroês
Cosroês. See Chosroes
Le feint véritable. See Saint
Genesius
Saint Genesius. 1646?
Lockert, L., tr. LOCU
Variant titles: Le feint
véritable; Saint Genest;
Le véritable Saint Genest
Saint Genest. See Saint
Genesius
Venceslas. See Wenceshaus
Le véritable Saint Genest. See
Saint Genesius

Wenceshaus. 1647.
Lockert, L., tr. LOCR
Variant title: Venceslas

ROTTER, FRITZ, and VINCENT,
ALLEN
Letters to Lucerne. 1941.
BES41

ROUSSIN, CLAUDE, 1941-
Une job. See Looking for a
job
Looking for a job. 1972.
Van Meer, A., tr. KAL5
Variant title: Une job

ROWE, NICHOLAS, 1674-1718
Ambitious step-mother. (1700)
BELK16
The fair penitent. 1703.
BELK3, DOB, MAND, MANF,
WILE
Lady Jane Gray. 1715. BELK7
The royal convert. 1707.
BELK7
Tamerlane. 1701. BELK3
The tragedy of Jane Shore.
1713. BELK1, EIGH, HAN,
MOSE2, NET, STM, TUQ
Ulysses. 1705. BELK18

ROWELL, GEORGE, 1923-
Sixty thousand nights (script,
research and lyrics by).
See May, Val. Sixty thousand
nights
--See Woods, Aubrey, jt. auth.

ROWLEY, WILLIAM, 1585?-1642?
The birth of Merlin (sometimes
attributed to). See Anonymous
Plays. The birth of Merlin
--See also Ford, John; Middleton,
Thomas, jt. auths.

ROYLE, EDWIN MILTON, 1862-1942
The squaw man. 1905. BES99

RÓŻEWICZ, TADEUSZ, 1921-
Birth rate: The biography of
a play for the theatre. 1968.
Gerould, D., and Gerould, E.,
trs. TWEN
Variant title: Przyrost
Naturalny
Przyrost Naturalny. See Birth
rate: The biography of a

play for the theatre

ROZOV, VICTOR SERGEEICH, 1913-
In search of happiness. 1955.
Daglish, R., tr. CLKX
Variant title: V poiskach
radosti
V poiskach radosti. See In
search of happiness

RUBENSTEIN, KEN
Icarus. NEWA4

RUDKIN, DAVID, 1936-
Afore night come. 1962. NEWE7
Ashes. 1974. BES76, WES1

RUEDA, LOPE DE, 1506-1565
Las aceitunas. See The olives
La carátula. See The mask
The mask. 1551?
Starkie, W., tr. SSTW
Variant title: La carátula
The olives. 1560?
Flores, A., tr. FLOS
Variant titles: Las aceitunas;
El paso de las olivas
El paso de las olivas. See The
olives
Paso séptimo. NOR. See also
The seventh farce
The seventh farce. 16th cent.
Chambers, W., tr. BAT6,
PATT
Variant title: Paso séptimo

RUIBAL, JOSE, 1925-
El asno. See The jackass
The jackass.
Seward, T., tr. WELL
Variant title: El asno
El hombre y la mosca. See
The man and the fly
The man and the fly. 1968.
Zelonis, J., tr. WELL, WELT
Variant title: El hombre y la
mosca

RUIZ, JUAN (ARCIPRESTE DE HITA),
1283?-1351?
Dialogue between Don Melón Ortiz
and Doña Endrina. See The
gallant, the bawd and the fair
lady
The gallant, the bawd and the
fair lady (adapted from El libro
de buen amor). 1343?

Starkie, W., tr. and adapter.
SSTW
Variant title: Dialogue between
Don Melón Ortiz and Doña
Endrina
El libro de buen amor (The book
of good love). See The gallant,
the bawd and the fair lady
(adapted from El libro de buen
amor)

RUIZ DE ALARCON Y MENDOZA,
JUAN, 1581?-1639
No hay mal que por bien no venga
(Don Domingo de Don Blas).
161-? HILL
Las paredes oyen. 161-? PATT
The suspecting truth. See La
verdad sospechosa
The truth suspected. See La
verdad sospechosa
La verdad sospechosa. 1619.
ALP
Ryan, R., tr. FLOS
Variant titles: The suspecting
truth; The truth suspected

RUMMO, PAUL-EERIK, 1942-
Cinderellagame. 1969.
Männix, A., and Valgemäe, M.,
trs. CONF
Variant title: Tukkatriinumäng
Tukkatriinumäng. See Cinderel-
lagame

RUNYON, DAMON, 1884-1946
Idyll of Miss Sarah Brown.
See Swerling, Jo and Burrows,
Abe. Guys and dolls (based
on the story by)

RUSHDY, RASHAD
A journey outside the wall.
(1963) ABL

RUSS, JOANNA, 1937-
Window dressing. 1969. NEWVM

RUSSELL, CHARLES L., 1932-
Five fingers on the black hand
side. 1969? SCV

RUSSELL, GEORGE WILLIAM (A. E.,
pseud.), 1867-1935
Deirdre. 1902. CAP

RUSSELL, LAWRENCE, 1941-

Penetration. 1969. ALI

RUSTEBUEF. See Rutebeuf

RUTEBEUF, fl.1248-1277
Le miracle de Theophile. 13th
cent. AXT

RUTEBEUF. See Rutebeuf

RUZZANTE. See Beolco, Angelo

RYALL, WILLIAM BOLITHO
(William Bolitho, pseud.), 1890-1930
Overture. 1930. BES30

RYE, ELIZABETH
The three-fold path. 1935. FIN

RYERSON, FLORENCE, 1892-1965
(MRS. COLIN CLEMENTS), and
CLEMENTS, COLIN CAMPBELL.
Harriet. 1943. BES42

RYGA, GEORGE, 1932-
Indian. (Television play)
1962. OXFC, PENG

RYSKIND, MORRIE, 1895-1985
See Kaufman, George S., jt. auth.

RYTON, ROYCE, 1924-
Crown Matrimonial. 1972.
PLAN43

"S., MR., MR. OF ART," See
Stevenson, William

SA-AMI-YASUKIYO, HIYOSHI.
See Hiyoshi, Sa-Ami Yasukiyo

SAAVEDRA, GUADALUPE DE
Justice. ASF

SAAVEDRA, MIGUEL DE CERVANTES.
See Cervantes Saavedra, Miguel

SAAVEDRA RIVAS, ANGEL PEREZ DE.
See Rivas, Angel Pérez de Saavedra

SACHS, HANS, 1494-1576
Der fahrende schüler im Paradies.
See The wandering scholar from
Paradise
Der fahrende schüller mit dem

Hotel Universe. WES10
The independent female; or, A
 man has his pride, a melodrama.
 1970. SAN
San Fran scandals; a vaudeville
 exposé. 1973. SAN
Los siete. 1970. SAN

SAN SECONDO, PIERMARIA ROSSO
DI. See Rosso di San Secondo,
Piermaria

SANCHEZ, FLORENCIO, 1875-1910
Los derechos de la salud. 1907.
 ALPE
The foreign girl. See La gringa
La gringa. 1904.
 Coester, A., tr. SSTE
 Variant title: The foreign
 girl

SANCHEZ, SONIA, 1934-
Uh, uh, but how do it free us?
 (1973) NEWL

SANCHEZ GARDEL, JULIO, d.1937
La montaña de las brujas.
 See The witches' mountain
The witches' mountain. 1912?
 Fassett, J., tr. BIE
 Variant title: La montaña de
 las brujas

SANDEAU, JULES, 1811-1883. See
Augier, Emile, jt. auth.

SANFORD, JEREMY
The whelks and the cromium.
 1958. NEWE12

SAPINSLEY, ALVIN, 1921-
Even the weariest river. 1957?
 GREAB

SARDOU, VICTORIEN, 1831-1908
Fatherland. See Patrie!
Patrie! 1869.
 Clark, B., tr. LEV, LEVE
 Variant title: Fatherland
Les pattes de mouche. 1860.
 Gilmour, L., tr. DRA2,
 PLAB2, SSTG
 Variant title: A scrap of
 paper
A scrap of paper. See Les
 pattes de mouche

-- and NAJAC, EMILE DE
Divorçons. See Let's get a
 divorce!
Let's get a divorce! 1880.
 Davies, F., tr. LAB
 Goldsby, A., and R., trs.
 BENSC, PLAN31
 Variant title: Divorçons

SARMENT, JEAN, 1897-1976
The most beautiful eyes in the
 world. See Les plus beaux yeux
 du monde
Le pêcheur d'ombres. 1921. HART
 Variant title: The shadow
 fisher
Les plus beaux yeux du monde.
 1925. RHO
 Variant title: The most beautiful eyes in the world
The shadow fisher. See Le pêcheur
 d'ombres

SAROYAN, WILLIAM, 1908-1981
The cave dwellers. 1956. GARSA
Hello out there. 1942. ELKE,
 HOLP, WATE
The human comedy. See Estabrook,
 Howard. The human comedy
 (screen play based on the book
 by)
The man with the heart in the
 Highlands. See My heart's in
 the highlands
My heart's in the highlands.
 1939. BART, BENT4, ROYE,
 TREBA, TREBJ, TREC2,
 TREE3, TREI3, VOAD
 Variant title: The man with
 the heart in the highlands
The oyster and the pearl. 1953.
 THOD
The people with light coming out
 of them. 1942. GALB
The time of your life. 1939.
 BES39, BIER, BLOC, CET,
 CLUR, COTQ, CRIT, DAVM,
 FAMAL, GARZ, GATB3,
 GAVE, HATA, KERN, LAV,
 MERU, SCAR, STEI

SARTRE, JEAN-PAUL, 1905-1980
Crime passionel. See Les mains
 sales
Dirty hands. See Les mains
 sales

The flies. 1943.
  Gilbert, S., tr. TREBA,
  TREBJ, TREC2, TREE2
  Variant title: Les mouches
Huis clos. 1944. CLOU
  Anon. tr. FOUA
  Gilbert, S., tr. BRZA,
  CLKJ, MALI2, MALN2,
  NORG2, TREI2
  Stuart, S., tr. BLOC,
  GARZH, HAMI
  Variant titles: In camera;
  No exit
In camera. See Huis clos
Les mains sales. 1948. PUCC
  Variant titles: Crime pas-
  sionel; Dirty hands; Red
  gloves
Les mouches. See The flies
Men without shadows. See
  The victors
Morts sans sépulture. See
  The victors
No exit. See Huis clos
Red gloves. See Les mains
  sales
The victors. 1946.
  Abel, L., tr. COTQ
  Variant titles: Men without
  shadows; Morts sans
  sépulture

SASTRE, ALFONSO, 1926-
Ana Kleiber. See Anna
  Kleiber
Anna Kleiber. 1961.
  Pronko, L., tr. COTQ,
  COTR
  Variant title: Ana Kleiber
Condemned squad. See Death
  squad
Death squad. 1953.
  Pronko, L., tr. HOLT
  Variant titles: Condemned
  squad; Escuadra hacia
  la muerte
Death thrust. 1961.
  Pronko, L., tr. COTP
Escuadra hacia la muerte.
  See Death squad
Guillermo Tell tiene los ojos
  tristes. See Sad are the eyes
  of William Tell
Sad are the eyes of William Tell.
  Pronko, L., tr. WELL
  Variant titles: Guillermo
  Tell tiene los ojos tristes;

William Tell has sad eyes
William Tell has sad eyes. See
  Sad are the eyes of William
  Tell

SAUNDERS, JAMES, 1925-
Bodies. 1977. PLAN48
Next time I'll sing to you. 1962.
  BES63

SAUNDERS, LOUISE, 1893-
The knave of hearts. BEAC7,
  COOK1

SAVORY, GERALD, 1909-
George and Margaret. 1937.
  FIP, THH

SAVOY(!), GERALD. See Savory,
  Gerald

SAYEMON, ENAMAI NO. See Enami
  Sayemon

SAYERS, DOROTHY LEIGH (MRS.
DOROTHY FLEMING), 1893-1957
The zeal of thy house. 1937.
  FAML

-- and BYRNE, MURIEL ST. CLARE
Busman's honeymoon. 1936.
  FAMK

SCALA, FLAMINO, fl.1620
The faithful friend. 17th cent.?
  Chambers, W., tr. BAT5
  Variant title: Il fido amico
Il fido amico. See The faithful
  friend
The portrait. 1575?
  Leverton, G., tr. TREB
  Van Der Meer, E., tr. CLF2,
  LEV, LEVE
  Variant title: Il rittrato
Il rittrato. See The portrait

SCHARY, DORE, 1905-1980
The devil's advocate (based on
  the novel by Morris L. West).
  1961. BES60
Sunrise at Campobello. 1958.
  AMB, BES57, CES

SCHAUFFLER, MRS. ELSIE
(TOUGH), 1888-1935
Parnell. 1936. FAMJ

SCHEFFAUER, HERMAN GEORGE,
1878-1927
The sons of Baldur. 1908.
BOH1

SCHEHADE, GEORGES, 1910-
Histoire de Vasco. See Vasco
The history of Vasco. See
Vasco
Vasco. 1956.
Victor, L., tr. and adapter.
COTS
Variant titles: Histoire de
Vasco; The history of
Vasco

SCHENKAR, JOAN, 1942-
Signs of life. 1979. WOMA

SCHEVILL, JAMES ERWIN, 1920-
American power. See The master;
The space fan (cover title of
two unrelated 1-act plays)
The master. 1964. BALLE1
The space fan. 1964. BALLE1

SCHILDT, RUNAR, 1888-1925
Galgamannen; en midvintersaga.
See The gallows man: a mid-
winter story
The gallows man; a midwinter
story. 1922.
Alexander, H., tr. SCAN1
Variant title: Galgamannen:
en midvintersaga

SCHILLER, JOHANN CHRISTOPH
FRIEDRICH VON, 1759-1805
The camp of Wallenstein. 1798.
Churchill, J., tr. BAT10
Variant titles: Das lager;
Wallenstein; Wallensteins
lager
The death of Wallenstein. 1799.
Coleridge, S., tr. ESS,
FRA3, KRE
Variant titles: Wallenstein;
Wallensteins tod
Don Carlos. 1787.
Kirkup, J., tr. BENR2
The homage of the arts. 1804.
Coleman, A., tr. FRA3
Variant title: Die huldigung
des künste
Die huldigung des künste. See
The homage of the arts
Das lager. See The camp of

Wallenstein
Mary Stuart. 1801.
Goldstone, J., and Reich, J., trs.
HOUK
Lamport, F., tr. LAMP
Lustig, T., tr. LUST, TREB
Mellish, J., tr. and Bentley,
E., adapter. BENR2,
DRA2, PLAB2
Wallenstein (trilogy). See The
camp of Wallenstein; The death
of Wallenstein
Wallensteins lager. See The camp
of Wallenstein
Wallensteins tod. See The death
of Wallenstein
Wilhelm Tell. See William Tell
William Tell. 1804.
Martin, T., tr. CLF2, FRA3,
GREA, HARC26, MAU, SMK,
STA, WEAV2
Variant title: Wilhelm Tell

SCHISGAL, MURRAY, 1926-
All over town. 1974. BES74
The Chinese. 1970. RICK
Luv. 1963. BES64, CEQA
The typists. 1960. MARO

SCHLITT, R.
The egg. See Marceau, Felicien.
The egg (tr. and adapted by)

SCHLOSS, MARTIN F.
Totentanz. See Anonymous plays.
Totentanz (from the German
text of)

SCHLUTER, KARL, 1883-
Afsporet. See Off the rails
Off the rails. 1932.
Born, A., tr. CONT
Variant title: Afsporet

SCHMIDMAN, JO ANN
Babes in the big house (struc-
ture by). See Terry, Megan.
Babes in the big house
Running gag. 1979. (lyrics by
Megan Terry; music by Mari-
anne de Pury and Lynn Her-
rick). HIJ

SCHMIDT, HARVEY, 1929-
Celebration (music by). See
Jones, Tom. Celebration

SCHNEEMANN, CAROLEE, 1939-
Meat joy. ASF

SCHNIBBE, HARRY. See Breen,
Richard, jt. auth.

SCHNITZLER, ARTHUR, 1862-1931
The affairs of Anatol. See
Anatol
Anatol. 1893.
Colbron, G., tr. CEW
Granville-Barker, H., tr.
BENS3
Variant title: The affairs of
Anatol
--See also A farewell supper
(from Anatol)
The duke and the actress. See
The green cockatoo
Der einsame weg. See The
lonely way
A farewell supper (from Anatol).
1893.
Granville-Barker, H., tr.
MIKL
Flirtation. See Light-o'-love
Die frage an das schicksal.
See Questioning the irrevo-
cable
The game of love. See Light-
o'-love
The green cockatoo. See Der
gruene kakadu
Der gruene kakadu. 1899.
FEFH2
Samuel, H., tr. FRA20
Van Der Meer, E., tr.
LEV, LEVE
Variant titles: The duke and
the actress; The green
cockatoo
Hands around. See Round dance
Intermezzo. 1905.
Björkman, E., tr. STE
Variant title: Zwischenspiel
Lebendige stunden. 1902. STI1
Colbron, G., tr. DID
Variant title: Living hours
Liebelei. See Light-o'-love
Light-o'-love. 1895.
Morgan, B., tr. DIK1, TUCG,
TUCM, TUCN, TUCO, WATI,
WATL1
Mueller, C., tr. COTKJ
Variant titles: Flirtation; The
game of love; Liebelei; Play-
ing with love; The reckoning

Literatur. See Literature
Literature. 1902.
Coleman, A., tr. FRA20
Variant title: Literatur
Living hours. See Lebendige
stunden
The lonely way. 1904.
Björkman, E., tr. MOSQ
Leigh, J., tr. WHI
Variant title: Der einsame
weg
Merry go round. See Round
dance
Playing with love. See Light-
o'-love
Professor Bernhardi. 1912.
Borell, L., and Adam, R.,
trs. FAMJ
Questioning the irrevocable.
1893.
Chambers, W., tr. BAT12
Variant title: Die frage an
das schicksal
The reckoning. See Light-o'-
love
Reigen. See Round dance
La ronde. See Round dance
Round dance. 1897.
Bentley, E., tr. BENT2,
WELT
Mueller, C., tr. ANTH,
COTKJ, COTQ, WEIP
Wallis, K., tr. BENS1
Weigert, H., and Newhall,
P., trs. BLOC
Variant titles: Hands around;
Merry go round; Reigen;
La ronde
Zwischenspiel. See Intermezzo

SCHONHERR, KARL, 1869-1943
Faith and fireside. 1910.
Mach, E., tr. FRA16
Variant title: Glaube und
heimat
Glaube und heimat. See Faith
and fireside

SCHROCK, GLADDEN
Glutt. See Two for the silence
Madam Popov. 1970. BALLE9
Taps. See Two for the silence
Two for the silence: Glutt, and
Taps. GUTR

SCHULBERG, BUDD, 1914- , and
BREIT, HARVEY

The disenchanted (adapted from the novel by Budd Schulberg). 1958. BES58

SCHULL, (JOHN) JOSEPH. See Schull, Joseph

SCHULL, JOSEPH, 1916-1980
The Vice President. (1973)
KAL3

SCHWARTZ, DELMORE, 1913-1966
Choosing company. 1936? AME5
Paris and Helen. 1941? NEWD41
Shenandoah. 1941? KRE

SCHWARTZ, JOEL
Psalms for two Davids. 1971.
BALLE9

SCHWARTZ, YEVGENY, 1897-
The dragon. 1944.
Hayward, M., and Shukman, H., trs. GLE

SCHWEFFELBRENNER, PIT. See Rauch, Edward H. (pseud. of)

SCOTT, DUNCAN CAMPBELL, 1862-1947
Pierre. 1921. MAS1

SCOTT, MUNROE
Wu-feng. (1970) KAL1

SCOTT, PAUL, 1920-1978
Pillars of salt. 1947? RUA

SCOTTI, TOMMASO GALLARATI.
See Gallarati-Scotti, Tommaso

"SCRIBBLE, SAM"
Dolorsolatio, a local political burlesque. 1865. WAGN1

SCRIBE, AUGUSTIN EUGENE, 1791-1861
Les doigts de fée. 1858.
BENZ
Variant titles: Frocks and thrills; Lady Margaret
Frocks and thrills. See Les doigts de fée
A glass of water. See Le verre d'eau
Lady Margaret. See Les doigts de fée

Le verre d'eau. 1840. BOR
Bodee, D., tr. SSTG
Variant title: A glass of water

-- and BAYARD, J. F. A.
La frontière de savoie. See A peculiar position
A peculiar position. 1837.
Planche, J., tr. SSTG
Variant title: La frontière de savoie

SCRIBE, EUGENE. See Scribe, Augustin Eugène

SCRIBLERUS SECUNDUS, pseud.
See Fielding, Henry

SEAMI, MOTOKIYO, 1363-1443
Aoi no Uye (sometimes attributed to). See Zenchiku, Ujinobu.
Aoi no Uye
Ashikara. See The reed cutter
Atsumori. 14th cent.
Waley, A., tr. ANDI, TAV, YOHA
The brocade tree.
French, C., tr. KEE
Variant title: Nishikigi
The deserted crone.
Jones, S., tr. ANDI, KEE
Variant title: Obasute
The dwarf trees.
Waley, A., tr. ANDI, PATM, PATP
Variant title: Hachi no ki
Hachi no ki. See The dwarf trees
Haku Rakuten. 14th cent.
Waley, A., tr. ANDF
Hnajo. See Lady Han
The imperial visit to Ohara (attributed to).
Hochstedler, C., tr. KEE
Variant title: Ohara gokō
Kanehira (attributed to).
Jones, S., tr. KEE
Komachi at Sekidera
Brazell, K., tr. ANDI, KEE
Variant title: Sekidera Komachi
Lady Han.
Tyler, R., tr. KEE
Variant title: Hanjo
Nakamitsu. 15th cent.
Chamberlain, B., tr. CLF1, KRE, ORI2

Nishikigi. See The brocade tree
Obasute. See The deserted crone
Ohara gokō. See The imperial
  visit to Ohara
The reed cutter.
  O'Brien, J., tr.   KEE
  Variant title: Ashikara
Sekidera Komachi. See Komachi
  at Sekidera
Semimaru.
  Matisoff, C., tr.   KEE

SEBASTIAN, ELLEN V.
Your place is no longer with us.
1982. WES13/14

SEBIRE, FRANÇOIS DESSANDRAIS.
See Dessandrais-Sebire, François

SEBREE, CHARLES, 1914-
The dry August. 1949. HARY

SECOND, LOUIS, pseud.
Apollinaris. 1942? NEWD42

SECONDO, PIERMARIA ROSSO DI
SAN. See Rossi di San Secondo,
Piermaria

SECUNDUS, H. SCRIBLERUS, pseud.
See Fielding, Henry

SEDAINE, MICHEL JEAN, 1719-1797
Le philosophe sans le savoir.
1765. BRE, ZDA

SEDLEY, SIR CHARLES, 1639-1701
The mulberry garden. 1668.
DAVR, JEFF1

SEDLEY, WILLIAM HENRY
See Smith, William Henry

SEGURA, MANUEL ASCENSIO, 1805-
1871
Na Catita. 1856. ALPE

SEJOUR, VICTOR, 1817-1874
The brown overcoat. 1858.
HARY

SELBY, CHARLES, 1802?-1863
Kinge Richard ye Third; or, Ye
Battel of Bosworth Field.
1844. NIN2

SELWYN, EDGAR, 1875-1944, and

GOULDING, EDMUND
Dancing mothers. 1924. BES24

SENECA, LUCIUS ANNAEUS, 4?
B.C.-65 A.D.
Agamemnon. 1st cent.
  Miller, F., tr.   DUC2
Hercules furens. See Mad Her-
  cules
Hercules Oetaeus. See Hercules
  on Oeta
Hercules on Oeta. 1st cent.
  Harris, E., tr.   DUC2
  Variant title: Hercules
    Oetaeus
Mad Hercules. 1st cent.
  Miller, F., tr.   DUC2
  Variant title: Hercules furens
Medea. 1st cent.
  Anon. tr.   MALR2
  Hadas, M., tr.   COTU, ROM
  Harris, E., tr.   CROS,
    CROV, GUIN, HAPV
  Miller, F., tr.   CLF1, DUC2,
    LIDE, SANM
  Taylor, J., tr.   TAV
Octavia. 1st cent.
  Miller, F., tr.   DUC2, HOWJ,
    HOWK
Oedipus. 1st cent.
  Hadas, M., tr.   ROM
  Mendell, C., tr.   LEVI
  Miller, F., tr.   DUC2, LIDE,
    SANO
Phaedra. 1st cent.
  Bradshaw, W., tr.   MIK8
  Harris, E., tr.   HAPV
  Miller, F., tr.   DUC2, LIDE,
    SANL
The Phoenician women. 1st cent.
  Harris, E., tr.   DUC2
  Variant title: Phoenissae
Phoenissae. See The Phoenician
  women
Thyestes. 1st cent.
  Hadas, M., tr.   ROM
  Harris, E., tr.   DUC2, HAPV,
    PAR
  Harris, E., tr., and Gassner,
    J., adapter.   TREB
  Heywood, L., tr.   MAKG
  Parker, D., tr.   TENN
Troades. See The Trojan women
The Trojan women. 1st cent.
  Miller, F., tr.   DUC2
  Variant title: Troades

SENTONGO, NUWA
The invisible bond. 1972.
AFR

SERLING, ROD, 1924-1975
Patterns. 1955. HUNT
Requiem for a heavyweight.
1957. CORB, SUT3
The shelter. SUT2

SERRANO, LYNNETTE M.
The bronx zoo. 1982. YOUP

SETTLE, ELKANAH, 1648-1724
The Empress of Morocco.
1673. DOA

SEWELL, STEPHEN, 1953-
The father we loved on a beach
by the sea. 1978. THUG

SEYMOUR, ALAN, 1927-
The one day of the year. 1961.
FIO, THOP

SHA, CH'ING-CH'IEN. See Lao,
Sheh, pseud.

SHA, SEH; FU, TO; MA, YUNG;
and LI, CHI-HUANG
Letters from the south. (1964)
Shapiro, S., tr. MESE

SHA, YEH-HSIN; LI, SHOU-
CH'ENG: and YAO, MING-TE
Chia-ju wo shih chen-ti. See
If I were real
If I were real. 1979.
Gunn, E., tr. TWEN (Scene
5 only; others summarized)
Variant title: Chia-ju wo
shih chen-ti

SHA YEXIN. See Sha, Yeh-hsin

SHABAKA
Blow this mother up (song by).
See San Francisco Mime Troupe.
Factwino vs. Armageddonman

SHADOW PLAYS. See Anonymous
Plays. The death of Karna; Irawan's
wedding; The reincarnation of Rama

SHADWELL, CHARLES, d.1726
The fair quaker of Deal; or
The humours of the navy.

1710. BELK17
The humours of the navy. See
The fair quaker of Deal

SHADWELL, THOMAS, 1642?-1692
Bury fair. 1689? MOR, STM
The Lancashire witches and
Tegue O. Divelly, the Irish
priest. 1681? BAT22
The libertine. 1676. MARL
The squire of Alsatia. 1688.
JEFF3, MAND, MANF

SHAFFER, ANTHONY, 1926-
Sleuth. 1970. BES70, BEST,
RICI

SHAFFER, PETER LEVIN, 1926-
Amadeus. 1979. BES80
Black comedy. 1967. BES66,
HAVL
Equus. 1973. ALLM, BARL,
BES74, SSSI
Five finger exercise. 1958.
BES59, NEWE4
The private ear. 1962. ENG
The royal hunt of the sun. 1964.
BES65, PLAJ1, RICIS
White liars. See White lies
White lies. 1967. RICJ
Variant title: White liars

SHAIRP, MORDAUNT, 1887-1939
The green bay tree. 1933.
BES33, CEU, GAW

SHAKESPEARE, WILLIAM, 1564-1616
All's well that ends well. 1595?
GRDB27
Antony and Cleopatra. 1606?
BROI, BROH, BROJ, BUR,
CROS, DIT, DOWN, ELK, EVC2,
GOLH, GRDB27, GUTH, GUTL,
LID, MANP, MIL, OLI2, SHR,
WELT, WOOE1
Variant title: The tragedy of
Antony and Cleopatra
Arden of Feversham (sometimes at-
tributed to). See Anonymous
Plays. Arden of Feversham
As you like it. 1599? BARJ,
BARK, BRIK, CASA, GRDB26,
HOUS, OLI1, SCW1, SOU
The birth of Merlin (sometimes
attributed to). See Anonymous
Plays. The birth of Merlin
The comedy of errors. 1592?

Much ado about nothing. 1598?
GRDB26
Othello, the Moor of Venice.
1604? ACE, ANT, AUB,
BARIC, BARJ, BEAR, BENU,
BIER, BLON, BLOND, BLOO,
BOW, COOP, COTKIR, DOV,
FREG, GLO, GRDB27, GREC1,
HAE, HAVL, HOGN, JAFF,
KNIG, LEVI, LITJ, LITL,
MESS, MOL, MON, OLI1,
PERS, PERT, PERU, PERV,
REIO, SCNN, SCNO, SCNP,
SCNPL, SCNQ, SIN, SMP,
SSSI, SUTL, TAUJ, VOLI,
VOLP, VON
Variant title: The tragedy of
Othello
Pericles, Prince of Tyre. 1609?
BELG7, GRDB27
The puritan; or, The widow of
Watling street (sometimes at-
tributed to). See Anonymous
Plays. The puritan; or, The
widow of Watling street
The reign of King Edward the
third (sometimes attributed to).
See Anonymous plays. The
reign of King Edward the third
Richard II. See King Richard II
Romeo and Juliet. 1594? BARO,
BLAH, CARMI, EDAD, EVA2,
EVB2, GASS, GATS, GLO,
GPA, GRDB26, GRIF, HOLP,
JORG, OLI1, PIC, REF, SHAW,
SMN, SOM, SOMA, STS, THO,
TOB
The taming of the shrew.
1593? GRDB26, SMR
The tempest. 1611? ADV, CALD,
CONN, FEL, GRDB27, HAPS1,
HAPT1, HARC46, KER, SSST,
SSSU
Timon of Athens. 1607? GRDB27
Titus Andronicus. 1593?
GRDB26
The tragedy of Antony and Cleo-
patra. See Antony and
Cleopatra
The tragedy of Hamlet, Prince
of Denmark. See Hamlet
The tragedy of King Lear. See
King Lear
The tragedy of King Richard II.
See King Richard II
The tragedy of King Richard III.
See King Richard III

The tragedy of Macbeth. See
Macbeth
The tragedy of Othello. See
Othello, the Moor of Venice
Troilus and Cressida. 1602?
BENSB1, GRDB27, WEAN
Twelfth night; or, What you will.
1599. BARB, BENU, BIER,
COTKI, DITA, FEFL, FOT,
GOLD, GRDB27, HILP, JOHO,
MIL, OLI1, STY, WALJ
The two gentlemen of Verona.
1594? GRDB26
The winter's tale. 1610. GRDB27,
OLI2, PRAT1
A Yorkshire tragedy (sometimes
attributed to). See Anonymous
Plays. A Yorkshire tragedy
--See Fletcher, John, jt. auth.

SHAMIR, MOSHE, 1921-
He walked through the fields.
1948
Hodes, A., tr. MOADE

SHANGE, NTOZAKE (b.Paulette
Williams), 1948-
for colored girls who have considered suicide/when the rainbow is enuf. 1976. BERS

SHANK, ADELE EDLING, 1940-
Sand castles. 1982. WES15/16
Sunset/sunrise. 1979. WES4
Winter play; a hyperreal comedy
in two acts. 1980. NEWQ

SHAPIRO, MEL, 1937- . See
Guare, John, jt. auth.

SHARP, ALAN, 1934-
The long-distance piano player.
1962. NEWE12

SHARP, ANTHONY, 1915-
Nightmare abbey (adapted from
the frolic by Thomas Love
Peacock). 1952. PLAN7

SHAW, ELIZABETH LLOYD. See
Hensel, Karen, jt. auth.

SHAW, GEORGE BERNARD, 1856-
1950
Androcles and the lion. 1913.
CARN, KRM, SAND, STRB,
WISF

Arms and the man. 1894.
ABRA, ABRB2, ABRE, ABRF,
ANT, BAC, BARB, BARU,
BARV, BEAL, BEAM, BEAR,
BLON, BLOND, BOWY, CALD,
CASE, COTKIR, COTKIS,
CUBG, DOD, GASS, GATS,
GOLD, HAVI, JORG, JORH,
KERP, KNIE, KNIG, LOOF,
MANP, MIJB, MORXD, REIN,
REIP, SATJ, SCAR, SCNN,
SCNO, SCNP, SCNPL, SHAX,
WEAN, WHFM
Caesar and Cleopatra. 1899.
BAIC, BIER, DIP, DIT, FREI,
GREAB, GOLH, JOHN, KET,
KON, LOR, MORT, REIL,
REIO, REIT, WEIS, WEIW
Candida. 1895. BARR, BONA,
BONB, COOP, DITA, HAVG,
KNIC, KNID, LOCLB, PERT,
PERU, PERV, STEI, TRE,
TREA1, TREBA, TREBJ,
TREC2, TREE3, TREI3
The devil's disciple. 1897.
BAUL, BOY, BOYN, CAPU,
CLM, CLN, CUBH, FREH, KIN,
LOCLA, PIC, SUL
The doctor's dilemma. 1906.
LID, TRI, TRIA, WARI, WARL
Don Juan in hell (from Man and
superman). 1907. BALL
Getting married. 1909. ULAN,
WEAL
Heartbreak house. 1920. BONB,
BONC, COTKIT, DOT, FOUX,
SEN, TREBJ, WEIP
How he lied to her husband.
1904. HOGI
John Bull's other island. 1904.
BARF, GREJ (act I, only)
Major Barbara. 1905. ABC,
ABRH, BAIC, BAIE, BARG,
BARJ, BARK, BARL, BENSB2,
BLOC, BOW, BUR, CLLC,
COK, COTKR, COTQ, GORE,
HAVHA, HEA, HEAL, LIEF,
LIEG, LITC, RAI, REIW,
REIWE, SALE, SCNQ, SSSI,
WAIU, WAIW, WEIM
Man and superman. 1903. AUG,
BLOC, HAPS2, HAPT2, ROET,
WATA
The man of destiny. 1897.
ALTE, DANI, FEFL, STEI
Misalliance. 1919. COTKI
Mrs. Warren's profession. 1902.

ABRJ, CLKY, SIXB, WELT,
WOM
Passion, poison and petrifaction;
or, The fatal gazogene. 1905.
THOD
Pygmalion. 1912. BARIC, BROI,
BROY, COX, DAI, DEAR,
EAVE, FOUK, FOUM, GOLK,
GOO, HEIS, KEN, KRM, LITI,
LITJ, MAE, ROHR, SDQ, SEVT,
SHAV, SHAW, SIN, SOU, WATE,
WISE
--See Lerner, Alan Jay. My fair
lady (adapted from)
Saint Joan. 1923. ALLK, ALLM,
BENSB2, BROI, CLL, COTX,
DOV, HAE, HIG, KER, MALN2,
SWA, THF, WAGC4
The shewing up of Blanco Posnet.
1909. BARH
The six of Calais. 1934. HOGF
Widowers' houses. 1892. BAI

SHAW, IRWIN, 1912-1984
Bury the dead. 1936. AMB,
AND, BENSPB, EDAD, FAMJ,
GAS, GATB2, KOZ

SHAW, ROBERT, 1927-1978
The man in the glass booth.
1968. BES68, PLAN34

SHAWN, WALLACE, 1943-
Mr. Frivolous. See A thought in
three parts
Summer evening. See A thought
in three parts
A thought in three parts (three
one-act plays: Summer evening; The youth hostel; Mr.
Frivolous). 1977. WOQ2
Youth hostel. See A thought in
three parts

SHAY, FRANK, 1888-1954
A Christmas carol (adapted from
the story by Charles Dickens).
1929? LEV, LEVE

SHEEAN, JOHN J.
Babes in the bighouse (music by).
See Terry, Megan. Babes in
the bighouse

SHEH, LU. See Lao, Sheh

SHEIN, BRIAN, 1947-

Cowboy island. (1972) FIFVE

SHEINEN, LEV ROMANOVICH,
1905- . See Tur, Leonid
Davidovich, jt. auth.

SHELDON, EDWARD BREWSTER,
1886-1946
The boss. 1911. QUIJ, QUIJR,
QUIK, QUIL, QUIM, QUIN
The jest. See Benelli, Sem.
The jest (tr. and adapted by)
"Man's extremity is God's op-
portunity." See Salvation
Nell
Romance. 1913. BAK, BES09
Salvation Nell. 1908. GARX,
GATB1
Variant title: "Man's extremity
is God's opportunity"

SHELLEY, ELSA (MRS. IRVING
KAYE DAVIS)
Pick-up girl. 1944. BES43

SHELLEY, PERCY BYSSHE, 1792-
1822
The Cenci. 1886. ASG, ENGL,
HARC18, KAU, KRE, MOSE2,
SMP, TAT, TAU, TRE
Prometheus unbound. 1820.
BERN, ENGL, GREB2, HAPT2,
PRAT2, SML

SHEN, TUAN-HSIEN. See Hsia, Yen

SHEPARD, SAM (pseud. of Samuel
Shepard Rogers), 1943-
Buried child. 1978. BERS,
FAMAD
Chicago. 1965. ORZ
Fool for love; a full-length play
in one act. 1983. BES83
Forensic and the navigators.
1967. SMC
The holy ghostly. 1972. OFF
Red cross. 1968. OFF
The tooth of crime. 1973. OBG

SHEPP, ARCHIE, 1937-
Junebug graduates tonight.
KINH

SHERIDAN, MRS. FRANCES, 1724-
1766
The discovery. 1763. BELG4

SHERIDAN, RICHARD BRINSLEY
BUTLER, 1751-1816
The critic; or, A tragedy re-
hearsed. 1779. ASH, COP,
COPC1, FEFL, NET, STM
The duenna. 1775. STM
The rivals. 1775. ALLI, ALLJ,
ALLK, ALLM, ANT, BENP,
CLK1, CLKY, DEM, DRA2,
EIGH, HIG, HOUS, KEY, LITL,
MOR, NET, PLAB2, REIO,
ROB, SCAR, SHAI2, SHAJ2,
SNYD1, STM, TUP, TUQ,
TWE, UHL, WEAT1, WOO1
Saint Patrick's Day, or The
scheming lieutenant. 1775.
GOODE
Variant title: The scheming
lieutenant
The scheming lieutenant. See
Saint Patrick's Day, or the
scheming lieutenant
The school for scandal. ABRB1,
ALT, ALTE, BAC, BAUG,
BENY, BONC, BRIG, BRIX,
BRIY, BRIZ, BROJ, BROK,
CLF1, CLKW, COF, COJ,
CONP, COTKI, DAV1, DEM,
FOUB, GASS, GATS, GRE,
GREB1, GREC1, HARC18,
HAVH, HUD, KRM, KRO, LIE,
LIED1, LIEE1, MACL, MAND,
MANF, MANH, MAX, MON,
MOO, MORR, MOSE2, NET,
PIC, RUB, RUSS, SHRO, SIG,
SMO, SPD, SPDB, SPEF1,
SSSI, STA, STM, TAT, TAU,
THO, TREB, TREC, TREE1,
TREI1, TUP, TUQ, TWE, UHL,
WATT2, WILE, WOOD1, WOOE1
A trip to Scarborough. 1777.
INCA7

SHERIDAN, THOMAS, 1719-1788
The brave Irishman; or, Captain
O'Blunder (sometimes attributed
to John Preston). 1746.
BELC3, HUGH
Variant title: Captain O'Blun-
der; or, The brave Irishman
Captain O'Blunder; or, The brave
Irishman. See The brave Irish-
man
The spirit of contradiction (by a
gentleman of Cambridge). 1760.
BELC4

SHERMAN, MARTIN
Bent. 1978. BES79
Passing by. 1974. GAW

SHERRIFF, ROBERT CEDRIC,
1896-1975
Badger's green. 1930. SIXD
The colonel's lady (screenplay
based on the story by W.
Somerset Maugham). JORG
Home at seven. 1950. BARV
Journey's end. 1928. BES28,
CEU, CHA, CHAN, CHAR,
FAO, FREI, FUL, HUDS2,
LOV, MOD, PLAD, STAT,
STAU, STAV, TRE, TREA1,
TREBA, TREC2, TREE3,
TREI3
The long sunset. 1955. PLAN12
A shred of evidence. 1960.
PLAN22
The telescope. 1957. PLAN15

-- and DE CASÁLIS, JEANNE
St. Helena. 1935. BES36,
FAMI

SHERWOOD, ROBERT EMMET, 1896-
1955
Abe Lincoln in Illinois. 1938.
BES38, BIER, BROX, CALG,
CALP, CASS, CLH, COOJ,
CORF, COTE, COTH, GARZ,
GATB2, GOW, GOWA, HAT,
HATA, HAVD, HAVE, NAGE,
PROD, ROLF, WAT1, WATO
Idiot's delight. 1936. BES35,
CLUR, CORE, CORF, FAMAL,
GAS, HIL, MERU, MOSH,
SIXP
The petrified forest. 1935.
BES34, CET, DOWM, MOSL,
WATC2
Reunion in Vienna. 1931.
BES31, FAME, THF
The road to Rome. 1926.
BES26, GASB
The rugged path. 1945. BES45
Second threshold. See Barry,
Philip. Second threshold
(revised by)
There shall be no night. 1940.
BES39, CORB, DUR
Tovarich. See Deval, Jacques.
Tovarich (tr. and adapted by)

SHEVELOVE, BURT, 1915-1982, and

GELBART, LARRY
A funny thing happened on the
way to the Forum. 1962.
(Adapted from Plautus'
Pseudolus.) GOODE

SHEZI, MTHULI, d.1972
Shanti. 1973. SOUT

SHI, JUNBAO, 1192-1276
Qui Hu tries to seduce his own
wife. 13th cent.
Dolby, W., tr. EIG
Variant title: Qiu Hu xi-gi
Qiu Hu xi-gi. See Qui Hu tries
to seduce his own wife

SHIELS, GEORGE, 1886-1949
The new gossoon. 1930. CAN

SHIELS, JOHN WILSON, 1871-1929
Nec-natama. 1914. BOH3

SHIH, YÜ-CHO
Picking up the jade. See
Picking up the jade bracelet
Picking up the jade bracelet.
Scott, A., tr. SXC3
Variant title: Picking up the
jade

SHIKO, OKAMURA. See Okamura,
Shikō

SHINE, TED, 1931-
Contribution, 1969. BRAS
Herbert III. 1974. HARY
Morning, noon and night.
(1964) REAG
The woman who was tampered with
in youth. (1980) CEN

SHIOMI, R. A.
Yellow fever. 1982. WES13/14

SHIPLEY, LISA
The bathtub. 1979. WES5

SHIRLEY, JAMES, 1596-1666
The cardinal. 1641. BAS,
BROC, LAWT, NEI, PAR, WALL
The gamester. See Gamesters
Gamesters. 1634. BELK19
Hyde Park. (1637) DPR2
The lady of pleasure. 1635.
BAS, HAPRA2, HAPRB2,
KNOW, NEI, SCH, SCI,

SCJ, SPE
The royall master. 1638. GAY3
The traitor. 1631. OLH, OLI2,
TAV
Triumph of peace. 1634. ETO
The wedding. 1626. KNOW

SHIRLEY, WILLIAM, 1739-1780
Edward the black prince.
(1750) BELK16

SHKVARKIN, VASILII VASIL'-
EVICH, 1893-
Father unknown. 1933.
Bakshy, H., tr. BAKS

SHOVELLER, BROCK
Westbound 12:01. 1970. KAL2

SHŌZŌ I, NAMIKI. See Namiki,
Shōzō I

SHUDRAKA (KING), 1st cent.
B.C.-1st cent. A.D.?
The little clay cart (attributed
to). 1st cent. B.C.-1st
cent. A.D.?
Lal, P., tr. BRA, LAL
Oliver, R., tr. WEL, PLAN29
Ryder, A., tr. ANDF
Wilson, H., tr. DOWS
Variant title: The toy
cart
The toy cart. See The little
clay cart

SHUE, LARRY, 1946-1985
The foreigner. 1983. BES84

SHULMAN, MAX, 1919-   , and
SMITH, ROBERT PAUL
The tender trap. 1954. THEA55

SHVARTS, EVGENII L'VOVICH,
1897-1958
The shadow. 1940.
Reeve, F., tr. REEV2

SICAM, GERONIMO D., and
CASINO, JESUS
Mir-i-nisa (based on the story
by José García Villa).
195-? EDAD

SIDDONS, HENRY, 1774-1815
Time's a tell-tale. 1807. INCA10

SIDNEY, SIR PHILIP, 1554-1586

The lady of May. 1579? PAR

SIERRA, GREGORIO MARTINEZ.
See Martínez Sierra, Gregorio

SIERRA, MARIA MARTINEZ. See
Martínez Sierra, María

SIERRA, RUBÉN
La raza pura, or racial, racial.
1969. CONR

SIEVEKING, LANCELOT DE
GIBERNE, 1896-1972
The strange case of Dr. Jekyll
and Mr. Hyde (adapted from
the novel by Robert Louis
Stevenson). 1956. PLAN15

SIFTON, CLAIRE, 1897-1980, and
SIFTON, PAUL
Give all thy terrors to the wind.
1936? KOZ

SIFTON, PAUL, 1898-1972. See
Sifton, Claire, jt. auth.

SIGURJONSSON, JOHANN, 1880-
1919
Bjaerg-Ejvind og hans hustru.
See Eyvind of the hills
Eyvind of the hills. 1911.
Schanche, H., tr. DIE
Variant title: Bjaerg-
Ejvind og hans hustru
Galtra-Loftur. See The wish
Loftor the magician. See The
wish
Ønsket. See The wish
The wish. 1914.
Haugen, E., tr. HAVHN
Variant titles: Galtra-Loftur;
Loftur the magician; Ønsket

SIMARD, ANDRÉ, 1949-
En attendant Gaudreault. See
Waiting for Gaudreault
Waiting for Gaudreault. 1976.
Beissel, H., and Francière,
A., trs. KAL5
Variant title: En attendant
Gandreault

SIMON, (MARVIN) NEIL, 1927-
Barefoot in the park. 1963.
BES63, MOST
Biloxi blues. 1985. BES84
California suite; a comedy in two

acts and four playlets:
Visitor from New York;
Visitor from Philadelphia;
Visitors from London;
Visitors from Chicago. 1976.
BES76
Chapter two. 1977. BERS,
BES77
Come blow your horn. 1961.
LITJ
The gingerbread lady. 1970.
BES70
The good doctor. 1973. BES73
I ought to be in pictures. 1980.
BES79
Last of the red hot lovers. 1969.
BES69
The odd couple. 1965. BES64,
COLT, GAT, GATB4, RICIS,
SSSI
Plaza suite. 1968. BES67
(3 one-act plays: Visitor from
Forest Hills; Visitor from
Hollywood; Visitor from Mamar-
oneck)
The prisoner of Second Avenue.
1971. BES71, GARTL
The sunshine boys. 1972.
BES72, BEST, KNIH
Visitor from Forest Hills (part of
Plaza Suite). 1968. RICK
Visitor from Hollywood. See
Plaza suite
Visitor from Mamaroneck. See
Plaza suite
Visitor from New York. See
California suite
Visitor from Philadelphia. See
California suite
Visitors from London. See
California suite
Visitors from Chicago. See
California suite

SIMONOV, KONSTANTIN MIKHAILO-
VICH, 1915-1979
The Russian people. See
The Russians
The Russians. 1942.
Odets, C., tr. SEVP
Shelley, G., and Guthrie, T.,
trs. FOUT
Variant titles: The Russian
people; Russkie lyndie
Russkie lyndie. See The Russians

SIMPSON, ELIZABETH. See

Inchbald, Mrs. Elizabeth (Simpson)

SIMPSON, NORMAN FREDERICK,
1919-
Oh! 1961. PLAAB
One way pendulum. 1959. POP
A resounding tinkle. 1957.
NEWE2, OBSE

SINGER, CAMPBELL, 1909- .
See Ross, George, jt. auth.

SIROIS, SERGE, 1953-
Dodo. 1971?
Van Burek, J., tr. KAL5
Variant title: Dodo l'enfant do
Dodo l'enfant do. See Dodo

SISSON, ROSEMARY ANNE, 1923-
The queen and the Welshman.
1957. PLAN18
The splendid outcasts. 1959.
PLAN19

SKELTON, JOHN, 1460-1529
Magnyfycence. 1516? FOUN,
POLL

ŠKĖMA, ANTANAS, 1911-1961
The awakening; a play in three
sequences: Footsteps; La
Cumparsita; The awakening.
(1956)
Škėma-Snyder, K., tr. CONF
Variant titles: La Cumparsita;
Footsteps; Pabudimas
La Cumparsita. See The awaken-
ing
Footsteps. See The awakening
Pabudimas. See The awakening

SKINNER, CORNELIA OTIS, 1901-
1979. See Taylor, Samuel, jt. auth.

SKOLNIK, WILLIAM, 1950-
Hoarse muse. See Campbell,
Paddy. Hoarse muse (music
by)

SLADE, BERNARD, 1930-
Same time, next year. 1975.
BERS, BES74, FAMAD, MOST
Tribute. 1978. BES77

SLADE, JULIAN, 1930-
Sixty thousand nights (music
and lyrics by). See May,

Val. Sixty thousand nights
Trelawny, a musical play (music
by). See Woods, Aubrey,
and Rowell, George. Trelawny,
a musical play

SLOMAN, ROBERT. See Dobie,
Laurence, jt. auth.

SLOVES, CHAIM, 1905-
Haman's downfall. 1944.
Rosenfeld, M., tr. LIFS

SŁOWACKI, JULIUSZ, 1809-1849
Fantazy. 1867.
Segel, H., tr. POB
Variant titles: The incor-
rigible; The new
Deianira; Niepoprawni;
Nowa Dejanira
The incorrigible. See Fantazy
The new Deianira. See Fantazy
Niepoprawni. See Fantazy
Nowa Dejanira. See Fantazy

SMALL, CHARLIE
The Wiz (music and lyrics by).
See Brown, William F. The
Wiz

SMEE, LILLIAN
No thoroughfare. 1935. FIN

SMITH, ALBERT RICHARD, 1816-
1860
The cricket on the hearth
(adapted from the story by
Charles Dickens). 1859.
CARP

SMITH, BETTY, 1904-1972
Fun after supper. 1940. GALB

SMITH, CHARLOTTE (TURNER),
1749-1806
What is she? 1799. INCA10

SMITH, DODIE, pseud. See Smith,
Dorothy Gladys

SMITH, DOROTHY GLADYS
(Dodie Smith; C. L. Anthony,
pseuds.), 1896-
Autumn crocus. 1931. FAMAN,
PLAD, PLAL2
Call it a day. 1935. BES35,
FAMI

Dear octopus. 1938. PLAL1
Service. 1932. FAMC
Touch wood. 1934. FAMF

SMITH, EDMUND (Edmund "Rag"
Smith), 1672-1710
Phaedra and Hippolitus. 1706.
BELK10

SMITH, HARRY JAMES, 1880-1918
Mrs. Bumpstead-Leigh. 1911.
BES09, MOSJ, MOSK, MOSL

SMITH, HOWARD FORMAN
Blackberryin'. 1922? SHAY

SMITH, JOHN, 1752-1809
A dialogue between an Englishman
and an Indian. 1781? MONR
A little teatable chitchat, ala-
mode; or an ancient discovery
reduced to modern practice;--
Being a dialogue, and a dish
of tea. 1781? MONR

SMITH, MARIAN SPENCER
An American grandfather.
(1924) IFKO

SMITH, MICHAEL, 1935-
Captain Jack's revenge. 1970.
NEWA4
The next thing. 1966. SMC

SMITH, RICHARD PENN, 1799-1854
The bombardment of Algiers.
1829? AMP13
The last man; or, The cock of
the village (adapted from
Le coq de village, by Charles
Décour and Anne Théodore).
1822. AMP13
The sentinels; or, The two
sergeants. 1829. AMP13
Shakespeare in love (adapted from
Shakespeare amoureux, by
Alexandre Duval). 1804.
AMP13
The triumph at Plattsburg. 1830.
QUIJ, QUIK
A wife at a venture. 1829.
AMP13
William Penn. 1829. AMP13

SMITH, ROBERT PAUL, 1915- .
See Shulman, Max, jt. auth.

SMITH, WILLIAM HENRY, 1806-
1872
  The drunkard; or, The fallen
    saved. 1844. MONR, VIC

SMITH, WINCHELL, 1871-1933, and
BACON, FRANK
  Lightnin'. 1918. CEY

SMOLIN, DMITRY
  Lysistrata. See Aristophanes.
  Lysistrata (tr. and adapted
    by)

SMOLLETT, TOBIAS GEORGE, 1721-
1771
  The reprisal. 1757. BELC2

SNEIDER, VERN, 1916-
  The teahouse of the August
    moon. See Patrick, John.
  The teahouse of the August
    moon (adapted from the novel
    by)

SNOW, ANDREA
  Factperson (script and songs by).
    See San Francisco Mime
    Troupe. Factperson

SOBOL, YEHOSHUA
  The night of the twentieth.
    Salkind, M., tr. MOADE

SOLLY, BILL, 1931- , and WARD,
DONALD
  Boy meets boy. 1975. HOF

SOLOMON, PETER
  Factwino meets the moral
    majority (script by). See
    San Francisco Mime Troupe.
  Factwino meets the moral
    majority

SOLOVEV, VLADIMIR ALEK-
SANDROVICH, 1907-
  Field Marshal Kutuzov. 1939.
    Robbins, J., tr. SEVP

SOLOVYOV, VLADIMIR A. See
Solovev, Vladimir Aleksandrovich

SOMIN, WILLI OSCAR, 1898-
  Attentat. See Close quarters
  Close quarters. 1935.
    Lennox, G., tr. and adapter.

    FAMH
    Variant title: Attentat

SØNDERBY, KNUD, 1909-1966
  En kvinde er overflødig. See
    A woman too many
  A woman too many. 1942.
    Roughton, A., tr. CONT
    Variant title: En kvinde er
    overflødig

SONDHEIM, STEPHEN, 1930-
  Company (music and lyrics by).
    See Furth, George.
    Company
  Follies (music and lyrics by).
    See Goldman, James. Follies
  A funny thing happened on the
    way to the Forum (music and
    lyrics by). See Shevelove,
    Burt. A funny thing happened
    on the way to the Forum
  Gypsy (lyrics by). See Laurents,
    Arthur. Gypsy
  A little night music (music and
    lyrics by). See Wheeler,
    Hugh. A little night music
  Pacific overtures (music and
    lyrics by). See Weidman,
    John. Pacific overtures
  Sunday in the park with George
    (music and lyrics by). See
    Lapine, James. Sunday in the
    park with George
  Sweeney Todd, the demon barber
    of Fleet Street (music and
    lyrics by). See Wheeler,
    Hugh. Sweeney Todd, the
    demon barber of Fleet Street
  West side story (lyrics by). See
    Laurents, Arthur. West side
    story

SOPHOCLES, 496-406 B.C.
  Ajax. 5th cent. B.C.
    Jebb, R., tr. GRDB5
    Moore, J., tr. GREP2
    Trevelyan, R., tr. OAT1
  Antigone. 441 B.C.
    Anon. tr. BLON, BRIT, CARN,
      EVB1, WORM
    Arnott, P., tr. HAVH, HAVHA
    Banks, T., tr. MALI1, MALN1,
      NORG1, NORI, SOM, SOMA,
      VON
    Cocteau, J., adapter, and
      Wildman, C., tr. BENU, CLM

Fitts, D., and Fitzgerald, R.,
trs. ABC, ADV, ALT,
ALTE, ANT, BARI, BARIA,
BARIC, BARU, BAUL,
BEAR, BONA, BONB,
BONC, CONG, CONP,
COOP, COX, CRAF, DIT,
DOV, DOWS, FIFT, GOLD,
GOLH, GUTH, GUTL, HIG,
HOGF, HOLP, JOHO, KERN,
KERO, LEVJ, LITL, MON,
MONA, MORT, MORV,
MORW, MORX, PERU, REIO,
ROHR, SCNP, SIN, SSST,
SSSU, SUL, TAUJ
Francklin, T., tr. MIK7
Gassner, J., tr. GATS
Jebb, R., tr. GLO, GRDB5,
GREE, HUD, KNID, KNIE,
OAT1, OAM, OATH, SHAV,
SHAX, THO, TRE, TREA2
Jebb, R., tr. and Rapp, A.,
modifier. GRDG, KNIG,
KNIH
Kitto, H., tr. CARLG
Lucas, F., tr. LUCA, LUCAB,
LUCAF
Neufeld, M., tr. MALR1
O'Sheel, S., tr. FREH, LIND
Plumptre, E., tr. BAT1,
BUCK, BUCL, BUCM,
EVA1, HARC8, HAVI, HIB,
HIBB, HOUS, HUDS2,
HUDT, INGW, MAST, THOM,
THON
Robinson, C., tr. ROBK
Roche, P., tr. BARH
Townsend, M., tr. CASE,
KOTKIR, COTY, SUTL
Watling, E., tr. BLOND,
BLOO, KON, PATM, PATP,
REF
Way, A., tr. STA
Whitelaw, R., tr. ATTI,
CLM, FEFT, ROBI, ROBJA,
TEN
Wyckoff, E., tr. GREP2,
GRER1
Young, G., tr. CLF1, CROS,
PLAG, SEBO, SEBP
Electra. 5th cent.
Anon. tr. HAPD, WED
Campbell, L., tr. FEFT
Ferguson, F., tr. FIFT,
FOR
Grene, D., tr. GREP2,
GRER2

Jebb, R., tr. GRDB5, OAT1
Kitto, H., tr. CLL, REA
Plumptre, E., tr. CLKW
Whitelaw, R., tr. ATT3
Young, G., tr. PLAG
King Oedipus. See Oedipus the
king
Oedipus at Colonus. 401 B.C.
Anon. tr. GRER3
Campbell, L., tr. FEFT,
ROBJA
Fitzgerald, R., tr. FIFT,
GREP2, MALI1
Jebb, R., tr. GRDB5, OAT1
Moebius, W., tr. COOA
Plumptre, E., tr. ROBJ
Young, G., tr. KRE
Variant title: Oedipus
coloneus
Oedipus coloneus. See Oedipus
at Colonus
Oedipus, King of Thebes. See
Oedipus the king
Oedipus rex. See Oedipus the
king
Oedipus the king. 5th cent.
Anon. tr. BEAS, CASA,
EVB1, MABC, SANK, SATJ,
SCNN, SCNPL, STS
Arnott, P., tr. HAPRL, MOL,
REIW, REIWE
Banks, T., tr. BOY, MALI1
Berkowitz, L., tr. BAIC,
MALN1
Berkowitz, L., and Brunner,
T., trs. BAIG, NORG1,
NORI
Bywater, I., tr. SCNO
Cavender, K., tr. GOU1,
SEVT, SMA, WEIS, WEIW
Cook, A., tr. COOA, DAVK,
HAPO, LIND
Fitts, D., and Fitzgerald, R.,
trs. ACE, ALLI, ALLJ,
ALLK, ALLM, ALS, BARI,
BARIA, BARIC, BARJ,
BEAM, BIER, BOW, BRIX,
BRIY, BRIZ, BROI, BUR,
CALD, CLKJ, CONO, DEAR,
DEAS, DIP, DIT, DITA,
DOV, DOWN, DUH, ELK,
FIFR, FREG, GOLD, GORE,
HEA, HEAL, HOGI, HOGN,
JAFF, JOHN, KEN, KINN,
KNO, KNOJ, LEVI, LID,
LITC, LITI, LITJ, LITN,
MADB, MORXB, MORXD,

Two threads. 1943.
Anon. tr. (revised by P. N.
Furbank) CONT
Variant title: To traade

SPARK, MURIEL SARAH, 1918-
Doctors of philosophy. 1962.
RHE
The party through the wall
(radio play). 1901. PLAAB

SPEARS, STEVE J., 1951-
King Richard. 1978. THUG

SPENCE, EULALIE, 1894-
The starter. 1927. LOC
Undertow. 1928. HARY

SPENCER, JAMES
A bunch of the gods were sitting
around one day. 1973.
BALLE12

SPENSLEY, PHILIP
Hell's bells. 1967. ALJ

SPEWACK, MRS. BELLA (COHEN),
1899- , and SPEWACK, SAMUEL
Boy meets girl. 1935.
BES35, CET, FAMJ, GAS,
SAFF
Kiss me Kate (adapted from
The taming of the shrew,
by William Shakespeare; music
and lyrics by Cole Porter).
1948. RICO
Leave it to me! (Music and
lyrics by Cole Porter).
1938. RICM
My 3 angels (adapted from La
cousine des anges, by Albert
Husson). 1953. BES52,
GARZH, THEA53

SPEWACK, SAMUEL, 1899-1971
Two blind mice. 1949. BES49
Under the sycamore tree. 1952.
PLAN7
--See also Spewack, Mrs. Bella
(Cohen), jt. auth.

SPINETTI, VICTOR, 1933-
See Kennedy, Adrienne, jt. auth.

SPUNDE, WALTER G.
The mercenary. SHAT

SRI-HARSHADEVA. See Harsha,
son of Hira

STAFF OF THE LIVING NEWSPAPER
Triple-A plowed under. 1936.
FEF

STALLINGS, LAURENCE, 1894-1968.
See Anderson, Maxwell, jt. auth.

STARKWEATHER, DAVID, 1935-
The poet's papers. (1970) NEWA3

STEELE, SIR RICHARD, 1672-1729
The conscious lovers. 1722.
BELK4, COF, EIGH, JEFF4,
MAND, MANF, MANH, MOR,
MOSE1, NET, STM, TAT, TAU,
TAY, TUP, TUQ, WILE
The funeral, or Grief a la mode.
1701. BELK8
Grief a la mode. See The funeral.
The tender husband. 1705.
BELK8, SIG

STEELE, RUFUS, 1877-1935
The fall of Ug. 1913. BOH3

STEELE, SILAS SEXTON
The crock of gold; or, The toiler's
trials. 1845. AMP14

STEELE, WILBUR DANIEL, 1886-1970
The giant's stair. 1924? THO

STEFFANSSON, DAVID JOHANN,
1895-1964
The golden gate. 1941.
Gathorne-Hardy, G., tr.
FIL, HAVHN
Variant title: Gullna hlidid
Gullna hlidid. See The golden
gate

STEIN, GERTRUDE, 1874-1946
Daniel Webster eighteen in America.
1937? NEWD37, SPC

STEIN, JOSEPH, 1912-
Fiddler on the roof (music by
Jerry Bock, lyrics by Sheldon
Harnick). 1964. BES64,
GAT, GATB4, RICIS, RICO

STEINBECK, JOHN, 1902-1968
The moon is down. 1942. BES41

Of mice and men. 1937.
BENPB, BES37, CLUR, CRIT,
FAMAL, GAS, GAVE, SATI

STEPHENS, HENRY MORSE, 1857-
1919
St. Patrick at Tara. 1909.
BOH2

STEPPLING, JOHN, 1951-
Neck. 1982. PLACE

STERLING, GEORGE, 1869-1926
The triumph of Bohemia. 1906.
BOH1

STERNHEIM, CARL, 1878-1942
Die Kassette. See The strongbox
Die marquise von Arcis. See
The mask of virtue
The mask of virtue. 1920.
Dukes, A., tr. and adapter.
FAMH
Variant title: Die marquise
von Arcis
A pair of drawers. See The
underpants
A place in the world. 1913.
Bentley, E., tr. BENS1
Clark, B., and Katzin, W.,
trs. KAT
Variant title: Der snob;
The snob
Der snob. See A place in the
world
The snob. See A place in the
world
The strongbox. 1912.
Edwards, M., and Reich, V.,
trs. SOK
Variant title: Die Kassette
The underpants. 1911.
Bentley, E., tr. BENT6
Variant title: A pair of
drawers

STEVENSON, ROBERT LOUIS, 1850-
1894
The strange case of Jekyll and
Mr. Hyde. See Sieveking,
Lance. The strange case of
Dr. Jekyll and Mr. Hyde
(adapted from)

STEVENSON, WILLIAM ("MR. S.
MR. of ART." pseud.), 1521-1575
Gammer Gurton's nedle. See

Gammer Gurton's needle
Gammer Gurton's needle (supposed
author). 1552? ADA, BAS,
BOA, CRE, DPR1, FAR,
GARZB, GAY1, HEIL, LEV,
LEVE, MARG, NES, THWO,
WATT2
Variant title: Gammer Gurton's
nedle

STEWART, DONALD OGDEN, 1894-
1980
Rebound. 1930. BES29

STEWART, DOUGLAS, 1913-
Ned Kelly. 1943? THOP

STEWART, DOUGLAS ALEXANDER,
1913-
The golden lover (radio play).
1943. FIO

STEWART, MICHAEL, 1924-1987
Hello, Dolly! (music and lyrics
by Jerry Herman; based on
The matchmaker, by Thornton
Wilder). 1964. BES63

-- and BRAMBLE, MARK
42nd Street (music and lyrics
by Harry Warren and Al Dubin;
based on the novel by Bradford
Ropes). 1980. BES80

STILES, THELMA JACKSON, 1939-
No one man show. 1971. CEN

STITT, MILAN, 1941-
The runner stumbles. 1976.
BES75

STONE, ARNOLD M. See Freed,
Donald, jt. auth.

STONE, JOHN AUGUSTUS, 1800-
1834
Metamora; or, The last of the
Wampanoags. 1829.
AMP14, CLA, COY, MONR
Tancred, King of Sicily; or,
The archives of Palermo.
1831. AMP14

STONE, PETER H., 1930- .
1776. (music and lyrics by
Sherman Edwards) 1969.
BES67, GARTL, RICO

-- and MAYER, TIMOTHY S.
My one and only (music by
George Gershwin; lyrics by
Ira Gershwin; "The score
is a collection of Gershwin
numbers from previous
Broadway shows ... unless
otherwise noted.."). 1983.
BES82

STOPPARD, TOM (b. Tomas
Straussler), 1937-
Jumpers. 1974. BES73
The real inspector hound. 1968.
LITJ
The real thing; a play in two
acts. 1982. BES83
Rosencrantz and Guildenstern
are dead. 1966. BES68,
NIL
Travesties. 1975. BES75

STORACE, STEPHEN, 1763-1796
No song no supper (music by).
See Hoare, Prince. No song
no supper

STOREY, DAVID MALCOLM, 1933-
The changing room. 1971.
BES72, PLAN44
The contractor. 1969. BES73,
PLAN40
Home. 1970. BES70, PLAN40
In celebration. 1969. PLAN38
The restoration of Arnold
Middleton. 1967. PLAN35

STOREY, ROBERT
Touch it light. 1957. PLAN18

STORM, LESLEY (pseud. of Mrs.
Mabel Margaret (Cowie) Clark),
1903-1971
Black chiffon. 1949. PLAN2

STOWE, MRS. HARRIET ELIZABETH
(BEECHER), 1811-1896
Uncle Tom's cabin. See Aiken,
George L. Uncle Tom's Cabin
(based on the novel by)

STRACHAN, ALAN, 1946-
See Guinness, Alec, jt. auth.

STRAMM, AUGUST, 1874-1915
Awakening. 1915?
Ritchie, J., and Garten, H.,

trs. RITS

STRANACK, JOHN
With malice aforethought. 1966.
BALLE3

STRATTON, ALLAN, 1951-
Rexy! 1981. PENG

STRAUSS, BOTHO, 1944-
Three acts of recognition. 1980.
WES8

STRINDBERG, AUGUST, 1849-1912
Brott och brott. See There are
crimes and crimes
Comrades. 1888.
Oland, E., and W., trs.
TUCG, TUCM, TUCN, TUCO
Variant title: Kamraterna;
Marodörer
Countess Julie. See Miss Julia
Creditors. 1889.
Sprigge, E., tr. PLAN21
Variant title: Fordringsägare
Crimes and crimes. See There are
crimes and crimes
The dance of death. 1901?
Ginsberg, N., tr. PLAN32
Locock, C., tr. ROET
A dream play. 1902.
Björkman, E., tr. WALJ,
WATA, WATI, WATL3
Goodman, R., tr. GOO
Locock, C., tr. DIK2
Paulson, A., tr. TREBA,
TREBJ, TREI3, WEIP
Sprigge, E., tr. AUG, BAUL,
CAPU, ROHR, WEIS
Variant titles: The dream
play; Ett drömspel
The dream play. See A dream
play
Ett drömspel. See A dream
play
Fadren. See The father
The father. 1887.
Erichsen, M., tr. DIC, SMI
Meyer, M., tr. FOUX
Oland, E., and W., trs. TRE,
TREA1, TREBA, TREBJ,
TREC2, TREE2, TREI2,
WHI
Sprigge, E., tr. FREG, GLO,
KERP
Variant title: Fadren
Fordringsägare. See Creditors

Fröken Julie. See Miss Julia
The ghost sonata. 1907.
Anon. tr. REIP
Goodman, R., tr. GOODE
Palmstierna, E., and Fagan,
J., trs. HAV
Sprigge, E., tr. BENY,
BLOC, KERP, NORG1,
REIL, REIN, REIT, REIWE,
SEN
Sprinchorn, E., tr. ALLK,
ALLM, COTQ, SEVT, WAIW
Variant titles: Spogelses-
sonaten; Spöksonaten; The
spook sonata
The great highway. 1910.
Paulson, A., tr. MODS
Variant title: Stora lands-
vägen
Kamraterna. See Comrades
Lady Julie. See Miss Julia
Marodörer. See Comrades
Miss Julia. 1888.
Anon. tr. BLON, CLN
Björkman, E., tr. CARP,
HAV, WARL
Locock, C., tr. BARK,
INTE, SATI, WOM
Sprigge, E., tr. AUG,
BLOC, CLM, COTX, DOV,
GLO, HEA, HOGN, KNIH,
LITL, REIO, REIW, SILK,
SILKI, SILN, SILO, SSSI,
STY, WEIM
Sprinchorn, E., tr. BLOND,
BONC, COTQ, COTY,
DOT, HAVH, HAVHA,
HOUP
Variant titles: Countess
Julie; Fröken Julie; Lady
Julie; Miss Julie
Miss Julie. See Miss Julia
Moderskärlek. See Motherly love
Motherly love. 1893.
Ziegler, F., tr. SHAY
Variant title: Moderskärlek
Spogelses-sonaten. See The ghost
sonata
Spöksonaten. See The ghost
sonata
The spook sonata. See The ghost
sonata
Stora landsvägen. See The great
highway
The stronger. See The stronger
woman
The stronger woman. 1890.

Anon. tr. PERS, PERT, PERU,
PERV, SCNPL, SHAY
Oras, A., tr. MORT, MORV,
MORW, MORXB, MORXD
Sprigge, E., tr. BUR, DITA,
KERN, KERO, LITN, ROY,
SCNQ
Variant title: The stronger
There are crimes and crimes.
1899.
Björkman, E., tr. MOSG,
MOSH, TREBA, TREC2,
TREE2, TREI2
Sprinchorn, E., tr. SPR
Variant titles: Brott och brott;
Crimes and crimes
To Damascus, part 1. 1900.
Paulson, A., tr. ULAN
Sprinchorn, E., tr. SPR

STRODE, WARREN CHETHAM. See
Chetham-Strode, Warren

STRONG, AUSTIN, 1881-1952
The drume of Oude. 1906.
LEV, LEVE, MIL

STROUSE, CHARLES, 1928-
Annie (music by). See Meehan,
Thomas. Annie; a musical in
two acts
Applause (music by). See
Comden, Betty and Green,
Adolph. Applause
"It's a bird, it's a plane, it's
superman" (music by).
See Newman, David and
Benton, Robert. "It's a bird,
it's a plane, it's superman"

STUART, MRS. AIMEE (McHARDY),
1886?-1981
Jeannie. 1940. FIR
Lace on her petticoat. 1950.
PLAN5
Sixteen. 1934. FAME

STUKALOV, N. F. See Pogodin,
Nikolai Federovich, pseud.

STURGES, PRESTON, 1898-1959
Strictly dishonorable. 1929.
BES29, GASB

STYNE, JULE, 1905-
Gypsy (music by). See Laurents,
Arthur. Gypsy

SUDERMANN, HERMANN, 1857-
1928
Casa paterna. See Magda
The fires of St. John. 1900.
Swickard, C., tr. MOSQ
Variant title: Johannisfeuer
Das glück im winkel. See The
vale of content
Happiness in a nook. See The
vale of content
Heimat. See Magda
Home. See Magda
Johannes. See John the Baptist
Johannisfeuer. See The fires
of St. John
John the Baptist. 1898.
Marshall, B., tr. FRA17
Variant title: Johannes
Magda. 1893.
Winslow, C., tr. WATI,
WATL2
Variant titles: Casa paterna;
Heimat; Home
The vale of content. 1895.
Leonard, W., tr. DIC
Variant titles: Das glück im
winkel; Happiness in a
nook

SUDRAKA (KING). See Shudraka
(King)

SUGIMORI, NOBUMORI. See Chikamatsu, Monzaemon

SULLIVAN, SIR ARTHUR SEYMOUR,
1842-1900 (composer). See Gilbert,
William Schwenck

SULLIVAN, L. M.
Baron's night, or Catch as
catch-can. 1973. NEWP

SUN, YU
The women's representative.
1953
Tang, S., tr. MESE

SUNDGAARD, ARNOLD, 1909-
Spirochete. 1938. FEF

SUNDUKIANTS, GAVRILL NIKI-
TOVICH, 1825-1911
The ruined family. 1888.
Collins, F., tr. ARM
Variant title: Die ruinerte
Familie

Die ruinerte Familie. See The
ruined family

SUTHERLAND, EFUA THEODORA,
1924-
Edufa. 1964. LITT

SUTRO, ALFRED, 1863-1933
John Glayde's honour. 1907.
DIG
A marriage has been arranged.
1902. PEN
The walls of Jericho. 1904.
MART

SVEINBJORNSSON, TRYGGI, 1891-
Bishop Jón Arason. 1950.
Hollander, L., tr. MODS

SWERLING, JOSEPH, 1897- ;
BURROWS, ABRAM; and LOESSER,
FRANK
Guys and dolls (based on the
story, Idyll of Miss Sarah
Brown, by Damon Runyan).
1950. BENT4, BES50

SWINBURNE, ALGERNON CHARLES,
1837-1909
Atlanta in Calydon. (1865). KAU

SYLVAINE, VERNON, 1897-1957
As long as they're happy. 1953.
PLAN9

SYLVANUS, ERWIN, 1917-
Dr. Korczak and the children.
1957.
Wellwarth, G., tr. BENB
Variant title: Korczak und
die Kinder
Korczak und die Kinder. See
Dr. Korczak and the children

SYNGE, JOHN MILLINGTON, 1871-
1909
Deirdre of the sorrows. 1910.
BARF
In the shadow of the glen. 1903.
BALL, LOCLA, MERC, STY
The playboy of the Western world.
1907. AUG, BAC, BENSB2,
BLOC, CEW, CLKW, CLKWI,
CLKY, CLLC, COK, COL2,
COTKI, COTM, COTQ, CUBE,
CUBG, DOT, DUR, FIG, FOS,
FOUX, GREAB, GREC2, HAU,

Variant title: Un geste pour
un autre
Un geste pour un autre. See
One way for another

TARKINGTON, BOOTH, 1869-1946
Clarence. 1919. BES19,
GARU
The intimate strangers. 1921.
COH
Monsieur Beaucaire. 1901.
PEN, PROB
The trysting-place. 1923?
SCWE, SCWG

-- and WILSON, HARRY LEON
The Gibson upright. 1919.
WEB
The man from home. 1908.
BES99, CEY

TARLO, LUNA. See Aaron, Joyce,
jt. auth.

TARLTON, RICHARD, d.1588
The famous victories of Henry
the fifth (sometimes attributed to). See Anonymous
Plays. The famous victories
of Henry the fifth

TASSO, TORQUATO, 1544-1595
Aminta. 1573.
Hunt, L., tr. BENSA
Oldmixon, J., tr. HAYD
Variant title: Amyntas
Amyntas. See Aminta

TATE, NAHUM, 1652-1715
A duke and no duke; or, Trapo-
lin's vagaries (adapted from
Trappolin suppos'd a prince,
by Sir Aston Cokain). 1684.
HUGH
The history of King Lear. 1681?
SUMB

TATHAM, JOHN, fl.1600
Grim the collier of Croydon;
or, The devil and his dame
(sometimes attributed to).
See Anonymous Plays. Grim
the collier of Croydon; or, The
devil and his dame

TAVEL, RONALD, 1941-
Boy on the straight-back chair.

1969. WOQ1
Gorilla queen. 1967. SMC

TAYLEURE, CLIFTON W., 1832-1891
Horse-shoe Robinson. 1856.
MOSS2

TAYLOR, CECIL (C. P.), 1929-1981
And a nightingale sang ... a play
in two acts. 1977. BES83
Bread and butter. 1966. NEWE10
Getting by, and going home. See
Walter
Good; a play with music in two
acts. 1981. BES82
Happy days are here again. 1967.
NEWE12
Walter. 1977. DEC
Variant title: Getting by, and
going home

TAYLOR, CHARLES A., 1864-1942
From rags to riches. 1903. AMP8

TAYLOR, CHRISTOPHER
The wings of the dove (based on
the novel by Henry James).
1963. PLAN28

TAYLOR, DON, 1936-
Paradise restored. 1972. CLKY

TAYLOR, RON
The unreasonable act of Julian
Waterman. KAL3

TAYLOR, SAMUEL, 1912-
The happy time (based on the
novel by Robert Fontaine).
1950. BES49
Sabrina fair. 1953. THEA54

-- and SKINNER, CORNELIA OTIS
The pleasure of his company.
1958. BES58

TAYLOR, TOM, 1817-1880
Our American cousin. 1858. BAI
New men and old acres. 1869.
BOOA3
The ticket-of-leave man. 1863.
BOOA2, MOSN, MOSO, ROWE

-- and READE, CHARLES
Masks and faces; or, Before and
behind the curtain. 1852.
ROWE

TCHEKOFF, ANTON. See
Chekhov, Anton Pavlovich

TCHING, TSE. See Kao, Ming

TEH-HUI, CHENG. See Cheng,
Teh-Hui

TEH-YAO, JEN. See Jen, Teh-Yao

TEICHMANN, HOWARD, 1916-1987,
and KAUFMAN, GEORGE S.
The solid gold Cadillac. 1953.
GART, THEA54

TEIXIDOR, JORDI
The legend of the piper.
Wellwarth, G., tr. WELV
Variant title: El retaule
del flautista
El retaule del flautista. See
The legend of the piper

TEJADA, LUIS VARGAS. See
Vargas Tejada, Luis

TELLEZ, GABRIEL (TIRSO DE
MOLINA, pseud.), 1570?-1648
El burlador de Sevilla. 1630.
ALP, HILL
Campbell, R., tr. BENR3,
FLOR, MALI1
O'Brien, R., tr. FLOS
Schizzano, A., and Mandel,
O., trs. MARL
Starkie, W., tr. SSTW
Variant titles: The love-rogue
The playboy of Seville; or,
Supper with a statue; The
rogue of Seville; The
trickster of Seville; The
trickster of Seville and his
guest of stone
The love-rogue. See El burlador
de Sevilla
The playboy of Seville; or, Sup-
per with a statue. See El
burlador de Sevilla
The rogue of Seville. See El
burlador de Sevilla
The trickster of Seville. See
El burlador de Sevilla
The trickster of Seville and his
guest of stone. See El burla-
dor de Sevilla

TEMBECK, ROBERT, 1940-

Baptism. 1972. SHAT

TEMPLE, JOAN, d.1965
No room at the inn. 1945. EMB2

TENNYSON, ALFRED, 1809-1892
Becket. 1893. KAU, MOSN,
SMK

TERENCE. See Terentius Afer,
Publius

TERENTIUS AFER, PUBLIUS, 195?-
159 B.C.
Adelphi. 160 B.C.
Anon. tr. DUC2, TREB,
TREC1, TREE1, TREI1
Casson, L., tr. CASU
Copley, F., tr. ROM
Held, W., tr. COTU
Lieberman, S., tr. LIDE
Oldfather, W., tr. GUI,
GUIN, HAPV
Riley, H., tr. MIK8
Suskin, A., tr. HOWK
Variant title: The brothers
The Andria. See The woman of
Andros
Andria, the fair Andrian. See
The woman of Andros
The brothers. See Adelphi
The eunuch. 161 B.C.
Anon. tr. DUC2
Colman, G., tr. BAT2
Parker, D., tr. BOVI
Variant title: Eunuchus
Eunuchus. See The eunuch
Heautontimorumenos. 163 B.C.
Anon. tr. DUC2
Riley, H., tr. MIK8
Variant titles: The self-
avenger; The self-tormentors
Hecyra. See The mother-in-law
The mother-in-law. 165 B.C.
Anon. tr. DUC2
Variant title: Hecyra
Phormio. 161 B.C.
Anon. tr. CLF1, HOWJ,
POR
Casson, L., tr. CASU, COTU
Clark, B., tr. DUC2, WEAV1
Copley, F., tr. ROM
Lieberman, S., tr. LIDE
Morgan, M., tr. CLKW, MAU
Oldfather, W., tr. GUI, GUIN,
HAPV
Parker, D., tr. BOVI

The self-avenger. See Heautonti-
morumenos
The self-tormentors. See Heauton-
timorumenos
The woman of Andros. 166 B.C.
Anon. tr. DUC2, MALR2
Copley, F., tr. ROM
Lieberman, S., tr. LIDE
Riley, H., tr. CROS, SEBO,
SEBP
Variant titles: The Andria;
Andria, the fair Andrian

TERKEL, LOUIS "STUDS," 1912-
Monologues from "Division Street,
USA" - a series of dramatic
interviews of disinherited
Americans. (1967) RAVA

TERRY, MEGAN, 1932-
American King's English for
queens (music by Lynn Her-
rick). 1978. HIJ
Approaching Simone. 1970.
WOM
Babes in the big house (struc-
ture by JoAnn Schmidman;
music by John J. Sheean).
(1974) HIJ
Calm down, Mother. 1965.
BAYM, SUB
Ex-Miss Copper Queen on a set
of pills. (1966) BALLE1
The gloaming, oh my darling.
1965. BAIC, BAIE
The magic realists. 1968. DIZ
Running gag (lyrics by). See
Schmidman, JoAnn. Running
gag
Sanibel and Captiva. OWE

TERSON, PETER, 1932-
The mighty reservoy. 1964.
NEWE14
A night to make the angels weep.
1964. NEWE11

TESICH, STEVE, 1942-
The carpenters. 1970. SCV

THARP, NEWTON J.
The quest of the Gorgon. 1905.
BOH1

THEOBALD, LEWIS, 1688-1744
Electra. (1714) BELK16

THEODORE, ANNE. See Décour,
Charles Hébert, jt. auth.

THEOTOKAS, GEORGE, 1906-1966
The game of folly vs. wisdom.
Gianos, M., tr. GIA

THOMA, LUDWIG, 1867-1921
Champions of morality. See
Moral
Moral. 1908.
Recht, C., tr. DID
Variant title: Champions of
morality

THOMAS, ALBERT ELLSWORTH,
1872-1947
No more ladies. 1934. BES33

THOMAS, AUGUSTUS, 1857-1934
As a man thinks. 1911. BAK
The copperhead. 1918. COH
In Mizzoura. 1893. MOSS3
The witching hour. 1907.
BES99, DIC, GARX, MOSJ,
MOSK, MOSL, QUIJ, QUIJR,
QUIK, QUIL, QUIM, QUIN

THOMAS, DYLAN, 1914-1953
The doctor and the devils.
1959. BEAR
Under milk wood. 1953. BES57

THOMAS, GWYN, 1913-
Jackie the jumper. 1963. PLAN26
The keep. 1961. PLAN24

THOMPSON, DENMAN, 1833-1911
Joshua Whitcomb. See The old
homestead
The old homestead. 1875. CEY
Variant title: Joshua Whitcomb

THOMPSON, ERNEST, 1949-
On Golden Pond. 1978. BES78

THOMPSON, FLORA JANE (TIMMS),
1876-1948
Lark rise to Candleford (v. 1
of her trilogy, Lark rise).
See Dewhurst, Keith. Lark
rise (based on)

THOMSON, JAMES, 1700-1748
Edward and Eleonora. (1739)
BELG2

Sophonisba. 1729. BELK18
Tancred and Sigismunda. 1745.
BELK5

THORDARSON, AGNAR, 1917-
Atoms and madams. 1955.
Haugen, E., tr. HAVHN
Variant title: Kjarnorka og
kvenkylli
Kjarnorka og kvenkylli. See
Atoms and madams

THURBER, JAMES, 1894-1961
A Thurber carnival. 1960.
BES59

-- and NUGENT, ELIOT
The male animal. 1940.
BES39, BLOO, GARZ, HARB,
KRM, LOCK, MIJY, ROLF,
WISD

THURSTON, ELLA L.
Family cooperative. DRU

THURY, FRED, and GALBRAITH,
ROBERT
Nuts and bolts and rusty things.
1974. KAL4

TIECK, JOHANN LUDWIG, 1773-1853
Der gestiefelte kater. 1844.
CAM
Winter, L., tr. FRA4
Variant title: Puss in boots
Puss in boots. See Der ge-
stiefelte kater

TIEN, HAN
The white snake.
Chang, D., tr., and Packard,
W. (English verse adapta-
tion) MIT

T'IEN, HAN. See T'ien, Shou-
ch'ang

T'IEN, SHOU-CH'ANG, 1898-1968
Kuen Han-ch'ing. (1958-1961)
Foreign Languages Press,
Peking, tr. TWEH (Scenes 3,
5, 9, and 11 have been
omitted)

TING, HSI-LIN, 1893-1974
Oppression. (1925)
Lau, J., tr. TWEH

Variant title: Ya-p'o Ya-p'o.
See Oppression

TING, YI. See Ho, Ching-chih, jt.
auth.

TIRSO DE MOLINA, pseud. See
Téllez, Gabriel

TO, FU. See Fu, To

TOBIN, JOHN, 1770-1804
The honeymoon. 1805. BAT16

TOFFENETTI, LAURA. See Hensel,
Karen, jt. auth.

TOLLER, ERNST, 1893-1939
Hinkelmann. 1922?
Ritchie, J., and Stowell, J.,
trs. RITV
Hoppla! See Hoppla! Such is
life!
Hoppla! Such is life! 1927?
Ould, H., tr. ULAN
Variant titles: Hoppla!;
Hoppla, wir leben
Hoppla, wir leben. See Hoppla!
Such is life
The machine-wreckers. 1922.
Dukes, A., tr. MOSG, MOSH
Variant title: Die maschinen-
stuermer
Man and the masses. See Masse
mensch
Die maschinen-stuermer. See
The machine-wreckers
Masse mensch. 1921. STI2
Untermeyer, L., tr. DUK,
WAT1, WATL4
Variant title: Man and the
masses
Nie wieder friede. See No more
peace!
No more peace! 1937.
Crankshaw, E., and Auden,
W., trs. CALM, WELG
Variant title: Nie wieder
friede
Transfiguration. 1919.
Crankshaw, E., tr. HAV
Variant titles: Transformation;
Wandlung
Transformation. See Transfigura-
tion
Wandlung. See Transfiguration

TOLSTOI, ALEKSIEI KONSTANTINO-
VICH, 1817-1875
The death of Iván the terrible.
1867.
Noyes, G., tr. NOY
Tsar Fyodor Ivanovitch. 1868?
Covan, J., tr. MOS
--See also Prutkov, Koz'ma,
pseud.

TOLSTOI, LEV NICHOLAEVICH,
1828-1910
Condemnation. 18-?
Maude, L., and Aylmer, trs.
COUR
The dominion of darkness. See
The power of darkness
The live corpse. 1911.
Anon. tr. GARZH
Maude, L., and A., trs.
CHA, CHAN
Variant titles: The living
corpse; The man who was
dead; Redemption
The living corpse. See The live
corpse
The man who was dead. See
The live corpse
The power of darkness; or, If
a claw is caught the bird is
lost. 1895.
Anon. tr. DIK1
MacAndrew, A., tr. GARZE,
MACD
Magarshack, D., tr. MAP
Noyes, G., and Patrick, G.,
trs. HOUG, NOY,
TREBA, TREBJ, TREC2,
TREE2, TREI2
Reeve, F., tr. REEV1
Variant title: The dominion of
darkness
Redemption. See The live corpse
Taxes. 18-?
Maude, L., and Aylmer, trs.
COUR

TOLSTOY. See Tolstoi

TOMPKINS, FRANK GEROW, 1879-
Sham. 1920? MIJA1

TONG KIA, KAO. See Kao, Ming

TOOMER, JEAN, 1894-1967
Balo. 1924. HARY, LOC
Kabnis. (1923) CARR

TOPOR, TOM, 1938-
Nuts. 1974. BES79

TORRENCE, FREDERICK RIDGELY,
1875-1950
The danse Calinda. 1922. LOC
Granny Maumee. 1917. LOC
The rider of dreams. 1917. LOC

TORRES NAHARRO, BARTOLOME DE,
fl. 1517
Comedia Himenea. See Hymen
Hymen. 1517?
Chambers, W., tr. BAT6
Variant title: Comedia
Himenea

TOTHEROH, DAN, 1894-1976
Wild birds. 1925. BES24

TOUGH, ELSIE. See Schauffler,
Mrs. Elsie (Tough)

TOURNEUR, CYRIL, 1575?-1626
The atheist's tragedy. 1610?
GOM
The revenger's tragedy. 1606?
DPR2, GOM, HAPRA2,
HARPB2, HUST, OLH, OLI2,
RYL, SALG

TOWNLEY, JAMES, 1714-1778
High life below stairs. 1759.
BAT16, MOR

TOWNSHEND, PETER, 1945- , and
THE WHO
Tommy, a rock opera. 1969.
GREAA

TREADWELL, SOPHIE (MRS. SOPHIE
McGEEHAN), 1891-1970
Hope for a harvest. 1941. BES41
Machinal. 1928. BES28, GASB,
PLAAD

TREMBLAY, RENALD, 1943- .
La céleste Gréta. See Greta,
the divine
Greta, the divine. 1973.
Van Meer, A., tr. KAL5
Variant title: La céleste
Gréta

TRENEV, KONSTANTIN FEDOROVICH,
1900-
Lyubov Yarovaya. 1926.

Bakshy, A., tr. BAKS

TRENYOV, KONSTANTIN FYODORO-
VICH. See Trenev, Konstantin
Fedorovich

TREPASSI, PIETRO. See Metastasio,
Pietro Antonio Domenico Buonaventura, pseud.

TRIANA, JOSE, 1931-
The criminals. 1964.
Fernandez, P., and Kustow,
M., trs. WOOG
Variant title: La noche de
los asesinos
La noche de los asesinos. See
The criminals

TRISTAN l'HERMITE, FRANÇOIS,
1601-1655
The death of Seneca. 1643?
Lockert, L., tr. LOCU
Variant title: La mort de
Seneque
Mariamne. 1636.
Lockert, L., tr. LOCR
Variant title: La mariane
La mariane. See Mariamne
La mort de Seneque. See
The death of Seneca
La mort du grand Osman. See
Osman
Osman. 1646-1647?
Lockert, L., tr. LOCU
Variant title: La mort du
grand Osman

TROTTER, CATHERINE, 1679-1749
The fatal friendship. 1698.
FEFO

TROUBETSKOY, AMELIE (RIVES)
CHANLER, 1863-1945
Herod and Mariamne. 1888?
KOH2

TRUMBO, DALTON, 1905-1976
Opening sequence. 1969.
BAYM

TRYE, JEAN GUILLAUME ANTOINE
CUVELIER DE. See Cuvelier de
Trye, Jean Guillaume Antoine

TRZEBIŃSKI, ANDRZEJ, 1922-1943
Aby podnieśc różę. See To pick

up the rose
To pick up the rose. 1942.
Gerould, D., and Gerould, E.,
trs. TWEN
Variant title: Aby podnieść
różę

TS'AO, YÜ (pseud. of Wan Chia-Pao),
1910-
Lei-yü. See Thunderstorm
Thunderstorm. 1933.
Wang, T., and Barnes, A.,
trs. MESH
Variant title: Lei-yü

TSE-TCHING. See Kao, Ming

TSUNG, FU-HSIEN, 1947?-
In a land of silence. (1978)
Shu-ying, T., tr. TWEH
Variant title: Yü wu-sheng
ch'u
Yü wu-sheng ch'u. See In a
land of silence

TSURUYA, NAMBOKU IV, 1755-1829,
SAKURADA, JISUKE II, and
TSUUCHI, GENSHICHI
Sukara Hime Azuma Bunshō. See
The scarlet princess of Edō
The scarlet princess of Edō. 1817.
Brandon, J., tr. KAB
Variant title: Sakura Hime
Azuma Bunsho

TSUUCHI, GENSHICHI. See Tsuruya, Namboku IV, jt. auth.

TSUUCHI, HANEMON. See Tsuuchi,
Jihei II, jt. auth.

TSUUCHI, HANJURO, YASUDA,
ABUN, and NAKADA, MANSUKE
Narukami Fudō Kityama Zakura.
See Saint Narukami and the
God Fudō
Saint Narukami and the God Fudō.
1684. (Based on: Saint
Narukami, by Danjūrō I; The
God Fudo, by Danjūrō I; and
The whisker tweezers, Anony-
mous Plays.)
Brandon, J., tr. KAB
Variant titles: The God Fudo;
Narukami Fudō Kityama
Zakura; Saint Narukami;
The whisker tweezers

TSUUCHI, JIHEI II, and TSUUCHI, HANEMON
Protection of the cherries of Flower Mansion. See Sukeroku: Flower of Edo
Sukeroku: Flower of Edo. 1713.
Brandon, J., tr. KAB
Variant titles: Protection of the cherries of Flower Mansion; Sukeroku yukari no Edo zakura
Sukeroku yukari no Edo zakura. See Sukeroku: Flower of Edo

TUCHOLSKY, KARL. See Hasenclever, Walter, jt. auth.

TUNG, YANG-SHENG. See Chou, Wei-po, jt. auth.

TUR, LEONID DAVIDOVICH, 1905-1961; TUR, PETR DAVIDOVICH; and SHEININ, LEV ROMANOVICH
Smoke of the fatherland. 1942.
Feinberg, A., tr. SEVP

TUR, PETR DAVIDOVICH, 1907-
See Tur, Leonid Davidovich, jt. auth.

TURGENEV, IVAN SERGIEEVICH, 1818-1883
A month in the country. 1872.
MacAndrew, A., tr. GARZE, MAB
Mandell, M., tr. FAMK
Newnham, R., tr. COTO
Nicolaeff, A., tr. PLAN45
Noyes, G., tr. NOY, TREB, TREC1, TREE1, TREI1
Williams, E., adapter. GARZH, HOUG

TURNEY, CATHERINE, 1906-
Bitter harvest. 1936. FOUP

TURNEY, ROBERT, 1900-
Daughter of Atreus. 1936. BES36

TURQUE, MICHAEL, 1933-
Shoptalk. 19-? GREAB

TYAN, HAN. See Tien, Han

TYLER, ROYALL, 1757-1826
The contrast. 1787. BLAI1, BPD1, CADY, DOWM, ELLI1, GARX, GATB1, HAL, HOWP1, MONR, MOSS1, QUIJ, QUIK, QUIL, QUIM, QUIN, QUIO1, SPI, STL1
The island of Barrataria. 18th cent. AMP15
Joseph and his brethren. 18th cent. AMP15
The judgment of Solomon. 18th cent. AMP15
The origin of the feast of Purim; or, The destinies of Haman and Mordecai. 18th cent. AMP15

TZARA, TRISTAN, 1896-1963
Le coeur à gaz. See The gas heart
The gas heart. 1920.
Benedikt, M., tr. BEN
Variant title: Le coeur à gaz

UDALL, NICHOLAS, 1505-1556
Jack Juggler (attributed to). See Anonymous Plays. Jack Juggler
Ralph Roister Doister. 1566?
ADA, BAS, BAT13, BOA, CRE, GARZB, GAY1, MAX, MIN2, MIO2, NES, PAR, SCW, TAV, THWO
Variant titles: Roister Doister; Royster Doyster
Respublica (attributed to). See Anonymous Plays Respublica
Roister Doister. See Ralph Roister Doister
Royster Doyster. See Ralph Roister Doister
Thersites (attributed to). See Anonymous Plays. Thersites

UDENSI, UWA
Monkey on the tree. AFR

UDOFF, YALE M., 1935-
A guy play. 1971. BALLE8

UHDE, MILAN, 1936-
A blue angel.
Pech, V., tr. and Stenberg, P., adapter. DBG

UJINOBU, ZENCHIKU. See
Zenchiku, Ujinobu

UKRAINKA, LESYA, psued. See
Kosach, Larisa Petrovna

UNRUH, FRITZ VON, 1885-1970
Heinrich aus Andernach. 1925.
STI2

UPSON, WILLIAM HAZLETT, 1891-
1975
The master salesman. 1924.
GALB

URISTA, ALBERTO H. (ALURISTA,
pseud.), 1947-
Dawn. CONR

USSEAU, ARNAUD D'. See
D'Usseau, Arnaud

USTINOV, PETER, 1921-
The love of four colonels.
1951. BES52, THEA53
The unknown soldier and his
wife. 1968. PLAN36

UYS, PIETER-DIRK
Paradise is closing down.
1977. THI

VALDEZ, LUIS, 1940-
Bernabé. CONR
The shrunken head of Pancho
Villa. 1965. WES11/12
Los Vendidos. 1967. CHG,
CONR

VALENCY, MAURICE JACQUES,
1903-
The Apollo of Bellac. See
Giraudoux, Jean. The
Apollo of Bellac (adapted by)
The enchanted. See Giraudoux,
Jean. The enchanted
(adapted by)
The madwoman of Chaillot. See
Giraudoux, Jean. The mad-
woman of Chaillot (adapted by)
Ondine. See Giraudoux, Jean.
Ondine (adapted by)
The visit. See Duerrenmatt,
Friedrich. The visit (tr. and
adapted by)

VALLE-INCLAN, RAMON MARIA DEL,
1870-1936
La cabeza del Bautista. 1924.
MARLI2
Divinas palabras. See Divine
words
Divine words. 1933.
Williams, E., tr. BENA
Variant title: Divinas palabras

VALLEJO, ANTONIO BUERO. See
Buero Vallejo, Antonio

VANBRUGH, SIR JOHN, 1664-1726
City wives confederacy. See
The confederacy
The confederacy. 1705. BELK15,
KRM
Variant title: City wives con-
federacy
A journey to London (ms. com-
pleted by C. Cibber). 1728.
BAT15, BELK6, TICK
Variant title: The provoked
husband
Mistake. 1705. BELK19
The provoked husband. See A
journey to London
The provok'd wife. 1697. BELK2,
FIS, GAY4, GOS, GOSA, JEFF3,
MAX, MOSE1, RES, RUB, TWE
The relapse; or, Virtue in danger.
1696. BELK11, DAVR, JEFF3,
MAND, MANF, MOR, NET,
REST, TUQ

VAN DOREN, MARK, 1894-1972
The last days of Lincoln. 1961.
AMB, SWI

VAN DRUTEN, JOHN, 1902-1957
After all. FAMAN, MYB, PLAD
Behold we live. 1932. FAMC
Bell, book and candle. 1950
BES50, GARW
The distaff side. 1933. BES34,
FAME
Flowers of the forest. 1934.
FAMG
I am a camera (adapted from the
Berlin stories by Christopher
Isherwood). 1951. BES51,
FAMO, GART, GAVE
Variant title: Sally Bowles
--See also Masteroff, Joe.
Cabaret (adapted from I am a
camera and the stories of

Christopher Isherwood)
I remember mama (based on the
book Mama's bank account by
Kathryn Forbes). 1944.
BES44, DAVI, GARZ, GRIH,
MERS, REDM, SPES, STAV
London wall. 1931. FAMAN
Sally Bowles. See I am a camera
Somebody knows. 1932. FAMB
There's always Juliet. 1931.
FAMB
The voice of the turtle. 1943.
BES43, GARZ, KRM
Young Woodley. 1925. BES25,
FAO, PLAD

-- and MORRIS, LLOYD
The damask cheek. 1942. BES42

VAN ITALLIE, JEAN-CLAUDE, 1936-
America hurrah. 1966.
BES66, CLN, ORZ, SANE
Interview. 1966. BAIC, GLI
Variant title: Pavane pro-
duced...
A masque for three dolls. See
Mot al
Motel; a masque for three dolls
(part of America hurrah).
1965. HAVL, RAVA
Naropa [being the incredibly
frustrating adventures of a
middle-aged university pro-
fessor on his way to perfect
enlightenment]; a play for
puppets and people adapted
from the translation by
Herbert V. Guenther of
Tibeton Texts. WOQ1
Pavane produced.... See Inter-
.view
The serpent: a ceremony. 1970.
BES69
Where is de queen? 1966.
BALLE3

VANE, SUTTON, 1888-1943
Outward bound. 1923.
BES23, CEU, MART

VARESI, GILDA, 1887- , and
BYRNE, MRS. DOLLY
Enter madame. 1920. BES20

VARGAS TEJADA, LUIS, 1802-
1829
Las convulsiones. 1828.

Bailey, W., tr. SSTE
Variant title: My poor nerves
My poor nerves. See Las con-
vulsiones

VEGA, RICARDO DE LA, 1829-1910
Pepa la frescachona. 190-?
BRET

VEGA, VENTURA DE LA, 1807-1865
El hombre de mundo. 1845.
BRET
Variant title: A man of the
world
A man of the world. See El
hombre de mundo

VEGA CARPIO, LOPE FELIX DE,
1562-1635
El caballero de Olmedo. 1620-
1622? MARLI1
The dog in the manger. 1613?
Chambers, W., tr. BAT6
Variant titles: The gardener's
dog; El perro del hortelano
La estrella de Sevilla. 1617?
ALP
Hayden, P., tr. CLKW, CROV,
MAU
Variant title: The star of
Seville
Fuente ovejuna. 1619. ALP
Campbell, R., tr. BENR3,
BENSB1
Flores, A., and Kittel, M.,
trs. FLOR, FLOS, HOUE,
TREB, TREC1, TREE1,
TREI1
Underhill, J., tr. ALPF,
DOWN, KRE, WARN2
Variant title: The sheep well
The gardener's dog. See The
dog in the manger
The king, the greatest Alcalde.
1620?
Underhill, J., tr. CLF2,
LOCM1, WEAV1
Variant title: El mejor Alcal-
de el rey
El mejor Alcalde el rey. See The
king, the greatest Alcalde
Peribanez and the commander of
Ocana. See Peribáñez y el
comendador de Ocaña
Peribáñez y el comendador de
Ocaña. 1610? HILL
Starkie, W., tr. SSTW

CHARLES MESSAGER), 1882-1971
   Michel Auclair. 1922.
   Howard, S., tr. LEV, LEVE
   Le paquebot Tenacity. 1920.
   HART, HARV
   Howard, S., tr. TUCG,
     TUCM
   Newberry, J., tr. DIE
   Variant titles: S. S. Tenacity;
     The steamer Tenacity; The
     steamship Tenacity
   S.S. Tenacity. See Le paquebot
     Tenacity
   The steamer Tenacity. See Le
     paquebot Tenacity
   The steamship Tenacity. See Le
     paquebot Tenacity

VILLA, JOSE GARCIA, 1914-
   Mir-i-nisa. See Sicam, Geronimo
   D., and Casiño, Jesús. Mir-
   i-nisa (based on the story by)

VILLA, LILIA A.
   Educating Josefina. 195-?
   EDAD

VILLIERS, CLAUDE DESCHAMPS,
1600?-1681
   L'apoticaire devalisê. 1658? LAN

VILLIERS, GEORGE. See
Buckingham, George Villiers

VINCENT, ALLEN. See Rotter,
Fritz, jt. auth.

VISE, JEAN DONNEAU DE. See
Donneau de Visé, Jean

VISHAKADATTA. 9th cent.
   Rākshasa's ring. See The
     signet ring of Rakshasa
   The signet ring of Rakshasa.
     9th cent.
     Coulson, M., tr. THWI
     Lal, P., tr. LAL
     Variant title: Rākshasa's
       ring

VISHĀKHADATTA. See Vishakadatta

VISHNEVSKII, VSEVOLOD VITALE-
VICH, 1900-1951
   Optimicheskaya tragediya. See
   An optimistic tragedy

An optimistic tragedy. 1933.
   Scott, H., and Carr, R., trs.
   FOUS
   Variant title: Optimicheskaya
     tragediya

VITRAC, ROGER, 1899-1952
   Les mystères de l'amour. See
     The mysteries of love
   The mysteries of love. 1927.
     Goldstone, R., tr. BEN
     Variant title: Les mystères
     de l'amour

VIZIN, DENIS VON. See Fonvízin,
Dinís Ivanovich

VOADEN, HERMAN, 1903-
   Hill-land. 1934. MAJ
   Murder pattern. 1936. WAGN3
   Wilderness; a play of the north.
     1931. WAGN3

VODAHOVIC, SERGIO VINA
   Three beach plays. 1964.
     Oliver, W., tr. OLIW

VOLLMER, LULA, 1898-1955
   Sun-up. 1923. BES23, LOW,
     QUIJR, QUIK, QUIL, QUIM,
     QUIN, TUCD, TUCM

VOLLMOLLER, KARL GUSTAV, 1878-
1948
   Uncle's been dreaming. 192-?
     Katzin, W., tr. KAT

VOLTAIRE, FRANÇOIS MARIE
AROUET DE, 1694-1778
   Candide. See Hellman, Lillian.
     Candide (based on)
   --See also McTaggart, James.
     Candide (translated and adapted
     for television by)
   Mahomet. 1741.
     Leigh, O., tr. BAT8
   Nanine. 1749. BRE
   Oedipe. See Oedipus
   Oedipus. 1718.
     Smollett, T., tr. SANO
     Variant title: Oedipe
   Socrates. 1759.
     Leigh, O., tr. BAT8
   Zaire. 1732. BRE, LOCR, SEA

VONNEGUT, KURT, JR., 1922-
   Fortitude. 1968. REA

VULPIUS, PAUL
Youth at the helm. 1934.
Griffith, H., tr. and adapter.
FAMH

WADDELL, SAMUEL (RUTHERFORD
MAYNE, pseud.), 1878-1967
Bridge head. 1934. CAN

WAGER, WILLIAM, fl. 1566
Enough is as good as a feast.
ca.1560-1570. SCAT

WAKEFIELD, JACQUES
Perceptual movement. (1979)
CEN

WAKEFIELD, LOU, and THE
WOMEN'S THEATRE GROUP
Time pieces. 1982. PLABE3

WAKEMAN, ALAN
Ships. 1975. HOM

WALKER, GEORGE F., 1947-
Ambush at Tether's End. 1971.
BRIN
The art of war. 1982. PENG
Prince of Naples. 1971. BRIP

WALKER, JOHN
The factory lad. 1832. BOOA1,
BOOM, VIC

WALKER, JOSEPH A., 1935-
Ododo. 1970. KINH
The River Niger. 1973. BERS,
BES72, RICT

WALKER, STUART, 1880-1941
The medicine show. 1917.
BEAC11

WALLACK, LESTER, 1820-1888
Rosedale; or, The rifle ball.
1863. AMP4

WALPOLE, SIR HUGH, 1884-1941
Kind lady. See Chodorov, Edward. Kind lady (adapted
from a story by)

WALTER, EUGENE, 1874-1941
The easiest way. 1908.
BESO9, DID, GARX, MOSS3

WALTER, NANCY
Rags. BALLE7

WAN, CHIA-PAO. See Ts'ao, Yü,
pseud.

WANDOR, MICHELENE
Aurora Leigh. 1979. PLABE1
Care and control (scripted by).
See Gay Sweatshop

WANG, CHING-KSIEN, 1940-
Wu Feng. (1979)
Kwok, C., and Yang, M., trs.
TWEH

WANG, JIUSI, 1468-1551
Wolf of Mount Zhong.
Dolby, W., tr. EIG
Variant title: Zhong-shan lang
Zhong-shan lang. See Wolf of
Mount Zhong

WANG SHIH-FU, 13th cent.
The west chamber. 13th cent.
Irwin, V., tr. IRW

WAPUL, GEORGE. See Wapull,
George

WAPULL, GEORGE, fl.1576
The tide tarrieth no man.
1576. SCAT

WARD, DONALD. See Solly, Bill,
jt. auth.

WARD, DOUGLAS TURNER, 1930-
Brotherhood. 1970. KINH
Day of absence. 1965. ACE,
BAC, BOYN, BRAS, GRIH,
HARY, OLIV, PFR, RAI, RICK
Happy ending. 1965. BARI,
BARIA, BARIC, BRAS, HOLP,
OLIV

WARD, Julia. See Howe, Mrs. Julia
(Ward)

WARD, THEODORE, 1902-1983
Big white fog. 1938. HARY
Our lan'. 1946. TUQT

WARREN, HARRY, 1893-1981
42nd Street (music and lyrics by).
See Stewart, Michael. 42nd
Street

WARREN, MRS. MERCY (OTIS),
1728-1814
The blockheads; or, The affrighted officers (attributed
to). See Anonymous Plays.
The blockheads; or, The
affrighted officers
The group. 1775? MOSS1
The motley assembly (attributed
to). See Anonymous Plays.
The motley assembly

WARREN, RUTH. See Hawthorne,
Ruth (Warren)

WASHBURN, DERIC
Ginger Anne. (1961) NEWA1

WASSERMAN, DALE, 1917-
Man of La Mancha (music by
Mitch Leigh, lyrics by Joe
Darion). 1965. BES65,
RICM

WATERHOUSE, KEITH, 1929- ,
and HALL, WILLIS
Billy liar. 1960. PLAJ1

WATKIN, LAWRENCE EDWARD,
1901-
On borrowed time. See
Osborn, Paul. On borrowed
time (based on the novel by)

WATKINS, ARTHUR THOMAS
LEVY. See Watkyn, Arthur, pseud.

WATKINS, MAURINE DALLAS, 1901-
1969
Chicago. 1926. BES26
--See also Ebb, Fred, and
Fosse, Bob. Chicago
(adapted from)

WATKYN, ARTHUR (pseud. of
Arthur Thomas Levy Watkins),
1907-1965
Not in the book. 1958. PLAN17
For better, for worse. 1952.
PLAN8

WATSON, HARMON C., 1943-
Those golden gates fall down.
(1971). FORD

WATSON, MARJORIE R.
The dogs of war. BRNB

WATSON-TAYLOR, GEORGE, d.1841
England preserved. 1795. INCA8

WATTERS, GEORGE MANKER, 1891-
1943, and HOPKINS, ARTHUR
MELANCTHON
Burlesque. 1927. BES27

WAUGH, EVELYN, 1903-1966
The man who liked Dickens
(television version by Robert
Tallman). SUT1

WEBBER, CECIL EDWIN
Be good, sweet maid. 1957.
PLAN15

WEBBER, JAMES PLAISTED, 1878-
1930
Frances and Francis. 1923.
WEB

WEBER, MARY FELTHAUS. See
Felthaus-Weber, Mary

WEBSTER, JOHN, 1580?-1625?
The Duchess of Malfi. 1613.
ABRH, ABRJ, ALLK, ALLM,
BALD, BAS, BAUL, BENQ,
BROC, CLKY, COTKIR, DEAN,
DEAO, DOWS, DPR2, DUN,
FOUD, HARC47, HOW, HUST,
MAKJ, MAX, NEI, OLH, OLI2,
ROET, SCH, SCI, SCJ, SEN,
SPD, SPDB, SPEF1, SSSI,
TAT, TAU, THA, TRE, TREA2,
TREB, TREC1, TREE1, TREI1,
WATT2, WHE, WINE, WRIH
Variant title: The tragedy of
the Duchess of Malfi
The tragedy of the Duchess of
Malfi. See The Duchess of
Malfi
The white devil; or, Vittoria
Corombona. 1612? BENY,
DPR2, HAPRA1, HAPRB1,
KRE, OLH, OLI2, ORNT, PAR,
RUB, RYL, SALG, SPE, WALL,
WHE

WEDEKIND, FRANK, 1864-1918
The court singer. See Der kam-
mersänger
The earth-spirit. See Erdgeist
The epicurean. See The Marquis
of Keith
Erdegeist. 1895.

Eliot, S., tr. DIK2
Variant title: The earth-
spirit
Frühlingserwachen. See
Spring's awakening
Der kammersänger. 1899. STI1
Boesche, A., tr. FRA20
Tridon, A., tr. HUDE,
TREBA, TREBJ, TREC2,
TREE2, TREI2
Variant titles: The court
singer; The tenor
King Nicolo. See Such is life
König Nikolo. See Such is life
The Marquis of Keith. 1900?
Gottlieb, B., tr. BENS2,
BLOC
Mueller, C., tr. COTL,
COTQ
Variant title: The epicurean
So ist das leben. See Such is
life
Spring's awakening. 1906.
Bentley, E., tr. BENT6
Variant title: Frühlingser-
wachen
Such is life. 1902.
Esslin, M., tr. ESS
Ziegler, F., tr. DIE, TUCG
Variant titles: King Nicolo;
König Nikolo; So ist das
leben
The tenor. See Der kammersänger

WEETMAN, MARTIN
Estonia you fall. 1983. WES13/
14

WEIDMAN, JEROME, 1913- , and
ABBOTT, GEORGE
Fiorello! (music by Jerry Bock;
lyrics by Sheldon Harnick).
1959. BES59, RICM

WEIDMAN, JOHN, 1946-
Pacific overtures (additional
material by Hugh Callingham
Wheeler). 1976. BES75

WEILL, KURT, 1900-1950
He who says yes. See Brecht,
Bertolt, jt. auth.
Johnny Johnson. See Green,
Paul. Johnny Johnson (music
by)
Lady in the dark (music by).
See Hart, Moss. Lady in the
dark
Lost in the stars. See Anderson,
Maxwell, jt. auth.
One touch of Venus (music by).
See Perelman, S. J., and Nash,
Ogden. One touch of Venus
The threepenny opera. See
Brecht, Bertolt. The three-
penny opera (music by)

WEINSTOCK, JACK, 1909- . See
Burrows, Abram S., jt. auth.

WEISS, PETER, 1916-1982
Marat/Sade. See The persecution
and assassination of Jean Paul
Marat...
The persecution and assassination
of Jean Paul Marat as performed
by the inmates of the Asylum of
Charenton under the direction
of the Marquis de Sade. 1964.
Skelton, G., tr. and adapter,
and Mitchell, A., verse
adapter. BES65, DITA,
REIL, REIWE
Variant titles: Marat/Sade;
The persecution and assas-
sination of Marat...; Die
Verfolgung und Ermordung
Jean Paul Marats, dargestellt
durch die Schauspielgruppe
des Hospizes zu Charenton
unter Anleitung des Herrn
de Sade
The persecution and assassination
of Marat... See The persecu-
tion and assassination of Jean
Paul Marat...
The tower. (1948)
Anon. tr. RICJ
Benedikt, M., and Heine, M.,
trs. BENB
Variant title: Der Turm
Der Turm. See The tower
Die Verfolgung und Ermordung
Jean Paul Marats, dargestellt
durch die Schauspielgruppe des
Hospizes zu Charenton unter
Anleitung des Herrn de Sade.
See The persecution and assas-
sination of Jean Paul Marat...

WEITZENKORN, LOUIS, 1893-1943
Five star final. 1930. BES30

WELCH, LEONA NICHOLAS, 1942-

Hands in the mirror. (1979)
CEN

WELLER, MICHAEL, 1942-
The bodybuilder. 1969. OFF
Loose ends. 1979. BERS,
BES78, BES79
Moonchildren. 1970. BES71,
FAMAD
Now there's just the three of us.
1969. OFF

WELLES, ORSON, 1915-1985. See
Mankiewicz, Herman J., jt. auth.

WELLMAN, JOHN
Starluster. 1979. WOQ1

WELLS, HERBERT GEORGE, 1866-
1946
Ann Veronica. See Gow, Ronald.
Ann Veronica (adapted from
the novel by)

WELTY, EUDORA, 1909-
The ponder heart. See Fields,
Joseph and Chodorov, Jerome.
The ponder heart (adapted
from the novel by)

WERFEL, FRANZ, 1890-1945
Goat song. 1921.
Langner, R., tr. ANTH, THF
Variant title: Bockgesang
Jacobowsky and the Colonel. See
Behrman, Samuel Nathaniel.
Jacobowsky and the Colonel
(adapted from the play by)

WERNER, FRIEDRICH LUDWIG
ZACHARIAS, 1768-1823
The twenty-fourth of February.
See Der vierundzwanzigste
Februar
Der vierundzwanzigste Februar.
1809. CAM
Chambers, W., tr. BAT10
Variant title: The twenty-
fourth of February

WERTENBAKER, TIMBERLAKE
New anatomies. 1981. PLACI

WESKER, ARNOLD, 1932-
Chicken soup with barley. 1958.
NEWE1
Chips with everything. 1962?

BES63, NEWE7
The four seasons. 1965. NEWE9
The kitchen. 1959. CONB, NEWE2
Roots. 1959. POP
Their very own and golden city.
1966. NEWE10

WESLEY, RICHARD, 1945-
Black terror. 1972. NEWL
The sirens. 1976. CEN

WESSON, KENNETH ALAN
Miss Cegenation. (1979) CEN

WEXLEY, JOHN, 1902-1985
The last mile. 1930. BES29
Running dogs. 1938? KOZ
They shall not die. 1934. BES33

WHARTON, MRS. EDITH NEWBOLD
(JONES), 1862-1937
Ethan Frome. See Davis, Owen
and Davis, Donald. Ethan
Frome (based on the novel by)

WHEELER, ANDREW CARPENTER,
1835-1903. See Alfriend, Edward.
M., jt. auth.

WHEELER, HUGH CALLINGHAM.
1916-
Big fish, little fish. 1961. BES60
A little night music (suggested by
Smiles of a summer night, film
by Ingmar Bergman; title from
Mozart's Eine Kleine Nacht-
musik; music and lyrics by
Stephen Sondheim). 1973.
BERS, RICM
Look: we've come through. 1961.
SSTY
Pacific overtures (additional mate-
rial by). See Weidman, John.
Pacific overtures
Sweeney Todd, the demon barber
of Fleet Street. (Music and
lyrics by Stephen Sondheim.
Based on the play by Christo-
pher Bond). 1979. BES78

WHITE, JOSEPH, 1933-
The leader. 1969. JON

WHITE, LUCY
The bird child. 1922. LOC

WHITE, TERENCE HANBURY, 1906-

1964
   The once and future king. <u>See</u>
   Lerner, Alan Jay. Camelot
   (based on the novel by)

WHITEHEAD, WILLIAM
   And if that mockingbird don't
   sing. 1977. WES3

WHITEHEAD, WILLIAM, 1715-1785
   Creusa, Queen of Athens. 1754.
   BELK20
   The Roman father. 1750.
   BELK20
   School for lovers. 1762.
   BELG16

WHITEMORE, HUGH, 1936-
   Pack of lies. 1983. BES84

WHITING, JOHN, 1917-1963
   The devils. 1961. NEWE6
   Marching song. 1954. NEWE3
   Saint's day. 1951. PLAN6

WHITTINGTON, ROBERT, 1912-
   The death of García Lorca.
   1940. CROZ1

WHO, THE
   Tommy, a rock opera. <u>See</u>
   Townshend, Peter, jt. auth.

WIEAND, PAUL R.
   Die huchzich um kreitz waig?
   18-? BUFF
   Der parra kumpt. 18-? BUFF
   Tzu forwitsich. 18-? BUFF

WEICHERT, ERNST EMIL, 1887-
1950
   Das spiel vom deutschen bettelmann. 1933. STI2

WIED, GUSTAV JOHANNES, 1858-
1914
   Ranke viljer. <u>See</u> 2 x 2 = 5
   2 x 2 = 5. 1906.
   Boyd, E., and Koppel, H.,
   trs. LEG
   Variant title: Ranke viljer

WIESE, ANNE PIERSON
   Coleman, S. D. 1982. YOUP

WILBRANDT, ADOLF VON, 1837-
1911

The master of Palmyra. 1889.
   Stork, C., tr. FRA16
   Variant title: Der meister
   von Palmyra
Der meister von Palmyra.
   <u>See</u> The master of Palmyra

WILBUR, RICHARD, 1921-
   Candide. <u>See</u> Hellman, Lillian.
   Candide (lyrics by)

WILCOX, ANNA JANE. <u>See</u> Harnwell, Mrs. Anna Jane (Wilcox)

WILCOX, MICHAEL
   Accounts. 1981. GAW

WILDE, OSCAR, 1854-1900
   An ideal husband. 1895. JAFF
   The importance of being earnest.
   1895. ABRJ, ACE, ALLM,
   ANT, ASG, ASH, BAIG, BARB,
   BARG, BARR, BENSB2, BENU,
   BOWY, BROG, CARP, CARPA,
   CASA, CEU, COLT, COTKI,
   COTKIS, COTKR, COTY, CRAF,
   CRAN2, EDAD, FEFL, FOUM,
   GREB2, GREC2, HILP, HOUS,
   KER, KRM, LOO, LOOA, MON,
   MOSN, MOSO, NEV1, REIWE,
   SAFF, SALE, SATI, SHAJ2,
   SIG, SMR, STE, STEI, STJN,
   STRB, STY, THOM, THON,
   TRE, TREA1, TREBA, TREBJ,
   TREC2, TREE3, TREI3, TUCD,
   TUCM, TUCN, TUCO, WATA,
   WHFM, WHI, WOO2, WOOD2,
   WOOE2
   Lady Windermere's fan. 1892.
   BAUG, BENY, BROJ, BROK,
   DAV1, DIC, HUD, LIE, LIED2,
   LIEE2, MACL, MAX, MOO,
   RUB, SMO, TAT, TAU
   A woman of no importance. 1893.
   COT

WILDE, PERCIVAL, 1887-1953
   Blood of the martyrs. 191-?
   STAU
   Confessional. 1916. BENP, PEN
   The traitor. 19-? RICH

WILDENBRUCH, ERNST VON, 1845-
1909
   Heinrich und Heinrich's geschlecht.
   <u>See</u> King Henry
   Henry IV of Germany, pt. I. <u>See</u>

King Henry
King Henry. 1896.
Wernaer, R., tr. FRA17
Variant titles: Heinrich
und Heinrich's geschlecht;
Henry IV of Germany, pt. I

WILDER, THORNTON NIVEN, 1897-
1975
The angel on the ship. 1928?
CHU
The happy journey to Trenton
and Camden. 1931. COOP,
GALB, WATE
The long Christmas dinner.
1931. DOWM, MIKL, SHAW,
SHAX
The matchmaker. 1955. BARJ,
BARS, BES55, BLOC, CASE,
GART, GATB2, GOLH, SHRO,
THEA56, WEAN
Variant title: The merchant
of Yonkers
--See Stewart, Michael. Hello,
Dolly! (adapted from)
The merchant of Yonkers. See
The matchmaker
Our town. 1938. BES37, BLOD1,
BONB, BONC, BRR1, BRS,
CARL, CARLE, CATH, CET,
COK, COOF, COOJ, CORB,
CORF, CROX, EDAD, FULT,
GOLK, HAT, ING, INGA,
INGB, LAM, MADG, NAGE,
ROGE, SIM, SUT3, TREBA,
TREBJ, TREC2, TREE3,
TREI3, WORL3
Pullman car Hiawatha. 1931?
BENT4, ELKE, MANL
The skin of our teeth. 1942.
BES42, BROE, BROI, COTQ,
CUBE, CUBG, CUBH, DOWS,
HEWE, HOWP2, JOHO, JORH,
KERO, LIEF, LIEG, MORXD,
SCNO, SCNT, WATA

WILHELM, PETER, 1943-
Conspiracy. See Frame work
Frame work. 1975. CONZI
(Act I only)
Variant title: Conspiracy

WILKINS, JOHN H., 1836?-1853
Signor Marc. 1854. AMP14

WILLARD, JOHN, 1885-1942
The cat and the canary. 1922.
CART

WILLCOX, HELEN LIDA, 1883-
Larola. 1917? FED1

WILLIAMS, ANITA JANE
A Christmas story. (1980) CEN
Variant title: A turkey tale
A turkey tale. See A Christmas
story

WILLIAMS, ARTHUR
The poor little watch girl. 1968.
SME

WILLIAMS, CHARLES, 1886-1945
Thomas Cranmer of Canterbury.
1936. BRZ

WILLIAMS, EMLYN, 1905-1987
The corn is green. 1938.
BES40, CEU, EDAD, GREC2,
PROX
The late Christopher Bean. See
Fauchois, René. The late
Christopher Bean (tr. and
adapted by)
A month in the country. See
Turgenev, Ivan. A month in
the country (adapted by)
Night must fall. 1935. CART,
FAMH

WILLIAMS, HUGH, 1904-1969, and
WILLIAMS, MARGARET (VYNER)
By accident (part of Double yoke).
1960. PLAN21
Variant title: Special providence
Double yoke (By accident; With
intent). 1960. PLAN21
Father's match. See The happy
man
The grass is greener. 1958.
PLAN19
The happy man. 1957. PLAN17
Variant title: Father's match
The irregular verb to love. 1961.
PLAN23
Plaintiff in a pretty hat. 1956.
PLAN15
A sparrow falls. See With intent
Special providence. See By ac-
cident
With intent (part of Double yoke).
1960. PLAN21
Variant title: A sparrow falls

WILLIAMS, JESSE LYNCH, 1871-
1929
And so they were married.
See Why marry?
Why marry? 1917. BES09,
CORD, CORE, CORF, QUI
Variant title: And so they
were married
Why not? 1922. BES22

WILLIAMS, LAUREN
Over fourteen: and single. DRU

WILLIAMS, MARGARET (VYNER),
1914- . See Williams, Hugh,
jt. auth.

WILLIAMS, MARY ANN, 1945-
Cinder, Tell-It. (1976) AUB

WILLIAMS, NORMAN
The mountain. GREG

WILLIAMS, PAULETTE. See
Shange, Ntozake

WILLIAMS, SAMM-ART, 1946-
Home. 1979. BES79

WILLIAMS, TENNESSEE (b.
Thomas Lanier Williams), 1914-1983
Camino real. 1953. CES, FAM,
MIJY, SANK, ULAN
The case of the crushed petu-
nias. (1948) COOF
Cat on a hot tin roof. 1955.
BES54, GART, GAVE,
GOODE, LITN, SCNPL,
SCNQ, SSSI, THEA55
The confessional. (1966) RICK
Dos ranchos; or, The purifica-
tion. 1944? NEWD44
The glass menagerie. 1944.
ALLM, AUB, BAIG, BARI,
BARIA, BARIC, BARS,
BES44, BLOC, BLON, BLOND,
BONA, BONB, BONC, BOYN,
BPD2, BPE, BROY, CASA,
CLH, COK, COOP, CORB,
COTQ, CUBE, CUBG, CUBH,
DEAS, DIT, DOWM, ELK,
GARZ, GATB3, GATS, GAVE,
HAPO, HATA, HAVH, HAVI,
HEA, KNIC, KNID, KNIG, LAV,
LIEG, LITC, LITJ, MAEC,
MABC, MANK, MANL, MON,
MONA, PERS, PERT, PIC,

REIP, REIT, ROHR, SDQ,
SHRO, SILK, SILKI, SILN,
SILO, SILP, SIXB, SIXC,
SOM, SOMA, SOU, SPES,
SSSF, STEI, STY, TREBA,
TREBJ, TREC2, TREE3,
TREI3, WAIT, WAIU, WALB,
WARH, WARL, WATE, WEIM,
WEIS, WEIW
Hello from Bertha. RAVA
I rise in flame, cried the Phoenix.
(1951). NEWW1
The last of my solid gold watches.
1947. BUR, PLAAB
The long goodbye. 1940. BAIG
A lovely Sunday for Creve
Coeur. 1979. BERS
The milk train doesn't stop here
anymore. 1962. BES62
The night of the iguana. 1961.
BES61, GARSA, RICIS, SEVT
Orpheus descending. 1957.
BES56, GARSA, GORE
Period of adjustment. 1960.
BES60
The rose tattoo. 1951. BES50,
CLM, CLN, COTY, GART,
GREAB, RICT
Small craft warnings. 1972.
BES71
Something unspoken. 1953? SUL
A streetcar named desire. 1947.
BARJ, BES47, CEQA, CLL,
CLLC, FOUX, GARW, GATB3,
GAVE, GOOD, NEWV, TUCO
Suddenly last summer. 1958.
LIEF, MESS
Summer and smoke. 1948.
GARW, GOLH, HAVG, TAUJ
Sweet bird of youth. 1959.
BES58
Talk to me like the rain and let
me listen. 1970. RAVA
27 Wagons full of cotton. 1955.
HALU, SPC

WILLIAMS, THOMAS LANIER. See
Williams, Tennessee

WILLIAMS, WILLIAM CARLOS, 1883-
1963
The first president. 1936? AME5
Trial horse no. 1: Many loves.
1942? NEWD42

WILLIAMSON, DAVID, 1942-
What if you died tomorrow. 1973.

FIO

WILLIAMSON, HAROLD
Peggy. 1919. HUD

WILLIAMSON, HUGH ROSS, 1901-
1978
Diamond cut diamond. 1952.
PLAN7
Gunpowder, treason and plot.
1951. PLAN6
Heart of Bruce. 1959.
PLAN20
A question of obedience. See
Teresa of Avila
Teresa of Avila. 1961.
PLAN24
Variant title: A question
of obedience

WILLIS, ANTHONY ARMSTRONG
(ANTHONY ARMSTRONG, pseud.),
1897-1976
Ten minute alibi. 1933. FAMD

WILLIS, NATHANIEL PARKER,
1806-1867
Bianca Visconti; or, The heart
overtasked. 1837. HAL
Tortesa, the usurer. 1839.
MOSS2, QUIJ, QUIK, QUIL,
QUIM, QUIN

WILLS, WILLIAM GORMAN, 1828-1891
Eugene Aram. 1873. KILG

WILMOT, ROBERT, fl.1568-1608
Tancred and Gismund; or,
Gismond of Salerne. 1591?
CUN

WILMURT, ARTHUR. See Obey,
André. Noah (tr. and adapted by)

WILSON, ANGUS FRANK JOHNSTONE,
1913-
The mulberry bush. 1955. RHE

WILSON, AUGUST, 1945-
Ma Rainey's black bottom.
1985. BES84

WILSON, FRANK H., 1886-1956
Sugar cane. 1925. LOC

WILSON, HARRY LEON, 1867-1939
Merton of the movies. See

Kaufman, George S., and Connelly, Marc. Merton of the
movies (based on the novel by)
--See Tarkington, Booth, jt. auth.

WILSON, JOHN, 1921-
Hamp. 1966. BES66

WILSON, LANFORD, 1937-
Angels fall. 1982. BES82
The fifth of July. 1978. BES77
The Hot 1 Baltimore. 1973.
BES72, OBG
Lemon sky. 1970. GARTL
The madness of Lady Bright.
1964. HOF, ORZ
Serenading Louie. 1976. BES75
Talley's folly. 1979. BERS,
BES79

WILSON, ROBERT, d.1600
Sir John Oldcastle, pt. I
(sometimes attributed to).
See Anonymous plays.
Sir John Oldcastle, pt. I.

WILSON, ROBERT, 1928-
A letter for Queen Victoria.
1974. THG

WILSON, SANDY, 1924-
The boyfriend. 1953. BES54

WILSON, THEODORA WILSON, d.1941
Champion north. 1933. FIT

WILTSE, DAVID, 1940-
Doubles. 1985. BES84

WINCELBERG, SHIMON, 1924-
The enemy. See Kataki
Kataki. 1959. BES58
Variant title: The enemy
Resort 76 (based on the novella,
A cat in the ghetto, by
Rachmil Bryks). 1969. THL
Variant title: The windows of
heaven
The windows of heaven. See
Resort 76

WINSLOE, CHRISTA
Children in uniform. 1932.
Burnham, B., tr. and adapter.
FAMC
Variant titles: Gestern und
heute; Girls in uniform;

Maedchen in uniform
Gestern und heute. See
Children in uniform
Girls in uniform. See Children
in uniform
Maedchen in uniform. See
Children in uniform

WINTER, JOHN KEITH, 1906-
The rats of Norway. 1933.
SIXH
The shining hour. 1934. BES33,
SEV

WISE, ERNEST GEORGE (ERNEST
GEORGE, pseud.), 1894-
Down our street. 1930. SIXD

WISHENGRAD, MORTON, 1913-1963
The rope dancers. 1957.
BES57, GARSA

WITHERSPOON, KATHLEEN
Jute. 1930. THX

WITKIEWICZ, STANISŁAW IGNACY,
1885-1939
The anonymous work: four acts
of a rather nasty nightmare.
1921.
Gerould, D., and Gerould, E.,
trs. TWEN
The cuttlefish. 1922.
Gerould, D., and Gerould,
E., trs. TREBJ
Kurka wodna. See The water
hen
The water hen. 1922.
Gerould, D., and Durer, C.,
trs. DUK
Variant title: Kurka wodna

WODEHOUSE, PELLHAM GRENVILLE,
1881-1975
The play's the thing. See
Molnár, Ferenc. The play's
the thing (adapted by)

WOLFE, HUMBERT, 1885-1940
The silent knight. 1939. SIXP

WOLFE, THOMAS, 1900-1938
Look homeward, angel. See
Frings, Ketti. Look homeward,
angel (based on the novel by)

WOLFF, RUTH

The abdication. 1971? NEWVM

WOLFSON, VICTOR, 1910-
Excursion. 1937. BES36

WOLLENWEBER, LUDWIG AUGUST,
1807-1888
Ein gesprach. 18-? BUFF
Das lied von der union. 18-?
BUFF
Die margareth und die Lea. 18-?
BUFF
Eb Refschneider un Susu Leim-
bach. 18-? BUFF
Die Sara und die Bets. 18-?
BUFF

WOMEN'S THEATRE GROUP
My mother says I never should.
1975. STR
--See also Wakefield, Lou, jt. auth.

WONG, OU-HUNG, and AH, CHIA
The Red lantern. See Anonymous
Plays. The Red lantern (adapted from the Shanghai opera
version by)

WOOD, CHARLES, 1932-
Cockade. 1963. NEWE8
Fill the stage with happy hours.
1966. NEWE11

WOOD, MRS. HENRY, 1813-1887
East Lynne. 1963. BAI, CEY
Variant title: The marriage
bells; or, The cottage on
the cliff
The marriage bells; or, The
cottage on the cliff. See
East Lynne

WOOD, O. HICKORY, 1858-1913, and
COLLINS, ARTHUR
The sleeping beauty and the beast.
1900. BOOA5

WOODBRIDGE, ELIZABETH. See
Morris, Elizabeth (Woodbridge)

WOODES, NATHANIEL, fl.1580?
The conflict of conscience. 1581.
SCAT

WOODS, AUBREY, 1928- , and
ROWELL, GEORGE

Trelawny, a musical play (based
on Trelawny of the "Wells" by
Sir Arthur Wing Pinero;
music and lyrics by Julian
Slade). 1972. PLAN41

WOODS, GRAHAME, 1934-
Vicky. KAL3

WOODS, W.
The twins; or, Which is which?
1780. BELC4

WOODS, WALTER
Billy the kid. 1906. AMP8

WOODWORTH, SAMUEL, 1785-1842
The forest rose. 1825. MONR

WOOLF, BENJAMIN EDWARD,
1836-1901
The almighty dollar. See The
mighty dollar
The mighty dollar. 1875. CLA
Variant title: The almighty
dollar

WOOLL, EDWARD, 1878-1970
Libel! 1934? SEV

WORDSWORTH, WILLIAM, 1770-1850
The borderers. 1797. ENGL,
KAU

WORKSHOP '71 THEATRE COMPANY,
1975-
Survival. 1976. SOUT

WOUK, HERMAN, 1915-
The Caine mutiny court-martial.
1953. BES53, GART, NEWV,
RED, THEA54

WRIGHT, RICHARD, 1908-1960,
and GREEN, PAUL
Native son. 1941. AMB, BES40,
HARY

WU, CH'UN-HAN, 1909-1966
Hai Jui dismissed from office.
(1961)
Huang, C., and Gunn, E.,
trs. TWEH (Acts III, VI
and IX in full; others summarized)
Variant title: Hai Jui pa-kuan
Hai Jui pa-kuan. See Hai Jui
dismissed from office

WU, HAN. See Wu, Ch'un-han

WUCHTER, ASTOR CLINTON
An der lumpa parti. See Barba,
Preston Albert (based on the
poem by)

WYCHERLEY, WILLIAM, 1640?-1716
The country wife. 1674? ALLK,
ALLM, BAUL, BELK17, DAVR,
ENC, FAL, FOUB, GOS, GOSA,
HAVL, JEFF1, KRM, MANH,
RES, REST, SALR, SEN, SEVT,
TAUJ, TUQ, TWE, WEAN, WILS,
WRIR
The plain dealer. 1676. FIS,
GAY4, JEFF2, MANF, MAX,
MOR, MOSE1, NET
--See also Bickerstaffe, I.
The plain dealer (altered by)

WYMARK, OWEN
Find me. 1977. PLABE2

XENOPOULOS, GREGORIUS, 1867-
1951
Divine dream.
Gianos, M., tr. GIA

YAFA, STEVEN H. 1941-
Passing shots. 1976. WES1

YAFFE, JAMES, 1927-
The deadly game (adapted from
the novel Trapps by Friedrich
Deurrenmatt). 1960. BES59

YAGORO, KONGO. See Kongō Yagorō

YAMAUCHI, WAKAKO
And the soul shall dance. 1977.
WES11/12

YANG, CHIANG. See Yang, Chi-
K'ang

YANG, CHI-K'ANG, 1911-
Feng-hsü. See Windswept blossoms
Windswept blossoms. (1945-46)
Gunn, E., tr. TWEH
Variant title: Feng-Hsü

YANG, HSIEN-CHIH, fl.1246

Rain on the Hsiao-Hsiang (attributed to).
Crump, J., tr. CRU

YANG, LÜ-FANG
Cuckoo sings again. (1957)
Talmadge, D., and Gunn, E.,
trs. TWEH (Acts I-III in
full; Act IV summarized)
Variant title: Pu-ku-niao
yu chiao-le
Pu-ku-niao yu chiao-le. See
Cuckoo sings again

YANG, MU, pseud. See Wang,
Ching-Ksien

YANKOWITZ, SUSAN, 1941-
Boxes. (1972) BALLE11
Slaughterhouse. 1971? NEWA4
Terminal. c1974. OPE

YAO, HSIN-NUNG, 1905-
Ch'ing kung yüan. See The
malice of empire
The malice of empire (act I,
scene 1). 1941?
Anon. tr. BIR2
Variant title: Ch'ing kung
yüan

YAO MINGDE. See Yao, Ming-te

YAO, MING-TE. See Sha, Yeh-
Hsin, jt. auth.

YASUDA, ABUN. See Tsuuchi,
Hanjurō, jt. auth.

YASUKIYO, HYOSHI SA-AMI.
See Hiyoshi, Sa-ami Yasukiyo

YEATS, JACK BUTLER, 1871-1957
La la noo. 1942. BARF

YEATS, WILLIAM BUTLER, 1865-
1939
At the hawk's well. 1916?
BLOC
Variant title: The well of im-
mortality
The cat and the moon. 1926.
HAE
Cathleen ni Houlihan. 1902.
DUR, MERC, MIKL, MOSN,
MOSO
The Countess Cathleen. 1892.

ASG, BOWY, CLKWI, COTM,
SECK
Deirdre. 1906. SALE, SSTA
The dreaming of the bones. 1931.
STEI
A full moon in March. 1935.
BENS1
The hour-glass. 1903. DIC,
REIT
The king's threshold. 1903. KRE
The land of heart's desire.
1894. BURR, DOV, HUD,
MACN, WATT2
On Baile's strand. 1904.
AUG, BARC, CAP, COTQ,
ULAN
The only jealousy of Emer.
1921? CAP, COK
Purgatory. 1939? ALT, BARH,
BEAM, BENT2, CALD, LITL,
REIN, REIP, REIWE, TAUJ,
TRI, TRIA, TREBJ, ULAN
The resurrection. 1934. MERC
The well of immortality. See
At the hawk's well
The words upon the windowpane.
1935. ALT, BARF, CAN, SHR

YEH, HSIAO-NAN. See Chou, Wei-po,
jt. auth.

YEHOSHUA, ABRAHAM B., 1936-
The lover. See Chilton, Nora.
Naim (based on the novel by)

YERBY, LOREES, 1930-
The golden bull of boredom.
NEWA1

YESTON, MAURY, 1945-
Nine (music and lyrics by).
See Kopit, Arthur Lee. Nine

YEVREINOV, NIKOLAI. See
Evreinov, Nikolaĭ

YI-PING, CHUNG. See Chung, Yi-
ping

YORDAN, PHILIP, 1914-
Anna Lucasta. 1944. BES44

YOSHIMURA, JAMES
Mercenaries. 1982. NEWQA

YOUNG, SIR CHARLES LAWRENCE,
1839-1887, and HOWARD, BRONSON

scenes

ZOLA, EMILE, 1840-1902
   Thérèse Raquin. 1873.
      Boutall, K., tr. BENS3,
      HOUP

ZORRILLA, FRANCISCO DE ROJAS.
See Rojas Zorrilla, Francisco de

ZORRILLA Y MORAL, JOSE,
1817-1893
   Don Juan Tenorio. 1844.
      BRET, MARLI1, TRES
      Oliver, W., tr. MARL

ZUBER, RON
   Three X love. KINH

ZUCKMAYER, CARL, 1896-1977
   The Captain from Koepenick.
      See The Captain of Köpenick.
   The Captain of Köpenick. 1931.
      Mueller, C., tr. WELG
      Variant titles: The Captain
        from Koepenick; Der
        hauptmann von Koepenick
   The devil's general. 1946.
      Gilbert, I., and W., trs.
      BLOC
      Variant title: Des Teufels
        General
   Der Hauptmann von Koepenick.
      See The Captain of Köpenick
   Des Teufels General. See The
      devil's general

ZWEIG, STEFAN, 1881-1942
   Volpone (adapted from the play
      by Ben Jonson).
      Langner, R., tr. GARZH

LIST OF COLLECTIONS ANALYZED
AND KEY TO SYMBOLS

ABC Abcarian, Richard, and
     Klotz, Marvin, eds. Litera-
     ture: the human experience.
     New York, St. Martins, 1973.
     971p
     Bergman, I. The seventh seal
     Everyman
     Ibsen, H. An enemy of the
     people
     Lowell, R. Benito Cereno
     Molière, J. The misanthrope
     Shakespeare, W. Othello
     Shaw, G. Major Barbara
     Sophocles. Antigone

ABL Abd al-Wahhab, Fārūq, comp.
     Modern Egyptian drama: an
     anthology/Farouk Abdel Wahab.
     Minneapolis: Biblioteca Islami-
     ca, 1974. 493p (Studies in
     Middle Eastern literature;
     no. 3)
     al-Hakim, T. The sultan's
     dilemma
     Idris, Y. The farfoors
     Roman, M. The new arrival
     Rushdy, R. A journey outside
     the wall

ABRA Abrams, Meyer Howard;
     Donaldson, E. Talbot; Smith,
     Hallett; Adams, Robert M.;
     Monk, Samuel Holt; Ford,
     George H. and Daiches,
     David, eds. The Norton
     anthology of English litera-
     ture; major authors edition.
     New York, W. W. Norton
     [c1962] 2024p
     Dryden, J. The secular masque
     Jonson, B. The vision of de-
     light
     Shakespeare, W. King Henry
     the fourth, pt. I
     Shaw, G. Arms and the man

ABRB Abrams, Meyer Howard;
      Donaldson, E. Talbot; Smith,
      Hallett; Adams, Robert M.;
      Monk, Samuel Holt; Ford,
      George H. and Daiches, David,
      eds. The Norton anthology of
      English literature...New York,
      W. W. Norton [c1962] 2v
Congreve, W. The way of the
  world 1
Everyman 1
Jonson, B. The vision of de-
  light 1
Marlowe, C. The tragical history
  of the life and death of Doctor
  Faustus 1
The second shepherds' play 1
Shakespeare, W. King Henry the
  fourth, pt. I 1
Shaw, G. Arms and the man 2
Sheridan, R. The school for
  scandal 1

ABRE Abrams, Meyer Howard, et
      al., eds. The Norton an-
      thology of English literature.
      Rev. ed. New York, Norton
      [c1968] 2658p
Dryden, J. The secular masque
Jonson, B. Vision of delight
Shakespeare, W. Henry IV, pt.
  I
Shaw, G. Arms and the man

ABRF Abrams, Meyer Howard, ed.
      Norton anthology of English
      literature. Rev. ed. New
      York, Norton, 1968. 2v
Congreve, W. The way of the
  world 1
Dryden, J. The secular masque
  1
Everyman 1
Jonson, B. The vision of de-
  light 1
Marlowe, C. Dr. Faustus 1
Second shepherds' play 1
Shakespeare, W. Henry IV,
  pt. I 1
Shaw, G. Arms and the man 2

ABRH Abrams, Meyer Howard, ed.
      Norton anthology of English
      literature. 3d ed. New York,
      Norton, 1974. 2v
The Brome play of Abraham and
  Isaac 1

Congreve, W. The way of the
  world 1
Dryden, J. The secular masque
  1
Everyman 1
Jonson, B. Pleasure reconciled
  to virtue 1
Marlowe, C. Dr. Faustus 1
The second shepherds' play 1
Shakespeare, W. Henry IV,
  pt. I 1
Shakespeare, W. King Lear 1
Shaw, G. Major Barbara 2
Webster, J. The Duchess of
  Malfi 1

ABRJ Abrams, Meyer Howard, ed.
      The Norton anthology of Eng-
      lish literature. 4th ed. New
      York, Norton, 1979. 2v
Byron, G. Manfred 2
Congreve, W. Love for love 1
Dryden, J. The secular masque
  1
Everyman 1
Jonson, B. Pleasure reconciled
  to virtue 1
Jonson, B. Volpone 1
Marlowe, C. Dr. Faustus 1
Pinter, H. Dumbwaiter 2
The second shepherds' play 1
Shakespeare, W. Henry IV,
  pt. I 1
Shakespeare, W. King Lear 1
Shaw, G. Mrs. Warren's pro-
  fession 2
Webster, J. The Duchess of
  Malfi 1
Wilde, O. The importance of
  being Earnest 2

ACE Access to literature; under-
     standing fiction, drama, and
     poetry; ed. by Elliott L.
     Smith and Wanda V. Smith.
     St. Martin Press, 1981. 819p.
Chekhov, A. A marriage proposal
Glaspell, S. Trifles
Holcroft, T. A tale of mystery
Ionesco, E. The gap
Miller, A. A memory of two Mon-
  days
Shakespeare, W. Othello
Sophocles. Oedipus rex
Ward, D. Day of absence
Wilde, O. The importance of
  being earnest

ADA   Adams, Joseph Quincy, ed.
        Chief pre-Shakespearean
        dramas...Boston, Houghton
        Mifflin [c1924] 712p
      Banns
      The betraying of Christ
      The birth of Jesus
      The castle of perseverance
      Christ's ministry
      The conversion of St. Paul
      The creation of Eve, with the ex-
        pelling of Adam and Eve out of
        Paradise
      The deluge
      Duk Moraud
      Edwards, R.   Damon and Pithias
      Everyman
      The fall of Lucifer
      The famous victories of Henry the
        fifth
      Gammer Gurton's nedle
      Gascoygne, G.   Supposes
      George a Greene, the pinner of
        Wakefield
      The harrowing of hell
      Heywood, J.   A mery play be-
        twene Johan Johan, the husband,
        Tyb his wife and Syr Johan the
        preest
      Heywood, J.   The playe called the
        four pp
      Heywood, J.   The play of the
        wether
      The judgment day
      The killing of Abel
      Leicestershire St. George play
      Lyly, J.   Campaspe
      The magi, Herod, and the
        slaughter of the innocents
      Mankind
      Mary Magdalene
      Noah
      Norton, T., and Sackville, T.
        Gorboduc; or, Ferrex and
        Porrex
      Oxfordshire St. George play
      Pharaoh
      The play of the sacrament
      Preston, T.   Cambises, king of
        Persia
      The prophets
      The resurrection of Christ
      The Revesby sword play
      Robin Hood and the friar
      Robin Hood and the sheriff of
        Nottingham
      The sacrifice of Isaac

      The salutation and conception
      The shepherds
      Shetland sword dance
      The trial of Christ
      Udall, N.   Roister Doister
      Wyt and science

ADV   Adventures in world litera-
        ture, [by] James Earl Apple-
        gate, [and others] classic ed.
        New York, Harcourt, Brace,
        Jovanovich, 1970. 1046p
      Ibsen, H.   An enemy of the
        people
      Molière, J.   The misanthrope
      Shakespeare, W.   The tempest
      Sophocles.   Antigone

AFR   African plays for playing;
        selected and edited by Michael
        Etherton.   London, Heinemann,
        1975-1976. 2v (African
        writers series)
      Ajibade, S.   Rakinyo 1
      Hevi, J.   Amavi 1
      Kasoma, G.   Black mamba two 2
      Musinga, V.   The tragedy of
        Mr. No-Balance 2
      Sentongo, N.   The invisible
        bond 1
      Udensi, U.   Monkey on the
        tree 2

ALD   Aldington, Richard, ed.
        French comedies of the
        XVIIIth century...London,
        Routledge [1923] 347p
      Destouches, P.   The conceited
        count
      Le Sage, A.   Turcaret; or, The
        financier
      Marivaux, P.   The game of love
        and chance
      Regnard, J.   The residuary
        legatee

ALI   Alive Theatre Workshop.
        Dialogue and dialectic: a
        Canadian anthology of short
        plays.   Guelph, Ontario,
        Alive Press [1972] 199p
      Bullock, M.   Not to Hong Kong
      Farmiloe, D.   What do you save
        from a burning building?
      Gilbert, S.   A glass darkly
      Leeds, C.   The love song of
        Rotten John Calabrese

Libman, C. Follow the leader
Pluta, L. Little guy Napoleon
Russell, L. Penetration
Spensley, P. Hell's bells
Szablowski, J. Subsidiary vice-
president

ALL Allen, John, ed. Four con-
tinental plays. London, Heine-
mann [1964] 149p
Chekhov, A. A wedding
Kleist, H. The broken jug
Niccodemi, D. The poet
Pirandello, L. The jar

ALLE Allen, John, ed. Three
medieval plays...London...
Heineman [c1953] 54p
The farce of Master Pierre
Pathelin
The pageant of the shearmen and
taylors
The summoning of Everyman

ALLI Allison, Alexander W.;
Carr, Arthur J., and Eastman,
Arthur M., eds. Masterpieces
of the drama...New York, Mac-
millan [c1957] 693p
Chekhov, A. The cherry orchard
Euripides. Alcestis
García Lorca, F. The house of
Bernarda Alba
Giraudoux, J. The madwoman of
Chaillot
Ibsen, H. Hedda Gabler
Jonson, B. Volpone; or, The
fox
Molière, J. The miser
O'Casey, S. Juno and the pay-
cock
Sheridan, R. The rivals
Sophocles. Oedipus rex
Synge, J. Riders of the sea

ALLJ Allison, Alexander Ward;
Carr, Arthur J. and Eastman,
Arthur M., eds. Master-
pieces of the drama. 2d ed...
New York, Macmillan [1966]
814p
Beckett, S. Act without words
Beckett, S. All that fall
Brecht, B. The Caucasian
chalk circle
Chekhov, A. The cherry or-
chard

Euripides. The bacchae
García Lorca, F. The house of
Bernarda Alba
Giraudoux, J. The madwoman of
Chaillot
Ibsen, H. Hedda Gabler
Jonson, B. Volpone; or, The
fox
Molière, J. The miser
O'Casey, S. Juno and the pay-
cock
Sheridan, R. The rivals
Sophocles. Oedipus
Synge, J. Riders to the sea

ALLK Allison, Alexander Ward;
Carr, Arthur J. and East-
man, Arthur M., eds. Master-
pieces of the drama. 3d ed...
New York, Macmillan, 1974.
937p
Aeschylus. Agamemnon
Aristophanes. Lysistrata
Beckett, S. Act without words
Beckett, S. All that fall
Brecht, B. Good woman of Set-
zuan
Chekhov, A. The cherry or-
chard
Congreve, W. The way of the
world
Davis, O. Purlie victorious
Euripides. The Bacchae
García Lorca, F. The house
of Bernarda Alba
Giraudoux, J. The madwoman
of Chaillot
Ibsen, H. Hedda Gabler
Jones, L. The toilet
Jonson, B. Volpone; or, The
fox
Miller, A. Death of a salesman
Molière, J. The miser
O'Casey, S. Juno and the pay-
cock
O'Neill, E. Desire under the
elms
Pirandello, L. Six characters in
search of an author
Racine, J. Phaedra
The second shepherd play
Shaw, G. Saint Joan
Sheridan, R. The rivals
Sophocles. Oedipus rex
Strindberg, A. The ghost sonata
Synge, J. Riders to the sea
Webster, J. The Duchess of Malfi

Wycherley, W. The country wife

ALLM Allison, Alexander W., Carr,
Arthur J., and Eastman,
Arthur M., eds. Masterpieces
of the drama. 4th ed. New
York, Macmillan, 1979.
Aeschylus. Agamemnon
Aristophanes. Lysistrata
Beckett, S. Act without words
Beckett, S. All that fall
Brecht, B. Good woman of Set-
zuan
Chekhov, A. Cherry orchard
Euripides. Bacchae
García Lorca, F. The house of
Bernarda Alba
Ibsen, H. Hedda Gabler
Jones, L. Dutchman
Jonson, B. Volpone; or, The fox
Miller, A. Death of a salesman
Molière, J. The miser
O'Casey, S. Juno and the pay-
cock
O'Neill, E. Desire under the
elms
Pirandello, L. Six characters in
search of an author
Racine, J. Phaedra
Second shepherds' play
Shakespeare, W. Henry IV,
Part 1
Shaffer, P. Equus
Shaw, G. St. Joan
Sheridan, R. The rivals
Sophocles. Oedipus rex
Strindberg, A. Ghost sonata
Synge, J. Rdiers to the sea
Webster, J. Duchess of Malfi
Wilde, O. Importance of being
earnest
Williams, T. Glass menagerie
Wycherley, W. Country wife

ALP Alpern, Hymen and Martel,
José, eds. Diez comedias
del siglo de oro...New York,
Harper [c1939] 859p
Calderón de la Barca, P.
La vida es sueño
Castro y Bellvis, G. Las moce-
dades del Cid
Cervantes Saavedra, M. La
Numancia
Mira de Amescua, A. El esclavo
del demonio
Moreto y Cabaña, A. El des-

dén con el desdén
Rojas Zorilla, F. Del rey abajo,
ninguno
Ruiz de Alarcón y Mendoza, J.
La verdad sospechosa
Téllez, G. El burlador de
Sevilla
Vega Carpio, L. La estrella
de Sevilla
Vega Carpio, L. Fuenteovejuna

ALPE Alpern, Hymen and Martel,
José, eds. Teatro hispano-
americano...[1st ed.] New
York, Odyssey Press [c1956]
412p
Alsina, A. La marca de fuego
Eichelbaum, S. Divorcio nupcial
Moock Bousquet, A. La serpiente
Rojas, R. Ollántay
Sánchez, F. Los derechos de la
salud
Segura, M. Na Catita

ALPF Alpern, Hymen, ed.
Three classic Spanish plays.
New York, Washington Square
Press [1963] 229p (The ANTA
Series of Distinguished Plays)
Calderón de la Barca, P. Life is
a dream
Rojas Zorilla, F. None beneath
the king
Vega Carpio, L. The sheep

ALPJ Alphonso-Karkala, John Baptist, ed. An anthology of Indian literature. Harmondsworth, Middlesex, Penguin,
1971. 630p
Bhasa. The vision of Vasavadat-
ta

ALS Altenbernd, Lynn, ed.
Exploring literature; fiction,
poetry, drama, criticism. New
York, Macmillan, 1970. 702p
Hansberry, L. A raisin in the
sun
Ibsen, H. Hedda Gabler
Lowell, R. My kinsman, Major
Molineux
Shakespeare, W. A midsummer
night's dream
Sophocles. Oedipus Rex

ALT Altenbernd, Lynn and Lewis,

ALT (cont.)
Leslie L., eds. Introduction to literature: plays. New York, Macmillan, 1963. 440p
Anouilh, J. Becket; or, The honor of God
Chekhov, A. The cherry orchard
Everyman
García Lorca, F. Blood wedding
Ibsen, H. Ghosts
Ionesco, E. The chairs
Molière, J. The miser
O'Neill, E. Desire under the elms
Pirandello, L. It is so (if you think so)
Sheridan, R. The school for scandal
Sophocles. Antigone
Synge, J. Riders to the sea
Yeats, W. Purgatory
Yeats, W. The words upon the window-pane

ALTE Altenberndt, Lynn and Lewis, L. L., eds. Introduction to literature: plays. 2d ed. New York, Macmillan, 1969. 546p
Anouilh, J. Becket; or, The honor of God
Chekhov, A. The cherry orchard
Everyman
García Lorca, F. Blood wedding
Ibsen, H. Ghosts
Ionesco, E. The chairs
Molière, J. The misanthrope
O'Neill, E. Desire under the elms
Pirandello, L. It is so (if you think so)
Plautus, T. Amphitryon
Shakespeare, W. The tragedy of Hamlet, Prince of Denmark
Shaw, G. The man of destiny
Sheridan, R. The school for scandal
Sophocles. Antigone
Synge, A. Riders to the sea

AMB America on stage: 10 great plays of American history. Edited with preface and introductory note by Stanley Richards. New York, Doubleday, 1976. 939p
Anderson, M. Valley Forge

Kingsley, S. The patriots
Koch, H. In time to come
Lawrence, J., and Lee, R. Inherit the wind
Levitt, S. The Andersonville trial
Miller, A. The crucible
Schary, D. Sunrise at Campobello
Shaw, I. Bury the dead
Van Doren, M. The last days of Lincoln
Wright, R. Native son

AME American caravan, a yearbook of American literature... Edited by Van Wyck Brooks, Alfred Kreymborg, Lewis Mumford and Paul Rosenfeld. New York, Macaulay [c1927-c1936] 5v Title varies: 1927, The American caravan; 1928, The second American Caravan; 1929, The new American caravan; 1931, American caravan IV; 1936, The new caravan
Basshe, E. The dream of the dollar 5
Frank, W. New Year's eve 2
Geddes, V. The stable and the grove 4
Gold, M. Hoboken blues 1
Green, P. Supper for the dead 1
Green, P. Tread the green grass 3
Kreymborg, A. The dead are free 5
Schwartz, D. Choosing company 5
Williams, W. The first president 5

AMEM American melodrama. Ed... by Daniel C. Gerould. N.Y., Performing Arts Journal Publications, 1983. 247
Aiken, G. Uncle Tom's Cabin
Belasco, D. The girl of the golden West
Boucicault, D. The poor of New York
Daly, A. Under the gaslight

AMERICAN LITERATURE: a period anthology; Oscar Cargill, general editor. See

AMP (cont.)
MacKaye, S. An arrant knave 11
MacKaye, S. In spite of all 11
MacKaye, S. Rose Michel 11
MacKaye, S. Won at last 11
Mitchell, L. Becky Sharp 16
Mortimer, L. No mother to guide
    her 8
Murdock, F. Davy Crockett; or,
    Be sure you're right, then go
    ahead 4
Payne, J. The black man; or,
    The spleen 6
Payne, J. The boarding schools;
    or, Life among the little folk 5
Payne, J. The Italian bride 6
Payne, J. The last duel in Spain
    6
Payne, J. Mazeppa; or, The wild
    horse of Tartary 5
Payne, J. Mount Savage 5
Payne, J. Romulus, the shepherd
    king 6
Payne, J. The Spanish husband;
    or, First and last love 5
Payne, J. Trial without jury; or,
    The magpie and the maid 5
Payne, J. The two sons-in-law 5
Payne, J. Woman's revenge 6
Smith, R. The bombardment of
    Algiers 13
Smith, R. The last man; or,
    The cock of the village 13
Smith, R. The sentinels; or,
    The two sergeants 13
Smith, R. Shakespeare in love 13
Smith, R. A wife at a venture 13
Smith, R. William Penn 13
Steele, S. The crock of gold; or,
    The toiler's trials 14
Stone, J. Metamora; or, The last
    of the Wampanoags 14
Stone, J. Tancred, King of Sicily;
    or, The archives of
    Palermo 14
Taylor, C. From rags to
    riches 8
Tyler, R. The island of Bar-
    rataria 15
Tyler, R. Joseph and his
    brethren 15
Tyler, R. The judgment of
    Solomon 15
Tyler, R. The origin of the
    feast of Purim; or, The
    destinies of Haman &
    Mordecai 15

Wallach, L. Rosedale; or, The
    rifle ball 4
Wilkins, J. Signor Marc 14
Woods, W. Billy the Kid 8
Young, C., and Howard, B.
    Knave and queen 10

AMPA America's lost plays. v21.
    Satiric comedies; Meserve,
    Walter J. and Reardon,
    William R., eds. Bloomington,
    Ind., Indiana University
    Press, 1969. 158p
The battle of Brooklyn
Brougham, J. Po-ca-hon-tas
Dunlap, W. Darby's return
Hunter, G. Androboros
The trial of Atticus before Judge
    Beau, for a rape

AND Anderson, George Kumler and
    Walton, Edna Lou, eds. This
    generation...Chicago, Scott,
    Foresman [c1939] 975p
Dunsany, E. The queen's ene-
    mies
Green, P. Johnny Johnson
O'Neill, E. The hairy ape
Shaw, L. Bury the dead

ANDE Anderson, George Kumler
    and Walton, Edna Lou, eds.
    This generation. Revised
    edition...Chicago, Scott,
    Foresman [c1949] 1065p
Coward, N. Fumed oak
Galsworthy, J. Loyalties
Green, P. Johnny Johnson
MacNeice, L. The dark tower
O'Neill, E. The hairy ape

ANDF Anderson, George Lincoln,
    ed. The genius of the
    Oriental theatre. New York,
    New American Library [1966]
    416p
Chikamatsu, M. The courier for
    hell
Hiyoshi, S. Benkei on the bridge
Kālidāsa. Shakuntalā and the
    ring of recognition
Miyamasu. The hatmaker
Namiki, G., III. The subscription
    list
Seami, M. Haku Rakuten
Shudraka. The little clay cart
Zembō, M. Atsumori at Ikuta

Zembo, M. Early snow
Zenchiku, U. Aoi no Uye

ANDI Anderson, George L., ed.
Masterpieces of the Orient...
Enlarged edition. New York,
Norton, 1977. 834p
Chikamatsu, M. The courier for
hell
The deserted crone
The dwarf tree
Kālidāsa. Shakuntalā and the
ring of recognition
Komachi at Sekidera
The red lantern
Seami, M. Atsumori
Zembō, M. Early snow
Zenchiku, U. Princess Hollyhock

ANG Andrews, John Douglass
and Smith, Albert Reginald
Wilson, eds. Three Elizabethan
plays...London, Nelson [1929]
287p
Beaumont, F., and Fletcher, J.
The knight of the burning
pestle
Jonson, B. Everyman in his
humour
Massinger, P. A new way to pay
old debts

ANSORGE, ELIZABETH FRANCES.
See
PROC Prose and poetry for
appreciation...

ANT Anthology; an introduction to
literature: fiction, poetry,
drama. Edited by Lynn Alten-
bernd. New York, Macmillan,
1977. 1669p
Arrabal, F. Picnic on the battle-
field
Brecht, B. Mother Courage and
her children
Hansberry, L. A raisin in the
sun
Ibsen, H. A doll's house
Miller, A. Death of a salesman
O'Neill, E. The hairy ape
Shakespeare, W. Othello
Shaw, G. Arms and the man
Sheridan, R. The rivals
Sophocles. Antigone
Wilde, O. The importance of
being earnest

ANTH An anthology of Austrian
drama, ed. with an introduc-
tion by Douglas A. Russell.
Rutherford, N.J., Fairleigh
Dickinson University Press,
c1982. 442p
Grillparzer, F. King Ottocar,
his rise and fall
Hochwälder, F. The raspberry
picker
Hofmannsthal, H. Electra
Nestroy, J. The talisman
Schnitzler, A. La Ronde
Werfel, F. Goat song

ANTM An anthology of modern
Belgian theatre: Maurice
Maeterlinck, Fernand Crom-
melynck, and Michel de
Ghelderode. Troy, N.Y.,
Whitston Pub. Co., 1981.
288p
Crommelynck, F. The sculptor
of masks
Ghelderode, M. Escurial
Ghelderode, M. The magpie on
the gallows
Maeterlinck, M. The blind
Maeterlinck, M. The intruder
Maeterlinck, M. Pelleas and
Melisande

ARM Armenian literature comprising
poetry, drama, folklore and
classic traditions...introduction
by Robert Arnot...Rev. ed.
New York, Colonial press
[c1901] 142p (The world's
great classics)
Sundukianz, G. The ruined
family

ARMS Armstrong, William A., ed.
Elizabethan history plays...New
York, Oxford University Press,
1965. 428p
Bale, J. King John
Davenport, R. King John and
Matilda
Edward the third
Ford, J. Perkin Warbeck
Woodstock

ARNOT, ROBERT. See
ARM Armenian literature...

ASF Ashley, Leonard R. N., comp.

ASF (cont.)
Mirrors for man: 26 plays of world drama. Cambridge, Mass., Winthrop Pubs., 1974. 967p
Anouilh, J. Antigone
Brecht, B. The three penny opera
Büchner, G. Woyzeck
Chekhov, A. The cherry orchard
Dumas, A., fils. Lady of the camellias
Everyman
Ibsen, H. The wild duck
Jarry, A. Ubu the King
Kennedy, A. The owl answers
Marlowe, C. The tragical history of Doctor Faustus
Molière, J. The miser
Namiki, G., III. The subscription scroll
O'Neill, E. The long voyage home
Pirandello, L. Six characters in search of an author
Plautus. Pot of gold
Saavedra, G. Justice
Schneeman, C. Meat joy
Shakespeare, W. Macbeth
Shaw, G. Mrs. Warren's profession
Sheridan, R. The School for scandal
Sophocles. Antigone
Strindberg, A. Miss Julie
Synge, J. Riders to the sea
Van Itallie, J. America Hurrah
Williams, T. The glass menagerie
Wycherley, W. The country wife

ASG Ashley, Leonard R. N., comp. Nineteenth-century British drama...[Glenview, Ill.] Scott, Foresman [1967] 700p
Boucicault, D. London assurance
Bulwer-Lytton, E. The lady of Lyons
Gilbert, W. H.M.S. Pinafore
Jerrold, D. Black-ey'd Susan
Jones, H. Michael and his lost angel
Lewis, L. The bells
Palmer, T. East Lynne
Pinero, A. The second Mrs. Tanqueray
Robertson, T. Caste
Shelley, P. The Cenci

Wilde, O. The importance of being earnest
Yeats, W. The Countess Cathleen

ASH Ashton, John William, ed. Types of English drama... New York, Macmillan, 1940. 750p
Abraham and Melchizedek and Lot, with the sacrifice of Isaac
Browning, R. A blot in the 'scutcheon
Congreve, W. The way of the world
Everyman
Gay, J. The beggar's opera
Greene, R. Friar Bacon and Friar Bungay
Heywood, T. A woman killed with kindness
Jonson, B. The alchemist
Marlowe, C. Edward II
O'Neill, E. Anna Christie
Sheridan, R. The critic
Wilde, O. The importance of being earnest

ATKINSON, BROOKS. See
FOUB Four great comedies of the restoration and 18th century;
NEWV New voices in the American theatre...

ATT Attic tragedies...Boston, Bibliophile society, 1927. 3v
Aeschylus. Prometheus bound 3
Euripides. Hippolytus 2
Euripides. Medea 2
Sophocles. Antigone 1
Sophocles. Electra 3
Sophocles. Oedipus the king 1

AUB Auburn, Mark S., and Burkman, Katherine H., comps. Drama through performance. Boston, Houghton Mifflin, 1977. 775p
Chekhov, A. The cherry orchard
Congreve, W. Love for love
Ibsen, H. The wild duck
Jellicoe, A. The knack
Pinter, H. A slight ache
Racine, J. Phaedra

Second shepherds' play
Shakespeare, W. A midsummer
night's dream
Shakespeare, W. Othello
Sophocles. Oedipus the king
Williams, M. Cinder, Tell-It
Williams, T. The glass menagerie

AUDE Auden, Wystan Hugh, ed.
The portable Greek reader...
New York, Viking, 1948.
726p
Aeschylus. Agamemnon
Aeschylus. Choephoroe
Aeschylus. Eumenides

AUG AUGHTRY, Charles Edward,
ed. Landmarks in modern
drama, from Ibsen to Ionesco.
Boston, Houghton Mifflin
[c1963] 726p
Brecht, B. The good woman of
Setzuan
Ibsen, H. A doll's house
Ionesco, E. The bald soprano
Maeterlinck, M. Pelléas and
Mélisande
Miller, A. Death of a salesman
Pirandello, L. Six characters in
search of an author
Shaw, G. Man and superman
Strindberg, A. A dream play
Strindberg, A. Miss Julie
Synge, J. The playboy of the
western world
Yeats, W. On Baile's strand

AXT Axton, Richard, and Stevens,
John, comps. and trs.
Medieval French plays. Oxford,
Blackwell, 1971. 313p
Adam de la Halle. Le jeu de la
feuillée
Adam de la Halle. Le jeu de
Robin et de Marion
Bodel, J. Le jeu de Saint
Nicolas
Courtois d'Arras
Le garçon et l'aveugle
Le jeu d'Adam: Adam and
Eve; Cain and Abel
Rutebeuf. Le miracle de
Théophile
La seinte resureccion

AYLIFF, H. K. See
MAL Malvern festival plays...

BAC Bach, Bert C. and Browning,
Gordon, comps. Drama for
composition. Glenview, Ill.,
Scott, Foresman, 1973. 507p
Everyman
Fry, C. A phoenix too frequent
Jonson, B. Volpone; or, the
fox
O'Neill, E. Desire under the
elms
Shakespeare, W. Hamlet
Shaw, G. Arms and the man
Sheridan, R. The school for
scandal
Synge, J. The playboy of the
western world
Ward, D. Day of absence

BAI Bailey, James Osler, ed.
British plays of the nine-
teenth century...New York,
Odyssey Press [1966] 535p
Boucicault, D. After dark
Boucicault, D. London assurance
Browning, R. Pippa passes
Buckstone, J. Luke the
labourer; or, The lost son
Bulwer-Lytton, E. Richelieu;
or, The conspiracy
Gilbert, W. Engaged
Holcroft, T. A tale of mystery
Jerrold, D. The rent-day
Jones, H. The masqueraders
Jones, H. The silver king
Marston, J. The patrician's
daughter
Maturin, C. Bertram; or, The
castle of St. Aldobrand
Pinero, A. The notorious Mrs.
Ebbsmith
Robertson, T. Caste
Shaw, G. Widowers' houses
Taylor, T. Our American cousin
Wood, H. East Lynne

BAIC Bain, Carl E., ed. Drama.
New York, Norton, 1973. 592p
Bullins, E. A son, come home
Chekhov, A. The three sisters
Euripides. The bacchae
Ibsen, H. The wild duck
Miller, A. A view from the bridge
Molière, A. The misanthrope
Pirandello, L. Six characters in
search of an author
Shakespeare, W. Hamlet
Shaw, G. Caesar and Cleopatra

BAIC (cont.)
Shaw, G. Major Barbara
Sophocles. Oedipus tyrannus
Terry, M. The gloaming, oh my
  darling
Van Itallie, C. Interview

BAIE Bain, Carl E., and others,
  comps. The Norton introduc-
  tion to literature...New York,
  Norton, 1973. 1191p
Bullins, E. A son, come home
Chekhov, A. The three sisters
Euripides. The bacchae
Ibsen, H. The wild duck
Pirandello, L. Six characters in
  search of an author
Shakespeare, W. Hamlet
Shaw, G. Major Barbara
Terry, M. The gloaming, oh my
  darling

BAIG Bain, Carl E., et al., eds.
  The Norton introduction to
  literature. 2d ed. New York,
  Norton, 1977. 1403p
Bullins, E. A son, come home
Chekhov, A. Three sisters
Euripides. The bacchae
Ibsen, H. The wild duck
Pirandello, L. Six characters in
  search of an author
The sacrifice of Isaac
Shakespeare, W. Hamlet
Sophocles. Oedipus tyrannus
Wilde, O. The importance of
  being Earnest
Williams, T. The glass menagerie
Williams, T. The long goodbye

BAK Baker, George Pierce,
  comp. Modern American
  plays...New York, Harcourt,
  Brace and Howe, 1920. 544p
Anspacher, L. The unchastened
  woman
Belasco, D. The return of Peter
  Grimm
Massey, E. Plots and playwrights
Sheldon, E. Romance
Thomas, A. As a man thinks

BAKS Bakshy, Alexander, comp.
  and tr. Soviet scene; six
  plays of Russian life...New
  Haven, Yale University Press,
  1946. 348p

Afinogenov, A. Far taiga
Ilyenkov, V. The square of
  flowers
Marshak, S. Twelve months
Pogodin, N. The chimes of the
  Kremlin
Shkvarkin, V. Father unknown
Trenyov, K. Lyubov Yarovaya

BALD Bald, Robert Cecil, ed. Six
  Elizabethan plays...Boston,
  Houghton Mifflin [c1963]
Beaumont, F., and Fletcher,
  J. The knight of the burning
  pestle
Dekker, T. The shoemakers'
  holiday
Ford, J. The broken heart
Jonson, B. Epicoene; or, The
  silent woman
Marlowe, C. Tamburlaine the
  great (Part 1)
Webster, J. The duchess of
  Malfi

BALL Ball, John, ed. From
  Beowulf to modern British
  writers. Based on Robert
  Shafer's From Beowulf to
  Thomas Hardy. [One-volume
  ed.] New York, Odyssey
  Press [1959] 1364p
Eliot, T. Murder in the cathe-
  dral
Everyman
Marlowe, C. The tragical history
  of Doctor Faustus
Shaw, G. Don Juan in hell
Synge, J. in the shadow of the
  glen

BALLE Ballet, Arthur Harold, ed.
  Playwrights for tomorrow; a
  collection of plays. Minneapo-
  lis, University of Minnesota
  Press, c1966-1975. 13v
Auletta, R. Stops 10
Ball, D. Assassin 7
Barber, P. I, Elizabeth Otis,
  being of sound mind 3
Bernard, K. The unknown
  Chinaman 10
Boretz, N. Shelter area 2
Bosakowski, P. Bierce takes on
  the railroad 11
Coyle, M. The root 12
Feldhaus-Weber, M. The world

BARD Barnet, Sylvan; Berman,
Morton and Burto, William,
eds. The genius of the
early English theatre...[New
York] New American Library
[c1962] 453p
Abraham and Isaac
Everyman
Jonson, B. Volpone
Marlowe, C. Doctor Faustus
Milton, J. Samson Agonistes
The second shepherds' play
Shakespeare, W. Macbeth

BARF Barnet, Sylvan; Berman,
Morton and Burto, William,
eds. The genius of the Irish
theatre...[New York] New
American Library [c1960]
366p
Gregory, I. The Canavans
O'Casey, S. Purple dust
O'Donovan, M. In the train
Shaw, G. John Bull's other
island
Synge, J. Deirdre of the sor-
rows
Yeats, J. La la noo
Yeats, W. The words upon the
windowpane

BARG Barnet, Sylvan; Berman,
Morton and Burto, William
eds. The genius of the
later English theater...
[New York] New American
Library [c1962] 536p
Byron, G. Cain
Congreve, W. The way of the
world
Golding, W. The brass butter-
fly
Goldsmith, O. She stoops to
conquer; or, The mistakes
of a night
Shaw, G. Major Barbara
Wilde, O. The importance of
being earnest

BARH Barnet, Sylvan; Berman,
Morton and Burto, William,
eds. An introduction to
literature...Boston, Little,
Brown [c1961] 491p
Quem quaeritis
Sophocles. Antigone
Shaw, G. The shewing up of

Blanco Posnet
Yeats, W. Purgatory

BARI Barnet, Sylvan, [and others]
comps. An introduction to
literature...4th ed. Boston,
Little, Brown, 1971. 961p
Ibsen, H. A doll's house
Ionesco, E. The gap
Molière, J. The misanthrope
Quem quaeritis
Shakespeare, W. The tragedy of
Hamlet: Prince of Denmark
Sophocles. Antigone
Sophocles. Oedipus Rex
Synge, J. Riders to the sea
Ward, D. Happy ending
Williams, T. The glass menagerie

BARIA Barnet, Sylvan, et al., eds.
An introduction to literature:
fiction, poetry, drama. 5th
ed. Boston, Little, Brown,
1973. 963p
Ibsen, H. A doll's house
Ionesco, E. The gap
Molière, J. The misanthrope
Quem quaeritis
Shakespeare, W. The tragedy of
Hamlet: Prince of Denmark
Sophocles. Antigone
Sophocles. Oedipus Rex
Synge, J. Riders to the sea
Ward, D. Happy ending
Williams, T. The glass menagerie

BARIC Barnet, Sylvan, et al., eds.
An introduction to literature:
fiction, poetry, drama. 6th
ed. Boston, Little, Brown,
1977. 1092p
Ibsen, H. A doll's house
Ionesco, E. The gap
Miller, A. Death of a salesman
Quem quaeritis
Shakespeare, W. The tragedy of
Othello
Shaw, B. Pygmalion
Sophocles. Antigone
Sophocles. Oedipus Rex
Synge, J. Riders to the sea
Williams, T. The glass menagerie

BARJ Barnet, Sylvan; Berman,
Morton and Burto, William, eds.
Tragedy and comedy...Boston,
Little, Brown [1967] 764p

Aristophanes. The birds
Ibsen, H. Hedda Gabler
Molière, J. The misanthrope
Pirandello, L. Henry IV
Shakespeare, W. As you like
   it
Shakespeare, W. The tragedy
   of Othello
Shaw, G. Major Barbara
Sophocles. Oedipus the king
Wilder, T. The matchmaker
Williams, T. A streetcar named
   desire

BARK Barnet, Sylvan, Berman,
   Morton, and Burto, William,
   eds. Types of drama:
   plays and essays. Boston,
   Little, Brown, 1972. 674p
Aristophanes. The birds
Bergman, I. Wild strawberries
Brecht, B. Good woman of
   Setzuan
Chekhov, A. Cherry orchard
Ibsen, H. Hedda Gabler
Ionesco, E. The gap
Jones, L. Dutchman
Miller, A. Death of a salesman
Molière, J. Misanthrope
O'Neill, E. Emperor Jones
Pirandello, L. Henry IV
Shakespeare, W. As you like it
Shakespeare, W. King Lear
Shaw, G. Major Barbara
Sophocles. Oedipus the king
Zindel, P. The effect of gamma
   rays on man-in-the-moon
   marigolds

BARL Barnet, Sylvan, et al.,
   comps. Types of drama:
   plays and essays. 2nd ed.
   Boston, Little, Brown, 1977.
   708p
Aristophanes. Lysistrata
Bergman, I. Wild strawberries
Brecht, B. Good woman of
   Setzuan
Chekhov, A. Cherry orchard
Ibsen, H. Hedda Gabler
Ionesco, E. The gap
Jones, L. Dutchman
Miller, A. Death of a salesman
Molière, J. Misanthrope
O'Neill, E. Emperor Jones
Pirandello, L. Six characters
   in search of an author

Shaffer, P. Equus
Shakespeare, W. King Lear
Shakespeare, W. A midsummer
   night's dream
Shaw, G. Major Barbara
Sophocles. Oedipus the king
Zindel, P. The effect of gamma
   rays on man-in-the-moon mari-
   golds

BARO Barranger, Milly Slater
   and Dodson, Daniel B. New
   York, Harcourt, Brace, Jo-
   vanovich, 1971. 431p
Arrabal, F. Picnic on the battle-
   field
Hansberry, L. A raisin in the
   sun
Ibsen, H. Ghosts
Miller, A. All my sons
Molière, J. The miser
Shakespeare, W. Romeo and
   Juliet
Sophocles. Antigone

BARR Barrows, Herbert; Heffner,
   Hubert; Ciardi, John and
   Douglas, Wallace, eds. An
   introduction to literature...
   Boston, Houghton Mifflin
   [c1959] 1331p
Chekhov, A. The cherry orchard
Ibsen, H. The wild duck
O'Casey, S. Juno and the pay-
   cock
Pirandello, L. Six characters in
   search of an author
Shaw, G. Candida
Wilde, O. The importance of
   being earnest

BARS Barrows, Marjorie Wescott,
   and others, eds. The American
   experience: Drama. New York,
   Macmillan, 1968. 371p (Rev.
   ed. of Contemporary American
   Drama)
Albee, E. The sandbox
Anderson, M. Barefoot in Athens
Hellman, L. The little foxes
Wilder, T. The matchmaker
Williams, T. The glass menagerie

BART Barrows, Marjorie
   Wescott, comp. Currents in
   drama. Rev. ed. New York,
   Macmillan [1968] 327p

BART (cont.)
  Benêt, S. The devil and
  ˅ Daniel Webster
  Čapek, K. R.U.R.
  Chekhov, A. The boor
  Milne, A. The ugly duckling
  Saroyan, W. The man with
    the heart in the highlands
  Shakespeare, W. A midsummer
    night's dream
  Tagore, R. The post office

BARU Barrows, Marjorie Wescott,
    ed. The English tradition:
    Drama. New York, Macmillan,
    1968. 477p
  Goldsmith, O. She stoops to
    conquer
  O'Casey, S. The plough and
    the stars
  Osborne, J. A subject of scan-
    dal and concern
  Shakespeare, W. Macbeth
  Shaw, G. Arms and the man

BARV Barrows, Marjorie Wescott
    and Dolkey, Matthew, eds.
    Modern English drama. New
    York, Macmillan [c1964]
    358p
  Dane, C. Wild Decembers
  Priestley, J. They came to
    the city
  Shaw, G. Arms and the man
  Sherriff, R. Home at seven

BAS Baskervill, Charles Read;
    Heltzel, Virgil B., and
    Nethercot, Arthur H., eds.
    Elizabethan and Stuart plays
    ...New York, Holt [c1934]
    1660p
  Arden of Feversham
  Attowell's jig (Francis' new jig)
  Beaumont, F., and Fletcher, J.
    The knight of the burning
    pestle
  Beaumont, F., and Fletcher, J.
    The maid's tragedy
  Beaumont, F., and Fletcher, J.
    Philaster
  Chapman, G. Bussy d'Ambois
  Dekker, T. The honest whore,
    pt. I
  Dekker, T. The shoemakers'
    holiday
  Fletcher, J. The faithful

  shepherdess
  Ford, J. The broken heart
  Ford, J. Perkin Warbeck
  Ford, J. Dekker, T., and
    Rowley, W. The witch of Ed-
    monton
  Gascoigne, G. Supposes
  Greene, R. Friar Bacon and
    Friar Bungay
  Greene, R. George a Greene
  Heywood, T. A woman killed
    with kindness
  Jonson, B. The alchemist
  Jonson, B. Every man in his
    humor
  Jonson, B. The hue and cry after
    cupid
  Jonson, B. The sad shepherd
  Jonson, B. Sejanus, his fall
  Jonson, T. Volpone
  Kyd, T. The Spanish tragedy
  Lyly, J. Endymion
  Marlowe, C. Doctor Faustus
  Marlowe, C. Edward II
  Marlowe, C. Tamburlaine, pt. I
  Marston, J., and Webster, J. The
    malcontent
  Massinger, P. The maid of honor
  Massinger, P. A new way to pay
    old debts
  Middleton, T. A trick to catch
    the old one
  Middleton, T., and Rowley, W.
    The changeling
  Mucedorus
  Norton, T., and Sackville, T.
    Gorboduc
  Peele, G. The arraignment of
    Paris
  Peele, G. The old wives' tale
  Preston, T. Cambises
  Shirley, J. The cardinal
  Shirley, J. The lady of pleasure
  Stevenson, W. Gammer Gurton's
    needle
  Udall, N. Roister Doister
  Webster, J. The Duchess of Malfi

BAT Bates, Alfred...The drama;
    Its history, literature and in-
    fluence on civilization...London,
    Athenian society, 1903-04. 22v
  Aeschylus. Eumenides 1
  Alfieri, V. Myrrha 5
  Aristophanes. The clouds 2
  Aristophanes. Ecclesiazusae 21
  Babo, J. Dagobert, king of the

BAT (cont.)

Udall, N. Ralph Roister Doister 13

Vanbrugh, J. The provoked husband 15

Vega Carpio, L. The dog in the manger 6

Voltaire, F. Mahomet 8

Voltaire, F. Socrates 8

The wept of the wish-ton-wish 19

Werner, F. The twenty-fourth of February 10

BAUG Baugh, Albert C., and McClelland, George W., eds. English literature...New York, Appleton-Century-Crofts [c1954] 1480p

Dryden, J. All for love

Marlowe, C. The tragical history of Doctor Faustus

Wilde, O. Lady Windermere's fan

BAUL Bauland, Peter and Ingram, William, comps. The tradition of the theatre. Boston, Allyn and Bacon, 1971. 633p

Brecht, B. The Caucasian chalk circle

Chekhov, A. The cherry orchard

Dürrenmatt, F. The visit

Ibsen, H. Hedda Gabler

Miller, A. The crucible

Molière, J. The would-be gentleman

The second shepherds' play

Shaw, G. The devil's disciple

Sophocles. Antigone

Strindberg, A. A dream play

Webster, J. The duchess of Malfi

Wycherley, W. The country wife

BAYLISS, JOHN See
NEWR New road...

BAYM Baylor, Robert and Moore, James, ed. In the presence of this continent; American themes and ideas...New York, Holt, Rinehart and Winston, 1971. 551p

Gurney, A. The golden fleece

Humphrey, H., and Baldwin, J. My childhood

Lamb, M. But what have you

done for me lately?

Terry, M. Calm down, Mother

Trombo, D. Opening sequence

BEAC Beacon lights of literature... [Edited by] Marquis E. Shattuck...Rudolph W. Chamberlain...Edwin B. Richards... [Books six-twelve] Syracuse, N.Y., Iroquois, 1940. 7v

Coppée, F. The violin maker of Cremona 8

Down, O. The maker of dreams 12

Dunsany, E. A night at an inn 11

Glaspell, S. Trifles 11

Goldsmith, O. She stoops to conquer 11

Gregory, I. The rising of the moon 12

Gregory, I. Spreading the news 8

Hall, H., and Middlemass, R. The valiant 10

Kaufman, G., and Connelly, M. Merton of the movies 12

MacKaye, P. Sam Average 11

Moeller, P. Helena's husband 12

Moorhouse, A. The grand cham's diamond 10

O'Neill, E. Ile 12

Saunders, L. The knave of hearts 7

Shakespeare, W. Julius Caesar 11

Shakespeare, W. Macbeth 12

Shakespeare, W. The merchant of Venice 10

Shakespeare, W. A midsummer night's dream 9

Walker, S. The medicine show 11

BEAL Beal, Richard S., and Korg, Jacob, eds. The complete reader. Englewood Cliffs, N.J., Prentice-Hall, 1961. 630p

Shakespeare, W. The chronicle history of King Henry the fourth, pt. one

Shaw, G. Arms and the man

Sophocles. Oedipus the King

BEAM Beal, Richard S. and Korg, Jacob, eds. The complete reader. 2d ed. Englewood

Cliffs, N.J., Prentice-Hall
[1967] 627p
Shakespeare, W. Henry IV,
pt. 1
Shaw, G. Arms and the man
Sophocles. Oedipus
Yeats, W. Purgatory

BEAR Beardsley, Monroe C.;
Daniel, Robert and Leggett,
Glenn, eds. Theme and
form...Englewood Cliffs, N.J.,
Prentice-Hall, 1956. 725p
Shakespeare, W. Othello
Shaw, G. Arms and the man
Sophocles. Antigone
Thomas, D. The doctor and the
devils

BEAS Beardsley, Monroe C., et
al., eds. Theme and form:
an introduction to literature.
4th ed. Englewood Cliffs,
N.J., Prentice-Hall, 1975.
Brecht, B. Life of Galileo
McNally, T. Botticelli
Sophocles. Oedipus the king

BECHHOFER, CARL ERIC. See
ROE Roberts, Carl Eric
Bechhofer, tr. Five Russian
plays...

BELC Bell, John, ed. Bell's
British theatre, farces--1784;
with a new introduction by
Byrne R. S. Fone; and with
new author and play indexes.
New York, AMS Press, 1977.
4v
Bate, H. The rival candidate 4
Bickerstaffe, I. The padlock 3
Bickerstaffe, I. The sultan 1
Bickerstaffe, I. Thomas and
Sally 2
Burney, C. Cunning man 2
Carey, H. Chrononhotonthologos
2
Carey, H. The contrivances 4
Cibber, C. Flora 4
Coffey, C. The devil to pay 2
Colman, G. Comus 4
Colman, G. The deuce is in him
1
Colman, G. The musical lady 2
Colman, G. Polly Honeycombe 3
Dibdin, C. The deserter 4

Dodsley, R. The miller of Mans-
field 3
Dodsley, R. The toy-shop 3
Fielding, H. The intriguing
chambermaid 3
Fielding, H. The lottery 2
Fielding, H. The mock doctor 1
Fielding, H. The virgin un-
masked 2
Foote, S. The author 3
Foote, S. The commissary 4
Foote, S. The Englishman in
Paris 3
Foote, S. The Englishman re-
turn'd from Paris 3
Foote, S. The knights 1
Foote, S. The lyar 2
Foote, S. The mayor of Garrat
2
Foote, S. The orators 4
Foote, S. The patron 4
Foote, S. Taste 1
Garrick, D. Bon ton 4
Garrick, D. Bucks, have at ye
all 4
Garrick, D. Catharine and
Petruchio 3
Garrick, D. Cymon 3
Garrick, D. The guardian 1
Garrick, D. High life below stairs
1
Garrick, D. Lethe 1
Garrick, D. The lying valet 2
Garrick, D. Miss in her teens 1
Garrick, D. Neck or nothing 2
Hawkesworth, J. Edgar and Em-
meline 4
Jackman, I. All the world's a
stage 4
Mendez, M. The chaplet 1
Murphy, A. The apprentice 1
Murphy, A. The citizen 3
Murphy, A. The old maid 2
Murphy, A. Three weeks after
marriage 4
Murphy, A. The upholsterer 1
O'Hara, K. The golden pippin 3
O'Hara, K. Midas 2
Ravenscroft, E. The anatomist 1
Reed, J. The register-office 3
Shakespeare, W. Florizel and
Perdita (altered from) 1
Sheridan, T. Captain O'Blunder
3
The spirit of contradiction (by a
Gentleman of Cambridge) 4
Smollet, T. The reprisal 2

BELC (cont.)
Woods, W. The twins 4

BELG Bell, John, ed. Bell's
British theatre; selected plays,
1791-1802, 1797; 49 plays un-
represented in eds. of 1776-
1781 and 1784; with a new in-
troduction and preface by
Byrne R. S. Fone and with
new author and play indexes.
New York, AMS Press, 1977.
16v
Bickerstaffe, I. The hypocrite,
altered from Colley Cibber 1
Bickerstaffe, I. The plain dealer,
altered from William Wycher-
ley 1
Bickerstaffe, I. The school for
fathers 1
Cibber, C. Love makes a man 2
Colman, G. Bonduca, altered
from Beaumont and Fletcher 3
Colman, G. The jealous wife 3
Cowley, H. Albina, Countess
Raimond 14
Cumberland, R. Battle of
Hastings 6
Cumberland, R. The brothers 5
Cumberland, R. The Carmelite 5
Cumberland, R. The choleric
man 6
Cumberland, R. The fashionable
lover 6
Cumberland, R. The natural son
6
Cumberland, R. The West In-
dian 5
Dodsley, R. Cleone 15
Foote, S. The minor 15
Franklin, T. Earl of Warwick 16
Garrick, D. The clandestine mar-
riage 7
Garrick, D. Cymon 7
Glover, R. Medea 15
Goldsmith, O. The good natured
man 8
Goldsmith, O. She stoops to con-
quer 8
Griffiths, E. School for rakes 2
Hartson, H. The Countess of
Salisbury 11
Hoole, J. Cyrus 9
Hoole, J. Timanthes 9
Hull, T. Henry II 4
Johnson, S. Irene 8
Jonson, B. The alchemist 16

Kelly, H. False delicacy 10
Kelly, H. School for wives 10
Kelly, H. A word to the wise 10
Kendrick, W. Falstaff's wedding
3
Lee, N. Chapter of accidents 11
Lee, N. Lucius Junius Brutus
11
Lillo, G. The fatal curiosity 9
Macklin, C. Man of the world 4
Mason, W. Caractacus 12
Mason, W. Elfrida 12
Milton, J. Samson Agonistes 12
Murphy, A. Grecian daughter
13
Murphy, A. The orphan of China
14
Murphy, A. School for guardians
14
Murphy, A. A way to keep him
13
Murphy, A. Zenobia 13
Shakespeare, W. Pericles (al-
tered from) 7
Sheridan, F. The discovery 4
Thomson, J. Edward and Eleonora
2
Whitehead, W. School for lovers
16

BELK Bell, John, ed. Bell's British
theatre, 1776-1781; with a new
introduction and preface by
Byrne R. S. Fone and with new
author and play indexes. New
York, AMS Press, 1977. 21v
Contains 105 plays, each with
special title page and separate
pagination. [Repr. of the
1776-1781 ed. pub. by J. Bell,
London]
Addison, J. Cato 3
Addison, J. The drummer 11
Banks, J. The Albion queens 14
Banks, J. Anna Bullen 14
Beaumont, F., and Fletcher, J.
Jovial crew 21
Beaumont, F., and Fletcher, J.
Philaster 18
Beaumont, F., and Fletcher, J.
Rule a wife and have a wife 4
Bickerstaffe, I. Lionel and
Clarissa 21
Bickerstaffe, I. Love in a village
21
Bickerstaffe, I. Maid of the mill
21

BELK (cont.)
confederacy 15
Vanbrugh, J. Mistake 19
Vanbrugh, J. The provok'd
wife 2
Vanbrugh, J. The relapse 11
Vanbrugh, J., and Cibber, C.
The provok'd husband 6
Villiers, G. The rehearsal 15
Whitehead, W. Creusa, Queen
of Athens 20
Whitehead, W. The Roman
father 20
Wycherley, W. The country
wife 17
Young, E. The brothers 14
Young, E. Busiris 16
Young, E. The revenge 12

BEN Benedikt, Michael and Well-
warth, George E., eds. and
trs. Modern French Theatre:
the avant-garde, Dada, and
surrealism; an anthology of
plays. New York, Dutton,
1964. 406p
Anouilh, J. and Aurenche, J.
Humulus the mute
Apollinaire, G. The beasts of
Tiresias
Aragon, L. The mirror-wardrobe
one fine evening
Artaud, A. Jet of blood
Breton, A. and Soupault, P. If
you please
Cocteau, J. The wedding on the
Eiffel Tower
Daumal, R. En gggarrrde!
Desnos, R. La Place de l'Etoile
Gilbert-Lecomte, R. The odyssey
of Ulysses the Palmiped
Ionesco, E. The painting
Jarry, A. King Ubu
Pinget, R. Architruc
Radiguet, R. The pelicans
Salacrou, A. A circus story
Tardieu, J. One way for another
Tzara, T. The gas heart
Vitrac, R. The mysteries of
love

BENA Benedikt, Michael and
Wellwarth, George E., eds.
Modern Spanish theatre; an
anthology of plays. New
York, Dutton, 1968. 416p
Alberti, R. Night and war in the

Prado Museum
Arrabal, F. First communion
Bellido, J. Football
Casona, A. Suicide prohibited in
springtime
García Lorca, F. The shoemaker's
prodigious wife
Mihura, M. Three top hats
Olmo, L. The news item
Valle-Inclán, R. Divine words

BENB Benedikt, Michael and Well-
warth, George E., eds. and
trs. Postwar German theatre:
an anthology of plays. New
York, Dutton, 1967. 348p
Borchert, W. The outsider
Dorst, T. Freedom for Clemens
Dürrenmatt, F. Incident at twi-
light
Frisch, M. The great fury of
Philip Hotz
Grass, G. Rocking back and
forth
Hildesheimer, W. Nightpiece
Kaiser, G. The raft of the
Medusa
Laszlo, C. The Chinese icebox
Laszlo, C. Let's eat hair!
Sylvanus, E. Dr. Korczak and
the children
Weiss, P. The tower

BENET, WILLIAM ROSE. See
OXF Oxford anthology of
American literature...edited
by William Rose Benét and
Norman Holmes Pearson

BENN Bennett, Henry Garland, ed.
...English literature...N.Y.,
American book company [c1935]
603p
Goldsmith, O. She stoops to con-
quer
Shakespeare, W. Macbeth

BENP Bennett, Henry Garland
...On the high road...N.Y.,
American book company
[c1935] 600p
Dowson, E. The Pierrot of the
minute
Everyman
Maeterlinck, M. The intruder
O'Neill, E. Where the cross is
made

Riggs, L. Knives from Syria
Shakespeare, W. Julius Caesar
Sheridan, R. The rivals
Wilde, P. Confessional

BENPB Bens, John H., ed.
Facing some problems...
New York, Holt, Rinehart,
and Winston, 1970. 306p
Rattigan, T. Table number seven
Shaw, I. Bury the dead
Steinbeck, J. Of mice and men

BENQ Benson, Carl Frederick and
Littleton, Taylor, eds. The
idea of tragedy. Glenview,
Ill., Scott Foresman [1966]
370p
Aeschylus. Agamemnon
Chekhov, A. Uncle Vanya
Ibsen, H. Rosmersholm
Shakespeare, W. King Lear
Sophocles. King Oedipus
Webster, J. The Duchess of Malfi

BENR Bentley, Eric Russell, ed.
The classic theatre [1st ed.]
...Garden City, N.Y., Double-
day [1958-61] 4v
Beaumarchais, P. Figaro's mar-
riage; or, One mad day 4
Beolco, A. Ruzzante returns
from the wars 1
Calderón de la Barca, P. Life is
a dream 3
Calderón de la Barca, P. Love
after death 3
Calderón de la Barca, P. The
wonder-working magician 3
Castro y Bellvis, G. Exploits of
the Cid 4
Cervantes Saavedra, M. The
siege of Numantia 3
Corneille, P. The cid 4
Goethe, J. Egmont 2
Goldoni, C. Mirandolina 1
Goldoni, C. The servant of two
masters 1
Gozzi, C. The king stag 1
Kleist, H. Penthesilea 2
Kleist, H. The Prince of Hom-
burg 2
Lesage, A. Turcaret 4
Michiavelli, N. The mandrake 1
Marivaux, P. The false confes-
sions 4
Molière, J. The misanthrope 4

Racine, J. Phaedra 4
Rojas, F. Celestina; or, The
tragi-comedy of Calisto and
Melibea 3
Schiller, J. Don Carlos 2
Schiller, J. Mary Stuart 2
Téllez, G. The trickster of Se-
ville and his guest of stone 3
The three cuckolds 1
Vega Carpio, L. Fuente Ovejuna
3

BENS Bentley, Eric Russell, ed.
From the modern repertoire.
Series one - three. [Denver,
Col.] University of Denver
press; Bloomington, Ind.,
Indiana University Press.
[c1949-1956] 3v
Anouilh, J. Cecile; or, The
school for fathers 3
Becque, H. La Parisienne 1
Brecht, B. Galileo 2
Brecht, B. Saint Joan of the
stockyards 3
Brecht, B. The threepenny opera 1
Büchner, G. Danton's death 1
Büchner, G. Leonce and Lena 3
Cocteau, J. The infernal ma-
chine 1
Cocteau, J. Intimate relations 3
Cummings, E. him 2
Eliot, T. Sweeney Agonistes 1
Fergusson, F. The king and the
duke 2
García Lorca, F. The love of
Don Perlimplin and Belisa in
the garden 1
Giraudoux, J. Electra 2
Jeffers, R. The Cretan woman 3
MacNeice, L. The dark tower 2
Mirbeau, O. The epidemic 2
Musset, A. A door should be
either open or shut 3
Musset, A. Fantasio 1
Obey, A. Venus and Adonis 2
Ostrovsky, A. Easy money 2
Pinero, A. The magistrate 3
Romains, J. Dr. Knock 3
Schnitzler, A. Anatol 3
Schnitzler, A. Round dance 1
Sternheim, C. The snob 1
Wedekind, F. The Marquis of
Keith 2
Yeats, W. A full moon in March
1
Zola, E. Thérèse Raquin 3

BENSA Bentley, Eric Russell, ed.
The genius of the Italian
theater. New York, New
American Library [1964]
584p
Bruno, G. The candle bearer
The deceived
Dovizi da Bibiena, B. The
follies of Calandro
Filippo, E. Filumena Marturano
Gozzi, C. Turandot
Pirandello, L. The emperor
Tasso, T. Amyntas

BENSB Bentley, Eric Russell,
ed. The great playwrights:
25 plays with commentaries by
critics and scholars...Garden
City, N.Y., Doubleday, 1972.
2v
Aeschylus. Prometheus bound 1
Brecht, B. The Caucasian chalk
circle 2
Brecht, B. Mother Courage 2
Calderón de la Barca, P. Life
is a dream 1
Chekhov, A. The three sisters
2
Euripides. The bacchae 1
Ibsen, H. Rosmersholm 2
Ibsen, H. The wild duck 2
Jonson, B. Volpone; or, The
fox 1
Kleist, H. Prince Frederick of
Hamburg 1
Molière, J. Don Juan; or, The
stone guest 1
Molière, J. The misanthrope 1
Pirandello, L. Right you are 2
Pirandello, L. Six characters in
search of an author 2
Racine, J. Phaedra 1
Shakespeare, W. King Lear 1
Shakespeare, W. Troilus and
Cressida 1
Shaw, G. Major Barbara 2
Shaw, G. Saint Joan 2
Sophocles. Antigone 1
Sophocles. King Oedipus 1
Strindberg, A. Miss Julie 2
Synge, J. The playboy of the
western world 2
Vega Carpio, L. Fuente ovejuna
1
Wilde, O. The importance of
being earnest 2

BENSC Bentley, Eric Russell, ed.
Let's get a divorce! and other
plays. New York, Hill and
Wang [c1958] 364p
Courteline, G. These cornfields
Feydeau, G. Keep an eye on
Amélie!
Labiche, E. and Martin, E. A
trip abroad
Prévert, J. A united family
Sardou, V. and Najac, E. Let's
get a divorce!

BENT Bentley, Eric Russell, ed.
The modern theatre. [Plays]
Garden City, N.Y., Doubleday
[c1955-1960] 6v
Anouilh, J. Medea 5
Anouilh, J. Thieves' carnival 3
Becque, H. Woman of Paris 1
Beerbohm, M. A social success
6
Brecht, B. The measures taken
6
Brecht, B. Mother courage 2
Brecht, B. The threepenny opera
1
Büchner, G. Woyzeck 1
Büchner, G. Danton's death 5
Conrad, J. One day more 3
Fitch, C. Captain Jinks of the
horse marines 4
Ghelderode, M. Escurial 5
Giraudoux, J. Electra 1
Giraudoux, J. Judith 3
Gogol, N. Gamblers 3
Gogol, N. The marriage 5
Labiche, E., and Marc-Michel. An
Italian straw hat 3
Mitchell, L. The New York idea
4
Musset, A. Fantasio 2
Musset, A. Lorenzaccio 6
O'Casey, S. Cock-a-doodle dandy
5
Ostrovsky, A. The diary of a
scoundrel 2
Saroyan, W. The man with the
heart in the Highlands 4
Schnitzler, A. La ronde 2
Sternheim, C. The underpants 6
Swerling, J., Burrows, A., and
Loesser, F. Guys and dolls 4
Verga, G. Cavalleria rusticana 1
Wedekind, F. Spring's awakening
6

Wilder, T. Pullman car Hiawatha 4

Yeats, W. Purgatory 2

BENU Bentley, Eric Russell, ed.
The play; a critical antholo-
gy...New York, Prentice-
Hall, 1951. 774p
Ibsen, H. Ghosts
Miller, A. Death of a salesman
Molière, J. The miser
Rostand, E. Cyrano de Bergerac
Shakespeare, W. Othello
Shakespeare, W. Twelfth night
Sophocles. Antigone
Strindberg, A. The ghost sonata
Wilde, O. The importance of
being earnest

BENY Bentley, Gerald Eades, ed.
The development of English
drama...New York, Appleton-
Century-Crofts [c1950] 823p
Abraham and Isaac
Beaumont, F., and Fletcher, J.
The knight of the burning
pestle
Boucicault, D. London assurance
Congreve, W. Love for love
Congreve, W. The way of the
world
Cumberland, R. The West Indian
Dekker, T. The shoemakers' holi-
day
The deluge; or, Noah's flood
Dryden, J. All for love; or, The
world well lost
Dryden, J., and Howard, R. The
Indian queen
Everyman
Fletcher, J. The wild-goose
chase
Ford, J. 'Tis a pity she's a
whore
Goldsmith, O. She stoops to
conquer
Greene, R. Friar Bacon and
Friar Bungay
Jonson, B. The alchemist
Lillo, G. The London merchant
Marlowe, C. Doctor Faustus
Pinero, A. The second Mrs.
Tanqueray
The second shepherds' play
Sheridan, R. The school for
scandal
Webster, J. The white devil

Wilde, O. Lady Windermere's fan

BENZ Benton, Charles William, ed.
Easy French plays...Chicago,
Scott, Foresman, 1901. 236p
Girardin, E. de. La joie fait
peur
Labiche, E. La grammaire
Scribe, E. Les doigts de fée

BERGH, ALBERT ELLERY. See
DRA Dramatic masterpieces...

BER Bergin, Thomas Goddard and
Anderson, Theodore, eds.
French plays...New York,
American book co. [c1941]
452p
Brieux, E. Les trois filles de
M. Dupont
Hervieu, P. La course du flam-
beau
Mirbeau, O. Les affaires sont
les affaires

BERKLEY, JAMES. See PATM,
PATP Patterns of literature...

BERM Bermel, Albert, ed. The
genius of the French theater
...New York, New American
Library [c1961] 574p
Anouilh, J. The lark
Beaumarchais, P. The barber of
Seville
Giraudoux, J. Song of songs
Hugo, V. Hernani
Labiche, E., and Delacour, A.
Pots of money
Molière, J. The imaginary invalid
Racine, J. Andromache
Rostand, E. The romantics

BERN Bernbaum, Ernest, ed.
Anthology of romanticism...New
York, Ronald [c1948] 1238p
Byron, G. Manfred
Shelley, P. Prometheus unbound

BERS Best American Plays: Eighth
Series, 1974-1982. Edited by
Clive Barnes Crown Publishers,
Inc., 1983. 548p
Babe, T. A prayer for my
daughter
Henley, B. Crimes of the heart
Kopit, A. Wings

BERS (cont.)

McNally, T. The Ritz
Mamet, D. American buffalo
Miller, J. That championship
season
Pomerance, B. The elephant man
Rabe, D. Streamers
Shange, N. For colored girls who
have considered suicide/when
the rainbow is enuf
Shepard, S. Buried child
Simon, N. Chapter two
Slade, B. Same time, next year
Walker, J. The River Niger
Weller, M. Loose ends
Wheeler, H. A little night music
Williams, T. A lovely Sunday
for Creve Coeur
Wilson, L. Talley's folly

BES Best plays of 1894/1899-
1985/85; and The yearbook of
the drama in America...Edited
by R. B. Mantle...G. P. Sher-
wood...John Chapman...Louis
Kronenberger...Henry Hewes...
Otis L. Guernsey, Jr...New
York, Dodd, Mead, 1920-85.
68v
Note: Excerpts and synopses
only. Numbers following titles
indicate volumes by years, e.g.,
27 indicates volume for 1927/28;
28 for 1928/29; etc.
Abbott, G., and Bridgers, A.
Coquette 27
Abbott, G., and Gleason, J.
The fall guy 24
Ableman, P. Green Julia 72
Ade, G. The county chairman
99
Akins, Z. Declassee 19
Akins, Z. The old maid 34
Albee, E. A delicate balance 66
Albee, E. The lady from Dubuque
79
Albee, E. Seascape 74
Albee, E. Tiny Alice 64
Albee, E. Who's afraid of
Virginia Woolf? 62
Alfred, W. Hogan's goat 65
Allen, J. Forty carats 68
Allen, R. Sugar babies 79
Allen, W. The floating light bulb
80
Anderson, M. Anne of the
thousand days 48

Anderson, M. Bad seed 54
Anderson, M. Barefoot in Athens
51
Anderson, M. Both your houses
32
Anderson, M. Candle in the
wind 41
Anderson, M. Elizabeth the
queen 30
Anderson, M. The eve of St.
Mark 42
Anderson, M. Gypsy 28
Anderson, M. High Tor 36
Anderson, M. Joan of Lorraine
46
Anderson, M. Key largo 39
Anderson, M., and Weill, K.
Lost in the stars 49
Anderson, M. Mary of Scotland
33
Anderson, M. Saturday's chil-
dren 26
Anderson, M. The starwagon 37
Anderson, M. Storm operation
43
Anderson, M. Valley Forge 34
Anderson, M. Winterset 35
Anderson, M., and Stallings, L.
What price glory? 24
Anderson, R. I never sang for
my father 67
Anderson, R. Tea and sympathy
53
Anderson, R. You know I can't
hear you when the water's
running 66
Andreyev, L. He who gets
slapped 21
Anouilh, J. Becket; or, The
honor of God 60
Anouilh, J. The lark 55
Anouilh, J. Poor Bitos 64
Anouilh, J. The rehearsal 63
Anouilh, J. Time remembered 57
Anouilh, J. The waltz of the
toreadors 56
Anouilh, J., and Galantière, L.
Antigone 45
Ansky, S. The dybbuk 25
Anspacher, L. The unchastened
woman 09
Archer, W. The green goddess
20
Archibald, W. The innocents 49
Ardrey, R. Stone and star 61
Arlen, M. The green hat 25
Atlas, L. Wednesday's child 33

and Key to Symbols / 261

St. Lambrecht)
The visit to the sepulchre (from
the Tenth-Century troper of
Winchester)
The woman taken in adultery (N
Town)

BEVI Bevis, Richard W., ed.
Eighteenth century drama:
afterpieces. London, Oxford
University Press, 1970. 286p
Colman, G. Polly Honeycombe
Fielding, H. The historical
register for year 1736
Foote, S. The commissary
Garrick, D. Miss in her teens
The kept mistress
Macklin, C. A will and no will
Murphy, A. The upholsterer
Murphy, A. The way to keep
him

BIER Bierman, Judah; Hart, James
and Johnson, Stanley, eds.
The dramatic experience...
Englewood Cliffs, N.J., Pren-
tice Hall, 1958. 549p
Everyman
García Lorca, F. Blood wedding
Ibsen, H. The wild duck
Hayes, J. The desperate hours
Miller, A. Death of a salesman
Saroyan, W. The time of your
life
Shakespeare, W. Othello
Shakespeare, W. Twelfth night;
or, What you will
Shaw, G. Caesar and Cleopatra
Sherwood, R. Abe Lincoln in Il-
linois
Sophocles. Oedipus rex

BIES Bierstadt, Edward Hale, ed.
Three plays of the Argentine...
New York, Duffield, 1920.
147p
Bayón Herrera, L. Santos Vega
Manco, S. Juan Moreira
Sánchez Gardel, P. The witches'
mountain

BIN Bingham, Joel Foote, comp.
Gemme della letteratura
italiane...London, Frowde,
1904. 1016p
Alfieri, V. Saul
Goldoni, C. Un curioso accidente

Metastasio, P. Attilio rigolo

BIR Birch, Cyril, ed. Anthology
of Chinese literature. New
York, Grove, 1972. 2v (v1,
From early times to the 14th
century; v2, From the 14th
century to the present day)
K'ang, C. Li K'uei carries
thorns 1
Ma, C. Autumn in the palace of
Han 1
T'ang, H. Peony pavilion 1
Yao, H. The malice of empire 2

BLA A Black quartet: 4 new Black
plays by Ben Caldwell, and
others...New York, New Ameri-
can Libraries, 1970. 158p
Bullins, E. The gentleman caller
Caldwell, B. Prayer meeting; or,
The first militant minister
Jones, L. Great goodness of life
Milner, R. The warning, a theme
for Linda

BLAG Blair, Walter, and Gerber,
John C., eds....Literature
(Better Reading vol. 2). Chi-
cago, Scott, Foresman [c1949]
778p
Note: Also published in one
volume under the title, The Col-
lege Anthology
Chekhov, A. The swan song
Dunsany, E. A night at an inn
Ibsen, H. Hedda Gabler
Molière, J. Tartuffe
O'Neill, E. Anna Christie
Sophocles. Oedipus the king

BLAH Blair, Walter and Gerber,
John, eds. Repertory...Chi-
cago, Scott, Foresman[1960]
1173p
Chekhov, A. The cherry orchard
Chekhov, A. The swan song
Chayefsky, P. Marty
Dunsany, E. A night at an inn
Fry, C. A phoenix too frequent
O'Neill, E. Bound east for Car-
diff
Shakespeare, W. Romeo and
Juliet
Sophocles. Oedipus the king

BLAI Blair, Walter; Hornberger,

BLAI (cont.)
    Theodore, and Stewart,
    Randall, eds. The literature
    of the United States...Chicago,
    Scott, Foresman [c1946-47] 2v
    Aiken, G. Uncle Tom's cabin; or,
      Life among the lowly 2
    Mitchell, L. The New York idea
      2
    O'Neill, E. The hairy ape 2
    Tyler, R. The contrast 1

BLAJ Blair, Walter; Hornberger,
    Theodore and Stewart, Randall.
    The literature of the United
    States...Single volume edition.
    Chicago, Scott, Foresman
    [c1949] 1313p
    O'Neill, E. The hairy ape

BLOC Block, Haskell M., and
    Shedd, Robert G., eds.
    Masters of modern drama...
    New York, Random House
    [c1962] 1198p
    Anouilh, J. Antigone
    Anouilh, J. Thieves' carnival
    Beckett, S. Endgame
    Brecht, B. The good woman of
      Setzuan
    Brecht, B. Mother courage and
      her children
    Camus, A. Caligula
    Chayefsky, P. Marty
    Chekhov, A. The cherry orchard
    Chekhov, A. The sea gill
    Cocteau, J. Orphée
    Duerrenmatt, F. The visit
    Frisch, M. Biedermann and the
      firebugs
    García Lorca, F. Blood wedding
    Giraudoux, J. Electra
    Giraudoux, J. The madwoman of
      Chaillot
    Gorki, M. The lower depths
    Hauptmann, G. The weavers
    Hofmannstahl, H. Death and the
      fool
    Ibsen, H. Ghosts
    Ibsen, H. Peer Gynt
    Ionesco, E. The bald soprano
    Kaiser, G. From morn to mid-
      night
    Maeterlinck, M. The intruder
    Miller, A. Death of a salesman
    O'Casey, S. Cock-a-doodle dandy
    O'Casey, S. Juno and the pay-

      cock
    Odets, C. Awake and sing!
    O'Neill, E. The Emperor Jones
    O'Neill, E. The iceman cometh
    Osborne, J. Look back in anger
    Pirandello, L. Henry IV
    Saroyan, W. The time of your
      life
    Sartre, J. No exit
    Schnitzler, A. La ronde
    Shaw, G. Major Barbara
    Shaw, G. Man and superman
    Strindberg, A. The ghost
      sonata
    Strindberg, A. Miss Julie
    Synge, J. The playboy of the
      western world
    Synge, J. Riders to the sea
    Wedekind, F. The Marquis of
      Keith
    Wilder, T. The matchmaker
    Williams, T. The glass menagerie
    Yeats, W. At the hawk's well
    Zuckmayer, C. The devil's
      general

BLOD Blodgett, Harold William and
    Johnson, Burges, eds.
    Readings for our times...
    Boston, Ginn [c1942] 2v
    Rostand, E. Cyrano de Bergerac
      1
    Wilder, T. Our town 1

BLON Bloomfield, Morton Wilfred,
    and Elliott, Robert C., eds.
    Great plays, Sophocles to
    Brecht. New York, Holt, Rine-
    hart and Winston [1965] 614p
    Brecht, B. The Caucasian chalk
      circle
    Chekhov, A. Three sisters
    Congreve, W. The way of the
      world
    Ibsen, H. Hedda Gabler
    Molière, J. The misanthrope
    O'Neill, E. The hairy ape
    Shakespeare, W. Othello
    Shaw, G. Arms and the man
    Sophocles. Antigone
    Strindberg, A. Miss Julie
    Williams, T. The glass menagerie

BLOND Bloomfield, Morton Wilfred,
    and Elliott, Robert C., eds.
    Great plays, Sophocles to Al-
    bee. 3d ed. New York, Holt,

1975. 701p
Albee, E. The American dream
Brecht, B. The Caucasian chalk
circle
Chekhov, A. Three sisters
Congreve, W. The way of the
world
Frisch, M. The firebugs
Ibsen, H. Hedda Gabler
Molière, J. The misanthrope
O'Neill, E. The hairy ape
Shakespeare, W. Othello
Shaw, G. Arms and the man
Sophocles. Antigone
Strindberg, A. Miss Julie
Williams, T. The glass menagerie

BLOO Bloomfield, Morton Wilfred,
and Elliott, Robert C., eds.
Ten plays...New York, Rine-
hart [c1951] 719p
Chekhov, A. Three sisters
Dekker, T. The shoemakers'
holiday
Farquhar, G. The beaux'
stratagem
Hellman, L. The little foxes
Ibsen, H. Hedda Gabler
O'Neill, E. The hairy ape
Rostand, E. Cyrano de Bergerac
Shakespeare, W. Othello
Sophocles. Antigone
Thurber, J., and Nugent, E.
The male animal

BOA Boas, Frederick Samuel, ed.
Five pre-Shakespearean come-
dies (early Tudor period)...
London, Oxford University
Press [1934] 343p (The
world's classics)
Gascoigne, G. Supposes
Heywood, J. The four pp
Medwall, H. Fulgens and Lu-
crece
"Mr. S. Mr. of Art." Gammer
Gurton's needle
Udall, N. Ralph Roister Doister

BOGO Bogorad, Samuel N. and
Trevithick, Jack, eds. The
college miscellany...New York,
Rinehart [c1952] 621p
Barrie, J. The twelve-pound
look
Rattigan, T. The Winslow
boy

Shakespeare, W. King Henry the
fourth, pt. I

BOH Bohemian club, San Francisco.
The Grove plays of the Bohe-
mian club; edited by Porter
Garnett...San Francisco, The
club, 1918. 3v
Crocker, C. The land of happi-
ness 3
Field, C. The cave man 2
Field, C. The man in the forest
1
Field, C. The owl and cave 1
Garnett, P. The green knight 2
Irwin, W. The Hamadryads 1
Myrtle, F. Gold 3
Pixley, F. Apollo 3
Redding, J. The atonement of
Pan 2
Robertson, L. Montezuma 1
Scheffauer, H. The sons of
Baldur 1
Shiels, J. Nec-natama 3
Steele, R. The fall of Ug 3
Stephens, H. St. Patrick at Tara
2
Stirling, G. The triumph of Bo-
hemia 1
Tharp, N. The quest of the Gor-
gon 1

BONA Bonazza, Blaze O., and Roy,
Emil, eds. Studies in drama...
New York, Harper & Row
[c1963] 344p
Ibsen, H. An enemy of the people
Shakespeare, W. A midsummer
night's dream
Shaw, G. Candida
Sophocles. Antigone
Williams, T. The glass menagerie

BONB Bonazza, Blaze Odell, and
Roy, Emil, eds. Studies in
drama. New York, Harper &
Row [c1963-64] 378p
Chekhov, A. The cherry or-
chard
Ibsen, H. An enemy of the people
Ibsen, H. The master builder
O'Neill, E. Desire under the elms
Shakespeare, W. King Lear
Shakespeare, W. A midsummer
night's dream
Shaw, G. Candida
Shaw, G. Heartbreak house

BONB (cont.)
 Sophocles. Antigone
 Wilder, T. Our town
 Williams, T. The glass menagerie

BONC Bonazza, Blaze Odell, and
 Roy, Emil, eds. Studies in
 drama. 2d ed. New York,
 Harper and Row [1968] 583p
 Brecht, B. Mother Courage and
 her children
 Chekhov, A. Cherry orchard
 Ibsen, H. An enemy of the
 people
 O'Neill, E. Desire under the elms
 Shakespeare, W. King Lear
 Shaw, G. Heartbreak house
 Sheridan, R. The school for scan-
 dal
 Sophocles. Antigone
 Strindberg, A. Miss Julie
 Synge, J. Riders to the sea
 Wilder, T. Our town
 Williams, T. The glass menagerie

BOND Bond, Richard Warwick, ed.
 Early plays from the Italian.
 Oxford, Clarendon Press, 1911.
 332p
 The buggbears
 Gascoigne, G. Supposes
 Misogonus

BOO Booth, Michael R., ed.
 Eighteenth century tragedy...
 London, New York, Oxford
 University Press, 1965. 394p
 Colman, G., the Younger. The
 iron chest
 Home, J. Douglas
 Johnson, S. Irene
 Lillo, G. The London merchant
 Moore, E. The gamester

BOOA Booth, Michael, R., ed.
 English plays of the nineteenth
 century. New York, Oxford
 University Press, 1969-1976.
 5v
 Blanchard, E. Aladdin; or, Harlequin and the wonderful lamp
 5
 Boucicault, D. The Corsican
 brothers 2
 Boucicault, D. The Shaughraun
 2
 Brough, W. The field of the

cloth of gold 5
 Brough, W., and Brough, R.
 The enchanted isle 5
 Brough, W., and Halliday, A.
 The area belle 4
 Bulwer-Lytton, E. Richelieu; or,
 The conspiracy 1
 Bulwer-Lytton, E. Money 3
 Byron, H. Robinson Crusoe;
 or, Harlequin Friday and the
 King of the Caribbee Islands
 5
 Chambers, C. The tyranny of
 tears 3
 Colman, G., the Younger. John
 Bull 3
 Coyne, J. How to settle accounts
 with your laundress 4
 Dibdin, T. Harlequin Harper;
 or, a jump from Japan 5
 Dibdin, T. Harlequin in his ele-
 ment 5
 Gilbert, W. Engaged 3
 Gilbert, W. Tom Cobb 4
 Jerrold, D. Black-eyed Susan;
 or, All in the downs 1
 Jerrold, D. Mr. Paul Pry 4
 Jones, H. Mrs. Dane's defence
 2
 Kenney, K. Raising the wind 4
 Knowles, J. Virginius 1
 Mathews, C. Patter versus clatter
 4
 Morton, J. Box and Cox 4
 Murray, W. Diamond cut diamond
 4
 Pinero, A. The magistrate 4
 Pinero, A. The second Mrs. Tan-
 queray 2
 Planché, J. Fortunio and his seven
 gifted servants 5
 Planché, J. The island of jewels
 5
 Pocock, I. The miller and his men
 1
 Taylor, T. New men and old
 acres 3
 Taylor, T. The ticket-of-leave
 man 2
 Walker, J. The factory lad 1
 Wood, J., and Collins, A. The
 sleeping beauty and the beast
 5

BOOB Booth, Michael R., comp.
 Hiss the villain, six English
 and American melodramas.

New York, Benjamin Blom,
1964. 390p
Daly, A. Under the gaslight
Haines, J. My Poll and my
partner Joe
Lewis, L. The bells
Phillips, W. Lost in London
Pocock, I. The miller and his
men
Pratt, W. Ten nights in a bar-
room

BOOM Booth, Michael R., ed. The
magistrate, and other nine-
teenth-century plays. London,
Oxford University Press, 1974.
464p
Boucicault, D. The Corsican
brothers
Colman, G. John Bull
Coyne, J. How to settle accounts
with your laundress
Gilbert, W. Engaged
Jones, H. Mrs. Dane's defence
Morton, J. Box and Cox
Pinero, A. The magistrate
Pocock, I. The miller and his
men
Walker, J. The factory lad

BOR Borgerhoff, Joseph Leopold,
ed.... Nineteenth century
French plays...New York,
Century [c1931] 790p
Augier, E. Le mariage d'Olympe
Augier, E. et Sandeau, J. Le
gendre de M. Poirier
Balzac, H. Mercadet
Becque, H. Les corbeaux
Brieux, E. Les trois filles de
M. Dupont
Curel, F. L'envers d'une sainte
Delavigne, C. Marino Faliero
Dumas, A. père. Antony
Dumas, A. père. Henri III et sa
cour
Dumas, A. fils. La dame aux
camélias
Dumas, A. fils. Les idées de
Madame Aubray
Hugo, V. Hernani
Musset, A. Les caprices de
Marianne
Pailleron, E. Le monde où l'on
s'ennuie
Picard, L. Les ricochets
Pixérécourt, R. Coelina; ou,

L'enfant du mystère
Rostand, E. Cyrano de Bergerac
Scribe, E. Le verre d'eau
Vigny, A. Chatterton

THE BORZOI READER. See
VAN Van Doren, Carl Clinton,
ed.

BOV Bovée, Arthur Gibbon; Cat-
tanès, Hélène and Robert,
Osmond Thomas, eds. Prome-
nades littéraires et historiques
...New York, Harcourt, Brace,
1940. 750p
Beaumarchais, P. Le barbier de
Séville
Pailleron, E. Le monde où l'on
s'ennuie

BOVE Bovée, Arthur Gibbon;
Cattanès, Hélène and Robert,
Osmond Thomas, eds. Prome-
nades littéraires et historiques
...Nouvelle édition. New York,
Harcourt Brace, 1948. 658p
Beaumarchais, P. Le barbier de
Séville
Legouvé, E., and Labiche, E. La
cigale chez les fourmis

BOVI Bovie, Smith Palmer, ed. Five
Roman comedies; in modern
English verse...New York, Dut-
ton, 1970. 329p
Plautus. Amphitryon
Plautus. Mostellaria
Plautus. Poenulus; or, The little
Carthaginian
Terence. The eunuch
Terence. Phormio

BOW Bowen, James K., and Van
Der Beets, Richard, comps.
Drama...New York, Harper and
Row, 1971. 761p
Aristophanes. Lysistrata
Chekhov, A. The cherry orchard
Dürrenmatt, F. The visit
Everyman
Ibsen, H. Ghosts
Molière, J. The misanthrope
O'Neill, E. Desire under the elms
Racine, J. Phaedra
Shakespeare, W. Othello
Shaw, G. Major Barbara
Sophocles. Oedipus Rex

BOW (cont.)
Strindberg, A. Miss Julie

BOWY Bowyer, John Wilson, and
Brooks, John Lee, eds.
The Victorian Age...Second
edition. New York, Appleton-
Century-Crofts [c1954] 1188p
Gilbert, W. Iolanthe; or, The
peer and the peri
Jones, H. Michael and his lost
angel
Pinero, A. The second Mrs.
Tanqueray
Robertson, T. Caste
Shaw, G. Arms and the man
Wilde, O. The importance of
being earnest
Yeats, W. The Countess
Cathleen

BOY Boynton, Robert Whitney
and Mack, Maynard, eds.
Introduction to the play.
New York, Hayden Book, 1969.
386p
Cocteau, J. The infernal machine
Ibsen, H. Ghosts
Shakespeare, W. Henry the
fourth, Pt. I
Shaw, G. The devil's disciple
Sophocles. Oedipus the King

BOYN Boynton, Robert Whitney,
and Mack, Maynard, comps.
Introduction to the play: in
the theater of the mind. Rev.
2d ed. Rochelle Park, N.J.,
Hayden Book Company, 1976.
262p
Cocteau, J. The infernal machine
McNally, T. Botticelli
Shaw, G. The devil's disciple
Ward, D. Day of absence
Williams, T. The glass menagerie

BPD Bradley, Edward Sculley, et
al., eds. The American tradition in literature. 4th ed.
New York, Grosset and Dunlap,
1974. 2v
O'Neill, E. The hairy ape 2
Tyler, R. The contrast 1
Williams, T. The glass menagerie
2

BPE Bradley, Edward Sculley, et

al., eds. The American tra-
dition in literature. 4th ed.
Shorter ed. in one volume.
New York, Grosset and Dun-
lap, 1974. 2001p
Williams, T. The glass menagerie

BQA Brandon, James R., ed. On
thrones of gold; three Javanese
shadow plays. Cambridge,
Massachusetts, Harvard Uni-
versity Press, 1970. 407p
Death of Karna
Irawan's wedding
The reincarnation of Rama

BRA Brandon, James R., comp.
Traditional Asian plays. New
York, Hill and Wang, 1972.
308p
Manohra
Namiki G., III. The subscription
list
Okamura, S. The Zen substitute
The price of wine
Shudraka, K. The toy cart
Zembō, M. Ikkaku sennin

BRAS Brasmer, William, and Consolo,
Dominick Peter, eds. Black
drama; an anthology...Columbus,
Ohio, Charles E. Merrill Pub-
lishing Company, 1970. 393p
Davis, O. Purlie victorious
Green, P. Native son
Hughes, L. Mulatto
Kennedy, A. Funny house of a
Negro
Shine, T. Contribution
Ward, D. Day of absence
Ward, D. Happy ending

BRE Brenner, Clarence Dietz, and
Goodyear, Nolan, A., eds.
Eighteenth century French
plays...New York, Century
[c1927] 561p
Beaumarchais, P. Le mariage
de Figaro
Crébillon, P. Rhadamiste et
Zénobie
Dancourt, F. Le chevalier à la
mode
Destouches, P. Le glorieux
Diderot, D. Le père de famille
Gresset, J. Le méchant
La Chaussée, P. Le préjugé à la

mode
Laya, J. L'ami des lois
Lesage, A. Turcaret
Marivaux, P. Le jeu de l'amour
et du hazard
Palissot de Montenoy, C. Les
philosophes
Regnard, J. Le légataire uni-
versel
Sedaine, M. Le philosophe sans
le savoir
Voltaire, F. Nanine
Voltaire, F. Zaire

BRET Brett, Lewis Edward ed.
...Nineteenth century Spanish
plays...New York, Appleton-
Century [c1935] 889p
Benavente y Martínez, J. El
nido ajeno
Bréton de los Herreros, M.
Muérete ¡y verás!
Echegaray y Eizaguirre, J. El
gran Galeoto
García Gutiérrez, A. Juan Loren-
zo
Gil y Zárate, A. Guzmán el
Bueno
Hartzenbusch, J. Los amantes de
Teruel
López de Ayala, A. Consuelo
Maratín, L. El sí de las niñas
Núñez de Arce, G. El haz de
leña
Pérez Galdós, B. La de San
Quintín
Rivas, A. Don Alvaro
Tamayo y Baus, M. Un drama
nuevo
Vega, R. Pepa la frescachona
Vega, V. El hombre de mundo
Zorrilla y Moral, J. Don Juan
Tenorio

BRIG Briggs, Thomas Henry;
Herzberg, Max J., and
Bolenius, Emma Miller, eds.
...English literature...Boston,
Houghton Mifflin [c1934] 770p
(Literature in the senior high
school. v4)
Shakespeare, W. The tragedy of
Macbeth
Sheridan, R. The school for
scandal
Synge, J. Riders to the sea

BRIK Briggs, Thomas Henry; Herz-
berg, Max J., and Bolenius,
Emma Miller, eds. ...Romance
...Boston, Houghton Mifflin
[c1932] 770p (Literature in
the senior high school. v2)
Peabody, J. The piper
Shakespeare, W. As you like it

BRIN Brissenden, Connie, ed. The
Factory Lab anthology. Van-
couver, Talon Books, Ltd.,
1974. 316p
Canale, R. The jingo ring
Greenland, B. We three, you and
I
Hollingsworth, M. Strawberry
fields
Kardish, L. Brussels sprouts
Walker, G. Ambush at Tether's
end

BRIP Brissenden, Connie, ed. Now
in paperback: six Canadian
plays of the 1970's. Toronto,
Fineglow Plays, 1973. 102p
Alianak, H. Mathematics
Alianak, H. Western
Del Grande, L. So who's Goldberg
Fineberg, L. Death
Petch, S. The general
Walker, G. Prince of Naples

BRIQ Brissenden, Connie, ed.
West Coast plays. Vancouver,
New Play Centre, 1975. 160p
Angel, L. Forthcoming wedding
Cone, T. Cabistique
Grainger, T. The helper
Hollingsworth, M. Operators
Rosen, S. The box

BRIT Britisch, Ralph A., and
others. Literature as art.
Provo, Utah, Brigham Young
University Press, 1972. 743p
Chekhov, A. The master builder
Goethe, J. Faust, Part I
Sophocles. Antigone

BRIU Brittin, Norman A., comp.
A reading apprenticeship lit-
erature. New York, Holt,
Rinehart, and Winston, 1971.
469p
Miller, A. A view from the bridge

A Yorkshire tragedy

BROC Brooke, Charles Frederick
Tucker and Paradise,
Nathaniel Burton, eds.
English drama, 1580-1642
...Boston, Heath [c1933]
1044p
Beaumont, F., and Fletcher, J.
The knight of the burning
pestle
Beaumont, F., and Fletcher, J.
The maid's tragedy
Beaumont, F., and Fletcher, J.
Philaster
Chapman, G. Bussy d'Ambois
Chapman, G., Johnson, B., and
Marston, J. Eastward ho!
Dekker, T. The shoemakers'
holiday
Fletcher, J. The island princess
Fletcher, J., and Massinger, P.
Beggars' bush
Ford, J. The broken heart
Greene, R. Friar Bacon and
Friar Bungay
Heywood, T. A woman killed
with kindness
Jonson, B. The alchemist
Jonson, B. Epicoene; or, The
silent woman
Jonson, B. Every man in his
humor
Jonson, B. The gipsies metamor-
phosed
Jonson, B. Volpone; or, The
fox
Kyd, T. The Spanish tragedy
Lyly, J. Endymion
Marlowe, C. Doctor Faustus
Marlowe, C. Edward II
Marlowe, C. The Jew of Malta
Marlowe, C. Tamburlaine, pt. I
Marston, J. The malcontent
Massinger, P. A new way to pay
old debts
Middleton, T. A game at chess
Middleton, T., and Rowley, W.
The changeling
Peele, G. The arraignment of
Paris
Peele, G. The old wives' tale
Shirley, J. The cardinal
Webster, J. The Duchess of Malfi

BROE Brooks, Cleanth, et al.,
comps. American literature;

the makers and the making.
New York, St. Martins, 1974.
2v
Odets, C. Waiting for Lefty 2
O'Neill, E. Desire under the
elms 2
Wilder, T. The skin of our teeth
2

BROF Brooks, Cleanth; Purser,
John Thibaut and Warren,
Robert Penn. An approach to
literature. Baton Rouge,
Louisiana University Press,
1936. 578p
Čapek, K. R.U.R. (Rossum's
universal robots)
Ibsen, H. Hedda Gabler

BROG Brooks, Cleanth; Purser,
John Thibaut and Warren,
Robert Penn. An approach to
literature. Rev. ed. New
York, Crofts, 1939. 634p
Čapek, K. R.U.R. (Rossum's
universal robots)
Ibsen, H. Hedda Gabler
Shakespeare, W. Antony and
Cleopatra
Wilde, O. The importance of
being earnest

BROH Brooks, Cleanth; Purser,
John Thibaut and Warren,
Robert Penn. An approach to
literature. Third edition.
New York, Appleton-Century-
Crofts [c1952] 820p
Eliot, T. Murder in the cathedral
Ibsen, H. Hedda Gabler
Maugham, W. The circle
Miller, A. All my sons
Shakespeare, W. Antony and
Cleopatra

BROI Brooks, Cleanth, et al.,
comps. An approach to liter-
ature. 5th ed. Englewood
Cliffs, N.J., Prentice-Hall,
1975. 902p
Beckett, S. Act without words
Eliot, T. Murder in the cathedral
Ibsen, H. Hedda Gabler
Shakespeare, W. Antony and
Cleopatra
Shaw, G. Pygmalion
Shaw, G. Saint Joan

BROI (cont.)
Sophocles. Oedipus rex
Wilder, T. The skin of our teeth

BROJ Brooks, Cleanth, and Heilman,
Robert B., eds. Understand-
ing drama...New York, Holt
[c1945] 515p
Congreve, W. The way of the
world
Everyman
Lillo, G. The London merchant
Ibsen, H. Rosmersholm
Plautus. The twin Menaechmi
Shakespeare, W. Henry IV, pt. I
Sheridan, R. The school for
scandal
Wilde, O. Lady Windermere's fan

BROK Brooks, Cleanth and Heilman,
Robert B. Understanding
drama; twelve plays...New
York, Holt [c1948] 674, +64p
Chekhov, A. The sea gull
Congreve, W. The way of the
world
Everyman
Ibsen, H. Rosmersholm
Lillo, G. The London merchant;
or, The history of George
Barnwell
Marlowe, C. Dr. Faustus
Plautus. The twin Menaechmi
Shakespeare, W. Henry IV, pt. I
Shakespeare, W. King Lear
Sheridan, R. The school for scan-
dal
Sophocles. Oedipus the king
Wilde, O. Lady Windermere's fan

BROOKS, VAN WYCK. See
AME American caravan...

BROTA Brown, Ashley and
Kimmey, J. L., eds.
Tragedy. Columbus, Ohio,
Merrill, 1968. 268p
Lowell, R. Benito Cereno
Shakespeare, W. King Lear
Sophocles. King Oedipus

BROWN, IVOR. See
FOUP Four plays of 1936...

BROW Brown, Leonard Stanley, and
Perrin, Porter Gale, eds. A
quarto of modern literature...

New York, Scribner [c1935]
436p
Barrie, J. Dear Burtus
Galsworthy, J. Justice
Howard, S. The silver cord
O'Neill, E. In the zone

BROX Brown, Leonard Stanley, and
Perrin, Porter Gale, eds. A
quarto of modern literature...
Third edition. New York,
Scribner [c1950] 631p
Galsworthy, J. Loyalties
Giraudoux, J. The madwoman
of Chaillot
Howard, S. The silver cord
Miller, A. Death of a salesman
O'Neill, E. The Emperor Jones
Sherwood, R. Abe Lincoln in Il-
linois

BROY Brown, Leonard Stanley and
Perrin, P. G., eds. A quarto
of modern literature. 5th ed.
New York, Scribner, 1964.
606p
Giraudoux, J. The madwoman of
Chaillot
Miller, A. Death of a salesman
Shaw, G. Pygmalion
Williams, T. The glass menagerie

BROZ Brown, Leonard Stanley;
Waite, Harlow O., and Atkinson,
Benjamin P., eds. Literature
for our time...New York, Holt
[c1947] 951p
Anderson, M. Winterset
Barry, P. The Philadelphia story
Behrman, S. Biography
Čapek, K. R.U.R.
Corwin, N. We hold these truths
MacLeish, A. The fall of the city
O'Neill, E. The hairy ape

BRR Brown, Sharon Osborne, ed.
Present tense...New York,
Harcourt, Brace, 1941. 3v
Čapek, K. R.U.R. (Rossum's
universal robots) 3
MacLeish, A. The fall of the city
3
Wilder, T. Our town 1

BRS Brown, Sharon Osborne, ed.
Present tense. Rev. ed. New
York, Harcourt, Brace, 1945.

762p
Corwin, N. Good heavens
Wilder, T. Our town

BRZ Browne, Elliott Martin, ed.
Four modern verse plays...
[Harmondsworth, Middlesex]
Penguin Books [1957] 269p
Eliot, T. The family reunion
Fry, C. A phoenix too frequent
MacDonagh, D. Happy as Larry
Williams, C. Thomas Cranmer of
Canterbury

BRZA Browne, Elliott Martin, ed.
Three European plays...
[Harmondsworth, Middlesex]
Penguin Books [1958] 190p
Anouilh, J. Ring round the moon
Betti, U. The queen and the
rebels
Sartre, J. In camera

BRZE Browne, Elliott Martin, ed.
Three Irish plays...Baltimore,
Penguin Books [1960, c1959]
236p
Johnston, D. The moon in the
Yellow river
MacDonagh, D. Step-in-the-
hollow
O'Conor, J. The iron harp

BROWNE, ELLIOTT MARTIN.
See also NEWE New English
dramatists...

BRYSON, LYMAN. See
THP Three great Greek
plays...

BUCK Buck, Philo M., jr., ed.
An anthology of world litera-
ture...New York, Macmillan,
1934. 1016p
Aeschylus. Agamemnon
Aeschylus. Prometheus bound
Aristophanes. The frogs
Euripides. Iphigenia at Aulis
Goethe, J. Faust, pts. I and II
Hauptmann, G. The sunken bell
Hebbel, F. Maria Magdalena
Ibsen, H. An enemy of the
people
Kālidāsa. Sakoontalá
Molière, J. The misanthrope
Molière, J. Tartuffe

Pèrez Galdós, B. Electra
Racine, J. Athaliah
Sophocles. Antigone
Sophocles. Oedipus the king

BUCL Buck, Philo M., jr., and
Alberson, Hazel, eds. An
anthology of world literature.
Revised edition...New York,
Macmillan, 1940. 1148p
Aeschylus. Agamemnon
Aeschylus. Prometheus bound
Aristophanes. The frogs
Book of Job
Euripides. Iphigenia at Aulis
Euripides. Medea
Goethe, J. Faust, pts. I and II
Hauptmann, G. The sunken bell
Hebbel, F. Maria Magdalena
Ibsen, H. An enemy of the
people
Kālidāsa. Sakoontalá
Molière, J. The misanthrope
Molière, J. Tartuffe
Racine, J. Athaliah
Sophocles. Antigone
Sophocles. Oedipus the king

BUCM Buck, Philo M., jr., and
Albertson, Hazel Stewart, eds.
An anthology of world litera-
ture. Third edition...New
York, Macmillan [c1951] 1150p
Aeschylus. Agamemnon
Aeschylus. Prometheus bound
Aristophanes. The frogs
Book of Job
Euripides. Iphigenia at Aulis
Euripides. Medea
Goethe, J. Faust
Hauptmann, G. The sunken bell
Hebbel, F. Maria Magdalena
Ibsen, H. An enemy of the
people
Kālidāsa. Shakuntalä
Molière, J. The misanthrope
Molière, J. Tartuffe
Plautus. Aulularia
Racine, J. Athaliah
Sophocles. Antigone
Sophocles. Oedipus the king

BUFF Buffington, Albert F., ed.
The Reichard collection of
early Pennsylvania German
plays...Lancaster, Pa., 1962.
439p (v61, Pennsylvania

BUFF (cont.)
  German Society)
Barba, P. An der lumpa parti
Barba, P. Die verrechelte
  rechler
Birmelin, J. Der gnopp
Birmelin, J. Em Docktor
  Fogel sei offis schtunn
Brendle, T. Di hoffning
Brendle, T. Die mutter
Fink, E. Noshions duhn
Grumbine, E. Die insurance
  business
Iobst, C. Die Calline
  browierts
Iobst, C. Es Heller's
  Chrischtdag
Miller, D. Per Peter soll en
  handwerk lernen
Miller, D. En gespräch zwischen
  zweb demokrate über politiks
Miller, D. Noch eppes vom Peter
  seim handwerk
Moss, A., and Newhard, E.
  H.M.S. Pinafore; oder, Das
  maedle und ihr sailor kerl
Rauch, E. Rip Van Winkle;
  oder, Die shpooks fum Blowa
  Barrick
Wieand, P. Der parra kumpt
Wieand, P. Die huchzich um
  kreitz waig
Wieand, P. Tzu forwitsich
Wollenweber, L. Das lied von
  der union
Wollenweber, L. Die Margareth
  und die Lea
Wollenweber, L. Die Sära und
  die Betz
Wollenweber, L. Eb Refschneider
  un Susi Leimbach
Wollenweber, L. Ein gespräch

BUL Bullen, Arthur Henry, ed.
  A collection of old English
  plays. New York, B. Blom,
  1964. 7v. in 4v
Davenport, R. The city night-
  cap 4
Davenport, R. A crowne for
  a conquerour 4
Davenport, R. King John and
  Matilda 4
Davenport, R. A new trick to
  cheat the divell 4
Davenport, R. A survey of the
  sciences 4

Davenport, R. Too late to call
  backe yesterday 4
The distracted emperor 2
The martyr'd souldier 1
The mayde's metamorphosis 1
Nabbes, T. Covent Garden 3
Nabbes, T. Hannibal and Scipio
  3
Nabbes, T. Tottenham Court 3
The noble souldier 1
Sir Gyles Goosecappe 2
Tragedy of Nero 1
The tryall of chevalry 2
The wisdom of Dr. Dodypoll 2

BUR Burgess, Charles Owen.
  Drama; literature on stage.
  Philadelphia, Lippincott, 1969.
  598p
Beach, L. The clod
Brecht, B. The good woman of
  Setzuan
Chekhov, A. The sea-gull
Ibsen, H. An enemy of the
  people
Lowell, R. Benito Cereno
Molière, J. The misanthrope
O'Neill, E. In the zone
Shakespeare, W. Antony and
  Cleopatra
Shaw, G. Major Barbara
Sophocles. Oedipus rex
Strindberg, A. The stronger
Williams, T. The last of my solid
  gold watches

THE BURNS MANTLE YEARBOOK...
  See
  BES Best plays of 1894/99...
  etc.

BURR Burrows, David James, and
  others, eds. Myth and motifs
  in literature. New York, Free
  Press, 1973. 470p
Aeschylus. Prometheus bound
Büchner, G. Woyzeck
Yeats, W. The land of the
  heart's desire

CADY Cady, Edwin H., ed. Litera-
  ture of the early republic...New
  York, Rinehart [c1950] 495p
Tyler, R. The contrast

CAL   Calamus; male homosexuality
       in twentieth century literature,
       an international anthology.
       Edited by David Galloway and
       Christian Sabisch. New York,
       William Morrow, 1982. 503p
  Inge, W. The boy in the basement
  Jones, L. The toilet

CALD   Calderwood, James Lee and
       Tollver, H. E., eds. Forms
       of drama. Englewood Cliffs,
       N.J., Prentice-Hall, 1969.
       601p
  Beckett, S. All that fall
  Chekhov, A. The cherry orchard
  Dürrenmatt, F. The visit
  Everyman
  Ibsen, H. The master builder
  Molière, J. Tartuffe
  Orton, J. Entertaining Mr.
    Sloane
  Racine, J. Phaedra
  The second shepherds' pageant
  Shakespeare, W. Henry the
    fourth, pt. I
  Shakespeare, W. The tempest
  Shakespeare, W. The tragedy
    of Macbeth
  Shaw, G. B. Arms and the man
  Sophocles. Oedipus rex
  Yeats, W. Purgatory

CALG   Campbell, Gladys and
       Thomas, Russell Brown, eds.
       Reading American literature...
       Boston, Little, Brown, 1944.
       912p
  Sherwood, R. Abe Lincoln in Il-
    linois

CALM   Campbell, Oscar James; Van
       Gundy, Justine and Shrodes,
       Caroline, eds. Patterns for
       living. New York, Macmillan,
       1940. 1306p
  Anderson, M. Winterset
  Carroll, P. Shadow and sub-
    stance
  Milne, A. Mr. Pim passes by
  Toller, E. No more peace!

CALN   Campbell, Oscar James; Van
       Gundy, Justine and Shrodes,
       Caroline, eds. Patterns for
       living...Alternate edition...New
       York, Macmillan [c1943, c1947]

       2v
  Anderson, M. Winterset 2
  Capek, K. R.U.R. 1
  Franken, R. Claudia 1
  Hellman, L. Watch on the Rhine
    2

CALP   Campbell, Oscar James; Van
       Gundy, Justine and Shrodes,
       Caroline, eds. Patterns for
       living...Third edition. New
       York, Macmillan, 1949. 951p
  Hellman, L. Watch on the Rhine
  Sherwood, R. Abe Lincoln in
    Illinois

CALQ   Campbell, Oscar James; Van
       Gundy, Justine and Shrodes,
       Caroline, eds. Patterns for
       living...Fourth edition. New
       York, Macmillan [c1955] 975p
  Hellman, L. Watch on the Rhine
  Miller, A. Death of a salesman

CAM   Campbell, Thomas Moody, ed.
       German plays of the nineteenth
       century...New York, Crofts,
       1930. 437p
  Anzengruber, L. Das vierte ge-
    bot
  Grillparzer, F. König Ottokars
    glück und ende
  Hauptmann, G. Einsame menschen
  Hebbel, C. Agnes Bernauer
  Hebbel, C. Herodes und Mariamne
  Hebbel, C. Maria Magdalene
  Kleist, B. Der zerbrochene krug
  Kleist, B. Prinz Friedrich von
    Homburg
  Ludwig, O. Der erbförster
  Tieck, J. Der gestiefelte kater
  Werner, Z. Der vierundzwanzigste
    Februar

CANADIAN PLAYS FROM HART
     HOUSE THEATRE. See
     MAS Massey, Vincent, ed.

CAN   Canfield, Curtis, ed. Plays
       of changing Ireland. New
       York, Macmillan, 1936. 481p
  Johnston, D. The old lady says
    'No!'
  Longford, C. Mr. Jiggins of
    Jigginstown
  Longford, E. Yahoo
  Manning, M. Youth's the

CAN (cont.)
season...?
Mayne, R. Bridge head
Robinson, L. Church street
Shiels, G. The new gossoon
Yeats, W. The words upon the
windowpane

CAP Canfield, Curtis, ed.
Plays of the Irish renais-
sance, 1880-1930...New York,
Ives Washburn, 1929. 436p
Colum, P. The land
Fitzmaurice, G. The dandy dolls
Gregory, I. Hyacinth Halvey
Hyde, D. The twisting of the
rope
Martyn, E. Maeve
Murray, T. Birthright
O'Casey, S. Juno and the pay-
cock
Pearse, P. The singer
Robinson, L. The big house
Russell, G. Deirdre
Synge, J. Riders to the sea
Yeats, W. On Baile's strand
Yeats, W. The only jealousy of
Emer

CAPU Caputi, Anthony Francis, ed.
Modern drama; authoritative
texts...backgrounds, and
criticism. New York, Norton
[1966] 494p
Chekhov, A. The three sisters
Ibsen, H. The wild duck
O'Neill, E. Desire under the elms
Pirandello, L. Henry IV
Shaw, G. The devil's disciple
Strindberg, A. A dream play

CARGILL, OSCAR. See
American literature: a period
anthology; Oscar Cargill,
general editor

CARL Carlsen, George Robert.
American literature; themes and
writers. St. Louis, Mo., Web-
ster, 1967. 788p
Lardner, R. Thompson's vacation
O'Neill, E. In the zone
Rose, R. Twelve angry men
Wilder, T. Our town

CARLE Carlsen, George Robert, et
al., comps. American liter-

ature: themes and writers.
3d ed. New York, McGraw-
Hill, 1978. 787p
Lardner, R. Thompson's vacation
Rose, R. Twelve angry men
Wilder, T. Our town

CARLG Carlsen, George Robert, and
Folkert, Miriam, comps. Brit-
ish and Western literature. 3d
ed. New York, McGraw-Hill,
1979. 786p
Ibsen, H. An enemy of the
people
Molière, J. The miser
Shakespeare, W. Macbeth
Sophocles. Antigone

CARM Carlsen, George Robert.
Encounters; themes in litera-
ture. St. Louis, Mo., Webster,
1967. 758p
Glaspel, S. Trifles
Goodrich, F., and Hackett, A.
The diary of Anne Frank
Shakespeare, W. Julius Caesar

CARME Carlsen, George Robert,
and Carlsen, Ruth Christoffer,
comps. Encounters: themes
in literature. 3d ed. New
York, McGraw-Hill, 1979.
754p
Daviot, G. The pen of my aunt
Goodrich, F., and Hackett, A.
The diary of Anne Frank
Shakespeare, W. Julius Caesar

CARMI Carlsen, George Robert, et
al., comps. Insights; themes
in literature. 3d ed. New
York, McGraw-Hill, 1979. 757p
Benét, S. The devil and Daniel
Webster
Gibson, W. The miracle worker
Shakespeare, W. Romeo and
Juliet

CARN Carlsen, George Robert.
Western literature; themes and
writers. St. Louis, Mo., Web-
ster, 1967. 786p
Shakespeare, W. Macbeth
Shaw, G. Androcles and the lion
Sophocles. Antigone

CARP Carpenter, Bruce, comp. A

book of dramas, an anthology
of nineteen plays...New York,
Prentice-Hall, 1929. 1111p
Aeschylus. Agamemnon
Archer, W. The green goddess
Behrman, S. The second man
Chekhov, A. The cherry orchard
Congreve, W. Love for love
Dickens, C. The cricket on the
  hearth
Euripides. The Trojan women
The farce of the worthy master
  Pierre Patelin
Hugo, V. Hernani
Ibsen, H. Hedda Gabler
Kaufman, G., and Connelly, M.
  Beggar on horseback
Maeterlinck, M. The intruder
Molière, J. The misanthrope
Parker, L. A minuet
Racine, J. Phaedra
Sophocles. Oedipus, King of
  Thebes
Strindberg, A. Miss Julia
Synge, J. Riders to the sea
Wilde, O. The importance of
  being earnest

CARPA Carpenter, Bruce, ed.
  A book of dramas...[Rev. ed.]
  New York, Prentice-Hall,
  1949. 992p
Aeschylus. Agamemnon
Behrman, S. The second man
Chekhov, A. The cherry orchard
Congreve, W. Love for love
Euripides. The Trojan women
Ibsen, H. Hedda Gabler
Kaufman, G., and Connelly, M.
  Beggar on horseback
Maeterlinck, M. The intruder
Molière, J. The misanthrope
O'Neill, E. The long voyage
  home
Racine, J. Phaedra
Rostand, E. Cyrano de Bergerac
Sophocles. Oedipus, King of
  Thiebes
Synge, J. Riders to the sea
Wilde, O. The importance of
  being earnest

CARR Carter-Harrison, Paul, comp.
  Kuntu drama: plays of the
  African continuum. New York,
  Grove, 1974. 352p
Brown, L. Devil Mas'

Carter-Harrison, P. The great
  MacDaddy
Césaire, A. A season in the
  Congo
Goss, C. Mars: Monument of
  the last black eunuch
Jones, L. Great goodness of
  life: a coon show
Kennedy, A. Cities in Bezique:
  The owl answers and A beast
  story
Toomer, J. Kabnis

CART Cartmell, Van H., and Cerf,
  Bennett Alfred, comps.
  Famous plays of crime and de-
  tection...Philadelphia,
  Blakiston, 1946. 910p
Cohan, G. Seven keys to Bald-
  pate
Chodorov, E. Kind lady
Dell, J. Payment deferred
Dunning, P., and Abbott, G.
  Broadway
Gillettte, W. Sherlock Holmes
Hamilton, P. Angel street
Megrue, R. Under cover
Rice, E. On trial
Rinehart, M., and Hopwood, A.
  The bat
Veiller, B. The thirteenth chair
Veiller, B. Within the law
Willard, J. The cat and the
  canary
Williams, E. Night must fall

CARTMELL, VAN H. See also
  CET...Cerf, Bennett Alfred
  and Cartmell, Van H., comps.

CASA Cassady, Marshall, and Cas-
  sady, Pat, comps. An intro-
  duction to theatre and drama.
  Skokie, Ill., National Textbook
  Company, 1975. 618p
Everyman
Gay, J. The beggar's opera
Hansberry, L. A raisin in the
  sun
Ibsen, H. An enemy of the
  people

CASE Cassell, Richard A. and
  Knepler, Henry, eds. What
  is the play? Glenview, Ill.,
  Scott, Foresman [1967] 751p
Anouilh, J. Antigone

CASE (cont.)
Dürrenmatt, F. The visit
Ghelderode, M. Christopher
  Columbus
Ibsen, H. An enemy of the
  people
Jonson, B. The alchemist
Lowell, R. My kinsman,
  Major Molineux
Molière, J. Scapin
O'Neill, I. Hughie
Shakespeare, W. King Henry IV,
  pt. I
Shaw, G. Arms and the man
Sophocles. Antigone
Wilder, T. The matchmaker

CASS Cassidy, Frederic G., ed.
  Modern American plays...New
  York, Longmans, Green, 1949.
  501p
Anderson, M. Winterset
Hellman, L. Watch on the Rhine
Lindsay, H., and Crouse, R.
  Life with father
Odets, C. Waiting for Lefty
O'Neill, E. Anna Christie
Sherwood, R. Abe Lincoln in
  Illinois

CASU Casson, Lionel, ed. and tr.
  Masters of ancient comedy...
  New York, Macmillan, 1960.
  424p
Aristophanes. The Acharnians
Menander. The arbitration
Menander. The grouch
Menander. She who was shorn
Menander. The woman of Samos
Plautus, T. The haunted house
Plautus, T. The rope
Terentius Afer, P. The brothers
Terentius Afer, P. Phormio

CATH Catholic University of America. Committee for the revision
  of English curricula...American
  profile. (The Catholic high
  school literature series. Book
  III) New York, W. H. Sadlier
  [c1944] 752p
Barry, P. The joyous season
Wilder, T. Our town

CAWL Cawley, Arthur C., ed.
  Everyman and medieval miracle
  plays...New York, Dutton

[c1959] 266p
Abraham and Isaac (Brome)
The annunciation (Coventry)
Cain and Abel (N Town)
The creation, and the fall of
  Lucifer (York)
The creation of Adam and Eve
  (York)
The crucifixion (York)
The death of Pilate (Cornish)
Everyman
The fall of man (York)
The harrowing of hell (Chester)
Herod the great (Wakefield)
The judgment (York)
Noah's flood (Chester)
The resurrection (York)
The second shepherds' pageant
  (Wakefield)
The woman taken in adultery (N
  Town)

CAWM Cawley, Arthur C., ed.
  The Wakefield pageants in the
  Towneley cycle...[Manchester]
  Manchester (University Press
  (c1958] 187p (Old and Middle
  English texts)
Coliphizacio
Mactacio Abel
Magnus Herodes
Prima pastorum
Processus Noe cum filiis
Secundus pastorum

CEN Center stage: an anthology of
  21 contemporary Black-American
  plays. Edited by Eileen Joyce
  Ostrow. Oakland, CA, Sea
  Urchin Press [c1981] 309p
Alexander, R. The hourglass
Cooper, J. Loners
Edwards, G. Three fallen angels
Foreman, F. Daddy's seashore
  blues
Hobbes, D. You can't always
  sometimes never tell
Houston, D. The fishermen
Hunkins, L. Revival
Jackson, C. In the master's
  house there are many mansions
Martin, S. The moving violation
Mason, C. The verandah
Molette, C. and Molette, B.
  Noah's ark
Owa. The Soledad tedrad, Part
  II: Transitions for a mime poem

Rhodes, C. The trip
Rivers, L. More bread and the circus
Shine, T. The woman who was tampered with in youth
Stiles, T. No one man show
Wakefield, J. Perceptual movement
Welch, L. Hands in the mirror
Wesley, R. The sirens
Wesson, K. Miss Cegenation
Williams, A. A Christmas story (A turkey tale)

CERF, BENNETT ALFRED. See also CART Cartmell, Van H., and Cerf, Bennett Alfred, comps. Famous plays of crime and detection...

CEQ Cerf, Bennett Alfred, comp. Four contemporary American plays...New York, Vintage Books [c1961] 386p
Chayefsky, P. The tenth man
Hansberry, L. A raisin in the sun
Hellman, L. Toys in the attic
Levitt, S. The Andersonville trial

CEQA Cerf, Bennett Alfred, comp. Plays of our time...New York, Random House [1967] 782p
Bolt, R. A man for all seasons
Hansberry, L. A raisin in the sun
Heggen, T. and Logan, J. Mister Roberts
Inge, W. Come back, little Sheba
Miller, A. Death of a salesman
O'Neill, E. The iceman cometh
Osborne, J. Look back in anger
Schisgal, M. Luv
Williams, T. A streetcar named desire

CER Cerf, Bennett Alfred, ed. The pocket book of modern American plays...New York, Pocket books [1942] 430p
Behrman, S. No time for comedy
Boothe, C. Margin for error
Odets, C. Awake and sing
Rice, E. Street scene

CES Cerf, Bennett Alfred, ed.

Six American plays for today ...New York, Modern Library [c1961] 599p
Chayefsky, P. The tenth man
Hansberry, L. A raisin in the sun
Hellman, L. Toys in the attic
Inge, W. The dark at the top of the stairs
Schary, D. Sunrise at Campobello
Williams, T. Camino Real

CET Cerf, Bennett Alfred and Cartmell, Van H., eds. Sixteen famous American plays... Garden City, N.Y., Garden City publishing co. [c1941] 1049p
Behrman, S. Biography
Boothe, S. The women
Connelly, M. The green pastures
Hart, M., and Kaufman, G. The man who came to dinner
Hecht, B., and MacArthur, C. The front page
Hellman, L. The little foxes
Howard, S. They knew what they wanted
Kingsley, S. Dead end
Kober, A. "Having wonderful time"
Lindsay, H., and Crouse, R. Life with father
Odets, C. Waiting for Lefty
O'Neill, E. Ah, wilderness!
Saroyan, W. The time of your life
Sherwood, R. The petrified forest
Spewack, B., and Spewack, S. Boy meets girl
Wilder, T. Our town

CEU Cerf, Bennett Alfred and Cartmell, Van H., comps. Sixteen famous British plays...Garden City, N.Y., Garden City publishing co. [1942] 1000p
Archer, W. The green goddess
Barrie, J. What every woman knows
Bennett, A., and Knoblock, E. Milestones
Besier, R. The Barretts of Wimpole street

CEU (cont.)
Coward, N. Cavalcade
Galsworthy, J. Loyalties
Housman, L. Victoria Regina
Maugham, W. The circle
Milne, A. Mr. Pim passes by
Pinero, A. The second Mrs.
   Tanqueray
Priestley, J. Dangerous
   corner
Shairp, M. The green bay
   tree
Sherriff, R. Journey's end
Vane, S. Outward bound
Wilde, O. The importance of
   being earnest
Williams, E. The corn is green

CEW Cerf, Bennett Alfred, and
   Cartmell, Van H., comps.
   Sixteen famous European plays
   ...Garden City, N.Y., Garden
   City publishing co. [1943]
   1052p
Ansky, S. The dybbuk
Baum, V. Grand hotel
Čapek, K. R.U.R.
Carroll, P. Shadow and sub-
   stance
Chekhov, A. The sea gull
Deval, J. Tovarich
Giraudoux, J. Amphitryon 38
Gorky, M. The lower depths
Hauptmann, G. The weavers
Ibsen, H. The wild duck
Martínez Sierra, G. The cradle
   song
Molnár, F. Liliom
Pirandello, L. Six characters in
   search of an author
Rostand, E. Cyrano de Bergerac
Schnitzler, A. Anatol
Synge, J. The playboy of the
   western world

CEY Cerf, Bennett Alfred, and
   Cartmell, Van H., comps.
   S.R.O.; the most successful
   plays in the history of the
   American stage...Garden City,
   N.Y., Doubleday, Doran,
   1944. 920p
Aiken, G. Uncle Tom's cabin
Boucicault, D. Rip Van Winkle
D'Ennery, A., and Cormon, E.
   The two orphans
Hammerstein, O., and Rodgers, R.

Oklahoma!
Kesselring, J. Arsenic and old
   lace
Kirkland, J. Tobacco road
Lindsay, H., and Crouse, R.
   Life with father
Manners, J. Peg o' my heart
Nichols, A. Abie's Irish Rose
Rinehart, M., and Hopwood, A.
   The bat
Smith, W., and Bacon, F.
   Lightnin'
Tarkington, B., and Wilson, H.
   The man from home
Thompson, D. The old homestead
Wood, Mrs. H. East Lynne

CHA Chandler, Frank Wadleigh and
   Cordell, Richard Albert, eds.
   Twentieth century plays...New
   York, Nelson, 1934. v.p.
Alvarez Quintero, S., and Alvarez,
   Quintero, J. Doña Clarines
Anderson, M., and Stallings, L.
   What price glory
Čapek, K., and Čapek, J. And
   so ad infinitum
Chlumberg, H. The miracle at
   Verdun
Connelly, M. The green pastures
Coward, N. Private lives
Crothers, R. As husbands go
Ervine, St. J. John Ferguson
Hankin, St. J. The last of the
   De Mullins
Jones, H. Dolly reforming herself
Lenormand, H. The coward
Maugham, W. The breadwinner
Molnár, F. The swan
O'Neill, E. Marco Millions
Pinero, A. The thunderbolt
Pirandello, L. Each in his own
   way
Rice, E. Street scene
Robinson, L. The far-off hills
Sherriff, R. Journey's end
Tolstoy, L. The live corpse

CHAN Chandler, Frank Wadleigh
   and Cordell, Richard Albert,
   eds. Twentieth century
   plays...Rev. New York, Nelson, 1939. v.p.
Alvarez Quintero, S., and
   Alvarez Quintero, J. Doña
   Clarines
Anderson, M. Winterset

Behrman, S. Rain from heaven
Čapek, K., and Čapek, J. And
so ad infinitum
Chlumberg, H. The miracle at
Verdun
Connelly, M. The green pastures
Coward, N. Private lives
Ervine, St. J. John Ferguson
Hankin, St. J. The last of the
De Mullins
Howard, S. The silver cord
Jones, H. Dolly reforming her-
self
Kaufman, G., and Connelly, M.
Beggar on horseback
Lenormand, H. The coward
Maugham, W. The breadwinner
Molnár, F. The swan
O'Neill, E. Anna Christie
Pinero, A. The thunderbolt
Pirandello, L. Each in his own
way
Rice, E. Street scene
Robinson, L. The far-off hills
Sherriff, R. Journey's end
Tolstoy, L. The live corpse

CHAP Chandler, Frank Wadleigh,
and Cordell, Richard Albert,
eds. Twentieth century plays,
American...Rev. New York,
Nelson, 1939. 295p
Anderson, M. Winterset
Behrman, S. Rain from heaven
Connelly, M. The green pastures
Howard, S. The silver cord
Kaufman, G., and Connelly, M.
Beggar on horseback
O'Neill, E. Anna Christie
Rice, E. Street scene

CHAR Chandler, Frank Wadleigh,
and Cordell, Richard Albert,
eds. Twentieth century plays,
British...Rev. and enl. New
York, Nelson, 1941. 399p
Barrie, J. The admirable Crichton
Coward, N. Private lives
Ervine, St. J. John Ferguson
Galsworthy, J. The silver box
Hankin, St. J. The last of the
De Mullins
Jones, H. Dolly reforming herself
Maugham, S. The breadwinner
Pinero, A. The thunderbolt
Robinson, L. The far-off hills
Sherriff, R. Journey's end

CHAPMAN, JOHN ARTHUR. See
BES Best plays of 1894/99...
etc.;
THEA Theater, 1953/56...

CHARLTON, J. M. See
PLAJ Plays of the sixties...;
PLAL Plays of the thirties...

CHEL The Chester Mystery Cycle.
Edited by Robert M. Lumiansky
and David Mills. V.1, Text:
published for the Early English
Text Society. London, Oxford,
1974. 624p
Abraham and Isaac - The Barbers
Abraham, Lot and Melchysedeck -
The Barbers
Adam and Eve - The Drapers
The annunciation and the nativity -
The Wrights
Antichrist - The Dyers
The ascension - The Tailors
Balaack and Balaam - The Cappers
The betrayal of Christ - The
Bakers
The blind Chelidonian - The
Glovers
Cain and Abel - The Drapers
Christ and the doctors - The
Blacksmiths
Christ and the moneylenders -
The Corvisors
Christ at the house of Simon the
Leper - The Corvisors
Christ on the road to Emmaus -
The Saddlers
Doubting Thomas - The Saddlers
The fall of Lucifer - The Tanners
The harrowing of hell - The
Cooks
Judas' plot - The Corvisors
The last judgment - The Websters
The last supper - The Bakers
Moses and the law - The Cappers
Noah's flood - The Waterleaders
and Drawers of Dee
The offerings of the three kings -
The Mercers
The passion - The Ironmongers
The pentecost - The fishmongers
The prophets of antichrist - The
Clothworkers
The purification - The Blacksmiths
The raising of Lazarus - The
Glovers
The resurrection - The Skinners

CHEL (cont.)
The slaughter of the innocents –
The Goldsmiths
The shepherds – The Painters
The temptation – The Butchers
The three kings – The Vintners
The trial and flagellation – The
Fletchers, Bowyers, Coopers,
and Stringers
The woman taken in adultery –
The Butchers

CHES The Chester mystery plays
...Adapted into modern English
by Maurice P. Hussey. London,
William Heinemann [c1957]
160p
Abraham and Isaac
The adoration of the magi
The adoration of the shepherds
Antichrist
The betrayal of Christ
Christ's ascension
Christ's passion
Christ's resurrection
The creation of man: Adam and
Eve
The fall of Lucifer
The last judgment
The magi's oblation
The nativity
Noah's deluge
Simon the leper
The slaying of the innocents

CHESE The Chester mystery plays;
seventeen pageant plays from
the Chester Craft Cycle.
Adapted into modern English
by Maurice Hussey. 2nd ed.
London, Heinemann, 1975.
170p
Abraham and Isaac
The adoration of the magi
The adoration of the shepherds
Antichrist
The betrayal of Christ
Christ's ascension
Christ's passion
Christ's resurrection
The creation of man: Adam and
Eve
The fall of Lucifer
The last judgment
The magi's oblation
The nativity
Noah's deluge

Simon the leper
The slaying of the innocents
The temptation

CHG Chicano voices [ed. by]
Carlota Cardenas de Dwyer;
Tino Villaneuva, editorial ad-
viser. Boston, Houghton
Mifflin, 1975. 189p
(Multi-ethnic literature series)
Valdez, L. Los vendidos

CHI Child, Clarence Griffin, ed.
and tr. The second shepherds'
play, Everyman, and other ear-
ly plays...Boston, Houghton
Mifflin [c1910] 138p
The Brome Abraham and Isaac
Everyman
The Oxfordshire St. George
play
The Quem quaeritis
Robin Hood and the friar
Robin Hood and the knight
Robin Hood and the potter
The second shepherds' play

CHR Christy, Arthur, and Wells,
Henry Willis, eds. World
literature...Freeport, N.Y.,
Books for Libraries, 1971.
1115p (Reprint)
Aeschylus. Agamemnon
Andreyev, L. An incident
Molnár, F. Still life
Pirandello, L. The jar

CHU Church, Mrs. Virginia
Woodson (Frame), ed. Curtain!
A book of modern plays...
New York, Harper, 1932.
504p
Bennett, A. The great adventure
Church, V. What men live by
Dunsany, E. The lost silk hat
Green, P. The man who died at
twelve o'clock
MacKaye, P. Napoleon crossing
the Rockies
Millay, E. Aria da capo
Milne, A. The great Broxopp
Morley, C. Good theatre
Nichols, R., and Brown, M.
Wings over Europe
O'Neill, E. The Emperor Jones
Wilder, T. The angel on the
ship

CLARK, BARRETT HARPER. See
also
AMP America's lost plays.

CLA Clark, Barrett Harper, ed.
Favorite American plays of the
nineteenth century...Princeton,
N.J., Princeton University
Press, 1943. 553p
Alfriend, E., and Wheeler, A.
The great diamond robbery
Belasco, D. The heart of Mary-
land
Boucicault, D. Flying scud; or,
A four-legged fortune
Campbell, B. My partner
Fechter, C. Monte Cristo
Howard, B. The banker's
daughter
Hoyt, C. A trip to Chinatown;
or, An idyll of San Francisco
Murdoch, F. Davy Crockett; or,
Be sure you're right, then go
ahead
Stone, J. Metamora; or, The
last of the Wampanoags
Woolf, B. The mighty dollar

CLD Clark, Barrett Harper, tr.
Four plays of the Free
theater...Cincinnati, Stewart
& Kidd, 1915. 257p
Ancey, G. The dupe
Curel, F. The fossils
Julien, J. The serenade
Porto-Riche, G. Françoise'
luck

CLDM Clark, Barrett Harper, ed.
Masterpieces of modern Spanish
drama...New York, Cuffield,
1917. 290p
Echegaray [y Eizaguirre], J.
The great Galeoto
Guimerá, A. Daniela
Pérez Galdós, B. The Duchess of
San Quentin

CLF Clark, Barrett Harper, ed.
World drama...New York,
Appleton, 1933. 2v
Abstraction 1
Adam 1
Aeschylus. Prometheus bound 1
Alfieri, V. Saul 2
Aristophanes. The clouds 1
Augier, E., and Sandeau, J.

M. Poirier's son-in-law 2
Beaumarchais, P. The barber of
Seville 2
Beaumont, F., and Fletcher, J.
The maid's tragedy 1
Beolco, A. Bilora 2
Calderón de la Barca, P. The
constant prince 2
Cervantes Saavedra, M. The
cave of Salamanca 2
The chalk circle 1
Chikamatsu Monzaemon. Fair
ladies at a game of poemcards
1
Corneille, P. The cid 2
Dumas, A. fils. The demimonde
2
Euripides. Alcestis 1
Everyman 1
The farce of the worthy Master
Pierre Patelin 1
Farquhar, G. The beaux' strata-
gem 1
Goethe, J. Egmont 2
Goldoni, C. The fan 2
Goldsmith, O. She stoops to
conquer 1
Heywood, T. A woman killed
with kindness 1
Holberg, L. Jeppe of the hill 2
Hugo, V. Hernani 2
Ibsen, H. A doll's house 2
Jonson, B. Every man in his
humour 1
Kālidāsa. Sakoontalá 1
Lessing, G. Miss Sara Sampson 2
Marlowe, C. The tragical history
of Dr. Faustus 1
Molière, J. The cit turned gentle-
man 2
Ostrovsky, A. The thunderstorm
2
Plautus, T. The captives 1
The play of St. George 1
Racine, J. Berenice 2
Sachs, H. The wandering scholar
from Paradise 1
Scala, F. The portrait 2
Schiller, J. William Tell 2
Seami, M. Nakamitsu 1
The second shepherds' play 1
Seneca. Medea 1
Sheridan, R. The school for
scandal 1
Sophocles. Antigone 1
Terence. Phormio 1
Vega Carpio, L. The king, the

CLF (cont.)
    greatest Alcalde 2
    The wise virgins and the
        foolish virgins 1

CLH Clark, Barrett Harper, and
        Davenport, William H., eds.
        Nine modern plays...New
        York, Appleton-Century-
        Crofts [c1951] 432p
    Anderson, M. High Tor
    Ferber, E., and Kaufman, G.
        Stage door
    Haines, W. Command decision
    Hart, M., and Kaufman, G.
        You can't take it with you
    O'Neill, E. The hairy ape
    Rice, E. Street scene
    Riggs, L. Green grow the
        lilacs
    Sherwood, R. Abe Lincoln in
        Illinois
    Williams, T. The glass menagerie

CLK Clark, David Lee; Gates,
        William Bryan and Leisy, Ernest
        Erwin, eds. The voices of
        English and America...New
        York, Nelson, 1939. 2v
    Dryden, J. All for love 1
    Everyman 1
    Farquhar, G. The beaux'
        stratagem 1
    Jonson, B. Every man in his
        humor 1
    Marlowe, C. The tragical history
        of Doctor Faustus 1
    Milton, J. Comus 1
    O'Neill, E. The Emperor Jones
        2
    Pinero, A. The second Mrs.
        Tanqueray 2
    The second shepherds' play 1
    Sheridan, R. The rivals 1

CLKJ Clark, Justus Kent and
        Piper, Henry D., eds. Dimen-
        sions in drama; six plays of
        crime and punishment. New
        York, Scribner [1964] 573p
    Gay, J. The beggar's opera
    Ibsen, H. Rosmersholm
    Miller, A. All my sons
    Sartre, J. No exit
    Shakespeare, W. Macbeth
    Sophocles. Oedipus rex

CLKW Clark, William Smith II, ed.
        Chief patterns of world
        drama...[Boston] Houghton
        Mifflin [c1946] 1152p
    Aeschylus. Prometheus bound
    Anderson, M. Mary of Scotland
    Aristophanes. The birds
    Barrie, J. The admirable Crichton
    Beaumont, F., and Fletcher, J.
        The maid's tragedy
    Čapek, J., and Čapek, K. The
        life of the insects
    Chekhov, A. The sea-gull
    Dekker, T. The shoemakers'
        holiday
    Euripides. Alcestis
    Etherege, G. The man of mode;
        or, Sir Fopling Flutter
    Glasworthy, J. The silver box
    Gogol, N. The inspector-general
    Green, P. Roll sweet chariot
    Hebbel, J. Maria Magdalena
    Ibsen, H. Hedda Gabler
    Jonson, B. Epicoene; or, The
        silent woman
    Marlowe, C. The troublesome
        reign and lamentable death of
        Edward the Second
    Molière, J. The miser
    Nice wanton
    O'Neill, E. The hairy ape
    Pirandello, L. Naked
    Plautus. The pot of gold
    Racine, J. Andromache
    The second shepherds' play
    Sheridan, R. The school for
        scandal
    Sophocles. Electra
    Synge, J. The playboy of the
        western world
    Terence. Phormio
    Vega, Lope de. The star of
        Seville

CLKWI Classic Irish drama, intro-
        duced by W. A. Armstrong.
        Harmondsworth: Penguin,
        1964 (1979 [printing]) 224p
        (Penguin plays)
    O'Casey, S. cock-a-doodle Dandy
    Synge, J. The playboy of the
        Western world
    Yeats, W. The Countess Cathleen

CLKX Classic Soviet plays; compiled
        by Alla Mikhailova; translated

from the Russian. Moscow,
Progress Publishers, 1979.
829p [Dist. in U.S. by Im-
ported Pubs.]
Arbuzov, A. Tanya
Bulgakov, M. The days of
the Turbins
Gorky, M. Yegor Bulychov
and others
Leonov, L. Invasion
Mayakovsky, V. Mystery-
bouffe
Pogodin, N. Kremlin chimes
Rozov, V. In search of hap-
piness

CLKY Classic theatre: the hu-
manities in drama; [ed. by]
Sylvan Barnet [and others]
Boston, Educ. Assocs., 1975.
682p
Chekhov, A. Three sisters
Goldsmith, O. She stoops to
conquer
Ibsen, H. Hedda Gabler
Ibsen, H. The wild duck
Marlowe, C. Edward the second
Pinero, A. Trelawny of the
"Wells"
Shakespeare, W. The tragedy
of Macbeth
Shaw, B. Mrs. Warren's pro-
fession
Sheridan, R. The rivals
Synge, J. The playboy of the
western world
Taylor, D. Paradise restored
Voltaire, F. Candide
Webster, J. The Duchess of
Malfi

CLL Clayes, Stanley A., ed.
Drama and discussion...New
York, Appleton-Century-
Crofts [1967] 651p
Aeschylus. Libation bearers
Anouilh, J. The lark
Beckett, S. All that fall
Brecht, B. Mother Courage
and her children
Chekhov, A. The cherry orchard
Euripides. The Trojan women
García Lorca, F. Blood wedding
Giraudoux, J. Tiger at the
gates
Ibsen, H. Ghosts
Shakespeare, W. Hamlet

Shaw, G. Saint Joan
Sophocles. Electra
Synge, J. Riders to the sea
Williams, T. A streetcar named
desire

CLLC Clayes, Stanley A., ed.
Drama and discussion. 2nd ed.
Englewood Cliffs, N.J.,
Prentice-Hall, 1978. 664p
Aeschylus. The libation bearers
(Chöephori)
Beckett, S. All that fall
Brecht, B. Mother Courage and
her children
Synge, J. The playboy of the
western world
Williams, T. A streetcar named
desire

CLM Clayes, Stanley A., and
Spencer, David G., eds.
Contemporary drama...New
York, Scribner [c1962] 512p
Chekhov, A. Uncle Vanya
García Lorca, F. The house of
Bernarda Alba
Giraudoux, J. Ondine
Hellman, L. The autumn garden
Ibsen, H. The wild duck
Maugham, W. The circle
Miller, A. A view from the
bridge
O'Casey, S. Juno and the pay-
cock
Odets, C. The country girl
Shaw, G. The devil's disciple
Sophocles. Antigone (Cocteau,
J. adapter)
Sophocles. Antigone
Strindberg, A. Miss Julie
Williams, T. The rose tattoo

CLN Clayes, Stanley and Spencer,
David G., eds. Contemporary
drama: 13 plays. 2nd ed.
New York, Scribner, 1970.
512p
Brecht, B. The Caucasian chalk
circle
Bullins, E. A son come home
Chekhov, A. Uncle Vanya
García Lorca, F. The house of
Bernarda Alba
Giraudoux, J. Ondine
Ibsen, H. The wild duck
Itallie, J. America hurrah

CLN (cont.)
Miller, A. A view from the bridge
O'Casey, S. Juno and the paycock
Odets, C. The country girl
Shaw, G. The devil's disciple
Strindberg, A. Miss Julie
Williams, T. The rose tattoo

CLOU Clouard, Henri, and Leggewie, Robert, eds. Anthologie de la litterature française. Tome II...New York, Oxford University Press, 1960. 468p
Giraudoux, J. La guerre de Troie n'aura pas lieu
Musset, A. Fantasio
Sartre, J. Huis clos

CLUR Clurman, Harold, ed. Famous American plays of the 1930s...[New York, Dell publishing co. c1959] 480p (Lauren drama series)
Behrman, S. End of summer
Odets, C. Akake and sing!
Saroyan, W. The time of your life
Sherwood, R. Idiot's delight
Steinbeck, J. Of mice and men

CLURMAN, HAROLD. See also SEVD Seven plays of the modern theatre

COD Coffman, George Raleigh, ed. ...A book of modern plays... Chicago, Scott, Foresman [c1925] 490p
Bennett, A., and Knoblock, E. Milestones
Gregory, I. The workhouse ward
Ibsen, H. An enemy of the people
O'Neill, E. Where the cross is made
Robertson, T. Caste
Rostand, E. The romancers
Synge, J. Riders to the sea

COF Coffman, George Raleigh, ed. Five significant English plays ...New York, Nelson, 1930. 433p

Dekker, T. The shoemakers' holiday
Marlowe, C. Dr. Faustus
Pinero, A. The second Mrs. Tanqueray
Sheridan, R. The school for scandal
Steele, R. The conscious lovers

COH Cohen, Helen Louise, ed. Longer plays by modern authors (American)...New York, Harcourt, Brace [c1922] 353p
Fitch, C. Beau Brummell
Kaufman, G., and Connelly, M. Dulcy
Tarkington, B. The intimate strangers
Thomas, A. The copperhead

COJ Cohen, Helen Louise, ed. Milestones of the drama. New York, Harcourt, Brace [1940] 580p
Everyman
Ibsen, H. A doll's house
Marlowe, C. Doctor Faustus
O'Neill, E. The Emperor Jones
Rostand, E. Cyrano de Bergerac
Sheridan, R. The school for scandal
Sophocles. Oedipus, king of Thebes

COK Cohn, Ruby; Dukore, Bernard F. and Block, Haskett M., eds. Twentieth century drama: England, Ireland [and] The United States...New York, Random House [1966] 692p
Albee, E. The zoo story
Beckett, S. Embers
Eliot, T. Murder in the cathedral
Odets, C. Awake and sing
O'Neill, E. The iceman cometh
Osborne, J. Look back in anger
Pinter, H. The dumb waiter
Shaw, G. Major Barbara
Synge, J. The playboy of the western world
Wilder, T. Our town
Williams, T. The glass menagerie
Yeats, W. The only jealousy of Emer

CONG (cont.)
Shakespeare, W. Richard III
Sophocles. Antigone

CONN Connolly, Francis Xavier,
ed. Literature, the chan-
nel of culture...New York,
Harcourt, Brace, 1948.
714p
Connelly, M. The green pastures
Shakespeare, W. The tempest
Synge, J. Riders to the sea

CONO Connolly, Francis Xavier,
ed. Man and his measure.
New York, Harcourt, Brace
& World [1964] 139p
Betti, U. Corruption in the
palace of justice
Marlowe, C. The tragical
history of Doctor Faustus
Molière, J. The misanthrope
Sophocles. Oedipus rex

CONP Connolly, Francis X., ed.
The types of literature...New
York, Harcourt, Brace
[c1955] 810p
Barrie, J. The twelve-pound
look
Eliot, T. Murder in the cathe-
dral
O'Neill, E. Bound east for
Cardiff
Sheridan, R. The school for
scandal
Sophocles. Antigone

CONR Contemporary Chicano
theatre; Roberto J. Garza,
editor. Notre Dame, Indiana,
University of Notre Dame
Press, 1976. 248p
Alurista. Dawn
Garza, R. No nos venceremos
Macias, Y. Mártir Montezuma
Macias, Y. The ultimate pendeja-
da
Portillo, E. The day of the swal-
lows
Sierra, R. La raza pura, or ra-
cial, racial
Valdez, L. Bernabé
Valdez, L. Los vendidos

CONT Contemporary Danish plays

...London, Thames and Hud-
son, 1955. 557p
Abell, K. The Queen on tour
Branner, H. The judge
Clausen, S. The bird of conten-
tion
Fischer, L. The mystery tour
Locher, J. Tea for three
Munk, K. Herod the king
Schüter, K. Off the rails
Sønderby, K. A woman too many
Soya, C. Two threads

CONZ Contemporary New Zealand
plays; selected...by Howard
McNaughton. Wellington and
London, Oxford, 1974. 153p
Baxter, J. The wide open cage
Bowman, E. Salve Regina
Campbell, A. When the bough
breaks
Mason, B. Hongi

CONZI Contemporary South African
plays/Edited and introduced by
Ernest Pereira. Johannesburg,
Ravan Press, 1977. 293p
Ferguson, I. Ritual 2378
Gray, S. An evening at the
Vernes
Leshoai, B. Lines draw monsters
(Act I)
Livingstone, D. A rhino for the
boardroom; a radio play
Maclennan, D. An enquiry into
the voyage of the Santiago
Roberts, S. Weekend
Wilhelm, P. Frame work

CONTINENTAL DRAMA. See
HARC Harvard classics,
v26

COOA Cook, Albert Spaulding,
and Dolin, Edwin, eds. An
anthology of Greek tragedy.
Indianapolis, Ind., Bobbs-
Merrill, 1972. 400p
Aeschylus. Agamemnon
Aeschylus. Prometheus bound
Euripides. Andromache
Euripides. The bacchae
Euripides. The Trojan women
Sophocles. Oedipus at Colonus
Sophocles. Oedipus Rex
Sophocles. Philoctetes

COOF Cook, David M., and
Wanger, Craig G., comps.
The small town in American
literature. New York, Dodd,
Mead, 1969. 253p
Wilder, T. Our town
Williams, T. The case of the
crushed petunias

COOJ Cook, Luella Bussey;
Loban, Walter; McDowell,
Tremaine and Stauffer,
Ruth M., eds. America
through literature...Harcourt,
Brace, 1948. 750p (Living
literature)
Sherwood, R. Abe Lincoln in
Illinois
Wilder, T. Our town

COOK Cook, Luella Bussey;
Norvell, George W., and
McCall, William A., eds.
Hidden treasures in literature.
...New York, Harcourt, Brace,
1934. 3v
Coppée, F. The violin-maker
of Cremona 1
Dunsany, E. A night at an inn
3
Field, R. The patchwork quilt
2
Fitch, C. Nathan Hale 2
Monkhouse, A. The grand
cham's necklace 2
Pillot, E. Two crooks and a lady
3
Rostand, E. The romancers 2
Saudners, L. The knave of
hearts 1
Shakespeare, W. Julius Caesar
3

COOP Cooper, Charles W. Preface
to drama...New York, Ronald
press [c1955] 773p
Coward, N. Fumed oak
Gilbert, W. H.M.S. Pinafore
Housman, L. "A good lesson!"
Ibsen, H. Hedda Gabler
Lindsay, H., and Crouse, R.
Life with father
Miller, A. The crucible
Molière, J. The ridiculous

précieuses
O'Neill, E. The long voyage
home
Shakespeare, W. Othello
Shaw, G. Candida
Sophocles. Antigone
Wilder, T. The happy journey
to Trenton and Camden
Williams, T. The glass menagerie

COOPA Cooper, Joshua, ed., and
tr. Four Russian plays.
Harmondsworth, Middlesex,
Penguin, 1972. 394p
Fonvizin, D. The infant
Gogol, N. The inspector
Griboiedov, A. Chatsky
Ostrovskiĭ, A. Thunder

COOPER, LANE. See
TEN Ten Greek plays

COP Copeland, Charles Townsend,
ed. The Copeland reader.
New York, Scribner, 1926.
1687p
Sheridan, R. The critic; or,
A tragedy rehearsed

COPB Copeland, Charles Townsend,
ed. The Copeland translations
...New York, Scribner, 1934.
1080p
Molière, J. The physician in
spite of himself

COPC Copeland, Charles Townsend,
ed. Copeland's treasury for
booklovers...New York,
Scribner, 1927. 5v
Sheridan, R. The critic; or, A
tragedy rehearsed 1

CORB Corbin, Richard K. and Balf,
Miriam, eds. Twelve American
plays, 1920-1960. New York,
Scribner, 1969. 480p
Albee, E. The sandbox
Chase, M. Harvey
Hellman, L. The little foxes
Kesselring, J. Arsenic and old
lace

CORB (cont.)
Nash, R. The rainmaker
O'Neill, E. Beyond the horizon
Patrick, J. The teahouse of
the August moon
Rodgers, R. and Hammerstein, O.
The king and I
Serling, R. Requiem for a
heavyweight
Sherwood, R. There shall be
no night
Wilder, T. Our town
Williams, T. The glass menagerie

CORD Cordell, Kathryn (Coe)
and Cordell, William Howard,
eds. The Pulitzer prize
plays, 1918-1934...New York,
Random House [1935] 856p
Anderson, M. Both your houses
Connelly, M. The green pastures
Davis, O. Icebound
Gale, Z. Miss Lulu Bett
Glaspell, S. Alison's house
Green, P. In Abraham's bosom
Howard, S. They knew what they
wanted
Hughes, H. Hell-bent fer heaven
Kaufman, G., and Ryskind, M.
Of thee I sing
Kelly, G. Craig's wife
Kingsley, S. Men in white
O'Neill, E. Anna Christie
O'Neill, E. Beyond the horizon
O'Neill, E. Strange interlude
Rice, E. Street scene
Williams, J. Why marry?

CORE Cordell, Kathryn (Coe) and
Cordell, William Howard, eds.
The Pulitzer prize plays...
New ed. New York, Random
house [1938?] 983p
Anderson, M. Both your houses
Connelly, M. The green
pastures
Davis, O. Icebound
Gale, Z. Miss Lulu Bett
Glaspell, S. Alison's house
Green, P. In Abraham's bosom
Hart, M., and Kaufman, G.
You can't take it with you
Howard, S. They knew what
they wanted
Hughes, H. Hell-bent fer
heaven
Kaufman, G., and Ryskind, M.

Of thee I sing
Kelly, G. Craig's wife
Kingsley, S. Men in white
O'Neill, E. Anna Christie
O'Neill, E. Beyond the horizon
O'Neill, E. Strange interlude
Rice, E. Street scene
Sherwood, R. Idiot's delight
Williams, J. Why marry?

CORF Cordell, Kathryn (Coe)
and Cordell, William Howard,
eds. A new edition of the
Pulitzer prize plays...New
York, Random house [1940]
1091p
Anderson, M. Both your houses
Connelly, M. The green pastures
Davis, O. Icebound
Gale, Z. Miss Lulu Bett
Glaspell, S. Alison's house
Green, P. In Abraham's bosom
Hart, M., and Kaufman, G. You
can't take it with you
Howard, S. They knew what they
wanted
Hughes, H. Hell-bent fer heaven
Kaufman, G., and Ryskind, M.
Of thee I sing
Kelly, G. Craig's wife
Kingsley, S. Men in white
O'Neill, E. Anna Christie
O'Neill, E. Beyond the horizon
O'Neill, E. Strange interlude
Rice, E. Street scene
Sherwood, R. Abe Lincoln in Il-
linois
Sherwood, R. Idiot's delight
Wilder, T. Our town
Williams, J. Why marry?

COT Cordell, Richard Albert, ed.
Representative modern plays...
New York, Nelson, 1929. 654p
Ade, G. The college widow
Bennett, A. The great adventure
Crothers, R. Expressing Willie
Dane, C. A bill of divorcement
Fitch, C. The climbers
Gilbert, W. Sweethearts
Hughes, H. Hell-bent fer heaven
Jones, H. Mrs. Dane's defence
Kaufman, G., and Connelly, M.
Beggar on horseback
Maugham, W. The circle
Milne, A. Success
O'Casey, S. Juno and the paycock

O'Neill, E. Diff'rent
Pinero, A. Iris
Robertson, T. Caste
Wilde, O. A woman of no importance

COTE Cordell, Richard Albert, ed.
Twentieth century plays,
American...Third edition.
New York, Ronald press
[c1947] 329p
Anderson, M. Winterset
Connelly, M. The green pastures
Hellman, L. The little foxes
Howard, S. The silver cord
Marquand, J., and Kaufman, G.
The late George Apley
O'Neill, E. Anna Christie
Rice, E. Street scene
Sherwood, R. Abe Lincoln in Illinois

COTH Cordell, Richard Albert, ed.
Twentieth century plays,
British, American, Continental...Third edition. New
York, Ronald press [c1947]
447p
Anderson, M. Winterset
Barrie, J. The admirable
Crichton
Čapek, K. R.U.R.
Galsworthy, J. The silver box
Hellman, L. The little foxes
Maugham, W. The circle
Marquand, J., and Kaufman, G.
The late George Apley
O'Neill, E. Anna Christie
Rice, E. Street scene
Rostand, E. Cyrano de Bergerac
Sherwood, R. Abe Lincoln in
Illinois

COTK Cordell, Richard Albert,
and Matson, Lowell, eds.
The off-Broadway theatre...
New York, Random house
[c1959] 481p
Anouilh, J. Ardèle
Barkentin, M. Ulysses in Nighttown
Forsyth, J. Héloise
Hayes, A. The girl on the Via
Flaminia
Lee, J. Career
O'Casey, S. Purple dust
Priestley, J., and Hawkes, J.

Dragon's mouth

CORDELL, RICHARD ALBERT. See
also
CHA, CHAN, CHAP, CHAR
Chandler, Frank Wadleigh and
Cordell, Richard Albert, eds.
Twentieth century plays...

COTKI Corrigan, Robert Willoughby,
ed. Comedy; a critical anthology. Boston, Houghton
Mifflin, 1971. 769p
Aristophanes. Lysistrata
Bellow, S. The last analysis
Brecht, B. Puntila and his hired
man
Chekhov, A. The cherry orchard
Giraudoux, J. The madwoman of
Chaillot
Jonson, B. Volpone
Molière, J. Tartuffe
Shakespeare, W. Twelfth night
Shaw, G. Misalliance
Sheridan, R. The school for
scandal
Synge, J. The playboy of the
western world
Wilde, O. The importance of
being earnest

COTKIR Corrigan, Robert Willoughby, comp. The forms of
drama. Boston, Houghton
Mifflin, 1972. 746p
Büchner, G. Woyzeck
Congreve, W. The way of the
world
Ibsen, H. Ghosts
Jellicoe, A. The knack
Labiche, E., and Michel, M.
An Italian straw hat
Miller, A. A view from the
bridge
Molière, J. The miser
Plautus, T. The Menaechmi
Shakespeare, W. Othello
Shaw, G. Arms and the man
Sophocles. Antigone
Webster, J. The duchess of
Malfi

COTKIS Corrigan, Robert Willoughby, comp. Laurel British
drama: the nineteenth century.
[New York, Dell, 1967] 464p
Boucicault, D. London assurance

COTKIS (cont.)
Gilbert, W. Patience
Lewis, L. The bells
Pinero, A. The second Mrs.
  Tanqueray
Shaw, G. Arms and the man
Wilde, O. The importance of
  being earnest

COTKIT Corrigan, Robert Wil-
  loughby, ed. Laurel
  British drama: the twentieth
  century. [New York, Dell,
  1965] 511p
Bagnold, E. The chalk garden
Bolt, R. A man for all seasons
Coward, N. Private lives
Galsworthy, L. Loyalties
Jellicoe, A. The knack
Shaw, G. Heartbreak house

COTKJ Corrigan, Robert Willoughby, ed. Masterpieces of the
  modern central European
  theatre; five plays. New
  York, Collier Books, 1967.
  382p
Čapek, K. R.U.R.
Hofmannstal, H. Electra
Molnár, F. The play's the
  thing
Schnitzler, A. The game of
  love
Schnitzler, A. La ronde

COTKR Corrigan, Robert Willough-
  by, ed. Masterpieces of the
  modern English theatre. New
  York, Collier Books, 1967.
  476p
Barrie, J. Dear Brutus
Galsworthy, J. Loyalties
Kops, B. Enter Solly Gold
Shaw, G. Major Barbara
Wilde, O. The importance of
  being earnest

COTKW Corrigan, Robert Willough-
  by, ed. Masterpieces of the
  modern French theatre; 6 plays.
  New York, Collier Books, 1967.
  442p
Anouilh, J. Euridice
Becque, H. The Parisian woman
Ghelderode, M. Christopher
  Columbus
Giraudoux, J. Electra

Ionesco, E. Improvisation; or,
  The shepherd's chameleon
Montherlant, H. Queen after
  death

COTL Corrigan, Robert Willoughby,
  ed. Masterpieces of the modern
  German theatre; five plays.
  New York, Collier Books, 1967.
  416p
Brecht, B. The Caucasian chalk
  circle
Büchner, G. Woyzeck
Hauptmann, G. The weavers
Hebbel, F. Maria Magdalena
Wedekind, F. The Marquis of
  Keith

COTM Corrigan, Robert Willoughby,
  ed. Masterpieces of the modern
  Irish theatre; five plays. New
  York, Collier Books, 1967.
  317p
O'Casey, S. Cock-a-doodle dandy
O'Casey, S. The silver tassie
Synge, J. The playboy of the
  western world
Synge, J. Riders to the sea
Yeats, W. The Countess Cahtleen

COTN Corrigan, Robert Willoughby,
  ed. Masterpieces of the modern
  Italian theatre; six plays. New
  York, Collier Books [1967]
  352p
Betti, U. Crime on Goat Island
Filippo, E. Filumena Marturano
Fratti, M. The academy
Fratti, M. The return
Pirandello, L. The pleasure of
  honesty
Pirandello, L. Six characters in
  search of an author

COTO Corrigan, Robert Willoughby,
  ed. Masterpieces of the modern
  Russian theatre; five plays.
  New York, Collier Books
  [c1967] 414p
Chekhov, A. The cherry orchard
Chekhov, A. Uncle Vanya
Gorki, M. The lower depths
Mayakovsky, V. The bed bug
Turgenev, I. A month in the
  country

COTP Corrigan, Robert Willoughby,

ed. Masterpieces of the
modern Spanish theatre.
New York, Collier Books,
1967. 384p
Benavente y Martínez, J.
The witches' sabbath
Buero Vallejo, A. The dream
weaver
García Lorca, F. The love of
Don Perlimplín and Belisa
in the garden
Martínez Sierra, G. The cradle
song
Sastre, A. Death thrust

COTQ Corrigan, Robert Willoughby,
ed. The modern theatre. New
York, Macmillan, 1964. 1267p
Anouilh, J. Eurydice
Beckett, S. Endgame
Betti, U. The queen and the
rebels
Brecht, B. The Caucasian chalk
circle
Büchner, G. Woyzeck
Chekhov, A. The cherry orchard
Chekhov, A. Uncle Vanya
Duerrenmatt, F. The visit
Eliot, T. Murder in the cathedral
Frisch, M. The Chinese wall
Fry, C. A sleep of prisoners
García Lorca, F. Yerma
Genêt J. Deathwatch
Giraudoux, J. Electra
Gorki, M. The lower depths
Hauptmann, G. The weavers
Hebbel, F. Maria Magdalena
Hellman, L. The little foxes
Hofmannsthal, H. Electra
Ibsen, H. Hedda Gabler
Ibsen, H. The wild duck
Ionesco, E. The chairs
Miller, A. A view from the
bridge
O'Casey, S. The plough and
the stars
O'Neill, E. Desire under the
elms
Pirandello, L. The emperor
Pirandello, L. Six characters
in search of an author
Saroyan, W. The time of your
life
Sartre, J. The victors
Sastre, A. Anna Kleiber
Schnitzler, A. La ronde
Shaw, G. Major Barbara

Strindberg, A. The ghost sonata
Strindberg, A. Miss Julie
Synge, J. Playboy of the western
world
Synge, J. Riders to the sea
Wedekind, F. The marquis of
Keith
Wilder, T. The skin of our teeth
Williams, T. The glass menagerie
Yeats, W. On Baile's strand

COTR Corrigan, Robert W., ed.
The new theatre of Europe...
[New York, Dell Publishing Co.,
c1962] 399p
Betti, U. Corruption in the palace
of justice
Bolt, R. A man for all seasons
Ghelderode, M. Pantagleize
Peryalis, N. Masks of angels
Sastre, A. Anna Kleiber

COTS Corrigan, Robert Willoughby,
ed. The new theatre of
Europe, 2; 5 contemporary
plays from the European stage
...New York, Dell, 1964.
320p
Brecht, B. Mother Courage
Fratti, M. The cage
Fratti, M. The suicide
Grass, G. The wicked cooks
Schehadé, G. Vasco

COTT Corrigan, Robert Willoughby,
ed. The new theatre of
Europe, 3; 4 contemporary
plays from the European stage
...New York, Dell, 1968.
309p
Dorst, T. The curve
Forssell, L. The Sunday
promenade
Guerdon, D. The laundry
Osborne, J. Inadmissable evi-
dence

COTU Corrigan, Robert Willoughby,
ed. Roman drama, in modern
translations. [New York, Dell,
1966] 380p
Horatius Flaccus, Q. Ars poetica
Plautus, T. The Menaechmi
Plautus, T. The merchant
Seneca, L. Medea
Terentius Afer, P. Adelphi
Terentius Afer, P. Phormio

COTX Corrigan, Robert Willough-
by, comp. Tragedy: a
critical anthology. Boston,
Houghton Mifflin, 1971.
787p
Coxe, L., and Chapman, R.
Billy Budd
Dryden, J. All for love
Euripides. The bacchae
Ibsen, H. The master builder
MacLeish, A. J.B.
Marlowe, C. Doctor Faust
Miller, A. Death of a salesman
Racine, J. Phaedra
Shakespeare, W. The tragedy
of King Lear
Shaw, G. Saint Joan
Sophocles. Oedipus the King
Strindberg, A. Miss Julie

COTY Corrigan, Robert Willoughby
and Rosenberg, James L., eds.
The art of the theatre, a
critical anthology of drama...
San Francisco, Chandler
[1964] 609p
Aristophanes. Lysistrata
Chekhov, A. Uncle Vanya
Ionesco, E. The new tenant
Molière, J. Tartuffe
Shakespeare, W. Macbeth
Sophocles. Antigone
Strindberg, A. Miss Julie
Synge, J. Riders to the sea
Wilde, O. The importance of
being earnest
Williams, T. The rose tattoo

CORRIGAN, ROBERT WILLOUGHBY.
See also
NEWA New American plays...

COUR Cournos, John, ed. A
treasury of classic Russian
literature...New York,
Capricorn Books [c1961]
580p and index
Gogol, N. The inspector-
general
Ostrovskiĭ, A. A domestic picture
Tolstoi, L. Condemnation
Tolstoi, L. Taxes

COUS Cournos, John, ed. A
treasury of Russian life and
humor...New York, Coward-
McCann [c1943] 676p

Gogol, N. The inspector

COX Cox, Martha Heasley, ed.
Image and value; an invitation
to literature. New York, Har-
court, Brace & World [1966]
630p
Arrabal, F. Picnic on the battle-
field
Giraudoux, J. The Apollo of
Bellac
O'Neill, E. A touch of the poet
Shaw, G. Pygmalion
Sophocles. Antigone

COY Coyle, William and Damaser,
H. G., eds. Six early Ameri-
can plays, 1798-1890. Colum-
bus, Ohio, Merrill, 1968.
313p
Boucicault, D. The octoroon
Dunlap, W. André
Herne, J. Margaret Fleming
Howard, B. Shenandoah
Mowatt, A. Fashion
Stone, J. Metamora

CRAF Craft, Harry M., comp.
Logic, style and arrangement
...Beverly Hills, Calif.,
Glencoe Press, 1971. 501p
Shakespeare, W. King Lear
Sophocles. Antigone
Wilde, O. The importance of
being earnest

CRAN Crane, William Garrett [and
others] eds. Twelve hundred
years; the literature of England...Harrisburg, Pa.
Stackpole and Heck [c1949]
2v
Wilde, O. The importance of
being earnest 2

CRE Creeth, Edmund, comp.
Tudor plays; an anthology of
early English drama. Garden
City, New York, Anchor
Books (Doubleday) [1966]
569p
Bale, J. Kyng Johan
Heywood, J. Johan Johan the
husbande
Medwall, H. Fulgens and Lucres
Preston, T. Cambises
Sackville, T., and Norton, T.

Ferrex and Porrex; or,
Gorboduc
Stevenson, W. Gammer Gurton's
nedle
Udall, N. Royster Doyster

CRIT The Critics' prize plays.
Introduction by George Jean
Nathan. Cleveland, Ohio,
World publishing co. [c1945]
377p
Anderson, M. High Tor
Anderson, M. Winterset
Hellman, L. Watch on the Rhine
Kingsley, S. The patriots
Saroyan, W. The time of your
life
Steinbeck, J. Of mice and men

CROS Cross, Ethan Allen, ed.
World literature. New York,
American book co. [c1935]
1396p
Aeschylus. PJrometheus bound
Bulwer-Lytton, E. Richelieu; or,
The conspiracy
Euripides. Iphigenia in Aulis
Galsworthy, J. The silver box
Ibsen, H. The master builder
Molière, J. The miser
Plautus. Menaechmi; or, The
twin brothers
Seneca. Medea
Shakespeare, W. Antony and
Cleopatra
Sophocles. Antigone
Terence. Andria

CROV Cross, Tom Peete and
Slover, Clark H., eds.
Heath readings in the litera-
ture of Europe...Boston,
Heath [c1933] 1194p
Adam, The play of
Aeschylus. Prometheus bound
Aristophanes. The birds
Corneille, P. Le cid
Goethe, J. Faust, pt. I
Goldoni, C. A curious mishap
Ibsen, H. Ghosts
Lessing, G. Minna von Barnhelm
Molière, J. The misanthrope
Plautus. The captives
Seneca. Medea
Vega Carpio, L. The star of
Seville

CROX Cross, Tom Peete; Smith,
Reed; Stauffer, Elmer C., and
Collette, Elizabeth. American
writers. Revised edition...
Boston, Ginn [c1955] 708p
Wilder, T. Our town

CROZ Cross-section...Edited by
Edwin Seaver. New York,
L. B. Fischer [c1944-48]
4v
Miller, A. The man who had
all the luck 1
Peters, P. Nat Turner 1
Whittington, R. The death of
García Lorca 1

CRU Crump, James Irving, comp.
Chinese theater in the days of
Kublai Khan. University of
Arizona Press, 1980. 429p
K'ang, C. Li K'uei carries
thorns
Meng, H. The Mo-ho-lo doll
Yang, H. Rain on the Hsiao-
hsiang

CUBE Cubeta, Paul M., ed....
Modern drama for analysis. New
York, William Sloane Associates
[c1950] 584p
Chekhov, A. The cherry orchard
Hellman, L. Watch on the Rhine
Ibsen, H. The wild duck
O'Casey, S. Juno and the
paycock
O'Neill, E. The Emperor Jones
Synge, J. The playboy of the
western world
Wilder, T. The skin of our
teeth
Williams, T. The glass menagerie

CUBG Cubeta, Paul M. Modern
drama for analysis. Revised
edition. [New York, Dryden,
c1955] 785p
Chekhov, A. The cherry orchard
Ibsen, H. The wild duck
Inge, W. Come back, little Sheba
O'Casey, S. Juno and the paycock
O'Neill, E. Anna Christie
Shaw, G. Arms and the man
Synge, J. The playboy of the
western world
Wilder, T. The skin of our teeth
Williams, T. The glass menagerie

CUBH Cubeta, Paul M. Modern
      drama for analysis...3d ed.
      New York, Holt, Rinehart
      and Winston [c1962] 613p
Albee, E. The sandbox
Anouilh, J. Becket; or, The
      honor of God
Chekhov, A. The cherry orchard
Eliot, T. Murder in the cathedral
Ibsen, H. Rosmersholm
Miller, A. A view from the bridge
O'Neill, E. Desire under the elms
Shaw, G. The devil's disciple
Wilder, T. The skin of our teeth
Williams, T. The glass menagerie

CUN Cunliffe, John William, ed.
     Early English classical trage-
     dies...Oxford, Clarendon
     Press, 1912. 352p
Gascoigne, G., and Kinwelmersh,
     F. Jocasta
Hughes, T. The misfortunes of
     Arthur
Norton, T., and Sackville, T.
     Gorboduc; or, Ferrex and
     Porrex
[Wilmot, R., and others] Gismond
     of Salerne

DAI Daiches, David; Jewett, Arno;
     Havighurst, Walter and Searles,
     John, comps. English litera-
     ture. Boston, Houghton
     Mifflin, 1968. 848p
Goldsmith, O. She stoops to con-
     quer
Shakespeare, W. Macbeth
Shaw, G. Pygmalion
Synge, J. Riders to the sea

DANA, H. W. L. See
     SEVP Seven Soviet plays...

DANI Daniel, Robert Woodham,
      and Leggett, G. H., eds.
      The written word...Englewood
      Cliffs, N.J., Prentice Hall,
      1960. 726p
Shaw, G. The man of destiny

DAV Davenport, William H.;
     Wimberley, Lowry C., and
     Shaw, Harry, eds. Dominant
     types in British and American

     literature...New York, Harper
     [c1949] 2v
Anderson, M. Winterset 1
Barrie, J. The 12-pound look 1
O'Neill, E. The hairy ape 1
Rice, E. The adding machine 1
The second shepherds' play 1
Shakespeare, W. King Henry
     the fourth 1
Sheridan, R. The school for
     scandal 1
Synge, J. Riders to the sea 1
Wilde, O. Lady Windermere's fan
     1

DAVI David, Sister Mary Agnes.
      Modern American Drama...New
      York, Macmillan [c1961] 235p
      (The pageant of literature)
Barry, P. The joyous season
Coxe, L., and Chapman, R.
     Billy Budd
Van Druten, J. I remember mama

DAVJ Davies, Reginald Trevor, ed.
      The Corpus Christi play of
      the English middle ages. To-
      towa, N.J., Rowman and
      Littlefield, 1972. 458p
Abraham (Wakefield)
Abraham (York)
Abraham and Isaac (Brome)
Abraham and Isaac (Dublin)
Abraham and Isaac (Ludus Coven-
     triae)
Abraham, Melchisedec and Isaac
     (Chester)
The apostles at the tomb
Appearance to Cleopas and Luke
Appearance to Mary Magdalen
Appearance to Thomas
Ascension
Assumption
Birth of the Son
Cain and Abel
Creation and fall of Lucifer
Creation and fall of man
Doomsday
Harrowing of Hell II
Herod and the three kings
Jesse
Jesus and the doctors
Matthias
Moses
Mother of Mercy: Conception
Mother of Mercy: Joseph
Mother of Mercy: Parliament of

Heaven and Annunciation
Mother of Mercy: Salutation
Noah
Passion I: Agony at Olivet
--I: Betrayal
--I: Council of Jews I
--I: Council of Jews II
--I: Entry into Jerusalem
--I: Maundy I
--I: Maundy II
--I: Maundy III
--I: Prologues
--I: Taking of Jesus
Passion II: Before Annas and
   Caiphas
--II: Before Herod II
--II: Before Pilate
Passion II: Before Pilate II
--II: Centurion
--II: Crucifixion
--II: Dream of Pilate's wife
--II: Harrowing of Hell I
--II: Jesus before Herod
--II: Longeus and burial
--II: Peter's denial
--II: Prologue
--II: Setting of watch
--II: Way of the cross
Pentecost
Presentation and purification
Raising of Lazarus
Resurrection and appearance
   to mother
The shepherds' play
Slaughter of the innocents
Story of the watch
Three Marys at the tomb
Trial of Joseph and Mary
Woman taken in adultery

DAVK Davis, Earle R., and
   Hummel, William C., eds.
   Readings for enjoyment.
   Englewood Cliffs, N.J.,
   Prentice-Hall, 1959. 611p
The book of Job
Kaufman, G., and Hart, M.
   The man who came to dinner
O'Neill, E. Ah, wilderness
Shakespeare, W. Hamlet,
   Prince of Denmark
Sophocles. Oedipus rex

DAVM Davis, Muriel, comp.
   Inscape; stories, plays,
   poems...Philadelphia, Lippincott, 1971. 632p

Aristophanes. Lysistrata
Chayefsky, P. Marty
Saroyan, W. The time of your
   life
Williams, T. The glass menagerie

DAVN Davis, Norman, ed. Non-
   cycle plays and fragments.
   Edited...by N. Davis. Sup-
   plementary Text No. 1; pub-
   lished for the Early English
   Text Society. London, Oxford,
   1970. 168p
Abraham and Isaac (Brome)
Abraham and Isaac (Northampton)
The Ashmole fragment
The Cambridge prologue
The Durham prologue
Dux moraud
The newcastle play (Noah's ark;
   or, The Shipwrights ancient
   play, or dirge).
The Norwich Grocers' play (The
   story of the creation of Eve,
   or the expelling of Adam and
   Eve out of paradise); Text A
   and Text B
The play of the sacrament
The pride of life
The Shrewsbury fragments: Of-
   ficium pastorum; Officium resur-
   rectionis; Officium peregrinorum
The Reynes extracts
The Rickinghall (Bury St. Ed-
   munds) fragment

DAVR Davison, Dennis, ed.
   Restoration comedies. London,
   Oxford, 1970. 399p
Dryden, J. Marriage a la mode
Etherege, G. She would if she
   could
Sedley, C. The mulberry garden
Vanbrugh, J. The relapse
Wycherley, W. The country wife

DBG Drama contemporary Czech-
   oslovakia; plays by Milan
   Kundera, Václav Havel, Pavel
   Kohout, Milan Uhde, Pavel
   Landovský, Ivan Klíma. Edited,
   with an introduction by Marketa
   Goetz-Stankiewicz. New York,
   Performing Arts Journal Pub-
   lications, 1985. 224p
Havel, V. Protest
Klíma, I. Games

DBG (cont.)
  Kohout, P. Fire in the basement
  Kundera, M. Jacques and his
    master
  Landovský, P. The detour
  Uhde, M. A blue angel

DEAN Dean, Leonard [Fellows],
  ed...
  Elizabethan drama...New York,
  Prentice-Hall, 1950. 334p
  (English masterpieces. v2)
  Marlowe, C. Doctor Faustus
  Shakespeare, W. Henry the
    fourth, pt. I
  Shakespeare, W. King Lear
  Webster, J. The Duchess of
    Malfi

DEAO Dean, Leonard Fellows, ed.
  Elizabethan drama...Second
  edition. Englewood Cliffs,
  N.J., Prentice-Hall, 1961.
  364p (English masterpieces.
  v2)
  Jonson, B. Volpone; or, The fox
  Marlowe, C. The tragical history
    of Doctor Faustus
  Shakespeare, W. King Lear
  Webster, J. The Duchess of Malfi

DEAP Dean, Leonard Fellows, ed.
  Nine great plays from
  Aeschylus to Eliot. New York,
  Harcourt, Brace [c1950] 595p
  Aeschylus. Agamemnon
  Chekhov, A. The cherry orchard
  Congreve, W. The way of the
    world
  Eliot, T. Murder in the cathedral
  Ibsen, H. The wild duck
  Jonson, B. Volpone; or, The fox
  Molière, J. The misanthrope
  O'Neill, E. The Emperor Jones
  Sophocles. King Oedipus

DEAR Dean, Leonard [Fellows], ed.
  Nine great plays, from
  Aeschylus to Eliot. Revised
  edition...New York, Harcourt
  Brace [c1956] 695p
  Aeschylus. Agamemnon
  Chekhov, A. The cherry orchard
  Congreve, W. The way of the
    world
  Eliot, T. Murder in the cathedral
  Ibsen, H. An enemy of the people

Jonson, B. Volpone
Molière, J. The would-be invalid
Shaw, G. Pygmalion
Sophocles. Oedipus Rex

DEAS Dean, Leonard [Fellows], ed.
  Twelve great plays. New
  York, Harcourt, Brace,
  Jovanovich, 1970. 789p
  Abse, D. House of cowards
  Aeschylus. Agamemnon
  Brecht, B. The Caucasian
    chalk circle
  Chekhov, A. The cherry orchard
  Ibsen, H. Ghosts
  Jonson, B. The alchemist
  Marlowe, C. The Jew of Malta
  Molière, J. Tartuffe
  Pirandello, L. Six characters in
    search of an author
  Shakespeare, W. Henry IV,
    Part 1
  Sophocles. Oedipus Rex
  Williams, T. The glass menagerie

DEBENHAM, A. H. See
  SEVE Seven sacred plays

DEC A decade's drama: six Scot-
  tish plays. Todmorden,
  Lancashire, Woodhouse Books,
  1980. 330p
  Byrne, J. Threads
  Conn, S. Play donkey
  Eveling, S. Mister
  Macdonald, R. Chinchilla
  MacMillan, H. The rising
  Taylor, C. Walter

DEM De Mille, Alban Bertram, ed.
  Three English comedies...Boston,
  Allyn and Bacon [c1924] 479p
  Goldsmith, O. She stoops to con-
    quer
  Sheridan, R. The rivals
  Sheridan, R. The school for
    scandal

DENSMORE, H. B. See
  TEN Ten Greek plays...

DIC Dickinson, Thomas Herbert, ed.
  Chief contemporary dramatists...
  [first series] Boston, Hough-
  ton, Mifflin [c1915] 676p
  Barker, G. The Madras house
  Bjørnson, B. Beyond human

power
Brieux, E. The red robe
Chekhov, A. The cherry orchard
Fitch, C. The truth
Galsworthy, J. Strife
Gregory, A. The rising of the
moon
Hauptmann, G. The weavers
Hervieu, P. Know thyself
Jones, H. Michael and his lost
angel
MacKaye, P. The scarecrow
Maeterlinck, M. Pélléas and
Mélisande
Moody, W. The great divide
Pinero, A. The second Mrs.
Tanqueray
Strindberg, A. The father
Sudermann, H. The vale of
content
Synge, J. Riders to the sea
Thomas, A. The witching
hour
Wilde, O. Lady Windermere's
fan
Yeats, W. The hour-glass

DID Dickinson, Thomas Herbert,
ed. Chief contemporary
dramatists, second series...
Boston, Houghton Mifflin
[c1921] 734p
Annunzio, G. d'. Gioconda
Gahr, H. The concert
Benavente (y Martínez), J.
The bonds of interest
Bennett, A., and Knoblock, E.
Milestones
Drinkwater, J. Abraham Lincoln
Dunsany, E. King Argimenes
and the unknown warrior
Ervine, St. J. Mixed marriage
Gorki, M. The lower depths
Guitry, S. Pasteur
Hazelton, G., and Benrimo, J.
The yellow jacket
Heiberg, G. The tragedy of love
Maugham, W. Our betters
Peabody, J. The piper
Porto-Riche, G. de. A loving
wife
Rostand, E. Cyrano de Bergerac
Schnitzler, A. Living hours
Thoma, L. Moral
Walter, E. The easiest way

DIE Dickinson, Thomas Herbert, ed.

Chief contemporary dramatists,
third series...Boston, Hough-
ton, Mifflin [c1930] 698p
Alvarez Quintero, S., and
Alvarez Quintero, J. Malvaloca
Andreyev, L. He who gets
slapped
Ansky, S. The dybbuk
Benelli, S. The love of the three
kings
Čapek, K. R.U.R.
Green, P. In Abraham's bosom
Hofmannsthal, H. von. Electra
Howard, S. The silver cord
Kaiser, G. From morn to midnight
Lenormand, H. Time is a dream
Martínez Sierra, G., and
Martínez Sierra, M. A lily
among thorns
Milne, A. The Dover road
Molnár, F. Liliom
O'Casey, S. Juno and the pay-
cock
O'Neill, E. The Emperor Jones
Pirandello, L. Naked
Sigurjónsson, J. Eyvind of the
hills
Vildrac, C. The steamship
Tenacity
Wedekind, F. Such is life
Yevreinov, N. The theatre of
soul

DIG Dickinson, Thomas Herbert,
and Crawford, Jack Randall,
eds. Contemporary plays...
Boston, Houghton Mifflin
[c1925] 650p
Anspacher, L. The unchastened
woman
Baker, E. Chains
Crothers, R. Mary the third
Davies, H. The mollusc
Davis, O. Icebound
Drinkwater, J. Oliver Cromwell
Granville-Barker, H. The Voysey
inheritance
Hankin, St. J. The Cassilis en-
gagement
Houghton, S. Hindle wakes
Kenyon, C. Kindling
Maugham, W. The circle
O'Neill, E. The hairy ape
Phillips, S. Paolo and Francesca
Rice, E. The adding machine
Sowerby, G. Rutherford and son
Sutro, A. John Gladye's honour

DIK Dickinson, Thomas Herbert,
ed. ... Continental plays
...Boston, Houghton Mifflin
[c1935] 2v (Types contem-
porary drama)
Alvarez Quintero, S., and
Alvarez Quintero, J. A
bright morning 1
Andreyev, L. The life of man
2
Annunzio, G. d'. Francesca da
Rimini
Bernard, J. L'invitation au
voyage 2
Brieux, E. The red robe 2
Capek, K. R.U.R. 1
Chekhov, A. The cherry orchard
1
Claudel, P. The tidings brought
to Mary 1
Echegaray [y Eizaguirre], J.
The great Galeoto 2
Gorky, M. The lower depths 2
Hauptmann, G. The weavers 1
Kaiser, G. The coral 2
Maeterlinck, M. Pelléas and
Mélisande 1
Molnár, F. Liliom 1
Pirandello, L. Six characters in
search of an author 2
Rostand, E. Cyrano de Bergerac
2
Schnitzler, A. Light-o'-love 1
Strindberg, A. A dream play 2
Tolstoy, L. The power of dark-
ness 1
Wedekind, F. Erdgeist 2

DIP Dietrich, Richard Farr, comp.
The realities of literature.
Waltham, Mass., Xerox College
Publications, 1971. 656p
Hansberry, L. A raisin in the
sun
Ionesco, E. The picture
Pirandello, L. Six characters
in search of an author
Shaw, G. Caesar and Cleopatra
Sophocles. Oedipus Rex

DIT Dietrich, Richard Farr, and
others, comps. The art of
drama. New York, Holt,
1969. 669p
Brecht, B. The Caucasian chalk
circle
Chekhov, A. The cherry orchard

Hansberry, L. Raisin in the sun
Ibsen, H. The wild duck
Miller, A. A view from the bridge
Molière, J. The misanthrope
Osborne, J. Luther
Pirandello, L. Six characters in
search of an author
Shakespeare, W. Antony and
Cleopatra
Shaw, G. Caesar and Cleopatra
Sophocles. Antigone
Sophocles. Oedipus
Williams, T. The glass menagerie

DITA Dietrich, Richard F., et al.,
comps. The art of drama. 2nd
ed. New York, Holt, 1976.
781p
Beckett, S. Act without words II
Chekhov, A. The cherry orchard
Hansberry, L. A raisin in the
sun
Ibsen, H. A doll's house
Ionesco, E. The gap
Miller, A. Death of a salesman
Molière, J. The misanthrope
Nichols, P. Joe Egg
O'Neill, E. The hairy ape
Pirandello, L. Six characters in
search of an author
Shakespeare, W. Twelfth night
Shaw, B. Candida
Sophocles. Oedipus rex
Strindberg, A. The stronger
Weiss, P. Marat/Sade
Zindel, P. The effect of gamma
rays on man-in-the-moon mari-
golds

DIV The Digby plays, rendered into
modern English. By Alice J.
Brock and David G. Byrd.
Dallas, Texas, Paon Press,
1973. 144p
Christ's burial and resurrection
The conversion of St. Paul
Herod's killing of the children
Mary Magdalene
A morality of wisdom, who is
Christ

DIZ Disch, Robert, and Schwartz,
Barry N., eds. Killing time;
a guide to life in the happy
valley. Englewood Cliffs,
N.J., Prentice-Hall, 1972.
500p

Aeschylus. Agamemnon
Chekhov, A. The cherry orchard
Davis, O. Purlie victorious
Fratti, M. The bridge
Terry, M. The magic realists

DOA Dobrée, Bonamy, ed.
     Five heroic plays...London,
     Oxford University Press, 1960.
     417p
Crowne, J. The destruction of
   Jerusalem
Dryden, J. Aureng-zebe
Lee, N. Sophonisba
Orrery, R. The tragedy of
   Mustapha, the son of Solyman
   the magnificent
Settle, E. The Empress of
   Morocco

DOB Dobrée, Bonamy, ed. Five
     restoration tragedies...[London]
     Oxford university press [1928]
     450p (The world's classics)
Addison, J. Cato
Dryden, J. All for love
Otway, T. Venice preserv'd
Rowe, N. The fair penitent
Southerne, T. Oroonoko

DOD Dodge, Richard H., and
     Lindblom, Peter D., comps.
     Of time and experience:
     literary themes. Cambridge,
     Mass., Winthrop Publishers,
     1972. 725p
Chayefsky, P. Marty
Dolan, H. Losers weepers
Lowell, R. My kinsman, Major
   Molineaux
Richardson, J. Gallows humor
Shaw, G. Arms and the man

DOT Dodson, Daniel Boone, comp.
     Twelve modern plays. Bel-
     mont, Calif., Wadsworth Pub-
     lishers, 1970. 471p
Anouilh, J. Antigone
Brecht, B. The good woman of
   Setzuan
Chekhov, A. The three sisters
García Lorca, F. The house of
   Bernarda Alba
Giraudoux, J. Tiger at the gates
Hellman, L. The little foxes
Ibsen, H. The wild duck
Miller, A. The crucible

Pirandello, L. Henry IV
Shaw, G. Heartbreak house
Strindberg, A. Miss Julie
Synge, J. The playboy of the
   western world

DOV Dolan, Paul J., and Dolan,
     Grace M., eds. Introduction
     to drama. New York, Wiley,
     1974. 642p
Chekhov, A. The cherry orchard
Ibsen, H. An emeny of the
   people
Jones, L. Dutchman
Lowell, R. Benito Cereno
Molière, J. The misanthrope
Pirandello, L. Henry IV
Racine, J. Phaedre
The second shepherds' play
Shakespeare, W. Othello
Shaw, G. Saint Joan
Sophocles. Antigone
Sophocles. Oedipus
Strindberg, A. Miss Julie
Yeats, W. Purgatory

DOWM Downer, Alan S., ed.
      American drama...New York,
      Thomas Y. Crowell [c1960]
      261p (American literary forms)
Herne, J. Shore acres
Moody, W. The great divide
O'Neill, E. The hairy ape
Sherwood, R. The petrified
   forest
Tyler, R. The contrast
Wilder, T. The long Christmas
   dinner
Williams, T. The glass menagerie

DOWN Downer, Alan S. The art of
      the play...New York, Henry
      Holt [c1955] 451p
Aeschylus. Prometheus bound
Chekhov, A. The sea-gull
Ibsen, H. Ghosts
Marlowe, C. Doctor Faustus
Molière, J. Tartuffe
O'Neill, E. The Emperor Jones
Shakespeare, W. Antony and
   Cleopatra
Sophocles. Oedipus rex
Vega Carpio, L. Fuente ovejuna

DOWS Downer, Seymour, ed.
      Great world theatre; an intro-
      duction to drama. New York,

DOWS (cont.)
   Harper & Row [1964]   867p
   Chekhov, A. The three sisters
   Euripides. The Bacchae
   Everyman
   Ibsen, H. Solness, the master
      builder
   Giraudoux, J. Tiger at the
      gates
   Goldsmith, O. She stoops to con-
      quer
   Miller, A. A view from the bridge
   Molière, J. The misanthrope
   Pirandello, A. Six characters in
      search of an author
   Plautus, T. The little ghost
   Shudraka. The toy cart
   Sophocles. Antigone
   Webster, J. The Duchess of Malfi
   Wilder, T. The skin of our teeth

DPR   Drama of the English Renais-
      sance; edited by Russell A.
      Fraser and Norman C. Rabkin.
      New York, Macmillan, 1976. 2v
      (V.1, Tudor period; V.2,
      Stuart period)
   Arden of Feversham 1
   Beaumont, F., and Fletcher, J.
      A king and no king 2
   Beaumont, F., and Fletcher, J.
      The knight of the burning
      pestle 2
   Chapman, G. Bussy D'Ambois 2
   Chapman, G. The widow's tears
      2
   Dekker, T., and Middleton, T.
      The roaring girl 2
   Dekker, T. The shoemakers'
      holiday 1
   Fletcher, J. The wild-goose
      chase 2
   Ford, J. Perkin Warbeck 2
   Ford, J. 'Tis a pity she's a
      whore 2
   Gascoigne, G. Supposes 1
   Greene, R. Friar Bacon and
      Friar Bungay 1
   Heywood, J. The four pp 1
   Heywood, T. A woman killed
      with kindness 1
   Jonson, B. The alchemist 2
   Jonson, B. Bartholomew Fair 2
   Jonson, B. Epicoene 2
   Jonson, B. Volpone 2
   Kyd, T. Spanish tragedy 1
   Lodge, T., and Greene, R. A

   looking glass for London and
      England 1
   Lyly, J. Gallathea 1
   Marlowe, C. The Jew of Malta 1
   Marlowe, C. Tamburlaine the
      Great, Pt. 1 and Pt. 2 1
   Marlowe, C. The tragical history
      of Doctor Faustus 1
   Marlowe, C. The troublesome
      reign and lamentable death of
      Edward the second 1
   Marston, J. The Dutch courtesan
      2
   Massinger, P. A new way to pay
      old debts 2
   Massinger, P. The Roman actor
      2
   Middleton, T. A chaste maid in
      Cheapside 2
   Middleton, T., and Rowley, W.
      The changeling 2
   Mucedorus 1
   Nashe, T. Summer's last will and
      testament 1
   Peele, G. David and Bethsabe 1
   Preston, T. Cambyses 1
   Sackville, T., and Norton, T.
      Gorboduc 1
   Shirley, J. Hyde Park 2
   Stevenson, W. Gammer Gurton's
      needle 1
   Tourneur, C. The revenger's
      tragedy 2
   Webster, J. The Duchess of Malfi
      2
   Webster, J. The white devil 2

DRA   Dramatic masterpieces by
      Greek, Spanish, French, Ger-
      man and English dramatists;
      with a special introduction by
      Albert Ellery Bergh. Rev. ed.
      New York, Collier [c1900] 2v
      (The world's greatest litera-
      ture)
   Aeschylus. Prometheus bound 1
   Aristophanes. The knights 1
   Calderón de la Barca, P. Life is
      a dream 1
   Euripides. Medea 1
   Goethe, J. Faust 2
   Goldsmith, O. She stoops to con-
      quer 1
   Ibsen, H. A doll's house 2
   Molière, J. The misanthrope 1
   Racine, J. Phaedra 1
   Sardou, V. Les pattes de

mouche 2
Schiller, F. Mary Stuart 2
Sophocles. Oedipus rex 1
Sheridan, R. The rival 2

DRU Drummond, Alexander Magnus,
and Gard, Robert E., eds.
The lake guns of Seneca and
Cayuga and eight other plays
of upstate New York. Port
Washington, N.Y., Kennikat
Press, 1972. 273p (Reprint)
Baker, E., and Drummond, A.
A day in the vineyard
Drummond, A. The lake guns of
Seneca and Cayuga
Gard, R. Let's get on with the
marrin'
Gard, R. Raisin' the devil
Gard, R. Mixing up the rent
Kamarck, E. Chenango crone
O'Connell, L. Donalds O'Rourk
Thurston, E. Family cooperative
Williams, L. Over fourteen: and
single

DUC Duckworth, George Eckel, ed.
The complete Roman drama...
New York, Random house
[c1942] 2v
Plautus. Amphytryon 1
Plautus. The braggart warrior 1
Plautus. The captives 1
Plautus. The Carthaginian 1
Plautus. Casina 1
Plautus. The casket 1
Plautus. The comedy of asses 1
Plautus. Curculio 1
Plautus. Epidicus 1
Plautus. The girl from Persia 1
Plautus. The haunted house 1
Plautus. The merchant 1
Plautus. The pot of gold 1
Plautus. Pseudolus 1
Plautus. The rope 1
Plautus. Stichus 2
Plautus. The three penny day 2
Plautus. Truculentus 2
Plautus. The twin Menaechmi 1
Plautus. The two bacchides 1
Querolus 2
Seneca. Agamemnon 2
Seneca. Hercules on Oeta 2
Seneca. Mad Hercules 2
Seneca. Medea 2
Seneca. Octavia 2
Seneca. Oedipus 2

Seneca. Phaedra 2
Seneca. The Phoenician women 2
Seneca. Thyestes 2
Seneca. The Trojan women 2
Terence. The brothers 2
Terence. The eunuch 2
Terence. The mother-in-law 2
Terence. Phormio 2
Terence. The self-tormentor 2
Terence. The woman of Andros 2

DUH Duhamel, Pierre Albert and
Hughes, Richard E., eds.
Literature: form and func-
tion...Englewood Cliffs, N.J.,
Prentice-Hall, 1965. 634p
Chekhov, A. The cherry orchard
Goldsmith, O. She stoops to con-
quer
Shakespeare, W. Richard II
Sophocles. Oedipus rex

DUK Dukore, Bernard F. and
Gerould Daniel C., eds. Avant
garde drama: a casebook,
(1918-1939). New York, Thomas
Y. Crowell, 1976. 592p
(Originally published by Bantam
in 1969 as Avant-garde drama:
Major plays and documents post
World War I)
Brecht, B. St. Joan of the stock-
yards
Cummings, E. him
Ghelderode, M. Chronicles of hell
Olesha, Y. The conspiracy of
feelings
Pirandello, L. Each in his own
way
Toller, E. Man and the masses
Witkiewicz, S. The water hen

DUN Dunn, Esther Cloudman, ed.
Eight famous Elizabethan
plays...New York, Modern
library [1932] 721p
Beaumont, F., and Fletcher, J.
The maid's tragedy
Dekker, T. The shoemakers'
holiday
Ford, J. 'Tis a pity she's a
whore
Heywood, T. A woman killed
with kindness
Jonson, B. Volpone; or, The fox

DUN (cont.)

Marlowe, C. The tragical history of Doctor Faustus

Massinger, P. A new way to pay old debts

Webster, J. The Duchess of Malfi

DUP Duran, Lee, tr. Plays of old Japan. Folcroft, Pa., Folcroft Library Editions, 1973. 127p (Reprint)

The Daimyo

Forsaken love

The hands in the box

The honor of Danzo

The horns

DUR Durham, Willard Higley and Dodds, John W., eds. British and American plays. 1830-1945...New York, Oxford university press, 1947. 796p

Anderson, M. Winterset

Barrie, J. The admirable Crichton

Bulwer-Lytton, E. Richelieu

Carroll, P. Shadow and substance

Connelly, M. The green pastures

Ervine, St. J. John Ferguson

Galsworthy, J. Strife

Ibsen, H. An enemy of the people

Jones, H. The liars

Kaufman, G., and Ryskind, M. Of thee I sing

Maugham, W. The circle

O'Casey, S. Juno and the paycock

Odets, C. Waiting for Lefty

O'Neill, E. The great god Brown

Pinero, A. The second Mrs. Tanqueray

Rice, E. The adding machine

Robertson, T. Caste

Sherwood, R. There shall be no night

Synge, J. The playboy of the western world

Yeats, W. Cathleen ni Houlihan

DUSE, ELEONORA. See
SAY Sayler, Oliver Martin, ed. The Eleonora Duse series of plays...

EAVE Eaves, Thomas Cary Duncan and Kimpe, Ben D., eds. The informal reader...New York, Appleton-Century-Crofts [c1955] 743p

Shaw, G. Pygmalion

EDAD Edades, Jean and Fosdick, Carolyn E., eds. Drama of the east and west. Manila, Bookman, 1956. 656p

Alvarez Quintero, S., and J. A sunny morning

Chekhov, A. The cherry orchard

Euripides. Medea

Guerrero, W. Forever

Ibsen, H. A doll's house

Joaquín, N. A portrait of the artist as Filipino

Kālidāsa. Shakuntalā

Molière, J. The misanthrope

Montano, S. Sabina

Palarca, J. Other tomorrows

Plautus. The Menaechmi

Shakespeare, W. Romeo and Juliet

Shaw, I. Bury the dead

Sicam, G., and Casiño, J. Mir-i-nisa

The sorrows of Han

Villa, L. Educating Josefina

Wilde, O. The importance of being earnest

Wilder, T. Our town

Williams, E. The corn is green

EIG Eight Chinese plays; from the 13th century to the present; translated with an introduction by William Dolby. New York, Columbia University Press, 1978. 164p

Buying rouge

Grandee's son takes the wrong career

Hegemon King says farewell to his queen

Identifying footprints in the snow

Liang, C. Washing silk

Liu, T. Cai Shun shares the mulberries

Shi, J. Qiu Hu tries to seduce his own wife

Wang, J. Wolf of Mount Zhong

EIGH Eighteenth-century plays with

an introduction by Ricardo
Quintana...New York, Modern
library [c1952] 484p
Addison, J. Cato
Fielding, H. The tragedy of
  tragedies
Gay, J. The beggar's opera
Goldsmith, O. She stoops to
  conquer
Lillo, G. The London merchant
Rowe, N. The tragedy of Jane
  Shore
Sheridan, R. The rivals
Steele, R. The conscious
  lovers

THE ELEONORA DUSE SERIES OF
  PLAYS. See
SAY Sayler, Oliver Martin,
  ed.

ELEVEN PLAYS OF THE GREEK
  DRAMATISTS. See
PLAG Plays of the Greek
  dramatists...

ELIOT, CHARLES W. See
HARC Harvard classics...

ELIZABETHAN DRAMA. See
HARC Harvard classics,
  v46-7

ELK Elkins, William R. and others,
  comps. Literary reflections.
  New York, McGraw, 1967.
  757p
Shakespeare, W. Antony and
  Cleopatra
Sophocles. Oedipus rex
Williams, T. The glass menagerie

ELKE Elkins, William R. and others,
  comps. Literary reflections.
  3d ed. New York, McGraw,
  1976. 501p
Anouilh, J. Antigone
O'Neill, E. Bound East for Cardiff
Saroyan, W. Hello out there
Wilder, T. Pullman car Hiawatha

ELLI Ellis, Harold Milton; Pound,
  Louise, and Spohn, George
  Weida, eds. A college book
  of American literature...New
  York, American book co.

[c1939] 2v
Boker, G. Francesca da Rimini
  1
O'Neill, E. The rope 2
Tyler, R. The contrast 1

ELLK Ellis, Harold Milton; Pound,
  Louise; Spohn, George Weida
  and Hoffman, Frederick J.,
  eds. A college book of American literature...Second edition.
  New York, American book co.
  [c1949] 1107p
O'Neill, E. The Emperor Jones

ELLIS, HAVELOCK. See
NER Nero (Tragedy); Nero
  and other plays...

EMB Embassy successes...London,
  Sampson, Low, Marston
  [1946-48] 3v
Bagnold, E. National velvet 2
Delderfield, R. Peace comes to
  Peckham 3
Delderfield, R. Worm's eye view
  1
Doherty, B. Father Malachy's
  miracle 1
Gielgud, V. Away from it all 3
Hartog, J. Skipper next to God
  2
Hay, I. "Let my people go!" 3
Pollock, R. Zoo in Silesia 1
Temple, J. No room at the inn 2

ENC Enclosure: a collection of
  plays, edited by Robert J.
  Nelson and Gerald Weales. New
  York, McKay, 1975. 282p
García Lorca, F. The house of
  Bernarda Alba
Odets, C. Awake and sing!
Racine, J. Athaliah
Wycherley, W. The country wife

ENG England, Alan William, ed. Two
  ages of man. Edinburgh, Oliver
  and Boyd, 1971. 206p
Cooper, G. Unman, Wittering and
  Zigo
Kaiser, G. The raft of Medusa
Leonard, H. Stephen D
Shaffer, P. The private ear

ENGLISH MASTERPIECES. v2. See
DEAN Dear, Leonard, ed.

ENGLISH MASTERPIECES (cont.)
    Elizabethan drama; v5. See
    MACI Mack, Maynard, ed.
    The Augustans...

ENGE English mystery plays: a
    selection, edited...by Peter
    Happé. Baltimore, Penguin,
    1975. 713p
    Abraham and Isaac (Brome)
    Abraham and Isaac (Chester)
    The adoration (York)
    The ascension (Chester)
    The assumption and coronation of
        the Virgin (York)
    Balaam, Balak and the prophets
        (Chester)
    Banns (Chester)
    The buffeting (Towneley)
    Christ's appearances to the dis-
        ciples (N Town)
    The creation, and Adam and Eve
        (Chester)
    The crucifixion (York)
    The death and burial (York)
    The death of Herod (N Town)
    The dream of Pilate's wife (York)
    The fall of Lucifer (Chester)
    The first shepherds' play (Towne-
        ley)
    The flight into Egypt (Towneley)
    The harrowing of hell (York)
    John the Baptist (York)
    Joseph (N Town)
    Judgement Day (York)
    The killing of Abel (Towneley)
    Lazarus (Towneley)
    Moses (York)
    The nativity (N Town)
    Noah (Chester)
    Noah (Towneley)
    The parliament of Heaven, the
        salutation and conception
        (N Town)
    The passion play I: The council
        of the Jews; The last supper;
        The betrayal (N Town)
    Pentecost (York)
    The purification, and Christ with
        the doctors (Chester)
    The resurrection (Towneley)
    The scourging (Towneley)
    The second shepherds' play
        (Towneley)
    The shearmen and tailors' play
        (Coventry)
    The temptation of Christ, and

the woman taken in adultery
    (Chester)
The three kings (introduction to)
    (York)

ENGL English romantic drama: an
    anthology, the major Romantics.
    Edited...by Charles J. Clancy.
    Norwood, 1976. 414p
    Blake, W. King Richard the
        Third
    Blake, W. The ghost of Abel
    Byron, G. Cain
    Byron, G. Manfred
    Byron, G. Sardanapalus
    Coleridge, S. Remorse
    Keats, J. King Stephen
    Keats, J., and Brown, C. Otho
        the Great
    Shelley, P. The Cenci
    Shelley, P. Prometheus unbound
    Wordsworth, W. The borderers

ERN Ernst, Earle, ed. Three
    Japanese plays from the tradi-
    tional theatre. Westport,
    Conn., Greenwood, 1976. 199p
    Kawatake, M. Benten the thief
    Kwanze, K. The maple viewing
    Takeda, I.; Miyoshi, S.; and
        Namiki, S. The house of
        Sugawara

ESA The essential self: an intro-
    duction to literature [edited by]
    Paul Berry. New York,
    McGraw, 1976. 439p
    Gardner, H. A thousand clowns
    In an oval office (from the Water-
        gate Transcripts)
    Sophocles. King Oedipus

ESS Esslin, Martin, ed. The genius
    of the German theater...New
    York, New American Library,
    1968. 638p
    Brecht, B. The Caucasian chalk
        circle
    Büchner, G. Leonce and Lena
    Goethe, J. Faust, a tragedy,
        pt. I
    Kleist, H. Prince Frederick of
        Homburg
    Lessing, G. Emilia Galotti
    Schiller, J. The death of Wallen-
        stein
    Wedekind, F. King Nicolo; or,

Such is life

ETO Evans, Herbert A., ed.
English masques...Norwood,
1976. 245p
Beaumont, F. Masque of the
Inner-Temple and Gray's Inn
Campion, T. Lords' masque
Daniel, S. Vision of the twelve
goddesses
D'Avenant, W. Salmacida spolia
Jonson, B. Fortunate isles, and
their union
Jonson, B. Golden age restored
Jonson, B. Lovers made men
Jonson, B. Masque at Lord Had-
dington's marriage
Jonson, B. Masque of Augurs
Jonson, B. Masque of Queens
Jonson, B. Neptune's triumph for
the return of Albion
Jonson, B. News from the New
World discovered in the moon
Jonson, B. Oberon
Jonson, B. Pan's anniversary,
or The shepherd's Holyday
The masque of flowers
Shirley, J. Triumph of peace

EVA Everett, Edwin Mallard; Brown,
Calvin S., and Wade, John D.,
eds. Masterworks of world lit-
erature...New York, Dryden
press [c1947] 2v
Euripides. Medea 1
Goethe, J. Faust, pt. I 2
Ibsen, H. An enemy of the
people 2
Molière, J. Tartuffe 2
Racine, J. Phaedra 2
Shakespeare, W. Romeo and
Juliet 2
Sophocles. Antigone 1
Sophocles. Oedipus the king 1

EVB Everett, Edwin Mallard; Brown,
Calvin S., and Wade, John D.,
eds. Masterworks of world lit-
erature...Revised edition...
New York, Dryden [c1955] 2v
Aeschylus. Agamemnon 1
Euripides. Medea 1
Goethe, J. Faust, Pt. I 2
Ibsen, H. The enemy of the
people 2
Molière, J. Tartuffe 2
Racine, J. Phaedra 2

Shakespeare, W. Romeo and
Juliet 2
Sophocles. Antigone 1
Sophocles. Oedipus the king 1

EVC Everett, Edwin Mallard, and
others, ed. Masterworks of
world literature. 3d ed. New
York, Holt, Rinehart, and
Winston, 1970. 2v
Aeschylus. Agamemnon 1
Aristophanes. Lysistrata 1
Euripides. Medea 1
Goethe, J. Faust 2
Molière, J. Tartuffe 2
Racine, J. Phaedra 2
Shakespeare, W. Antony and
Cleopatra 2
Sophocles. Oedipus the King 1

EVE Everyman and other plays.
[London] Chapman and Hall,
1925. 201p
Everyman
The nativity
The shepherds' play

EVER "Everyman," with other inter-
ludes, including eight miracle
plays. London, Dent [1928]
198p (Everyman's library)
Abraham, Melchisedec, and Isaac
Bale, J. God's promises
The crucifixion
The deluge
Everyman
The harrowing of hell
Mary Magdalene
Pageant of shearmen and taylors
St. George and the dragon
Second shepherds' play
The three Maries

FAD Faderman, Lillian and Bradshaw,
Barbara, comps. Speaking for
ourselves: American ethnic
writing. 2d ed. Glenview, Ill.,
Scott Foresman, 1975. 625p
Davis, O. Purlie victorious
Nemerov, H. Cain

FAL Falle, George C., ed. Three
restoration comedies...London,
Macmillan, 1964. 342p
Buckingham, G. The rehearsal

FAL (cont.)
Congreve, W. The way of the
world
Wycherley, W. The country wife

FALE The fallen crown: three
French Mary Stuart plays of
the seventeenth century/
introd. notes, critical comments, and editing, Michael
G. Paulson. Washington:
University Press of America,
c1980. 199p
Boursault, E. Marie Stuard,
reine d'Ecosse
Montchrestien, A. La reine
d'Ecosse
Regnault, C. Marie Stuard,
reyne d'Ecosse

FAM Famous American plays of the
1950's. Selected and intro-
duced by Lee Strasberg. [New
York, Dell, c1962] 415p
Albee, E. The zoo story
Anderson, R. Tea and sympathy
Gazzo, M. A hatful of rain
Hellman, L. The autumn
garden
Williams, T. Camino real

FAMAD Famous American plays of
the 1970s; with an introduction
by Ted Hoffman. New York,
Dell, 1981. 460p (The Laurel
Drama Series)
Bullins, E. The taking of Miss
Janie
Innaurato, A. Gemini
Rabe, D. The basic training of
Pavlo Hummel
Shepard, S. Buried child
Slade, B. Same time, next year
Weller, M. Moonchildren

FAMAH Famous American plays of
the 1960s; selected and intro-
duced by Harold Clurman. New
York, Dell, 1972. 395p (The
Laurel Drama Series)
Alfred, W. Hogan's goat
Crowley, M. The boys in the
band
Heller, J. We bombed in New
Haven
Horovitz, I. The Indian wants
the Bronx

Lowell, R. Benito Cereno

FAMAL Famous American plays of
the 1930's. Selected and in-
troduced by Harold Clurman.
[N.Y., Dell, c1959] 480p
Behrman, S. End of summer
Odets, C. Awake and sing!
Saroyan, W. The time of your
life
Sherwood, R. Idiot's delight
Steinbeck, J. Of mice and men

FAMAN Famous plays of 1931...
London, Gollancz [1931]
672p
Anthony, C. Autumn crocus
Besier, R. The Barretts of
Wimpole street
Delafield, E. To see ourselves
Fagan, J. The improper duchess
Van Druten, J. After all
Van Druten, J. London wall

FAMB Famous plays of 1932...Lon-
don, Gollancz, 1932. 654p
Bax, C. The rose without a
thorn
Hart, M., and Kaufman, G.
Once in a life time
Mackenzie, R. Musical chairs
Rice, E. See Naples and die
Van Druten, J. Somebody knows
Van Druten, J. There's always
Juliet

FAMC Famous plays of 1932-33...
London, Gollancz, 1933.
727p
Ackland, R. Strange orchestra
Anthony, C. Service
Chlumberg, H. Miracle at Ver-
dun
Rice, E. Counsellor-at-law
Van Druten, J. Behold we live
Winsloe, C. Children in uniform

FAMD Famous plays of 1933...Lon-
don, Gollancz, 1933. 702p
Armstrong, A. Ten-minute alibi
Chetham-Strode, W. Sometimes
even now
Daviot, G. Richard of Bordeaux
Fauchois, R. The late Christo-
pher Bean
Howard, S. Alien corn
Kaufman, G., and Ryskind, M.

Of thee I sing

FAME Famous plays of 1933-34...
London, Gollancz, 1934. 712p
Daviot, G. The laughing woman
Hodge, M. The wind and the
rain
Lipscomb, W., and Minney, R.
Clive of India
Sherwood, R. Reunion in Vienna
Stuart, A., and Stuart, P. Six-
teen
Van Druten, J. The distaff side

FAME Famous plays of 1934...Lon-
don, Gollancz, 1934. 688p
Anthony, C. Touch wood
Daviot, G. Queen of Scots
Harwood, H. Old folks at home
Jennings, G. Family affairs
Kingsley, S. Men in white
Mackenzie, R. The Maitlands

FAMG Famous plays of 1934-35...
London, Gollancz, 1935. 695p
Ackland, R. The old ladies
Egan, M. The dominant sex
Ginsbury, M. Viceroy Sarah
Johnson, P. Lovers' leap
Pryce, R. Frolic wind
Van Druten, J. Flowers of the
forest

FAMH Famous plays of 1935...Lon-
don, Gollancz, 1935. 622p
Hodge, M. Grief goes over
Raphaelson, S. Accent on youth
Somin, W. Close quarters (At-
tentat)
Sternheim, C. The mask of
virtue
Vulpius, P. Youth at the helm
Williams, E. Night must fall

FAMI Famous plays of 1935-36...
London, Gollancz, 1936. 701p
Ackland, R. After October
Anthony, C. Call it a day
Deevy, T. Katie Roche
Hodson, J. Red night
Odets, C. Awake and sing
Sherriff, R., and De Casalis, J.
St. Helena

FAMJ Famous plays of 1936...Lon-
don, Gollancz, 1936. 568p
Farjeon, E., and Farjeon, H.

The two bouquets
Odets, C. Till the day I die
Schauffler, E. Parnell
Schnitzler, A. Professor Bern-
hardi
Shaw, I. Bury the dead
Spewack, B., and Spewack, S.
Boy meets girl

FAMK Famous plays of 1937...Lon-
don, Gollancz, 1937. 775p
Boothe, C. The women
Lenormand, H. In Theatre street
Reid, A. People in love
Rice, E. Judgment day
Sayers, D., and Byrne, M. Bus-
man's honeymoon
Turgenev, I. A month in the
country

FAML Famous plays of 1938-39
...London, Gollancz, 1939.
661p
Egan, M. To love and to cherish
Hodson, J. Harvest in the north
MacOwan, N. Glorious morning
Malleson, M., and Brooks, H.
Six men of Dorset
Odets, C. Golden boy
Sayers, D. The zeal of thy
house

FAMO Famous plays of 1954...Lon-
don, Gollancz, 1954. 592p
Christie, A. Witness for the
prosecution
Christie, D., and C. Carrington,
V. C.
Hunter, N. A day by the sea
Odets, C. The big knife
Van Druten, J. I am a camera

FAO Famous plays of to-day...
London, Gollancz, 1929. 671p
Berkeley, R. The lady with a
lamp
Dukes, A. Such men are danger-
ous
Hoffe, M. Many waters
Levy, B. Mrs. Moonlight
Sherriff, R. Journey's end
Van Druten, J. Young Woodley

FAOS Famous plays of today...Lon-
don, Gollancz, 1953. 373p
Hunter, N. Waters of the moon
Knott, F. Dial "M" for murder

FAOS (cont.)
Priestley, J., and Hawkes, J.
Dragon's mouth
Rattigan, T. The deep blue
sea

FAR Farmer, John Stephen, ed.
...Anonymous plays. 3rd
series...London, Early English
drama society, 1906. 302p
(Early English dramatists)
Gammer Gurton's needle
Jack Juggler
King Darius
New custom
Trial of treasure

FARM Farmer, John Stephen, ed.
...Five anonymous plays. 4th
series...London, Early English
drama society, 1908. 328p
(Early English dramatists)
Appius and Virginia
Common conditions
Grim the collier of Croydon
The marriage of wit and science
The marriage of wit and wisdom

FARN Farmer, John Stephen, ed.
...Recently recovered "lost"
Tudor plays with some others.
London, Early English drama
society, 1907. 427p (Early
English dramatists)
An interlude of impatient poverty
The interlude of John the
evangelist
An interlude of wealth and health
Mankind
Medwall, H. Nature
Redford, J. The play of wit and
science
Respublica

FARO Farmer, John Stephen, ed.
...Six anonymous plays. 1st
series (c1510-1537)...London,
Early English drama society,
1905. 286p (Early English
dramatists)
The beauty and good properties
of women (commonly called
Calisto and Melibaea)
Hickscorner
The nature of the four elements
The summoning of Every man
Thersites

The world and the child

FARP Farmer, John Stephen, ed.
...Six anonymous plays. 2d
series...London, Early English
drama society, 1906. 478p
(Early English dramatists)
A comedy called Misogonus
The history of Jacob and Esau
An interlude of godly Queen
Hester
The interlude of youth
A moral play of Albion, knight
Tom Tyler and his wife

FAY, W. G. See
FIT Five three-act plays...

FED Federal council of the churches
of Christ in America. Commit-
tee on religious drama. Reli-
gious dramas, 1924-25...New
York, Century [c1923-26] 2v
Bates, E. The two thieves 2
Cropper, M. Two sides of the
door 2
Currie, C. Whither goest thou?
2
Goodman, K. Dust of the road
1
Goold, M. The quest divine 2
Goold, M. St. Claudia 2
Goold, M. The shepherds 2
Hamlin, M. The rock 1
Harnwell, A., and Meaker, I.
The alabaster box 2
Kimball, R. The resurrection 1
Leamon, D. Barabas 2
McCauley, C. The seeker 1
MacKaye, P. The pilgrim and the
book 1
Mason, H. At the gate beautiful
2
Mygatt, T. The sword of the
Samurai 2
Osgood, P. A sinner beloved 1
Willcox, H. Larola 1
Woodbridge, E. The crusade of
the children 1

FEDERAL THEATRE PLAYS. See
FEE, FEF Federal theatre
project

FEE Federal theatre project.
Federal theatre plays...
["Edited for the Federal

Theatre by Pierre de Rohan"]
New York, Random house
[c1938] v.p.
Arent, A., ed. One-third of a
nation
Conkle, E. Prologue to glory
Dubois, W. Haiti

FEF Federal theatre project.
Federal theatre plays...
["Edited for the Federal
theatre by Pierre de Rohan."]
New York, Random house
[c1938] v.p.
Arent, A. Power, a living news-
paper
Sundgaard, A. Spirochete
Triple-A plowed under, by
the staff of the Living news-
paper

FEFH Feise, Ernst and Steinhauer,
Harry, eds. German literature
since Goethe...Boston, Houghton
Mifflin [c1958] 2v
Brecht, B. Das verhör des
Lukullus 2
Grillparzer, F. Der traum ein
leben 1
Hauptmann, G. Michael Kramer 2
Hebbel, F. Maria Magdalene 1
Hofmannsthal, H. Das Salzburger
grosse welttheater 2
Kaiser, G. Gas II 2
Schnitzler, A. Der grüne kakadu
2

FEFL Felheim, Marvin, ed. Comedy;
plays, theory, and criticism...
New York, Harcourt, Brace
[c1962] 288p
Aristophanes. The birds
Chekhov, A. A wedding; or,
A joke in one act
Fry, C. A phoenix too frequent
Molière, J. The misanthrope
Shakespeare, W. Twelfth night;
or, What you will
Shaw, G. The man of destiny
Sheridan, R. The critic; or, A
tragedy rehearsed
Wilde, O. The importance of being
earnest

FEFM Felperin, Howard Michael, ed.
Dramatic romance...New York,
Harcourt, Brace, Jovanovich,

1973. 258p
Brecht, B. The Caucasian chalk
circle
Eliot, T. The cocktail party
Euripides. Alcestis
Gay, J. The beggar's opera
Ibsen, H. When we dead awaken
Shakespeare, W. The tempest

FEFO The female wits; women play-
wrights on the London stage,
1660-1720, by Fidelis Morgan.
London, Virago Press, 1981.
468p [cover title: The female
wits; women playwrights of the
Restoration]
Behn, A. The lucky chance, or:
An alderman's bargain
Centlivre, S. The wonder: a
woman keeps a secret
Manley, M. The royal mischief
Pix, M. The innocent mistress
Trotter, C. The fatal friendship

FEFT Fifteen Greek plays translated
into English...New York, Ox-
ford University Press, 1943.
794p
Aeschylus. Agamemnon
Aeschylus. Choephoroe
Aeschylus. The Eumenides
Aeschylus. Prometheus bound
Aristophanes. The birds
Aristophanes. The clouds
Aristophanes. The frogs
Euripides. Electra
Euripides. Hippolytus
Euripides. Iphigenia in Tauris
Euripides. Medea
Sophocles. Antigone
Sophocles. Electra
Sophocles. Oedipus at Colonus
Sophocles. Oedipus, king of
Thebes

FIF Fifteenth century prose and
verse, with an introduction by
Alfred W. Pollard. New York,
Dutton [1903] 324p (An
English garner. [v1])
Everyman
The pageant of the shearmen and
tailors

FIFR Fitts, Dudley, ed. Four Greek
plays...New York, Harcourt,
Brace [c1960] 310p

FIFR (cont.)
  Aeschylus. Agamemnon
  Aristophanes. The birds
  Euripides. Alcestis
  Sophocles. Oedipus rex

FIFT Fitts, Dudley, ed. Greek
    plays in modern translation
    ...New York, Dial press,
    1947. 596p (The permanent
    library series)
  Aeschylus. Agamemnon
  Aeschylus. Eumenides
  Aeschylus. Prometheus bound
  Euripides. Alcestis
  Euripides. Hippolytus
  Euripides. Medea
  Euripides. The Trojan women
  Sophocles. Antigone
  Sophocles. King Oedipus
  Sophcoles. Oedipus at Colonus

FIFV Fitts, Dudley, ed. Six Greek
    plays in modern translation...
    New York, Dryden [c1955]
    294p
  Aeschylus. Agamemnon
  Aeschylus. Choephoroe
  Aeschylus. Eumenides
  Aristophanes. The birds
  Euripides. Andromache
  Sophocles. Philoctetes

FIFVE Five Canadian plays. Toron-
    to, Playwrights Co-op, 1978.
    152p
  Gass, K. Hurray for Johnny
    Canuck
  Hubert, C. The twin sinks of
    Allan Sammy
  Lazarus, J. Babel rap
  Mitchell, K. Heroes
  Shein, B. Cowboy island

FIFW Five Chinese Communist plays;
    edited by Martin Ebon. New
    York, Day, 1975. 328p
  Azalea Mountain
  Ho, C., and Ting, Y. The white-
    haired girl
  The Red detachment of women
  The Red lantern
  Taking the bandits' stronghold

FIG Five great modern Irish plays
    ...with a foreword by George
    Jean Nathan. New York,

    Modern Library [1941] 332p
  Carroll, P. Shadow and sub-
    stance
  Gregory, I. Spreading the news
  O'Casey, S. Juno and the pay-
    cock
  Synge, J. The playboy of the
    western world
  Synge, J. Riders to the sea

FIJ Five Italian Renaissance come-
    dies; ed. by Bruce Penman.
    Harmondsworth, Middlesex,
    Penguin, 1978. 443p
  Aretino, P. The stablemaster
  Ariosto, L. Lena
  Gl'Intronati de Siena. The de-
    ceived
  Guarini, G. The faithful shep-
    herd
  Machiavelli, N. Mandragola

FIL Five modern Scandinavian plays.
    New York, Twayne Publishers.
    1971. 424p
  Chorell, W. The sisters
  Grieg, N. Our power and our
    glory
  Lagerkvist, P. The man who
    lived his life over
  Soya, C. Lion with corset
  Stefánsson, D. The golden gate

FIN Five new full-length plays for
    all-women casts...London,
    Dickson & Thompson [1935]
    375p
  Box, M. Angels of war
  Box, S. The woman and the
    walnut tree
  Popplewell, O. This bondage
  Rye, E. The three-fold path
  Smee, L. No thoroughfare

FIO Five plays for stage, radio,
    and television; ed. by Alrene
    Sykes, Brisbane, University of
    Queensland Press, 1977. 279p
  Esson, L. The drovers
  Roberts, T. Lindsay's boy
  Seymour, A. The one day of the
    year
  Stewart, D. The golden lover
  Williamson, D. What if you died
    tomorrow

FIP Five plays of 1937...[London]

Hamilton [1937] v.p.
Hellman, L. The children's
hour
Jerome, H. Charlotte Corday
Lyndon, B. They came by night
Rattigan, T. French without
tears
Savory, G. George and Mar-
garet

FIR Five plays of 1940...London,
Hamilton [1940] v.p.
Ardrey, R. Thunder rock
Boothe, C. Margin for error
Ginsbury, N. The first gentleman
Morgan, D. A house in the square
Stuart, A. Jeannie

FIS Five Restoration comedies/intro-
duced by Brian Gibbon. Lon-
don, A. & C. Black [c1984]
727p (The new mermaids)
Congreve, W. Love for love
Etherege, G. The man of mode
Farquhar, G. The recruiting of-
ficer
Vanbrugh, J. The provok'd wife
Wycherley, W. The plain-dealer

FIT Five three-act plays; foreword
by W. G. Fay. [London]
Rich and Cowan [1933] 448p
Bennett, A. Flora
Gielgud, V. Chinese white
Holme, C. "I want!"
Pertwee, R. Heat wave
Wilson, T. Champion north

FLAN Flanagan, John Theodore
and Hudson, Arthur Palmer,
eds. Folklore in American
literature...Evanston, Ill.,
Rowe, Peterson [c1958] 511p
Green, P. Unto such glory
MacKaye, P. The scarecrow; or,
The glass of truth

FLOR Flores, Angel, ed. Masterpieces of the Spanish golden
age...New York, Rinehart
[c1957] 395p
Calderón de la Barca. The great
theater of the world
Téllez, G. The trickster of
Seville and the guest of stone
Vega Carpio, L. Fuenteovejuna

FLOS Flores, Angel, ed. Spanish
drama...New York, Bantam
Books [c1962] 473p (Library
of world drama)
Benavente y Martínez, J. The
bonds of interest
Calderón de la Barca, P. Life is
a dream
Cervantes Saavedra, M. The
vigilant sentinel
Echegaray y Eizaguirre, J. The
great Galeoto
García Lorca, F. Blood wedding
Moratín, L. When a girl says yes
Rueda, L. The olives
Ruiz de Alarcón y Mendoza, J.
The truth suspected
Téllez, G. The rogue of Seville
Vega Carpio, L. Fuenteovejuna

FOL Folsom, Marcia McClintock and
Kirschner, Linda Heinlein, eds.
By women: an anthology of
literature. Boston, Houghton
Mifflin, 1976. 478p
Glaspell, S. Trifles
Hansberry, L. A raisin in the
sun

FOR Force, William M., comp.
Orestes and Electra; myth and
dramatic form...Boston,
Houghton Mifflin [1968]
329p
Aeschylus. The libation-
bearers
Euripides. Electra
Giraudoux, J. Electra
Richardson, J. The prodigal
Sophocles. Electra

FORD Ford, Nick Aaron, ed.
Black insights: significant
literature by Black Americans -
1760 to the present. Boston,
Ginn, 1971. 373p
Hansberry, L. A raisin in the
sun (Act I only)
Peterson, L. Take a giant step
Watson, H. Those golden gates
fall down

FOS Foulke, Robert, and Smith,
Paul, comps. An anatomy of
literature. New York, Harcourt, Brace, Jovanovich,
1972. 1125p

FOS (cont.)
Jonson, B. Volpone; or, The
fox
Shakespeare, W. King Lear
Synge, J. The playboy of the
western world

FOT Foundations of drama [ed. by]
C. J. Gianakaris. Boston,
Houghton Mifflin, 1975. 437p
Euripides. Medea
Hansberry, L. A raisin in the
sun
Ibsen, H. An enemy of the
people
Miller, A. The crucible
O'Neill, E. A touch of the poet
Shakespeare, W. Twelfth night

FOUA Four contemporary French
plays...New York, Modern
library, 1967. 265p
Anouilh, J. Antigone
Camus, A. Caligula
Giraudoux, J. The madwoman
of Chaillot
Sartre, J. No exit

FOUAC Four Australian plays.
Harmondsworth, Middlesex,
Penguin, 1977. 320p
Buzo, A. The front room boys
Hibberd, J. White with wire
wheels
Hibberd, J. Who?
Romeril, J. Chicago, Chicago

FOUAF Four French Renaissance
plays; in translation with in-
troductions and notes...by
Arthur P. Stabler, general
editor. [Pullman] Washing-
ton State University Press,
1978. 368p
Garnier, R. The Hebrew women
Jodelle, E. Eugene
Larivey, P. The spirits
Montchrestien, A. The Queen of
Scots

FOUB Four great comedies of the
restoration and 18th century
...With an introduction by
Brooks Atkinson. New York,
Bantam Books [c1958] 321p
Congreve, W. The way of the
world

Goldsmith, O. She stoops to conquer; or, The mistakes of a
night
Sheridan, R. The school for
scandal
Wycherley, W. The country wife

FOUD Four great Elizabethan plays.
With an introduction by John
Gassner. New York, Bantam
Books [c1960] 316p
Dekker, T. The shoemakers'
holiday; or, A pleasant comedy
of the gentle craft
Jonson, B. Volpone; or, The
fox
Marlowe, C. The tragical history
of Doctor Faustus
Webster, J. The Duchess of
Malfi

FOUF Four modern French come-
dies...With an introduction by
Wallace Fowlie. New York,
Capricorn Books [c1960] 256p
Adamov, A. Professor Toranne
Aymé, M. Clérambard
Courteline, G. The commissioner
Jarry, A. Ubu Roi

FOUK Four modern plays; first
series...rev. ed. New York,
Holt, Rinehart and Winston,
1963. 292p
Chekhov, A. The cherry orchard
Ibsen, H. Hedda Gabler
O'Neill, H. Emperor Jones
Shaw, B. Pygmalion

FOUM Four modern verse plays.
First [and] second series...ed.
by Henry Popkin. New York,
Holt, Rinehart and Winston
[c1957, 1961] 2v
Gorky, M. The lower depths
Ibsen, H. Hedda Gabler
Ibsen, H. Rosmersholm
Miller, A. Death of a salesman
O'Neill, E. The Emperor Jones
Rostand, E. Cyrano de Bergerac
Shaw, G. Pygmalion
Wilde, O. The importance of
being earnest

FOUN Four morality plays/edited
with an introduction and notes
by Peter Happé. Harmonds-

worth, Middlesex, England,
Penguin Books. c1979. 709p
Bale, J. King Johan
The castle of perseverance
Lindsay, D. Ane satire of the
thrie estaitis
Skelton, J. Magnyfycence

FOUP Four plays of 1936...with
an introduction by Ivor
Brown. [London] Hamilton
[1936] 624p
Jerome, H. Jane Eyre
Jerome, H. Pride and prejudice
Lyndon, B. The amazing Dr.
Clitterhouse
Turney, C. Bitter harvest

FOUR Four Renaissance tragedies;
with an introduction and
glossary by Donald Stone,
Jr. Cambridge, Mass., Harvard University Press, 1966.
224p
Bèze, T. Abraham sacrifiant
Buchanan, G. Jephté; ou, Le
voeu
Jodelle, E. Didon se sacrifiant
Taille, J. Saul le furieux

FOUS Four...Soviet...plays...New
York, International publishers,
1937. 427p
Gorky, M. Yegor Bulichov and
others
Kocherga, I. Masters of time
Pogodin, N. Aristocrats
Vishnevskiĭ, V. An optimistic
tragedy

FOUT Four Soviet war plays...Lon-
don, Hutchinson [1944] 208p
Korneichuk, A. The front
Korneichuk, A. Guerillas of the
Ukrainian Steppes
Leonov, L. Invasion
Simonov, K. The Russians

FOUX Fourteen great plays. London, [Heinemann] [Octopus
Books], [1977] 859p (jointly
published by Heinemann, Octopus, and Martin Secker and
Warburg, Ltd.)
Albee, E. Who's afraid of Virginia Woolf?
Bolt, R. A man for all seasons

Chekhov, A. The sea-gull
Coward, N. Private lives
García Lorca, F. Blood wedding
Ibsen, H. A doll's house
Maugham, W. The circle
Miller, A. Death of a salesman
O'Neill, E. The great god Brown
Priestley, J. An inspector calls
Shaw, G. Heartbreak house
Strindberg, A. The father
Synge, J. The playboy of the
western world
Williams, T. A streetcar named
desire

FOWL Fowlie, Wallace, ed., and tr.
Classical French drama...New
York, Bantam Books [c1962]
277p
Beaumarchais, P. The barber of
Seville
Corneille, P. The cid
Marivaux, P. The game of love
and chance
Molière, J. The intellectual ladies
Racine, J. Phaedra

FOWLIE, WALLACE. See also
FOUF Four modern French
comedies...

FRA Francke, Kuno, ed. The Ger-
man classics of the nineteenth
and twentieth centuries...New
York, German publication so-
ciety [c1913-14] 20v
Anzengruber, L. The farmer
foresworn 16
Freytag, G. The journalists 12
Fulda, L. Tête-à-tête 17
Goethe, J. Faust, pt. I 1
Goethe, J. Faust, pt. II 1
Goethe, J. Iphigenia in Tauris 1
Grillparzer, F. The Jewess of
Toledo 6
Grillparzer, F. Medea 6
Gutzkow, K. Sword and queue 7
Halbe, M. Mother earth 20
Hardt, E. Tristram the jester 20
Hauptmann, G. Michael Kramer
18
Hauptmann, G. The sunken bell
18
Hauptmann, G. The weavers 18
Hebbel, F. Maria Magdalena 9
Hebbel, F. Siegfried's death 9
Hofmannsthal, H. Death and the

FRA (cont.)
fool 17
Hofmannsthal, H. The death of
Titian 17
Hofmannsthal, H. The marriage
of Sobeide 20
Kleist, H. The prince of Hom-
burg 4
Ludwig, O. The hereditary
forester 9
Schiller, F. The death of
Wallenstein 3
Schiller, F. The homage of the
arts 3
Schiller, F. William Tell 3
Schnitzler, A. The green cocka-
too 20
Schnitzler, A. Literature 20
Schönherr, K. Faith and fire-
side 16
Sudermann, H. John the Baptist
17
Tieck, J. L. Puss in boots 4
Wedekind, F. The court
singer 20
Wilbrandt, A. The master of
Palmyra 16
Wildenbruch, E. King Henry
17

FRAN Franklin, Alexander, ed.
Seven miracle plays. New
York, Oxford University
Press, 1963. 158p
Abraham and Isaac
Adam and Eve
Cain and Abel
King Herod
Noah's flood
The shepherds
The three kings

FREE Freedley, George, ed.
Three plays about crime and
criminals...New York, Washington Square Press [c1962]
278p
Chodorov, E. Kind lady
Kesselring, J. Arsenic and old
lace
Kingsley, S. Detective story

FREG Freedman, Morris, ed.
Tragedy; texts and commenta-
ry...New York, Scribner, 1969.
641p
Aeschylus. Agamemnon

Betti, U. Corruption in the
palace of justice
Chekhov, A. The three sisters
Dryden, J. All for love
Euripides. Medea
Everyman
García Lorca, F. Yerma
Ibsen, H. Ghosts
Marlowe, C. The tragic history
of Doctor Faustus
Milton, J. Samson Agonistes
O'Neill, E. Desire under the
elms
Pirandello, L. Henry IV
Racine, J. Phaedra
Shakespeare, W. Othello, The
Moor of Venice
Sophocles. Oedipus rex
Strindberg, A. The father

FREH Freedman, Morris and Davis,
P. B., eds. Controversy in
literature; fiction, drama and
poetry with related criticism.
New York, Scribner, 1968.
750p
Abraham and Isaac (Brome)
Ferlinghetti, L. Our little trip
Ibsen, H. An enemy of the people
Kopit, A. Oh dad, poor dad,
mamma's hung you in the closet
and I'm feelin' so sad
Shaw, G. The devil's disciple
Sophocles. Antigone

FREI Freier, Robert; Lazarus,
Arnold Leslie and Potell, Her-
bert, eds. Adventures in
modern literature. Fourth
edition. New York, Harcourt
Brace [c1956] 690p (Adven-
tures in literature series)
Glaspell, S. Trifles
O'Casey, S. The end of the be-
ginning
Shaw, G. Caesar and Cleopatra
Sherriff, R. Journey's end

FRO From classroom to stage. Three
new plays. London, Longmans,
1966. 214p
Grant, D. The king cat
Holt, B. Noah's ark
Mitson, R. Beyond the bourn;
or, The night time stood still

FUL Fullington, James Fitz-James;

Reed, Harry B., and McCorkle, Julia Norton, eds. The new college omnibus...New York, Harcourt, Brace, 1938. 1241p
Connelly, M. The green pastures
Howard, S. The silver cord
O'Neill, E. The hairy ape
Sherriff, R. Journey's end

FULLINGTON, JAMES FITZ-JAMES.
See also MCCA, MCCB, MCCD, MCCF, MCCG McCallum, James Dow, ed. The college omnibus...

FULT Fulton, Albert Rondthaler, ed. Drama and theatre, illustrated by seven modern plays...New York, Holt [c1946] 556p
Barrie, J. A well-remembered voice
Coward, N. Blithe spirit
Lawson, J. Roger Bloomer
O'Neill, E. Beyond the horizon
Pinero, A. The second Mrs. Tanqueray
Rice, E. Street scene
Wilder, T. Our town

GALB Galbraith, Esther E., ed. Plays without footlights...New York, Harcourt, Brace [c1945] 358p
Anderson, M. Journey to Jerusalem
Greene, P. Papa is all
Niggli, J. This bull ate nutmeg
Reely, M. Flittermouse
Rickert, V. The bishop's candlesticks
Roberts, C. Tails up
Saroyan, W. The people with light coming out of them
Smith, B. Fun after supper
Upson, W. The master salesman
Wilder, T. The happy journey to Trenton and Camden

GARNETT, PORTER. See BOH Bohemian club, San Francisco. The Grove plays of the Bohemian club...

GARSA Gassner, John, ed. Best American plays; 5th ser., 1957-1963...New York, Crown, 1963. 678p
Albee, E. Who's afraid of Virginia Woolf?
Anderson, R. Silent night, lonely night
Chayefsky, P. Gideon
Frings, K. Look homeward, angel
Gardner, H. A thousand clowns
Gibson, W. Two for the see-saw
Inge, W. The dark at the top of the stairs
Kerr, J. Mary, Mary
Kopit, A. Oh dad, poor dad, mamma's hung you in the closet and I'm feelin' so sad
MacLeish, A. J. B.
Mosel, T. All the way home
O'Neill, E. A touch of the poet
Saroyan, W. The cave dwellers
Vidal, G. The best man
Williams, T. The night of the iguana
Williams, T. Orpheus descending
Wishengrad, M. The rope dancers

GART Gassner, John, ed. Best American plays. Fourth series ...1951-57...New York, Crown [c1958] 648p
Anderson, R. Tea and sympathy
Axelrod, G. The seven year itch
Gazzo, M. A hatful of rain
Hartog, J. The fourposter
Inge, W. Bus stop
Inge, W. Picnic
Kaufman, G., and Teichman, H. The solid gold Cadillac
Lawrence, J., and Lee, R. Inherit the wind
Levin, I. No time for sergeants
Miller, A. The crucible
Miller, A. A view from the bridge
O'Neill, E. A moon for the misbegotten
Van Druten, J. I am a camera
Wilder, T. The matchmaker
Williams, T. Cat on a hot tin roof
Williams, T. The rose tattoo
Wouk, H. The Caine mutiny

GARTL [Gassner, John] ed. Best American plays: 7th series, 1967-1973; ed. with an introduction by Clive Barnes. New York, Crown, 1975. 585p

GARTL (cont.)
Albee, E. All over
Allen, W. Play it again, Sam
Crowley, M. The boys in the
band
Elder, L. Ceremonies in dark
old men
Feiffer, J. Little murders
Foster, P. Tom Paine
Friedman, B. Scuba duba
Guare, J. The house of blue
leaves
Horovitz, I. Morning
Kopit, A. Indians
McNally, T. Noon
Melfi, L. Night
Miller, A. The price
Montgomery, R. Subject to fits
Rabe, D. Sticks and bones
Sackler, H. The great white
hope
Simon, N. The prisoner of
Second Avenue
Stone, P., and Edwards, S.
1776
Wilson, L. Lemon sky

GARU Gassner, John, ed. Best
American plays; supplementary
vol., 1918-58...New York,
Crown [c1961] 687p
Barry, P. Here come the clowns
Behrman, S. Biography
Chase, M. Harvey
Colton, J. Rain
Davis, O., and Davis, D. Ethan
Frome
Goodrich, F., and Hackett, A.
The diary of Anne Frank
Green, P. The house of Connelly
Howard, S., and DeKruif, P.
Yellow jack
Kingsley, S. Men in white
Mayer, E. Children of darkness
Odets, C. Awake and sing
Osborn, P. Morning's at seven
Osborn, P. On borrowed time
Patrick, J. The teahouse of the
August moon
Rice, E. The adding machine
Riggs, L. Green grow the lilacs
Tarkington, B. Clarence

GARW Gassner, John, ed. Best
American plays. Third series -
1945-51...New York, Crown
[c1952] 707p

Anderson, M. Anne of the
thousand days
Coxe, L., and Chapman, R.
Billy Budd
Euripides. Medea
Heggen, T., and Logan, J.
Mister Roberts
Hellman, L. The autumn garden
Herbert, F. The moon is blue
Inge, W. Come back, little Sheba
Kingsley, S. Darkness at noon
Kingsley, S. Detective story
Lindsay, H., and Crouse, R.
State of the union
McCullers, C. The member of
the wedding
Miller, A. All my sons
Miller, A. Death of a salesman
O'Neill, E. The iceman cometh
Van Druten, J. Bell, book and
candle
Williams, T. A streetcar named
desire
Williams, T. Summer and smoke

GARX Gassner, John, comp. Best
plays of the early American
theatre; from the beginning to
1916...New York, Crown
[1967] 716p
Aiken, G. Uncle Tom's cabin
Barker, J. Superstition
Boucicault, D. The octoroon
Fechter, C. The Count of Monte
Cristo
Fitch, C. The truth
Gillette, W. Secret service
Howells, W. The mousetrap
MacKaye, P. The scarecrow
Mitchell, L. The New York idea
Moody, W. The great divide
Mowatt, A. Fashion
Payne, J. and Irving, W. Charles
the second
Sheldon, E. Salvation Nell
Thomas, A. The witching hour
Tyler, R. The contrast
Walter, E. The easiest way

GARZ Gassner, John, ed. Best
plays of the modern American
theatre: Second series...New
York, Crown [c1947] 776p
Barry, P. The Philadelphia story
Gow, J., and D'Usseau, A. To-
morrow the world
Hellman, L. Watch on the Rhine

Kanin, G. Born yesterday
Kaufman, G., and Hart, M.
  The man who came to dinner
Kesselring, J. Arsenic and old
  lace
Kingsley, S. The patriots
Laurents, A. Home of the brave
Lindsay, H., and Crouse, R.
  Life with father
Patrick, J. The hasty heart
Rice, E. Dream girl
Saroyan, W. The time of your
  life
Sherwood, R. Abe Lincoln in
  Illinois
Thurber, J., and Nugent, E.
  The male animal
Van Druten, J. I remember
  mama
Van Druten, J. The voice of
  the turtle
Williams, T. The glass menagerie

GARZAL Gassner, John, ed. Four
  new Yale playwrights. New
  York, Crown [1965] 235p
Eisenstein, M. The fighter
Ingham, R. A simple life
Kleb, W. Honeymoon in Haiti
Murray, R. The good lieutenant

GARZB Gassner, John, ed.
  Medieval and Tudor drama...
  New York, Bantam Books
  [c1963] 457p (Library of
  world drama)
Abraham and Isaac
The betrayal of Christ
A Christmas mumming; the play
  of Saint (Prince) George
The creation and the fall of
  Lucifer
The crucifixion
The death of Herod
The death of Pilate
The deluge
An Easter resurrection play
Everyman
Man's disobedience and the fall
  of man
The murder of Abel
The Orléans sepulcher
The pageant of the shearmen and
  tailors
A pantomime for Easter day
The quem quaeritis
The resurrection, harrowing of

hell, and the last judgment
The second shepherds' play
Heywood, J. The play called
  the four pp
Hrotsvit. Dulcitius
Hrotsvit. Paphnutius
Sackville, T., and Norton, T.
  Gorboduc
Stevenson, W. Gammer-Gurton's
  needle
Udall, N. Ralph Roister Doister

GARZE Gassner, John, ed. 19th
  century Russian drama...with
  introduction and prefaces by
  Marc Slonin. New York,
  Bantam Books [c1963] 342p
  (Library of world drama)
Gogol, N. The inspector general
Ostrovsky, A. The thunderstorm
Pushkin, A. The stone guest
Tolstoy, L. The power of dark-
  ness
Turgenev, I. A month in the
  country

GARZG Gassner, John, ed. 20th
  century Russian drama. Trans-
  lated with an introduction and
  prefaces by Andrew R. Mac-
  Andrew. New York, Bantam
  Books [c1963] 376p (Library
  of world drama)
Andreyev, L. He who gets slapped
Chekhov, A. The three sisters
Gorky, M. The lower depths
Mayakóvsky, V. The bathhouse
Olesha, Y. A list of assets

GARZH Gassner, John, ed. Twenty
  best European plays on the
  American stage...New York,
  Crown [c1957] 733p
Anouilh, J. The lark
Behrman, S. Jacobowsky and the
  Colonel
Benavente y Martínez, J. The
    passion flower
Čapek, J., and Capek, K. The
  world we live in
Chekhov, A. The sea gull
Giraudoux, J. The madwoman of
  Chaillot
Giraudoux, J. Ondine
Giraudoux, J. Tiger at the gates
Heijermans, H. The good hope
Howard, S. The late Christopher

GARZH (cont.)
Bean
Kaiser, G. From morn to midnight
Molnár, F. The play's the thing
Obey, A. Noah
Pirandello, L. As you desire me
Rappaport, S. The dybbuk
Sartre, J. No exit
Spewack, S. My three angels
Tolstoy, L. Redemption
Turgenev, I. A month in the country
Zweig, S. Volpone

GAS Gassner, John, ed. Twenty best plays of the modern American theatre...New York, Crown [c1939] 874p
Abbott, G., and Holm, J. Three men on a horse
Anderson, M. High Tor
Anderson, M. Winterset
Barry, P. The animal kingdom
Behrman, S. End of summer
Boothe, C. The women
Connelly, M. Green pastures
Ferber, E., and Kaufman, G. Stage door
Green, P. Johnny Johnson
Hart, M., and Kaufman, G. You can't take it with you
Hellman, L. The children's hour
Kingsley, S. Dead end
Kirkland, J., and Caldwell, E. Tobacco road
MacLeish, A. The fall of the city
Odets, C. Golden boy
Reed, M. Yes, my darling daughter
Shaw, I. Bury the dead
Sherwood, R. Idiot's delight
Spewack, B., and Spewack, S. Boy meets girl
Steinbeck, J. Of mice and men

GASB Gassner, John, ed. Twenty-five best plays of the modern American theatre: Early series...New York, Crown [c1949] 756p
Anderson, M., and Hickerson, H. Gods of the lightning
Anderson, M. Saturday's children
Balderston, J. Berkeley Square
Barry, P. Paris bound
Beach, L. The clod

Behrman, S. The second man
Conkle, E. Minnie Field
Dunning, P., and Abbott, G. Broadway
Glaspell, S. Trifles
Green, P. White dresses
Hecht, B., and MacArthur, C. The front page
Heyward, D., and Heyward, D. Porgy
Howard, S. They knew what they wanted
Kaufman, G., and Connelly, M. Beggar on horseback
Kelly, G. Craig's wife
Kelly, G. Poor Aubrey
Millay, E. Aria da Capo
O'Neill, E. Desire under the elms
O'Neill, E. The hairy ape
O'Neill, E. Ile
Rice, E. Street scene
Sherwood, R. The road to Rome
Stallings, L., and Anderson, M. What price glory?
Sturges, P. Strictly dishonorable
Treadwell, S. Machinal

GASY Gassner, John, ed. The Yale School of Drama presents...[1st ed.] New York, Dutton, 1964. 315p
Hailey, O. Hey you, light man!
Hill, E. Man better man
Oliansky, J. Here comes Santa Claus

GAT Gassner, John, and Barnes, Olive, eds. Best American plays. 6th series, 1963-1967. New York, Crown, 1971. 594p
Albee, E. Tiny Alice
Alfred, W. Hogan's goat
Anderson, R. You know I can't hear you when the water's running
Baldwin, J. Blues for Mister Charlie
Bellow, S. The last analysis
Duberman, M. In white America
Gilroy, F. The subject was roses
Goldman, J. The lion in winter
Hanley, W. Slow dance on the killing ground
Hansberry, L. The sign in Sidney Brustein's window
Jones, L. The toilet

GATS (cont.)
York, Holt, Rinehart and
Winston [1963] 583p
Besier, R. The Barretts of
Wimpole Street
Chekhov, A. Then and now
Dunsany, E. A night at an inn
Everyman
Giraudoux, J. The Apollo of
Bellac
Howard, S. The late Christopher
Bean
Ibsen, H. An enemy of the
people
Mackaye, P. The scarecrow
Molière, J. The pretentious
ladies
Shakespeare, W. Romeo and Juliet
Shaw, G. Arms and the man
Sheridan, R. The school for scan-
dal
Sophocles. Antigone
Williams, T. The glass menagerie

GATT Gassner, John and Sweetkind,
Morris, comps. Tragedy, his-
tory and romance. New York,
Holt, Rinehart and Winston,
1968. 419p
Miller, A. The crucible
Rostand, E. Cyrano de Bergerac
Shakespeare, W. Henry IV, pt. I
Sophocles. Oedipus the king

GASSNER, JOHN. See also
FOUD Four great Elizabethan
plays; TRE, TREA, TREB,
TREBA, TREC, TREE, TREI
A treasury of the theatre...

GAUB Gaubert, Helen A. Four
classic French plays...New
York, Washington Square
Press [c1961] 260p
Corneille, P. The cid
Molière, J. The would-be
gentleman
Racine, J. Athaliah
Racine, J. Phaedra

GAVE Gaver, Jack, ed. Critics'
choice. New York Drama
Critics' Circle prize plays
1935-55...New York, Haw-
thorn books [c1955] 661p
Anderson, M. High tor
Anderson, M. Winterset

Hellman, L. Watch on the Rhine
Inge, W. Picnic
Kingsley, S. Darkness at noon
Kingsley, S. The patriots
McCullers, C. The member of
the wedding
Miller, A. All my sons
Miller, A. Death of a salesman
Patrick, J. The teahouse of the
August moon
Saroyan, W. The time of your
life
Steinbeck, J. Of mice and men
Van Druten, J. I am a camera
Williams, T. Cat on a hot tin
roof
Williams, T. The glass menagerie
Williams, T. A streetcar named
desire

GAW Gay plays/edited and intro-
duced by Michael Wilcox. Lon-
don, Methuen, 154p
McClenaghan, T. Submariners
Shairp, M. The green bay tree
Sherman, M. Passing by
Wilcox, M. Accounts

GAY Gayley, Charles Mills, ed.
Representative English come-
dies...New York, Macmillan,
1903-36. 4v
Brome, R. The antipodes 3
Chapman, G.; Jonson, B., and
Marston, J. Eastward hoe 2
Congreve, W. The way of the
world 4
Cowley, A. Cutter of Coleman-
street 4
Dekker, T. The shoemaker's
holiday 3
Dryden, J. The Spanish fryar
4
Farquhar, G. The recruiting
officer 4
Fletcher, J. Rule a wife and
have a wife 3
Greene, R. The honorable
historie of Frier Bacon and
Frier Bungay 1
Heywood, J. A mery play
betweene Johan Johan, Tyb,
his wyfe, and Syr Jhan the
preest 1
Heywood, J. The play of the
wether 1
Jonson, B. The alchemist 2

Jonson, B. Epicoene; or, The
silent woman 2
Jonson, B. Every man in his
humour 2
Lyly, J. Alexander and Cam-
paspe 1
Massinger, P. A new way to
pay old debts 3
The merry devill of Edmonton
2
Middleton, T., and Rowley, W.
The Spanish gipsie 3
Peele, G. The old wives' tale
1
Porter, H. The two angry
women of Abington 1
Shirley, J. The royall master
3
Stevenson, W. Gammer Gurton's
nedle 1
Udall, N. Roister Doister 1
Vanbrugh, J. The provok'd
wife 4
Wycherley, W. The plain-
dealer 4

GEST, MORRIS. See
MOSA Moscow art theatre
series of Russian plays...

GIA Gianos, Mary P., ed. and tr.
Introduction to modern Greek
literature; an anthology of
fiction, drama, and poetry.
New York, Twayne, 1969. 548p
Akritas, L. Hostages
Prevelakis, P. The last tourna-
ment
Theotokas, G. The game of folly
vs. wisdom
Xenopoulos, G. Divine dream

GLE Glenny, Michael, ed. Three
Soviet plays. [Middlesex,
Eng.] Penguin Books [1966]
217p
Babel, I. Marya
Mayakóvsky, V. The bedbug
Schwartz, Y. The dragon

GLI Gliner, Robert and Raines,
Robert Arnold, eds. Munching
on existence; contemporary
American society through literature. New York, Free Press,
1971. 465p
Koch, K. The academic murders

McNally, T. Tour
Pinter, H. Trouble in the works
Van Itallie, J. Interview

GLO Glorfeld, Louis E., and others,
eds. Plays by four tragedians.
Columbus, Ohio, Merrill, 1968.
529p
Ibsen, H. Ghosts
Ibsen, H. Hedda Gabler
Shakespeare, W. Othello
Shakespeare, W. Romeo and Juliet
Sophocles. Antigone
Sophocles. Oedipus the king
Strindberg, A. The father
Strindberg, A. Miss Julie

GOL Goldberg, Isaac, tr.
Plays of the Italian theatre...
Boston, Luce, 1921. 202p
Lopez, S. The sparrow
Morselli, E. Gastone the animal
tamer
Morselli, E. Water upon fire
Pirandello, L. Sicilian limes
Verga, G. The wolf-hunt

GOLB The golden steed: seven
Baltic plays/edited by Alfreds
Straumanis. Prospect Heights,
Ill.: Waveland Press, c1979.
383p
Boruta, K. Whitehorn's windmill
Brigadere, A. Maija and Paija
Kitzberg, A. The werewolf
Lutz, O. The spirit of Lake
Ulemiste
Luts, O. The will-o'-the-wisp
Rainis, J. The golden steed
Saja, K. The village of nine
woes

GOLD Goldman, Mark and Traschen,
Isadore, eds. The drama;
traditional and modern...Rock-
leigh, N.J., Allyn and Bacon
[1968] 690p
Beckett, S. Happy days
Brecht, B. Mother Courage
Chekhov, A. The cherry orchard
Ibsen, H. The wild duck
Molière, J. The misanthrope
Pirandello, L. Six characters in
search of an author
Shakespeare, W. King Lear
Shakespeare, W. Twelfth night
Shaw, G. Arms and the man

GOLD (cont.)
Sophocles. Oedipus rex

GOLH Goldstone, Richard Henry,
comp. Contexts of the
drama...New York, McGraw-
Hill [1968] 775p
Albee, E. The zoo story
Anouilh, J. Becket
Chekhov, A. Three sisters
Euripides. Hippolytus
Ibsen, H. Hedda Gabler
Molière, J. The miser
O'Neill, E. Hughie
Shakespeare, W. Antony and
Cleopatra
Shaw, G. Caesar and Cleopatra
Sophocles. Antigone
Wilder, T. The matchmaker
Williams, T. Summer and smoke

GOLK Goldstone, Richard Henry,
comp. Mentor masterworks of
modern drama: five plays.
New York, New American
Library, 1969. 478p
Ibsen, H. An enemy of the
people
Miller, A. The crucible
Rostand, E. Cyrano de Bergerac
Shaw, G. Pygmalion
Wilder, T. Our town

GOM Gomme, Andor Harvey, ed.
Jacobean tragedies...New
York, Oxford University
Press, 1969. 398p
Marston, J. The malcontent
Middleton, T. Women beware
women
Middleton, T., and Rowley, W.
The changeling
Tourneur, C. The atheist's
tragedy
Tourneur, C. The revenger's
tragedy

GOO Goodman, G., ed. From
script to stage: eight modern
plays. San Francisco, Rinehart Press, 1971. 623p
Aspenström, W. The apes shall
inherit the earth
Brecht, B. The seven deadly
sins of the lower middle
classes
Chekhov, A. The seagull

Ibsen, H. Hedda Gabler
O'Neill, E. Desire under the elms
Pinget, R. The old tune
Shaw, G. Pygmalion
Strindberg, A. A dream play

GOOD Goodman, Randolph, ed.
Drama on stage...New York,
Holt, Rinehart and Winston
[c1961] 475p
Everyman
Duerrenmatt, F. The visit
Euripides. Medea
Molière, J. The misanthrope
Shakespeare, W. The tragedy
of Macbeth
Williams, T. A streetcar named
desire

GOODE Goodman, Randolph, ed.
Drama on stage...2d ed.
New York, Holt, 1978. 658p
Beckett, S. Krapp's last tape
Duerrenmatt, F. The visit
Euripides. Medea
Everyman
Ibsen, H. An enemy of the people
Molière, J. Le misanthrope
Shakespeare, W. Macbeth
Sheridan, R. St. Patrick's Day,
or The scheming lieutenant
Shevelove, B., and Gelbart, L.
A funny thing happened on the
way to the Forum
Strindberg, A. The ghost sonata
Williams, T. Cat on a hot tin
roof

GORDON, DUDLEY CHADWICK. See
TOD Today's literature

GORDP Gordon, Edward J., comp.
Introduction to tragedy.
Rochelle Park, N.J., Hayden
Books, 1973. 349p
Anouilh, J. Antigone
Ibsen, H. Hedda Gabler
O'Neill, E. Beyond the horizon
Sophocles. Oedipus the king

GORE Gordon, Walker K., ed.
Literature in critical per-
spectives: an anthology. New
York, Appleton-Century-Crofts.
1968. 795p
Shakespeare, W. The tragedy of
Hamlet, Prince of Denmark

Shaw, G. Major Barbara
Sophocles. Oedipus rex
Williams, T. Orpheus descend-
    ing

GOS Gosse, Edmund William.
    Restoration plays from
    Dryden to Farquhar. London,
    Dent [1929] 431p (Every-
    man's library)
Congreve, W. The way of the
    world
Dryden, J. All for love
Farquhar, G. The beaux' strata-
    gem
Otway, T. Venice preserved
Vanbrugh, J. The provok'd
    wife
Wycherley, W. The country wife

GOSA Gosse, Edmund William.
    Restoration plays from Dryden
    to Farquhar. London, Dent
    [1932] 509p (Everyman's
    library)
Congreve, W. The way of the
    world
Dryden, J. All for love
Etherege, G. The man of mode
Farquhar, G. The beaux' strata-
    gem
Otway, T. Venice preserved
Vanbrugh, J. The provok'd wife
Wycherley, W. The country wife

GOU Gould, James Adams, and
    Kiefer, Harry Christian, eds.
    The western humanities. New
    York, Holt, Rinehart, and
    Winston, 1971. 2v
Aristophanes. Lysistrata 1
Brecht, B. The Caucasian chalk
    circle 2
Goethe, J. Faust, Part I 2
Goldsmith, O. She stoops to con-
    quer; or, The mistakes of a
    night 2
Ibsen, H. Hedda Gabler 2
Racine, J. Phaedra 2
Sophocles. Oedipus the king 1

GOW Gow, J. Rodger and Hanlon,
    Helen J., eds. Five Broadway
    plays...New York, Harper
    [c1948] 432p
Anderson, M. High Tor
Besier, R. The Barretts of

Wimpole Street
Chodorov, J., and Fields, J.
    Junior miss
Osborn, P. On borrowed time
Sherwood, R. Abe Lincoln in
    Illinois

GOWA Gow, J. Rodger and Hanlon,
    Helen J., eds. Five Broadway
    plays. 2d ed. New York,
    Globe Book Co., 1968. 432p
Anderson, M. High Tor
Besier, R. The Barretts of Wim-
    pole Street
Chodorov, J., and Fields, J.
    Junior miss
Osborn, P. On borrowed time
Sherwood, R. Abe Lincoln in
    Illinois

GPA Graham, Gary B. Freshman
    English program...Chicago,
    Scott, Foresman [c1960]
    946p
Ibsen, H. Hedda Gabler
O'Neill, E. Bound east for Car-
    diff
Shakespeare, W. Romeo and
    Juliet
Sophocles. Oedipus the king

GRA Grant, Elliott Mansfield, ed.
    Chief French plays of the
    nineteenth century...New
    York, Harper, 1934. 934p
Augier, E. Le gendre de M.
    Poirier
Becque, H. Les corbeaux
Brieux, E. La robe rouge
Dumas, A. fils. La dame aux
    camélias
Dumas, A. père. Henri III et
    sa cour
Hugo, V. Hernani
Hugo, V. Ruy Blas
Musset, A. On ne badine pas
    avec l'amour
Rostand, E. Cyrano de Bergerac
Vigny, A. Chatterton

GRAF Grant, Elliott Mansfield, ed.
    Four French plays of the
    twentieth century...New York,
    Harper [c1949] 338p
Anouilh, J. Antigone
Bernard, J. Le secret d'Arvers
Giraudoux, J. Siegfried

GRAF (cont.)
Pagnol, M., and Nivoix, P. Les
marchands de gloire

GRD   Great American parade.
Garden City, N.Y., Doubleday,
Doran, 1935. 611p
Connelly, M. The green pastures

GRDB Great books of the western
world...[Robert Maynard Hut-
chins, editor in chief]...[Chi-
cago] W. Benton [1952] 54v
Aeschylus. Agamemnon 5
Aeschylus. Choephoroe 5
Aeschylus. Eumenides 5
Aeschylus. The Persians 5
Aeschylus. Prometheus bound 5
Aeschylus. The seven against
Thebes 5
Aeschylus. The suppliant
maidens 5
Aristophanes. Acharnians 5
Aristophanes. Birds 5
Aristophanes. Clouds 5
Aristophanes. Ecclesiazusae 5
Aristophanes. Frogs 5
Aristophanes. Knights 5
Aristophanes. Lysistrata 5
Aristophanes. Peace 5
Aristophanes. Plutus 5
Aristophanes. Thesmaphoriazusae
5
Aristophanes. Wasps 5
Euripides. Alcestis 5
Euripides. Andromache 5
Euripides. The bacchantes 5
Euripides. The cyclops 5
Euripides. Electra 5
Euripides. Hecuba 5
Euripides. Helen 5
Euripides. Heracleidae 5
Euripides. Heracles mad 5
Euripides. Hippolytus 5
Euripides. Ion 5
Euripides. Iphigenia among the
Tauri 5
Euripides. Iphigenia at Aulis 5
Euripides. Medea 5
Euripides. The Phoenician
maidens 5
Euripides. Rhesus 5
Euripides. The suppliants 5
Euripides. The Trojan women 5
Goethe, J. Faust 47
Shakespeare, W. All's well that
ends well 27

Shakespeare, W. Antony and
Cleopatra 27
Shakespeare, W. As you like it
26
Shakespeare, W. The comedy of
errors 26
Shakespeare, W. Coriolanus 27
Shakespeare, W. Cymbeline 27
Shakespeare, W. Hamlet, Prince
of Denmark 27
Shakespeare, W. Julius Caesar
26
Shakespeare, W. King Henry the
eighth 27
Shakespeare, W. King Henry the
fifth 26
Shakespeare, W. King Henry IV,
Part 1 26
Shakespeare, W. King Henry IV,
Part 2 26
Shakespeare, W. King Henry VI,
Part 1 26
Shakespeare, W. King Henry VI,
Part 2 26
Shakespeare, W. King Henry VI,
Part 3 26
Shakespeare, W. King John 26
Shakespeare, W. King Richard II
26
Shakespeare, W. King Richard III
26
Shakespeare, W. King Lear 27
Shakespeare, W. Love's labour's
lost 26
Shakespeare, W. Macbeth 27
Shakespeare, W. Measure for
measure 27
Shakespeare, W. The merchant
of Venice 26
Shakespeare, W. The merry wives
of Windsor 27
Shakespeare, W. A midsummer
night's dream 26
Shakespeare, W. Much ado about
nothing 26
Shakespeare, W. Othello, the
Moor of Venice 27
Shakespeare, W. Pericles, Prince
of Tyre 27
Shakespeare, W. Romeo and Juliet
26
Shakespeare, W. The taming of
the shrew 26
Shakespeare, W. The tempest 27
Shakespeare, W. Timon of Athens 27
Shakespeare, W. Titus Andronicus
26

Shakespeare, W. Troilus and
Cressida 27
Shakespeare, W. Twelfth night
27
Shakespeare, W. The two gentle-
men of Verona 26
Shakespeare, W. The winter's
tale 27
Sophocles. Ajax 5
Sophocles. Antigone 5
Sophocles. Electra 5
Sophocles. Oedipus at Colonus
5
Sophocles. Oedipus the king 5
Sophocles. Philoctetes 5
Sophocles. Trachiniae 5

GRDG Greek drama/edited by Moses
Hadas. Toronto; London; Ban-
tam, 1965 (1982 printing).
337p (A Bantam classic)
Aeschylus. Agamemnon
Aeschylus. Eumenides
Aristophanes. Frogs
Euripides. Hippolytus
Euripides. Medea
Euripides. Trojan women
Sophocles. Antigone
Sophocles. Oedipus the king
Sophocles. Philoctetes

GRE Great plays (English)...
with biographical notes and
a critical introduction by
Joseph O'Connor...[Aldine
ed.] New York, Appleton,
1900. 421p (The world's
great books)
Browning, R. A blot in the
'scutcheon
Fletcher, J. The faithful
shepherdess
Jonson, B. The alchemist
Marlowe, C. Edward the second
Payne, J. Brutus; or, The fall
of Tarquin
Sheridan, R. The school for
scandal

GREA Great plays (French and
German)...with biographical
notes, and a critical introduc-
tion by Brander Matthews...
[Aldine ed.] New York,
Appleton, 1901. 504p (The
world's great books)
Corneille, P. The cid

Hugo, V. Ruy Blas
Lessing, G. Minna von Barnhelm
Molière, J. Tartuffe
Racine, J. Athaliah
Schiller, J. Wilhelm Tell

GREAA Great rock musicals; ed.,
with an introduction...by
Stanley Richards. New York,
Stein and Day, 1979. 562p
Brown, W. The Wiz
Driver, D. Your own thing
Fornés, M. Promenade
Guare, J., and Shapiro, M. Two
gentlemen of Verona
Jacobs, J., and Casey, W.
Grease
Ragni, G., and Rado, J. Hair
Rice, T. Jesus Christ superstar
Townshend, P., and The Who.
Tommy

GREAB Grebanier, Bernard D. N.,
and Reiter, Seymour, eds.
Introduction to imaginative
literature. New York, Thomas
Y. Crowell Company...[c1960]
969p
Coward, N. Brief encounter
Milton, J. Samson Agonistes
O'Neill, E. In the zone
Sapensley, A. Even the weariest
river
Shakespeare, W. King Lear
Shaw, G. Caesar and Cleopatra
Synge, J. The playboy of the
western world
Turque, M. Shoptalk
Williams, T. The rose tattoo

GREB Grebanier, Bernard D. N.,
and Thompson, Stith, eds.
English literature and its
backgrounds...New York,
Cordon co. [c1939-40] 2v
Aeschylus. Prometheus bound 2
Byron, G. Manfred 2
Congreve, W. The way of the
world 1
Everyman 1
Marlowe, C. The tragical history
of Doctor Faustus 1
Milton, J. Samson Agonistes 1
Molière, J. The misanthrope 1
Shelley, P. Prometheus unbound 2
Sheridan, R. The school for scan-
dal 1

GREB (cont.)
Wilde, O. The importance of
being earnest 2

GREC Grebanier, Bernard D. N.;
Middlebrook, Samuel;
Thompson, Stith, and Watt,
William, eds. English litera-
ture and its backgrounds.
Revised edition...New York,
Dryden Press [c1949] 2v
Abraham and Isaac 1
Browning, R. In a balcony 2
Congreve, W. The way of the
world 1
Dekker, T. The shoemaker's
holiday 1
Everyman 1
Marlowe, C. Doctor Faustus 1
Milton, J. Samson Agonistes 1
Molière, J. The misanthrope 1
Shakespeare, W. Othello 1
Sheridan, R. The school for
scandal 1
Sophocles. Oedipus the king 1
Synge, J. The playboy of the
western world 2
Wilde, O. The importance of
being earnest 2
Williams, E. The corn is green
2

GREE Greek dramas...with biograph-
ical notes and a critical intro-
duction by Bernadotte Perrin...
[Aldine ed.] New York,
Appleton, 1900. 390p (The
world's great books)
Aeschylus. Agamemnon
Aeschylus. Prometheus bound
Aristophanes. The clouds
Aristophanes. Plutus
Euripides. Alcestis
Euripides. Medea
Sophocles. Antigone
Sophocles. Oedipus tyrannus

GREG Greenfield, Ralph, and Side,
Ronald K., eds. Temper of
the times;...New York,
McGraw-Hill, 1969. 557p
Hailey, A. Shadow of suspicion
Odets, C. Waiting for Lefty
Synge, J. Riders to the sea
Williams, N. The mountain

GREJ Greenspan, Charlotte L., and

Hirsch, Lester M., eds. All
those voices: The minority
experience. New York,
Macmillan, 1971. 484p
Nkosi, L. The rhythm of
violence
Shakespeare, W. The merchant
of Venice
Shaw, G. John Bull's other
island. (Act I only)

GREN Grene, David, tr. Three
Greek tragedies in transla-
tion...Chicago, University of
Chicago Press [c1942] 228p
Aeschylus. Prometheus bound
Euripides. Hippolytus
Sophocles. Oedipus the king

GREP Grene, David, and Lattimore,
Richmond, eds. The complete
Greek tragedies...[Chicago]
University of Chicago Press
[1959] 4v
Aeschylus. Agamemnon 1
Aeschylus. The eumenides 1
Aeschylus. The libation bearers
1
Aeschylus. The Persians 1
Aeschylus. Prometheus bound 1
Aeschylus. Seven against Thebes
1
Aeschylus. The suppliant
maidens 1
Euripides. Alcestis 3
Euripides. Andromache 3
Euripides. The bacchae 4
Euripides. The cyclops 3
Euripides. Electra 4
Euripides. Hecuba 3
Euripides. Helen 3
Euripides. The Heracleidae 3
Euripides. Heracles 3
Euripides. Hippolytus 3
Euripides. Ion 4
Euripides. Iphigenia in Aulis 4
Euripides. Iphigenia in Tauris
3
Euripides. The Medea 3
Euripides. Orestes 4
Euripides. The Phoenician women
4
Euripides. Rhesus 4
Euripides. The suppliant women
4
Euripides. The Trojan women 3
Sophocles. Ajax 2

Sophocles. Antigone 2
Sophocles. Electra 2
Sophocles. Oedipus at Colonus
2
Sophocles. Oedipus the king 2
Sophocles. Philoctetes 2
Sophocles. The women of
Trachis 2

GRER Grene, David, and Latti-
more, Richmond, eds.
Greek tragedies...[Chicago]
University of Chicago Press
[1960] 3v
Aeschylus. Agamemnon 1
Aeschylus. The eumenides 3
Aeschylus. The libation bearers
2
Aeschylus. Prometheus bound 1
Euripides. Alcestis 3
Euripides. The bacchae 3
Euripides. Electra 2
Euripides. Hippolytus 1
Euripides. Iphigenia in Tauris
2
Euripides. The Trojan women 2
Sophocles. Antigone 1
Sophocles. Electra 2
Sophocles. Oedipus at Colonus 3
Sophocles. Oedipus the king 1
Sophocles. Philoctetes 3

GRIF Griffin, Alice Sylvia (Venezky),
ed. Living theatre...New
York, Twayne [c1953] 510p
Aeschylus. Oresteia
Anderson, M. Winterset
Chekhov, A. The sea gull
Everyman
Giraudoux, J. The madwoman
of Chaillot
Hebbel, F. Maria Magdalena
Ibsen, H. Hedda Gabler
Marlowe, C. Faustus
Molière, J. The misanthrope
Odets, C. Awake and sing
Plautus, T. Mostellaria
Rice, E. Street scene
Shakespeare, W. Romeo and
Juliet

GRIH Griffith, Francis, and
Mersand, Joseph, eds. Eight
American ethnic plays. New
York, Scribner's, 1974. 386p
Alfred, W. Hogan's goat
Apstein, T. Wetback run

Hansberry, L. A raisin in the
sun
Marqués, R. The oxcart
Rose, R. Dino
Van Druten, J. I remember Mama
Ward, D. Day of absence

GROS Gross, Theodore, L. The
literature of American Jews.
New York, Free Press, 1973.
510p
Odets, C. Awake and sing

THE GROVE PLAYS OF THE BOHE-
MIAN CLUB. See
BOH Bohemian club, San
Francisco

GROV Grove Press modern drama;
6 plays by Brecht, Baraka,
Feiffer, Genêt, Mrożek,
Ionesco; John Lahr, editor.
New York, Grove, 1975. 446p
Brecht, B. The Caucasian chalk
circle
Feiffer, J. The White House
murder case
Genêt, J. The blacks: a clown
show
Ionesco, E. Rhinoceros
Jones, E. The toilet
Mrożek, S. Tango

GUE Guerney, Bernard Guilbert, ed.
A treasury of Russian litera-
ture...New York, Vanguard
Press [c1943] 1048p
Chekhov, A. The three sisters
Gogol, N. The inspector general
Gorki, M. The lower depths

GUI Guinagh, Kevin and Dorjahn,
Alfred Paul, eds. Latin
literature in translation...New
York, Longmans, Green, 1942.
822p
Platus, T. The menaechmi
Plautus, T. The rudens; or, The
rope
Terence. The Adelphi; or, The
brothers
Terence. The Phormio

GUIN Guinagh, Kevin and Dorjahn,
Alfred P., eds. Latin literature
in translation...Second edition.
New York, Longmans, Green

GUIN (cont.)
[c1952] 822p
Plautus. The menaechmi
Plautus. The rudens
Seneca. Medea
Terence. The Adelphi
Terence. The Phormio

GUSTAFSON, ALRIK. See
SCAN Scandinavian plays
of the twentieth century...

GUTH Guth, Hans Paul. Idea
and image...Belmont,
Calif., Wadsworth Pub. Co.
[c1962] 838p
Ibsen, H. The master builder
Miller, A. The crucible
Molière, J. The misanthrope
Shakespeare, W. Antony and
Cleopatra
Sophocles. Antigone

GUTL Guth, Hans Paul, comp.
Literature. 2d ed...Belmont,
Calif., Wadsworth Pub. Co.
[1968] 923p
Ibsen, H. The master builder
Miller, A. The crucible
Shakespeare, W. Antony and
Cleopatra
Sophocles. Antigone

HAE Hall, Donald, comp. To read
literature: fiction, poetry,
drama. New York, Holt,
Rinehart & Winston, 1981.
1508p
Albee, E. The zoo story
Ibsen, H. Hedda Gabler
Miller, A. Death of a salesman
Shakespeare, W. Othello, The
Moor of Venice
Shaw, G. Saint Joan
Yeats, W. The cat and the
moon

HAH Halliday, Frank Ernest, ed.
The legend of the rood...Lon-
don, Gerald Duckworth [c1955]
142p
The death of Pilate
The legend of the rood
The three Maries

HAL Halline, Allan Gates, ed.
American plays. New York,
American book co. [c1935]
787p
Barker, J. Superstition
Barry, P. You and I
Bird, R. The gladiator
Boker, G. Francesca da Rimini
Daly, A. Horizon
Davis, O. Icebound
Dunlap, W. André
Green, P. The field god
Howard, B. The Henrietta
Miller, J. The Danites in the
Sierras
Mitchell, L. The New York idea
Moeller, P. Madame Sand
Mowatt, A. Fashion
O'Neill, E. The great god Brown
Paulding, J. The bucktails; or,
Americans in England
Tyler, R. The contrast
Willis, N. Bianca Visconti

HALLINE, ALLAN GATES. See also
SIXC Six modern American
plays...

HALM Halman, Talat Sait, ed.
Modern Turkish drama, an
anthology of plays in transla-
tion. Edited, with an intro-
duction by T. Halman. Minnea-
polis, Bibliotheca Islamica,
1976. 415p
Cumali, N. Dry summer
Dilmen, G. The ears of Midas
Oflazoğlu, A. Ibrahim the mad
Taner, H. The ballad of Ali of
Keshan

HALU Hamalian, Leo, and Volpe,
Edmond L., eds. Pulitzer
prize reader...New York,
Popular Library [c1961]
607p
Williams, T. 27 wagons full of
cotton

HAM Hamilton, Edith, tr. Three
Greek plays...New York,
Norton [c1937] 239p
Aeschylus. Agamemnon
Aeschylus. Prometheus bound
Euripides. The Trojan women

HAMI Hamilton (Hamlish) ltd.,

London Majority: 1931-52...
London, Hamish Hamilton
[1952] 1035p
Rattigan, T. The Browning
version
Sartre, J. In camera

HAN Hampden, John, comp.
Eighteenth century plays...
London, Dent [1928] 408p
(Everyman's library)
Addison, J. Cato
Colman, G., and Garrick, D.
The clandestine marriage
Cumberland, R. The West Indian
Fielding, H. The tragedy of
tragedies; or, Tom Thumb the
great
Gay, J. The beggar's opera
Lillo, G. The London merchant;
or, George Barnwell
Rowe, N. Jane Shore

HANG Hanger, Eunice, comp.
Three Australian plays.
Minneapolis, Minn., Univ. of
Minnesota Press, 1968. 274p
Elliott, S. Rusty bugles
McKinney, J. The well
Mathew, R. We find the bunyip

HAO Happé, Peter, ed. Tudor in-
terludes. New York, Penguin,
1972. 434p
Apius and Virginia
Fulwell, U. Like will to like
Heywood, J. The play of the
wether
Medwall, H. Fulgens and
Lucres. (Extracts)
Redford, J. Wit and science
Respublica. (Extracts)
Youth

HAP Harbrace omnibus...edited by
H. B. Reed, J. N. McCorcle,
W. H. Hildreth, and J. D.
McCallum. New York, Har-
court, Brace, 1942. v.p.
Anderson, M. High Tor
O'Neill, E. In the zone

HAPD Harding, Helen Elizabeth,
ed...Tragedies old and new...
New York, Noble & Noble
[c1939] 486p
Note: Also published under the

title, Hamlet and other tragedies
O'Neill, E. Beyond the horizon
Shakespeare, W. Hamlet
Sophocles. Electra

HAPO Hardison, Osborne Bennett,
and Mills, Jerry Leath, eds.
The forms of imagination...
Englewood Cliffs, N.J.,
Prentice-Hall, 1972. 615p
Chekhov, A. Uncle Vanya
Hansberry, L. A raisin in the
sun
Sophocles. Oedipus Rex
Williams, T. The glass menagerie

HAPRA Harrier, Richard C., ed.
The Anchor anthology of
Jacobean drama...Garden City,
N.Y., Doubleday (Anchor
Books). 1963. 2v
Chapman, G. Bussy D'Ambois 1
Ford, J. The broken heart 2
Jonson, B. Everyman in his
humour 1
Marston, J. and Webster, J. The
malcontent 1
Middleton, T. and Rowley, W.
The changeling 2
Shirley, J. The lady of pleasure
2
Tourneur, C. The revenger's
tragedy 2
Webster, J. The white devil 1

HAPRB Harrier, Richard C., ed.
Jacobean drama; an anthology
...New York, Norton, 1968.
2v
Chapman, G. Bussy D'Ambois 1
Ford, J. The broken heart 2
Jonson, B. Everyman in his
humour 1
Marston, J. and Webster, J. The
malcontent 1
Middleton, T. and Rowley, W.
The changeling 2
Shirley, J. The lady of pleasure
2
Tourneur, C. The revenger's
tragedy 2
Webster, J. The white devil 1

HARRIS, BRICE. See REST
Restoration plays...

HAPRL Harris, Stephen LeRoy, comp.

HAPRL (cont.)
The humanist tradition in world literature: an anthology of masterpieces from Gilgamesh to the divine comedy. Columbus, Ohio, Merrill, 1970. 1008p
Aeschylus. Agamemnon
Aeschylus. Prometheus bound
Aristophanes. Lysistrata
Euripides. The bacchae
Euripides. Media
Sophocles. Oedipus the King
Sophocles. Philoctetes

HAPS Harrison, G. B., ed. Major British writers...New York, Harcourt [c1954] 2v
Shakespeare, W. Hamlet, Prince of Denmark
Shakespeare, W. King Henry the fourth, pt. I
Shakespeare, W. The tempest
Shaw, G. Man and superman

HAPT Harrison, George Bagshawe [and others], eds. Major British writers...Enl. ed., New York, Harcourt, Brace [c1959] 2v
Byron, G. Manfred 2
Dryden, J. The secular masque 1
Milton, J. Samson Agonistes 1
Shakespeare, W. Hamlet 1
Shakespeare, W. Henry IV, part I 1
Shakespeare, W. The tempest 1
Shaw, G. Man and superman 2
Shelley, P. Prometheus unbound 2

HAPV Harsh, Philip Whaley, ed. An anthology of Roman drama ...New York, Holt, Rinehart and Winston [c1960] 317p
Plautus, T. The rope
Plautus, T. The twin Menaechmi
Seneca, L. The Medea
Seneca, L. The Phaedra
Seneca, L. The Thyestes
Terentius Afer, P. The brothers
Terentius Afer, P. The Phormio

HARA Hart, James David, and Gohdes, Clarence, eds.
America's literature. New York. Dryden [c1955] 958p
O'Neill, E. The hairy ape

HARB Hartley, Lodwick Charles and Ladu, Arthur Irish, eds. Patterns in modern drama...New York, Prentice-Hall, 1948. 496p
Chekhov, A. Uncle Vanya
Galsworthy, J. The pigeon
Hellman, L. The little foxes
Ibsen, H. An enemy of the people
Kelly, G. Craig's wife
O'Neill, E. The Emperor Jones
Thurber, J., and Nugent, E. The male animal

HARC Harvard classics, edited by Charles W. Eliot. New York, Collier [c1909-10] 50v
Aeschylus. Agamemnon 8
Aeschylus. The furies 8
Aeschylus. The libation-bearers 8
Aeschylus. Prometheus bound 8
Aristophanes. The frogs 8
Beaumont, F., and Fletcher, J. Philaster 47
Browning, R. A blot in the 'scutcheon 18
Byron, R. Manfred 18
Calderón de la Barca, P. Life is a dream 26
Corneille, P. Polyeucte 26
Dekker, T. The shoemaker's holiday 47
Dryden, J. All for love; or, The world well lost 18
Euripides. The bacchae 8
Euripides. Hippolytus 8
Goethe, J. Egmont 19
Goethe, J. Faust, pt. I 19
Goldsmith, O. She stoops to conquer 18
Jonson, B. The alchemist 47
Lessing, G. Minna von Barnhelm; or, The soldier's fortune 26
Marlowe, C. Doctor Faustus 19
Marlowe, C. Edward the second 46
Massinger, P. A new way to pay old debts 47
Milton, J. Comus 4
Milton, J. Samson Agonistes 4

HAT   Hatcher, Harlan Henthorne,
       ed. Modern American
       dramas...New York, Har-
       court, Brace, 1941. 394p
Anderson, M. Winterset
Howard, S. Dodsworth
Odets, C. Awake and sing
O'Neill, E. Beyond the horizon
Rice, E. The adding machine
St. Joseph, E. A passenger to
    Bali
Sherwood, R. Abe Lincoln in
    Illinois
Wilder, T. Our town

HATA   Hatcher, Harlan Henthorne,
       ed. Modern American dramas.
       New edition...New York, Har-
       court, Brace [c1949] 378p
Anderson, M. Winterset
Heggen, T. Mister Roberts
Miller, A. All my sons
O'Neill, E. The Emperor Jones
Rice, E. The adding machine
Saroyan, W. The time of your
    life
Sherwood, R. Abe Lincoln in Il-
    linois
Williams, T. The glass menagerie

HAU   Hatcher, Harlan Henthorne,
       ed. Modern British dramas...
       New York, Harcourt, Brace,
       1941. 374p
Dunsany, E. If
Galsworthy, J. Justice
Maugham, W. The constant wife
Monkhouse, A. The conquering
    hero
O'Flaherty, L. The informer
Pinero, A. Mid-channel
Synge, J. The playboy of the
    western world

HAV   Hatcher, Harlan Henthorne,
       ed. Modern continental
       dramas...New York, Harcourt,
   ˇ   Brace, 1941. 747p
Capek, K. R.U.R.
Chekhov, A. The cherry orchard
Claudel, P. The tidings brought
    to Mary
Gorky, M. The lower depths
Hauptmann, G. Hannele
Ibsen, H. Hedda Gabler
Katayev, V. Squaring the circle
Lenormand, H. Time is a dream

Maeterlinck, M. Pelléas and
    Mélisande
Martínez Sierra, G. The cradle
    song
Molnár, F. Liliom
Pirandello, L. As you desire me
Rostand, E. Cyrano de Bergerac
Strindberg, A. The ghost sonata
Strindberg, A. Miss Julia
Toller, E. Transfiguration

HAVD   Hatcher, Harlan Henthorne,
       ed. Modern dramas. Shorter
       edition...New York, Harcourt,
       Brace [c1944] 495p
Anderson, M. Winterset
Čapek, K. R.U.R.
Chekhov, A. Cherry orchard
Galsworthy, J. Justice
Hellman, L. Watch on the Rhine
Ibsen, H. Hedda Gabler
O'Flaherty, L. The informer
O'Neill, E. Beyond the horizon
Sherwood, R. Abe Lincoln in
    Illinois

HAVE   Hatcher, Harlan Henthorne,
       ed. Modern dramas. New
       shorter edition. New York,
       Harcourt, Brace [c1948]
       479p
Anderson, M. Winterset
Čapek, K. R.U.R.
Galsworthy, J. Justice
Hellman, L. The little foxes
Ibsen, H. Hedda Gabler
Katayev, V. Squaring the circle
Maugham, W. The circle
O'Neill, E. Beyond the horizon
Sherwood, R. Abe Lincoln in Il-
    linois

HAVG   Hatcher, Harlan Henthorne
       ...A Modern repertory. New
       York, Harcourt, Brace [c1953]
       714p
Coxe, L., and Chapman, R. Billy
    Budd
Eliot, T. Murder in the cathedral
Fry, C. Venus observed
Giraudoux, J. The madwoman of
    Chaillot
Kingsley, S. Detective story
O'Casey, S. Juno and the paycock
O'Neill, E. Ah, wilderness!
Shaw, G. Candida
Williams, T. Summer and smoke

HAVH Hatlen, Theodore W., comp.
Drama; principles and plays
...New York, Appleton-
Century-Crofts [1967] 552p
Beckett, S. Act without words,
I
Brecht, B. The Caucasian
chalk circle
Ibsen, H. An enemy of the
people
Ionesco, E. The leader
Molière, J. The miser
O'Neill, E. Desire under the
elms
Shakespeare, W. Hamlet
Shaw, G. Major Barbara
Sheridan, R. The school for
scandal
Sophocles. Antigone
Strindberg, A. Miss Julie
Williams, T. The glass menagerie

HAVHA Hatlen, Theodore W., ed.
Drama: principles and plays.
2nd ed. Englewood Cliffs,
N.J., Prentice-Hall, 1975.
660p
Beckett, S. Act without words
Brecht, B. The Caucasian chalk
circle
Congreve, W. The way of the
world
Durrenmatt, F. The physicists
Elder, L. Ceremonies in dark
old men
Ibsen, H. An enemy of the people
Ionesco, E. The leader
Molière, J. The miser
O'Neill, E. The Emperor Jones
Osborne, J. Look back in anger
Shakespeare, W. King Lear
Shaw, G. Major Barbara
Sophocles. Antigone
Strindberg, A. Miss Julie

HAVHN Haugen, Einar Ingvald, ed.
Fire and ice; 3 Icelandic plays
...Madison, University of
Wisconsin Press, 1967. 266p
Sigurjónsson, J. The wish
Stefánsson, D. The golden gate
Thórdarson, A. Atoms and
madams

HAVI Havighurst, Walter; Almy,
Robert F., Wilson, Gordon D.,
and Middlebrook, L. Ruth,

eds...Selection: a reader for
college writing. New York,
Dryden [c1955] 740p
Shaw, G. Arms and the man
Sophocles. Antigone
Synge, J. Riders to the sea
Williams, T. The glass menagerie

HAVL Hay, David L. and Howell,
James F., comps. Contact
with drama. Chicago, Science
Research Associates, 1974.
550p
Cornish, R. Open twenty-four
hours
Enrico, R. On Owl Creek
Ibsen, H. Hedda Gabler
Miller, A. Death of a salesman
O'Neill, E. The Emperor Jones
Pirandello, L. Six characters in
search of an author
Shaffer, P. Black comedy
Shakespeare, W. Othello
Synge, J. Riders to the sea
Van Itallie, J. Motel
Wycherley, W. The country wife
Zindel, P. The effect of gamma
rays on man-in-the-moon mari-
golds

HAY Haydn, Hiram Collins, ed.
The portable Elizabethan
reader...New York, Viking,
1946. 688p
Dekker, T. The shoemaker's
holiday; or, A pleasant comedy
of the gentle craft
Marlowe, C. Doctor Faustus

HAYD Haydn, Hiram Collins and
Nelson, John Charles, eds.
...A renaissance treasury...
New York, Doubleday, 1953.
432p
Machiavelli, N. Mandragola
Tasso, T. Aminta

HAYES, HELEN. See
GRIF Griffin, Alice Sylvia
(Venezky), ed. Living
theatre...

HAYE Hayes, Richard, ed. Port-
Royal and other plays...New
York, Hill and Wang [c1962]
267p (Mermaid dramabook)
Claudel, P. Tobias and Sara

HAYE (cont.)
  Copeau, J. The little poor man
  Mauriac, F. Asmodée
  Montherlant, H. Port-Royal

HEA The Heath introduction to
  drama, with a preface on
  drama and introductory notes
  by Jordan Y. Miller.
  Lexington, Mass., Heath,
  1976. 907p
  Aristophanes. Lysistrata
  Brecht, B. Mother courage
  Chekhov, A. The cherry orchard
  Ibsen, H. Hedda Gabler
  Miller, A. Death of a salesman
  Molière, J. The misanthrope
  O'Neill, E. Desire under the elms
  Pinter, H. The dumb waiter
  Pirandello, L. Six characters in
    search of an author
  The second shepherds' play
  Shakespeare, W. Hamlet
  Shaw, G. Major Barbara
  Sophocles. Oedipus rex
  Strindberg, A. Miss Julie
  Williams, T. The glass menagerie

HEAL Heath introduction to litera-
  ture. Compiled by Alice
  Landy. Lexington, Mass.,
  Heath, c1980.
  Miller, A. Death of a salesman
  The second shepherds' play
  Shakespeare, W. Hamlet
  Shaw, G. Major Barbara
  Sophocles. Oedipus rex

HEIL Heilman, Robert B., ed. An
  anthology of English drama be-
  fore Shakespeare...New York,
  Rinehart [c1952] 405p
  The betrayal
  The crucifixion
  Everyman
  Greene, R. The honorable
    history of Friar Bacon and
    Friar Bungay
  Kyd, T. The Spanish tragedy
  Marlowe, C. The tragical history
    of Dr. Faustus
  Noah
  The second shepherds' play
  Stevenson, W. Gammer Gurton's
    needle

HEIS Heisch, Elizabeth, ed.

Discovery and recollection; an
  anthology of literary types.
  New York, Holt, Rinehart and
  Winston, 1970. 566p
  Benét, S. The devil and Daniel
    Webster
  Chayevsky, P. Marty
  Fletcher, L. Sorry, wrong num-
    ber
  Hansberry, L. A raisin in the
    sun
  Shaw, G. Pygmalion

HEWE Hewes, Henry, ed. Famous
  American plays of the 1940's
  ...[New York, Dell, c1960]
  447p (Laurel drama series)
  Anderson, M., and Weil, K. Lost
    in the stars
  Laurents, A. Home of the brave
  McCullers, C. The member of
    the wedding
  Miller, A. All my sons
  Wilder, T. The skin of our teeth

HEWES, HENRY. See also
  BES Best plays of 1894/99-
  1961/62...

HIB Hibbard, Clarence Addison, ed.
  Writers of the western world.
  Boston, Houghton, Mifflin
  [c1942] 1261p
  Aeschylus. Agamemnon
  Aristophanes. The frogs
  Euripides. Medea
  Evreinov, N. The theatre of the
    soul
  Goethe, J. Faust, pt. I
  Ibsen, H. The master builder
  Molière, J. The misanthrope
  O'Neill, E. The hairy ape
  Racine, J. Phaedra
  Shakespeare, W. King Lear
  Sophocles. Antigone

HIBA Hibbard, Clarence Addison,
  ed...Writers of the western
  world...[Rev. ed.] Boston,
  Houghton, Mifflin [c1946]
  1033p (United States Naval
  Academy edition edited by
  Cyril B. Judge)
  Aeschylus. Agamemnon
  Aristophanes. The frogs
  Evreinov, N. The theatre of the
    soul

Goethe, J. Faust, pt. I
Ibsen, H. The master builder
Molière, J. The misanthrope
O'Neill, E. The hairy ape
Shakespeare, W. King Lear

HIBB Hibbard, Clarence Addison,
and Frenz, Horst, eds.
Writers of the western world
...Second edition...Boston,
Houghton Mifflin [c1954]
1239p
Aeschylus. Agamemnon
Aristophanes. The frogs
Chekhov, A. The cherry orchard
Claudel, P. The satin slipper;
or, The worst is not the
surest
Euripides. Medea
Goethe, J. Faust, pt. I
Ibsen, H. The master builder
Molière, J. The misanthrope
O'Neill, E. The hairy ape
Pirandello, L. The jar
Racine, J. Phaedra
Shakespeare, W. King Lear
Sophocles. Antigone

HIBH Hibbett, Howard, ed. Contemporary Japanese literature:
an anthology of fiction, film,
and other writing since 1945.
New York, Knopf, 1977.
468p
Abe, Kōbō (Kimifusa). Friends
Kurosawa, Akira. Ikiru
Ozu, Yasujirō. Tokyo story

HIG Higgins, V. Louise and Kerr,
Walter, eds. Five world
plays. New York, Harcourt,
Brace and World, 1964. 550p
Chekhov, A. The cherry orchard
Shakespeare, W. Hamlet
Shaw, G. Saint Joan
Sheridan, R. The rivals
Sophocles. Antigone

HIJ High energy musicals from the
Omaha Magic Theatre. New
York, N.Y., Broadway Play
Publishing, c1983. 212p
Schmidman, J. Running gag
Terry, M. American king's
English for queens
Terry, M. Babes in the big-
house

HILDRETH, WILLIAM HENRY. See
also
HAP Harbrace omnibus...

HIL Hildreth, William Henry and
Dumble, Wilson Randle, eds.
Five contemporary American
plays...New York, Harper
[c1939] 410p
Anderson, M. Winterset
Kaufman, G., and Ryskind, M.
Of thee I sing
Odets, C. Waiting for Lefty
O'Neill, E. Ah, wilderness
Sherwood, R. Idiot's delight

HILL Hill, John McMurray and
Harlan, Mabel Margaret, eds.
Cuatro comedias...New York,
Norton [c1941] 699p
Calderón de la Barca, P. No
siempre lo peor es cierto
Ruiz de Alarcón y Mendoza, J.
No hay mal que por bien no
venga (Don Domingo de Don
Blas)
Téllez, G. (Tirso de Molina
[pseud.]). El burlador de
Sevilla
Vega [Carpio], L. de. Peribáñez
y el comendador de Ocaña

HILP Hill, Philip George, comp.
The living art; an introduction
to theatre and drama. New
York, Holt, Rinehart and
Winston, 1971. 578p
Brecht, B. Galileo
Hellman, L. The little foxes
MacLeish, A. J.B.
Miller, A. A view from the bridge
Molière, J. Tartuffe
Oldenburg, C. Fotodeath
Rostand, E. Cyrano de Bergerac
Shakespeare, W. Twelfth night
Sophocles. Oedipus Rex
Wilde, O. The importance of
being earnest

HOF Hoffman, William M., ed. Gay
plays: the first collection.
New York, Avon, 1979. 493p
Chambers, J. A late snow
Hoffman, W., and Holland, A.
Cornbury: The queen's
governor
Marcus, F. The killing of Sister

HOF (cont.)
George
Miller, S. Confessions of a
female disorder
Orton, J. Entertaining Mr.
Sloane
Patrick, R. T-shirts
Solly, B., and Ward, D. Boy
meets boy
Wilson, L. The madness of
Lady Bright

HOFFMAN, WILLIAM M. See
NEWA New American plays...

HOGE Hogan, Robert Goode,
comp. Seven Irish plays,
1946-1964...Minneapolis,
University of Minnesota
Press [1967] 472p
Byrne, S. Design for a head-
stone
Douglas, J. The ice goddess
Keane, J. Many young men of
twenty
Keane, J. Sharon's grave
MacMahon, B. Song of the anvil
Molly, M. The visiting house
O'Donovan, J. Copperfaced Jack

HOGF Hogan, Robert Goode and
Molin, Sven Eric, eds.
Drama; the major genres...
New York, Dodd, Mead, 1962.
652p
Chekhov, A. The three sisters
García Lorca, F. The house of
Bernarda Alba
Gorky, M. Yegor Bulychov and
the others
Inge, W. Bus stop
James, H. The American
Jonson, B. The silent woman
Molière, J. Tartuffe
O'Casey, S. The plough and the
stars
Shakespeare, W. The tragedy of
King Lear
Shaw, G. The six of Calais
Sophocles. Antigone

HOGI Hogins, James B., comp.
Literature; a collection of
mythology and folklore, short
stories, poetry, drama...Chi-
cago, Science Research
Associates, 1973. 962p

Arrabal, F. Picnic on the battle-
field
Bullins, E. The electornic nigger
Miller, A. A view from the
bridge
Molière, J. Sganarelle
Shakespeare, W. Macbeth
Shaw, G. How he lied to her
husband
Sophocles. Oedipus Rex
Synge, J. Riders to the sea

HOGN Hogins, James B., comp.
Literature; a collection of
mythology and folklore, short
stories, poetry, and drama.
2nd ed. Chicago, Science
Research Associates, 1977.
974p
Arrabal, F. Picnic on the battle-
field
Henshaw, J. The jewels of the
shrine
Miller, A. A view from the bridge
O'Neill, E. Ile
Pirandello, L. The man with the
flower in his mouth
Shakespeare, W. Othello
Sophocles. Oedipus rex
Strindberg, A. Miss Julie

HOLM Holmes, John Albert and
Towle, Carroll S., eds. A
complete college reader...Bos-
ton, Houghton, Mifflin
[c1950] 1063p
Anderson, M. Winterset
Ibsen, H. An enemy of the people
O'Neill, E. Ah, wilderness!

HOLP Holmes, Paul C., and
Lehman, A. J., eds. Keys to
understanding; receiving and
sending; drama. New York,
Harper and Row, 1970. 459p
Aristophanes. Lysistrata
Cowen, R. Summertime
Gardner, H. A thousand clowns
Ionesco, E. The gap
Jones, L. Dutchman
Saroyan, W. Hello out there
Shakespeare, W. Romeo and
Juliet
Sophocles. Antigone
Ward, D. Happy ending

HOLT Holt, Marion P., ed. The

modern Spanish stage: four
plays. New York, Hill and
Wang, 1970. 388p
Buero Vallejo, A.   The concert
    at Saint Ovide
Casona, A.   The boat without
    fisherman
López Rubio, J.   The blindfold
Sastre, A.   Condemned squad

HOM   Homosexual acts; five short
    plays from The Gay Season
    at The Almost Free Theatre,
    ed. by Ed Berman.   London,
    Inter-Action Inprint, 1975.
    142p   (Ambiance/Almost Free
    playscripts, 1)
Collinson, L.   Thinking straight
Patrick, R.   Fred and Harold
Patrick, R.   The haunted host
Patrick, R.   One person
Wakeman, A.   Ships

HOPP   Hopper, Vincent Foster, and
    Lahey, Gerald B., eds.
    Medieval mystery plays...
    morality plays...and interludes.
    Great Neck, N.Y., Barron's
    Educational Series   [c1962]
    299p
Abraham and Isaac
The castle of perseverance
Everyman
Noah's flood
The second shepherds' play
Heywood, J.   Johan Johan
Heywood, J.   The play called the
    four pp

HORN   Horn, Gunnar.   A cavalcade
    of world writing...Boston,
 v Allyn and Bacon, 1961.   718p
Capek, K.   R.U.R.   (Rossum's
    universal robots)

HORNE, HERBERT P.   See
    NER   Nero (Tragedy).   Nero
    & other plays...

HOUE   Houghton, Norris, ed.   The
    golden age...[New York,
    Dell, 1963]   349p   (Laurel
    masterpieces of continental
    drama, v1)
Calderón de la Barca, P.   Life
    is a dream
Corneille, P.   The cid

Molière, J.   The misanthrope
Racine, J.   Phaedra
Vega Carpio, L.   The sheep
    well

HOUG   Houghton, Norris, ed.
    Great Russian plays...[New
    York, Dell, c1960]   511p
    (Laurel drama series)
Andreyev, L.   He who gets
    slapped
Chekhov, A.   The cherry orchard
Gogol, N.   The inspector general
Gorky, M.   The lower depths
Tolstoy, L.   The power of dark-
    ness
Turgenev, I.   A month in the
    country

HOUK   Houghton, Norris, ed.   The
    romantic influence.   [New York,
    Dell, 1963]   542p   (Laurel mas-
    terpieces of continental drama,
    v2)
Goethe, J.   Faust, pt. 1
Hugo, V.   Hernani
Rostand, E.   Cyrano de Bergerac
Schiller, F.   Mary Stuart

HOUP   Houghton, Norris, ed.   Seeds
    of modern drama.   [New York,
    Dell, 1963]   413p   (Laurel
    masterpieces of continental
    drama, v3)
Chekhov, A.   The sea gull
Hauptmann, G.   The weavers
Ibsen, H.   An enemy of the people
Strindberg, A.   Miss Julie
Zola, E.   Thérèse Raquin

HOUR   The hour of one: six Gothic
    melodramas, edited and intro-
    duced by Stephen Wischhusen.
    London, Gordon Fraser Gallery,
    1975.   173p
Fitz-Ball, E.   The devil's elixir
Fitz-Ball, E.   The flying Dutch-
    man; or, The phantom ship;
    a nautical drama
Holcroft, T.   A tale of mystery
Lewis, M.   The castle spectre
Milner, H.   Frankenstein; or,
    The man and the monster
Planché, J.   The vampire; or,
    The bride of the isles

HOUS   Houston, Percy Hazen and

HOUS (cont.)
Smith, Robert Metcalf, eds.
Types of world literature...
Garden City, N.Y., Doubleday,
Doran [c1930] 1200p
Aeschylus. Agamemnon
Aristophanes. The birds
Euripides. Hippolytus
Everyman
Ibsen, H. A doll's house
Molière, J. The misanthrope
Plautus. T. The captives
Racine, J. Athaliah
Shakespeare, W. As you like it
Shakespeare, W. King Lear
Sheridan, R. The rivals
Sophocles. Antigone
Wilde, O. The importance of
being earnest

HOW Howard, Edwin Johnson, ed.
Ten Elizabethan plays...New
York, Nelson, 1931. 451p
Beaumont, F., and Fletcher, J.
The knight of the burning
pestle
Beaumont, F., and Fletcher, J.
Philaster
Dekker, T. The shoemaker's
holiday
Greene, R. The honorable his-
tory of Friar Bacon and Friar
Bungay
Jonson, B. The alchemist
Kyd, T. The Spanish tragedy
Marlowe, C. Tamburlaine the
great
Marlowe, C. The tragical history
of Dr. Faustus
Massinger, P. A new way to pay
old debts
Webster, J. The Duchess of
Malfi

HOWE Howe, George and Harrer,
Gustave Adolphus, eds...
Greek literature in translation
...New York, Harper [c1924]
642p
Aeschylus. Agamemnon
Aristophanes. The clouds
Euripides. Alcestis
Euripides. Medea
Menander. The arbitration
Sophocles. Oedipus the king

HOWF Howe, George, and Harrer,

Gustave Adolphus, eds.
Greek literature in translation
...Revised edition by Preston
Herschel Epps. New York,
Harper [c1948] 903p
Aeschylus. Agamemnon
Aristophanes. The clouds
Aristophanes. The frogs
Euripides. Alcestis
Euripides. Medea
Menander. The arbitration
Sophocles. Oedipus the king

HOWJ Howe, George, and Harrer,
Gustave, eds...Roman litera-
ture in translation...New York,
Harper, 1924. 630p
Plautus. Menaechmi
Seneca. Octavia
Terence. Phormio

HOWK Howe, George, and Harrer,
Gustave, eds. Roman litera-
ture in translation...Revised
by Albert Suskin...New York,
Harper [c1959] 649p
Horatius Flaccus, Q. The bore;
a dramatic version of Horace
(Satires I, 9)
Plautus, T. The braggart sol-
dier
Seneca, L. Octavia
Terentius Afer, P. The brothers

HOWP Howe, Irving, [and others],
comps. The literature of
America. New York, McGraw-
Hill, 1971. 2v
Albee, E. The zoo story 2
Jones, L. Dutchman 2
O'Neill, E. Desire under the elms
2
Tyler, R. The contrast 1
Wilder, T. The skin of our teeth
2

HUB Hubbell, Jay Broadus, ed.
American life in literature...
New York, Harper [c1936]
849p
O'Neill, E. Marco millions

HUBA Hubbell, Jay Broadus, ed.
American life in literature...
New York, Harper [c1949] 2v
O'Neill, E. The Emperor Jones
2

HUD Hubbell, Jay Broadus and
Beatty, John Owen, eds.
An introduction to drama...
New York, Macmillan, 1927.
838p
Abraham and Isaac
Beaumont, F., and Fletcher,
J. Philaster
Chekhov, A. The boor
Dunsany, E. A night at an
inn
Everyman
Farquhar, G. The beaux'
stratagem
Gerstenberg, A. Overtones
Gilbert, W., and Sullivan, A.
Iolanthe
Glaspell, S. Trifles
Goldsmith, O. She stoops to
conquer
Hauptmann, G. The assumption
of Hannele
Ibsen, H. A doll's house
Jones, H. The goal
Jonson, B. Volpone
Maeterlinck, M. The intruder
Marlowe, C. Doctor Faustus
Molière, J. Tartuffe
O'Neill, E. The Emperor Jones
Pinero, A. The second Mrs.
Tanqueray
Plautus, T. Menaechmi
Quem quaeritis
Rostand, E. Cyrano de Bergerac
The second shepherds' play
Sheridan, R. The school for
scandal
Sophocles. Antigone
Synge, J. Riders to the sea
Wilde, O. Lady Windermere's fan
Williamson, H. Peggy
Yeats, W. The land of heart's
desire

HUDE Huberman, Edward, and
Raymo, Robert R., eds.
Angels of vision...Boston,
Houghton Mifflin [c1962]
679p
Harburg, E., and Saidy, F.
Finian's rainbow
Inge, W. The dark at the top
of the stairs
Priestley, J. An inspector calls
Shakespeare, W. A midsummer
night's dream
Wedekind, F. The tenor

HUDS Hudson, Arthur Palmer;
Hurley, Leonard Buswell and
Clark, Joseph Deadrick, eds.
Nelson's college caravan...
New York, Nelson, 1936. 4v
Green, P. Unto such glory 2
O'Neill, E. Marco millions 2
Rostand, E. Cyrano de
Bergerac
Sherriff, R. Journey's end 2
Sophocles. Antigone 2

HUDT Hudson, Arthur Palmer;
Hurley, Leonard Buswell and
Clark, Joseph Deadrick, eds.
Nelson's college caravan...3rd
ed. New York, Nelson, 1942.
1418p (4v in 1)
Čapek, K. R.U.R.
O'Neill, E. Marco millions
Sophocles. Antigone

HUGH Hughes, Leo, and Scouten,
A. H., eds. Ten English
farces...Austin, Texas, Uni-
versity of Texas Press, 1948.
286p
Behn, A. The emperor of the
moon
The bilker bilk'd
Dogget, T. Hob; or, The
country wake
Hoare, P. No song no supper
Inchbald, E. Appearance is
against them
Jevon, T.; Coffey, C.; Mottley,
J., and Cibber, T. The
devil to pay; or, The wives
metamorphos'd
Johnson, C. The cobbler of
Preston
Ravenscroft, E., and Motteux,
P. The anatomist; or, The
sham doctor
Sheridan, T. The brave Irish-
man
Tate, N. A duke and no duke

HUNG Hung, Josephine Huang,
comp. Classical Chinese
plays. 2nd ed. London,
Vision Press, 1972. 277p
The faithful harlot
One missing head
The price of wine
Twice a bride
Two men on a string

HUNT   Hunt, Kellogg, W., and
       Stoakes, Paul, eds. Our
       living language...Boston,
       Houghton Mifflin [c1961]
       631p
Miller, A. Death of a salesman
Serling, R. Patterns

HUSSEY, MAURICE P. See
       CHES Chester mystery plays

HUST   Huston, John Dennis and
       Kernan, A. B., comps.
       Classics of the renaissance
       theater: English plays. New
       York, Harcourt, 1969. 735p
Ford, J. 'Tis a pity she's a
       whore
Jonson, B. Volpone
Kyd, T. The Spanish tragedy
Marlowe, C. Tamburlaine the
       Great
Middleton, T. and Rowley, W.
       The changeling
Tourneur, C. The revenger's
       tragedy
Webster, J. The Duchess of
       Malfi

HUTC   Hutchens, John K., ed.
       The American twenties...
       Philadelphia, Lippincott
       [c1952] 480p
O'Neill, E. The Emperor Jones

HUTCHINS, ROBERT MAYNARD.
       See
       GRDB Great books of the
       western world...

IFKO   Ifkovic, Edward, comp.
       American letter: immigrant
       and ethnic writing, ed. by
       Edward Ifkovic. Englewood
       Cliffs, N.J., Prentice-Hall
       [1975] 386p
Lawson, J. Processional
Smith, M. An American grand-
       father

INCA   Inchbald, Mrs. Elizabeth
       (Simpson), comp. The modern
       theatre; a collection of plays.
       (First published in London,
       1811, in ten volumes; reissued

in 1968 in five volumes). New
York, Benjamin Blom, Inc.,
1968. 10v in 5
Cobb, J. Ramah Droog 6
Cobb, J. The wife of two hus-
bands 6
Colman, G. The English merchant
9
Colman, G., the younger. Who
wants a guinea? 3
Cowley, Mrs. H. Which is the
man? 10
Cumberland, R. The box-lobby
challenger 5
Cumberland, R. The Carmelite 5
Cumberland, R. False impres-
sions 5
Cumberland, R. The imposters
6
Cumberland, R. The mysterious
husband 5
Cumberland, R. The natural
son 5
Dibdin, T. The school for pre-
judice 4
He's much to blame 4
Holcroft, T. Duplicity 4
Holcroft, T. The school for
arrogance 4
Holcroft, T. Seduction 4
Holman, J. The votary of wealth
3
Hull, T. Henry the Second, or
The fall of Rosamond 9
Inchbald, Mrs. E. I'll tell you
what 7
Inchbald, Mrs. E. Next door
neighbors 7
Inchbald, Mrs. E. The wise man
of the East 7
Jephson, R. Braganza 6
Jephson, R. The law of Lombardy
6
Kelly, H. School for wives 9
Lee, Miss. The chapter of acci-
dents 9
Macnally, L. Fashionable
levities 10
Macready, W. The bank note 9
Matilda 8
More, H. Percy 7
Morton, T. Secrets worth know-
ing 3
Morton, T. Zorinski 3
O'Keeffe, J. Lie of a day 10
Philon, F. He would be a sol-
dier 8

Reynolds, F. The delinquent 2
Reynolds, F. Folly as it flies 2
Reynolds, F. Fortune's fool 2
Reynolds, F. The fugitive 8
Reynolds, F. How to grow rich 1
Reynolds, F. Laugh when you can 2
Reynolds, F. Life 1
Reynolds, F. Notoriety 1
Reynolds, F. The rage 1
Reynolds, F. Speculation 2
Reynolds, F. Werter 3
Reynolds, F. The will 1
St. John, J. Mary Queen of Scots 8
Sheridan, R. A trip to Scarborough 7
Siddon, H. Time's a tell-tale 10
Smith, C. What is she? 10
Watson, G. England preserved 8

INDI The Indiana experience: an anthology; compiled and edited by Arnold Leslie Lazarus. Bloomington, Ind., Indiana University Press, 1977. 426p
McCutcheon, G. The double doctor: a farce
Phillips, D. The worth of a woman

ING Inglis, Rewey Belle; Gehlmann, John; Bowman, Mary Rives and Foerster, Norman, eds. Adventures in American literature. 3rd ed...New York, Harcourt, Brace, 1941. v.p.
Anderson, S. Textiles
O'Neill, E. Where the cross is made
Wilder, T. Our town

INGA Inglis, Rewey Belle; Bowman, Mary Rives; Gehlmann, John and Schramm, Wilbur. Adventures in American literature... Fourth...edition. New York, Harcourt, Brace [c1947] 811p
Buck, P. Will this earth hold?
Gallico, P. The snow goose
O'Neill, E. Where the cross is made
Wilder, T. Our town

INGB Inglis, Rewey Belle; Gehlmann, John; Bowman, Mary Rives and Schramm, Wilbur, eds. Adventures in American literature. Mercury edition. [5th edition] New York, Harcourt, Brace, 1952. 783p
Clarke, W. The ghost patrol
Gallico, P. The snow goose
Wilder, T. Our town

INGE Inglis, Rewey Belle; Cooper, Alice Cecilia; Sturdevant, Marion A., and Benét, William Rose, eds. Adventures in English literature. Rev. ed. ...New York, Harcourt, Brace, 1938. 1178p
Galsworthy, J. Strife
Shakespeare, W. Macbeth
Synge, J. Riders to the sea

INGG Inglis, Rewey Belle; Cooper, Alice Cecilia; Oppenheimer, Celia, and Benét, William Rose, eds. Adventures in English literature...Fourth edition. New York, Harcourt, Brace [c1946] 775p
Barrie, J. The old lady shows her medals
Galsworthy, J. Strife
Shakespeare, W. Macbeth
Synge, J. Riders to the sea

INGH Inglis, Rewey Belle; Stauffer, Donald A., and Larsen, Cecil Evva, eds. Adventures in English literature. Mercury edition. New York, Harcourt, Brace. 1952. 782p
Barrie, J. The old lady shows her medals
Besier, R. The Barretts of Wimpole Street
Synge, J. Riders to the sea

INGW Inglis, Rewey Belle, and Stewart, William Kilbourne, eds. Adventures in world literature...New York, Harcourt, Brace, 1936. 1268p
Benavente y Martínez, J. No smoking
The bird-catcher in hell

INGW (cont.)

Ibsen, H. An enemy of the
people

Molière, J. The physician in
spite of himself

Sachs, H. The horse thief

Sophocles. Antigone

INTE International modern
plays...London, Dent [1950]
304p (Everyman's library)

Čapek, K., and Čapek, J. The
life of the insects

Chiarelli, L. The mask and the
face

Cocteau, J. The infernal machine

Hauptmann, G. Hannele

Strindberg, A. Lady Julie

IRW Irwin, Vera Rusforth, comp.
and tr. Four classical Asian
plays in modern translation.
Baltimore, Penguin, 1972.
333p

Bhasa. The vision of Vasavan-
datta

Danjuro I. Narukami

Wang, S. The west chamber

Zembō, M. Ikkaku sennin

JACKSON, SIR BARRY. See
MAL Malvern festival plays...

JAFF Jaffe, Adrian H., and
Weisinger, Herbert, eds.
The laureate fraternity...
Evanston, Ill., Row, Peterson
[c1960] 720p

Goldsmith, O. She stoops to
conquer; or, The mistakes
of a night

Kingsley, S. Detective story

O'Neill, E. Ah, wilderness!

Shakespeare, W. Othello, the
Moor of Venice

Sophocles. Oedipus rex

Wilde, O. An ideal husband

JEFF Jeffares, Alexander N., ed.
Restoration comedy. Totowa,
N.J., Rowman & Littlefield,
1974. 4v

Behn, A. The lucky chance; or,
An alderman's bargain 3

Behn, A. The rover; or, The

banished cavaliers 2

Cibber, C. The careless husband 4

Cibber, C. Love's last shift 3

Congreve, W. Love for love 3

Congreve, W. The way of the
world 4

Crowne, J. Sir Courtly Nice 2

Dryden, J. The kind keeper, or,
Mr. Limberham 2

Dryden, J. Sir Martin Mar-all,
or, The feigned innocence 1

D'Urfey, T. Madam Fickle, or,
The witty false one 2

Etherege, G. The man of mode
1

Etherege, G. She would if she
could 1

Farquhar, G. The beaux' stratagem 4

Farquhar, G. The constant
couple, or, A trip to the Jubilee 4

Farquhar, G. The recruiting
officer 4

Killigrew, T. The parson's
wedding 1

Ravenscroft, E. The London
cuckolds 2

Sedley, C. The mulberry garden
1

Shadwell, T. The Squire of Alsatia 3

Steele, R. The conscious lovers
4

Vanbrugh, J. The provok'd wife
3

Vanbrugh, J. The relapse 3

Wycherley, W. The country wife
1

Wycherley, W. The plain dealer
2

THE JOHNS HOPKINS STUDIES IN
ROMANCE LITERATURE AND
LANGUAGES v29. See
LAN Lancaster, Henry Car-
rington, ed. Five French
farces, 1655-1694?...

JOH [Johnson, Rossiter] ed. An
anthology of Italian authors
from Cavalcanti to Fogazzaro
(1270-1907)...[New York]
National alumni [c1907] 388p
(The literature of Italy, 1265-
1907)

Metastasio, P. Achilles in Scyros

JOHN Johnson, Stanley Lewis;
Bierman, Judah and Hart,
James, eds. The play and
the reader. Englewood
Cliffs, N.J., Prentice-Hall,
1966. 442p
Aristophanes. Lysistrata
Brecht, B. Mother Courage
Giraudoux, J. The madwoman of
Chaillot
Ibsen, H. Rosmersholm
Ionesco, E. The chairs
Pirandello, L. Henry IV
Shakespeare, W. King Lear
Shaw, G. Caesar and Cleopatra
Sophocles. Oedipus rex

JOHO Johnson, Stanley Lewis,
[and others], eds. The play
and the reader. Englewood
Cliffs, N.J., Prentice-Hall,
1971. 583p
Anouilh, J. Antigone
Brecht, B. The Caucasian chalk
circle
Frisch, M. Firebugs
Ibsen, H. An enemy of the
people
Molière, J. Tartuffe
Pirandello, L. Right you are if
you think you are
Shakespeare, W. Hamlet
Shakespeare, W. Twelfth night
Sophocles. Antigone
Wilder, T. The skin of our teeth

JON Jones, Le Roi, and Neal,
Larry, eds. Black fire: an
anthology of Afro-American
writing. New York, Apollo
Eds., 1969. 670p
Bullins, E. How do you do
Caldwell, B. Prayer meeting;
or, The first militant minister
Drayton, R. Notes from a strange
God
Freeman, C. The suicide
Garrett, J. We own the night
Jackson, M. Flowers for the
trash-man
Jones, L. Madheart
Patterson, C. Black ice
White, J. The leader

JONA Jones, Willis Knapp, tr.

and comp. Men and angels:
three South American comedies.
Carbondale, Ill., Southern Illinois University Press, 1970.
191p
Darthes, J., and Damel, C. The
quack doctor
Frank, M. The man and the century
Matto, J. The fate of Chipi
González

JORG Jorgenson, Paul A., and
Shroyer, Frederick B., eds.
A college treasury...New York,
Charles Scribner's sons
[c1956] 598p
Howard, S. The silver cord
Rice, E. The adding machine
Shakespeare, W. Romeo and
Juliet
Shaw, G. Arms and the man
Sherriff, R. The colonel's lady

JORH Jorgensen, Paul A., and
Shroyer, Frederick B., eds.
A college treasury: prose,
fiction, drama, poetry...2nd
ed. New York, Scribner
[1967] 604p
Shakespeare, W. The tragedy of
Hamlet, Prince of Denmark
Shaw, G. Arms and the man
Sophocles. Oedipus rex
Wilder, T. The skin of our teeth

KAB Kabuki: 5 classic plays; trans-
lated by James R. Brandon.
Cambridge, Mass., Harvard
University Press, 1975. 378p
Love letter from the licensed
quarter
Namiki, S.; Namiki, S. I.; Namiki,
G., and Asada, I. Chronicle
of the Battle of Ichinotani
Tsuruya, N. IV; Sakurada, J. II,
and Tsuuchi, G. The scarlet
princess of Edo
Tsuuchi, H.; Yasuda, A., and
Nakada, M. Saint Narukami
and the god Fudō
Tsuuchi, J. II and Tsuuchi, H.
Sukeroku: Flower of Edo

KAL Kalman, Rolf, ed. A collection

KAL (cont.)
    of Canadian plays. Toronto,
    Bastet Books, 1972-1978.
    5v

Ball, A., and Bradbury, P.
    Professor Fuddle's fantastic
    fairy-tale machine 4
Bolt, C. Cyclone Jack 4
Boston, S. Counsellor extra-
    ordinary 1
Cameron, R. Masque 4
Cook, M. Colour the flesh the
    colour of dust 1
Denison, M. Marsh hay 3
Fruet, W. Wedding in white
    2
Gerneau, M. Four to four 5
Garner, H. Three women 2
Ibbitson, J. Catalyst 4
Jack, D. Exit muttering 1
Kemp, D. King Grumbletum and
    the magic pie 4
Lavigne, L. Are you afraid of
    thieves? 5
McMaster, B. Which witch is
    which? 4
Mercier, S. A little bit left 5
Mitchell, W. The devil's instru-
    ment 2
Moore, M. The pile, the store,
    inside out 2
Nicol, E. The clam made a face
    4
Peterson, L. Billy Bishop and
    the Red Baron 4
Ravel, A. The twisted loaf;
    Soft voices (two short plays)
    3
Rosen, S. Two plays: Love
    mouse; Meyer's room 1
Roussin, C. Looking for a job
    5
Schull, J. The vice president
    3
Scott, M. Wu-feng 1
Shoveller, B. Westbound 12:01
    2
Simard, A. Waiting for Gaudre-
    ault 5
Sirois, S. Dodo
Taylor, R. The unreasonable
    act of Julian Waterman 3
Thury, F., and Galbraith, R.
    Nuts and bolts and rusty
    things 4
Tremblay, R. Greta, the divine
    5

Woods, G. Vicky 3
Zacharko, L. Land of magic
    spell 4

KAT Katzin, Mrs. Winifred, comp.
    Eight European plays...New
    York, Brentano, 1927. 426p
Bernard, J. Glamour
Bernard, J. Martine
Harlan, W. The Nüremberg egg
Kaiser, G. The fire in the opera
    house
Mann, H. Madame Legros
Rosso di san Secondo, P. The
    stairs
Sternheim, C. A place in the
    world
Vollmöller, K. Uncle's been
    dreaming

KAU Kauver, Gerald B., and
    Sorensen, Gerald Charles,
    comps. Nineteenth century
    English verse drama. Cran-
    bury, N.J., Fairleigh Dickinson
    University Press, 1973. 355p
Arnold, M. Empedocles on Etna
Browning, R. King Victor and
    King Charles
Coleridge, S. Remorse
Gordon, G. Manfred
Keats, J. Otho the Great
Shelley, P. The Cenci
Swinburne, A. Atlanta in Calydon
Tennyson, A. Becket
Wordsworth, W. The borderers

KEE Keene, Donald, ed. and comp.
    Twenty plays of the Nō theatre.
    New York, Columbia University
    Press, 1970. 336p
The iron crown
Komparu-Zenchiku. The queen
    mother of the West
Komparu-Zenchiku. Yōkihi
Kongō, Y. The bird-scaring boat
Kwanze, K. K. Komachi and the
    hundred nights
Kwanze, K. K. Matsukaze
Kwanze, K. K. The sought-for
    grave
Kwanze, K. N. Dōjōji
Kwanze, K. N. The priest and
    the willow
Seami, M. The brocade tree
Seami, M. The deserted crone
Seami, M. The imperial visit to

Ohara
Seami, M. Kanehira
Seami, M. Komachi at Sekidera
Seami, M. Lady Han
Seami, M. The reed cutter
Seami, M. Semimaru
Shōkun
The shrine in the fields
The valley rite

KER Kermode, John Frank, ed.
The anthology of English
literature. New York, Oxford
University Press, 1973. 2v
Congreve, W. The way of the
world 1
Everyman 1
Gay, J. The beggar's opera 1
Marlowe, C. Doctor Faustus 1
The second shepherds' play 1
Shakespeare, W. The tempest 1
Shaw, G. Saint Joan 2
Wilde, O. The importance of
being earnest 2

KERN Kernan, Alvin B., ed.
Character and conflict: An
introduction to drama...New
York, Harcourt, Brace [c1963]
757p
Brecht, B. Mother Courage and
her children
Chekhov, A. The cherry orchard
Everyman
Ibsen, H. Hedda Gabler
MacLeish, A. The fall of the city
Molière, J. The misanthrope
Saroyan, W. The time of your
life
Shakespeare, W. King Henry the
fourth, part 1
Shakespeare, W. The tragedy of
Hamlet, Prince of Denmark
Sophocles. Antigone
Strindberg, A. The stronger

KERO Kernan, Alvin Bernard, ed.
Character and conflict; an in-
troduction to drama. 2d ed.
New York, Harcourt, Brace
and World, 1969. 721p
Arrabal, F. Picnic on the battle-
field
Brecht, B. Mother Courage and
her children
Chekhov, A. The cherry orchard
Everyman

Giraudoux, J. Tiger at the gates
Ibsen, H. Hedda Gabler
Molière, J. The misanthrope
Shakespeare, W. Hamlet
Sophocles. Antigone
Strindberg, A. The stronger
Synge, J. Riders to the sea
Wilder, T. The skin of our teeth

KERP Kernan, Alvin Bernard, ed.
Classics of the modern theater,
realism and after. New York,
Harcourt, Brace and World
[1965] 538p
Albee, E. The zoo story
Betti, U. Corruption in the
palace of justice
Brecht, B. Mother Courage
and her children
Chekhov, A. The cherry orchard
García Lorca, F. Blood wedding
Ibsen, H. Ghosts
Ionesco, E. The chairs
Pirandello, L. Six characters in
search of an author
Shaw, G. Arms and the man
Strindberg, A. The father
Strindberg, A. The ghost sonata

KET Ketchum, Roland and Billis,
Adolph, eds. Three masters
of English drama...New York,
Dodd, Mead, 1934. 469p
Dryden, J. All for love
Shakespeare, W. Julius Caesar
Shaw, G. Caesar and Cleopatra

KEY Keyes, Rowena Keith and Roth,
Helen M., eds...Comparative
comedies present and past. New
York, Noble & Noble [c1935]
628p
Barry, P. Holiday
Beach, L. The goose hangs high
Goldsmith, O. She stoops to con-
quer
Sheridan, R. The rivals

KILG Kilgarriff, Michael, comp. The
golden age of melodrama:
twelve 19th century melodramas.
Abridged and introduced by the
author. London, Wolfe Pub.,
1974. 499p
Buckstone, J. Luke the labourer
Byron, H., and Boucicault, D.
Lost at sea

KILG (cont.)
    Gilbert, W.   Dan'l Druce
    Haines, J.   The ocean of life
    Holcroft, T.   A tale of mystery
    Jerrold, D.   Fifteen years of a
        drunkard's life
    Maria Martin; or, The murder in
        the red barn
    Oxenford, J.   East Lynne
    Pitt, G.   The string of pearls
        (Sweeney Todd)
    Planché, J.   The vampire
    Potter, P.   Trilby
    Wills, W.   Eugene Aram

KIN   Kincheloe, Isabel Mary, and
    Cook, Lester H., comps.
    Adventures in values.   New
    York, Harcourt, Brace, Jo-
    vanovich, 1969.   784p
    Anderson, M.   Feast of Ortolans
    Hansberry, L.   A raisin in the
        sun
    Jeffers, R.   Medea
    Shakespeare, W.   Macbeth
    Shaw, G.   Devil's disciple
    Vidal, G.   Visit to a small planet

KING, VERNON RUPERT.   See
    TOD   Today's literature...

KINH   King, Woodie, and Milner,
    Ron, comps.   Black drama
    anthology.   New York, Colum-
    bia University Press, 1971.
    671p
    Branch, W.   A medal for Willie
    Bullins, E.   The corner
    Caldwell, B.   All white caste
    Charles, M.   Black cycle
    Dean, P.   The owl killer
    DeAnda, P.   Ladies in waiting
    Elder, L.   Charades on East
        Fourth Street
    Gordon, C.   The breakout
    Greaves, D.   The marriage
    Hill, E.   Strictly matrimony
    Hughes, L.   Mother and child
    Jackson, E.   Toe jam
    Jones, L.   Bloodrites
    Jones, L.   Junkies are full of
        (SHHH...)
    Mackey, W.   Requiem for
        Brother X
    Mason, C.   Gabriel
    Milner, R.   Who's got his own
    Mitchell, L.   Star of the morning

Pitcher, O.   The one
Shepp, A.   Junebug graduates
    tonight
Walker, J.   Ododo
Ward, D.   Brotherhood
Zuber, R.   Three X love

KINN   Kinney, Arthur Frederick,
    and others, eds.   Symposium
    on love.   Boston, Houghton,
    Mifflin, 1970.   268p
    Abraham and Isaac
    Molière, J.   Tartuffe
    Pirandello, L.   Six characters
        in search of an author
    Shakespeare, W.   The tragedy
        of King Lear
    Sophocles.   Oedipus the king
    Zembō, M.   Early snow

KNIC   Knickerbocker, Kenneth L.,
    and Reninger, H.   Willard,
    eds...Interpreting literature.
    New York, Henry Holt
    [c1955]   850p
    Chekhov, A.   The boor
    Connelly, M.   The green pastures
    Ibsen, H.   A doll's house
    O'Neill, E.   Ile
    Rostand, E.   Cyrano de Bergerac
    Shaw, G.   Candida
    Williams, T.   The glass menagerie

KNID   Knickerbocker, Kenneth L.
    and Reninger, H.   Willard, eds.
    Interpreting literature, Revised
    edition...New York, Holt, Rine-
    hart and Winston [c1960]   832p
    Chekhov, A.   The boor
    Connelly, M.   The green pastures
    Ibsen, H.   A doll's house
    O'Neill, E.   Ile
    Frost, R.   A masque of reason
    Shakespeare, W.   The tragedy of
        Macbeth
    Shaw, G.   Candida
    Sophocles.   Antigone
    Williams, T.   The glass menagerie

KNIE   Knickerbocker, Kenneth L.,
    and Reninger, H.   Willard.
    Interpreting literature...3rd
    ed., New York, Holt, Rinehart
    and Winston [1969]   908p
    Besier, R.   The Barretts of Wim-
        pole Street
    Chekhov, A.   The boor

Connelly, M. The green pastures
Ibsen, H. An enemy of the
people
Molière, J. The physician in spite
of himself
O'Neill, E. "Ile"
Shakespeare, W. The tragedy of
Macbeth
Shaw, G. Arms and the man
Sophocles. Antigone

KNIG Knickerbocker, Kenneth L.,
and Reninger, H. Willard, eds.
Interpreting literature: pre-
liminaries to literary judgment.
5th ed. New York, Holt,
1974. 909p
Brecht, B. The Caucasian chalk
circle
Chekhov, A. The boor
Duerrenmatt, F. The visit
Frisch, M. Biedermann and the
firebugs
Ibsen, H. An enemy of the people
Molière, J. The physician in spite
of himself
O'Neill, E. Ile
Shakespeare, W. The tragedy of
Othello
Shaw, G. Arms and the man
Sophocles. Antigone
Williams, T. The glass menagerie

KNIH Knickerbocker, Kenneth L.,
and Reninger, H. Willard, eds.
Interpreting literature...6th ed.
New York, Holt, 1978. 852p
Camus, A. Caligula
Duerrenmatt, F. The visit
Ibsen, H. Ghosts
Molière, J. The physician in
spite of himself
O'Neill, E. Ile
Shakespeare, W. The tragedy of
Hamlet, Prince of Denmark
Simon, N. The sunshine boys
Sophocles. Antigone
Strindberg, A. Miss Julie
Synge, J. The playboy of the
western world

KNO Knott, John Ray, and
Reaske, Christopher Russell,
eds. Mirrors; an introduction
to literature. San Francisco,
Canfield Press, 1972. 508p
Bergman, I. The seventh seal

Frisch, M. Biedermann and the
firebugs
Ibsen, H. Hedda Gabler
Jones, L. Dutchman
Sophocles. Oedipus rex

KNOJ Knott, John Ray, and Reaske,
Christopher Russell, eds.
Mirrors; an introduction to
literature. San Francisco,
Canfield Press [1975] 542p
Bergman, I. The seventh seal
Ibsen, H. Hedda Gabler
Jones, L. Dutchman
Shakespeare, W. King Lear
Sophocles. Oedipus rex

KNOW Knowland, A. S., ed. Six
Caroline plays...London,
Oxford University Press, 1962.
553p
Brome, R. The antipodes
Brome, R. The mad couple
well matched
D'Avenant, W. The wits
Killigrew, T. The parson's
wedding
Shirley, J. The lady of pleasure
Shirley, J. The wedding

KOH Kohut, George Alexander, ed.
A Hebrew anthology...Cincin-
nati, Bacharach, 1913. 2v
Byron, G. Cain 2
Byron, G. Heaven and earth 2
Cayzer, C. David and Bathshua
2
Davidson, R. Elijah 2
Ewing, T. Jonathan 2
Francis, A. The song of songs
which is Solomon's 2
Leavitt, J. The Jewish captives
2
Lessing, G. Nathan the wise 2
Milman, H. Belshazzar 2
Milman, H. The fall of Jerusalem
2
Milton, J. Samson Agonistes 2
More, H. Belshazzar 2
More, H. Daniel 2
More, H. David and Goliath 2
More, H. Moses in the bulrushes
2
Racine, J. Athaliah 2
Rives, A. Herod and Mariamne 2

KON Konick, Marcus, ed. Six

KON (cont.)
complete world plays and a
history of the drama. New
York, Globe [c1963] 701p
Chekhov, A. The cherry orchard
Everyman
Ibsen, H. An enemy of the
people
Rostand, E. Cyrano de Bergerac
Shaw, G. Caesar and Cleopatra
Sophocles. Antigone

KOZ Kozlenko, William, ed. The
best short plays of the social
theatre...New York, Random
house [c1939] 456p
Auden, W., and Isherwood, C.
The dog beneath the skin
Bengal, B. Plant in the sun
Blitzstein, M. The cradle will
rock
Green, P. Hymn to the rising
sun
Kozlenko, W. This earth is ours
Maltz, A. Private Hicks
Odets, C. Waiting for Lefty
Shaw, I. Bury the dead
Sifton, C., and Sifton, P.
Give all thy terrors to the
wind
Wesley, J. Running dogs

KREYMBORG, ALFRED. See also
AME American caravan...

KRE Kreymborg, Alfred, ed.
Poetic drama...New York,
Modern age [c1941] 855p
Abraham, Melchisedec, and
Isaac
Adam
Aeschylus. Agamemnon
Aristophanes. The Acharnians
Auden, W., and Isherwood, C.
The dog beneath the skin
Bottomley, G. Gruach
The chalk circle
Corneille, P. Cinna
Euripides. Ion
Everyman
Goethe, J. Torquato Tasso
Hauptmann, G. The white saviour
Jonson, B. Volpone
Kreymborg, A. Hole in the wall
MacLeish, A. The fall of the
city
Marlowe, C. Tamburlaine the

great, pt. I
Massinger, P. A new way to pay
old debts
Millay, E. Aria da capo
Molière, J. The misanthrope
Moody, W. The death of Eve
Racine, J. Athaliah
Rostand, E. The last night of
Don Juan
Sachs, H. The wandering
scholar from Paradise
Schiller, F. The death of Wallen-
stein
Schwartz, D. Shenandoah
Seami. Nakamitsu
The second shepherds' play
Shakespeare, W. Measure for
measure
Shelley, P. The Cenci
Sophocles. Oedipus coloneus
Vega Carpio, L. de. The sheep
well
Webster, J. The white devil
Yeats, W. The king's threshold

KRONENBERGER, LOUIS. See also
BES Best plays of 1894/99-
1961/62

KRM Kronenberger, Louis, ed.
Cavalcade of comedy...New
York, Simon and Schuster
[c1953] 715p
Congreve, W. Love for love
Congreve, W. The way of the
world
Coward, N. Blithe spirit
Etherege, G. The man of mode
Goldsmith, O. She stoops to con-
quer
Jonson, B. The alchemist
Jonson, B. Volpone
Kelly, G. The show-off
Maugham, W. The circle
Mayer, E. Children of darkness
O'Casey, S. Juno and the pay-
cock
Osborn, P. Morning's at seven
Shaw, G. Androcles and the lion
Shaw, G. Pygmalion
Sheridan, R. The school for
scandal
Synge, J. The playboy of the
western world
Thurber, J., and Nugent, E.
The male animal
Vanbrugh, J. The confederacy

Van Druten, J. The voice of
the turtle
Wilde, O. The importance of
being earnest
Wycherley, W. The country wife

KRO Kronenberger, Louis, ed.
An eighteenth century miscellany...New York, Putnam,
1936. 578p
Gay, J. The beggar's opera
Sheridan, R. The school for
scandal

KRON Kronenberger, Louis, ed.
The pleasure of their company...New York, Knopf,
1946. 653p
Congreve, W. The way of the
world

KUMU Kumu Kahua plays/edited
by Dennis Carroll. Honolulu:
University of Hawaii Press,
c1983. 249p
Amano, L. Ashes
Aw, A. All brand new classical
Chinese theatre
Benton, J. Twelf nite o wateva!
Inouye, B. Reunion
Kates, C. The travels of Heikiki
Lum, D. Oranges are lucky
Morris, R. Paradise tours
Sakamoto, E. In the alley

LAB Labiche, Eugène and Gondinet,
Edmond, eds. Three French
farces. [Le plus heureux des
trois] The happiest of the
three...Harmondsworth, Middlesex, Penguin, 288p
Labiche, E., and Gondinet, E.
The happiest of the three
Feydeau, G. Get out of my hair
Sardou, V., and Najac, E. Let's
get a divorce!

LAH Lahr, John, ed. Showcase 1;
plays from Eugene O'Neill foundation. New York, Grove,
1970. 220p
Gagliano, F. Father Uxbridge
wants to marry
Guare, J. Muzeeka
Hailey, O. Who's happy now?

Horovitz, I. The Indian wants
the Bronx

LAL Lal, Paul, ed. and tr. Great
Sanscrit plays...[New York,
New Directions, 1964] 396p
Bhāsa. The dream of Vāsavan-
datta
Bhavabhūti. The later story of
Rama
Harsha. Ratnavali
Kālidāsa. Shakuntalā
Shudraka, K. The toy cart
Vishakadatta. The signet ring of
Rakshasa

LAM Lambert, Robert and Lynn,
Kenneth S., eds. The range
of literature; drama. Boston,
Houghton, Mifflin, 1969.
502p
Duberman, M. In white America
Hart, M., and Kaufman, G. You
can't take it with you
Ibsen, H. An enemy of the
people
Rostand, E. Cyrano de Bergerac
Wilder, T. Our town

LAMP Lamport, Francis John, ed.
and tr. Five German tragedies.
Harmondsworth, Middlesex,
Penguin, 1969. 503p
Goethe, J. Egmont
Grillparzer, F. Medea
Kleist, H. Penthesilea
Lessing, G. Emelia Galotti
Schiller, J. Mary Stuart

LAN Lancaster, Henry Carrington,
ed...Five French farces,
1655-1694?...Baltimore, Johns
Hopkins Press, 1937. 141p
(The Johns Hopkins studies in
Romance literatures and
languages, v29)
Boisrobert, F. L'amant ridicule
Le docteur amoureux
Donneau de Visé, J. Le gentil-
homme guespin
Raisin, J. Merlin gascon
Villiers, C. L'apoticaire devalisé

LAO Landis, Joseph C., ed. and tr.
The dybbuk, and other great
Yiddish plays. New York,
Bantam Books [1966] 356p

LAO (cont.)
Anski, S. The dybbuk
Asch, S. God of vengeance
Hirshbein, P. Green fields
Leivick, H. The golem
Pinski, D. King David and his
wives

LAOG Landis, Joseph C., ed.
and tr. The great Jewish
plays. New York, Horizon,
1972. 356p
Asch, S. God of vengeance
Halper, L. The golem
Hirshbein, P. Green fields
Pinski, D. King David and
his wives
Rappoport, S. The dybbuk

LAP Landis, Paul Nissley, ed.
Four famous Greek plays...
New York, Modern library
[1929] 285p
Aeschylus. Agamemnon
Aristophanes. The frogs
Euripides. Medea
Sophocles. Oedipus the king

LAT The late Medieval religious
play of Bodleian MSS Digby
133 and e Museo 160/edited
by Donald C. Baker, John
L. Murphy and Louis B. Hall,
Jr. - Oxford: Published for
the Early English Text Society
by the Oxford University
Press, 1982. 284p (Early
English Text Society; no.
283)
Christ's burial
Christ's resurrection
The conversion of St. Paul
(Digby)
Killing of the children
Mary Magdalen (Digby)
Wisdom

LAUGHLIN, JAMES. See
NEWD New directions in prose
and poetry...

LAUREL DRAMA SERIES. See
FAM Famous American plays
of the 1950's; FAMAD Famous
American plays of the 1970s;
FAMAH Famous American
plays of the 1960s; FAMAL

Famous American plays of the
1930's; HEWE Hewes, Henry,
ed. Famous American plays of
the 1940's...HOUG Houghton,
Norris, ed. Great Russian
plays...MACG Macgowan, Kenneth, ed. Famous American
plays of the 1920's...

LAUREL MASTERPIECES OF CONTI-
NENTAL DRAMA, v1-3. See
HOUE, HOUK, NOUP Hough-
ton, Norris, ed.

LAV Laverty, Carroll D., and
others, comps. The unity of
English...New York, Harper,
1971. 556p
Hansberry, L. A raisin in the
sun
Saroyan, W. The time of your
life
Williams, T. The glass menagerie

LAW Law, Frederick Houk, ed.
Modern plays, short and long
...New York, Century, 1924.
429p
Archer, W. The green goddess
Church, V. What men live by
Corneau, P. Masks
Dean, A. Just neighborly
Gilbert, W. Iolanthe
Mackay, C. Benjamin Franklin
journeyman
MacMillan, D. Off Nags head
Macmillan, M. The pioneers
Mick, H. The maid who wouldn't
be proper
Rip van Winkle
Takeda, I. Bushido

LAWR Lawrence, Robert Gilford,
ed. Early seventeenth cen-
tury drama...New York,
Dutton [c1963] 390p
Dekker, T. The shoemaker's
holiday; or, The gentle craft
Heywood, T. A woman killed
with kindness
Marston, J., and Webster, J.
The malcontent
Massinger, P. A new way to pay
old debts
Middleton, T., and Rowley, W.
The changeling

LAWS Lawrence, Robert Gilford, ed.
Jacobean and Caroline comedies. London, Dent, 1973.
241p
Brome, R. A jovial crew
Ford, J., and Rowley, W. The
witch of Edmonton
Middleton, T. A trick to catch
the old one

LAWT Lawrence, Robert Gilford, ed.
Jacobean and Caroline trage-
dies. London, Dent, 1975.
265p
Ford, J. Perkin Warbeck
Middleton, T. Women beware
women
Shirley, J. The cardinal

LEG Le Gallienne, Eva, ed. Eva
Le Gallienne's Civic repertory
plays...New York, Norton
[c1928] 327p
Chekhov, A. Three sisters
Goldoni, C. La locandiera
Ibsen, H. Hedda Gabler
Wied, G. 2 x 2 = 5

LEIS Leishman, J. B., ed. The
three Parnassus plays (1598-
1601)...London, Ivor
Nicholson & Watson, 1949.
398p
The first part of the return
from Parnassus
The pilgrimage to Parnassus
The second part of the return
from Parnassus

LEV Leverton, Garrett Hasty, ed.
Plays for the college theater...
New York, French, 1932.
629p
Ames, W. A kiss in Xanadu
Atlas, L. "L"
Barry, P. Hotel Universe
Boucicault, D. Belle Lamar
Britton, K., and Hargrave, R.
Houseparty
Buckingham, G. The rehearsal
Elser, F. Low bridge
Everyman
France, A. The man who married
a dumb wife
Gammer Gurton's needle
Green, P. The Lord's will
Ibsen, H. The wild duck

Kaufman, G. The butter and egg
man
Kreymborg, A. Lima beans
Levy, B. Springtime for Henry
Martínez Sierra, G. The two
shepherds
Molière, J. The doctor in spite
of himself
Molnár, F. Liliom
O'Neill, E. The moon of the
Caribbees
Riggs, L. Green grow the lilacs
Rostand, E. Cyrano de Bergerac
Sardou, V. Patrie!
Scala, F. The portrait
Schnitzler, A. The green cocka-
too
Shay, F. A Christmas carol
Strong, A. The drums of Oude
Vildrac, C. Michel Auclair
The York nativity

LEVE Leverton, Garrett Hasty, ed.
Plays for the college theater...
New York, French, 1934. 601p
Ames, W. A kiss in Xanadu
Atlas, L. "L"
Barry, P. Hotel Universe
Boucicault, D. Belle Lamar
Britton, K., and Hargrave R.
Houseparty
Buckingham, G. The rehearsal
Everyman
France, A. The man who married
a dumb wife
Gammer Gurton's needle
Green, P. The Lord's will
Ibsen, H. The wild duck
Kaufman, G. The butter and egg
man
Kreymborg, A. Lima beans
Levy, B. Springtime for Henry
Martínez Sierra, G. The two
shepherds
Molière, J. The doctor in spite of
himself
Molnár, F. Liliom
O'Neill, E. The moon of the
Caribbees
Riggs, L. Green grow the lilacs
Rostand, E. Cyrano de Bergerac
Sardou, V. Patrie!
Scala, F. The portrait
Schnitzler, A. The green cocka-
too
Shay, F. A Christmas carol
Strong, A. The drums of Oude

LEVE (cont.)
  Vildrac, C. Michel Auclair
  The York nativity

LEVG Levin, David, and Gross,
  Theodore L., comps. America
  in literature. New York,
  Wiley [c1978] 2v
  Albee, E. The American dream
  O'Neill, E. The hairy ape

LEVI Levin, Richard Louis, ed.
  Tragedy; Plays, theory,
  criticism...New York, Harcourt,
  Brace & World [c1960] 217p
  Ibsen, H. Ghosts
  O'Neill, E. The hairy ape
  Seneca, L. Oedipus
  Shakespeare, W. Othello
  Sophocles. Oedipus rex

LEVJ Levin, Richard Louis, ed.
  Tragedy: plays, theory and
  criticism...Alternate ed...New
  York, Harcourt Brace and
  World [1965] 233p
  Eliot, T. Murder in the cathedral
  Ibsen, H. The wild duck
  Shakespeare, W. Coriolanus
  Sophocles. Antigone

LEWI Lewisohn, Ludwig, ed. Among
  the nations...New York, Farrar. Strauss [c1948] 270p
  Galsworthy, J. Loyalties

LIBRARY OF BEST AMERICAN
  PLAYS. See
  GARW, GARZ, GAS, GASB
  Gassner, John, ed...

LIBR Library of universal literature...New York, Alden bros.
  [c1906] [701]p
  Addison, J. Cato

LIBRARY OF WORLD DRAMA. See
  FLOS Flores, Angel, ed.
  Spanish drama...
  GARZB Gassner, John, ed.
  Medieval and Tudor drama...
  GARZE Gassner, John, ed.
  19th cent. Russian drama...
  GARZJ Gassner, John, ed.
  20th cent. Russian drama...
  MACD MacAndrew, Andrew
  Robert, tr. 19th century

Russian drama...
MACE MacAndrew, Andrew
  Robert, tr. 20th century
  Russian drama

LID Lid, Richard Wald and Bernd,
  Daniel, comps. Plays, classic
  and contemporary. Philadel-
  phia, Lippincott, [1967] 623p
  Chekhov, A. The cherry orchard
  Etherege, G. The man of mode;
  or, Sir Fopling Flutter
  Ibsen, H. Little Eyolf
  Ionesco, E. Maid to marry
  Molière, J. Don Juan
  Shakespeare, W. The tragedy of
  Antony and Cleopatra
  Shaw, G. The doctor's dilemma
  Sophocles. Oedipus rex

LIDE Lieberman, Samuel and Miller,
  Frank Justus, eds. and trs.
  Roman drama...New York,
  Bantam Books [1964] 376p
  Plautus, T. Menaechmi twins
  Plautus, T. Prisoners of war
  Plautus, T. The rope
  Seneca, L. Medea
  Seneca, L. Oedipus
  Seneca, L. Phaedra
  Terence, P. Adelphi
  Terence, P. Phormio
  Terence, P. The woman of Andros

LIE Lieder, Paul Robert; Lovett,
  Robert Morss and Root, Robert
  Kilburn, eds. British drama...
  Boston, Houghton Mifflin
  [c1929] 374p
  Beaumont, F., and Fletcher, J.
  Philaster; or, Love lies a-
  bleeding
  The Brome Abraham and Isaac
  Congreve, W. The way of the
  world
  Dryden, J. All for love; or, The
  world well lost
  Everyman
  Jonson, B. The alchemist
  Marlowe, C. The tragical history
  of Dr. Faustus
  The second shepherds' play
  Sheridan, R. The school for
  scandal
  Wilde, O. Lady Windermere's fan

LIED Lider, Paul Robert; Lovett,

Robert Morss and Root,
Robert Kilburn, eds. British
prose and poetry. Revised
ed. Boston, Houghton Mifflin
[c1938] 2v
Dryden, J. All for love 1
Jonson, B. Volpone 1
Marlowe, C. Dr. Faustus 1
Second shepherds' play 1
Sheridan, R. The school for
scandal 1
Synge, J. The playboy of the
western world 2
Wilde, O. Lady Windermere's
fan 2

LIEE Lieder, Paul Robert; Lovett,
Robert Morss and Root,
Robert Kilburn, eds. British
poetry and prose. Third
edition...Boston, Houghton
Mifflin [c1950] 2v
Dryden, J. All for love 1
Jonson, B. Alchemist 1
Marlowe, C. Dr. Faustus 1
The second shepherds' play 1
Sheridan, R. The school for
scandal 1
Synge, J. Playboy of the western
world 2
Wilde, O. Lady Windermere's fan
2

LIEF Lief, Leonard, and Light,
James Forest, [eds.]. The
modern age; literature. 2d ed.
New York, Holt, 1972. 744p
Feiffer, J. Little murders
Miller, A. A memory of two
Mondays
O'Neill, E. Desire under the
elms
Shaw, G. Major Barbara
Wilder, T. The skin of our teeth
Williams, T. Suddenly last sum-
mer

LIEG Lief, Leonard, and Light,
James Forest, comps. The
modern age: literature. 3d
ed. New York, Holt, 1976.
Feiffer, J. Little murders
O'Neill, E. Desire under the
elms
Shaw, G. Major Barbara
Wilder, T. The skin of our teeth
Williams, T. The glass menagerie

LIFS Lifson, David S., ed. and tr.
Epic and folk plays of the
Yiddish theatre. Rutherford,
N.J., Fairleigh Dickinson
University Press, 1975. 224p
Axenfeld, I., and Reznik, L.
Recruits; or, That's how it was
Hirshbein, P. Farvorfen vinkel
Kobrin, L. Yankel Boyla
Leivick, H. Hirsh Lekert
Sloves, C. Haman's downfall

LIND Lind, Levi Robert, ed. Ten
Greek plays in contemporary
translations...Boston, Houghton
Mifflin [c1957] 419p
Aeschylus. Agamemnon
Aeschylus. Prometheus bound
Aristophanes. Lysistrata
Euripides. Alcestis
Euripides. Andromache
Euripides. Bacchae
Euripides. Suppliants
Sophocles. Antigone
Sophocles. Oedipus rex
Sophocles. Philoctetes

LITC Literature; a college anthology
ed. by Patrick W. Shaw.
Boston, Houghton Mifflin,
1977. 1255p
Albee, E. The American dream
Brecht, B. The Caucasian chalk
circle
Bullins, E. A son, come home
Ibsen, H. Ghosts
Molière, J. The misanthrope
O'Neill, E. Desire under the elms
Shakespeare, W. The tragedy of
Hamlet, Prince of Denmark
Shaw, B. Major Barbara
Sophocles. Oedipus rex
Williams, T. The glass menagerie

LITI Literature: an introduction to
fiction, poetry and drama [comp.
by] X. J. Kennedy. Boston,
Little, 1976. 1447p
Albee, E. The zoo story
Bullins, E. A son, come home
Chekhov, A. The cherry orchard
Fielding, H. Tom Thumb
Gregory, I. The workhouse ward
Ibsen, H. A doll's house
Kopit, A. The hero
Miller, A. Death of a salesman
O'Neill, E. The hairy ape

LITI (cont.)
    Pirandello, L. Six characters in
        search of an author
    Shakespeare, W. The tragedy of
        Hamlet, Prince of Denmark
    Shaw, G. Pygmalion
    Sophocles. Oeidipus rex

LITJ Literature: an introduction
        to fiction, poetry and drama
        [comp. by] X. J. Kennedy.
        2d ed. Boston, Little, 1979.
        1412p
    Albee, E. The zoo story
    Brecht, B. Mother Courage and
        her children
    Chekhov, A. The marriage pro-
        posal
    Gregory, I. The workhouse ward
    Ibsen, H. A doll's house
    Pinter, H. The dumb waiter
    Shakespeare, W. The tragedy of
        Othello
    Shaw, G. Pygmalion
    Simon, N. Come blow your horn
    Sophocles. Oedipus rex
    Stoppard, T. The real inspector
        hound
    Williams, T. The glass menagerie

LITL Literature: fiction, poetry,
        drama [comp. by] Joseph K.
        Davis, et al. Glenview, Ill.,
        Scott, Foresman, 1977. 1157p
    Chekhov, A. The cherry orchard
    Hellman, L. The little foxes
    Ionesco, E. The gap
    O'Neill, E. The hairy ape
    Shakespeare, W. Othello
    Sheridan, R. The rivals
    Sophocles. Antigone
    Strindberg, A. Miss Julie
    Yeats, W. Purgatory

LITN Literature as experience; an
        anthology. Edited by Irving
        Howe, John Hollander, and
        David Bromwich. New York,
        Harcourt Brace Jovanovich.
        c1979. 1104p
    Hellman, L. The little foxes
    Ibsen, H. A doll house
    Molière, J. The school for wives
    Shakespeare, W. Hamlet
    Sophocles. Oedipus rex
    Strindberg, A. The stronger
    Williams, T. Cat on a hot tin roof

THE LITERATURE OF ITALY, 1265-
        1907. See
    JOH Johnson, Rossiter, ed.
        An anthology of Italian authors
        from Cavalcanti to Fogazzaro...

LITT Litto, Fredric M., ed. Plays
        from Black Africa...New York,
        Hill and Wang, 1968. 316p
    Clark, J. Song of a goat
    Henshaw, J. The jewels of the
        shrine
    Hutchinson, A. The rainkillers
    Nkosi, L. The rhythm of violence
    Ofori, H. The literary society
    Sutherland, E. Edufa

LIU Liu, Jung-en, comp. and tr.
        Six Yuan plays. Harmonds-
        worth, Middlesex, Penguin,
        1972. 285p
    Chêng, T. The soul of Ch'ien-
        nu leaves her body
    Chi, C. The orphan of Chao
    Kuan, H. The injustice done to
        Tou Ngo
    Li, H. Chang boils the sea
    Ma, C. Autumn in Han Palace
    A stratagem of interlocking rings

LOC Locke, Alain Le Roy, and
        Montgomery, Gregory, eds.
        Plays of Negro life...New
        York, Harper, 1927. 430p
    Bruce, R. Sahdji, an African
        ballet
    Culbertson, E. Rackey
    Duncan, T. The death dance
    Green, P. In Abraham's bosom
    Green, P. The no'count boy
    Green, P. White dresses
    Johnson, G. Plumes
    Matheus, J. 'Cruiter
    O'Neill, E. The dreamy kid
    O'Neill, E. The Emperor Jones
    Richardson, W. The broken banjo
    Richardson, W. The flight of the
        natives
    Rogers, J. Judge Lynch
    Spence, E. The starter
    Toomer, J. Balo
    Torrence, R. The danse Calinda
    Torrence, R. Granny Maumee
    Torrence, R. The rider of
        dreams
    White, L. The bird child
    Wilson, F. Sugar cane

LOCK Locke, Louis Glenn; Gibson,
William M., and Arms, George,
eds. Introduction to litera-
ture...New York, Rinehart
[c1948] 592p (Readings for
liberal education, v2)
Euripides. Alcestis
Marlowe, C. Doctor Faustus
O'Neill, E. The Emperor Jones
Thurber, J., and Nugent, E.
The male animal

LOCL Locke, Louis Glenn; Gibson,
William M., and Arms, George,
eds. Introduction to literature
...Revised edition. New
York, Rinehart [c1952] 749p
(Readings for liberal education,
v2)
Cocteau, J. The infernal machine
Ibsen, H. Hedda Gabler
Marlowe, C. The tragical history
of Doctor Faustus
O'Neill, E. The long voyage home
Sophocles. Oedipus the king

LOCLA Locke, Louis Glenn; Gibson,
William M., and Arms, George,
eds. Introduction to litera-
ture. Third edition...New
York, Rinehart [c1957] 864p
(Readings for liberal education,
v2)
Cocteau, J. The infernal machine
Ibsen, H. Hedda Gabler
Molière, J. The bourgeois
gentleman
O'Neill, E. The long voyage home
Shaw, G. The devil's disciple
Sophocles. Oedipus the king
Synge, J. In the shadow of the
glen

LOCLB Locke, Louis Glenn; Gibson,
William and Arms, George, eds.
Introduction to literature.
Fourth edition...New York,
Holt, Rinehart and Winston
[c1962] (Readings for liberal
education, v3)
Cocteau, J. The infernal machine
García Lorca, F. Blood wedding
Ibsen, H. Hedda Gabler
O'Neill, E. The long voyage home
Shaw, G. Candida
Sophocles. Oedipus the king

LOCM Locke, Louis Glenn; Kirby,
John P., and Porter, M. E.,
eds. Literature of western
civilization...New York, Ronald
[c1952] 2v
Aeschylus. Agamemnon 1
Aristophanes. Lysistrata 1
Euripides. Medea 1
Goethe, J. Faust, pt. I 2
Ibsen, H. Rosmersholm 2
Molière, J. The misanthrope 2
Plautus, T. Amphitryon 1
Racine, J. Phaedra 2
Shakespeare, W. Hamlet 1
Vega Carpio, L. The king the
greatest Alcalde 1
Sophocles. Oedipus the king 1

LOCR Lockert, Lacy, ed., and tr.
The chief rivals of Corneille
and Racine...Nashville,
Vanderbilt University Press,
c1956. 605p
Campistron, J. Andronicus
Corneille, T. The earl of Essex
Corneille, T. Laodice
Crebillon, P. Rhadamistus and
Zenobia
Du Ryer, P. Saul
Du Ryer, P. Scaevola
La Fosse, A. Manlius Capitolinus
Mairet, J. Sophonisba
Rotrou, J. Chosroes
Rotrou, J. Wenceshaus
Tristan l'Hermite, F. Mariamne
Voltaire, F. Zaire

LOCU Lockert, Lacy, ed. and tr.
More plays by rivals of Cor-
neille and Racine...Nashville,
Vanderbilt University Press,
1968. 694p
Boyer, C. Oropaste
Campistron, J. Tiridate
Corneille, T. Ariane
Corneille, T. Maximian
Corneille, T. Timocrate
Du Ryer, P. Esther
Hardy, A. Mariamne
La Grange-Chancel. Ino et
Mélicerte
Tristan l'Hermite, F. La mort de
Seneque
Tristan l'Hermite, F. Osman
Péchantré. Geta
Quinault, P. Astrate
Rotrou, J. Saint Genest

LOGG Loggins, Vernon, ed. Three
great French plays...Greenwich,
Connecticut, Fawcett [c1961]
256p
Corneille, P. Polyeucte
Molière, J. The hypochondriac
Racine, J. Phèdre

LOND London, Ephraim, ed. The
world of law; a treasury of
great writing about and in the
law, short stories, plays...New
York, Simon and Schuster
[1960] 2v
The farce of the worthy master 1
Mortimer, J. The dock brief 1
Rattigan, T. The Winslow boy 1

LONO London omnibus, with an in-
troduction by Carl Van Doren,
Garden City, N.Y., Doubleday,
Doran, 1932. v.p.
Coward, N. Private lives

LOO Loomis, Roger Sherman and
Clark, Donald Leman, eds.
Modern English readings...New
York, Farrar and Rinehart,
1934. 892p
Lawson, J. Success story
O'Neill, E. The moon of the
Caribbees
Wilde, O. The importance of
being earnest

LOOA Loomis, Roger Sherman, and
Clark, Donald Leman, eds.
Modern English readings. Rev.
ed...New York, Farrar and
Rinehart, 1936. 1074p
Anderson, M. Both your houses
Connelly, M. The green pastures
O'Neill, E. Beyond the horizon
Synge, J. Riders to the sea
Wilde, O. The importance of
being earnest

LOOB Loomis, Roger Sherman, and
Clark, Donald Leman, eds.
Modern English readings. 3rd
ed...New York, Farrar and
Rinehart, 1939. 1147p
Anderson, M. Both your houses
Connelly, M. The green pastures
MacLeish, A. The fall of the
city
O'Neill, E. Beyond the horizon

Synge, J. Riders to the sea

LOOC Loomis, Roger Sherman, and
Clark, Donald Leman, eds.
Modern English readings. 4th
ed...New York, Farrar and
Rinehart, 1942. 968p
Connelly, M. The green pastures
Hart, M., and Kaufman, G. You
can't take it with you
MacLeish, A. The fall of the city
O'Neill, E. Beyond the horizon
Synge, J. Riders to the sea

LOOD Loomis, Roger Sherman, and
Clark, Donald Leman, eds.
Modern English readings. Fifth
edition...New York, Rinehart
[c1946] 1062p
Connelly, M. The green pastures
Corwin, N. Good heavens
Hart, M., and Kaufman, G. You
can't take it with you
MacLeish, A. The fall of the city
O'Neill, E. Beyond the horizon
Synge, J. Riders to the sea

LOOE Loomis, Roger Sherman, and
Clark, Donald Leman, eds.
Modern English readings. Sixth
edition...New York, Rinehart
[c1950] 1061p
Connelly, M. The green pastures
Hart, M., and Kaufman, G. You
can't take it with you
MacLeish, A. The fall of the city
O'Neill, E. Beyond the horizon
Synge, J. Riders to the sea

LOOF Loomis, Roger Sherman; Clark,
Donald Leman, and Middendorf,
John Harlan, eds. Modern
English readings. Seventh
edition...New York, Rinehart
[c1956] 1097p
Hart, M., and Kaufman, G. You
can't take it with you
O'Neill, E. Beyond the horizon
Shaw, G. Arms and the man
Synge, J. Riders to the sea

LOOM Loomis, Roger Sherman and
Wells, Henry Willis, eds. Representative medieval and Tudor
plays, translated and modernized...New York, Sheed &
Ward, 1942. 301p

The annunciation
Heywood, J. John, Tyb, and
Sir John
Heywood, J. The pardoner and
the friar
Hilarius. The miracle of Saint
Nicholas and the image
La Vigne, A. The miracle of
the blind man and the cripple
The miracle of Saint Nicholas and
the school boys
The miracle of Saint Nicholas and
the virgins
The mystery of the redemption
The second shepherds' play
The summoning of Everyman

LOR Lovell, Ernest James, and
Pratt, Willis W., eds. Modern
drama: An anthology of nine
plays...Boston, Ginn [c1963]
425p
Anderson, M. The wingless vic-
tory
Duncan, R. The death of Satan
Euripides. Medea
Giraudeoux, J. Electra
Ibsen, H. Hedda Gabler
Maugham, W. The constant wife
Miller, A. The crucible
O'Neill, E. A moon for the mis-
begotten
Shaw, G. Caesar and Cleopatra

LOV Lovett, Robert Morss, and
Jones, Howard Mumford, eds.
The college reader...Boston,
Houghton Mifflin [c1936]
1099p
Archer, W. The green goddess
Sherriff, R. Journey's end

LOVR Lovrien, Marian; Potell,
Herbert and Bostwich, Pru-
dence, eds. Adventures in
living...New York, Harcourt,
Brace, 1955. 626p (Adven-
tures in literature series)
Corwin, N. Ann Rutledge
Duffield, B. The lottery
Law, W. Indomitable blacksmith
Lindsay, H., and Crouse, R.
Life with father
Martens, A. Blue beads
Richmond, S. Career for Ralph

LOW Lowe, Orton, ed. Our land

and its literature...New York,
Harper, 1936. 666p
Vollmer, L. Sun-up

LUCA Lucas, Frank Laurence, ed.
and tr. Greek drama for
everyman...London, J. M.
Dent [1954] 454p
Aeschylus. Agamemnon
Aeschylus. Prometheus bound
Aristophanes. The clouds
Euripides. The bacchae
Euripides. Hippolytus
Sophocles. Antigone
Sophocles. Oedipus the king

LUCAB Lucas, Frank Laurence,
ed. and tr. Greek drama for
the common reader; reissued
with corrections. London,
Chatto, 1967. 459p
Aeschylus. Agamemnon
Aeschylus. Prometheus bound
Aristophanes. The clouds
Euripides. The bacchae
Euripides. Hippolytus
Sophocles. Antigone
Sophocles. Oedipus the king

LUCAF Lucas, Frank Laurence, ed.
and tr. Greek tragedy and
comedy. New York, Viking,
1968. 454p
Aeschylus. Agamemnon
Aeschylus. Prometheus bound
Aristophanes. The clouds
Euripides. The bacchae
Euripides. Hippolytus
Sophocles. Antigone
Sophocles. Oedipus the king

LUCAS, HARRIET MARCELLA. See
PROD Prose and poetry for
appreciation...

LUST Lustig, Theodore H., tr.
Classical German drama...With
an introduction by Victor
Lange...New York, Bantam
Books [c1963] 466p
Büchner, G. Danton's death
Goethe, J. Egmont
Kleist, H. The prince of Homburg
Lessing, G. Nathan the wise
Schiller, J. Mary Stuart

LYMAN, WILLIAM WHITTINGHAM. See

LYMAN (cont.)
TOD Today's literature...

LYK Lyons, Eugene, ed...Six
Soviet plays...Boston,
Houghton Mifflin, 1934.
[469]p
Afinogenyev, A. Fear
Bulgakov, M. Days of the Tur-
bins
Glebov, A. Inga
Katayev, V. Squaring the circle
Krishon, V. Bread
Pogodin, N. Tempo

LYO Lyons, John Coriden and
Searles, Colbert, eds.
Eight French classic plays...
New York, Holt [c1932] 609p
Corneille, P. Le cid
Corneille, P. Le menteur
Corneille, P. Polyeucte
Molière, J. Le misanthrope
Molière, J. Les précieuses ridi-
cules
Molière, J. Le Tartuffe; ou
L'imposteur
Racine, J. Andromaque
Racine, J. Phèdre

MAB MacAndrew, Andrew Robert,
tr. 19th century Russian
drama...New York, Bantam
Books [1963] 342p (The
library of world drama)
Gogol, N. The inspector general
Ostrovsky, A. The thunderstorm
Pushkin, A. The stone guest
Tolstoy, L. The power of dark-
ness
Turgenev, I. A month in the
country

MABA MacAndrew, Andrew Robert,
tr. 20th century Russian
drama. New York, Bantam
Books [1963] 376p (The
library of world drama)
Andreyev, L. He who gets
slapped
Chekhov, A. The three sisters
Gorky, M. The lower depths
Mayakóvsky, V. The bathhouse
Olesha, Y. A list of assets

MABC McAvoy, William C., ed.
Dramatic tragedy. New York,
Webster Division, McGraw-Hill,
1971. 390p
Everyman
Ibsen, H. Ghosts
Marlowe, C. The tragical
history of Doctor Faustus
Miller, A. All my sons
Shakespeare, W. The tragedy
of Hamlet, Prince of Denmark
Sophocles. Oedipus rex
Williams, T. The glass menagerie

MAC McCallum, James Dow, ed.
The college omnibus...New
York, Harcourt, Brace, 1933.
832p
O'Neill, E. The Emperor Jones
Synge, J. Riders to the sea

MACB McCallum, James Dow, ed.
The college omnibus...New
York, Harcourt, Brace [c1934]
982p
Galsworthy, J. Strife
O'Neill, E. The Emperor Jones
Synge, J. Riders to the sea

MACC McCallum, James Dow, ed.
The 1936 college omnibus...in
collaboration with Marston
Balch, Percy Marks...[and
others]. New York, Harcourt,
Brace [c1936] 1193p
Galsworthy, J. Strife
O'Neill, E. The Emperor Jones
Rostand, E. Cyrano de Bergerac

MACE McCallum, James Dow, ed.
The revised college omnibus...
in collaboration with Marston
Balch, Ralph P. Boas, Percy
Marks [and others]. New
York, Harcourt, Brace, 1939.
1258p
Galsworthy, J. Strife
MacLeish, A. Air raid
O'Neill, E. The Emperor Jones
Rostand, E. Cyrano de Bergerac

MACF McCallum, James Dow, ed.
The college omnibus. 6th edi-
tion...in collaboration with
Marston Balch, Ralph P. Boas,
Percy Marks, Benfield Pressey,

Louis Untermeyer. New
York, Harcourt, Brace [c1947]
1288p
Galsworthy, J. Strife
Nichols, R., and Browne, M.
Wings over Europe
O'Neill, E. The Emperor Jones
Rostand, E. Cyrano de Bergerac

McCALLUM, JAMES DOW. See also
HAP Harbrace omnibus...

MACL MacClelland, George Williams,
and Baugh, Albert Croll, eds.
Century types of English
literature chronologically
arranged...New York, Century,
1925. 1144p
Dekker, T. The shoemaker's
holiday
Dryden, J. All for love
Sheridan, R. The school for
scandal
Wilde, O. Lady Windermere's fan

MACN McClintock, Marshall, ed.
The Nobel prize treasury...
Garden City, N.Y., Doubleday,
1948. 612p
Benavente, J. His widow's hus-
band
Bjørnson, B. Between the battles
Echegaray, J. The street singer
Hauptmann, G. The sunken bell
Maeterlinck, M. Interior
O'Neill, E. Desire under the elms
Pirandello, L. Our lord of the
ships
Yeats, W. The land of heart's
desire

McCORKLE, J. N. See
HAP Harbrace omnibus...

MACU MacCurdy, Raymond R., ed.
Spanish drama of the Golden
Age: twelve plays. New York,
Irvington, 1979. 634p
Calderón de la Barca, P. El gran
teatro del mundo
Calderón de la Barca, P. El
médico y su honra
Castro y Bellvís, G. Las moce-
dades del Cid
Cervantes, M. Entremés del
retablo de las maravillas
Mira de Amescua, A. La adversa

fortuna de don Alvaro de Luna
Moreto y Cabaña, A. El desdén
con el desdén
Rojas Zorilla, F. Entre bobos
anda el juego
Ruiz de Alarcón, J. El examen
de los maridos
Téllez, G. El burlador de
Sevilla
Téllez, G. El condenado por
desconfiado
Vega [Carpio], L. El caballero
de Olmedo
Velez de Guevara, L. Reinar
después de morir

MAD MacDermott, John Francis, ed.
Modern plays...New York,
Harcourt, Brace [c1932]
427p
Čapek, K. R.U.R.
Howard, S. They knew what they
wanted
Hughes, H. Hell bent fer heaven
Ibsen, H. A doll's house
Maugham, W. The circle
Milne, A. Mr. Pim passes by
O'Neill, E. The Emperor Jones

MADB MacDonald, J. W. and Saxton,
J. C. W., comps. Four
stages...New York, St. Martin's
Press [1967, c1966] 398p
Ibsen, H. Pillars of society
Marlowe, C. Doctor Faustus
Miller, A. All my sons
Sophocles. Oedipus rex

MADG McDowell, Tremaine, ed.
America in literature...New
York, Crofts, 1944. 540p
Connelly, M. The green pastures
Wilder, T. Our town

MADI McDowell, Tremaine, ed.
The romantic triumph; American literature from 1830 to
1860...New York, Macmillan,
1933. 744p (American literature: a period anthology;
Oscar Cargill, general editor.
v2)
Boker, G. Francesca da Rimini

MAE McFarland, Philip; Hynes,
Samuel, Benson, Larry D. and
Peckham, Mase, eds. Forms

MAE (cont.)
in English literature. Boston,
Houghton Mifflin, 1972.
Everyman
Pinter, H. A night out
Shakespeare, W. Macbeth
Shaw, G. Pygmalion

MAEC McFarland, Philip, Kirschner,
Allen and Peckham, Morse,
eds. Perceptions in literature.
Boston, Houghton Mifflin
[c1972] 783p
Shakespeare, W. Julius Caesar
Williams, T. The glass menagerie

MAF Macgowan, Kenneth, ed.
Famous American plays of
the 1920's...[New York, Dell,
c1959] 511p (Laurel drama
series)
Anderson, M., and Stallings, L.
What price glory?
Barry, P. Holiday
Heyward, D., and Heyward, D.
Porgy
Howard, S. They knew what
they wanted
O'Neill, E. The moon of the
Caribbees
Rice, E. Street scene

McGRAW, H. WARD. See
PROB Prose and poetry for
appreciation...PROF, PROG,
PROH Prose and poetry of
America...PROM, PRON
Prose and poetry of England...

MAH Machiz, Herbert, ed. Artists'
theatre: four plays...New
York, Grove [c1960] 224p
Abel, L. Absalom
Ashbery, J. The heroes
Merrill, J. The bait
O'Hara, F. Try! Try!

MAJ Major plays of the Canadian
theatre, 1934-1984/selected and
edited by Richard Perkyns;
foreword by Robertson Davies.
Toronto, Ontario, Irwin Publishing, 1984. 742p
Bolt, C. Buffalo jump
Cook, M. The head, guts and
soundbone dance
Coulter, J. Riel

Davies, R. At my heart's core
French, D. Of the fields, lately
Gélinas, G. Bousille and the just
Herbert, J. Fortune and men's
eyes
Pollock, S. Generations
Ravel, A. Dispossessed
Reaney, J. The Canadian brothers;
or The prophecy fulfilled
Ringwood, G. Drum song
Voaden, H. Hill-land

MAK McIlwraith, Archibald Kennedy,
ed. Five Elizabethan come-
dies...London, Oxford Univer-
sity Press [1934] 308p (The
world's classics)
Dekker, T. The shoemaker's
holiday
Greene, R. Friar Bacon and
Friar Bungay
Lyle, J. Campaspe
The merry devil of Edmonton
Peele, G. The old wives' tale

MAKG McIlwraith, Archibald Ken-
nedy, ed. Five Elizabethan
tragedies...London, Oxford
University Press [1938]
399p (The world's classics)
Arden of Feversham
Heywood, T. A woman killed with
kindness
Kyd, T. The Spanish tragedy
Norton, T., and Sackville, T.
Gorboduc
Seneca, L. Thyestes

MAKJ McIlwraith, Archibald Kennedy,
ed. Five Stuart tragedies...
London, Oxford University
Press [1953] 497p (The
world's classics)
Beaumont, F., and Fletcher, J.
The maid's tragedy
Chapman, G. Bussy D'Ambois
Ford, J. 'Tis a pity she's a whore
Massinger, P. The Roman actor
Webster, J. The Duchess of Malfi

MAL Mack, Maynard, ed...The
Augustans...New York,
Prentice-Hall, 1950. 343p
(English masterpieces, v5)
Gay, J. The beggar's opera

MALC Mack, Maynard [and others],

eds. The continental edition
of world masterpieces...New
York, W. W. Norton [c1962]
1971p
Aeschylus. Agamemnon
Euripides. Medea
Goethe, J. Faust, pts. I & 2
Ibsen, H. The wild duck
Molière, J. The bourgeois
gentleman
Racine, J. Phaedra
Sophocles. King Oedipus

MALG Mack, Maynard [and others],
eds. World masterpieces...
New York, W. W. Norton
[c1956] 2v
Aeschylus. Agamemnon 1
Euripides. Medea 1
Goethe, J. Faust, pts. 1 & 2
Ibsen, H. The wild duck 2
Molière, J. The bourgeois
gentleman 2
Racine, J. Phaedra 2
Shakespeare, W. Hamlet,
Prince of Denmark 1
Sophocles. King Oedipus 1
Synge, J. The playboy of the
western world 2

MALI Mack, Maynard [and others]
eds. World masterpieces...
Rev. ed. New York, Norton
[1965] 2v
Aeschylus. Agamemnon 1
Aeschylus. Prometheus bound
1
Aristophanes. Lysistrata 1
Brecht, B. The Caucasian chalk
circle 2
Calderón de la Barca, P. Life
is a dream 1
Eliot, T. Murder in the cathe-
dral 2
Euripides. Medea 1
Euripides. Trojan women 1
Everyman 1
Goethe, J. Faust (abridged ed.)
2
Ibsen, H. The wild duck 2
Marlowe, C. The tragical history
of the life and death of Doc-
tor Faustus 1
Molière, J. Tartuffe; or, The
imposter 2
Molina, T. The trickster of
Seville and his guest of

stone 1
Racine, J. Phaedra 2
Sartre, J. No exit 2
Shakespeare, W. Hamlet 1
Sophocles. Antigone 1
Sophocles. Oedipus at Colonus 1
Sophocles. Oedipus the king 1

MALN Mack, Maynard, and others,
eds. World masterpieces. 3d
ed. New York, Norton, 1973.
2v
Aeschylus. Agamemnon 1
Aristophanes. Lysistrata 1
Calderón de la Barca, P. Life is
a dream 1
Chekhov, A. The cherry orchard
2
Euripides. Medea 1
Goethe, J. Faust, Part 1 2
Ibsen, H. The wild duck 2
Marlowe, C. The tragical history
of the life and death of Doctor
Faustus 1
Molière, J. Tartuffe 2
Pirandello, L. Henry IV 2
Racine, J. Phaedra 2
Sartre, J. No exit 2
Shakespeare, W. Hamlet, Prince
of Denmark 1
Shaw, G. Saint Joan 2
Sophocles. Antigone 1
Sophocles. Oedipus tyrannus 1

MALR MacKendrick, Paul, and Howe,
Herbert M., eds. Classics in
translation. Madison, Wiscon-
sin. The University of Wis-
consin Press, 1952. 2v
Aeschylus. Agamemnon 1
Aristophanes. Frogs 1
Euripides. Medea 1
Plautus. The haunted house 2
Seneca. Medea 2
Sophocles. Antigone 1
Terence. Woman from Andros 2

MAM McLean, Hugh and Vickery,
Walter N., eds. and trs. The
year of protest, 1956: An
anthology of Soviet literary
materials...New York, Random
House [c1961] 269p
Alyoshin, S. Alone

MAMB McLeish, Kenneth, comp.
and tr. The frogs and other

MAMB (cont.)
> Greek plays. Harlow, Long-
> mans, 1970. 202p
> Aeschylus. Prometheus bound
> Aristophanes. The birds
> Aristophanes. The frogs
> Euripides. Medea

MANA McMahon, Agnes; Krauss,
> Franklin Brunell, and Carter,
> James Franklin, eds. Explora-
> tions in French literature...
> New York, Nelson, 1939. 538p
> Labiche, E. Le voyage de
> Monsieur Perrichon

MANC McMichael, George L., ed.
> Anthology of American litera-
> ture. General editor: George
> McMichael. Advisory editors:
> Frederick Crews [and others].
> New York, Macmillan, 1980.
> 2v (V. 1, Colonial through
> Romantic; V. 2, Realism to
> the Present)
> Albee, E. The zoo story 2
> Jones, L. Dutchman 2
> O'Neill, E. The hairy ape 2

MANCB McMichael, George L.,
> comp. Concise anthology of
> American literature. New
> York, Macmillan [c1974] 2007p
> (Abridged from his Anthology
> of American literature)
> Albee, E. The zoo story
> O'Neill, E. The hairy ape

MAND MacMillan, Dougald, and
> Jones, Howard Mumford, eds.
> Plays of the restoration and
> eighteenth century...New
> York, Holt, 1931. 986p
> Addison, J. Cato
> Cibber, G. Love's last shift
> Colman, G., and Garrick, D.
> The clandestine marriage
> Congreve, W. The way of the
> world
> Cumberland, R. The West Indian
> D'Avenant, W. The siege of
> Rhodes, pt. I
> Dryden, J. All for love
> Dryden, J., and Howard, R.
> The Indian queen
> Etherege, G. The man of mode
> Farquhar, G. The beaux' strata-

gem
> Gay, J. The beggar's opera
> Goldsmith, O. She stoops to con-
> quer
> Home, J. Douglas
> Kelly, H. False delicacy
> Kotzebue, A. The stranger
> Lee, N. The rival queens
> Lillo, G. The London merchant
> Otway, T. Venice preserved
> Rowe, N. The fair penitent
> Shadwell, T. The squire of
> Alsatia
> Sheridan, R. The school for
> scandal
> Steele, R. The conscious lovers
> Vanbrugh, J. The relapse
> Villiers, G., and others. The
> rehearsal

MANF MacMillan, Dougald and
> Jones, Howard Mumford, eds.
> Plays of the restoration and
> eighteenth century...New
> York, Holt [1938] 961p
> Addison, J. Cato
> Cibber, C. Love's last shift
> Colman, G., and Garrick, D.
> The clandestine marriage
> Congreve, W. The way of the
> world
> Cumberland, R. The West Indian
> D'Avenant, W. The siege of
> Rhodes, pt. I
> Dryden, J. All for love
> Dryden, J., and Howard, R.
> The Indian queen
> Etherege, G. The man of mode
> Farquhar, G. The beaux'
> stratagem
> Gay, J. The beggar's opera
> Goldsmith, O. She stoops to
> conquer
> Home, J. Douglas
> Kelly, H. False delicacy
> Kotzebue, A. The stranger
> Lee, N. The rival queens
> Lillo, G. The London merchant
> Otway, T. Venice preserved
> Rowe, N. The fair penitent
> Shadwell, T. The squire of
> Alsatia
> Sheridan, R. The school for
> scandal
> Steele, R. The conscious lovers
> Vanbrugh, J. The relapse
> Villiers, G., and others. The

rehearsal
Wycherley, W. The plaindealer

MANH McMillin, Scott, ed.
Restoration and eighteenth-
century comedy. New York,
Norton, 1973. 565p
Congreve, W. The way of the
world
Etherege, G. The man of mode
Sheridan, R. The school for
scandal
Steele, R. The conscious lovers
Wycherley, W. The country wife

MANK McNamee, Maurice B.;
Cronin, James E., and Rogers,
Joseph A., eds. Literary
types and themes. New York,
Rinehart [c1960] 705p
Anouilh, J. Antigone
Barrie, J. The twelve-pound look
Chayefsky, P. Marty
Miller, A. Death of a salesman
Williams, T. The glass menagerie

MANL McNamee, Maurice Basil [and
others], eds. Literary types
and themes. 2d ed. New
York, Rinehart and Winston,
1971. 773p
Albee, E. The American dream
Miller, A. Death of a salesman
Pirandello, L. Six characters in
search of an author
Wilder, T. Pullman car Hiawatha
Williams, T. Glass menagerie

MANM McNaughton, William, ed.
Chinese literature; an anthol-
ogy from the earliest times to
the present day. Rutland, Vt.,
Charles E. Tuttle, 1974. 836p
Kuan, H. The butterfly dream

MANN McNiff, William T., ed. The
beginnings of English literature...New York, Macmillan
[c1961] 198p
Everyman
Marlowe, C. The tragedy of
Doctor Faustus

MANP McNulty, John B., ed. Modes
of literature. Boston, Houghton
Mifflin, 1977. 630p
Shakespeare, W. Antony and

Cleopatra
Shaw, G. Arms and the man

MAP Magarshack, David, tr. The
storm, and other Russian
plays...New York, Hill and
Wang [c1960] 362p (Mermaid
dramabook)
Chekhov, A. Uncle Vanya
Gogol, N. The government inspec-
tor
Gorky, M. The lower depths
Ostrovsky, A. The storm
Tolstoy, L. The power of dark-
ness

MAR Malcolmson, Anne (Burnett),
adapter. Miracle plays; seven
medieval plays for modern
players...Boston, Houghton
Mifflin [c1956, 1959] 142p
Abraham and Isaac
Herod and the magi
The nativity
Noah's flood
Saint Nicholas and the three
scholars
The shepherds' play
Hilarius. The statue of Saint
Nicholas

MALINE, JULIAN L. See
PATM, PATP Patterns of
literature...PROI Prose
and poetry of America...

MALLON, WILFRED M. See
PROI Prose and poetry of
America...

MARG Malvern festival plays
MCMXXXIII, arranged for
production by H. K. Ayliff.
With an introduction by Hugh
Walpole and a preface by Sir
Barry Jackson. London,
Heath Cranton, 1933. 343p
The conversion of St. Paul
Dryden, J. All for love
Heywood, T. The fair maid of
the west
Jones, H. The dancing girl
Knowles, J. The love-chase
"Mr. S., master of arts." Gammer
Gurton's needle

MARK Mandel, Oscar, comp. and tr.

MARK (cont.)
Five comedies of medieval
France. New York, Dutton,
1970. 158p
The chicken pie and the chocolate
cake
Bodel, J. The play of Saint
Nicholas
Adam de la Halle. The play of
Robin and Marion
Peter Quill's shenanigans
The washtub

MARL Mandel, Oscar, ed. The
theatre of Don Juan; a collec-
tion of plays and views,
1630-1963...Lincoln, University
of Nebraska Press, c1963.
731p
Don Juan and Don Pietro; or, The
dead stone's banquet
Grabbe, C. Don Juan and Faust
Molière, J. Don Juan; or, The
libertine
Molina, T. The playboy of
Seville; or, Supper with a
statue
Moncrieff, W. Giovanni in Lon-
don; or, The libertine re-
claimed
Ponte, L. The punished libertine;
or, Don Giovanni
Rostand, F. The last night of
Don Juan
Shadwell, T. The libertine
Zorrilla y Moral, J. Don Juan
Tenorio

MANTLE, R. BURNS. See
BES Best plays of 1894/1899
...etc. See also TRE, TREA
A treasury of the theatre...

MARLI Marín, Diego, comp. Litera-
tura española; selección. In-
troducciones y notas por Diego
Marín. New York, Holt, Rinehart and Winston, 1968. 2v
(Tomo 1: Desde los orígenes
hasta el Romanticismo; Tomo 2:
Época moderna)
Benavente y Martínez, J. Los malhechores de bien 2
Buero Vallejo, A. Irene, o el
tesoro 2
Calderón de la Barca, P. La
vida es sueño 1

Cervantes, M. La cueva de
Salamanca 1
García Lorca, F. La zapatera pro-
digiosa 2
Moratín, L. El sí de las niñas 1
Valle-Inclán, R. La cabeza del
Bautista 2
Vega Carpio, L. El caballero de
Olmedo 1
Zorrilla, J. Don Juan Tenorio 1

MARNAU, FRED. See
NEWR New road...

MARO Marowitz, Charles, ed. New
American drama. Harmonds-
worth, Middlesex, Penguin,
[1966] 203p
Albee, E. The American dream
Miller, A. Incident at Vichy
Richardson, J. Gallows humour
Schisgal, M. The typists

MARR Marowitz, Charles, comp.
Open space plays. Harmonds-
worth, Middlesex, Penguin,
1974. 310p
Burgess, J., and Marowitz, C.
The Chicago conspiracy
Burns, A., and Marowitz, C.
Palach
Herbert, J. Fortune and men's
eyes
McCough, R. The puny little
life show
Marowitz, C. An Othello

MART Marriott, James William, ed.
Great modern British plays...
London, Harrap [1932] 1083p
Bennett, A., and Knoblock, E.
Milestones
Berkeley, R. The white château
Besier, R. The virgin goddess
Brighouse, H. Hobson's choice
Chapin, H. The new morality
Coward, N. The young idea
Dane, C. A bill of divorcement
Dukes, A. The man with a load
of mischief
Galsworthy, J. Strife
Gilbert, W. Pygmalion and
Galatea
Hankin, St. J. The return of the
prodigal
Jones, H. The liars
McEvoy, C. The likes of her

Maugham, W. The circle
Munro, C. At Mrs. Beam's
Pinero, A. Trelawny of the
"Wells"
Robertson, T. Caste
Sutro, A. The walls of Jericho
Vane, S. Outward bound

MAS Massey, Vincent, ed.
Canadian plays form Hart
house theatre...Toronto,
Macmillan, 1926-27. 2v
Aikins, C. The god of gods 2
Borsook, H. Three weddings of
a hunchback 1
Cooke, B. The translation of
John Snaith 1
Denison, M. Balm 1
Denison, M. Brothers in arms 1
Denison, M. The weather
breeder 1
Mackay, I. The second lie 1
Mackay, L. The freedom of Jean
Guichet 2
Osborne, M. The point of view
1
Reid, L. Trespassers 2
Scott, D. Pierre 1

MAST Masterpieces of Greek
literature...Supervising editor
John Henry Wright. Boston,
Houghton Mifflin [c1902]
456p
Aeschylus. Prometheus bound
Euripides. Alcestis
Sophocles. Antigone

MASW Batlow, Myron, comp. The
black crook, and other nine-
teenth century American
plays. New York, Dutton,
1967. 511p
Barras, C. The black crook
Boker, G. Francesca da Rimini
Boucicault, D. The octoroon; or,
Life in Louisiana
Herne, J. Margaret Fleming
Howard, B. Shenandoah
Mowatt, A. Fashion; or, Life in
New York
Rip Van Winkle

MAU Matthews, Brander, ed. The
chief European dramatists...
Boston, Houghton Mifflin
[c1916] 786p

Aeschylus. Agamemnon
Aristophanes. The frogs
Augier, E., and Sandeau, J. The
son-in-law of M. Poirier
Beaumarchais, P. The barber of
Seville
Calerón de la Barca, P. Life is
a dream
Corneille, P. The cid
Dumas, A. fils. The outer edge
of society
Euripides. Medea
Goethe, J. Goetz von Berlichingen
Goldoni, C. The mistress of the
inn
Holberg, L. Rasmus Montanus
Hugo, V. Hernani
Ibsen, H. A doll's house
Lessing, G. Minna von Barnhelm
Molière, J. Tartuffe
Plautus, T. The captives
Racine, J. Phaedra
Schiller, J. William Tell
Sophocles. Oedipus the king
Terence, P. Phormio
Vega Carpio, L. de. The star
of Seville

MATTHEWS, BRANDER. See also
GREA Great plays (French
and German)...

MAX Matthews, Brander and Lieder,
Paul Robert, eds. The chief
British dramatists excluding
Shakespeare...Boston, Hough-
ton Mifflin [c1924] 1084p
Beaumont, F., and Fletcher, J.
Philaster; or, Love lies a-
bleeding
Boucicault, D. London assurance
The Brome Abraham and Isaac
Bulwer-Lytton, E. Richelieu; or,
The conspiracy
Congreve, W. The way of the
world
Dryden, J. All for love; or, The
world well lost
Farquhar, G. The beaux' strata-
gem
Gilbert, W. Pygmalion and Galatea
Goldsmith, O. She stoops to con-
quer; or, The mistakes of a
night
Heywood, T. A woman killed with
kindness
Jones, H. The liars

MAX (cont.)
Jonson, B. Every man in his
humour
Kyd, T. The Spanish tragedy;
or, Hieronimo is mad again
Marlowe, C. The troublesome
reign and lamentable death of
Edward the second
Massinger, P. A new way to
pay old debts
Otway, T. Venice preserved; or,
A plot discovered
Pinero, A. The second Mrs.
Tanqueray
Robertson, T. Caste
The second shepherds' play
Sheridan, R. The school for
scandal
Udall, N. Ralph Roister Doister
Vanbrugh, J. The provoked
wife
Webster, J. The Duchess of
Malfi
Wilde, O. Lady Windermere's fan
Wycherley, W. The plain dealer

MELO Melodrama classics: six
plays and how to stage them
[edited by] Dorothy Mackin.
New York, Sterling, 1982.
384p
Boucicault, D. After dark; or,
Pardon-for-a-price
D'Ennery, A., and Corman, E.
The two orphans; or, In the
hands of heaven
MacKaye, S. Hazel Kirke; or,
Adrift from her father's love
The spoilers; or, There's never
a law of God or man runs north
of fifty-three
Taylor, T. The ticket-of-leave
man
Under two flags

MEN Mendenhall, John Cooper, ed.
English literature, 1650-1800...
Chicago, Lippincott [c1940]
1166p
Congreve, W. The way of the
world
Dryden, J. Aureng-zebe
Otway, T. Venice preserv'd

MERC Mercier, Vivian, and Greene,
David H., eds. 1000 years of
Irish prose. Part I. The

literary revival. New York,
Devin-Adair, 1952. 607p
O'Casey, S. The shadow of a
gunman
Synge, J. In the shadow of the
glen
Yeats, W. Cathleen ni Houlihan
Yeats, W. The resurrection

MERS Mersand, Joseph E., ed.
Three comedies of American
family life...New York,
Washington Square Press
[c1961] 314p
Kaufman, G., and Hart, M.
You can't take it with you
Lindsay, H., and Crouse, R.
Life with father
Van Druten, J. I remember
mama

MERT Mersand, Joseph, ed. Three
dramas of American individual-
ism...New York, Washington
Square Press [c1961] 266p
Anderson, M. High Tor
Lavery, E. The magnificent
Yankee
Odets, C. Golden boy

MERU Mersand, Joseph E., ed.
Three dramas of American
realism...New York, Washington Square Press [c1961]
312p
Rice, E. Street scene
Saroyan, W. The time of your
life
Sherwood, R. Idiot's delight

MERV Mersand, Joseph E., ed.
Three plays about doctors...
New York, Washington Square
Press [c1961] 294p
Howard, S., and DeKruif, P.
Yellow jack
Ibsen, H. An enemy of the people
Kingsley, S. Men in white

MERW Mersand, Joseph E., ed.
Three plays about marriage...
New York, Washington Square
Press [c1962] 298p
Barry, P. Holiday
Howard, S. They knew what they
wanted
Kelly, G. Craig's wife

MESERVE, WALTER J. See also
AMPA America's lost plays,
v21, edited by Walter J.
Meserve and William R.
Reardon

MESE Meserve, Walter J., Jr.,
and Meserve, Ruth, I., eds.
Modern drama from Communist
China. New York, New York
University Press, 1970. 368p
Chao, C.; Chang, P.; and
Chung, Y. Yesterday
Jen, T. Magic aster
Kuan, H. Snow in midsummer
Lao, S. Dragon beard ditch
Lu, H. The passer-by
The Red lantern
Sha, S.; Fu, T.; Ma, Y.; and
Li, C. Letters from the south
Sun, Y. The women's representa-
tive
Ting,Y., and Ho, C. The white-
haired girl

MESH Meserve, Walter J., Jr., and
Meserve, Ruth I., eds.
Modern literature from China.
New York, New York University
Press, 1974. 337p
Ts'ao, Y. Thunderstorm

MESS Messner, Nancy Shingler [and
others], comps. Collection:
literature for the seventies.
Lexington, Mass., Heath, 1972.
915p
Aristophanes. Lysistrata
Bermange, B. Scenes from family
life
Chekhov, A. Uncle Vanya
Ibsen, H. An enemy of the
people
Roemer, M., and Young, R.
Nothing but a man
Shakespeare, W. Othello
Williams, T. Suddenly last sum-
mer

METR Metropol: Literary almanac.
Edited by Vasily Aksyonov,
Viktor Yerofeyev, et al.
N.Y., Norton, c1982. 636p
Aksyonov, V. The four tempera-
ments: a comedy in ten
tableaux

MID Middle age, old age; short
stories, poems, plays, and
essays on aging. Edited by
Ruth Granetz Lyell. New
York, Harcourt, Brace Jo-
vanovich, 1980. 390p
Anderson, R. I never sang for
my father

MIG Mikasinovich, Branko, ed.
Five modern Yugoslav plays.
New York, Cyrco Press,
c1977. 339p
Casule, K. Darkness
Kozak, P. An affair
Lebović, D. Hallelujah
Marinković, R. Gloria
Obrenović, A. The bird

MIJ Miller, Edwin Lillie, ed. Ex-
plorations in literature...
Chicago, Lippincott [c1933-
34] 2v
Gilbert, W. The mikado 2
Shakespeare, W. Macbeth 2

MIJA Miller, Edwin Lillie, ed. Ex-
plorations in literature...Rev.
ed...Chicago, Lippincott
[c1937-38] 2v
O'Neill, E. The Emperor Jones 1
Shakespeare, W. Macbeth 2
Tompkins, F. Sham 1

MIJB Miller, James Edwin and Slate,
Bernice, comps. The dimen-
sions of literature...New York,
Random House [1967] 808p
Brecht, B. The Caucasian chalk
circle
O'Neill, E. In the zone
Shaw, G. Arms and the man
Sophocles. Oedipus rex

MIJE Miller, James Edwin [and
others], comps. Translations
from the French...Glenview,
Ill., Scott, Foresman, 1971.
402p
Anouilh, J. Antigone
Cocteau, J. The Eiffel Tower
wedding party
Duras, M. The rivers and forests
Giraudoux, J. The Apollo of Bel-
lac
Molière, J. The forced marriage

MIJY Miller, Jordan Yale, ed.
  American dramatic litera-
  ture...New York, McGraw-
  Hill, 1961. 641p
Behrman, S. Biography
Chase, M. Harvey
Haines, W. Command decision
Hellman, L. The little foxes
Heyward, D., and Heyward, D.
  Porgy
McCullers, C. The member of
  the wedding
Miller, A. The crucible
O'Neill, E. Desire under the elms
Thurber, J., and Nugent, E.
  The male animal
Williams, T. Camino real

MIK Miller, Marion Mills, ed. The
  classics, Greek & Latin...New
  York, V. Parke [c1909-10]
  15v
Aeschylus. Prometheus bound 7
Aristophanes. The clouds 7
Euripides. Medea 7
Plautus, T. Captivi 8
Plautus, T. Menaechmi 8
Plautus, T. Miles gloriosus 8
Seneca, L. The phaedra; or,
  Hippolytus 8
Sophocles. Antigone 7
Terence. Adelphi 8
Terence. Heautonimorumenos 8

MIKE Miller, Perry [and others],
  eds. Major writers of America
  ...New York, Harcourt, Brace
  & World [c1962] 2v
O'Neill, E. The iceman cometh 2

MIKL Millett, Fred Benjamin.
  Reading drama; a method of
  analysis with selections for
  study...New York, Harper
  [c1950] 252p
Barrie, J. The will
O'Neill, E. Beyond the horizon
Schnitzler, A. A farewell supper
Synge, J. Riders to the sea
Wilder, T. The long Christmas
  dinner
Yeats, W. Cathleen ni Houlihan

MIL Millett, Fred Benjamin, and
  Bentley, Gerald Eades, eds.
  The play's the thing...New
  York, Appleton-Century [c1936]

  571p
Belasco, D. The return of Peter
  Grimm
Chekhov, A. Uncle Vanya
Chester play of the deluge
Congreve, W. Love for love
Cumberland, W. The West
  Indian
Dryden, J. All for love
Euripides. Hippolytus
Gregory, I. Hyacinth Halvey
Howard, S. Ned McCobb's
  daughter
Ibsen, H. Ghosts
Maeterlinck, M. Interior
Marlowe, C. Doctor Faustus
Molière, J. The misanthrope
O'Neill, E. The hairy ape
Plautus, T. The haunted house
Racine, J. Phaedra
Rostand, E. Cyrano de Bergerac
Shakespeare, W. Antony and
  Cleopatra
Shakespeare, W. Twelfth night
Sophocles. Oedipus, king of
  Thebes
Strong, A. The drums of Oude

MIMN Minnesota showcase; four
  plays. Introduced by Michael
  Langham, with comments by
  Charles M. Nolte, et al.
  Minneapolis, University of
  Minnesota Press, 1975. 296p
  (Minnesota drama editions #9)
Ball, D. Georg Büchner's
  Woyzeck
Donahue, J. The cookie jar
Feldshuh, D. Fables here and
  then
Nolte, C. Do not pass go

MIN Minor Elizabethan drama...Lon-
  don, Dent [1913] 2v (Every-
  man's library)
Arden of Feversham 1
Greene, R. Friar Bacon and
  Friar Bungay 2
Greene, R. James the fourth 2
Kyd, T. The Spanish tragedy 1
Lyly, J. Endimion 2
Norton, T., and Sackville, T.
  (Lord Buckhurst) Gordobuc 1
Peele, G. David and Bethsabe 1
Peele, G. The old wives' tale 2
Udall, N. Ralph Roister Doister
  2

MIO Minor Elizabethan drama...
London, Dent [1939] 2v
(Everyman's library)
Arden of Feversham 1
Greene, R. Friar Bacon and
Friar Bungay 2
Greene, R. James the fourth 2
Kyd, T. The Spanish tragedy
1
Lyly, J. Endimion 2
Norton, T., and Sackville, T.
(Lord Buckhurst) Gorboduc
1
Peele, G. David and Bethsabe 1
Peele, G. The old wives' tale 2
Preston, T. Cambyses 1
Udall, N. Ralph Roister Doister
2

MIR Minor Elizabethan tragedies:
new edition with revised con-
tents; edited by T. W. Craik.
London, Dent, 1974. 285p
(Everyman's University Library
491; first published in 1910
as V. 1 of Minor Elizabethan
drama)
Arden of Feversham
Kyd, T. The Spanish tragedy
Norton, T., and Sackville, T.
Gorboduc
Preston, T. Cambises

MIT Mitchell, John D., ed. The red
pear garden: 3 great dramas
of revolutionary China. Boston, Godine, 1974. 285p
Li, S. The wild boar forest
Taking Tiger Mountain by strategy
Tien, H. The white snake

MODERN ENGLISH DRAMA. See
HARC Harvard classics, v18

MNOD Modern Nordic plays: Den-
mark. New York, Twayne,
c1974. 449p
Branner, H. Thermopylae
Olsen, E. The bookseller cannot
sleep
Rifbjerg, K. Developments
Ronild, P. Boxing for one

MNOF Modern Nordic plays: Fin-
land. New York, Twayne,
1973. 304p
Haavikko, P. The superintendent

Järner, V. Eva Maria
Manner, E. Snow in May
Meri, V. Private Jokinen's mar-
riage leave

MNOI Modern Nordic plays: Ice-
land...New York, Twayne,
c1973. 427p
Björnsson, O. Ten variations
Björnsson, O. Yolk-life
Halldórsson, E. Mink
Jakobsson, J. The seaway to
Baghdad
Laxness, H. The pigeon banquet

MNON Modern Nordic plays: Nor-
way. New York, Twayne,
1974. 431p
Borgen, J. The house
Havrevold, F. The injustice
Kielland, A. The lord and his
servants
Vesaas, T. The bleaching yard

MNOS Modern Nordic plays:
Sweden. New York, Twayne,
1973. 419p
Forssell, L. The madcap
Fridell, F. One man's bread
Görling, L. The sandwiching
Höijer, B. Isak Juntti had many
sons

MOAD Modern drama in America,
Volume I; edited by Alvin S.
Kaufman & Franklin D. Case.
New York, Washington Square
Press, 1982. 415p (Realism
from Provincetown to Broadway,
1915-1929)
Glaspell, S. Trifles
Green, P. In Abraham's bosom
Howard, S. Lucky Sam McCarver
Kelly, G. The show-off
O'Neill, E. Anna Christie

MOADE Modern Israeli drama: an
anthology. Edited by Herbert
S. Joseph. Rutherford, Fair-
leigh Dickinson University
Press, c1983. 267p
Bar-Yosef, Y. Difficult people
Chilton, N. Naïm
Horowitz, D. Cherli ka cherli
Megged, A. The first sin
Shamir, M. He walked through
the fields

MOADE (cont.)
   Sobol, Y. The night of the
      twentieth

MOD Modern plays...London, Dent
      [1937] 354p (Everyman's
      library)
   Bennett, A., and Knoblock, E.
      Milestones
   Coward, N. Hay fever
   Maugham, W. For services
      rendered
   Milne, A. The Dover road
   Sherriff, R. Journey's end

MODS Modern Scandinavian plays
      ...New York, Liveright
      [c1954] 366p
   Kielland, T. Queen Margaret of
      Norway
   Munk, K. Egelykke
   Strindberg, A. The great high-
      way
   Sveinbjörnsson, T. Bishop Jón
      Arason

MOL Mondala; literature for critical
      analysis [by] Wilfred L. Guerin
      [and others], eds. New York,
      Harper and Row, 1970. 766p
   Miller, A. A view from the bridge
   Shakespeare, W. Othello
   Sophocles. Oedipus the King

MON Montague, Gene and Henshaw,
      Marjorie, comps. The ex-
      perience of literature...Engle-
      wood Cliffs, N.J., Prentice-
      Hall [1966] 404p
   Shakespeare, W. Othello, the
      Moor of Venice
   Sheridan, R. The school for
      scandal
   Sophocles. Antigone
   Wilde, O. The importance of
      being earnest
   Williams, T. The glass menagerie

MONA Montague, Gene; Henshaw,
      Marjorie and Salerno, Nicholas
      A., comps. The experience
      of literature...2d ed. Engle-
      wood Cliffs, N.J., Prentice-
      Hall [1970] 803p
   Hansberry, L. A raisin in the
      sun
   Shakespeare, W. Hamlet

Sophocles. Antigone
Williams, T. The glass menagerie

MONR Moody, Richard, ed. Dramas
      from the American theatre,
      1762-1909. Cleveland, World
      [c1966] 873p (New World
      literature series, v1)
   Aiken, G. Uncle Tom's cabin
   Bird, R. The gladiator
   Boker, G. Francesca da Rimini
   Brougham, J. Po-ca-hon-tas
   Burk, J. Bunker-Hill
   Dunlap, W. The glory of Columbia
   Dunlap, W. A trip to Niagara
   Fitch, C. The city
   Harrigan, E. The Mulligan guard
      ball
   Herne, J. Shore acres
   Hopkinson, F. A dialogue and ode
   Howard, B. Shenandoah
   Howells, W. A letter of introduc-
      tion
   Hoyt, C. A temperance town
   McCloskey, J. Across the conti-
      nent
   Minstrel show
   Mitchell, L. The New York idea
   Moody, W. The great divide
   Mowatt, A. Fashion
   Munford, R. The candidates
   Noah, M. She would be a soldier
   Smith, J. A dialogue between an
      Englishman and an Indian
   Smith, J. A little teatable chit-
      chat
   Smith, W. The drunkard
   Stone, J. Metamora
   Tyler, R. The contrast
   Woodworth, S. The forest rose

MONV Moore, Harry Thornton, ed.
      Elizabethan age...[N.Y., Dell,
      1965] 544p
   Arden of Feversham
   Dekker, T. The shoemaker's
      holiday
   Marlowe, C. The tragical history
      of Doctor Faustus

MOO Moore, John Robert, ed. Rep-
      resentative English dramas...
      Boston, Ginn [c1929] 461p
   Dryden, J. All for love
   Everyman
   Goldsmith, O. She stoops to con-
      quer

Marlowe, C. The tragical history
of Doctor Faustus
Sheridan, R. The school for
scandal
Wilde, O. Lady Windermere's fan

MOR Morgan, Arthur Eustace, comp.
English plays, 1660-1820...New
York, Harper, 1935. 1157p
Addison, J. Cato
Buckstone, J. Luke, the labourer
Colman, G., and Garrick, D.
The clandestine marriage
Congreve, W. The way of the
world
Cumberland, R. The West Indian
Dryden, J. All for love; or, The
world well lost
Dryden, J. Almanzor and Alma-
hide; or, The conquest of
Granada by the Spaniards
Etherege, G. The man of mode;
or, Sir Fopling Flutter
Farquhar, G. The beaux'
stratagem
Foote, S. The mayor of Garret
Gay, J. The beggar's opera
Goldsmith, O. She stoops to con-
quer; or, The mistakes of a
night
Hoadly, B. The suspicious hus-
band
Home, J. Douglas
Lillo, G. The London merchant
Morton, T. Speed the plough
Murphy, A. All in the wrong
Otway, T. Venice preserv'd;
or, A plot discover'd
Reynolds, F. The dramatist; or,
Stop him who can!
Shadwell, T. Bury-fair
Sheridan, R. The rivals
Steele, R. The conscious lovers
Townley, J. High life below
the stairs
Vanbrugh, J. The relapse; or,
Virtue in danger
Wycherley, W. The plain-dealer

MORR Morrell, Janet M., ed. Four
English comedies of the 17th
and 18th centuries...Baltimore,
Penguin [Harmondsworth,
Middlesex, 1950,...1962]
414p
Congreve, W. The way of the
world

Goldsmith, O. She stoops to conquer; or, The mistakes of a
night
Jonson, B. Volpone; or, The fox
Sheridan, R. The school for
scandal

MORRIS, ALTON CHESTER. See also
WISD, WISE, WISF Wise, Jacob
Hooper [and others] eds. Col-
lege English...

MORT Morris, Alton Chester; Walker,
Biron; Bradshaw, Philip;
Hodges, John C. and Whitten,
Mary E., eds. College English:
the first year...4th ed. New
York, Harcourt, Brace and
World [1964] 944p
Hughes, R. The sister's tragedy
O'Casey, S. Red roses for me
Shaw, G. Caesar and Cleopatra
Sophocles. Antigone
Strindberg, A. The stronger

MORV Morris, Alton Chester; Walker,
Biron; Bradshaw, Philip;
Hodges, John C. and Whitten,
Mary E., eds. College English:
the first year...5th ed. New
York, Harcourt, Brace and
World [1968] 957p
Anouilh, J. Becket; or, The
honor of God
Miller, A. The crucible
Sophocles. Antigone
Strindberg, A. The stronger
Synge, J. The playboy of the
western world

MORW Morris, Alton Chester;
Walker, Biron; Bradshaw,
Philip; Hodges, John C. and
Whitten, Mary E., eds. Col-
lege English: the first year
...6th ed. New York, Har-
court Brace Jovanovich, 1973.
878p
Camus, A. Caligula
Miller, A. The crucible
Sophocles. Antigone
Strindberg, A. The stronger
Synge, J. The playboy of the
western world

MORX Morris, Alton Chester; Walker,
Biron and Bradshaw, Philip,

MORX (cont.)
comps. Imaginative literature;
fiction, drama, poetry...N.Y.,
Harcourt, Brace and World
[1968] 353p
Anouilh, J. Becket; or, The
honor of God
Miller, A. The crucible
Sophocles. Antigone
Synge, J. The playboy of the
western world

MORXB Morris, Alton Chester,
Walker, Biron and Bradshaw,
Philip, comps. Imaginative
literature; fiction, drama,
poetry. 2nd ed. New York,
Harcourt, Brace, Jovanovich
c1973 329p
Camus, A. Caligula
Miller, A. The crucible
Sophocles. Antigone
Strindberg, A. The stronger
Synge, J. The playboy of the
western world

MORXD Morris, Alton Chester,
Walker, Biron and Bradshaw,
Philip, comps. Imaginative
literature: fiction, drama,
poetry. 3d ed. New York,
Harcourt, Brace, Jovanovich,
1978. 402p
Chekhov, A. The cherry orchard
Miller, A. The crucible
Shaw, G. Arms and the man
Sophocles. Antigone
Strindberg, A. The stronger
Wilder, T. The skin of our teeth

MOS Moscow art theatre series of
Russian plays, ed. by Oliver
M. Sayler...New York, Bren-
tano [c1923] v.p.
Chekhov, A. The cherry orchard
Chekhov, A. The three sisters
Chekhov, A. Uncle Vanya
Gorky, M. The lower depths
Tolstoi, A. Tsar Fyodor Ivano-
vitch

MOSA Moscow art theatre series of
Russian plays, direction of
Morris Gest, ed. by Oliver M.
Sayler. [2nd series] New
York, Brentano [c1923] v.p.
Chekhov, A. Ivanoff

Dostoievsky, F. The brothers
Karamazoff
Goldoni, C. The mistress of the
inn
Ibsen, H. An enemy of the
people
Ostrovsky, A. Enough stupidity
in every wise man

MOSE Moses, Montrose Jonas, ed.
British plays from the restora-
tion to 1820...Boston, Little,
Brown, 1929. 2v
Cibber, C. The careless husband
1
Colman, G., and Garrick, D. The
clandestine marriage 2
Congreve, W. The way of the
world 1
Cumberland, R. The fashionable
lover 2
Dryden, J. The Spanish Fryar;
or, The double discovery 1
Etherege, G. The man of mode;
or, Sir Fopling Flutter 1
Farquhar, G. The beaux' strata-
gem 2
Gay, J. The beggar's opera 2
Goldsmith, O. She stoops to con-
quer; or, The mistakes of a
night 2
Home, J. Douglas 2
Otway, T. Venice preserv'd;
or, A plot discover'd 1
Rowe, N. Jane Shore 2
Shelley, P. The Cenci 2
Sheridan, R. The school for
scandal 2
Steele, R. The conscious lovers
1
Vanbrugh, J. The provok'd wife
1
Villiers, G. The rehearsal 1
Wycherley, W. The plain-dealer
1

MOSG Moses, Montrose Jonas, ed.
Dramas of modernism and their
forerunners...Boston, Little
Brown, 1931. 741p
Andreyev, L. He who has slapped
Čapek, K., and Čapek, J. Adam
the creator
Chekhov, A. The cherry orchard
Gorky, M. Night's lodging
(The lower depths)
Howard, S. The silver cord

Kaiser, G. From morn to mid-
night
Kelly, G. Craig's wife
Lenormand, H. The dream doctor
Maugham, W. The circle
Milne, A. The truth about
Blayds
Molnár, F. Liliom
Nichols, R., and Browne, M.
Wings over Europe
O'Neill, E. Desire under the elms
Pirandello, L. Right you are!
(If you think so)
Strindberg, J. There are crimes
and crimes
Toller, E. The machine-
wreckers

MOSH Moses, Montrose Jonas and
Campbell, Oscar James, eds.
Dramas of modernism and their
forerunners...Rev. ed...
Boston, Little, Brown, 1941.
946p
Anderson, M. Winterset
Andreyev, L. He who gets
slapped
Čapek, K., and Čapek, J. Adam
the creator
Carroll, P. Shadow and substance
Chekhov, A. The cherry orchard
Gorky, M. Night's lodging (The
lower depths)
Howard, S. The silver cord
Kaiser, G. From morn to midnight
Kelly, G. Craig's wife
Lenormand, H. The dream doctor
Maugham, W. The circle
Milne, A. The truth about Blayds
Molnár, F. Liliom
Nichols, R., and Browne, M.
Wings over Europe
Odets, C. Golden boy
O'Neill, E. Desire under the elms
Pirandello, L. Right you are!
(If you think so)
Sherwood, R. Idiot's delight
Strindberg, J. There are crimes
and crimes
Toller, E. The machine-
wreckers

MOSJ Moses, Montrose Jonas, ed.
Representative American dramas,
national and local...Boston,
Little, Brown, 1926. 681p
Belasco, D. The girl of the

golden west
Crothers, R. Nice people
Davis, O. The detour
Fitch, C. The city
Forbes, J. The famous Mrs. Fair
Hoyt, C. A Texas steer
Kaufman, G., and Connelly, M.
Dulcy
Kelly, G. The show-off
MacKaye, P. The scarecrow
Megrue, R., and Hackett, W. It
pays to advertise
O'Neill, E. The Emperor Jones
Peabody, J. The piper
Rice, E. The adding machine
Smith, H. Mrs. Bumpstead-
Leigh
Thomas, A. The witching hour

MOSK Moses, Montrose Jonas, ed.
Representative American dramas,
national and local...Rev. ed.
Boston, Little, Brown, 1933.
890p
Barry, P. Holiday
Behrman, S. The second man
Belasco, D. The girl of the
golden west
Connelly, M. The green pastures
Crothers, R. Nice people
Davis, O. The detour
Fitch, C. The city
Forbes, J. The famous Mrs. Fair
Howard, S. Lucky Sam McCarver
Hoyt, C. A texas steer
Kaufman, G., and Connelly, M.
Dulcy
Kelly, G. The show-off
MacKaye, P. The scarecrow
Megrue, R., and Hackett, W. It
pays to advertise
O'Neill, E. The Emperor Jones
Peabody, J. The piper
Rice, E. The adding machine
Smith, H. Mrs. Bumpstead-Leigh
Thomas, A. The witching hour

MOSL Moses, Montrose Jonas and
Krutch, Joseph Wood, eds.
Representative American
dramas, national and local...
Rev. and brought up-to-date
...Boston, Little, Brown, 1941.
1041p
Anderson, M. The masque of
kings
Barry, P. Holiday

MOSL (cont.)

Behrman, S. The second man
Belasco, D. The girl of the golden west
Connelly, M. The green pastures
Crothers, R. Nice people
Davis, O. The detour
Fitch, C. The city
Forbes, J. The famous Mrs. Fair
Howard, S. Lucky Sam McCarver
Hoyt, C. A Texas steer
Kaufman, G., and Connelly, M. Dulcy
Kelly, G. The show-off
MacKaye, P. The scarecrow
Megrue, R., and Hackett, W. It pays to advertise
Odets, C. Awake and sing
O'Neill, E. The Emperor Jones
Peabody, J. The piper
Rice, E. The adding machine
Sherwood, R. The petrified forest
Smith, H. Mrs. Bumpstead-Leigh
Thomas, A. The witching hour

MOSN Moses, Montrose Jonas, ed.
Representative British dramas, Victorian and modern...Boston, Little, Brown, 1918. 861p
Barker, G. The Madras house
Boucicault, D. London assurance
Browning, R. A blot in the 'scutcheon
Bulwer-Lytton, E. Richelieu; or, The conspiracy
Colum, P. Thomas Muskerry
Dunsany, E. The gods of the mountain
Galsworthy, J. The silver box
Gilbert, W. H.M.S. Pinafore; or, The lass that loved a sailor
Gregory, I. The workhouse ward
Hankin, St. J. The Cassilis engagement
Jerrold, D. Black-ey'd Susan; or, All in the downs
Jones, H. The masqueraders
Knowles, J. Virginius
Masefield, J. The tragedy of Pompey the Great
Pinero, A. The gay Lord Quex
Robertson, T. Caste
Synge, J. Riders to the sea
Taylor, T. The ticket-of-leave man
Tennyson, A. Becket
Wilde, O. The importance of being earnest
Yeats, W. Cathleen ni Houlihan

MOSO Moses, Montrose Jonas, ed.
Representative British dramas, Victorian and modern. New rev. ed...Boston, Little, Brown, 1931. 996p
Boucicault, D. London assurance
Browning, R. A blot in the 'scutcheon
Bulwer-Lytton, E. Richelieu; or, The conspiracy
Coward, N. Easy virtue
Dane, C. A bill of divorcement
Dunsany, E. The gods of the mountain
Galsworthy, J. The silver box
Gilbert, W. H.M.S. Pinafore; or, The lass that loved a sailor
Granville-Barker, H. The Madras house
Gregory, I. The workhouse ward
Hankin, St. J. The Cassilis engagement
Jerrold, D. Black-ey'd Susan; or, All in the downs
Jones, H. The masqueraders
Knowles, J. Virginius
Maugham, W. Our betters
Monkhouse, A. First blood
Munro, C. At Mrs. Beam's
Pinero, A. The gay Lord Quex
Robertson, T. Caste
Synge, J. Riders to the sea
Taylor, T. The ticket-of-leave man
Wilde, O. The importance of being earnest
Yeats, W. Cathleen ni Houlihan

MOSQ Moses, Montrose Jonas, ed.
Representative continental dramas, revolutionary and transitional...Boston, Little, Brown, 1924. 688p
Andreyeff, L. The life of man
Annunzio, G. d'. The daughter of Jorio
Becque, H. The vultures
Benavente y Martínez, J. The bonds of interest
Chekhov, A. The sea-gull
Donnay, M. Lovers

Giacosa, G. Like falling leaves
Hauptmann, G. The sunken bell
Ibsen, H. The wild duck
Maeterlinck, M. Monna Vanna
Nirdlinger, C. The world and
   his wife
Rostand, E. Cyrano de Bergerac
Schnitzler, A. The lonely way
Sudermann, H. The fires of St.
   John
Verhaeren, E. The dawn

MOSS Moses, Montrose Jonas, ed.
   Representative plays by
   American dramatists...New
   York, Dutton, 1918-25. 3v
Aiken, G. Uncle Tom's cabin 2
Barker, J. The Indian princess;
   or, La belle sauvage 1
Bateman, Mrs. S. Self 2
Belasco, D. The return of Peter
   Grimm 3
Boker, G. Francesca da Rimini
   3
Brackenridge, H. The battle of
   Bunkershill 1
Brown, D. Sertorius; or, The
   Roman patriot 2
Bunce, O. Love in '76 3
Burke, C. Rip Van Winkle 3
Conrad, R. Jack Cade 2
Dunlap, W. André 1
Fitch, C. The moth and the
   flame 3
Godfrey, T. The prince of
   Parthia 1
Howard, B. Shenandoah 3
Hutton, J. Fashionable follies 2
Jones, J. The people's lawyer
   2
Leacock, J. The fall of British
   tyranny; or, American liberty
   1
Low, S. The politician outwitted
   1
MacKaye, S. Paul Kauvar; or,
   Anarchy 3
Mitchell, L. The New York idea
   3
Mowatt, Mrs. A. Fashion 2
Noah, M. She would be a soldier;
   or, The plains of Chippewa 1
Payne, J. Brutus; or, The fall
   of Tarquin 2
Rogers, R. Ponteach; or, The
   savages of America 1
Tayleure, C. Horse-shoe

Robinson 2
Thomas, A. In Mizzoura 3
Tyler, R. The contrast 1
Walter, E. The easiest way 3
Warren, Mrs. M. The group 1
Willis, N. Tortesa, the usurer
   2

MOST The most popular plays of the
   American theatre: ten of
   Broadway's longest-running
   plays. Edited...by Stanley
   Richards. New York, Stein
   and Day, 1979. 703p
Burrows, A. Cactus flower
Chase, M. Harvey
Hamilton, P. Angel street
Kerr, J. Mary, Mary
Kesselring, J. Arsenic and old
   lace
Kirkland, J. Tobacco road
Lindsay, H., and Crouse, R.
   Life with father
Nichols, A. Abie's Irish rose
Simon, N. Barefoot in the park
Slade, B. Same time, next year

MUMFORD, LEWIS. See
   AME American caravan...

MURP Murphy, Charles T.;
   Guinagh, Kevin and Oates,
   Whitney, J., eds. Greek and
   Roman classics in translation...
   New York, Longmans, Green
   [c1947] 1052p
Aeschylus. Prometheus bound
Aristophanes. The clouds
Euripides. Hippolytus
Sophocles. Oedipus the king

MURRAY, GILBERT. See
   TEN Ten Greek plays...

MYB My best play...London, Faber
   & Faber [1934] 590p
Bax, C. The Venetian
Coward, N. Hay fever
Dane, C. Granite
Maugham, W. The circle
Milne, A. Success
Munro, C. The rumour
Robinson, L. The whiteheaded
   boy
Van Druten, J. After all

NAGE Nagelberg, Munjou Moses.
Drama in our time...New
York, Harcourt, Brace
[c1948] 478p
Arent, A. One-third of a nation
Čapek, K. R.U.R.
Corwin, N. El Capitan and the
corporal
Hellman, L. Watch on the Rhine
Howard, S. Yellow Jack
Saroyan, W. The human comedy
Sherwood, R. Abe Lincoln in
Illinois
Wilder, T. Our town

NATHAN, GEORGE JEAN. See
CRIT The Critics' prize
plays...FIG Five great modern
Irish plays...WORP World's
great plays...

NEI Neilson, William Allan, ed. The
chief Elizabethan dramatists,
excluding Shakespeare...Bos-
ton, Houghton Mifflin [1911]
878p
Beaumont, F., and Fletcher, J.
The knight of the burning
pestle
Beaumont, F., and Fletcher, J.
The maid's tragedy
Beaumont, F., and Fletcher, J.
Philaster
Chapman, G. Bussy D'Ambois
Dekker, T. The honest whore,
pt. I
Dekker, T. The honest whore,
pt. II
Dekker, T. The shoemaker's
holiday
Fletcher, J. The faithful
shepherdess
Fletcher, J. The wild-goose chase
Ford, J. The broken heart
Greene, R. The honourable his-
tory of Friar Bacon and Friar
Bungay
Heywood, T. A woman killed
with kindness
Jonson, B. The alchemist
Jonson, B. Every man in his
humour
Jonson, B. Sejanus, his fall
Jonson, B. Volpone; or, The
fox
Kyd, T. The Spanish tragedy;
or, Hieronimo is mad again

Lyly, J. Endymion, the man
in the moon
Marlowe, C. The Jew of Malta
Marlowe, C. Tamburlaine, pt. I
Marlowe, C. The tragical history
of Doctor Faustus
Marlowe, C. The troublesome
reign and lamentable death of
Edward the second
Marston, J. The malcontent
Massinger, P. A new way to pay
old debts
Middleton, T. A trick to catch
the old one
Middleton, T., and Rowley, W.
The changeling
Peele, G. The old wives' tale
Shirley, J. The cardinal
Shirley, J. The lady of pleasure
Webster, J. The Duchess of Malfi

NELS Nelson, John Herbert and
Cargill, Oscar, eds. Contemporary trends; American
literature since 1900. Revised
edition. New York, Macmillan
[c1949] 1263p (American
literature; a period anthology.
[v4] Oscar Cargill, gen. ed.)
Anderson, M. Winterset
MacLeish, A. The fall of the city
O'Neill, E. Bound east for Cardiff
O'Neill, E. Lazarus laughed

NER Nero (Tragedy)...Nero & other
plays; edited...by Herbert P.
Horne; Havelock Ellis; Arthur
Symons and A. Wilson Verity...
New York, Scribner [1904-48]
488p
Day, J. Humour out of breath
Day, J. The parliament of bees
Field, N. Amends for ladies
Field, N. Woman is a weathercock
Nero
Porter, H. The two angry women
of Abington

NES Nethercot, Arthur Hobart [and
others], eds. Elizabethan
plays. New York, Holt, 1971.
845p
Chapman, G. Bussy d'Ambois
Dekker, T. The honest whore,
pt. I
Dekker, T. The shoemaker's
holiday

Gascoigne, G. Supposes
Greene, R. George A. Greene, the pinner of Wakefield
Greene, R. The honorable history of Friar Bacon and Friar Bungay
Heywood, T. A woman killed with kindness
Kyd, T. The Spanish tragedy
Lyly, J. Endymion
Marlowe, C. Attowell's jig (Francis' new jig)
Marlowe, C. Edward the second
Marlowe, C. Doctor Faustus
Marlowe, C. Mucedorus
Marlowe, C. Tamburlaine, pt. I
Marston, J. The malcontent
Norton, T. and Sackville, T. Gorboduc
Peele, G. The arraignment of Paris
Peele, G. The old wives' tale
Preston, T. Cambises, King of Persia
Stevenson, W. Gammer Gurton's needle
Udall, N. Ralph Roister Doister

NET Nettleton, George Henry and Case, Arthur Ellicott, eds. British dramatists from Dryden to Sheridan...Boston, Houghton Mifflin [c1939] 957p
Addison, J. Cato
Buckingham, G. The rehearsal
Cibber, C. The careless husband
Colman, G. The jealous wife
Congreve, W. The way of the world
Cumberland, R. The West Indian
Dryden, J. All for love; or, The world well lost
Dryden, J. The conquest of Granada by the Spaniards, pt. I
Etherege, G. The man of mode; or, Sir Fopling Flutter
Farquhar, G. The beaux' stratagem
Fielding, H. Tom Thumb
Garrick, D. The lying valet
Gay, J. The beggar's opera
Goldsmith, O. She stoops to conquer; or, The mistakes of a night
Home, J. Douglas

Lillo, G. The London merchant; or, The history of George Barnwell
Otway, T. Venice preserved; or, A plot discovered
Rowe, N. The tragedy of Jane Shore
Sheridan, R. The critic; or, A tragedy rehearsed
Sheridan, R. The rivals
Sheridan, R. The school for scandal
Steele, R. The conscious lovers
Vanbrugh, J. The relapse; or, Virtue in danger
Wycherley, W. The plain dealer

NEVI Neville, Mary Anthony and Herzberg, Max J., eds. This England...Chicago, Rand McNally [c1956] 786p
Shakespeare, W. Macbeth
Wilde, O. The importance of being earnest

NEW AMERICAN CARAVAN. 1929. See
AME American caravan, v3

NEWA New American plays. Edited by Robert Willoughby Corrigan (v1) and William H. Hoffman (v2,v3,v4). New York, Hill and Wang, 1965-71. 4v
Barlow, A. Mr. Biggs 1
Bullins, E. The electronic nigger 3
Bush, J. French gray 2
Cameron, K. The hundred and first 1
Dey, J. Passacaglia 2
Estrin, M. An American playground sampler 3
Eyen, T. The white whore and the bit player 2
Fredericks, C. A summer ghost 1
Harris, T. Always with love 3
Heide, R. At war with the mongols 4
Herndon, V. Until the monkey comes 2
Hoffman, B. The king of Spain 3
Hoffman, W. Thank you, Miss Victoria 3
Jasudowicz, D. Blood money 1
Kennedy, A. The owl answers 2

NEWA (cont.)

Levinson, A. Socrates wounded 1

Magnuson, J. African Medea 4

Maljean, J. A message from cougar 2

Mee, C. Constantinople Smith 1

Molinaro, U. The abstract wife 2

Owens, R. Futz 2

Patrick, R. The golden circle 3

Peluso, E. Moby tick 4

Rosenberg, J. The death and life of Sneaky Fitch 1

Rubenstein, K. Icarus 4

Smith, M. Captain Jack's revenge 4

Starkweather, D. The poet's papers 3

Washburn, D. Ginger Anne 1

Yankowitz, S. Slaughterhouse 4

Yerby, L. The golden bull of boredom 1

NEW CARAVAN. 1936. See AME American caravan. v5

NEW DIRECTIONS. See NEWD New directions in prose and poetry...James Laughlin, ed. See also PLAA Playbook...; SPC Spearhead...

NEWD New directions in prose and poetry...James Laughlin, ed. Norfolk, Ct., New Directions, 1936-1955. 15v

Brecht, B. The exception and the rule 55

Brecht, B. Mother courage 41

Büchner, G. Woyzeck 50

Cocteau, J. Les maries de la Tour Eiffel 37

García Lorca, F. In the frame of Don Cristóbal 44

Goodman, P. The tower of Babel 40

Hutchins, M. The case of Astrolable 44

Hutchins, M. A play about Joseph Smith, jr. 44

Hutchins, M. The wandering Jew 51

Moss, H. No strings attached 44

Ortiz de Montellano, B. Salome's head 44

Reid, B. The fourth room 44

Rexroth, K. Iphigenia at Aulis 44

Rexroth, K. Phaedra 44

Schwartz, D. Paris and Helen 41

Second, L. Apollinaris 42

Stein, G. Daniel Webster, eighteen in America 37

Williams, T. Don ranchos; or, The purification 44

Williams, W. Trial horse no. 1: Many loves 42

NEWDE New drama one. Selected, edited and introduced by Lloyd Fernando. London, Oxford, 1972. 147p

Das, K. Lela Mayang

Dorall, E. A tiger is loose in our community

Lee, J. The happening in the bungalow

NEWE New English dramatists... Edited by E. Martin Browne... Tom Maschler...[Harmondsworth, Middlesex] Penguin Books [1958-1971] 14v

Arden, J., and D'Arcy, M. The happy haven 4

Arden, J. Live like pigs 3

Bermange, B. No quarter 12

Bolt, R. A man for all seasons 6

Churchill, C. The ants 12

Conn, S. The king 14

Cooper, G. Everything in the garden 7

Cooper, G. Happy family 11

Cooper, G. The object 12

Finley, I. The estate hunters 14

Finley, I. Walking through seaweed 14

Fugard, A. The blood knot 13

Hall, W. The long and the short and the tall 3

Hastings, M. Yes, and after 4

Howarth, D. A lily in little India 9

Johnson, B. You're human like the rest of them 14

Kops, B. The hamlet of Stepney Green 1

Lessing, D. Each his own wilder-

NEWR New road...edited by Fred
Marnau...Alex Comfort...
John Bayliss...1943-1947.
London, The grey walls
press [1943-1947] 5v
Carroll, P. The strings, my
Lord, are false 1
Gardiner, W. The last refuge 1

NEWV New voices in the American
theatre. Foreword by Brooks
Atkinson. New York, Modern
library [c1955] 559p
Anderson, R. Tea and sympathy
Axelrod, G. The seven year itch
Inge, W. Come back little Sheba
Miller, A. Death of a salesman
Williams, T. A streetcar named
desire
Wouk, H. The Caine mutiny
court-martial

NEWVM The new women's theatre:
10 plays by contemporary
American women. Edited by
Honor Moore. New York,
Vintage, 1977. 537p
Childress, A. Wedding band: a
love/hate story in black and
white
Howe, T. Birth and after birth
Jacker, C. Bits and pieces
Kraus, J. The ice wolf: a tale
of the Eskimos
Lamb, M. I lost a pair of gloves
yesterday
Merriam, E., Wagner, P. and
Hoffsiss, J. Out of our
fathers' house
Molinaro, U. Breakfast past
noon
Moore, H. Mourning pictures
Russ, J. Window dressing
Wolff, R. The abdication

NEW WORLD LITERATURE SERIES,
v1. See
MONR Moody, Richard, ed.
Dramas from the American
theatre, 1762-1909

NEWW New world writing...New
York, New American library,
1952-1956. 10v
Bellow, S. The wrecker 6
Bercovici, E. The heart of
age 4

Brunson, B. A bastard of the
blood 10
Denney, R. September lemonade
7
Eberhart, R. The visionary
farms 3
García Lorca, F. Don Cristobita
and Doña Rosita 8
Ionesco, E. The bald soprano 9
MacDonagh, D. Happy as Larry
6
Meldon, M. Purple path to the
poppy field 5
Picasso, P. Desire trapped by
the tail 2
Williams, T. I rise in flame,
cried the Phoenix 1

NIC Nicoll, Allardyce, ed.
Lesser English comedies of
the eighteenth century...
London, Oxford university
press [1927] [537]p (The
world's classics)
Colman, G. The jealous wife
Inchbald, E. Every one has his
fault
Morton, T. Speed the plough
Murphy, A. The way to keep him
Reynolds, F. The dramatist

NINE GREEK DRAMAS. See
HARC Harvard classics, v8

NIL Nine plays of the modern
theater; with an introduction
by Harold Clurman. New York,
Grove Press, 1981. 896p
Beckett, S. Waiting for Godot
Brecht, B. The Caucasian chalk
circle
Dürrenmatt, F. The visit
Genêt, J. The balcony
Ionesco, E. Rhinoceros
Mamet, D. American buffalo
Mrozek, S. Tango
Pinter, H. The birthday party
Stoppard, T. Rosencrantz and
Guildenstern are dead

NILS Nineteenth-century American
plays, edited by Myron Matlaw.
New York, Applause Theatre
Book Publishers, 1985. 270p.
[Originally appeared in, and is
reprinted from, The black
crook - MASW]

NORG (cont.)
    is a dream 1
    Chekhov, A. The cherry orchard
    2
    Euripides. Hippolytus 1
    Euripides. Medea 1
    Ibsen, H. Hedda Gabler 2
    Molière, J. Tartuffe, or The
    imposter 2
    Pirandello, L. Henry IV 2
    Racine, J. Phaedra 2
    Sartre, J. No exit (Huis clos) 2
    Sophocles. Antigone 1
    Sophocles. Oedipus tyrannus 1
    Strindberg, A. The ghost sonata
    2

NORI The Norton anthology of
    world masterpieces. Maynard
    Mack, General Editor. 4th
    ed. New York, Norton, 1979.
    1750p
    Aeschylus. Agamemnon
    Aristophanes. Lysistrata
    Calderón de la Barca, P. Life is
    a dream
    Euripides. Hippolytus
    Euripides. Medea
    Marlowe, C. The tragical history
    of the life and death of Doctor
    Faustus
    Shakespeare, W. Hamlet, Prince
    of Denmark
    Sophocles. Antigone
    Sophocles. Oedipus tyrannus

NOY Noyes, George Rapall, ed. and
    tr. Masterpieces of the Rus-
    sian drama...New York,
    Appleton-Century, 1933. 902p
    Andreyev, L. Professor
    Storitsyn
    Chekhov, A. The cherry orchard
    Fonvízin, D. The young hopeful
    Gogol, N. The inspector
    Gorky, M. Down and out
    Griboyedov, A. Wit works woe
    Mayakóvsky, V. Mystery-Bouffe
    Ostrovsky, A. The poor bride
    Pisemsky, A. A bitter fate
    Tolstoy, A. The death of Ivan
    the terrible
    Tolstoy, L. The power of dark-
    ness
    Turgenev, I. A month in the
    country

OAM Oates, Whitney Jennings and
    Murphy, Charles Theophilus,
    eds. Greek literature in
    translation...New York, Long-
    mans, Green, 1944. 1072p
    Aeschylus. Agamemnon
    Aeschylus. The Eumenides
    Aeschylus. Prometheus bound
    Aristophanes. Lysistrata
    Euripides. The bacchae
    Euripides. Hippolytus
    Menander. The arbitration
    Sophocles. Antigone
    Sophocles. Oedipus the king

OAT Oates, Whitney Jennings and
    O'Neill, Eugene Gladstone,
    eds. The complete Greek
    drama...New York, Random
    house [c1938] 2v
    Aeschylus. Agamemnon 1
    Aeschylus. The choephori 1
    Aeschylus. The eumenides 1
    Aeschylus. The Persians 1
    Aeschylus. Prometheus bound 1
    Aeschylus. The seven against
    Thebes 1
    Aeschylus. The suppliants 1
    Aristophanes. The Acharnians 2
    Aristophanes. The birds 2
    Aristophanes. The clouds 2
    Aristophanes. The ecclesiazusae
    2
    Aristophanes. The frogs 2
    Aristophanes. The knights 2
    Aristophanes. Lysistrata 2
    Aristophanes. Peace 2
    Aristophanes. Plutus 2
    Aristophanes. Thesmophoriazusae
    2
    Aristophanes. The wasps 2
    Euripides. Alcestis 1
    Euripides. Andromache 1
    Euripides. The bacchae 2
    Euripides. The cyclops 2
    Euripides. Electra 2
    Euripides. Hecuba 1
    Euripides. Helen 2
    Euripides. The Heracleidae 1
    Euripides. Heracles 1
    Euripides. Hippolytus 1
    Euripides. Ion 1
    Euripides. Iphigenia in Aulis 2
    Euripides. Iphigenia in Tauris
    1
    Euripides. Medea 1

OHL (cont.)
Vidal, G. Visit to a small planet

OLH Oliphant, Ernest Henry Clark,
ed. Elizabethan dramatists
other than Shakespeare...New
York, Prentice-Hall, 1931.
1511p
Arden of Feversham
Beaumont, F., and Fletcher, J.
The knight of the burning
pestle
Beaumont, F., and Fletcher, J.
The maid's tragedy
Beaumont, F., and Fletcher, J.
Philaster
Brome, R. A jovial crew
Dekker, T. The honest whore,
pt. II
Drayton, M. The merry devil of
Edmonton
Ford, J. The broken heart
Greene, R. Friar Bacon and
Friar Bungay
Heywood, T. A woman killed
with kindness
Jonson, B. The alchemist
Jonson, B. Bartholomew fair
Jonson, B. Volpone
Jonson, B. B., Chapman, G., and
Marston, J. Eastward hoe!
Kyd, T. The Spanish tragedy
Lyly, J. Campaspe
Marlowe, C. Edward II
Marlowe, C. Faustus
Massinger, P. A new way to pay
old debts
Middleton, T. Women, beware
women
Middleton, T., and Rowley, W.
The changeling
Milton, J. Comus
Peele, G. The old wives' tale
Porter, H. The two angry
women of Abington
Rowley, W., and Middleton, T.
A fair quarrel
Shirley, J. The traitor
Tourneur, C. The revenger's
tragedy
Webster, J. The Duchess of Malfi
Webster, J. The white devil
A Yorkshire tragedy

OLI Oliphant, Ernest Henry Clark,
ed. Shakespeare and his
fellow dramatists...New York,

Prentice-Hall, 1929. 2v
Arden of Feversham 1
Beaumont, F., and Fletcher, J.
The knight of the burning
pestle 2
Beaumont, F., and Fletcher, J.
The maid's tragedy 2
Beaumont, F., and Fletcher, J.
Philaster 2
Brome, R. A jovial crew 2
Dekker, T. The honest whore,
pt. II 1
Drayton, M. The merry devil of
Edmonton 1
Ford, J. The broken heart 2
Greene, R. Friar Bacon and Friar
Friar Bungay 1
Heywood, T. A woman killed with
kindness 1
Jonson, B. The alchemist 2
Jonson, B. Bartholomew fair 2
Jonson, B. Volpone 1
Jonson, B., Chapman, G., and
Marston, J. Eastward hoe! 1
Kyd, T. The Spanish tragedy 1
Lyly, J. Campaspe 1
Marlowe, C. Edward II 1
Marlowe, C. Faustus 1
Massinger, P. A new way to pay
old debts 2
Middleton, T. Women, beware
women 2
Middleton, T., and Rowley, W.
The changeling 2
Milton, J. Comus 2
Peele, G. The old wives' tale 1
Porter, H. The two angry women
of Abington 1
Rowley, W., and Middleton, T.
A fair quarrel 2
Shakespeare, W. Antony and
Cleopatra 2
Shakespeare, W. As you like it
1
Shakespeare, W. Coriolanus 2
Shakespeare, W. Cymbeline 2
Shakespeare, W. Hamlet 1
Shakespeare, W. Henry IV, pt. 1
1
Shakespeare, W. Julius Caesar 1
Shakespeare, W. King Lear 1
Shakespeare, W. Macbeth 2
Shakespeare, W. The merchant of
Venice 1
Shakespeare, W. Midsummer
night's dream 1
Shakespeare, W. Othello 1

Shakespeare, W. Romeo and
Juliet 1
Shakespeare, W. Twelfth night
1
Shakespeare, W. The winter's
tale 2
Shirley, J. The traitor 2
Tourneur, C. The revenger's
tragedy 2
Webster, J. The Duchess of
Malfi 2
Webster, J. The white devil 2
A Yorkshire tragedy 2

OLIV Oliver, Clinton S. and Sills,
Stephanie, eds. Contemporary
black drama...New York,
Scribner, 1970. 360p
Baldwin, J. Blues for Mr. Char-
lie
Bullins, E. Gentleman caller
Davis, O. Purlie victorious
Gordone, C. No place to be
somebody
Hansberry, L. A raisin in the
sun
Jones, L. Dutchman
Kennedy, A. Funnyhouse of a
Negro
Ward, D. Day of absence
Ward, D. Happy ending

OLIW Oliver, William Irvin, ed.
and tr. Voices of change in
the Spanish American theater.
Austin, Texas, University of
Texas Press, 1971. 294p
Buenaventura, E. In the right
hand of God the Father
Carbillido, E. The day they
let the lions loose
Gambargo, G. The camp
Hernández, L. The mullatto's
orgy
Maggi, C. The library
Vodáhovic, S. Three beach
plays

OPE Open Theater. Three works
by the Open Theater. New
York, Drama Book Specialists/
Publishers, 1974. 191p
Open Theater. The mutation show
Open Theater. Nightwalk
Yankowitz, S. Terminal

ORI Oriental literature...Rev. ed.

New York, Colonial Press
[c1960] 4v (The world's
great classics)
Abstraction 2
Kālidāsa. Sakoontalā 3
Nakamitsu 2
The sorrows of Han 4

ORNC Ornstein, Robert and Spen-
cer, Hazelton, eds. Eliza-
bethan and Jacobean comedy
...Boston, Heath [1964] 315p
(A companion volume to the
editors' Elizabethan and Jaco-
bean tragedy...)
Beaumont, F. The knight of
the burning pestle
Dekker, T. The shoemaker's
holiday
Gascoine, G. Supposes
Greene, R. Friar Bacon and
Friar Bungay
Jonson, B. The alchemist
Jonson, B. Every man in his
humour
Lyly, J. Endymion, the man in
the moon
Massinger, P. A new way to
pay old debts

ORNT Ornstein, Robert and Spen-
cer, Hazelton, eds. Eliza-
bethan and Jacobean tragedy...
Boston, Heath [1964] 308p
(A companion volume to the
editors' Elizabethan and
Jacobean comedy...)
Chapman, G. Bussy D'Ambois
Ford, J. The broken heart
Kyd, T. The Spanish tragedy
Marlowe, C. The tragical history
of Doctor Faustus
Middleton, T. and Rowley, W.
The changeling
Webster, J. The white devil

ORT Ortego, Philip D., comp. We
are Chicanos. New York,
Washington Square Press, 1973.
330p
Portillo, E. The day of the swallows

ORZ Orzel, Nick, and Smith,
Michael, eds. Eight plays
from off-Broadway. Indianapolis, Bobbs, Merrill, 1966. 281p

ORZ (cont.)
Fornés, M. The successful life of 3: a skit for vaudeville
Foster, P. Balls
O'Hara, F. The general returns from one place to another
Oppenheimer, J. The great American desert
Shepard, S. Chicago
Terry, M. Calm down, Mother
Van Itallie, J. America hurrah
Wilson, L. The madness of Lady Bright

OULD Ould, Herman, ed. The book of the P.E.N...London, Arthur Barker [1950] 254p
Farjeon, E. The plane-tree
Jameson, S. William the defeated
Johnson, P. The Duchess at sunset

OWE Owens, Rochelle, ed. Spontaneous combustion; 8 new American plays. New York, Winter House, 1972. 224p (Winter Repertory, 6)
Bovasso, J. Schubert's last serenade
Bullins, E. Dialect determinism
Hoffman, W. A quick nut bread to make your mouth water
Jones, L. Ba-Ra-Ka
Kennedy, A. Sun
Melfi, L. Cinque
Owens, R. He wants shih
Terry, M. Sanibel and Captiva

OXF Oxford anthology of American literature, chosen and edited by William Rose Benét and Norman Holmes Pearson. New York, Oxford University Press, 1938. 1705p
O'Neill, E. Lazarus laughed

OXFC The Oxford anthology of Canadian literature, edited by Robert L. Weaver and William Toye. Toronto, Oxford, 1973. 546p
Ryga, G. Indian

PAJ Parker, John W., ed. Adventures in playmaking; 4 plays

by Carolina playmakers. Chapel Hill, Univ. of North Carolina Press, c1968. 333p
Brower, B. A little to the left
Graves, R. The battle of the carnival and Lent
McDonald, C. and Mason, W. Spring for sure
Niggli, J. Singing valley

PAR Parks, Edd Winfield, and Beatty, Richard Croom, eds. The English drama, an anthology, 900-1642...New York, Norton [c1935] 1495p
Abraham and Isaac
Beaumont, F., and Fletcher, J. Philaster; or, Love lies a-bleeding
Daniel, S. The vision of the twelve goddesses
Dekker, T. The shoemaker's holiday
Everyman
Fletcher, J., and Shakespeare, W. Two noble kinsmen
Ford, J. 'Tis a pity she's a whore
Greene, R. The honorable history of Friar Bacon and Friar Bungay
Heywood, J. A merry play between John John the husband
Heywood, T. A woman killed with kindness
Jonson, B. Every man in his humour
Jonson, B. Oberon, the fairy prince
Jonson, B. Sejanus, his fall
Jonson, B. Volpone; or, The fox
Kyd, T. The Spanish tragedy
Lyly, J. Endymion
Marlowe, C. Edward II
Marlowe, C. The Jew of Malta
Marlowe, C. The tragical history of Dr. Faustus
Massinger, P. A new way to pay old debts
Milton, J. Comus
Oxfordshire St. George play
Peele, G. The old wives' tale
Plautus, T. The miles gloriosus
The quem quaeritis
Robin Hood and the friar
The second shepherds' play
Seneca L. Thyestes
Shetland sword dance

Shirley, J. The cardinal
Sidney, P. The Lady of May
Udall, N. Ralph Roister Doister
Webster, J. The white devil

PARNASSUS PLAYS (1598-1601)
...See
LEIS Leishman, J. B., ed.

PARR Parry, W. Dyfed. Old plays
for modern players...London,
Arnold [1930] 156p
Abraham and Isaac
Heywood, J. The four p's
Jonson, B. Volpone; or, The fox
Noah's flood
Peele, G. The old wives' tale
The shepherds' play

PARV Patt, Beatrice P., and
Nozick, Martin, eds. The
generation of 1898 and after
...New York, Dodd, Mead,
1961. 427p
García Lorca, F. La casa de
Bernarda Alba

PATM Patterns of literature. Edited
by Julian L. Maline and James
Berkley. New York, Singer-
Random House, 1967. 4v
(v3, Dramatic literature)
Chekhov, A. The boor 3
Ibsen, H. An enemy of the
people 3
McCullers, C. The member of the
wedding 3
Maeterlinck, M. The intruder 3
Mukerji, D. The judgment of
Indra 3
Rostand, E. The romancers 3
Seami, M. The dwarf trees 3
Shakespeare, W. Macbeth 3
Sophocles. Antigone 3
Synge, J. Riders to the sea 3

PATP Patterns of literature.
Edited by Julian L. Maline and
James Berkley. New York,
Singer-Random House [1969]
734p
Anouilh, J. Antigone
McCullers, C. The member of the
wedding
Mukerji, D. The judgment of
Indra
Seami, M. The dwarf trees

Shakespeare, W. Macbeth
Sophocles. Antigone
Synge, J. Riders to the sea

PATR Patterson, Lindsay, [comp.]
Black theatre; a 20th century
collection of the best play-
wrights. New York, Dodd,
Mead, 1971. 493p
Baldwin, J. The amen corner
Bontemps, A., and Cullen, C.
The St. Louis woman
Branch, W. In splendid error
Bullins, E. In the wine time
Childress, A. Trouble in mind
Davis, O. Purlie victorious
Elder, L. Ceremonies in dark old
men
Gordone, C. No place to be some-
body
Hansberry, L. A raisin in the
sun
Hughes, L. Simply heaven
Jones, L. Dutchman
Peterson, L. Take a giant step

PATT Pattison, Walter Thomas.
Representative Spanish authors
...New York, Oxford Univer-
sity Press, 1942. 2v in 1
Rivas, A. Don Alvaro; o, La
fuerza del sino
Rueda, L. Paso séptimo: de las
aceitunas
Ruiz de Alarcón y Mendoza, J.
Las paredes oyen

PEARSON, NORMAN HOLMES. See
OXF Oxford anthology of
American literature...edited by
William Rose Benét and Norman
Holmes Pearson

PEN Pence, Raymond Woodbury, ed.
Dramas by present-day
writers...New York, Scribner
[c1927] 690p
Bennett, A., and Knoblock, E.
Milestones
Davies, M. The slave with two
faces
Drinkwater, J. Cophetua
Dunsany, E. A night at an inn
Galsworthy, J. Loyalties
Glaspell, S. Trifles
Gregory, I. Spreading the news
Jacobs, W. A love passage

PEN (cont.)
    Jones, H. The goal
    Kaufman, G., and Connelly, M.
        Merton of the movies
    Mackay, C. Counsel retained
    Morley, C. Thursday evening
    O'Neill, E. "Ile"
    Sutro, A. A marriage has been
        arranged
    Tarkington, B. Monsieur Beau-
        caire
    Wilde, P. Confessional

PENG Penguin book of modern
    Canadian drama; edited by
    Richard Plant. Markham,
    Ontario, Canada, Penguin
    Books Canada Limited, 1984.
    904p
    Coulter, J. Riel
    Freeman, D. Creeps
    French, D. Of the fields, lately
    Fruet, W. Wedding in white
    Herbert, J. Fortune and men's
        eyes
    Hollingsworth, M. Ever loving
    Pollock, S. Blood relations
    Reaney, J. Handcuffs: (The
        Donnellys: Part Three)
    Ringwood, G. Garage sale
    Ryga, G. Indian
    Stratton, A. Rexy!
    Walker, G. The art of war

PENNSYLVANIA GERMAN SOCIETY.
    See
    BUFF Buffington, Albert F.,
    ed. The Richard collection of
    early Pennsylvania German
    plays...

PERRIN, BERNADOTTE. See
    GREE Greek dramas...

PERS Perrine, Laurence, comp.,
    Dimensions of drama. New
    York, Harcourt, Brace, Jo-
    vanovich, 1973. 567p
    Chekhov, A. The brute
    Everyman
    García Lorca, F. Blood wedding
    Ibsen, H. An enemy of the
        people
    Miller, A. Death of a salesman
    Molière, J. The misanthrope
    Shakespeare, W. Othello
    Sophocles. Oedipus rex

Strindberg, A. The stronger
Williams, T. The glass menagerie

PERT Perrine, Laurence, comp.
    Literature; structure, sound
    and sense. New York, Har-
    court, Brace, Jovanovich,
    1970. 1426p
    Albee, E. The sandbox
    Chekhov, A. The brute
    García Lorca, F. Blood wedding
    Ibsen, H. An enemy of the
        people
    Miller, A. Death of a salesman
    Molière, J. The misanthrope
    Shakespeare, W. Othello
    Shaw, G. Candida
    Sophocles. Oedipus rex
    Strindberg, A. The stronger
    Williams, T. The glass menagerie

PERU Perrine, Laurence, ed.
    Literature, structure, sound
    and sense. 2d ed. New
    York, Harcourt, Brace, Jo-
    vanovich, 1974. 1508p
    Albee, E. The sandbox
    Chekhov, A. The brute: A joke
        in one act
    Everyman
    García Lorca, F. Blood wedding
    Hansberry, L. A raisin in the
        sun
    Ibsen, H. An enemy of the
        people
    Miller, A. Death of a salesman
    Molière, J. The misanthrope
    Shakespeare, W. Othello
    Shaw, G. Candida
    Sophocles. Antigone
    Strindberg, A. The stronger

PERV Perrine, Laurence, ed.
    Literature; structure, sound,
    and sense. 3d ed. New York,
    Harcourt, Brace, Jovanovich,
    1978
    Albee, E. The sandbox
    Chekhov, A. The brute
    Giraudoux, J. The madwoman of
        Chaillot
    Hansberry, L. A raisin in the
        sun
    Hughes, L. Mother and child
    Ibsen, H. An enemy of the
        people
    Miller, A. Death of a salesman

Molière, J. The misanthrope
Shakespeare, W. Othello
Shaw, G. Candida
Sophocles. Oedipus rex
Strindberg, A. The stronger

PFR Perspectives: an anthology.
Edited by Marianne H. Russo,
Edward B. Groff. Dubuque,
Iowa, Kendall/Hunt Pub. Co.,
c1976. 390p
Shakespeare, W. Othello
Sophocles. Oedipus the king
Ward, D. Day of absence

PHI Philbrick, Norman, ed. Trum-
pets sounding: propaganda
plays of the American revolu-
tion. New York, 1972. 367p
The battle of Brooklyn, a farce
of two acts
The blockheads; or, The af-
frighted officers
Brackenridge, H. The death of
General Montgomery, in
storming the City of Quebec
A dialogue, between a Southern
delegate, and his spouse, on
his return from the grand
Continental Congress
The fall of British tyranny; or,
American liberty triumphant
The motley assembly
Munford, R. The patriots

PIC Pickering, Jerry V., ed. A
treasury of drama; classical
through modern. New York,
West, 1975. 515p
Dieb, R. The mating of Alice May
Chekhov, A. The cherry orchard
The farce of Master Pierre
Oathelin
Shakespeare, W. Romeo and
Juliet
Shaw, G. The devil's disciple
Sheridan, R. The school for
scandal
Sophocles. Oedipus the king
Williams, T. The glass menagerie

PIE Pierce, Frederick Erastus and
Schreiber, Carl Frederick, eds.
Fiction and fantasy of German
romance. New York, Oxford
University Press, 1927. 392p
Kleist, H. Kaethchen of Heilbronn

PIET Pieterse, Cosmo, ed. Five Af-
rican plays. London, Heine-
mann, 1972. 217p
Bart-Williams, G. The drug
Kay, K. Laughter and hubbub in
the house
Kimmel, H. The cell
Oyono, F. Houseboy

PLAYBOOK: FIVE PLAYS FOR A NEW
THEATRE (PLAA). See also
PLAC Plays for a new theater;
Playbook 2...

PLAA Playbook: Five plays for a
new theatre. [1] [New York]
New Directions [c1956] 298p
Abel, L. The death of Odysseus
Hivnor, R. The ticklish acrobat
Kinoshita, J. Twilight crane
Merrill, J. The immortal husband
Richards, I. A leak in the uni-
verse

PLAAB The playmakers one; com-
piled by Roger Mansfield, illus-
trated by Barry Davies. Hud-
dersfield [Eng.] Schofield &
Sims Ltd., 1976 120p
Arden, J. Death of a cowboy
Brecht, B. He who says yes
Campton, D. Incident
Jenkins, R. The whole truth
Livings, H. The gamecock
Pinter, H. Request stop
Simpson, N. Oh!
Spark, M. The party through the
wall
Williams, T. The last of my solid
gold watches

PLAAD Plays by American women:
the early years. Edited...by
Judith E. Barlow. New York,
Avon, 1981. 334p
Crothers, R. A man's world
Gale, Z. Miss Lulu Bett
Glaspell, S. Trifles
Mowatt, A. Fashion
Treadwell, S. Machinal

PLAB Plays by Greek, Spanish,
French, German and English
dramatists...Rev. ed. New
York, Colonial Press [c1900]
2v (The world's great
classics)

PLAB (cont.)

Aeschylus. Prometheus bound 1
Aristophanes. The knights 1
Calderón de la Barca, P. Life
a dream 1
Euripides. Medea 1
Goethe, J. Faust, pt. I 2
Goldsmith, O. She stoops to con-
quer 1
Ibsen, H. A doll's house 2
Molière, J. The misanthrope 1
Racine, J. Phaedra 1
Sardou, V. Les pattes de
mouche 2
Schiller, F. Mary Stuart 2
Sheridan, R. The rivals 2
Sophocles. Oedipus rex 1

PLABE Plays by women/[selected
and introduced by Michelene
Wandor].--London: Methuen,
1983-84. 3v
Churchill, C. Vinegar Tom 1
Duffy, M. Rites 2
Gems, P. Aunt Mary; scenes from
provincial life 3
Gems, P. Dusa, Fish, Stas and
Vi 1
Goldemberg, R. Letters home 2
Horsfield, D. Red devils 3
Luckham, C. Trafford Tanzi 2
Page, L. Tissue 1
Pollock, S. Blood relations 3
Wakefield, L., and The Women's
Theatre Group. Time pieces
3
Wandor, M. Aurora Leigh 1
Wymark, O. Find me 2

PLAC Plays for a new theater; play-
book 2...[New York] New
Directions [1966] 282p
Alvaro, C. The long night of
Medea
Goll, Y. Methusalem; or, The
eternal bourgeois
Hawkes, J. The wax museum
Hivnor, R. The assault upon
Charles Sumner
Vian, B. Knackery for all

PLACE Plays from Padua Hills 1982/
edited by Murray Mednick.
Claremont, Calif: Pomona
College, c1983. 169p
Epstein, M. Mysteries of the
bridal night

Fornes, M. The Danube
LaTempa, S. Sunset Beach
Martell, L. Hoss drawin'
Mednick, M. Coyote V: Listening
to old Nana
Monroe, M. Politesse: A piece
for tape and landscape
O'Keefe, J. Bercilak's dream
Steppling, J. Neck

PLACI Plays Introduction: Plays
by new writers. London,
Faber, 1984. 343p
Clough, D. In Kanada
Darke, N. High water
Fletcher, J. Babylon has fallen
Fox, E. Ladies in waiting
James, L. Trial and error
Wertenbaker, T. New anatomies

PLAD Plays of a half-decade...
[London] Gollancz [1933]
1008p
Anthony, C. Autumn crocus
Bax, C. The rose without a thorn
Berkeley, R. The lady with a
lamp
Besier, R. The Barretts of Wim-
pole street
Dealfield, E. To see ourselves
Fagan, J. The improper duchess
Hoffe, M. Many waters
Mackenzie, R. Musical chairs
Sherriff, R. Journey's end
Van Druten, J. After all
Van Druten, J. Young Woodley

PLAG ...Plays of the Greek
dramatists...New York, Caxton
House [c1946] 360p
Note: Variant title: Eleven plays
of the Greek dramatists...
Aeschylus. Agamemnon
Aeschylus. Choephoroe
Aeschylus. The Eumenides
Aristophanes. The clouds
Aristophanes. The frogs
Aristophanes. Lysistrata
Euripides. The cyclops
Euripides. Iphigenia in Tauris
Sophocles. Antigone
Sophocles. Electra
Sophocles. Oedipus, the king

PLAH Plays of the Moscow art
theatre musical studio...English
translation from the Russian by

George S., and Gilbert
Seldes, with introductions
by Oliver M. Sayler. New
York, Brentano [c1925]
v.p.
Aristophanes. Lysistrata
Lecocq, C. The daughter of
Madame Angot
Lipskeroff, C. Carmencita
and the soldier
Offenbach, J. La périchole
Pushkin, A. Love and death,
featuring "Aleko," by Rach-
maninoff

PLAJ Plays of the sixties. Se-
lected by J. M. Charlton.
London, Pan Books, 1966-1967.
2v
Campton, D. Soldier from the
wars returning 2
Chapman, J. Simple spymen 2
Lessing, D. Play with a tiger 1
Millar, R. The affair 2
Murdoch, I. and Priestley, J. A
severed head 2
Rattigan, T. Ross 1
Shaffer, P. The royal hunt of
the sun 1
Waterhouse, K. and Hall, W.
Billy Liar 1

PLAYS OF THE SOUTHERN AMERI-
CAS. See
SSTE Stanford University.
Dramatists' Alliance

PLAL Plays of the thirties. Selected
by J. M. Charlton. London,
Pan Books, 1966-1967. 2v
Besier, R. The Barretts of Wim-
pole Street 2
Bridie, J. Tobias and the angel
1
Coward, N. Private lives 2
Daviot, G. Richard of Bordeaux
1
Gow, R. and Greenwood, W. Love
on the dole 1
Rattigan, T. French without
tears 2
Smith, D. Autumn crocus 2
Smith, D. Dear Octopus 1

PLAN Plays of the year, chosen by
J. C. Trewin...London, Paul
Elek; New York, Frederick

Ungar [c1949-1980] 48v
Abse, D. House of cowards 23
Achard, M. Rollo 20
Ackland, R. Before the party 2
Ackland, R. A dead secret 16
Albery, P. Anne Boleyn 14
Anouilh, J. The ermine 13
Anouilh, J. Medea 15
Anouilh, J. The waltz of the
toreadors 8
Arden, J. The party 18
Arout, G. Beware of the dog 33
Babel, I. Marya 35
Bagnold, E. Call me Jacky 34
Boland, B. Cockpit 1
Boland, B. Gordon 25
Boland, B. The prisoner 10
Boland, B. The return 9
Braddon, R. Naked island 22
Browne, F. The family dance 46
Browne, W. The holly and the
ivy 3
Bryden, B. Willie Rough 43
Chekhov, A. Uncle Vanya 39
Chetham-Stroke, W. Background
4
Christie, D. and Christie, C.
His excellency 4
Coffee, L. and Cowen, W. Family
portrait 1
Cooper, G. Out of the crocodile
27
Corlett, W. Tinker's curse 34
Crabbe, K. The last romantic 45
Cross, B. The mines of sulphur
30
Dewhurst, K. Lark rise 48
Dewhurst, K. Rafferty's chant
33
Dighton, J. The happiest days
of your life 1
Dighton, J. Who goes there! 6
Dinner, W., and Morum, W. The
late Edwina Black 2
Dobie, L., and Sloman, R. The
tinker 24
Dowling, J., and Letton, F. The
young Elizabeth 7
Dyer, C. Rattle of a simple man
26
Exton, C. Have you any dirty
washing, mother dear? 37
Fairchild, W. The sound of mur-
der 20
Feely, T. Don't let summer come
29
Fletcher, J. The chances 25

PLAN (cont.)

Francis, W. Portrait of a queen 30

Frisby, T. There's a girl in my soup 32

Frost, R. Small hotel 13

Gear, B. The sky is green 27

Gilbert, M. The bargain 23

Gilbert, M. A clean kill 21

Gillette, W. Sherlock Holmes 44

Goldoni, C. The servant of two masters 36

Gow, R. Ann Veronica 2

Gow, R. The Edwardians 20

Green, J. Murder mistaken 8

Green, J. South 12

Guinness, A., and Strachan, A. Yahoo 46

Guitry, S. Don't listen ladies! 1

Guthrie, T. Top of the ladder 3

Hale, J. The black swan winter 37

Hale, J. Spithead 38

Hanley, J. Say nothing 27

Harrison, J. Knight in four acts 38

Harrison, J. Unaccompanied cello 40

Harvey, F. The day after the fair 43

Hastings, C. Bonaventure 3

Hastings, C. Uncertain joy 12

Hastings, C. Seagulls over Sorrento 4

Hellman, L. The children's hour 5

Hochwälder, F. The public prosecutor 16

Hochwälder, F. The strong are lonely 14

Home, W. The jockey club stakes 40

Home, W. Lloyd George knew my father 42

Home, W. The queen's highland servant 35

Home, W. The secretary bird 36

Horne, K. Trial and error 9

Horne, W. The thistle and the rose 4

Howarth, D. Three months gone 39

Ibsen, H. John Gabriel Borkman 23

Jeans, R. Count your blessings 5

Jeans, R. Young wives' tale 3

Jones, P. Birthday honours 9

Jones, P. The last meeting of the Knights of the White Magnolia 47

Jones, P., and Jowett, J. The party spirit 11

Kennaway, J. Country dance 33

Kimmins, A. The amorous prawn 21

King, N. The shadow of doubt 12

King, P. Serious charge 11

King, P. and Cary, F. Sailor, beware! 12

King, P. and Cary, F. Watch it, sailor! 22

Kleist, H. The Prince of Homburg 36

Launder, F. and Guilliat, S. Meet a body 10

Leigh, M. Abigail's party 47

Leonard, H. Da 44

Leonard, H. The Patrick Pearse motel 41

Leonard, H. The poker session 28

Lethbridge, N. The Portsmouth defence 32

Levy, B. The member for Gaza 32

Lewis, S. Siwan 21

Lonsdale, F. Let them eat cake 19

Luke, P. Hadrian VII 33

Macauley, P. The creeper 29

MacDougall, R. The gentle gunman 5

MacDougall, R. To Dorothy, a son 4

MacIlwraith, B. The anniversary 31

Mackie, P. The big killing 25

Mackie, P. The whole truth 13

Macrae, A. Both ends meet 10

Marcus, F. Beauty and the beast 46

Marcus, F. Formation dancers 28

Marcus, F. The killing of Sister George 31

Marcus, F. Mrs. Mouse are you within? 35

Marcus, F. Notes on a love affair 42

Massinger, P. The city madam 28

The sacrifice of Isaac
The salutation and conception
Secunda pastorum
Thersytes
Bale, J. King John
Heywood, J. The pardoner and
the frere
Skelton, J. Magnyfycence

POLLARD, ALFRED WILLIAM. See
also
FIF Fifteenth century prose
and verse

POOL Pooley, Robert C.; Farmer,
Paul; Thornton, Helen and
Anderson, George K., eds.
England in literature...Chica-
go, Scott, Foresman [c1953]
752p
Fry, C. The boy with a cart
Goldsmith, O. She stoops to
conquer
Shakespeare, W. Macbeth

POP Popkin, Henry, ed. The new
British drama...New York,
Grove Press [1964] 606p
Arden, J. Serjeant Musgrave's
dance
Behan, B. The hostage
Delaney, S. A taste of honey
Pinter, H. The caretaker
Simpson, N. One way pendulum
Wesker, A. Roots

POR The portable Roman reader.
Edited, and with an introduction, by Basil Davenport. Harmondsworth, Middlesex, Penguin,
1977. 656p
Plautus. Amphitryon
Terence. Phormio

PRAT Pratt, Robert A. [and
others] eds. Masters of
British literature...Second
edition. Boston, Houghton
Mifflin [c1958, 1962] 2v
Arnold, M. Empedocles on Etna 2
Arnold, M. The strayed reveler
2
Shakespeare, W. The first part
of Henry the fourth 1
Shakespeare, W. The tragedy of
King Lear 1
Shakespeare, W. The winter's

tale 1
Shelley, P. Prometheus unbound
2

PRO Pronko, Leonard Cabell, ed.
Three modern French plays
of the imagination...[New
York, Dell, 1966] 252p (The
Laurel language library,
French series)
Ghelderode, M. Christophe
Colomb
Ionesco, E. Les chaises
Neveux, G. Juliette ou la clé
des songes

PROB Prose and poetry for appre-
ciation...edited by H. Ward
McGraw...Syracuse, N.Y.,
Singer [c1934] 1971p (The
prose and poetry series)
Dunsany, E. A night at an inn
Gregory, A. The rising of the
moon
Monkhouse, A. The grand cham's
diamond
Tarkington, B. Monsieur Beau-
caire

PROC Prose and poetry for appre-
ciation, edited by Elizabeth
Frances Ansorge [and others]
Syracuse, N.Y., Singer
[c1942] 787p (The prose and
poetry series)
Corwin, N. They fly through the
air
Gregory, A. Spreading the news
Kaufman, G., and Hart, M. The
American way
Knight, E. Never come Monday
Knight, V. Cartwheel

PROD Prose and poetry for appre-
ciation, edited by Harriet
Marcelia Lucas [and others]
Fourth edition. Syracuse,
N.Y. Singer [c1950] 822p
(The prose and poetry series)
Corwin, N. The odyssey of
Runyon Jones
Gilbert, W. and Sullivan, A. The
Mikado
Glaspell, S. Trifles
Sherwood, R. Abe Lincoln in
Illinois

PROF   Prose and poetry of America;
      edited by H. Ward McGraw...
      Syracuse, N.Y., Singer
      [c1934] 1034p (The prose
      and poetry series)
Fitch, C.   Nathan Hale
Glaspell, S.   Trifles
Hopkins, A.   Moonshine

PROG   Prose and poetry of America
      ...edited by H. Ward McGraw
      ...Syracuse, N.Y., Singer
      [c1934] 1198p (The new prose
      and poetry series. South-
      western edition)
Bowen, M.   Crude and unrefined
Fitch, C.   Nathan Hale
Fortune, J.   The cavalier from
  France
Glaspell, S.   Trifles
Hopkins, A.   Moonshine
Rogers, J.   Judge Lynch

PROH   Prose and poetry of America;
      edited by H. Ward McGraw [and
      others] Catholic edition...Syra-
      cuse, N.Y., Singer [c1940]
      1133p (The new prose and
      poetry series)
Fitch, C.   Nathan Hale
Hopkins, A.   Moonshine
Kelly, G.   Poor Aubrey

PROI   Prose and poetry of America
      ...edited by Julian L. Maline...
      Wilfred M. Mallon [and others]
      Syracuse, N.Y., Singer
      [c1949] 822p (At head of
      title: The St. Thomas More
      series)
Connelly, M.   The green pastures
Hopkins, A.   Moonshine
Mulvey, T.   Letter to Tuffy

PROM   Prose and poetry of England
      ...edited by H. Ward McGraw.
      Syracuse, N.Y., Singer
      [c1934] 1196p (The new
      prose and poetry series)
Dunsany, E.   The lost silk hat
Goldsmith, O.   She stoops to con-
  quer
Shakespeare, W.   Macbeth

PRON   Prose and poetry of England;
      edited by H. Ward McGraw.
      Catholic edition...Syracuse,

N.Y., Singer [c1940] 1150p
  (The new prose and poetry
  series)
Benson, R.   The upper room
Dunsany, E.   The lost silk hat
Shakespeare, W.   Macbeth

PROW   Prose and poetry of the
      world; edited by John R.
      Barnes [and others] Syracuse,
      N.Y., Singer [c1941] 1010p
      (The prose and poetry series)
Euripides.   Medea
Ibsen, H.   A doll's house
O'Neill, E.   Where the cross is
  made
Sachs, H.   The wandering scholar
  from Paradise
Synge, J.   Riders to the sea

PROX   Prose and poetry of the
      world; edited by James K.
      Agnew and Agnes L. Mc-
      Carthy...Syracuse, N.Y.,
      Singer [c1954] 788p
Čapek, K.   R.U.R.
Miller, A.   Pussycat and the ex-
  pert plumber who was a man
Williams, E.   Corn is green

PUCC   Pucciani, Oreste, F., ed.
      The French theater since
      1930...Boston, Ginn and
      Company [c1954] 400p
Camus, A.   Le malentendu
Cocteau, J.   La machine infernale
Giraudoux, J.   La guerre de
  Troie n'aura pas lieu
Montherlant, H.   La reine morte
Sartre, J.   Les mains sales

THE PULITZER PRIZE PLAYS. See
      CORD, CORE, CORF Cordell,
      Kathryn (Coe) and Cordell,
      William Howard, eds.

QUI   Quinn, Arthur Hobson, ed.
      Contemporary American plays
      ...New York, Scribner
      [c1923] 382p
Crothers, R.   Nice people
Emery, G.   The hero
Kaufman, G., and Connelly, M.
  To the ladies!
O'Neill, E.   The Emperor Jones

Williams, J. Why marry?

QUIJ Quinn, Arthur Hobson, ed.
Representative American
plays...New York, Century,
1917. 968p
Barker, J. Superstition
Belasco, D. and Long, J.
Madame Butterfly
Bird, R. The broker of Bogota
Boker, G. Francesca da Rimini
Boucicault, D. The octoroon; or,
Life in Louisiana
Crothers, R. He and she
Custis, G. Pocahontas; or, The
settlers of Virginia
Dunlap, W. André
Fitch, C. Her great match
Gillette, W. Secret service
Godfrey, T. The prince of
Parthia
Howard, B. Shenandoah
Howe, J. Leonora; or, The
world's own
MacKaye, P. The scarecrow
MacKaye, S. Hazel Kirke
Mitchell, L. The New York idea
Moody, W. The faith healer
Payne, J. and Irving W. Charles
the second
Rip Van Winkle
Ritchie, A. Fashion
Sheldon, E. The boss
Smith, R. The triumph at Platts-
burg
Thomas, A. The witching hour
Tyler, R. The contrast
Willis, N. Tortesa the usurer

QUIJR Quinn, Arthur Hobson, ed.
Representative American
plays from 1880 to the present
day...Modern drama ed. New
York, Century [c1928]
495-1052p
Belasco, D., and Long, J.
Madame Butterfly
Crothers, R. He and she
Fitch, C. Her great match
Gillette, W. Secret service
Howard, B. Shenandoah
MacKaye, P. The scarecrow
MacKaye, S. Hazel Kirke
Mitchell, L. The New York idea
Moody, W. The faith healer
O'Neill, E. Beyond the horizon
Sheldon, E. The boss

Thomas, A. The witching hour
Vollmer, L. Sun-up

QUIK Quinn, Arthur Hobson, ed.
Representative American plays,
1767-1923...3rd ed. rev. and
enl. New York, Century,
1925. 1052p
Barker, J. Superstition
Belasco, D. and Long, J. Madame
Butterfly
Bird, R. The broker of Bogota
Boker, G. Francesca da Rimini
Boucicault, D. The octoroon; or,
Life in Louisiana
Crothers, R. He and she
Custis, G. Pocahontas; or, The
settlers of Virginia
Dunlap, W. André
Fitch, C. Her great match
Gillette, W. Secret service
Godfrey, T. The prince of Parthia
Howard, B. Shenandoah
Howe, J. Leonora; or, The world's
own
MacKaye, P. The scarecrow
MacKaye, S. Hazel Kirke
Mitchell, L. The New York idea
Moody, W. The faith healer
O'Neill, E. Beyond the horizon
Payne, J. and Irving, W. Charles
the second
Rip Van Winkle
Ritchie, A. Fashion
Sheldon, E. The boss
Smith, R. The triumph at Platts-
burg
Thomas, A. The witching hour
Tyler, R. The contrast
Vollmer, L. Sun-up
Willis, N. Tortesa the usurer

QUIL Quinn, Arthur Hobson, ed.
Representative American plays
from 1767 to the present day...
5th ed. rev. and enl. New
York, Century [c1930] 1107p
Barker, J. Superstition
Barry, P. Paris bound
Belasco, D. and Long, J.
Madame Butterfly
Bird, R. The broker of Bogota
Boker, G. Francesca da Rimini
Boucicault, D. The octoroon; or,
Life in Louisiana
Crothers, R. He and she
Custis, G. Pocahontas; or, the

QUIL (cont.)
  settlers of Virginia
Dunlap, W. André
Fitch, C. The girl with the
  green eyes
Gillette, W. Secret service
Godfrey, T. The prince of
  Parthia
Herne, J. Margaret Fleming
Howard, B. Shenandoah
Howard, S. The silver cord
MacKaye, P. The scarecrow
MacKaye, S. Hazel Kirke
Mitchell, L. The New York idea
Moody, W. The faith healer
O'Neill, E. Beyond the horizon
Payne, J., and Irving, W.
  Charles the second
Rip Van Winkle
Ritchie, A. Fashion
Sheldon, E. The boss
Thomas, A. The witching hour
Tyler, R. The contrast
Vollmer, L. Sun-up
Willis, N. Tortesa the usurer

QUIM Quinn, Arthur Hobson, ed.
  Representative plays from 1767
  to the present day...6th ed.
  rev. and enl. New York,
  Appleton-Century [c1938]
  1157p
Anderson, M. Winterset
Barker, J. Superstition
Barry, P. Paris bound
Belasco, D. and Long, J.
  Madame Butterfly
Bird, R. The broker of Bogota
Boker, G. Francesca da Rimini
Boucicault, D. The octoroon; or,
  Life in Louisiana
Crothers, R. He and she
Custis, G. Pocahontas; or, The
  settlers of Virginia
Dunlap, W. André
Fitch, C. The girl with the
  green eyes
Gillette, W. Secret service
Godfrey, T. The prince of
  Parthia
Herne, J. Margaret Fleming
Howard, B. Shenandoah
Howard, S. The silver cord
MacKaye, P. The scarecrow
MacKaye, S. Hazel Kirke
Mitchell, L. The New York idea
Moody, W. The faith healer

O'Neill, E. Beyond the horizon
Payne, J. and Irving, W. Charles
  the second
Rip Van Winkle
Ritchie, A. Fashion
Sheldon, E. The boss
Thomas, A. The witching hour
Tyler, R. The contrast
Vollmer, L. Sun-up
Willis, N. Tortesa the usurer

QUIN Quinn, Arthur Hobson, ed.
  Representative American plays
  from 1767 to the present day
  ...7th ed., rev. and enl.
  New York, Appleton-Century-
  Crofts [c1953] 1248p
Anderson, M. Winterset
Barker, J. Superstition
Barry, P. Paris bound
Belasco, D. and Long, J.
  Madame Butterfly
Bird, R. The broker of Bogota
Boker, G. Francesca da Rimini
Boucicault, D. The octoroon; or,
  Life in Louisiana
Crothers, R. He and she
Custis, G. Pocahontas; or, The
  settlers of Virginia
Dunlap, W. André
Fitch, C. The girl with the green
  eyes
Gillette, W. Secret service
Godfrey, T. The prince of Parthia
Haines, W. Command decision
Hammerstein II, O.; Rodgers, R.;
  Logan, J. and Michener, J.
  South Pacific
Herne, J. Margaret Fleming
Howard, B. Shenandoah
Howard, S. The silver cord
Jefferson, J. Rip Van Winkle
MacKaye, P. The scarecrow
MacKaye, S. Hazel Kirke
Mitchell, L. The New York idea
Moody, W. The faith healer
O'Neill, E. Beyond the horizon
Payne, J. Charles the second
Ritchie, A. Fashion; or, Life
  in New York
Sheldon, E. The boss
Thomas, A. The witching hour
Tyler, R. The contrast
Vollmer, L. Sun-up
Willis, N. Tortesa the usurer

QUIO Quinn, Arthur Hobson;

Baugh, Albert Croll and Howe,
Will David, eds. The litera-
ture of America...New York,
Scribner [c1929] 2v
Belasco, D. and Long, J.
Madame Butterfly 2
Boker, G. Francesca da Rimini
1
Howells, W. The unexpected
guests 2
O'Neill, E. Lazarus laughed 2
Tyler, R. The contrast 1

QUINTANA, RICARDO. See
EIGH Eighteenth century
plays...

RAI Raines, Robert Arnold, ed.
Modern drama and social
change. Englewood Cliffs,
N.J., Prentice-Hall, 1972.
339p
Brecht, B. Galileo
Camus, A. Caligula
Ionesco, E. The leader
O'Neill, E. The hairy ape
Shaw, G. Major Barbara
Ward, D. Day of absence

RAP Ramas, Wilhelmina Q.
Sugbuanon theatre from Sotto
to Rodriguez and Kabahar:
an introduction to pre-war
Sugbuanon drama. Quezon
City, University of the
Philippines Press, 1982.
369p
Kabahar, P. Babaye ug lalake
Kabahar, P. Miss Dolying
Rodriguez, B. Bomba Nyor!

RAV Ravicz, Marilyn Ekdahl, ed.
Early colonial religious
drama in Mexico: from
Tzompantli to Golgotha.
Washington, D.C., Catholic
University of America Press,
1970. 263p
The adoration of the kings
The destruction of Jerusalem
The final judgment
How the Blessed Saint Helen
found the holy cross
The merchant
The sacrifice of Isaac

Souls and testamentary executors

RAVA Ravitz, Abe C., ed. The
disinherited: plays; Myrna J.
Harrison and Robert J. Griffin,
consulting editors. Encino,
Calif., Dickenson Pub., 1974.
273p
Anderson, M. Winterset
Brown, W. The escape; or, A
leap for freedom
Caldwell, B. The king of soul;
or, The Devil and Otis Redding
The double Dutch act
The double Wop act
Figueroa, J. Everybody's a Jew
Green, P., and Green, E.
Fixin's: the tragedy of a
tenant farm woman
Hughes, L. Soul gone home
Jones, L. Great goodness of
life (A coon show)
Lamb, M. But what have you
done for me lately?
Levine, M., McNamee, G., and
Greenberg, D. The tales of
Hoffman--a series of excerpts
from the "Chicago Conspiracy"
trial
Miller, J. The Danites in the
Sierras
Moore, E. Angela is happening
O'Neill, E. All God's chillun got
wings
Rice, E. The adding machine
The school act
The straight and the Jew
Terkel, L. Monologues from
"Division Street, USA"
Van Itallie, C. Motel: a masque
for three dolls
Williams, T. Hello from Bertha
Williams, T. Talk to me like the
rain and let me listen

RAY Ray, Gordon Norton; Edel,
Leon; Johnson, Thomas H.;
Paul, Sherman and Simpson,
Claude, eds. Masters of
American literature...Boston,
Houghton [c1959] 2v
O'Neill, E. Desire under the elms
2
O'Neill, E. The long voyage home
2

READINGS FOR LIBERAL EDUCATION,

READINGS FOR LIBERAL EDUCATION,
(cont.)
 v.2. See
  LOCLA, LOCLB Locke, Louis
  Glenn [and others], eds.
  Introduction to literature...

REA Reality in conflict: literature
 of values in opposition. Glenview, Ill., Scott Foresman,
 1976. 511p
 Lawrence, J., and Lee, R. Inherit the wind
 Sophocles. Electra
 Vonnegut, K. Fortitude

REARDON, WILLIAM R. See also
 AMPA America's lost plays,
 v21, edited by Walter J.
 Meserve and William R. Reardon

REAG Reardon, William R., et al.,
 eds. The black teacher and
 the dramatic arts; a dialogue,
 bibliography, and anthology.
 Westport, Conn., Negro Uni-
 versities Press, 1970. 487p
 Davis, O. Curtain call, Mr.
  Aldridge, sir
 Jackson, C., and Hatch, J. Fly
  blackbird
 Mitchell, L. A land beyond the
  river
 Mitchell, L. Tell Pharaoh
 Shine, T. Morning, noon and
  night

RED Redman, Crosby E., comp.
 Designs in drama. Rev. ed.
 New York, Macmillan, 1968.
 365p
 Barrie, J. The admirable
  Crichton
 Rattigan, T. The Winslow boy
 Shakespeare, W. Julius Caesar
 Wouk, H. The Caine mutiny
  court martial

REDM Redman, Crosby E., comp.
 Drama II...New York, Mac-
 millan [c1962] 357p
 Barrie, J. The admirable
  Crichton
 Rattigan, T. The Winslow boy
 Shakespeare, W. Julius Caesar
 Van Druten, J. I remember
  mama

REED, HARRY B. See
 HAP Harbrace omnibus...

REEV Reeve, Franklin D., ed. and
 tr. An anthology of Russian
 plays...New York, Vintage
 Books [c1961, 1963] 2v
 Andreyev, L. He who gets
  slapped 2
 Blok, A. The puppet show 2
 Bulgakov, M. The days of the
  Turbins 2
 Chekhov, A. The sea gull 2
 Fonvizĭn, D. The minor 1
 Gogol, N. The inspector
  general 1
 Gorky, M. The lower depths 2
 Griboyedov, A. The trouble with
  reason 1
 Mayakóvsky, V. The bedbug 2
 Ostrovsky, A. The storm 1
 Pushkin, A. Boris Godunov 1
 Shvarts, E. The shadow 2
 Tolstoy, L. The power of dark-
  ness 1

REF Reflections in literature.
 Philip McFarland, et al., eds.
 Boston, Houghton Mifflin,
 c1975. 719p
 Shakespeare, W. Romeo and
  Juliet
 Sophocles. Antigone

REIL Reinert, Otto, ed. Classic
 through modern drama...Bos-
 ton, Little, Brown, 1970. 949p
 Albee, E. Who's afraid of Virginia
  Woolf?
 Brecht, B. The Caucasian chalk
  circle
 Chekhov, A. The three sisters
 Etherege, G. The man of mode;
  or, Sir Fopling Flutter
 Everyman
 Ibsen, H. The wild duck
 Jones, L. Dutchman
 Molière, J. Tartuffe
 O'Neill, E. The Emperor Jones
 Shakespeare, W. Hamlet
 Shaw, G. Caesar and Cleopatra
 Sophocles. Oedipus rex
 Strindberg, A. The ghost sonata
 Synge, J. Riders to the sea
 Weiss, P. The persecution and
  assassination of Jean-Paul
  Marat as performed by the in-

mates of the Asylum of
Charenton under the direction
of the Marquis de Sade

REIN Reinert, Otto, ed. Drama,
an introductory anthology...
Boston, Little, Brown
[c1961] 672p
Brecht, B. The good woman of
Setzuan
Chekhov, A. Three sisters
Everyman
Ibsen, H. The wild duck
Ionesco, E. The lesson
Miller, A. A view from the
bridge
Molière, J. Tartuffe
Shakespeare, W. Macbeth
Shaw, G. Arms and the man
Sophocles. Oedipus rex
Strindberg, A. The ghost so-
nata
Yeats, W. Purgatory

REIO Reinert, Otto, ed. Drama,
an introductory anthology.
Alternate ed. Boston, Little,
Brown [1964] 889p
Albee, E. The American dream
Brecht, B. The Caucasian chalk
circle
Chekhov, A. The cherry orchard
Ibsen, H. Hedda Gabler
Jonson, B. The alchemist
Molière, J. The misanthrope
Pirandello, L. Six characters in
search of an author
Shakespeare, W. Othello
Shaw, G. Caesar and Cleopatra
Sheridan, R. The rivals
Sophocles. Antigone
Strindberg, A. Miss Julie
Synge, J. The playboy of the
western world

REIP Reinert, Otto, ed. Modern
drama, nine plays...Boston,
Little, Brown [c1961, 1962]
491p
Brecht, B. The good woman of
Setzuan
Chekhov, A. Three sisters
Ibsen, H. The wild duck
Ionesco, E. The lesson
Pirandello, L. Six characters in
search of an author
Shaw, G. Arms and the man

Strindberg, A. The ghost sonata
Williams, T. The glass menagerie
Yeats, W. Purgatory

REIT Reinert, Otto, ed. Modern
drama. Alternate ed. Boston,
Little, Brown [1966] 630p
Albee, E. The zoo story
Brecht, B. The Caucasian chalk
circle
Chekhov, A. The cherry orchard
Ghelderode, M. Chronicles of
hell
Ibsen, H. The wild duck
Pirandello, L. Six characters in
search of an author
Shaw, G. Caesar and Cleopatra
Strindberg, A. The father
Synge, J. The playboy of the
western world
Williams, T. The glass menagerie
Yeats, W. The hour-glass

REIV Reinert, Otto, ed. Six plays,
an introductory anthology.
Boston, Little, Brown, 1973.
401p
Chekhov, A. The cherry orchard
Ibsen, H. Hedda Gabler
Molière, J. The misanthrope
Shakespeare, W. Othello
Sophocles. Antigone
Williams, T. The glass menagerie

REIW Reinert, Otto, and Arnott,
Peter, eds. Thirteen plays; an
introductory anthology. New
York, Little, Brown, 1978.
762p
Albee, E. Who's afraid of Virginia
Woolf?
Beckett, S. Act without words I
Chekhov, A. The cherry orchard
Ibsen, H. A doll's house
Jones, L. Dutchman
Miller, A. Death of a salesman
Molière, J. Tartuffe
Pinter, H. The dumb waiter
Pirandello, L. Six characters in
search of an author
Shakespeare, W. Hamlet
Shaw, G. Major Barbara
Sophocles. Oedipus the king
Strindberg, A. The ghost sonata

REIWE Reinert, Otto, and Arnott,
Peter, eds. Twenty-three

REIWE (cont.)
plays; an introductory anthology. New York, Little, Brown, 1978. 1232p
Albee, E. Who's afraid of Virginia Woolf?
Beckett, S. Act without words I
Brecht, B. The Caucasian chalk circle
Chekhov, A. The cherry orchard
Etherege, G. The man of mode
Everyman
Gilbert, W. S. Trial by jury
Ibsen, H. A doll's house
Jones, L. Dutchman
Miller, A. Death of a salesman
Molière, J. Tartuffe
O'Neill, E. Ah, wilderness!
Pinter, H. The dumb waiter
Pirandello, L. Six characters in search of an author
Racine, J. Phaedra
Shakespeare, W. Hamlet
Shaw, G. Major Barbara
Sophocles. Oedipus the king
Strindberg, A. The ghost sonata
Synge, J. Riders to the sea
Weiss, P. Marat/Sade
Wilde, O. The importance of being earnest
Yeats, W. Purgatory

RELIGIOUS DRAMAS, 1924-25. See
FED Federal council of the churches of Christ in America

RES Restoration plays/edited and introduction by Sir Edmund Gosse. London, Dent; New York, Dutton, 1974. 509p
Congreve, W. The way of the world
Dryden, J. All for love
Etherege, G. The man of mode
Farquhar, G. The beaux stratagem
Otway, T. Venice preserved
Vanbrugh, J. The provoked wife
Wycherley, W. The country wife

REST Restoration plays; with an introduction by Brice Harris... New York, Modern library [c1955] 674p
Congreve, W. The way of the world
Dryden, J. All for love

Etherege, G. The man of mode
Farquhar, G. The beaux' stratagem
Otway, T. Venice preserved
Vanbrugh, J. The relapse
Villiers, G. The rehearsal
Wycherley, W. The country wife

RET Restoration tragedies; edited... by James Sutherland, London, Oxford, 1977. 441p
Banks, J. The unhappy favourite
Dryden, J. All for love
Lee, N. Lucius Junius Brutus
Otway, T. Venice preserved
Southerne, T. Oroonoko

REV Revolution: a collection of plays. Edited by Gerald Weales and Robert J. Nelson. New York, McKay, 1975. 312p
Betti, U. The queen and the rebels
Lowell, R. Benito Cereno
O'Casey, S. The plough and the stars
Shakespeare, W. Coriolanus

RHE Rhode, Eric, ed. Novelists' theatre. Harmondsworth, Middlesex, Penguin, 1966. 279p
Dennis, N. August for the people
Spark, M. Doctors of philosophy
Wilson, A. The mulberry bush

RHO Rhodes, Solomon Alhadef, ed. The contemporary French theatre...New York, Crofts, 1942. 431p
Bernard, J. Martine
Claudel, P. L'annonce faite à Marie
Curel, F. Le repas du lion
Lenormand, H. L'homme et ses fantômes
Maeterlinck, M. Pelléas et Mélisande
Porto-Riche, G. Amoureuse
Raynal, P. Le tombeau sous l'Arc de triomphe
Romains, J. Cromedeyre-le-Vieil
Sarment, J. Les plus beaux yeux du monde

RICM (cont.)
  Hart, M. Lady in the dark
  Lerner, A. Camelot
  Masteroff, J. Cabaret
  Spewack, B., and Spewack, S.
    Leave it to me!
  Wasserman, D. Man of La Mancha
  Weidman, J., and Abbott, G.
    Fiorello!
  Wheeler, H. A little night music

RICN Richards, Stanley, ed. Ten
    classic mystery and suspense
    plays of the modern theatre.
    New York, Dodd, Mead, 1973.
    887p
  Archibald, W. The innocents
  Chodorov, E. King lady
  Christie, A. Ten little Indians
  Cohan, G. Seven keys to Bald-
    pate
  Hayes, J. The desperate hours
  Job, T. Uncle Harry
  Percy, E., and Denham, R.
    Ladies in retirement
  Priestley, J. An inspector calls
  Roffey, J. Hostile witness
  Williams, E. Night must fall

RICO Richards, Stanley, ed. Ten
    great musicals of the American
    theatre...Radnor, PA, Chilton,
    1973. 594p (See also RICM)
  Furth, G. Company
  Heyward, D., and Heyward, D.
    Porgy and Bess
  Kaufman, G., Ryskind, M., and
    Gershwin, I. Of thee I sing
  Laurents, A. Gypsy
  Laurents, A. West Side story
  Lerner, A. Brigadoon
  Perelman, S., and Nash, O.
    One touch of Venus
  Spewack, B., and Spewack, S.
    Kiss me, Kate
  Stein, J. Fiddler on the roof
  Stone, P. 1776

RICT Richards, Stanley, ed. The
    Tony winners: a collection of
    ten exceptional plays, winners
    of the Tony Award for the most
    distinguished play of the year.
    Garden City, N.Y., Doubleday,
    c1977. 935p
  Gilroy, F. The subject was roses
  Goodrich, F., and Hackett, A.

The diary of Anne Frank
  Hartog, J. de. The fourposter
  Heggen, T., and Logan, J.
    Mister Roberts
  McMahon, F. Brendan Behan's
    Borstal Boy
  Osborne, J. Luther
  Patrick, J. The teahouse of the
    August moon
  Rabe, D. Sticks and bones
  Walker, J. The River Niger
  Williams, T. The rose tattoo

RIL Richardson, Lyon Norman;
    Orians, George H., and Brown,
    Herbert R., eds. The heri-
    tage of American literature...
    Boston, Ginn [c1951] 2v
  O'Neill, E. Anna Christie 2

RIR Richardson, Willis, comp.
    Plays and pageants from the
    life of the Negro. Great Neck,
    N.Y., Core Collection Books,
    1979. 373p (Reprint of the
    1930 ed. published by Asso-
    ciated Publishers, Washington,
    D.C.)
  Burke, I. Two races
  Cuney-Hare, M. Antar of Araby
  Duncan, T. Sacrifice
  Guinn, D. Out of the dark
  Gunner, F. The light of the
    women
  McCoo, E. Ethiopia at the bar of
    justice
  Matheus, J. Ti Yette
  Miller, M. Graven images
  Miller, M. Riding the goat
  Richardson, W. The Black horse-
    man
  Richardson, W. The house of
    sham
  Richardson, W. The king's
    dilemma

RITS Ritchie, James M. and
    Garten, H. F., eds. and trs.
    Seven expressionist plays;
    Kokoschka to Barlach. London,
    Calder and Boyars [1968]
    201p
  Barlach, E. Squire Blue Boll
  Brust, A. The wolves
  Goll, I. Methusalem
  Kafka, F. The guardian of the
    tomb

Kaiser, T. The protagonist
Kokoschka, O. Murderer hope
  of womankind
Stramm, A. Awakening

RITV Ritchie, James M. and
  Stowell, J. D., eds. and trs.
  Vision and aftermath: four
  expressionist war plays...
  London, Calder and Boyars,
  1969. 208p
Goering, R. Naval encounter
Haesenclever, W. Antigone
Hauptmann, C. War, a Te Deum
Toller, E. Hinkelmann

ROB Robbins, Harry Wolcott and
  Coleman, William Harold, eds.
  Western world literature...
  New York, Macmillan, 1938.
  1422p
Aeschylus. Agamemnon
Aristophanes. The frogs
Calderón de la Barca, P. Keep
  your own secret
Euripides. Iphigenia at Aulis
Everyman
Goethe, J. Faust, pt. I
Ibsen, H. Ghosts
Molière, J. Misanthrope
O'Neill, E. Beyond the horizon
Plautus, T. The captives
Racine, J. Phaedra
Shakespeare, W. King Lear
Sheridan, R. The rivals

ROBE Robertson, Durant Waite,
  ed. The literature of medieval
  England. New York, McGraw-
  Hill, 1970. 612p
Everyman
Mactacio Abel
Secunda pastorum

ROBI Robinson, Charles Alexander,
  Jr., ed. An anthology of Greek
  drama, first series...New York,
  Rinehart [c1949] 269p (Rine-
  hart editions)
Aeschylus. Agamemnon
Aristophanes. Lysistrata
Euripides. Hippolytus
Euripides. Medea
Sophocles. Antigone
Sophocles. Oedipus the king

ROBJ Robinson, Charles Alexander,

Jr., ed. An anthology of
  Greek drama, second series...
  New York, Rinehart [c1954]
  398p (Rinehart editions)
Aeschylus. Choëphoroe
Aeschylus. Eumenides
Aeschylus. Prometheus bound
Aristophanes. The clouds
Aristophanes. The frogs
Euripides. The bacchae
Euripides. The Trojan women
Sophocles. Oedipus at Colonus
Sophocles. Philoctetes

ROBJA Robinson, Charles Alexander,
  Jr., ed. The spring of civili-
  zation, Periclean Athens. New
  York, Dutton, 1954. 464p
Aeschylus. Agamemnon
Euripides. Medea
Euripides. The Trojan women
Sophocles. Antigone
Sophocles. Oedipus at Colonus
Sophocles. Oedipus the king

ROBK Robinson, Cyril Edward, tr.
  The genius of the Greek
  drama...Oxford, Clarendon
  press, 1921. 96p
Aeschylus. Agamemnon
Euripides. Medea
Sophocles. Antigone

ROBM Robinson, Donald Fay,
  ed. The Harvard Dramatic
  Club miracle plays; ten plays
  translated and adapted by
  various hands...New York,
  French, 1928. 241p
The Benediktbeuren play
Bourlet, K. The nativity
The Hessian Christmas play
The Maastricht play
The pageant of the shearmen and
  the tailors
The provençal play
The star
The Towneley play
The Umbrian play
The wisemen

ROE Roberts, Carl Eric Bechhofer,
  tr. Five Russian plays, with
  one from the Ukrainian...New
  York, Dutton, 1916. 173p
Chekhov, A. The jubilee
Chekhov, A. The wedding

ROE (cont.)
  Evreinov, N. The beautiful
    despot
  Evreinov, N. A merry death
  Fonvizin, D. The choice of a
    tutor
  Ukrainka, L. [pseud.] The
    Babylonian captivity

ROET Roby, Robert C., and
  Ulanov, Barry, eds. Intro-
  duction to drama...New York,
  McGraw-Hill, 1962. 704p
  Chekhov, A. The cherry orchard
  Congreve, W. The way of the
    world
  Euripides. Medea
  Giraudoux, J. Tiger at the gates
  Ibsen, H. Rosmersholm
  Jonson, B. The alchemist
  Kaiser, G. From morn to midnight
  Lindsay, D. The satire of the
    three estates
  Molière, J. The misanthrope
  Plautus, T. Miles gloriosus
  Racine, J. Phaedra
  Shaw, G. Man and superman
  Sophocles. Oedipus rex
  Strindberg, A. The dance of
    death
  Webster, J. The Duchess of Malfi

ROGE Rogers, Winfield Heyser;
  Redinger, Ruby V., and Haydn
  II, Hiram C., eds. Explora-
  tions in living...New York,
  Reynal & Hitchcock [c1941]
  783p
  Ibsen, H. An enemy of the people
  Shakespeare, W. Hamlet
  Wilder, T. Our town

ROHAN, PIERRE DE. See
  FEE, FEF Federal theatre
  project. Federal theatre plays
  ...["Edited for the Federal
  theatre by Pierre de Rohan"]

ROHR Rohrberger, Mary; Woods,
  Samuel H., Jr., and Dukore,
  Bernard F., comps. An intro-
  duction to literature...New
  York, Random House [1968]
  983p
  Everyman
  Shakespeare, W. The tragedy of
    Macbeth

Shaw, G. Pygmalion
Sophocles. Antigone
Strindberg, A. A dream play
Williams, T. The glass menagerie

ROLF Rolfe, Franklin Prescott;
  Davenport, William H. and
  Bowerman, Paul, eds. The
  modern omnibus...New York,
  Harcourt, Brace [c1946]
  1071p
  Anderson, M. Key Largo
  Kaufman, G. and Ryskind, M.
    Of thee I sing
  Sherwood, R. Abe Lincoln in
    Illinois
  Thurber, J. and Nugent, E.
    The male animal

ROM Roman drama...Indianapolis
  Bobbs-Merrill [c1965] 463p
  Plautus, T. The Menaechmi
  Plautus, T. The haunted house
  Plautus, T. The rope
  Seneca, L. Medea
  Seneca, L. Oedipus
  Seneca, L. Thyestes
  Terence, P. The brothers
  Terence, P. Phormio
  Terence, P. The woman of
    Andros

ROMA Romano-V., Octavio I., and
  Rios C., Herminio, eds. El
  espejo--The morror: selected
  Chicano literature. Berkeley,
  CA, Quinto Sol, 1972.
  Portillo, E. The day of the
    swallows

ROSE, MARTIAL. See
  TOWN Towneley plays. The
  Wakefield mystery plays...

ROSENFIELD, JOHN. See
  THX Three Southwest plays...

ROSENFIELD, PAUL. See
  AME American caravan...

ROSS Ross, Ralph Gilbert; Berry-
  man, John and Tate, Allen,
  eds. The arts of reading.
  New York, Thomas Y. Crowell
  [c1960] 488p
  Chekhov, A. A marriage proposal
  Shakespeare, W. The tragedy of

Macbeth

Scott, P. Pillars of salt

ROWC Rowell, George, ed. Late
Victorian plays, 1890-1914.
New York, Oxford, 1968.
507p
Davies, H. The mollusc
Galsworthy, J. Justice
Granville-Barker, H. The Voy-
sey inheritance
Hankin, St. J. The Cassilis en-
gagement
Houghton, S. Hindle wakes
Jones, H. The liars
Pinero, A. The second Mrs.
Tanqueray

ROWE Rowell, George, ed.
Nineteenth century plays...
London, Oxford University
Press [c1953] 567p
Albery, J. Two roses
Boucicault, D. The colleen bawn
Bulwer-Lytton, E. Money
Grundy, S. A pair of spectacles
Hazelwood, C. Lady Audley's
secret
Jerrold, D. Black-ey'd Susan
Lewis, L. The bells
Robertson, T. Caste
Taylor, T. The ticket-of-leave
man
Taylor, T. and Reade, C. Masks
and faces

ROY Roy, Emil, and Roy, Sandra,
comps. Literary spectrum.
Boston, Allyn, 1974. 355p
Andreëv, L. An incident
Chekhov, A. The bear
O'Neill, E. Hughie
Strindberg, A. The stronger
Synge, J. Riders to the sea

ROYE Roy, Emil, and Roy, Sandra,
comps. Literature I. New York,
Macmillan, 1976. 669p
Saroyan, W. My heart's in the
highlands
Synge, J. Riders to the sea

RUA Rubinstein, Harold Frederick,
ed. Four Jewish plays...
London, Gollancz, 1948. 303p
Bernhard, E. The Marranos
Block, T. You must stay to tea
Hemro. Poor ostrich

RUB Rubinstein, Harold Frederick,
ed. Great English plays...
New York, Harper, 1928.
1136p
Beaumont, F. and Fletcher, J.
The maid's tragedy
Congreve, W. The way of the
world
Dekker, T. The shoemaker's
holiday
Everyman
Farquhar, G. The recruiting of-
ficer
Fletcher, J. The chances
Ford, J. 'Tis a pity she's a
whore
Goldsmith, O. She stoops to
conquer
Heywood, J. John, Tyb, and
the curate
Jones, H. Judah
Jonson, B. The silent woman
Jonson, B., Chapman, G., and
Marston, J. Eastward ho!
Kyd, T. The Spanish tragedy
Marlowe, C. Doctor Faustus
Marlowe, C. Edward the second
Massinger, P. The bondman
Massinger, P. A new way to pay
old debts
Otway, T. Venice preserved
Peele, G. The old wives' tale
Robertson, T. Society
Sheridan, R. The school for
scandal
Vanbrugh, J. The provoked wife
A Wakefield nativity
Webster, J. The white devil
Wilde, O. Lady Windermere's fan
A Yorkshire tragedy

RUSS Russell, Harry Kitsun; Wells,
William and Stauffer, Donald
A., eds. Literature in English
...New York, Holt [c1948]
1174p
Shakespeare, W. King Lear
Sheridan, R. The school for
scandal

RUSV Russell, John David, and
Brown, Ashley, eds. Satire
...Cleveland, World Books,
[c1967] 420p
Euripides. The cyclops

RUSV (cont.)
  Mayokóvsky, V. The bedbug
  Molière, J. Love is the best
    doctor

RVI Russian satiric comedy: six
  plays, ed. and trans. by
  Laurence Senelick. N.Y.,
  Performing Arts Journal Publi-
  cations, 1983. 198p
  Babel, I. Sundown
  Bulgakov, M. Ivan Vasilievich
  Evreinov, N. The fourth wall
  Ilf, I. The power of love
  Krylov, I. The milliner's shop
  Prutkov, K. The headstrong
    Turk, or, Is it nice to be a
    grandson?

RYL Rylands, George Humphrey
  Wolfestan, ed. Elizabethan
  tragedy...London, Bell, 1933.
  623p
  Chapman, G. Bussy d'Ambois
  Ford, J. 'Tis a pity she's a
    whore
  Heywood, T. A woman killed
    with kindness
  Marlowe, C. Tamburlaine the
    great, pt. I
  Tourneur, C. The revenger's
    tragedy
  Webster, J. The white devil

SAFF Saffron, Robert, ed. Great
  farces...New York, Collier
  Books, 1966. 316p
  Aristophanes. Lysistrata
  Gogol, N. The inspector
    general
  Molière, J. Le bourgeois
    gentilhomme
  Spewack, B. and Spewack, S.
    Boy meets girl
  Wilde, O. The importance of
    being earnest

SAFM Saffron, Robert, ed. Great
  melodramas...New York,
  Collier Books, 1966. 341p
  Dumas, A. Monte Cristo
  Gillette, W. Secret service
  Hamilton, P. Angel street
  Maugham, W. The letter

SALE Salerno, Henry Frank, ed.
  English drama in transition
  1880-1920...New York,
  Pegasus [1968] 544p
  Barrie, J. The admirable Crichton
  Galsworthy, J. The silver box
  Jones, H. The liars
  Maugham, W. Our betters
  Pinero, A. The second Mrs.
    Tanqueray
  Shaw, G. Major Barbara
  Synge, J. The playboy of the
    western world
  Wilde, O. The importance of
    being earnest
  Yeats, W. Deirdre

SALF Salgādo, Ramsay Gāmini Nor-
  ton, ed. Four Jacobean city
  comedies. Drayton, Middlesex,
  Penguin, 1975. 428p
  Jonson, B. The devil is an ass
  Marston, J. The Dutch courtesan
  Massinger, P. A new way to pay
    old debts
  Middleton, T. A mad world, my
    masters

SALG Salgādo, Ramsay Gāmini Nor-
  ton, ed. Three Jacobean
  tragedies...Baltimore, Penguin
  Books [1965] 363p
  Middleton, T. The changeling
  Tourneur, C. The revenger's
    tragedy
  Webster, J. The white devil

SALR Salgādo, Ramsay Gāmini Nor-
  ton, ed. Three restoration
  comedies...Baltimore, Penguin
  Books [1968] 365p
  Congreve, W. Love for love
  Etherege, G. The man of mode
  Wycherley, W. The country wife

SAN San Francisco Mime Troupe.
  By popular demand; plays and
  other works. San Francisco,
  The Troupe, 1980. 302p
  San Francisco Mime Troupe. The
    Dragon Lady's revenge
  San Francisco Mime Troupe. Eco-
    man
  San Francisco Mime Troupe. False
    promises/Nos engañaron
  San Francisco Mime Troupe.

Frijoles, or Beans to you
San Francisco Mime Troupe.
Frozen wages
San Francisco Mime Troupe. The
independent female; or, A
man has his pride, a melodrama
San Francisco Mime Troupe. Los
siete
San Francisco Mime Troupe. San
Fran scandals; a vaudeville ex-
posé

SAND Sanderlin, George. College
reading...Boston, Heath
[c1953] 849p
Ibsen, H. An enemy of the
people
O'Neill, E. Bound east for Cardiff
Shaw, G. Androcles and the lion

SANE Sanders, Charles [and
others] eds. Synthesis:
responses to literature. New
York, Knopf, 1971. 750p
Chekhov, A. The three sisters
Euripides. The bacchae
Ibsen, H. The master builder
Itallie, J. America hurrah
Molière, J. Tartuffe
Pirandello, L. Henry IV

SANK Sanders, Thomas S. The
discovery of drama. Glenview,
Ill., Scott, Foresman, 1968.
637p
Bellow, S. Orange souffle
Chayefsky, P. The latent hetero-
sexual
Giraudoux, J. Sodom and Gomor-
rah
Shakespeare, W. Macbeth
Sophocles. Oedipus rex
Synge, J. Riders to the sea
Williams, T. Camino real

SANL Sanderson, James L. and
Gopnik, Irwin, eds. Phaedra
and Hippolytus: myth and
dramatic form. Boston,
Houghton Mifflin, 1966. 338p
Euripides. Hippolytus
Jeffers, R. The Cretan woman
O'Neill, E. Desire under the elms
Racine, J. Phaedra
Seneca. Phaedra

SANM Sanderson, James L. and
Zimmerman, Everett, eds.
Medea: myth and dramatic
form...Boston, Houghton
Mifflin [1967] 337p
Anderson, M. The wingless
victory
Anouilh, J. Medea
Euripides. Medea
Jeffers, R. Medea
Seneca. Medea

SANO Sanderson, James L. and
Zimmerman, Everett, eds.
Oedipus: myth and dramatic
form...Boston, Houghton
Mifflin [1968] 341p
Cocteau, J. The infernal
machine
Gide, A. Oedipus
Seneca. Oedipus
Sophocles. King Oedipus
Voltaire. Oedipus

SATA Satan, Socialites, and Solly
Gold: Three new plays from
England. New York, Coward-
McCann [c1961] 280p
Duncan, R. The death of Satan
Jupp, K. The socialites
Kops, B. Enter Solly Gold

SATI Satin, Joseph Henry, comp.
Reading literature...Boston,
Houghton Mifflin [1964]
1338p (Pt. III, Reading
drama)
Albee, E. The sand box
Betti, U. Corruption in the
palace of justice
Chekhov, A. Uncle Vanya
Hill, F. The six degrees of crime
Molière, J. The physician in spite
of himself
Steinbeck, J. Of mice and men
Strindberg, A. Miss Julie
Wilde, O. The importance of
being earnest

SATJ Satin, Joseph Henry, ed.
Reading literature; stories,
plays and poems...Boston,
Houghton Mifflin [1968] 683p
Albee, E. The sand box
Chekhov, A. Uncle Vanya
Giraudoux, J. The tiger at the

SATJ (cont.)
  gates
  Shaw, G. Arms and the man
  Sophocles. Oedipus the king

SAYLER, OLIVER MARTIN, See also
  MOS, MOSA Moscow art
  theatre series of Russian plays
  ...and PLAM Plays of the
  Moscow art theatre musical
  studio...

SAY Sayler, Oliver Martin, ed.
  The Eleonora Duse series of
  plays...New York, Brentano
  [c1923] v.p.
  Annunzio, G. d'. The dead city
  Gallarati-Scotti, T. Thy will be
  done
  Ibsen, H. Ghosts
  Ibsen, H. The lady from the sea
  Praga, M. The closed door

SCAN ...Scandinavian plays of the
  twentieth century...Princeton,
  N.J., Princeton University
  Press, 1944-1951. 3v
  Abell, K. Anna Sophie Hedvig 2
  Bergman, H. Mr. Sleeman is
  coming 1
  Bergman, H. The Swedenhielms
  3
  Dagerman, S. The condemned 3
  Grieg, N. The defeat; a play
  about the Paris Commune 2
  Josephson, R. Perhaps a poet 1
  Krog, H. The sounding shell 2
  Lagerkvist, P. Let man live 3
  Lagerkvist, P. The man without
  a soul 1
  Munk, K. Niels Ebbesen 2
  Schildt, R. The Gallows man:
  a midwinter story 1

SCAR Scanlan, David, comp. 5
  comedies. Boston, Houghton,
  Mifflin, 1971. 343p
  Giraudoux, J. The madwoman of
  Chaillot
  Pritchard, B. Captain Fantastio
  meets the ectomorph
  Saroyan, W. The time of your
  life
  Shaw, G. Arms and the man
  Sheridan, R. The rivals

SCAT Schell, Edgar Thomas, ed.

English morality plays and
  moral interludes...New York,
  Holt, Rinehart and Winston,
  1969. 554p
The castle of perseverance
Everyman
The interlude of youth
Lupton, T. All for money
Redford, J. Wit and science
Respublica
Wager, W. Enough is as good as
  a feast
Wapull, G. The tide tarrieth
  no man
Woodes, N. The conflict of
  conscience
World and the child

SCH Schelling, Felix Emmanuel,
  ed. Typical Elizabethan
  plays...New York, Harper,
  1926. 797p
  Beaumont, F. and Fletcher, J.
  The maid's tragedy
  Beaumont, F. and Fletcher, J.
  Philaster; or, Love lies a-
  bleeding
  Chapman, G., Jonson, B. and
  Marston, J. Eastward ho!
  Dekker, T. The pleasant comedy
  of Old Fortunatus
  Fletcher, J. Rule a wife and
  have a wife
  Ford, J. The chronical history
  of Perkin Warbeck, a strange
  truth
  Greene, R. A pleasant conceited
  comedy of [George a Greene],
  the pinner of Wakefield
  Heywood, T. A woman killed with
  kindness
  Jonson, B. The hue and cry
  after cupid
  Jonson, B. The sad shepherd
  Jonson, B. Volpone; or, The fox
  The lamentable and true tragedy
  of Master Arden of Feversham
  in Kent
  Lyly, J. Endymion, the man in
  the moon
  Marlowe, C. The tragical history
  of Doctor Faustus
  Marlowe, C. The troublesome
  reign and lamentable death of
  Edward II
  Massinger, P. A new way to pay
  old debts

Middleton, T. and Rowley, W.
The changeling
Munday, A. Sir Thomas More
(An ill May-day)
The return from Parnassus; or,
The scourge of simony,
pt. II
Shirley, J. The lady of pleasure
Webster, J. The tragedy of The
Duchess of Malfi

SCI Schelling, Felix Emmanuel and
Black, Matthew, W., eds.
Typical Elizabethan plays...
Rev. and enl. ed. New York,
Harper [c1931] 1033p
Beaumont, F. and Fletcher, J.
The knight of the burning
pestle
Beaumont, F. and Fletcher, J.
The maid's tragedy
Beaumont, F. and Fletcher, J.
Philaster; or, Love lies a-
bleeding
Chapman, G., Jonson, B. and
Marston, J. Eastward ho!
Dekker, T. The pleasant comedy
of Old Fortunatus
Dekker, T. The shoemaker's
holiday; or, The gentle craft
Fletcher, J. The faithful
shepherdess
Fletcher, J. Rule a wife and
have a wife
Ford, J. The broken heart
Greene, R. The honorable history
of Friar Bacon and Friar Bun-
gay
Heywood, T. A woman killed
with kindness
Jonson, B. Every man in his
humour
Jonson, B. The hue and cry
after cupid
Jonson, B. Volpone; or, The
fox
Kyd, T. The Spanish tragedy
Lyly, J. Endymion, the man in
the moon
Marlowe, C. Tamburlaine the
great, pt. I
Marlowe, C. The tragical history
of Doctor Faustus
Marlowe, C. The troublesome
reign and lamentable death of
Edward II
Massinger, P. A new way to pay

old debts
Middleton, T. Michaelmas term
Middleton, T. and Rowley, W.
The changeling
Munday, A. Sir Thomas More
(An ill May-day)
Peele, G. The old wives' tale
The return from Parnassus; or,
The scourge of simony, pt. II
Shirley, J. The lady of pleasure
Webster, J. The tragedy of The
Duchess of Malfi

SCJ Schelling, Felix Emmanuel and
Black, Matthew W., eds.
Typical Elizabethan plays...
Third edition, revised and
enlarged...New York, Harper
[c1949] 1065p
Beaumont, F. and Fletcher, J.
The knight of the burning
pestle
Beaumont, F. and Fletcher, J.
The maid's tragedy
Beaumont, F. and Fletcher, J.
Philaster; or, Love lies a-
bleeding
Chapman, G., Jonson, B. and
Marston, J. Eastward ho!
Dekker, T. The shoemaker's
holiday; or, The gentle craft
Fletcher, J. The faithful
shepherdess
Ford, J. The broken heart
Greene, R. The honorable his-
tory of Friar Bacon and Friar
Bungay
Heywood, T. A woman killed
with kindness
Jonson, B. Every man in his
humour
Jonson, B. The hue and cry
after cupid
Jonson, B. Volpone; or, The fox
Kyd, T. The Spanish tragedy
Lyly, J. Endymion, the man in
the moon
Marlowe, C. Tamburlaine the
great, pt. I
Marlowe, C. The tragical history
of Doctor Faustus
Marlowe, C. The troublesome
reign and lamentable death of
Edward II
Massinger, P. A new way to pay
old debts
Middleton, T. Michaelmas term

SCJ (cont.)
Middleton, T. and Rowley, W.
The changeling
Munday, A. Sir Thomas More
(An ill May-day)
Peele, G. The old wives' tale
The return from Parnassus; or,
The scourge of simony, pt. II
Shirley, J. The lady of pleasure
Webster, J. The tragedy of the
Duchess of Malfi

SCN Schinz, Albert; Robert, Os-
mond Thomas and Giroud,
Pierre François, eds.
Nouvelle anthologie française.
New York, Harcourt, Brace,
1936. 680p
Corneille, P. Le cid
La farce de maître Pierre
Pathelin
Hugo, V. Ruy Blas
Labiche, E. et Martin, E. La
poudre aux yeux
Molière, J. Le bourgeois gentil-
homme
Racine, J. Andromaque

SCNN Schneider, Elizabeth W.;
Walker, Albert L. and Childs,
Herbert E., eds. The range
of literature...New York,
American Book Company
[c1960] 732p
Chekhov, A. The cherry orchard
Rice, E. The adding machine
Shakespeare, W. Othello, the
Moor of Venice
Shaw, G. Arms and the man
Sophocles. Oedipus rex

SCNO Schneider, Elizabeth Winter-
steen; Walker, Albert L. and
Childs, Herbert E., eds. The
range of literature...2d ed.
New York, American Book Co.
[1967] 702p
Beckett, S. All that fall
Chekhov, A. The cherry orchard
Ionesco, E. Improvisation; or,
The shepherd's chameleon
Shakespeare, W. Othello
Shaw, G. Arms and the man
Sophocles. Oedipus rex
Wilder, T. The skin of our teeth

SCNP Schneider, Elizabeth Winter-

steen [and others] eds. The
range of literature. 3d ed.
New York, Van Nostrand-
Reinhold, 1973. 1116p
Chekhov, A. The cherry orchard
Hansberry, L. A raisin in the
sun
Ibsen, H. A doll's house
MacLeish, A. J.B.
Mrożek, S. The police
Shakespeare, W. Othello
Shaw, G. Arms and the man
Sophocles. Antigone

SCNPL Scholes, Robert; Klaus,
Carl H. and Silverman,
Michael, eds. Elements of
literature: essay, fiction,
poetry, drama, film. New
York, Oxford University Press,
1978. 1356p
Aristophanes. Lysistrata
Bullins, E. In the wine time
Everyman
Ibsen, H. A doll's house
Molière, J. The misanthrope
Pinter, H. A slight ache
Shakespeare, W. Othello
Shaw, G. Arms and the man
Sophocles. Oedipus rex
Strindberg, A. The stronger
Williams, T. Cat on a hot tin
roof

SCNQ Scholes, Robert; Comley,
Nancy R.; Klaus, Carl H. and
Silverman, Michael, eds. Ele-
ments of literature five: fic-
tion, poetry, drama, essay,
film. Revised ed. New York,
Oxford University Press, 1982.
1504p
Aristophanes. Lysistrata
Beckett, S. Krapp's last tape
Brecht, B. The threepenny
opera
Everyman
Hughes, L. Mother and child
Ibsen, H. A doll's house
Mankiewicz, H., and Welles, O.
Citizen Kane
Molière, J. The misanthrope
Shakespeare, W. Othello
Shaw, G. Major Barbara
Sophocles. Oedipus Rex
Strindberg, A. The stronger
Williams, T. Cat on a hot tin roof

SCNR Schorer, Mark, comp.
Galaxy: literary modes and
genres. New York, Harcourt,
Brace and World [1967] 620p
Chekhov, A. The three sisters
Euripides. The Trojan women
Giraudoux, J. Tiger at the gates
Lowell, R. My kinsman, Major
Molineux

SCNT Schorer, Mark, comp.
The literature of America:
twentieth century...New York,
McGraw-Hill, 1970. 1159p
Albee, E. The zoo story
Jones, L. Dutchman
O'Neill, E. Desire under the elms
Wilder, T. The skin of our teeth

SCV Schotter, Richard, ed. The
American place theatre. New
York, Dell Publishing Company,
1973. 270p
Cameron, K. Papp
Ribman, R. Fingernails blue as
flowers
Russell, C. Five on the black
hand side
Tabori, G. The cannibals
Tesich, S. The carpenters

SCW Schweikert, Harry Christian,
ed. Early English plays...New
York, Harcourt, Brace [c1928]
845p
Abraham and Isaac
Banns
Dekker, T. The shoemaker's
holiday
Everyman
The fall of Lucifer
Greene, R. The honorable history
of Friar Bacon and Friar Bun-
gay
Jonson, B. Every man in his
humour
The judgment day
Kyd, T. The Spanish tragedy
Lyly, J. Endymion
Marlowe, C. Tamburlaine the
great, pts. I and II
Marlowe, C. The tragical history
of Doctor Faustus
Noah
Peele, G. The old wives' tale
Quem quaeritis
Robin Hood and the friar

Sackville, T. and Norton, T.
Gorboduc
Saint George and the dragon
The second shepherds' play
Udall, N. Ralph Roister Doister

SCWE Schweikert, Harry Christian;
Inglis, Rewey Belle and
Gehlmann, John, eds. Adven-
tures in American literature...
New York, Harcourt, Brace
[c1930] 1064p
Fitch, C. Nathan Hale
O'Neill, E. Where the cross is
made
Tarkington, B. The trysting
place

SCWG Schweikert, Harry Christian;
Inglis, Rewey Belle; Gehlmann,
John and Foerster, Norman,
eds. Adventures in American
literature. Rev. ed. New
York, Harcourt Brace, 1936.
1217p
Kelly, G. Poor Aubrey
O'Neill, E. The Emperor Jones
Tarkington, B. The trysting
place

SCWI Schweikert, Harry Christian;
Miller, Harry Augustus and
Cook, Luella Bussey, eds. Ad-
ventures in appreciation...New
York, Harcourt, Brace, 1935.
1965p
Dunsany, E. The lost silk hat
Howard, S. and DeKruif, P.
Yellow jack
Shakespeare, W. As you like it

SCX Scott, Adolphe Clarence, ed.
and tr. Traditional Chinese
plays. Madison, University
of Wisconsin Press, 1967-75.
3v
The butterfly dream (Hu tieh
meng) 1
Fifteen strings of cash (Shih wu
kuan) 2
Longing for worldly pleasures
(Ssu fan) 2
Nü, C. A girl setting out for
trial 3
Shih, Y. Picking up the jade
bracelet 3
Ssu Lang visits his mother (Ssu

SCX (cont.)
Lang t'an mu) 1

SDQ The Scribner quarto of
modern literature; edited by
A Walton Litz. New York,
Scribner, 1978. 597p
Albee, E. The zoo story
O'Neill, E. Desire under the
elms
Pinter, H. A slight ache
Shaw, G. Pygmalion
Williams, T. The glass menagerie

SEA Searles, Colbert, ed. Seven
French plays (1730-1897)...
New York, Holt [c1935] 749p
Augier, E. Le gendre de M.
Poirier
Beaumarchais, P. Le mariage de
Figaro
Becque, H. Les corbeaux
Hugo, V. Hernani
Marivaux, P. Le jeu de l'amour
et du hasard
Rostand, E. Cyrano de Bergerac
Voltaire, F. Zaire

SEAVER, EDWIN. See
CROZ Cross-section...

SEBO Seboyar, Gerald Edwin and
Brosius, Rudolph Frederic, eds.
Readings in European literature.
New York, Crofts, 1928. 876p
Aeschylus. Prometheus bound
Aristophanes. The frogs
Euripides. Medea
Ibsen, H. Ghosts
Molière, J. The high-brow ladies
Plautus. The crock of gold
Racine, J. Phaedra
Sophocles. Antigone
Terence. Andria; the fair Andrian

SEBP Seboyar, Gerald Edwin and
Brosius, Rudolph Frederic, eds.
Readings in European literature
[Second edition] New York,
Crofts, 1946. 900p
Aeschylus. Prometheus bound
Aristophanes. The frogs
Euripides. Medea
Ibsen, H. Ghosts
Molière, J. The high-brow ladies
Plautus. The Menaechmi
Racine, J. Phaedra

Sophocles. Antigone
Terence. Andria; the fair
Andrian

SECK Secker, Martin. The
eighteen-nineties...London,
Richards [1948] 616p
Dowson, E. The pierrot of the
minute
Yeats, W. The Countess
Cathleen

SECOND AMERICAN CARAVAN.
1928. See
AME American caravan, v2

SELDES, GEORGE S. See
PLAM Plays of the Moscow
art theatre musical studio...

SELDES, GILBERT. See
PLAM Plays of the Moscow
art theatre musical studio...

SEN Seng, Peter J., ed. Plays;
Wadsworth handbook and an-
thology. Belmont, Calif.,
Wadsworth Publishing Company,
1970. 487p
Chekhov, A. The cherry orchard
Everyman
García Lorca, F. The house of
Bernarda Alba
Ibsen, H. The wild duck
Jonson, B. Volpone, or; The
fox
O'Neill, E. Desire under the elms
Pirandello, L. Six characters in
search of an author
The second shepherds' play
Shakespeare, W. Macbeth
Shakespeare, W. A midsummer
night's dream
Shaw, G. Heartbreak house
Sophocles. Oedipus rex
Strindberg, A. The ghost sonata
Synge, J. Riders to the sea
Webster, J. The Duchess of Malfi
Wycherly, W. The country wife

SER Seronde, Joseph and Peyre,
Henri, eds...Nine classic French
plays...Boston, Heath [c1936]
748p
Corneille, P. Le cid
Corneille, P. Horace
Corneille, P. Polyeucte

Molière, J. Le précieuses ridi-
  cules
Molière, J. Le misanthrope
Molière, J. Le Tartuffe
Racine, J. Andromaque
Racine, J. Esther
Racine, J. Phèdre

SERD Seronde, Joseph and Peyre,
  Henri, eds...Three classic
  French plays...Boston, Heath
  [c1935] 253p
Corneille, P. Le cid
Molière, J. Les précieuses ridi-
  cules
Racine, J. Andromaque

SET Setchanove, L. J. Five
  French comedies...Boston,
  Allyn and Bacon [c1925]
  276p
Bernard, T. L'anglais tel qu'on
  le parle
La farce de maitre Pathelin
Forest, L. Par un jour de pluie
France, A. La comèdie de celui
  qui épousa une femme muette
Maurey, M. Rosalie

SEV Seven plays...London, Heine-
  mann [1935] 775p
Coward, N. Conversation piece
Dane, C. Moonlight is silver
Kennedy, M. Escape me never!
Lonsdale, F. Aren't we all?
Priestley, J. Laburnum grove
Winter, J. The shining hour
Wooll, E. Libel

SEVD Seven plays of the modern
  theatre. With an introduction
  by Harold Clurman. New York,
  Grove Press [c1962] 548p
Beckett, S. Waiting for Godot
Behan, B. The quare fellow
Delaney, S. A taste of honey
Gelber, J. The connection
Genêt, J. The balcony
Ionesco, E. Rhinoceros
Pinter, H. The birthday party

SEVE Seven sacred plays with an
  introduction by Sir Francis
  Younghusband and notes by
  A. H. Debenham. London,
  Methuen [1934] v.p.
Bulkley, A. The crown of light

Debenham, A. Good will toward
  men
Debenham, A. The Prince of
  Peace
Gonne, F. In the city of David
Hines, L. Simon
Mell, M. The apostle play
The passion play of Alsfeld

SEVP Seven Soviet plays...with
  introductions by H. W. L.
  Dana. New York, Macmillan,
  1946. 520p
Afinogenov, A. On the eve
Korneichuk, A. The front
Leonov, L. The orchards of
  Polovchansk
Rokk, V. Engineer Sergeyev
Simonov, K. The Russian people
Solovyov, V. Field Marshall
  Kutuzov
Tur, L., Tur, P. and Sheinin, L.
  Smoke of the fatherland

SEVT Seventeen plays: Sophocles
  to Baraka. Edited by
  Bernard F. Dukore. New
  York, Crowell, 1976. 808p
Aristophanes. Lysistrata
Brecht, B. Mother Courage and
  her children
Büchner, G. Woyzeck
Chekhov, A. The sea gull
Ibsen, H. A doll's house
Ionesco, E. The gap
Jones, L. The slave
Molière, J. The school for wives
Pirandello, L. Each in his own
  way
The second shepherds' play
Shakespeare, W. Hamlet
Shaw, G. Pygmalion
Sophocles. Oedipus the king
Strindberg, A. The ghost sonata
Synge, J. Riders to the sea
Williams, T. The night of the
  iguana
Wycherley, W. The country wife

SHA Shafer, Robert, ed. American
  literature...New York, Doubleday, Doran [c1926] 2v
Fitch, C. The girl with the green
  eyes 2
O'Neill, E. "The hairy ape" 2

SHAH Shafer, Robert, ed. From

SHAH (cont.)
Beowulf to Thomas Hardy...
New York, Doubleday, Page
[c1924] 2v
Dryden, J. All for love 1
Everyman 1
Goldsmith, O. She stoops to
conquer 1
Marlowe, C. The tragical his-
tory of Doctor Faustus 1

SHAI Shafer, Robert, ed. From
Beowulf to Thomas Hardy...
Rev. ed. New York, Double-
day, Doran [c1931] 2v
Congreve, W. The way of the
world 1
Everyman 1
Marlowe, C. The tragical history
of Doctor Faustus 1
Sheridan, R. The rivals 2

SHAJ Shafer, Robert, ed. From
Beowulf to Thomas Hardy.
New ed...New York, Doubleday,
Doran [c1939] 2v
Dekker, T. ·The shoemaker's
holiday 1
Dryden, J. All for love; or, The
world well lost 1
Everyman 1
Marlowe, C. The tragical history
of Doctor Faustus 1
The second shepherds' play 1
Sheridan, R. The rivals 2
Wilde, O. The importance of
being earnest 2

SHAK Shakespeare the sadist/
Wolfgang Bauer/Rainer Werner
Fassbinder. My foot my tutor/
Peter Handke. Stallerhof/
Franz Xaver Kroetz. Trans.
[from the German] by Renata
and Martin Esslin, Anthony
Vivis, Michael Roloff, and
Katharina Hehn. London, Eyre
Methuen, 1977. 96p
Bauer, W. Shakespeare the sadist
Fassbinder, R. Bremen coffee
Handke, P. My foot my tutor
Kroetz, F. Stallerhof

SHAR Sharp, Russell, A.; Brewton,
John E.; Lemon, Babette, and
Abney, Louise, eds. English
and continental literature...

Chicago, Laidlaw [c1950]
800p (Cultural Growth series)
Gregory, I. The rising of the
moon
Molière, J. The physician in
spite of himself
Shakespeare, W. Macbeth

SHAT Shaver, Joseph L., comp.
Contemporary Canadian drama.
Ottawa, Borealis Press, 1974.
231p
Dunn, T. Maada and Ulka
Godlovitch, C. Timewatch
Graves, W. The proper per-
spective
Ravel, A. Black dreams
Spunde, W. The mercenary
Tallman, J. Trans-Canada High-
way
Tembeck, R. Baptism

SHAV Shaw, Harry, ed. A collection of readings for writers;
book three of A complete
course in freshman English.
6th ed. New York, Harper
and Row [1967] 722p
Shakespeare, W. The tragedy of
Macbeth
Shaw, G. Pygmalion
Sophocles. Antigone

SHAW Shaw, Harry, ed. A com-
plete course in freshman
English...Fifth edition. New
York, Harper & Brothers
[c1959] 1306p
Shakespeare, W. The tragedy of
Romeo and Juliet
Shaw, G. Pygmalion
Wilder, T. The long Christmas
dinner

SHAX Shaw, Harry Lee, ed. A
complete course in freshman
English. 7th ed. New York,
Harper, 1973. 836p
Shaw, G. Arms and the man
Sophocles. Antigone
Wilder, T. The long Christmas
dinner

SHAY Shay, Frank, ed. A treasury
of plays for women...Boston,
Little, Brown, 1922. 443p
Clements, C. Columbine

Clements, C. The siege
Dransfield, J. The lost Pleiad
Emig, E. The china pig
Gerstenberg, A. Ever young
Gerstenberg, A. A patroness
Knox, F. For distinguished service
Kreymborg, A. Manikin and Minikin
Kreymborg, A. Rocking chairs
McCauley, C. The conflict
Maeterlinck, M. The death of Tintagiles
Millay, E. The lamp and the bell
Morley, C. Rehearsal
O'Neill, E. Before breakfast
Pillot, E. My lady dreams
Smith, H. Blackberryin'
Strindberg, A. Motherly love
Strindberg, A. The stronger woman

SHER Sheratsky, Rodney E. and Reilly, John L., eds. The lively arts; 4 representative types. New York, Globe Book Co. [1964] 544p
Agee, J. Abraham Lincoln, the early years
Chayefsky, P. Marty
Lawrence, J. and Lee, R. Inherit the wind

SHERWOOD, GARRISON P. See BEST plays of 1894/1899...etc.

SHR Shrodes, Caroline; Van Gundy, Justine and Dorius Joel, comps. Reading for understanding: fiction, drama, poetry...New York, Macmillan [1968] 716p
Albee, E. The zoo story
Chekhov, A. The sea-gull
Ibsen, H. Ghosts
Shakespeare, W. Antony and Cleopatra
Sophocles. King Oedipus
Yeats, W. The words upon the window pane

SHRO Shroyer, Frederick Benjamin, and Gardemal, Louis G., comps. Types of drama. Glenview, Ill., Scott, Foresman, 1970. 678p
Aristophanes. The frogs

Brecht, B. The good woman of Setzuan
Everyman
Molière, J. Tartuffe
Powell, A. The death of everymom
Rostand, E. Cyrano de Bergerac
Shakespeare, W. Hamlet
Sheridan, R. The school for scandal
Sophocles. Oedipus the king
Wilder, T. The matchmaker
Williams, T. The glass menagerie

SIG The Signet classic book of 18th- and 19th-century British drama; edited and with an introduction by Katharine Rogers. New York, New American Library, Inc., 1979. 580p
Boucicault, D. The octoroon
Farquhar, G. The beaux' stratagem
Gay, J. The beggar's opera
Gilbert, W. Ruddigore
Lillo, G. The London merchant
Sheridan, R. The school for scandal
Steele, R. The conscious lovers
Wilde, O. The importance of being earnest

SILK Simonson, Harold Peter, ed. Quartet: a book of stories, plays, poems and critical essays. New York, Harper and Row, 1970. 1019p
Chekhov, A. Uncle Vanya
Ibsen, H. Ghosts
Strindberg, A. Miss Julie
Synge, J. Riders to the sea
Williams, T. The glass menagerie

SILKI Simonson, Harold Peter, ed. Quartet: a book of stories, plays, poems and critical essays. New York, Harper and Row, 1973. 1092p
Hansberry, L. A raisin in the sun
Ibsen, H. Ghosts
Ionesco, E. The gap
Strindberg, A. Miss Julie
Synge, J. Riders to the sea
Williams, T. The glass menagerie

SILM Simonson, Harold Peter, ed. Trio; a book of stories, plays,

SILM (cont.)
   and poems...New York, Harper & Brothers [c1962] 489p
Chekhov, A. The cherry orchard
Ibsen, H. Ghosts

SILN Simonson, Harold Peter, ed.
   Trio: a book of stories, plays
   and poems. 3d ed. New York,
   Harper, 1970. 747p
Chekhov, A. Uncle Vanya
Ibsen, H. Ghosts
Strindberg, A. Miss Julie
Synge, J. Riders to the sea
Williams, T. The glass menagerie

SILO Simonson, Harold Peter, ed.
   Trio: a book of stories, plays
   and poems. 4th ed. New
   York, Harper, 1975. 743p
Chekhov, A. Uncle Vanya
Ibsen, H. A doll's house
Miller, A. All my sons
Strindberg, A. Miss Julie
Synge, J. Riders to the sea
Williams, T. The glass menagerie

SILP Simonson, Harold Peter, ed.
   Trio: a book of stories, plays
   and poems. 5th ed. New
   York, Harper, 1980.
Chekhov, A. The cherry orchard
Ibsen, H. Hedda Gabler
Ionesco, E. The chairs
Williams, T. The glass menagerie

SIM Simpson, Claude Mitchell and
   Nevins, Allan, eds. The
   American reader...Boston,
   Heath [c1941] 866p
Connelly, M. The green pastures
Riggs, L. Green grow the lilacs
Wilder, T. Our town

SIN Singleton, Ralph H. and Millet,
   Stanton, eds. An introduction
   to literature...Cleveland, World
   [1966] 1237p
Ibsen, H. Hedda Gabler
Shakespeare, W. Measure for
   measure
Shakespeare, W. Othello
Shaw, G. Pygmalion
Sophocles. Antigone
Sophocles. Oedipus rex

SIXB Six great modern plays...

   [New York, Dell, c1956] 512p
Chekhov, A. Three sisters
Ibsen, H. The master builder
Miller, A. All my sons
O'Casey, S. Red roses for me
Shaw, G. Mrs. Warren's profes-
   sion
Williams, T. The glass menagerie

SIXC Six modern American plays.
   Introduction by Allan G. Hal-
   line...New York, Modern
   library [c1951] 419p
Anderson, M. Winterset
Heggen, T. and Logan, J. Mister
   Roberts
Hellman, L. The little foxes
Kaufman, G. and Hart, M. The
   man who came to dinner
O'Neill, E. The Emperor Jones
Williams, T. The glass menagerie

SIXD Six plays...London, Gollancz,
   1930. 672p
Bax, C. Socrates
Connelly, M. The green pastures
George, E. Down our street
Glaspell, S. Alison's house
Rice, E. Street scene
Sherriff, R. Badger's green

SIXH Six plays...London, Heine-
   mann [1934] 746p
Coward, N. Design for living
Dane, C. Wild Decembers
Kaufman, G. and Ferber, E.
   Dinner at eight
Maugham, W. Sheppey
Priestley, J. Dangerous corner
Winter, K. The rats of Norway

SIXL Six plays of 1939...[London]
   Hamilton [1939] v.p.
Behrman, S. No time for comedy
Hellman, L. The little foxes
Jones, J. Rhondda roundabout
Lyndon, B. The man in Half
   moon street
McCracken, E. Quiet wedding
Rattigan, T. After the dance

SIXP Six plays of today...London,
   Heinemann [1939] 716p
Coppel, A. I killed the count
Coward, N. Point Valaine
Hodge, M. The island
Priestley, J. Cornelius

Sherwood, R. Idiot's delight
Wolfe, H. The silent knight

SMA Small, Norman M., and Sutton,
     Maurice Lewis, eds. The
     making of drama. Boston,
     Holbrook Press, 1972. 691p
Brecht, B. The Caucasian chalk
     circle
Chekhov, A. The cherry orchard
Goldoni, C. The servant of two
     masters
Gorki, M. The lower depths
Kopit, A. Oh dad, poor dad,
     mama's hung you in the closet
     and I'm feelin' so sad
Molière, J. Tartuffe
Rice, E. The adding machine
Shakespeare, W. Hamlet
Sophocles. Oedipus the king

SMC Smith, Michael Townsend, ed.
     The best off off-Broadway.
     New York, Dutton, 1969. 256p
Agenoux, S. Charles Dickens'
     Christmas carol
Fornés, M. Dr. Kheal
Heide, R. Moon
Kvares, D. Mushrooms
Shepard, S. Forensic and the
     navigators
Smith, M. The next thing
Tavel, R. Gorilla queen

SME Smith, Michael Townsend, ed.
     More plays from off off-
     Broadway. Indianapolis.
     Bobbs Merrill, 1972. 409p
Birmisa, G. Georgie porgie
Eyen, T. Grand tenement and
     November 22
Handler, W. Flite cage
Hoffman, W. X
                    X
            X   X
                 X
Kennedy, A. A rat's mass
Koutoukas, H. Tidy passions, or
     kill, kaleidoscope, kill
Ludlam, C. Bluebeard
Mednick, M. Willie the germ
Williams, A. The poor little watch
     girl

SMI Smith, Robert Metcalf, ed...
     Types of domestic tragedy...
     New York, Prentice-Hall, 1928.

     576p (World drama series)
Annunzio, G. d'. Gioconda
Hebbel, F. Maria Magdalena
Heywood, T. A woman killed
     with kindness
Ibsen, H. Hedda Gabler
Lillo, G. George Barnwell; or,
     The London merchant
Pinero, A. Mid-channel
Strindberg, A. The father

SMK Smith, Robert Metcalf, ed...
     Types of historical drama...
     New York, Prentice-Hall,
     1928. 635p (World drama
     series)
Hebbel, C. Agnes Bernauer
Ibsen, H. The pretenders
Kleist, H. The prince of Homburg
Schiller, F. William Tell
Shakespeare, W. King Henry the
     fourth, pt. I
Tennyson, A. Becket

SML Smith, Robert Metcalf, ed...
     Types of philosophic drama...
     New York, Prentice-Hall, 1928.
     524p (World drama series)
Aeschylus. Prometheus bound
Andreev, L. The life of man
The book of Job
Byron, G. Manfred
Everyman
Marlowe, C. Dr. Faustus
Milton, J. Samson Agonistes
Shelley, P. Prometheus unbound

SMN Smith, Robert Metcalf, ed...
     Types of romantic drama...New
     York, Prentice-Hall, 1928. 621p
     (World drama series)
Corneille, P. The Cid
Dryden, J. All for love
Grillparzer, F. Sappho
Maeterlinck, M. Pelléas and
     Mélisande
Phillips, S. Paolo and Francesca
Rostand, E. Cyrano de Bergerac
Shakespeare, W. Romeo and
     Juliet

SMO Smith, Robert Metcalf, ed...
     Types of social comedy...New
     York, Prentice-Hall, 1928.
     759p (World drama series)
Congreve, W. The way of the
     world

SMO (cont.)
Goldsmith, O. She stoops to conquer
Massinger, P. A new way to pay old debts
Maugham, W. Our betters
Molière, J. Tartuffe
Pinero, A. The gay Lord Quex
Sheridan, R. The school for scandal
Wilde, O. Lady Windermere's fan

SMP Smith, Robert Metcalf, ed...
Types of world tragedy...New York, Prentice-Hall, 1928.
667p (World drama series)
Euripides. Medea
Gorki, M. The lower depths
Hauptmann, G. The weavers
Ibsen, H. Ghosts
Racine, J. Phaedra
Shakespeare, W. Othello, the Moor of Venice
Shelley, P. The Cenci
Sophocles. Oedipus the king

SMR Smith, Robert Metcalf and Rhoads, Howard Garrett, eds.
...Types of farce comedy...New York, Prentice-Hall, 1928.
598p (World drama series)
Aristophanes. The frogs
France, A. The man who married a dumb wife
Gay, J. The beggar's opera
Gilbert, W. and Sullivan, A. Patience
Molière, J. The doctor in spite of himself
Pinero, A. The magistrate
Plautus, T. The Menaechmi
Shakespeare, W. The taming of the shrew
Wilde, O. The importance of being earnest

SNO Snow, Lois Wheeler, ed. and tr. China on stage; an American actress in the People's Republic. New York, Random House, 1972. 328p
Ou-hung, W., and Chia, A. Red lantern
Red detachment of women
Shachiapang
Taking Tiger Mountain by strategy

SNYD Snyder, Franklyn Bliss and Martin, Robert Grant, eds. A book of English literature...4th edition. New York, Macmillan [c1942-43] 2v
Abraham and Isaac 1
Dryden, J. All for love 1
Everyman 1
Galsworthy, J. Loyalties 2
Marlowe, C. Doctor Faustus 1
Noah's flood 1
O'Casey, S. Juno and the paycock 2
Sheridan, R. The rivals 1

SOK Sokel, Walter Herbert, ed. Anthology of German expressionist drama; a prelude to the absurd. Garden City, N.Y., Doubleday, 1963. 365p
Brecht, B. Baal
Goll, Y. The immortal one
Hasenclever, W. Humanity
Kaiser, G. Alkibiades saved
Kokoschka, O. Job
Kokoschka, O. Murderer the women's hope
Lauckner, R. Cry in the street
Sorge, R. The beggar
Sternheim, C. The strongbox

SOM Somer, John L., comp. Dramatic experience: the public voice. Glenview, Ill., Scott, Foresman, 1970. 282p
Ibsen, H. Hedda Gabler
Shakespeare, W. Romeo and Juliet
Sophocles. Antigone
Synge, J. The playboy of the western world
Williams, T. The glass menagerie

SOMA Somer, John L., and Cozzo, Joseph, comps. Literary experience: public and private voices. Glenview, Ill., Scott Foresman, 1971. 681p
Ibsen, H. Hedda Gabler
Shakespeare, W. Romeo and Juliet
Sophocles. Antigone
Synge, J. The playboy of the western world
Williams, T. The glass menagerie

SOME Somerset, J. A. B., ed. Four Tudor interludes. London,

Athlone Press, 1974. 184p
An enterlude called Lusty Juven-
tus
Fulwell, U. Like will to like
Heywood, J. A play of love
Mankind

SOU Soule, George, comp. The
theatre of the mind. Engle-
wood Cliffs, N.J., Prentice-
Hall, 1974. 665p
Aeschylus. Agamemnon
Aristophanes. Lysistrata
Chekhov, A. The cherry orchard
Ibsen, H. Hedda Gabler
Molière, J. The miser
Pinter, H. The dumb waiter
Shakespeare, W. As you like it
Shakespeare, W. King Lear
Shaw, G. Pygmalion
Williams, T. The glass menagerie

SOUT South African people's plays;
ons phola hi/Plays by Gibson
Kente, Credo V. Mutwa, Mthuli
Shezi and Workshop '71/
Selected with introductory mate-
rial by Robert Mshengu Kav-
anagh. London, Heinmann.
[c1981] 176p
Kente, G. Too late
Mutwa, C. uNosilimela
Shezi, M. Shanti
Workshop '71 Theatre Company.
Survival

SPC Spearhead. 10 years' experi-
mental writing in America [New
York, New directions, c1947]
604p
Hutchins, M. Aunt Julia's Caesar
Stein, G. Daniel Webster eighteen
in America
Williams, T. 27 wagons full of
cotton

SPD Spencer, Hazelton, ed. British
literature. Boston, Heath
[c1951] 2v (V.1: From
Beowulf to Sheridan; V.2:
From Blake to the present day)
Congreve, W. The way of the
world 1
Dekker, T. The shoemakers'
holiday 1
Marlowe, C. Dr. Faustus 1
The second shepherds' play 1

Sheridan, R. The school for
scandal 1
Webster, J. The Duchess of Malfi
1

SPDB Spencer, Hazelton, ed.
British literature. 2nd ed.
Boston, Heath [c1963] 2v
(V.1: From Beowulf to
Sheridan; V.2: From Blake
to the present day)
Congreve, W. The way of the
world 1
Marlowe, C. Dr. Faustus 1
The second shepherds' play 1
Sheridan, R. The school for
scandal 1
Webster, J. The Duchess of Malfi 1

SPE Spencer, Hazelton, ed.
Elizabethan plays...Boston,
Little, Brown, 1933. 1173p
Beaumont, F. [and Fletcher, J.]
The knight of the burning
pestle
Beaumont, F. and Fletcher, J.
The maid's tragedy
Beaumont, F. and Fletcher, J.
Philaster; or, Love lies a-
bleeding
Chapman, G. Bussy d'Ambois
Chapman, G.; Jonson, B. and
Marston, J. Eastward ho!
Dekker, T. The honest whore,
pt. I
Dekker, T. The honest whore,
pt. II
Dekker, T. The shoemaker's
holiday
Fletcher, J. The wild-goose
chase
Ford, J. The broken heart
Greene, R. The honourable his-
tory of Friar Bacon and Friar
Bungay
Heywood, T. A woman killed
with kindness
Jonson, B. The alchemist
Jonson, B. Bartholomew fair
Jonson, B. Every man in his hu-
mour
Jonson, B. Volpone; or, The
fox
Kyd, T. The Spanish tragedy;
or, Hieronimo is mad again
Lyly, J. Endymion, the man in
the moon

SPE (cont.)
Marlowe, C. The Jew of Malta
Marlowe, C. Tamburlaine, pt. I
Marlowe, C. The tragical history
of Doctor Faustus
Marlowe, C. The troublesome
reign and lamentable death of
Edward the second
Marston, J. The malcontent
Massinger, P. A new way to pay
old debts
Middleton, T. A trick to catch
the old one
Middleton, T. and Rowley, W.
The changeling
Shirley, J. The lady of pleasure
Webster, J. The white devil; or;
Vittoria Corombona

SPEF Spencer, Hazleton; Houghton,
Walter E. and Barrows, Her-
bert. British literature...
Boston, Heath [c1951, 1952]
2v
Congreve, W. The way of the
world 1
Dekker, J. The shoemaker's
holiday 1
Marlowe, C. Doctor Faustus 1
The second shepherds' play 1
Sheridan, R. The school for
scandal 1
Webster, J. The Duchess of
Malfi 1

SPER Sper, Felix, ed. Favorite
modern plays...New York,
Globe Book Company [c1953]
530p
Barrie, J. The admirable Crich-
ton
Besier, R. The Barretts of
Wimpole Street
Galsworthy, J. Loyalties
Lindsay, H. and Crouse, R.
Life with father
Rattigan, T. The Winslow boy

SPES Sper, Felix, ed. Living
American plays...New York,
Globe Book [c1954] 454p
Hart, M. and Kaufman, G. You
can't take it with you
Howard, S. The late Christopher
Bean
Lavery, E. The magnificent
Yankee

Van Druten, J. I remember Mama
Williams, T. The glass menagerie

SPI Spiller, Robert Ernest, ed.
The roots of national culture;
American literature to 1830...
New York, Macmillan, 1933.
758p (American literature: a
period anthology; Oscar Cargill,
general editor, v1)
Tyler, R. The contrast

SPR Sprinchorn, Evert, ed. The
genius of the Scandinavian
theater. New York, New
American Library [1964] 637p
Avell, K. Days on a cloud
Holberg, L. Jeppe of the hill
Ibsen, H. The master builder
Ibsen, H. The wild duck
Lagerkvist, P. The difficult hour
Strindberg, A. Crimes and
crimes
Strindberg, A. To Damascus,
Part I

SRY Srygley, Ola Pauline and Betts,
Otsie Verona, eds. Highlights
in English literature and other
selections...Dallas, Texas,
Banks, Upshaw [1940] 868p
Goldsmith, O. She stoops to
conquer
Milne, A. The boy comes home
Shakespeare, W. Macbeth

SRYG Srygley, Ola Pauline and
Betts, Otsie Verona, eds.
Highlights in English litera-
ture...Dallas, Texas, Banks
Upshaw [c1940] 868p
Goldsmith, O. She stoops to
conquer
Milne, A. The boy comes home
Shakespeare, W. Macbeth
Tolstoy, L. What men live by

SSSF Stafford, William T., ed.
Twentieth century American
writing...New York Odyssey
Press [1965] 712p (The
Odyssey surveys of American
writing)
O'Neill, E. Desire under the elms
Rice, E. The adding machine
Williams, T. The glass menag-
erie

SSSI Stages of drama: Classical
to contemporary theater.
[Compiled by] Carl H. Klaus,
Miriam Gilbert and Bradford
S. Field, Jr. N.Y., Wiley
[c1981] 1098p
Aeschylus. Agamemnon
Aristophanes. Lysistrata
Beckett, S. Endgame
Brecht, B., and Hauptmann, E.
The threepenny opera
Chekhov, A. The cherry orchard
Etherege, G. The man of mode
Euripides. The bacchae
Everyman
García Lorca, F. The house of
Bernarda Alba
Ibsen, H. A doll's house
Jones, L. Dutchman
Jonson, B. Volpone
La farce de Maître Pierre Pathelin
Marlowe, C. Edward II
Miller, A. Death of a salesman
Molière. The misanthrope
O'Neill, E. A moon for the misbe-
gotten
Pinter, H. The homecoming
Pirandello, L. Six characters in
search of an author
Second shepherds' play
Shaffer, P. Equus
Shakespeare, W. Othello
Shaw, G. Major Barbara
Sheridan, R. School for scandal
Simon, N. Odd couple
Sophocles. Oedipus Rex
Strindberg, A. Miss Julie
Synge, J. Playboy of the Western
world
Webster, J. Duchess of Malfi
Williams, T. Cat on a hot tin roof

SSST Stallman, R. W. and Watters,
R. E. The creative reader...
New York, Ronald [c1954]
923p
Chekhov, A. The cherry orchard
Coxe, L. and Chapman, R. Billy
Budd
Ibsen, H. The wild duck
Shakespeare, W. The tempest
Sophocles. Antigone

SSSU Stallman, R. W. and Watters,
R. E. The creative reader...
Second edition. New York,
Ronald [c1962] 992p

Anouilh, J. Antigone
Coxe, L. and Chapman, R. Billy
Budd
Ibsen, H. The wild duck
Shakespeare, W. The tempest
Sophocles. Antigone

SSTA Stamm, Rudolf, ed...Three
Anglo-Irish plays...Bern,
Switzerland, A. Francke,
1943. 114p (Bibliotheca
Anglicana...v5)
Gregory, I. The rising of the
moon
Synge, J. Riders to the sea
Yeats, W. Deirdre

SSTE Stanford University.
Dramatists' Alliance. Plays of
the southern Americas...Stan-
ford Univ., Dramatists' Alliance,
1942. v.p.
Acevedo Hernández, A. Cabrerita
Sánchez, F. La Gringa
Vargas Tejada, L. Las convulsiones

SSTF Stanley, Linda, and Gillespie,
Sheena, comps. The treehouse:
an introduction to literature.
Cambridge, Mass., Winthrop
Pubs., 1974. 368p
Čapek, K., and Čapek, J.
The insect play
Euripides. Medea
Miller, A. A memory of two Mon-
days

SSTG Stanton, Stephen S., ed.
Camille and other plays...New
York, Hill and Wang [1957]
306p (Mermaid dramabook)
Augier, E. Olympe's marriage
Dumas, A. Camille
Sardou, V. A scrap of paper
Scribe, E. The glass of water
Scribe, E. and Bayard, J. A
peculiar position

SSTW Starkie, Walter Fitzwilliam,
ed. and tr. Eight Spanish
plays of the golden age...
New York, Modern Library
[1964] 328p
Calderón de la Barca, P. The
mayor of Zalamea
Cervantes Saavedra, M. The

SSTW (cont.)
jealous old man
Cervantes Saavedra, M. Pedro,
the artful dodger
The mystery play of Elche
Rueda, L. The mask
Ruiz, J. The gallant, the bawd,
and the fair lady
Téllez, G. The playboy of Se-
ville
Vega Carpio, L. Peribáñez and
the commander of Ocaña

SSTY Stasio, Marilyn, ed. Broad-
way's beautiful losers. New
York, Delacorte Press, 1972.
425p
Bellow, S. The last analysis
Mercier, M. Johnny no-trump
Perelman, S. The beauty part
Richardson, J. Xmas in Las
Vegas
Wheeler, H. Look: we've come
through

STAUFFER, RUTH MATILDA. See
also
FREI Freier, Robert...Ad-
ventures in modern literature

STA Stauffer, Ruth Matilda, comp.
The progress of drama through
the centuries...New York,
Macmillan, 1927. 696p
Bulwer-Lytton, E. The lady of
Lyons; or, Love and pride
Calderón de la Barca, P. The
constant prince
Corneille, P. Polyeucte
Euripides. The Trojan women
Everyman
Fitch, C. The truth
Goldsmith, O. She stoops to con-
quer; or, The mistakes of a
night
Ibsen, H. An enemy of the
people
Jonson, B. Epicoene; or, The
silent woman
Marlowe, C. Faustus
Molière, J. L'avare
Plautus, T. Aulularia; or, The
pot of gold
Racine, J. Berenice
Schiller, J. William Tell
The second shepherds' play
Shakespeare, W. Hamlet

Sheridan, R. The school for
scandal
Sophocles. Antigone

STAT Stauffer, Ruth Matilda and
Cunningham, William H., eds.
Adventures in modern litera-
ture. New York, Harcourt,
Brace [c1939] 1170p
Anderson, M. The feast of Or-
tolans
Galsworthy, J. The silver box
Gibney, S. and Collings, P. The
story of Louis Pasteur
Glaspell, S. Trifles
Goodman, K. and Hecht, B. The
hand of Siva
Sherriff, R. Journey's end

STAU Stauffer, Ruth Matilda and
Cunningham, William H., eds.
Adventures in modern litera-
ture...Second edition. New
York, Harcourt, Brace, 1944.
1042p
Čapek, K. R.U.R.
Gibney, S. and Collings, P. The
story of Louis Pasteur
Glaspell, S. Trifles
Goodman, K. and Hecht, B. The
hand of Siva
Sherriff, R. Journey's end
Wilde, P. Blood of the martyrs

STAV Stauffer, Ruth Matilda; Cun-
ningham, William H., and Sulli-
van, Catherine J., eds. Ad-
ventures in modern literature.
Third edition...New York,
Harcourt, Brace, 1951. 747p
Corwin, N. My client Curley
Glaspell, S. Trifles
O'Casey, S. The end of the be-
ginning
Sherriff, R. Journey's end
Van Druten, J. I remember mama

STE Steeves, Harrison Ross, ed.
Plays from the modern theatre
...Boston, Heath [c1931]
526p
Chekhov, A. The cherry orchard
Donnay, M. Lovers
Hauptmann, G. The beaver coat
Ibsen, H. Ghosts
Molnár, F. Liliom
O'Neill, E. The great god Brown

Pinero, A. The second Mrs.
  Tanqueray
Schnitzler, A. Intermezzo
Wilde, O. The importance of
  being earnest

STEI Steinberg, M. W., ed.
  Aspects of modern drama...
  [New York] Henry Holt
  [c1960] 633p
Anderson, M. Elizabeth the
  queen
Galsworthy, J. Strife
Miller, A. Death of a salesman
O'Neill, E. The great god
  Brown
Saroyan, W. The time of your
  life
Shaw, G. Candida
Shaw, G. Man of destiny
Synge, J. The playboy of the
  western world
Synge, J. Riders to the sea
Wilde, O. The importance of
  being earnest
Williams, T. The glass menagerie
Yeats, W. The dreaming of the
  bones

STI Steinhauer, Harry, ed. Das
  Deutsche drama, 1880-1933...
  New York, Norton [c1938] 2v
Hauptmann, G. Das friedensfest
Hofmannsthal, H. Der tor und
  der tod 1
Kaiser, G. Gas I 2
Schnitzler, A. Lebendige
  stunden 1
Toller, E. Masse mensch 2
Unruh, F. Heinruch aus Ander-
  nach 2
Wedekind, F. Der kammersänger
  1
Wiechert, E. Das spiel vom
  deutschen bettelmann 2

STJ Steinhauer, Harry and Walter,
  Felix, eds. Omnibus of French
  literature...New York, Mac-
  millan, 1941. 2v
Beaumarchais, P. Le barbier de
  Seville 1
Becque, H. Les corbeaux 2
Corneille, P. Le cid 1
Hugo, V. Ruy Blas 2
Marivaux, P. Le jeu de l'amour
  et du hasard 1

Molière, J. Le misanthrope 1
Racine, J. Andromaque 1

STJM Steinmann, Martin, Jr.
  and Willen, Gerald, eds.
  Literature for writing...Bel-
  mont, Cal., Wadsworth Pub-
  lishing Co. [c1962] 692p
Gay, J. The beggar's opera
Miller, A. Death of a salesman
Shakespeare, W. Henry IV

STJN Steinmann, Martin and Willen,
  Gerald, ed. Literature for
  writing; an anthology of
  major British and American
  authors...2d ed. Belmont,
  Calif., Wadsworth [1967]
  719p
Miller, A. Death of a salesman
Shakespeare, W. Henry IV
Synge, J. Riders to the sea
  (one act only)
Wilde, O. The importance of
  being earnest

STL Stern, Milton R. and Cross,
  Seymour L., eds. American
  literature survey...New York,
  Viking [c1962] 4v
O'Neill, E. The hairy ape 4
Tyler, R. The contrast 1

STM Stevens, David Harrison, ed.
  Types of English drama,
  1660-1780...Boston, Ginn
  [c1923] 920p
Addison, J. Cato
Buckingham, G., and others. The
  rehearsal
Congreve, W. Love for love
Congreve, W. The way of the
  world
Dryden, J. All for love; or, The
  world well lost
Dryden, J. Aureng-Zebe
Etherege, G. The man of mode;
  or, Sir Fopling Flutter
Farquhar, G. The beaux' strata-
  gem
Feilding, H. The tragedy of
  tragedies; or, The life and
  death of Tom Thumb the
  great
Gay, J. The beggar's opera
Goldsmith, O. The goodnatured
  man

STM (cont.)
  Goldsmith, O. She stoops to
    conquer; or, The mistakes
    of a night
  Home, J. Douglas
  Lillo, G. The London merchant;
    or, The history of George
    Barnwell
  Otway, T. Venice preserved;
    or, A plot discovered
  Rowe, N. Jane Shore
  Shadwell, T. Bury fair
  Sheridan, R. The critic
  Sheridan, R. The duenna
  Sheridan, R. The rivals
  Sheridan, R. The school for
    scandal
  Steele, R. The conscious
    lovers

STOC Stock, Dora and Stock,
    Marie, eds...Recueil de
    lectures...Boston, Heath
    [c1950] 240p
  Labiche, E. La grammaire

STONE, DONALD, JR. See
  FOUR Four Renaissance
  tragedies...

STRANSBERG, LEE. See
  FAM Famous American
  plays of the 1950's...

STR Strike while the iron is hot;
    three plays on sexual politics
    edited and introduced by
    Michelene Wandor. London,
    The Journeyman Press, 1980.
    141p
  Gay Sweatshop. Care and control
  Red Ladder Theatre. Strike while
    the iron is hot
  Women's Theatre Group. My
    mother says I never should

STRB Stroud, Theodore Albert,
    and Gordon, E. J., eds. The
    literature of comedy; an
    anthology. Boston, Ginn, 1968.
    763p
  Day, C. Life with father
  Rostand, E. Cyrano de Bergerac
  Shaw, G. Androcles and the lion
  Wilde, O. The importance of being
    earnest

STS Structure and meaning: an
    introduction to literature [ed.]
    by Anthony Duke; John K.
    Franson; Russell E. Murphy
    and James W. Parins. Boston,
    Houghton, 1976. 1222p
  Anderson, R. Tea and sympathy
  Bullins, E. The electronic nigger
  Chayefsky, P. Marty
  Inge, W. Come back, little Sheba
  McCullers, C. The member of
    the wedding
  Miller, A. All my sons
  O'Neill, E. The Emperor Jones
  Shakespeare, W. Romeo and Juliet
  Sophocles. Oedipus rex
  Synge, J. Riders to the sea

STY Styan, J. L., comp. The
    challenge of the theatre. En-
    cino, Calif., Dickenson Publish-
    ing Co., 1972. 421p
  Aeschylus. Agamemnon
  Chekhov, A. The cherry orchard
  Everyman
  Frisch, M. The firebugs
  Ibsen, H. The wild duck
  Pirandello, L. Six characters in
    search of an author
  Shakespeare, W. King Lear
  Shakespeare, W. Twelfth night
  Sophocles. Oedipus the king
  Strindberg, A. Miss Julie
  Synge, J. The shadow of the glen
  Wilde, O. The importance of being
    earnest
  Williams, T. The glass menagerie

SUB Sullivan, Victoria, and Hatch,
    James V., eds. Plays by and
    about women. New York,
    Random House, 1973. 425p
  Boothe, C. The women
  Childress, A. Wine in the wilder-
    ness
  Duffy, M. Rites
  Gerstenberg, A. Overtones
  Ginsberg, N. Advertisement
  Hellman, L. The children's hour
  Lessing, D. Play with a tiger
  Terry, M. Calm down, Mother

SUL Summers, Hollis Spurgeon and
    Whan, Edgar, eds. Literature:
    An introduction. New York,
    McGraw-Hill, 1960. 706p

Jonson, B. Volpone; or, The
  fox
MacLeish, A. The music crept
  by me upon the waters
Miller, A. The crucible
Shaw, G. The devil's disciple
Sophocles. Antigone
Wilder, T. The matchmaker
Williams, T. Something unspoken

SUM Summers, Montague, ed.
  Restoration comedies...London,
  Cape, 1921. 400p
Crowne, J. Sir Courtly Nice; or,
  It cannot be
Killigrew, T. The parson's
  wedding
Ravenscroft, E. The London
  cuckolds

SUMB Summers, Montague, ed.
  Shakespeare adaptations...
  London, Cape, 1922. 282p
D'Avenant, W. and Dryden, J.
  The tempest; or, The en-
  chanted island
Duffett, T. The mock-tempest;
  or, The enchanted castle
Tate, N. The history of King
  Lear

SUT Sutton, John F. and others,
  comps. Ideas and patterns in
  literature...New York, Harcourt,
  Brace, Jovanovich, 1970. 4v
Agee, J. The bride comes to
  Yellow sky 3
Anouilh, J. Antigone 2
Chekhov, A. The marriage pro-
  posal 1
Gibson, W. The miracle worker 1
O'Casey, S. The end of the be-
  ginning 4
O'Neill, E. Ile 3
Serling, R. Requiem for a heavy-
  weight 3
Serling, R. The shelter 2
Shakespeare, W. Julius Caesar 2
Shakespeare, W. Macbeth 4
Shaw, G. Arms and the man 4
Waugh, E. The man who liked
  Dickens 1
Wilder, T. Our town 3

SUTL Sutton, Larry M. and others,
  comps. Journeys: an introduction to literature. Boston,

Holbrook Press, 1971. 510p
Hughes, R. The sister's tragedy
Odets, C. Waiting for Lefty
Shakespeare, W. Othello
Sophocles. Antigone

SWA Swander, Homer D., ed. Man
  and the gods; three tragedies.
  Harcourt, Brace and World
  [c1964] 215p
Aeschylus. Agamemnon
Marlowe, C. The tragical history
  of Doctor Faustus
Shaw, G. Saint Joan

SWI Swire, Willard, ed. Three dis-
  tinctive plays about Abraham
  Lincoln...New York, Washington
  Square Press [c1961] 208p
Conkle, E. Prologue to glory
Drinkwater, J. Abraham Lincoln
Van Doren, M. The last days of
  Lincoln

SWIT Switz, Theodore MacLean and
  Johnston, Robert A., eds.
  Great Christian plays...Green-
  wich, Conn., Seabury, 1956.
  306p
Abraham and Isaac
Conversion of St. Paul
Everyman
Resurrection
Totentanz

SYM Symes, Ken M., ed. Two
  voices: writing about literature.
  Boston, Houghton Mifflin,
  1976. 289p
Everyman
Hansberry, L. A raisin in the sun

SYMONS, ARTHUR. See
  NER Nero (Tragedy). Nero &
  other plays

TAFT Taft, Kendall B. Minor
  knickerbockers...New York,
  American book company [c1947]
  410p
Payne, J. Charles the second

TAK Takaya, Ted T., ed. and tr.
  Modern Japanese drama, an
  anthology. New York, Columbia

TAK (cont.)
University Press, 1979.
277p
Abe, Kōbō. You, too, are
guilty
Betsuyaku, Minoru. The move
Mishima, Yukio. Yoroboshi: the
blind young man
Yamazaki, Masakazu. The boat
is a sailboat
Yashiro, Seiichi. Hokusai sketch
books

TAT Tatlock, John Strong Perry
and Martin, Robert Grant, eds.
Representative English plays...
New York, Century, 1916.
838p
Abraham and Isaac
Addison, J. Cato
Beaumont, F. and Fletcher, J.
Philaster; or, Love lies a-
bleeding
Browning, R. A blot in the
'scutcheon
Bulwer-Lytton, E. The lady of
Lyons; or, Love and pride
Congreve, W. The way of the
world
Dekker, T. The shoemaker's
holiday; or, The gentle craft
Dryden, J. Almanzor and Alma-
hide; or, The conquest of
Granada
Everyman
Fielding, H. The tragedy of
tragedies; or, The life and
death of Tom Thumb the great
Fletcher, J. The wild-goose
chase
Goldsmith, O. She stoops to con-
quer; or, The mistakes of a
night
Heywood, T. A woman killed with
kindess
Jonson, B. The alchemist
Lyly, J. Mother Bombie
Marlowe, C. The troublesome
reign and lamentable death of
Edward the second
Middleton, R. and Rowley, W.
The changeling
Noah's flood
Otway, T. Venice preserved; or,
A plot discovered
The second shepherds' play
Shelly, P. The Cenci

Sheridan, R. The school for
scandal
Steele, R. The conscious lovers
Webster, J. The Duchess of Malfi
Wilde, O. Lady Windermere's fan

TAU Tatlock, John Strong Perry
and Martin, Robert Grant, eds.
Representative English plays...
2d ed. rev. and enl. New
York, Appleton-Century
[c1938] 914p
Abraham and Isaac
Addison, J. Cato
Beaumont, F. and Fletcher, J.
Philaster; or, Love lies a-
bleeding
Bulwer-Lytton, E. The lady of
Lyons; or, Love and pride
Congreve, W. The way of the
world
Dekker, T. The shoemaker's
holiday; or, The gentle craft
Dryden, J. Almanzor and
Almahide; or, The conquest of
Granada
Everyman
Fielding, H. The tragedy of
tragedies; or, The life and
death of Tom Thumb the great
Fletcher, J. The wild-goose
chase
Goldsmith, O. She stoops to con-
quer; or, The mistakes of a
night
Heywood, T. A woman killed with
kindness
Jonson, B. The alchemist
Lillo, G. The London merchant;
or, The history of George
Barnwell
Lyly, J. Mother Bombie
Marlowe, C. The troublesome
reign and lamentable death of
Edward the second
Middleton, T. and Rowley, W.
The changeling
Noah's flood
Otway, T. Venice preserved;
or, A plot discovered
Pinero, A. The second Mrs.
Tanqueray
Robertson, T. Caste
The second shepherds' play
Shelley, P. The Cenci
Sheridan, R. The school for
scandal

Steele, R. The conscious lovers
Webster, J. The Duchess of Malfi
Wilde, O. Lady Windermere's fan

TAUJ Taylor, John Chesley, and
Thompson, Gary Richard,
comps. Ritual, realism, and
revolt; major traditions in the
drama. New York, Scribner,
1972. 816p
Adamov, A. Professor Toranne
Camus, A. Caligula
Eliot, T. Murder in the cathedral
Euripides. Medea
Euripides. Orestes
Ibsen, H. Hedda Gabler
Jones, L. The slave
Middleton, T. and Rowley, W.
The changeling
Miller, A. The crucible
O'Neill, E. The great god Brown
Osborne, J. The entertainer
Shakespeare, W. Othello
Sophocles. Antigone
Synge, J. Riders to the sea
Williams, T. Summer and smoke
Wycherley, W. The country wife
Yeats, W. Purgatory

TAV Taylor, Joseph Richard, ed.
European and Asiatic plays...
Boston, Expression co., 1936.
730p
Aristophanes. The frogs
Calderón de la Barca, P. Life
is a dream
Corneille, P. The cid
Dekker, T. The shoemaker's
holiday
Enamai Sayemon. The cormorant
fisher
Esashi Jūō. The bird catcher in
hell
Euripides. Medea
Everyman
Heywood, J. The four p's
Hroswitha. Dulcitius
Kālidāsa. Shakuntalā
Massinger, P. A new way to pay
old debts
Plautus, T. The Menaechmi
Sackville, T. and Norton, T.
Gorboduc
Seami, M. Atsumori
The second shepherds' play
Seneca, L. Medea
Shakespeare, W. The comedy of

errors
Shirley, J. The traitor
The sorrows of Han
Udall, N. Ralph Roister Doister

TAY Taylor, William Duncan, ed.
Eighteenth century comedy...
London, Oxford University
Press [1929] 413p (The
world's classics)
Farquhar, G. The beaux' strata-
gem
Fielding, H. The tragedy of
tragedies; or, The life and
death of Tom Thumb the great
Gay, J. The beggar's opera
Goldsmith, O. She stoops to con-
quer
Steele, R. The conscious lovers

TEN Ten Greek plays, translated
into English by Gilbert Murray
and others; with an introduction
by Lane Cooper, and a preface
by H. B. Densmore. New York,
Oxford University Press, 1930.
475p
Aeschylus. Agamemnon
Aeschylus. The choephoroe
Aeschylus. The eumenides
Arisophanes. The frogs
Aristophanes. Plutus, the god of
riches
Euripides. Electra
Euripides. Iphigenia in Tauris
Euripides. Medea
Sophocles. Antigone
Sophocles. Oedipus, king of
Thebes

TENN Tenth muse: classical drama
in translation; edited...by
Chalres Doria. Athens, Ohio,
Ohio University Press, Swallow
Press, 1980. 587p
Aeschylus. Prometheus bound
Aeschylus. The suppliants
Aristophanes. Peace
Euripides. The bacchae
Euripides. The cyclops
Plautus, T. The rope
Seneca, L. Thyestes
Sophocles. Philoctetes

THA Thayer, William Roscoe, ed.
The best Elizabethan plays...
Boston, Ginn [c1890] 611p

THA (cont.)

Beaumont, F. and Fletcher, J.
Philaster; or, Love lies a-
bleeding
Fletcher, J. and Shakespeare, W.
The two noble kinsmen
Jonson, B. The alchemist
Marlowe, C. The Jew of Malta
Webster, J. The Duchess of Malfi

THEA Theatre. 1953-56. Edited
by John Chapman...New York,
Random House [c1953-56] 4v
Abbott, G. and Bissell, R.
The pajama game 54
Anderson, M. The bad seed 55
Anderson, R. Tea and sympathy
54
Axelrod, G. The seven year itch
53
Bagnold, E. The chalk garden 56
Behrman, S. and Logan, J.
Fanny 55
Chase, M. Bernardine 53
Chodorov, E. Oh, men! Oh,
women! 54
Christie, A. Witness for the
prosecution 55
Denker, H. and Berkey, R. Time
limit! 56
Eliot, T. The confidential clerk
54
Fields, J. and Chodorov, J. The
ponder heart 56
Fields, J. and Chodorov, J.
Wonderful town 53
Gazzo, M. A hatful of rain 56
Giraudoux, J. Ondine 54
Giraudoux, J. Tiger at the gates
56
Hackett, A. and Goodrich, F. The
diary of Anne Frank 56
Hart, M. The climate of Eden 53
Hayes, J. The desperate hours
55
Howard, S. Madam, will you walk
54
Inge, W. Bus stop 55
Inge, W. Picnic 53
Kingsley, S. Lunatics and lovers
55
Knott, F. Dial "M" for murder
53
Kober, A. and Logan, J. Wish
you were here 53
Kurnitz, H. Reclining figure 55
Latouche, J. The golden apple 54

Laurents, A. The time of the
cuckoo 53
Lawrence, J. and Lee, R. Inherit
the wind 55
Levin, I. No time for sergeants
56
Loesser, F. The most happy fella
56
Maurette, M. Anastasia 55
Menotti, G. The saint of Bleeker
Street 55
Miller, A. The crucible 53
Miller, A. A view from the bridge
56
O'Brien, L. The remarkable Mr.
Pennypacker 54
Patrick, J. The teahouse of the
August moon 54
Rosten, N. Mister Johnson 56
Shulman, M. and Smith, R. The
tender trap 55
Spewack, S. and Spewack, B. My
three angels 53
Taylor, S. Sabrina fair 54
Teichman, H. and Kaufman, G.
The solid gold Cadillac 54
Ustinov, P. The love of four
colonels 53
Wilder, T. The matchmaker 56
Williams, T. Cat on a hot tin roof
55
Wouk, H. The Caine mutiny court-
martial 54
Young, S. Mr. Pickwick 53

THEC Theatre for tomorrow...London,
Longmans, Green, 1940. 397p
Breen, R. and Schnibble, H.
"Who ride on white horses," the
story of Edmund Campion
Lavery, E. and Murphy, G.
Kamiano, the story of Damien
Nagle, U. Savonarola, the flame
of Florence

THF Theatre guild. The Theatre
guild anthology...New York,
Random house [c1936] 961p
Anderson, M. Mary of Scotland
Andreyev, L. He who gets
slapped
Barry, B. Hotel Universe
Behrman, S. Rain from heaven
Ervine, St. J. John Ferguson
Heyward, D. and Heyward, D.
Porgy
Howard, S. The silver cord

Milne, A. Mr. Pim passes by
Milnár, F. Liliom
O'Neill, E. Strange interlude
Rice, E. The adding machine
Shaw, G. Saint Joan
Sherwood, R. Reunion in Vienna
Werfel, F. Goat song

THG The theatre of images. Edited
   ...by Bonnie Marranca. New
   York, Drama Books, 1977.
   122p
Breuer, L. The red horse ani-
   mation
Foreman, R. Pandering to the
   masses: a misrepresentation
Wilson, R. A letter for Queen
   Victoria

THH Theatre omnibus...[London]
   Hamilton [1938] v.p.
Behrman, S. Amphitryon 38
Jerome, H. Jane Eyre
Jerome, H. Pride and prejudice
Lyndon, B. The amazing Dr.
   Clitterhouse
Rattigan, T. French without
   tears
Savoy(!), G. George and Mar-
   garet

THI Theatre one, new South African
   drama; edited by Stephen Gray.
   Johannesburg, Ad. Donker
   (Pty) Ltd., 1978. 181p
Bosman, H. Street-woman
Dike, F. The sacrifice of Kreli
Fugard, A. Orestes
Livingstone, D. The sea my
   winding sheet
Uys, P. Paradise is closing down

THL The theatre of the Holocaust:
   four plays, ed...by Robert
   Skloot. University of Wiscon-
   sin Press, 1982. 333p
Delbo, C. Who will carry the
   word?
Lieberman, H. Throne of straw
Tabori, G. The cannibals
Wincelberg, S. Resort 76

THO Thomas, Russell Brown, ed.
   Plays and the theatre...Boston,
   Little, Brown, 1937. 729p
Anderson, M. Elizabeth the
   queen

Besier, R. The Barretts of Wim-
   pole street
Ibsen, H. An enemy of the
   people
Kelly, G. Poor Aubrey
Master Pierre Patelin
Molière, J. The miser
Morton, J. Box and Cox
O'Neill, E. In the zone
Shakespeare, W. Romeo and
   Juliet
Sheridan, R. The school for
   scandal
Sophocles. Antigone
Steele, W. The giant's stair

THOD Thompson, David, ed.
   Theatre today. London,
   Longmans, 1965. 206p
Albee, E. The sand box
Campton, D. Then...
Donleavy, J. The interview
Ionesco, E. The new tenant
Mankowitz, W. It should happen
   to a dog
O'Casey, S. Hall of healing
Pinter, H. The black and white
Pinter, H. Last to go
Saroyan, W. The oyster and the
   pearl
Shaw, G. Passion, poison and
   petrifaction

THOM Thompson, Stith, ed. Our
   heritage of world literature...
   New York, Dryden Press
   [c1938] 1246p
Aeschylus. Agamemnon
Aristophanes. The frogs
Chekhov, A. The cherry orchard
Euripides. Alcestis
Goethe, J. Faust, pt. I
Ibsen, H. A doll's house
Molière, J. The miser
Plautus, T. The captives
Racine, J. Phaedra
Shakespeare, W. Hamlet
Sophocles. Antigone
Wilde, O. The importance of
   being earnest

THON Thompson, Stith and Gassner,
   John, eds. Our heritage of
   world literature...Rev. ed.
   New York, Dryden Press
   [c1942] 1416p
Aeschylus. Agamemnon

THON (cont.)
Aristophanes. The frogs
Chekhov, A. The cherry orchard
Euripides. Alcestis
Goethe, J. Faust, pt. I
Hauptmann, G. The weavers
Ibsen, H. A doll's house
Molière, J. The miser
Plautus, T. The captives
Racine, J. Phaedra
Shakespeare, W. Hamlet
Sophocles. Antigone
Wilde, O. The importance of
being earnest

THOP Three Australian plays...
Harmondsworth, Middlesex,
Penguin [1963] 311p
Porter, H. The tower
Seymour, A. The one day of
the year
Stewart, D. Ned Kelly

THOR Three East European plays.
Hammondsworth, Middlesex,
Penguin, 1970. 271p
Hay, J. The horse
Havel, V. The memorandum
Mrożek, S. Tango

THP Three great Greek plays...
Selected [with an introduction]
by Lyman Bryson. Greenwich,
Conn., Fawcett [c1960]
Aeschylus. Agamemnon
Euripides. Hippolytus
Sophocles. Oedipus the king

THQ Three late medieval morality
plays/Mankind, Everyman,
Mundus et infans; edited by
G. A. Lester. London/Ernest
Bean Limited; New York/W.W.
Norton & Co., Inc., 1981.
157p
Everyman
Mankind
Mundus et infans

THR Three modern plays from the
French...New York, Holt,
1914. 272p
Donnay, M. The other danger
Lavedan, H. The prince d'Aurec
Lemaître, J. The pardon

THT Three Negro plays...Harmonds-
worth, Middlesex, Penguin,
1969. 207p
Hansberry, L. The sign in
Sidney Brustein's window
Hughes, L. Mulatto
Jones, L. The slave

THTN Three Nigerian plays.
London, Longmans, 1967.
89p
Ijimere, O. Born with the fire
on his head
Ladipo, D. Moremi
Ogunyemi, W. The scheme

THU Three plays. London,
Gardner, Darton [1926] v.p.
Ouless, E. Our pageant
Pakington, M. The queen of
hearts
Paul, Mrs. C. The fugitive king

THUG Three political plays; ed. by
Alrene Maude Sykes. St.
Lucia [Australia] University
of Queensland Press, 1980.
156p. (Contemporary Australian
plays, 9)
Bradley, J. Irish stew
Sewell, S. The father we loved
on a beach by the sea
Spears, S. King Richard

THV Three popular French comedies.
Translated and notes by Albert
Bermel. New York, Ungar,
1975. 170p
Beaumarchais, P. The barber of
Seville
Courteline, G. The commissioner
has a big heart
Labiche, E., and Delacourt, A.
Pots of money

THW Three Rastell plays: Four
elements, Calisto and Melebea,
Gentleness and nobility/
Edited by Richard Axton.
Cambridge, D. S. Brewer Ltd.
and Totowa, N.J., Rowman and
Littlefield, 1979. 169p (Tudor
Interludes)
Calisto and Melebea
Four elements
Heywood, J. Gentleness and
nobility

THWI Three Sanskrit plays.
Translated by Michael
Coulson. Harmondsworth,
Penguin, 1981. 430p
Bhavabhūti. Mālati and Mād-
hava
Kālidāsa. Sakuntalā
Vishākhadatta. Rākshasa's
ring

THWO Three sixteenth-century
comedies/Gammer Gurton's
needle, Roister Doister, The
old wife's tale/Edited by
Charles Walters Whitworth.
London/Ernest Benn Ltd.;
New York/W. W. Norton &
Co. Inc. 1984. 272p
Peele, G. The old wife's tale
Stevenson, W. Gammer Gurton's
needle
Udall, N. Roister Doister

THX Three Southwest plays...
With an introduction by John
Rosenfield. Dallas, Southwest
review, 1942. 326p
Acheson, S. We are besieged
Rogers, J. Where the dear
antelope play
Witherspoon, K. Jute

THY Three Soviet plays...Moscow,
Foreign Language Publishing
House [1961] 247p
Arbuzov, A. It happened in
Irkutsk
Korneichuk, A. Platon Krechet
Pogodin, N. Kremlin chimes

THZ Three Tudor classical interludes: Thersites, Jacke
Jugeler, Horestes/edited by
Marie Axton. Cambridge
[Cambridgeshire], D. S.
Brewer; Totowa, N.J., Rowan
and Littlefield, 1982. 237p
A new enterlude called Thersytes:
Thys enterlude folowynge doth
declare howe that the greatest
boesters are not the greatest
doers
A new enterlude for chyldren to
playe named Jacke Jugeler:
both wytte, very playsent, and
merye
A new enterlude of vice conteyn-

ing the history of Horestes
with the cruell rengment of
his fathers death upon his
one naturall mother

TICK Tickner, Frederick James, ed.
Restoration dramatists...Lon-
don, Nelson [1930] 229p
Dryden, J. Aureng-zebe
Farquhar, G. The beaux' strata-
gem
Otway, T. Venice preserved; or,
A plot discovered
Vanbrugh, J. A journey to Lon-
don

TICO Tickner, Frederick James, ed.
Shakespeare's predecessors...
London, Nelson [1929] 278p
Greene, R. Friar Bacon and Friar
Bungay
Heywood, J. The four p's
Kyd, T. The Spanish tragedy
Marlowe, C. Tamburlaine the
great [pt. I]

TOB To be; identity in literature.
Edited by Edmund J. Farrell,
[et al] Glenview, Ill., Scott
Foresman, 1976. 510p
Anouilh, J., and Aurenche, J.
Augustus
Blinn, W. Brian's song
Shakespeare, W. Romeo and Juliet

TOBI Tobin, James Edward; Hamm,
Victor M. and Hines, William
H., eds. College book of
English literature...New York,
American Book Co. [c1949]
1156p
Marlowe, C. The tragical history
of Doctor Faustus
The second shepherds' play
Synge, J. Riders to the sea

TOD Today's literature...edited by
Dudley Chadwick Gordon,
Vernon Rupert King and
William Whittingham Lyman...
New York, American Book Co.
[c1935] 998p
Bernard, L. Lars killed his son
Flavin, M. Amaco
Ford, H. Youth must be served
Galsworthy, J. The silver box
Green, P. In Abraham's bosom

TOD (cont.)
  Gregory, I. The workhouse ward
  Hopkins, A. Moonshine
  Jennings, T. No more frontier
  O'Neill, E. Where the cross is
    made
  Riggs, L. Knives form Syria

TOWN Towneley plays. The Wake-
    field mystery plays. Ed. by
    Martial Rose...London, Evans,
    c1961. 464p
  Abraham
  The annunciation
  The ascension of the Lord
  The buffeting
  Caesar Augustus
  The conspiracy
  The creation
  The crucifixion
  The deliverance of souls
  The first shepherds' play
  The flight into Egypt
  The hanging of Judas
  Herod the Great
  Isaac
  Jacob
  John the Baptist
  The judgment
  The killing of Abel
  Lazarus
  Noah
  The offering of the magi
  Pharaoh
  The pilgrims
  The play of the doctors
  The procession of the prophets
  The purification of Mary
  The resurrection
  The salutation of Elizabeth
  The scourging
  The second shepherds' play
  The talents
  Thomas of India

TRE A treasury of the theatre...
    from Aeschylus to Eugene
    O'Neill; edited by Burns
    Mantle and John Gassner.
    New York, Simon and
    Schuster, 1935. 1643p
  Aeschylus. Agamemnon
  Anderson, M. Elizabeth the
    queen
  Anderson, M. and Stallings, L.
    What price glory?
  Aristophanes. Lysistrata

Chekhov, A. The cherry orchard
Congreve, W. The way of the
  world
Connelly, M. The green pastures
Euripides. Electra
Everyman
Galsworthy, J. Escape
Goethe, J. Faust, pt. I
Gorki, M. The lower depths
Hauptmann, G. The weavers
Ibsen, H. Hedda Gabler
Job
Jonson, B. Volpone
Kālidāsa. Shakuntalā
Kaufman, G. and Ryskind, M.
  Of thee I sing
Kwanze, K. Sotoba Komachi
Molière, J. The misanthrope
Molnár, F. Liliom
O'Neill, E. Anna Christie
Pirandello, L. Six characters
  in search of an author
Racine, J. Phaedra
Rostand, E. Cyrano de Bergerac
Shakespeare, W. Hamlet
Shaw, G. Candida
Shelley, P. The Cenci
Sherriff, R. Journey's end
Sophocles. Antigone
Strindberg, A. The father
Synge, J. Riders to the sea
Webster, J. The Duchess of Malfi
Wilde, O. The importance of
  being earnest

TREA A treasury of the theatre...
    [edited by Burns Mantle and
    John Gassner] rev. and
    adapted for colleges by Philo
    M. Buck, jr., John Gassner
    [and] H. S. Alberson. New
    York, Simon and Schuster
    [c1940] 2v (v1, From Ibsen
    to Odets; v2, Aeschylus to
    Hebbel)
  Abraham and Isaac 2
  Aeschylus. Agamemnon 2
  Anderson, M. Elizabeth the
    queen 1
  Anderson, M. and Stallings, L.
    What price glory? 1
  Aristophanes. Lysistrata 2
  Chekhov, A. The cherry orchard
    1
  Congreve, W. The way of the
    world 2
  Connelly, M. The green pas-

TREBA (cont.)
Hauptmann, G. The weavers
Hellman, L. The little foxes
Ibsen, H. Ghosts
Ibsen, H. Hedda Gabler
Ionesco, E. The chairs
Maeterlinck, M. The intruder
Maugham, W. The circle
Miller, A. Death of a salesman
Molnár, F. Liliom
O'Casey, S. The plough and
the stars
Odets, C. Golden boy
O'Neill, E. Anna Christie
O'Neill, E. The hairy ape
Pirandello, L. Six characters in
search of an author
Rostand, E. Cyrano de Bergerac
Saroyan, W. My heart's in the
highlands
Sartre, J. The flies
Shaw, G. Candida
Sherriff, R. Journey's end
Stallings, L. and Anderson, M.
What price glory?
Strindberg, A. A dream play
Strindberg, A. The father
Strindberg, A. There are crimes
and crimes
Synge, J. Riders to the sea
Tolstoy, L. The power of dark-
ness
Wedekind, F. The tenor
Wilde, O. The importance of
being earnest
Wilder, T. Our town
Williams, T. The glass menagerie

TREBJ A treasury of the theatre.
4th ed. Edited by John Gass-
ner and Bernard F. Dukore.
New York, Simon and Schuster,
1970. 1298p
Albee, E. Who's afraid of Virginia
Woolf?
Anderson, M. Elizabeth the queen
Anouilh, J. The lark
Artaud, A. The spurt of blood
Becque, H. The vultures
Brecht, B. Galileo
Brecht, B. The good woman of
Setzuan
Chekhov, A. The cherry orchard
Claudel, P. The tidings brought
to Mary
García Lorca, F. Blood wedding
Giraudoux, J. The madwoman of

Chaillot
Gorki, M. The lower depths
Hauptmann, G. The weavers
Hellman, L. The little foxes
Ibsen, H. Ghosts
Ibsen, H. Hedda Gabler
Jarry, A. Ubu the king
Jones, L. Dutchman
Lowell, R. Benito Cereno
Maeterlinck, M. The intruder
Maugham, W. The circle
Miller, A. Death of a salesman
O'Casey, S. The plough and
the stars
Odets, C. Golden boy
O'Neill, E. The hairy ape
O'Neill, E. A moon for the mis-
begotten
Osborne, J. and Creighton, A.
Epitaph for George Dillon
Pinter, H. A slight ache
Pirandello, L. Six characters
in search of an author
Rostand, E. Cyrano de Bergerac
Saroyan, W. My heart's in the
highlands
Sartre, J. The flies
Shaw, G. Candida
Shaw, G. Heartbreak house
Strindberg, A. A dream play
Strindberg, A. The father
Synge, J. Playboy of the
western world
Synge, J. Riders to the sea
Tolstoy, L. The power of dark-
ness
Wedekind, F. The tenor
Wilde, O. The importance of
being earnest
Wilder, T. Our town
Williams, T. The glass menagerie
Witkiewicz, S. The cuttlefish
Yeats, W. Purgatory

TREC A treasury of the theatre...
Revised edition for colleges.
Edited by John Gassner...
New York, Simon and
Schuster [c1950-51] 2v
(v1, From Aeschylus to Tur-
genev; v2, From Henrik Obsen
to Arthur Miller)
Abraham and Isaac 1
Aeschylus. Agamemnon 1
Anderson, M. Elizabeth the
queen 2
Aristophanes. The frogs 1

TREE (cont.)

Euripides. The Trojan women 1

Everyman 1

Galsworthy, J. Escape 3

García Lorca, F. Blood wedding 2

Goethe, J. Faust 1

Gogol, N. The inspector 1

Gorki, M. The lower depths 2

Gregory, I. The workhouse ward 3

Hauptmann, G. The weavers 2

Hebbel, F. Maria Magdalena 1

Hellman, L. The little foxes 3

Ibsen, H. Ghosts 2

Ibsen, H. Hedda Gabler 2

Jonson, B. Volpone 1

Kālidāsa. Shakuntalā 1

Kwanze, K. Sotoba Komachi 1

Maeterlinck, M. The intruder 2

Marlowe, C. The tragical history of Doctor Faustus 1

Maugham, W. The circle 3

Miller, A. Death of a salesman 3

Molière, J. The misanthrope 1

Molnár, F. Liliom 2

Musset, A. No trifling with love 1

O'Casey, S. The plough and the stars 3

Odets, C. Golden boy 3

O'Neill, E. Anna Christie 3

O'Neill, E. The hairy ape 3

Pirandello, L. Six characters in search of an author 2

Plautus. The Menaechmi 1

Racine, J. Phaedra 1

Rostand, E. Cyrano de Bergerac 2

Saroyan, W. My heart's in the highlands 3

Sartre, J. The flies 2

The second shepherds' play 1

Shakespeare, W. Hamlet 1

Shaw, G. Candida 3

Sheridan, R. The school for scandal 1

Sherriff, R. Journey's end 3

Sophocles. Oedipus the king 1

Stallings, L. and Anderson, M. What price glory? 3

Strindberg, A. The father 2

Strindberg, A. There are crimes and crimes 2

Synge, J. Riders to the sea 3

Terence. The brothers 1

Tolstoy, L. The power of darkness 2

Turgenev, I. A month in the country 1

Vega Carpio, L. Fuente ovejuna 1

Webster, J. The Duchess of Malfi 1

Wedekind, F. The tenor 2

Wilde, O. The importance of being earnest 3

Wilder, T. Our town 3

Williams, T. The glass menagerie 3

TREI A treasury of the theatre-- Revised edition, edited by John Gassner. New York, Simon, 1963. 3v (v1, World drama: From Aeschylus to Turgenev; v2, Modern European drama: From Henrik Ibsen to Jean-Paul Sartre; v3, Modern drama: From Oscar Wilde to Eugène Ionesco)...

Abraham and Isaac 1

Aeschylus. Agamemnon 1

Anderson, M. Elizabeth the queen 3

Anouilh, J. The lark 3

Aristophanes. The frogs 1

Barrie, J. The admirable Crichton 3

Becque, H. The vultures 2

Brecht, B. The private life of the master race [excerpts] 2

Büchner, G. Danton's death 1

Čapek, K. R.U.R. 2

Chekhov, A. The cherry orchard 2

Claudel, P. The tidings brought to Mary 3

Congreve, W. The way of the world 1

Connelly, M. The green pastures 3

Coward, N. Blithe spirit 3

Euripides. The Trojan women 1

Everyman 1

Galsworthy, J. Escape 3

García Lorca, F. Blood wedding 2

Genêt, J. The maids 3

Giraudoux, J. The madwomen of Chaillot 3

Goethe, J. Faust, pt. I 1

Gogol, N.   The inspector 1
Gorki, M.   The lower depths 2
Gregory, I.   The workhouse ward 3
Hauptmann, G.   The weavers 2
Hebbel, F.   Maria Magdalena 1
Hellman, L.   The little foxes 3
Ibsen, H.   Ghosts 2
Ibsen, H.   Hedda Gabler 2
Ionesco, E.   The chairs 3
Jonson, B.   Volpone 1
Kālidāsa.   Shakuntalā 1
Kwanze, K.   Sotoba Komachi 1
Maeterlinck, M.   The intruder 2
Marlowe, C.   The tragical history of Doctor Faustus 1
Maugham, W.   The circle 3
Miller, A.   Death of a salesman 3
Molière, J.   The misanthrope 1
Molnár, F.   Liliom 2
Musset, A.   No trifling with love 1
O'Casey, S.   The plough and the stars 3
Odets, C.   Golden boy 3
O'Neill, E.   Anna Christie 3
O'Neill, E.   The hairy ape 3
Pirandello, L.   Six characters in search of an author 2
Plautus.   The Menaechmi 1
Racine, J.   Phaedra 1
Rostand, E.   Cyrano de Bergerac 2
Saroyan, W.   My heart's in the highlands 3
Sartre, J.   The flies 2
The second shepherds' play 1
Shakespeare, W.   Hamlet 1
Shaw, G.   Candida 3
Sheridan, R.   The school for scandal 1
Sherriff, R.   Journey's end 3
Sophocles.   Oedipus the king 1
Stallings, L. and Anderson, M.
    What price glory? 3
Strindberg, A.   A dream play 3
Strindberg, A.   The father 2
Strindberg, A.   There are crimes and crimes 2
Synge, J.   Riders to the sea 3
Terence.   The brothers 1
Tolstoy, L.   The power of darkness 2
Turgenev, I.   A month in the country 1
Vega Carpio, L.   Fuente ovejuna 1

Webster, J.   The Duchess of Malfi 1
Wedekind, F.   The tenor 2
Wilde, O.   The importance of being earnest 3
Wilder, T.   Our town 3
Williams, T.   The glass menagerie 3

TRES   Tres dramas románticos...
    Garden City, New York,
    Doubleday, 1962.   319p
García Gutiérrez, A.   El trovador
Rivas, A.   Don Alvaro; ó, La fuerza del sino
Zorrilla y Moral, J.   Don Juan Tenorio

TREWIN, J. C.   See
    PLAN   Plays of the year...

TRI   Trilling, Lionel, comp.   The experience of literature...
    Garden City, N.Y., Doubleday, 1967.   1320p
Brecht, B.   Galileo
Chekhov, A.   The three sisters
Ibsen, H.   The wild duck
Pirandello, L.   Six characters in search of an author
Shakespeare, W.   The tragedy of King Lear
Shaw, G.   The doctor's dilemma
Sophocles.   Oedipus rex
Yeats, W.   Purgatory

TRIA   Trilling, Lionel, comp.   The experience of literature...New York, Holt, Rinehart and Winston [1967] 1320p
Brecht, B.   Galileo
Chekhov, A.   The three sisters
Ibsen, H.   The wild duck
Pirandello, L.   Six characters in search of an author
Shakespeare, W.   The tragedy of King Lear
Shaw, G.   The doctor's dilemma
Sophocles.   Oedipus rex
Yeats, W.   Purgatory

TUCD   Tucker, Samuel Marion, ed.
    Modern American and British plays...New York, Harper [c1931] 946p
Anderson, M.   Saturday's children

TUCD (cont.)
Barry, P. In a garden
Brighouse, H. Hobson's choice
Colton, J. and Randolph, C.
 Rain
Coward, N. The vortex
Crothers, R. Mary the third
Dane, C. Granite
Emery, G. The hero
Ervine, St. J. John Ferguson
Glover, H. The king's jewry
Granville-Barker, H. Waste
Green, P. The field god
Houghton, S. Hindle wakes
Howard, S. The silver cord
Kaufman, G. and Connelly, M.
 To the ladies!
Maugham, W. The circle
Millay, E. The king's henchman
Milne, A. The truth about
 Blayds
Moeller, P. Madame Sand
O'Neill, E. The great god Brown
Pinero, A. The thunderbolt
Vollmer, L. Sun-up
Wilde, O. The importance of
 being earnest

TUCG Tucker, Samuel Marion, ed.
 Modern continental plays...
 New York, Harper, 1929. 836p
Andreyev, L. He who gets
 slapped
Annunzio, G. d'. Francesca da
 Rimini
Benavente y Martínez, J. La
 malquerida
Bjørnson, B. Beyond our power
Bracco, R. Phantasms
Brieux, E. False gods
Čapek, K. R.U.R.
Chekhov, A. The cherry orchard
Claudel, P. The tidings brought
 to Mary
Gorki, M. The lower depths
Hauptmann, G. The rats
Kaiser, G. The coral
Kaiser, G. Gas, pt. I
Kaiser, G. Gas, pt. II
Maeterlinck, M. Pelléas and
 Mélisande
Molnár, F. Liliom
Pérez Galdós, B. Electra
Rostand, E. Cyrano de Bergerac
Schnitzler, A. Light-o'-love
Strindberg, A. Comrades
Vildrac, C. S. S. Tenacity

Wedekind, F. Such is life

TUCJ Tucker, Samuel Marion, ed.
 Modern plays...New York,
 Macmillan [c1932] 400p
Bennett, A. and Knoblock, E.
 Milestones
Crothers, R. Mary the third
Hughes, H. Hell bent fer
 heaven
Milne, A. The ivory door
O'Neill, E. The Emperor Jones

TUCM Tucker, Samuel Marion, ed.
 Twenty-five modern plays...
 New York, Harper [c1931]
 1045p
Andreyev, L. He who gets
 slapped
Annunzio, G. d'. Francesca
 da Rimini
Barry, P. In a garden
Benavente y Martínez, J. La
 malquerida
Čapek, K. R.U.R.
Chekhov, A. The cherry orchard
Coward, N. The vortex
Crothers, R. Mary the third
Ervine, St. J. John Ferguson
Green, P. The field god
Hauptmann, G. The rats
Howard, S. The silver cord
Kaiser, G. The coral
Kaiser, G. Gas, pt. I
Kaiser, G. Gas, pt. II
Maeterlinck, M. Pelléas and
 Mélisande
Maugham, W. The circle
Milne, A. The truth about
 Blayds
Molnár, F. Liliom
O'Neill, E. The great god
 Brown
Pinero, A. The thunderbolt
Rostand, E. Cyrano de Bergerac
Schnitzler, A. Light-o'-love
Strindberg, A. Comrades
Vildrac, C. S. S. Tenacity
Vollmer, L. Sun-up
Wilde, O. The importance of
 being earnest

TUCN Tucker, Samuel Marion and
 Downer, Alan S., eds.
 Twenty-five modern plays...
 Revised edition by Alan S.
 Downer. New York, Harper

[c1948] 1009p
Andreyev, L. He who gets
  slapped
Auden, W. and Isherwood, C.
  The ascent of F6
Benavente, [y Martínez, J.] La
  malquerida
Čapek, K. R.U.R.
Chekhov, A. The cherry orchard
Cocteau, J. The infernal machine
Ervine, St. J. John Ferguson
Gorki, M. The lower depths
Green, P. The field god
Haines, W. Command decision
Hauptmann, G. The rats
Howard, S. The silver cord
Ibsen, H. Rosmersholm
Kaiser, G. The coral
Kaiser, G. Gas I
Kaiser, G. Gas II
Maeterlinck, M. Pelléas and
  Mélisande
Molnár, F. Liliom
O'Casey, S. The plough and
  the stars
O'Neill, E. The great god Brown
Pinero, A. The thunderbolt
Riggs, L. Roadside
Rostand, E. Cyrano de Bergerac
Schnitzler, A. Light-o'-love
Strindberg, A. Comrades
Synge, J. Riders to the sea
Wilde, O. The importance of
  being earnest

TUCO Tucker, S. Marion and
  Downer, Alan S., eds.
  Twenty-five modern plays...
  Third edition...New York,
  Harper [c1953] 1008p
Andreyev, L. He who gets
  slapped
Benavente, J. La malquerida
Čapek, K. R.U.R.
Chekhov, A. The cherry orchard
Cocteau, J. The infernal machine
Eliot, T. Murder in the cathedral
Ervine, St. J. John Ferguson
Gorki, M. The lower depths
Hauptmann, G. The rats
Howard, S. The silver cord
Ibsen, H. Rosmersholm
Kaiser, G. The coral
Kaiser, G. Gas, Parts 1 and 2
Maeterlinck, M. Pelléas and
  Mélisande
Miller, A. Death of a salesman

Molnár, F. Liliom
O'Casey, S. The plough and
  the stars
O'Neill, E. The great god Brown
Pinero, A. The thunderbolt
Riggs, L. Roadside
Rostand, E. Cyrano de Bergerac
Schnitzler, A. Light-o'-love
Strindberg, A. Comrades
Synge, J. Riders to the sea
Wilde, O. The importance of
  being earnest
Williams, T. A streetcar named
  desire

TUP Tupper, Frederick and Tupper,
  James Waddell, eds. Repre-
  sentative English dramas from
  Dryden to Sheridan...New York,
  Oxford University Press, 1914.
  46─
Addison, J. Cato
Congreve, W. The way of the
  world
Dryden, J. All for love
Dryden, J. The conquest of
  Granada
Farquhar, G. The beaux' strata-
  gem
Fielding, H. Tom Thumb the
  great
Gay, J. The beggar's opera
Goldsmith, O. She stoops to
  conquer
Otway, T. Venice preserved
Sheridan, R. The rivals
Sheridan, R. The school for
  scandal
Steele, R. The conscious lovers

TUQ Tupper, Frederick and Tupper,
  James Waddell, eds. Repre-
  sentative English dramas from
  Dryden to Sheridan...New and
  enl. ed. New York, Oxford
  University Press [c1934] 722p
Addison, J. Cato
Cibber, C. Love's last shift
Congreve, W. The way of the
  world
Dryden, J. All for love
Dryden, J. The conquest of
  Granada
Etherege, G. The man of mode
Farquhar, G. The beaux' strata-
  gem
Fielding, H. Tom Thumb the great

TUQ (cont.)
Gay, J. The beggar's opera
Goldsmith, O. She stoops to
conquer
Lillo, G. The London merchant
Otway, T. Venice preserved
Rowe, N. The tragedy of Jane
Shore
Sheridan, R. The rivals
Sheridan, R. The school for
scandal
Steele, R. The conscious lovers
Vanbrugh, J. The relapse
Wycherley, W. The country wife

TUQH Turkish literature...tr. into
English for the first time, with
a special introduction by
Epiphanius Wilson...Rev. ed.
New York, Colonial Press
[1901] 462p (The world's
great classics)
Mirza Feth-Ali, A. The magistrates

TUQT Turner, Darwin, T., comp.
Black drama in America: an
anthology. Greenwich, Conn.,
Fawcett, 1971. 630p
Bass, K. We righteous bombers
Davis, O. Purlie victorious
Dodson, O. Bayou legend
Edmonds, R. Earth and stars
Hughes, L. Emperor of Haiti
Jones, L. The toilet
Peterson, L. Take a giant step
Richardson, W. The chip woman's
fortune
Ward, T. Our lan'

TUR Turrell, Charles Alfred, ed.
and tr. Contemporary Spanish
dramatists...Boston, Badger
[c1919] 397p
Alvarez Quintero, S. and Alvarez
Quintero, J. The women's
town
Dicenta y Benedicto, J. Juan
José
Linares Rivas, M. The claws
Marquina, E. When the roses
bloom again
Pérez Galdós, B. Electra
Zamacois, E. The passing of the
magi

TWE Twelve famous plays of the

restoration and eighteenth
century...New York, Modern
Library [c1933] 952p
Congreve, W. Love for love
Congreve, W. The way of the
world
Dryden, J. All for love; or,
the world well lost
Farquhar, G. The beaux' strata-
gem
Garrick, D. The clandestine
marriage
Gay, J. The beggar's opera
Goldsmith, O. She stoops to
conquer; or, The mistakes
of a night
Otway, T. Venice preserv'd;
or, A plot discover'd
Sheridan, R. The rivals
Sheridan, R. The school for
scandal
Vanbrugh, J. The provok'd
wife
Wycherley, W. The country wife

TWEH Twentieth-century Chinese
drama: an anthology/edited
by Edward M. Gunn. Bloom-
ington, Indiana University
Press, c1983.
Ch'en, P. Men and women in
wild times (Acts I and III in
full; Act III omitted)
Chou, W.; Tung, Y.; and Yeh, H.
The artillery commander's son
Hu, S. The greatest event in life
Hung, S. Yama chao
Li, C. Springtime
Ou-yang, Y. P'an Chin-lien
The Red lantern (Scenes 1-7
summarized; Scenes 8-11 in
full)
Sha, Y.; Li, S.; and Yao, M.
If I were real (Scene 5 in
full; others summarized)
Shen, T. Under Shanghai eaves
T'ien, H. Kuan Han-ch'ing
(Scenes 3, 5, 9, and 11 have
been omitted)
Ting, H. Oppression
Tsung, F. In a land of silence
Wang, C. Wu Feng
Wu, C. Hai Jui dismissed from
office (Acts III, VI and IX in
full; others summarized)
Yang, C. Windswept blossoms
Yang, L. Cuckoo sings again

(Acts I-III in full; Act IV
summarized)

TWEN Twentieth-century Polish
avant-garde drama: plays,
scenarios, critical documents,
by Stanislaw Ignacy Witkiewicz
[et al.] Translated by Daniel
Gerould in collaboration with
Eleanor Gerould. Ithaca
[N.Y.] Cornell University
Press, c1977. 287p
Afanasjew, J. "The world is not
such a bad place..." (selec-
tions from)
Afanasjew, J., and the Afanasjeff
Family Circus. Good evening,
clown
Afanasjew, J., and the Bim-Bom
Troupe. Faust
Afanasjew, J., and the Bim-Bom
Troupe. Snouts
Gałczyński, K. The green goose
(Twenty-two short plays from
The Little Theatre of The
Green Goose)
Mrożek, S. The professor
Różewicz, T. Birth rate: The
biography of a play for the
theatre
Trzebiński, A. To pick up the
rose
Witkiewicz, S. The anonymous
work: four acts of a rather
nasty nightmare

UHL Uhler, John Earle, ed.
The best eighteenth century
comedies...New York, Knopf,
1929. 480p
Farquhar, G. The beaux' strata-
gem
Gay, J. The beggar's opera
Goldsmith, O. She stoops to
conquer
Sheridan, R. The rivals
Sheridan, R. The school for
scandal

ULAN Ulanov, Barry, ed. Makers
of the modern theater...New
York, McGraw-Hill [c1961]
743p
Anouilh, J. Antigone
Betti, U. The queen and the
rebels
Chekhov, A. Ivanov
García Lorca, F. Yerma
Giraudoux, J. Sodom and
Gomorrah
Giraudoux, J. Song of songs
Hauptmann, G. Hannele
Ibsen, H. John Gabriel Borkman
Ionesco, E. The bald soprano
Marcel, G. Ariadne
Miller, A. A view from the
bridge
Motherlant, H. The master of
Santiago
O'Casey, S. Purple dust
O'Neill, E. The long voyage
home
Pirandello, L. Henry IV
Shaw, G. Getting married
Strindberg, A. To Damascus,
part 1
Synge, J. The well of the saints
Toller, E. Hoppla! Such is life!
Williams, T. Camino real
Yeats, W. On Baile's strand
Yeats, W. Purgatory

UNTE Untermeyer, Louis, ed. The
Britannica library of great
American writing...Chicago,
J. B. Lippincott [c1960]
2v
O'Neill, E. The Emperor Jones 2

VAN Van Doren, Carl Clinton, ed.
The Borzoi reader...New
York, Knopf, 1936. 1033p
Kaufman, G., Ryskind, M. and
Gershwin, I. Of thee I sing

VANM Van Doren, Carl Clinton, ed.
Modern American prose...New
York, Harcourt, Brace [c1934]
939p
Anderson, M. and Stallings, L.
What price glory?

VAN DOREN, CARL CLINTON.
See also
AMI American omnibus...;
LONO London omnibus...

VANV Van Ghent, Dorothy (Ben-
don) and Brown, Joseph S.,
eds. Continental literature;

VANV (cont.)
    an anthology...Philadelphia,
    Lippincott [1968] 2v
Aeschylus. Agamemnon 1
Aristophanes. Lysistrata 1
Brecht, B. The good woman of
    Setzuan 2
Euripides. Hippolytus 1
García Lorca, F. The king of
    Harlem 2
García Lorca, F. Lament for
    Ignacio Sánchez Mejías 2
Goethe, J. Faust, pt. I 2
Ibsen, H. Hedda Gabler 2
Molière, J. Tartuffe 2
Pirandello, L. Such is life 2
Racine, J. Phaedra 2
Sophocles. Oedipus rex 1

VENEZKY, ALICE. See
    GRIF Griffin, Alice Sylvia
    (Venezky), ed...

VIC Victorian melodramas: seven
    English, French, and American
    melodramas; edited and intro-
    duced by James L. Smith.
    London, Dent; Totowa, N.J.,
    Rowman and Littlefield, 1976.
    252p
Boucicault, D. The Corsican
    brothers
Dumas, A., fils. The lady of the
    camelias (adapted from)
Hamblin, L. Nick of the woods
London by night
Milner, H. Mazeppa
Smith, W. The drunkard
Walker, J. The factory lad

VOAD Voaden, Herman Arthur, ed.
    Four good plays to read and
    act...Toronto, Longmans
    Green [c1944] 297p
Coward, N. Cavalcade
Jerome, H. Price and prejudice
MacLeish, A. The fall of the
    city
Saroyan, W. My heart's in the
    highlands

VOLI Volpe, Edward Loris, and
    Magalaner, Marvin, comps.
    An introduction to literature:
    drama. New York, Random
    House, 1967. 467p
Chekhov, A. The cherry orchard

Ibsen, H. The wild duck
Molière, J. Tartuffe
O'Neill, E. Desire under the elms
Shakespeare, W. Othello
Sophocles. Oedipus rex

VOLP Volpe, Edward Loris [and
    others] eds. Poetry, drama,
    fiction...New York, Random
    House [c1967] 808p
O'Neill, E. Desire under the elms
Shakespeare, W. Othello
Sophocles. Oedipus rex

VON Von Staden, H., comp.
    Western literature...New York,
    Harcourt, Brace, Jovanovich,
    1971. 3v
Aeschylus. Agamemnon 1
Aristophanes. Lysistrata 1
Euripides. Bacchae 1
Goethe, J. Faust, Part 1 3
Ibsen, H. The master builder 3
Lowell, R. Old glory: Benito
    Cereno 3
Molière, J. The misanthrope 2
Pirandello, L. Six characters in
    search of an author 3
Shakespeare, W. Othello 2
Sophocles. Oedipus the king 1

WAGC Wagenheim, Harold H.; Brat-
    tig, Elizabeth Voris and Dolkey,
    Matthew, eds. Our reading
    heritage...New York, Henry
    Holt [c1956] 4v
Bennett, A. and Knoblock, E.
    Milestones 4
Cohan, G. Pigeons and people
    3
Foote, H. The dancers
Gilsdorf, F. and Gibson, P. The
    ghost of Benjamin Sweet 1
Gordon, R. Years ago 1
Kelly, G. Finders'-keepers 3
O'Neill, E. In the zone 2
Osborn, P. Point of no return 3
Rattigan, T. The Winslow boy 2
Shakespeare, W. Macbeth 4
Shaw, G. Saint Joan 4

WAGE Wagenheim, Harold H.; Brat-
    tig, Elizabeth Voris and Flesch,
    Rudolf, eds. Read up on life
    ...New York, Henry Holt, 1952.

507p (Holt literature series)
Gordon, R. Years ago

WAGN Canada's lost plays/edited
by Anton Wagner...Richard
Plant...Toronto: Canadian
Theatre Review Publications,
1978-80. 3v (V1, The nineteenth century; V2, Women
pioneers; V3, The developing
mosaic)
Bush, T. Santiago; a drama in
five acts 1
Candidus, C. The female consistory of Brockville; a melodrama in three acts 1
Coulter, J. The house in the
quiet glen 3
Curzon, S. Laura Secord, the
heroine of 1812 2
Curzon, S. The sweet girl
graduate; a comedy in four
acts 2
Cushing, E. The fatal ring; a
drama 2
Davies, R. Hope deferred 3
Davin, N. The fair grit; or,
The advantages of coalition,
a farce 1
Denison, M. The weather
breeder 3
Fuller, W. H.M.S. Parliament;
or, The lady who loved a
government clerk 1
Joudry, P. Teach me how to
cry; a drama in three acts 2
Kerr, L. Open doors 3
McIlwraith, J. Ptarmigan; or,
A Canadian carnival; an origi-
nal comic opera in two acts 1
Merritt, C. When George the
third was king; an historical
drama in three acts 2
Ringwood, G. Pasque flower; a
play of the Canadian prairie 2
Ringwood, G. The rainmaker 3
"Scribble, S." Dolorsolatio; a
local political burlesque 1
Voaden, H. Murder pattern 3
Voaden, H. Wilderness; a play
of the north 3

WAIT Waite, Harlow O. and Atkinson, Benjamin P., eds.
Literature for our time...
New York, Henry Holt [c1953]
998p

Anderson, M. Winterset
Barry, P. The Philadelphia story
Behrman, S. Biography
MacLeish, A. The fall of the city
O'Neill, E. The hairy ape
Williams, T. The glass menagerie

WAIU Waite, Harlow O. and Atkin-
son, Benjamin P., eds. Liter-
ature for our time...New York,
Henry Holt [c1958] 1009p
Barry, P. The Philadelphia story
Giraudoux, J. Tiger at the gates
O'Neill, E. The hairy ape
Shaw, G. Major Barbara
Williams, T. The glass menagerie

WAIW Waith, Eugene M., ed. The
dramatic moment...Englewood
Cliffs, N.J., Prentice-Hall
[1967] 505p
Albee, E. The zoo story
Brecht, B. Mother Courage and
her children
Chekhov, A. The seagull
Ibsen, H. Hedda Gabler
Jonson, B. Volpone; or, The
fox
Molière, J. The misanthrope
Pirandello, L. Six characters in
search of an author
Shakespeare, W. King Lear
Shaw, G. Major Barbara
Sophocles. Oedipus rex
Strindberg, A. The ghost sonata
Summoning of everyman

WALB Wall, Vincent and McCormick,
James Patton, eds. Seven
plays of the modern theater...
New York, American Book Co.
[c1950] 521p
Anderson, M. Winterset
Chekhov, A. Uncle Vanya
Coward, N. Blithe spirit
Ibsen, H. Hedda Gabler
Maugham, W. The circle
O'Neill, E. The hairy ape
Williams, T. The glass menagerie

WALJ Walley, Harold Reinoehl. The
book of the play...New York,
Scribner [c1950] 699p
Chekhov, A. The sea gull
Congreve, W. The way of the
world
Ibsen, H. An enemy of the people

WALJ (cont.)

Molière, J. The misanthrope

O'Neill, E. Desire under the elms

Racine, J. Phaedra

Rostand, E. Cyrano de Bergerac

Shakespeare, W. The tragedy of Hamlet, Prince of Denmark

Shakespeare, W. Twelfth night; or, What you will

Sophocles. Oedipus the king

Strindberg, A. The dream play

Synge, J. The playboy of the western world

WALL Walley, Harold Reinoehl and Wilson, John Harold, eds. Early seventeenth century plays, 1600-1642...New York, Harcourt, Brace [c1930] 1120p

Beaumont, F. and Fletcher, J. A king or no king

Brome, R. A mad couple well matched

Chapman, G. The revenge of Bussy D'Ambois

Chapman, G., Jonson, B. and Marston, J. Eastward ho!

D'Avenant, W. Love and honor

Dekker, T. and Middleton, T. The honest whore, pt. I

Fletcher, J. The wild-goose chase

Ford, J. 'Tis a pity she's a whore

Heywood, T. A woman killed with kindness

Jonson, B. Volpone; or, The fox

Marston, J. The Dutch courtesan

Massinger, P. A new way to pay old debts

Middleton, T. A chaste maid in Cheapside

Shirley, J. The cardinal

Webster, J. The white devil

WALPOLE, HUGH. See
MAL Malvern festival plays...

WAR Warfel, Harry Redcay; Gabriel, Ralph Henry and Williams, Stanley Thomas, eds. The American mind...New York, American Book Co. [c1937]

1520p

O'Neill, E. The Emperor Jones

WARH Warnock, Robert. Representative modern plays...American. Chicago, Scott, Foresman [c1952] 758p

Anderson, M. Valley Forge

Behrman, S. Biography

Howard, S. The late Christopher Bean

Kaufman, G. and Connelly, M. Beggar on horseback

Miller, A. Death of a salesman

Odets, C. Waiting for Lefty

O'Neill, E. Mourning becomes Electra

Williams, T. The glass menagerie

WARI Warnock, Robert, ed. Representative modern plays, British. Chicago, Scott, Foresman [1953] 710p

Barrie, J. The admirable Crichton

Coward, N. The blithe spirit

Eliot, T. Murder in the cathedral

Fry, C. A phoenix too frequent

Galsworthy, J. Loyalties

Maugham, W. The constant wife

O'Casey, S. Juno and the paycock

Shaw, G. The doctor's dilemma

Synge, J. Riders to the sea

WARL Warnock, Robert, comp. Representative modern plays: Ibsen to Tennessee Williams. Chicago, Scott, Foresman [1964] 696p

Behrman, S. Biography

Chekhov, A. The sea-gull

Fry, C. A phoenix too frequent

Ibsen, H. The master builder

Maugham, W. The constant wife

O'Casey, S. Juno and the paycock

O'Neill, E. Desire under the elms

Shaw, G. The doctor's dilemma

Strindberg, A. Miss Julie

Synge, J. Riders to the sea

Williams, T. The glass menagerie

WARN Warnock, Robert and Anderson, George K., eds. The world in literature...Chicago, Scott, Foresman [c1950] 2v in 1

Aeschylus. Agamemnon 1
Aristophanes. The clouds 1
Euripides. Hippolytus 1
Kālidāsa. Shakuntalā 1
Shakespeare, W. Hamlet,
    Prince of Denmark 2
Sophocles. Oedipus the king
    1
Vega Carpio, L. The sheep
    well 2

WAT Watrous, George Ansel, ed.
    Elizabethan dramatists...New
    York, Crowell [1903] 293p
Beaumont, F. and Fletcher, J.
    Philaster
Jonson, B. Every man in his
    humour
Marlowe, C. Dr. Faustus

WATA Watson, Ernest Bradlee and
    Pressey, Benfield, eds. Con-
    temporary drama: American,
    English and Irish, European...
    New York, Scribner [c1959]
    577p
Chekhov, A. Uncle Vanya
Eliot, T. Murder in the cathedral
Frings, K. Look homeward, angel
García Lorca, F. Blood wedding
Ibsen, H. Hedda Gabler
Inge, W. Comeback, little Sheba
Miller, A. The crucible
O'Casey, S. Purple dust
O'Neill, E. Ah, wilderness!
Pirandello, L. Henry IV
Shaw, G. Man and superman
Strindberg, A. The dream play
Synge, J. Riders to the sea
Wilde, O. The importance of
    being earnest
Wilder, T. The skin of our teeth

WATC Watson, Ernest Bradlee and
    Pressey, Benfield, comps. Con-
    temporary drama; American
    plays...New York, Scribner
    [c1931-38] 2v
Anderson, M. Elizabeth the
    queen 2
Barry, P. Hotel Universe 2
Howard, S. The silver cord 1
Kaufman, G. and Connelly, M.
    Beggar on horseback 1
Lawson, J. Processional 1
Mitchell, L. The New York idea
    1

O'Neill, E. The Emperor Jones
    1
O'Neill, E. The hairy ape 2
Rice, E. Street scene 2
Sherwood, R. The petrified
    forest 2

WATE Watson, Ernest Bradlee and
    Pressey, Benfield, eds. Con-
    temporary drama, eleven
    plays: American, English,
    European...New York, Scrib-
    ner's [c1956] 341p
Anouilh, J. Antigone
Connelly, M. The green pastures
Coward, N. Ways and means
Fry, C. Venus observed
Giraudoux, J. The madwoman of
    Chaillot
Hellman, L. Another part of the
    forest
Miller, A. Death of a salesman
Saroyan, W. Hello out there
Shaw, G. Pygmalion
Wilder, T. The happy journey to
    Trenton and Camden
Williams, T. The glass menagerie

WATF Watson, Ernest Bradlee and
    Pressey, Benfield, comps.
    Contemporary drama: English
    and Irish plays...New York,
    Scribner [c1931] 2v
Barrie, J. Dear Brutus 2
Barrie, J. What every woman
    knows 1
Dunsany, E. The glittering gate
    1
Galsworthy, J. Justice 1
Galsworthy, J. Loyalties 2
Gregory, I. Hyacinth Halvey 1
Maugham, W. The circle 2
Milne, A. Mr. Pim passes by 2
O'Casey, S. Juno and the pay-
    cock 2
Pinero, A. Mid-channel 1
Synge, J. Riders to the sea 1

WATI Watson, Ernest Bradlee and
    Pressey, Benfield, comps.
    Contemporary drama: Euro-
    pean, English and Irish,
    American plays...New York,
    Scribner [c1941] 1177p
Anderson, M. Elizabeth the
    queen
Andreyev, L. He who gets

WATI (cont.)
slapped
Barrie, J.   Dear Brutus
Barrie, J.   What every woman
knows
Barry, P.   Hotel Universe
Benavente y Martínez, J.   The
˅ passion flower
Čapek, K.   R.U.R.   (Rossum's
universal robots)
Chekhov, A.   The cherry orchard
Chekhov, A.   Uncle Vanya
Curel, F. de.   The fossils
Dunsany, E.   The glittering gate
Galsworthy, J.   Justice
Galsworthy, J.   Loyalties
Gorki, M.   Night's lodging; or,
The lower depths
Gregory, I.   Hyacinth Halvey
Hauptmann, G.   The beaver coat
Howard, S.   The silver cord
Ibsen, H.   A doll's house
Ibsen, H.   Hedda Gabler
Kaufman, G. and Connelly, M.
Beggar on horseback
Lawson, J.   Processional
Maeterlinck, M.   Pelléas and
Mélisande
Maugham, W.   The circle
Milne, A.   Mr. Pim passes by
O'Casey, S.   Juno and the pay-
cock
O'Neill, E.   The Emperor Jones
O'Neill, E.   "The hairy ape"
Pinero, A.   Mid-channel
Pirandello, L.   "Henry IV"
Rice, E.   Street scene
Rostand, E.   Cyrano de Bergerac
Schnitzler, A.   Light-o'-love
Sherwood, R.   Abe Lincoln in Il-
linois
Strindberg, A.   The dream play
Sudermann, H.   Magda
Synge, J.   Riders to the sea
Toller, E.   Man and the masses

WATL Watson, Ernest Bradlee and
Pressey, Benfield, comps.
Contemporary drama: European
plays...New York, Scribner
[c1931-34]   4v
Andreyev, L.   He who gets
slapped   4
Annunzio, G. d'.   Francesca da
Rimini   3
Becque, H.   The vultures   1
Benavente y Martínez, J.   The

˅ passion flower   3
Čapek, K.   R.U.R.   4
Chekhov, A.   The cherry orchard
1
Chekhov, A.   The sea gull   3
Chekhov, A.   Uncle Vanya   2
Curel, F. de.   The fossils   1
Gorki, M.   Night's lodging   3
Hauptmann, G.   The beaver coat
1
Ibsen, H.   A doll's house   1
Ibsen, H.   Hedda Gabler   2
Maeterlinck, M.   Pelléas and
Melisande   2
Pirandello, L.   Henry IV   4
Rostand, E.   Cyrano de Bergerac
2
Schnitzler, A.   Light-o'-love   1
Strindberg, A.   The dream play
3
Sudermann, H.   Magda   2
Toller, E.   Man and the masses
4

WATO Watson, Ernest Bradlee
and Pressey, Benfield, comps.
Contemporary drama, nine
plays: American, English,
European...New York, Scribner
[c1941]   362p
Barrie, J.   What every woman knows
Čapek, K.   R.U.R.   (Rossum's
universal robots)
Galsworthy, J.   Justice
Howard, S.   The silver cord
Maugham, W.   The circle
O'Neill, E.   "The hairy ape"
Rice, E.   Street scene
Rostand, E.   Cyrano de Bergerac
Sherwood, R.   Abe Lincoln in Il-
linois

WATR Watson, Ernest Bradlee and
Pressey, Benfield, comps.
Five modern plays...New York,
Scribner [c1933]   v.p.
Chekhov, A.   The cherry orchard
Galsworthy, J.   Justice
Ibsen, H.   Hedda Gabler
Maeterlinck, M.   Pelléas and
Mélisande
Rostand, E.   Cyrano de Bergerac

WATS Watt, Homer Andrew and
Cargill, Oscar, eds.   College
reader. New York, Prentice-
Hall, 1948.   949p

Behrman, S. End of summer
Corwin, N. Radio primer
Galsworthy, J. Strife
Gregory, A. Spreading the news

WATT Watt, Homer Andrew and
Munn, James Buell, eds. Ideas
and forms in English and
American literature...Chicago,
Scott, Foresman [c1932] 2v
Gregory, I. Hyacinth Halvey 2
Milne, A. The Dover road 2
Mr. S. Mr. of Art. Gammer Gur-
ton's needle 2
Pinero, A. The second Mrs.
Tanqueray 2
Sheridan, R. The school for
scandal 2
Synge, J. Riders to the sea 2
Webster, J. The Duchess of Malfi
2
Yeats, W. The land of heart's
desire 2

WEAL Weales, Gerald Clifford, ed.
Edwardian plays...New York,
Hill and Wang [1962] 429p
(Mermaid dramabook)
Granville-Barker, H. The
Madras house
Hankin, J. The return of the
prodigal
Maugham, W. Loaves and fishes
Pinero, A. Mid-channel
Shaw, G. Getting married

WEAN Weales, Gerald Clifford, ed.
Eleven plays...New York,
Norton [1964] 617p
Anouilh, J. The lark
Barker, G. Rococo
Euripides. Alcestis
Ibsen, H. The wild duck
Miller, A. All my sons
Musset, A. Camille and Perdican
Pirandello, L. Tonight we im-
provise
Shakespeare, W. Troilus and
Cressida
Shaw, G. Arms and the man
Wilder, T. The matchmaker
Wycherley, W. The country wife

WEAT Weatherley, Edward Howell;
Moffet, Harold Y.; Prouty,
Charles T. and Noyes, Henry
H. The English heritage...

Boston, Ginn [c1945] 2v
Barrie, J. The twelve-pound
look 2
Everyman 1
Farquhar, G. The beaux' strata-
gem 1
Marlowe, C. The tragical history
of Doctor Faustus 1
Noah's flood 1
Sheridan, R. The rivals 1
Synge, J. Riders to the sea 2

WEAV Weatherly, Edward Howell;
Wagener, A. Pelzer; Zeydel,
Edwin H. and Yarmolinsky,
Avrahm, eds. The heritage
of European literature. Boston,
Ginn [c1948-49] 2v
Aeschylus. Agamemnon 1
Chekhov, A. The cherry orchard
2
Euripides. Electra 1
Goethe, J. Faust, pt. I 2
Ibsen, H. The wild duck 2
Molière, J. Tartuffe; or, The
imposter 2
Molière, J. The physician in spite
of himself 2
Racine, J. Phaedra 2
Schiller, J. William Tell 2
Sophocles. Oedipus the king 1
Terence. Phormio 1
Vega Carpio, L. The king the
greatest Alcalde 1

WEB Webber, James Plaisted and
Webster, Hanson Hart, eds.
Typical plays for secondary
schools...Boston, Houghton
Mifflin [c1929] 343p
Note: Re-issued in 1930 as
Typical plays for young people,
291p. Same contents.
Baring, M. The rehearsal
Chapin, H. Augustus in search
of a father
Frank, M. A mistake at the
manor
Gilbert, W. Sweethearts
Gregory, I. The dragon
Healey, F. The copper pot
Hsiung, C. The thrice promised
bride
Kotzebue, A. Pharaoh's daughter
Mackay, C. The prince of court
painters
Tarkington, B. and Wilson, H.

WEB (cont.)
  The Gibson upright
  Webber, J. Frances and
  Francis

WED Wedeck, Harry Ezekiel, ed.
  Classics of Greek literature
  ...New York, Philosophical
  Library, 1963. 385p
  Aeschylus. The Persians
  Aristophanes. The birds
  Euripides. Iphigenia in Tauris
  Sophocles. Electra

WEE Week-end library. 3rd issue
  [1930] Garden City, N.Y.,
  Doubleday Page, 1930. v.p.
  Maugham, W. The circle
  Morley, C. Really, my dear...
  Morley, C. Wagon-lits

WEIM Weiss, Samuel Abba, ed.
  Drama in the modern world
  ...Boston, Heath [1964] 555p
  Arbuzov, A. It happened in
  Irkutsk
  Beckett, S. All that fall
  Brecht, B. The good woman of
  Setzuan
  Chekhov, A. The cherry orchard
  García Lorca, F. The house of
  Bernarda Alba
  Giraudoux, J. Ondine
  Ibsen, H. The wild duck
  Ionesco, E. The bald soprano
  O'Neill, E. Desire under the elms
  Pirandello, L. Six characters in
  search of an author
  Shaw, G. Major Barbara
  Strindberg, A. Miss Julie
  Synge, J. The playboy of the
  western world
  Williams, T. The glass menagerie

WEIP Weiss, Samuel Abba, ed.
  Drama in the modern world:
  plays and essays. Alternate
  ed. Lexington, Mass., Heath,
  1974. 614p
  Beckett, S. All that fall
  Brecht, B. Mother Courage and
  her children
  Chekhov, A. The three sisters
  Eisenstein, S. Ivan the Terrible:
  the screenplay, part one
  García Lorca, F. Blood wedding
  Gordone, C. No place to be

  somebody
  Ibsen, H. The master builder
  Ionesco, E. Jack; or, The sub-
  mission
  O'Neill, E. The hairy ape
  Pirandello, L. Henry IV
  The Red lantern
  Schnitzler, A. La ronde
  Shaw, G. Heartbreak house
  Strindberg, A. A dream play
  Synge, J. Riders to the sea

WEIS Weiss, Samuel Abba, comp.
  Drama in the western world;
  15 plays with essays. Bos-
  ton, Heath. 1968. 794p
  Aristophanes. Lysistrata
  Beckett, S. All that fall
  Brecht, B. The Caucasian chalk
  circle
  Chekhov, A. Uncle Vanya
  Euripides. The bacchae
  Ibsen, H. Ghosts
  Kleist, H. The Prince of Hom-
  burg
  Molière, J. The misanthrope
  O'Neill, E. Desire under the elms
  Pirandello, L. Six characters in
  search of an author
  Racine, J. Phaedra
  Shaw, G. Caesar and Cleopatra
  Sophocles. Oedipus the king
  Strindberg, A. A dream play
  Williams, T. The glass menagerie

WEIW Weiss, Samuel Abba, comp.
  Drama in the western world;
  9 plays with essays. Boston,
  Heath, 1968. 506p
  Aristophanes. Lysistrata
  Brecht, B. The Caucasian chalk
  circle
  Chekhov, A. Uncle Vanya
  Ibsen, H. Ghosts
  Molière, J. The misanthrope
  Pirandello, L. Six characters in
  search of an author
  Shaw, G. Caesar and Cleopatra
  Sophocles. Oedipus the king
  Williams, T. The glass menagerie

WEL Wells, Henry Willis, ed. Six
  Sanskrit plays, in English
  translation. New York, Asia
  Publishing House [1964] 487p
  Bhāsa. The vision of Vāsavadatta
  Bhavabhūti. Rama's later history

WES (cont.)

Gower, D. Daddies 1

Graham, B. Jacob's ladder 6

Hensel, K.; Johns, P.; Kent, E.; Meredith, S.; Shaw, E., and Toffenetti, L. Going to see the elephant 15/16

Hopkins, G., and Lindberg, W. Dinosaur 6

Horovitz, I. The widow's blind date 13/14

Innaurato, A. Earth worms 4

Kazan, N. Safe house 3

Kral, B. One to grow on 15/16

Larson, N. Imitations 5

Linfante, M. Pizza 6

Lynch, M. Sylvester the Cat vs Galloping Billy Bronco 6

McClure, M. Goethe: Ein fragment 2

Martell, L. Hoss drawin' 13/14

Mednick, M. Coyote V: Listening to old Nana 13/14

Mednick, M. Coyote IV: Other side camp 9

Mednick, M. Coyote I: Pointing 7

Mednick, M. Coyote III: Planet of the spider people 7

Mednick, M. Coyote II: The shadow ripens 7

Miller, A. The fox 13/14

Miller, S. Cross country 1

Patrick, R. Judas 5

Pezzulo, T. Skaters 4

Phillips, L. The last of the Marx Brothers' writers 2

Pifer, D. An evening in our century 10

Porter, J. St. George 3

Pritchard, B. The day Roosevelt died 10

Provisional Theatre, The. Inching through the Everglades 10

Puccioni, M. Two o'clock feeding 4

Rivers, S. Maud Gonne says no to the poet 3

Robinson, J. Wolves 2

Rudkin, D. Ashes 1

San Francisco Mime Troupe. Factperson 15/16

San Francisco Mime Troupe. Factwino meets the moral majority 15/16

San Francisco Mime Troupe. Fact-

wino vs. Armageddonman 15/16

San Francisco Mime Troupe. Ghosts 10

San Francisco Mime Troupe. Hotel Universe 10

Sebastian, E. Your place is no longer with us 13/14

Shank, A. Sand castles 15/16

Shank, A. Sunset/sunrise 4

Shiomi, R. Yellow fever 13/14

Shipley, L. The bathtub 5

Sossi, R., and Condon, F. The Chicago conspiracy trial 7

Strauss, B. Three acts of recognition 8

Valdez, L. The shrunken head of Pancho Villa 11/12

Weetman, M. Estonia you fall 13/14

Whitehead, W. And if that mockingbird don't sing 3

Yafa, S. Passing shots 1

Yamauchi, W. And the soul shall dance 11/12

Zahn, C. The reactivated man 11/12

WHE Wheeler, Charles Bickersteth, ed. Six plays by contemporaries of Shakespeare...London, Oxford University Press [1928] 595p (The world's classics)

Beaumont, F. and Fletcher, J. The knight of the burning pestle

Beaumont, F. and Fletcher, J. Philaster

Dekker, T. The shoemaker's holiday

Massinger, P. A new way to pay old debts

Webster, J. The Duchess of Malfi

Webster, J. The white devil

WHF White, Elizabeth A. and others, eds. Understanding literature. Boston, Ginn, 1967. 751p

Alvarez Quintero, S. and Alvarez Quintero, J. A sunny morning

Fletcher, L. Sorry, wrong number

MacLeish, A. The trojan horse

Shakespeare, W. The life of King Henry the fifth

WHFA White, Elizabeth A. and
others, eds. Understanding
literature. Boston, Ginn,
1970. 756p
Gibson, W. The miracle worker
Goodrich, F. and Hackett, A.
The diary of Anne Frank
Shakespeare, W. The life of
King Henry the fifth

WHFM White, Melvin R., and
Whiting, Frank M. Play-
reader's repertory: an an-
thology for introduction to
theatre. Glenview, Ill., Scott,
Foresman, 1970. 804p
Aristophanes. The birds
Chekhov, A. The cherry orchard
Everyman
Hansberry, L. A raisin in the
sun
Ibsen, H. Ghosts
Kopit, A. Oh dad, poor dad,
mamma's hung you in the
closet and I'm feelin' so sad
Molière, J. Tartuffe
O'Neill, E. Desire under the elms
Pirandello, L. Six characters in
search of an author
Shakespeare, W. Hamlet, Prince
of Denmark
Shaw, G. Arms and the man
Sophocles. King Oedipus
Wilde, O. The importance of
being earnest

WHITING, B. J. See
COL College survey of
English literature. [Edited by
B. J. Whiting...and others]

WHI Whitman, Charles Huntington,
ed. Representative modern
dramas...New York, Macmillan,
1936. 1121p
Anderson, M. Elizabeth the
queen
Barry, P. Hotel Universe
Behrman, S. Biography
Benavente y Martínez, J. The
bonds of interest
Brieux, E. The red robe
Chekhov, A. The cherry orchard
Galsworthy, J. Strife
Gorki, M. The lower depths
Green, P. In Abraham's bosom
Hauptmann, G. The weavers

Howard, S. The silver cord
Ibsen, H. The wild duck
Maeterlinck, M. Pelléas and
Mélisande
Maugham, W. Our betters
Molnár, F. Liliom
O'Casey, S. Juno and the pay-
cock
O'Neill, E. The hairy ape
Pinero, A. Mid-channel
Pirandello, L. Six characters in
search of an author
Rostand, E. Cyrano de Bergerac
Schnitzler, A. The lonely way
Strindberg, A. The father
Synge, J. Riders to the sea
Wilde, O. The importance of
being earnest

WHK Whitman, Charles Huntington,
ed. Seven contemporary plays
...Boston, Houghton Mifflin
[c1931] 565p
Chekhov, A. The cherry orchard
Galsworthy, J. Strife
Hauptmann, G. The sunken bell
Ibsen, H. An enemy of the people
O'Neill, E. Beyond the horizon
Rostand, E. Cyrano de Bergerac
Synge, J. Riders to the sea

WHT Whittaker, Charlotte C., ed.
Youth and the world...Chicago,
Ill., Lippincott [c1955] 512p
(Reading for life series)
Ibsen, H. A doll's house

WILSON, EPIPHANIUS. See
TUQH Turkish literature...

WILE Wilson, John Harold, ed. Six
eighteenth century plays.
Boston, Houghton Mifflin
[c1963] 374p
Gay, J. The beggar's opera
Goldsmith, O. She stoops to
conquer
Lillo, G. The London merchant
Rowe, N. The fair penitent
Sheridan, R. The school for
scandal
Steele, R. The conscious lovers

WILS Wilson, John Harold, ed. Six
Restoration plays...Boston,
Houghton Mifflin [c1959]
463p

WILS (cont.)
  Congreve, W. The way of the
    world
  Dryden, J. All for love; or,
    The world well lost
  Etherege, G. The man of
    mode; or, Sir Fopling Flutter
  Farquhar, G. The beaux' strata-
    gem
  Otway, T. Venice preserved; or,
    A plot discovered
  Wycherley, W. The country wife

WIM Wilson, Marian M., ed. Popu-
    lar performance plays of
    Canada. [Toronto, Simon &
    Pierre, 1976] Various pagings
    (V.1)
  Campbell, P. Hoarse muse
  Colley, P. The Donnellys
  Crips, J. A wife in the hand
  Grant, D. What glorious times
    they had--Nellie McClung
  McMaster, B. Put on the spot/
    When everybody cares (2 kid
    plays)

WINE Wine, Martin L., ed. Drama
    of the English renaissance.
    New York, Modern Library,
    1969. 786p
  Beaumont, F. and Fletcher, J.
    The knight of the burning
    pestle
  Beaumont, F. and Fletcher, J.
    Philaster; or, Love lies a-
    bleeding
  Dekker, T. The shoemaker's
    holiday: a pleasant comedy
    of a gentle craft
  Ford, J. The broken heart
  Jonson, B. The masque of
    blackness
  Jonson, B. Volpone; or, The
    fox
  Marlowe, C. The tragical his-
    tory of the life and death of
    Doctor Faustus
  Middleton, T. and Rowley, W.
    The changeling
  Webster, J. The Duchess of
    Malfi

WINN Winny, James, ed. Three
    Elizabethan plays...London,
    Chatto and Windus [c1959]
    223p

Lyly, J. Midas
Mucedorus
The reign of King Edward III

WISD Wise, Jacob Hooper; Congle-
    ton, J. E.; Morris, Alton C.
    and Hodges, John C...College
    English: the first year...New
    York, Harcourt, Brace [c1952]
    959p
  Kingsley, S. Darkness at noon
  Rostand, E. Cyrano de Bergerac
  Thurber, J. and Nugent, E. The
    male animal

WISE Wise, Jacob Hooper; Congleton,
    J. E.; Morris, Alton C. and
    Hodges, John C...College Eng-
    lish: the first year...Revised
    edition. New York, Harcourt,
    Brace [c1956] 982p
  Miller, A. Death of a salesman
  Rostand, E. Cyrano de Bergerac
  Shaw, G. Pygmalion

WISF Wise, Jacob Hooper; Morris,
    Alton C. and Hodges, John C.,
    eds. College English: the
    first year. Third edition...
    New York, Harcourt, Brace
    [c1960] 982p
  Anouilh, J. Antigone
  Capote, T. The grass harp
  Miller, A. Death of a salesman
  Shaw, G. Androcles and the lion

WOM Women in drama: an anthology.
    Edited by Harriet Kriegel.
    New York, New American Li-
    brary; London, New English
    Library, 1975. 408p
  Aristophanes. Lysistrata
  Euripides. Medea
  Glaspell, S. Trifles
  Ibsen, H. The lady from the sea
  Middleton, T. Women beware
    women
  Shaw, G. Mrs. Warren's profes-
    sion
  Strindberg, A. Miss Julie
  Terry, M. Approaching Simone

WOMA The women's project; seven
    new plays by women. Edited
    by Julia Miles. New York,
    Performing Arts Journal Pub-
    lications and American Place

Theatre, 1980. 372p
Aaron, J., and Tarlo, L. Acro-
batics
Collins, K. In the midnight
hour
Gilliatt, P. Property
Goldemberg, R. Letters home
Mueller, L. Killings on the last
line
Purscell, P. Separate ceremonies
Schenkar, J. Signs of life

WOMB The women's project 2/edited
by Julia Miles. New York,
Performing Arts Journal Pub-
lications, c1984. 182p
Cizmar, P. Candy & Shelley go
to the desert
Collins, K. The brothers
Galloway, T. Heart of a dog
Mack, C. Territorial rites
Mueller, L. Little victories

WOMR Women writers in Russian
modernism; an anthology.
Translated and edited by
Temira Pachmuss. Urbana,
University of Illinois Press,
1978. 340p
Verbitskaya, A. Mirage

WOO Woods, George Benjamin;
Watt, Homer Andrew and
Anderson, George Kumler,
eds. The literature of Eng-
land...Chicago, Scott, Fores-
man [c1936] 2v
Dekker, T. The shoemaker's
holiday 1
Galsworthy, J. Strife 2
Marlowe, C. The tragical his-
tory of Doctor Faustus 1
The second shepherds' play 1
Sheridan, R. The rivals 1
Wilde, O. The importance of
being earnest 2

WOOD Woods, George Benjamin;
Watt, Homer Andrew and
Anderson, George Kumler, eds.
The literature of England...
[Rev. ed.] Chicago, Scott,
Foresman [c1941] 2v
Everyman 1
Jonson, B. Epicoene; or, The
silent woman 1
Marlowe, C. Doctor Faustus 1

Sheridan, R. The school for
scandal 1
The second shepherds' play 1
Synge, J. Riders to the sea 1
Wilde, O. The importance of
being earnest 2

WOOE Woods, George Benjamin;
Watt, Homer A. and Anderson,
George K., eds...The literature
of England...[Third edition]
Chicago, Ill., Scott, Foresman
[1947] 2v
Congreve, W. The way of the
world 1
Dryden, J. All for love 1
Everyman 1
Marlowe, C. The tragical history
of Doctor Faustus 1
The second shepherds' play 1
Shakespeare, W. The tragedy of
Antony and Cleopatra 1
Sheridan, R. The school for
scandal 1
Synge, J. Riders to the sea 2
Wilde, O. The importance of
being earnest 2

WOOG Woodyard, George, ed. The
modern stage in Latin America:
six plays. New York, Dutton,
1971. 331p
Carballido, E. I too speak of
roses
Diaz, J. The place where the mam-
mals die
Dragún, O. And they told us we
were immortal
Gomes, A. Payment as pledged
Marqués, R. The fanlights
Triana, J. The criminals

WOQ Wordplays; an anthology of new
American drama. New York,
Performing Arts Journal Publi-
cations. 1981-1984. 4v
Akalaitis, J. Dressed like an egg
4
Babe, T. Kid champion 4
Bosakowski, P. Chopin in space
4
Breuer, L. Hajj; the performance
3
Fornes, M. Fefu and her friends
1
Hauptman, W. Domingo courts 1
Jenkin, L. Dark ride 2

WOQ (cont.)
Jones, J. Night coil 4
Kennedy, A. A movie star has to star in black and white 3
Kondoleon, H. The brides 2
Martin, J. Clear glass marbles 3
Martin, J. Rodeo 3
Mednick, M. Taxes 3
Mee, C. The investigation of the murder in El Salvador 4
Nelson, R. Vienna notes 1
O'Keefe, J. All night long 2
Overmyer, E. Native speech 3
Owens, R. Chucky's lunch 2
Shawn, W. A thought in three parts 2
Tavel, R. Boy on the straight-back chair 1
Van Itallie, J. Naropa 1
Wellman, J. Starluster 1

WORLD DRAMA SERIES. See
SMI, SMK, SML, SMN, SMO, SMP, SMR Smith, Robert Metcalf, ed.

WORL The world in literature [edited by] Elizabeth Collette; Tom Peete Cross and Elmer C. Stauffer. Boston, Ginn [c1949] 4v
Barrie, J. Shall we join the ladies? 4
Shakespeare, W. Julius Caesar 2
Shakespeare, W. Macbeth 4
Wilder, T. Our town 3

WORM The world of tragedy, edited by John Kimmey and Ashley Brown. N.Y., New American Library, 1981. 466p
Miller, A. A view from the bridge
Racine, J. Phaedra
Sophocles. Antigone
Shakespeare, W. Macbeth

WORN The world turned upside down; prose and poetry of the American revolution; ed. and with an introd. by James H. Pickering. Port Washington, N.Y., Kennikat, 1975.
"The Battle of Brooklyn"
Brackenridge, H. The battle of

Bunkers-Hill

THE WORLD'S GREAT BOOKS. See
GRE Great plays (English)...
GREA Great plays (French and German)...GREE Greek dramas...

THE WORLD'S GREAT CLASSICS. See
ORI Oriental literature...
PLAB Plays by Greek, Spanish, French, German and English dramatists...TUQH Turkish literature...

WORP World's great plays; with an introduction by George Jean Nathan. Cleveland, Ohio, World Publishing Co. [1944] 491p
Aristophanes. Lysistrata
Chekhov, A. The cherry orchard
Goethe, J. Faust
Ibsen, H. The master builder
O'Casey, S. The plough and the stars
O'Neill, E. The Emperor Jones
Rostand, E. Cyrano de Bergerac

THE WORLD'S GREATEST LITERATURE. See
DRA Dramatic masterpieces...

WRIGHT, JOHN HENRY. See
MAST Masterpieces of Greek literature...

WRIH Wright, Louis Booker and LaMar, Virginia A., eds. Four famous Tudor and Stuart plays. New York, Washington Square Press [1963] 422p
Dekker, T. The shoemaker's holiday
Jonson, B. Volpone
Marlowe, C. Doctor Faustus
Webster, J. The Duchess of Malfi

WRIR Wright, Louis Booker and LaMar, Virginia A., eds. Four great Restoration plays...New York, Washington Square Press [1964] 477p
Congreve, W. The way of the world
Dryden, J. All for love

Farquhar, G. The beaux' stratagem
Wycherley, W. The country wife

YOHA Yohannan, John D., ed. A
treasury of Asian literature...
New York, John Day [c1956]
487p
Kālidāsa. Shakuntalā
Motokiyo, S. Atsumori

YOUP The Young Playwrights Festival collection: ten plays by
young playwrights between the
ages of eight and eighteen/
compiled and edited by the
Foundation of the Dramatists
Guild, Inc.; preface by
Stephen Sondheim; introduction
by Gerald Chapman. New
York, N.Y.: Avon Books
[1983] 263p
Berger, A. It's time for a
change
Garson, J. So what are we gonna
do now?
Gutwillig, S. In the way
Litt, J. Epiphany

Lonergan, K. The Rennings
children
McNamara, J. Present tense
Marchand, S. Half fare
Murphy, P. Bluffing
Serrano, L. The Bronx Zoo
Wiese, A. Coleman, S. D.

ZDA Zdanowicz, Casimir Douglas,
ed. Four French comedies of
the eighteenth century...New
York, Scribner [c1933] 488p
(The modern student's library)
Beaumarchais, P. Le barbier de
Séville
Lesage, A. Turcaret
Marivaux, P. Le jeu de l'amour
et du hasard
Sedaine, M. Le philosophe sans
le savoir

ZIM Zimmermann, Armand, ed. Four
European plays...New York,
Macmillan [1965] 547p
Anouilh, J. Thieves' carnival
Chekhov, A. The cherry orchard
Ibsen, H. An enemy of the people
Rostand, E. Cyrano de Bergerac

life. Gems, P.
Auprès de ma blonde. Achard, M.
See Behrman, S. I know my
love
Aureng-zebe. Dryden, J.
Aurora Leigh. Wandor, M.
Die ausnahme und die regel.
See Brecht, B. The exception
and the rule
Author, The. Foote, S.
Autobiography of a pearl diver.
Epstein, M.
L'autre danger. See Donnay, M.
The other danger
Autumn crocus. Smith, D. G.
Autumn garden, The. Hellman, L.
Autumn in Han Palace. See
Ma, C. Autumn in the Palace
of Han
Autumn in the Palace of Han.
Ma, C.
Autumn morning, An. See
Alvarez Quintero, S. and
Alvarez Quintero, J. A bright
morning
L'avare. See Molière, J. The
miser
Avenger, The. See Bird, R.
Caridorf
Les avengles. See Maeterlinck,
M. The blind
Aves. See Aristophanes. The
birds
Awake and sing. Odets, C.
Awakening. Stramm, A.
Away from it all. Gielgud, V.
Azalea mountain. Anonymous
plays

Baal. Brecht, B.
Babaye ng lalake. See Kabahar, P.
Woman and man
Babel rap. Lazarus, J.
Babes in the big house. Terry, M.
Babylon has fallen. Fletcher, J.
Babylonian captivity, The. Kosach,
L.
Bacchae, The. Euripides
Bacchantes, The. See Euripides.
The bacchae
Back stage of the soul, The. See
Evreinov, N. The theatre of the
soul
Back to back. Brown, A.
Background. Chetham-Strode, W.

Bad habits. McNally, T.
Bad man. Edmonds, R.
Bad man, The. Brown, P.
Bad play for an old lady, A.
Johnson, E.
Bad seed, The. Anderson, M.
Badger's green. Sherriff, R.
Bait, The. Merrill, J.
Le bal des voleurs. See
Anouilh, J. Thieves' carnival
Balaack and Balaam (Chester).
Anonymous plays
Balaam, Balak and the prophets.
See Anonymous plays. Balaack
and Balaam
Le balcon. See Genêt, J. The
balcony
Balcony, The. Genêt, J.
Bald prima donna, The. See
Ionesco, E. The bald soprano
Bald soprano, The. Ionesco, E.
Ballad of Ali of Keshan. Taner, H.
Balls. Foster, P.
Balm. Denison, M.
Balo. Toomer, J.
Baltaragio malūnas. See Boruta, K.
Whitehorn's windmill
Banished cavaliers, The. See Behn,
A. The rover
Bank note, The. Macready, W.
Banker's daughter, The. Howard,
B.
Bankrupt, The. Boker, G.
Banns (Chester). Anonymous plays
Banns (Coventry). Anonymous plays
Banns, The (N Town). Anonymous
plays
Baptism. Tembeck, R.
Barabas. Leamon, D.
Ba-ra-ka. Jones, L.
Barbara Allen. See Richardson, H.
and Berney, W. Dark of the
moon
Barbara Frietchie. Fitch, C.
Barbarossa. Brown, J.
Barber of Seville, The. See
Beaumarchais, P. Le barbier de
Seville
Le barbier de Seville; ou, La pré-
caution inutile. Beaumarchais,
P.
La barca sin pescador. See
Rodríguez, A. The boat without
a fisherman
Barefoot in Athens. Anderson, M.
Barefoot in the park. Simon, N.
Bargain, The. Gilbert, M.

Bucktails, The; or, Americans in England. Paulding, J.

Buffalo jump. Bolt, C.

Buffeting, The (Wakefield). Anonymous plays

Buggbears, The. Jeffere, J.

Bunch of keys, A; or, The hotel. Hoyt, C.

Bunch of the gods were sitting around one day, A. Spencer, J.

Bunker-Hill; or, The death of General Warren. Burk, J.

Bunthorne's bride. See Gilbert, W. and Sullivan, A. Patience

Buñuelos, Los. Anonymous plays

Burial of a war criminal, The. Gałczyński, K.

Buried child. Shepard, S.

El burlador de Sevilla. Téllez, G.

Burlesque. Watters, G. and Hopkins, A.

Bury fair. Shadwell, T.

Bury the dead. Shaw, I.

Bus stop. Inge, W.

Bushido. Takeda, I.

Busie body, The. See Centlivre, S. The busy body

Business is business. See Mirbeau, O. Les affaires sont les affaires

Busiris. Young, E.

Busman's honeymoon. Sayers, D. and Byrne, M.

Bussy D'Ambois. Chapman, G.

Busy body, The. Centlivre, S.

But what have you done for me lately? See Lamb, M. Scyklon Z

Butley. Gray, S.

Butter and egg man, The. Kaufman, G.

Butterflies are free. Gershe, L.

Butterfly dream, The. Kuan, H.

Buying rouge. Anonymous plays

By accident. Williams, H. and Williams, M.

By ourselves. See Fulda, L. Tête-à-tête

Bygmester Solness. See Ibsen, H. The master builder

El caballero de Olmedo. Vega Carpio, L.

Cabaret. Masteroff, J.

La cabeza del Bautista. Valle-

Inclán, R.

Cabistique. Cone, T.

Cabrerita. Acevedo Hernández, A.

La caccia al lupo. See Verga, G. The wolfhunt

Cactus flower. Burrows, A.

Caesar and Cleopatra. Shaw, G.

Caesar Augustus (Wakefield). Anonymous plays

Cage, The. Fratti, M.

La cage aux folles. Fierstein, H.

La cage aux folles. Poiret, J. See Fierstein, H. La cage aux folles

La cagnotte. See Labiche, E. and Delacour, A. Pots of money

Cai Shun fen-shen. See Liu, T. Cai Shun shares the mulberries

Cai Shun shares the mulberries. Liu, T.

Cain. Byron, G.

Cain. Nemerov, H.

Cain and Abel. Anonymous plays

Cain and Abel (Chester). Anonymous plays

Caine mutiny court-martial, The. Wouk, H.

La Calandria. See Dovizi da Bibiena, B. The follies of Calandro

Caleb the degenerate. Cotter, J.

California suite. Simon, N.

Caligula. Camus, A.

Calisto and Melebea (a new commodye in englysh in maner of an enterlude). See Rojas, F. Celestina

Calisto and Melibaea. See Anonymous plays. The beauty and good properties of women

Call it a day. Smith, D.

Call me Jacky. Bagnold, E.

Calline browierts, Die. Iobst, C.

Calm down, Mother. Terry, M.

Cambises, King of Persia. Preston, T.

Cambridge prologue, The. Anonymous plays

Cambyses. See Preston, T. Cambises, King of Persia

Camelot. Lerner, A.

Camilla; or, The fate of a coquette. See Dumas, A., fils. La dame aux camélias

Camille. See Dumas, A., fils. La dame aux camélias

Camille and Perdican. Musset, A.

Adam and Eve; The adoration
of the Magi; The adoration of
the shepherds; The annunciation
and the nativity; Antichrist;
The ascension; Balaack and
Balaam; Banns; The betrayal of
Christ; The blind Chelidonian;
Cain and Abel; Christ and the
doctors; Christ and the moneylenders; Christ appears to the
disciples; Christ at the house of
Simon the leper; Christ on the
road to Emmaus; Christ's ascension; Christ's ministry; Christ's
passion; Christ's resurrection;
The creation of man: Adam and
Eve; The death of Herod; The
deluge; Doubting Thomas; The
fall of Lucifer; The harrowing of
hell; Judas' plot; The last judgment; The last supper; The magi's
oblation; Moses and the law; The
nativity; The passion; The pentecost; The prophets; The
prophets of Antichrist; The purification; The raising of Lazarus;
The resurrection, harrowing of
hell, and the last judgment; The
sacrifice of Isaac; The shepherds;
Simon the leper; The slaying of
the innocents; The temptation;
The three kings; The trial and
flagellation; The woman taken in
adultery
Chetvyortaya stena. See Evreinov,
N. The fourth wall
Le cheval Tartare. See Payne, J.
Mazeppa
Le chevalier à la mode. Dancourt,
F.
Chia-ju wo shih chen-ti. See
Sha, Y.; Li, S.; and Yao, M.
If I were real
Chicago. Ebb, F. and Fosse, B.
Chicago. Shepard, S.
Chicago. Watkins, M.
Chicago, Chicago. See Romeril, J.
The man from Chicago
Chicago conspiracy, The.
Burgess, J. and Marowitz, C.
Chicago conspiracy trial, The.
Sossi, R. and Condon, F.
Chicago "conspiracy" trials. See
Levine, M.; McNamee, G.;
and Greenberg, D. The tales
of Hoffman - a series of excerpts
from the "Chicago conspiracy"

trial
Chicken feed. Bolton, G.
Chicken pie and the chocolate cake,
The. Anonymous plays
Chicken soup with barley. Wesker,
A.
Child hath found his father. The.
See Anonymous plays. The birth
of Merlin
Child of Grace. See Funt, J. The
magic and the loss
Child wife, The. See Ibsen, H. A
doll's house
Children in uniform. Winsloe, C.
Children of a lesser God. Medoff,
M.
Children of darkness. Mayer, E.
Children of Heracles, The. See
Euripides. The Heracleidae
Children of nature. See Kobrin, L.
Yankel Boyla
Children of the kingdom. Opper, D.
Children of the wolf. Peacock, J.
Children's hour, The. Hellman, L.
Child's play. Marasco, R.
Chimes of the Kremlin, The.
Pogodin, N.
China pig, The. Emig, E.
Chinchilla. MacDonald, R.
Chinese, The. Schisgal, M.
Chinese icebox, The. Laszlo, C.
Chinese wall, The. Frisch, M.
Chinese white. Gielgud, V.
Der Chinesische Kühlschrank. See
Laszlo, C. The Chinese icebox
Die Chinesische Mauer. See Frisch,
M. The Chinese wall
Ch'ing-ch'un. See Li, C. Spring-
time
Ch'ing kung yüan. See Yao, H.
The malice of empire
Chip woman's fortune, The.
Richardson, W.
Chips with everyting. Wesker, A.
Chiu Keng t'ien. See Anonymous
plays. One missing head
Choephori, The. See Aeschylus.
Choephoroe
Choephoroe. Aeschylus
Choice of a tutor, The. Fonvizin,
D.
Choleric man, The. Cumberland, R.
Choosing company. Schwartz, D.
Chopin in space. Bosakowski, P.
Chorus line. Kirkwood, J. and
Dante, N.
Chosroes. Rotrou, J.

Christ and the doctors (Chester).
Anonymous plays
Christ and the moneylenders
(Chester). Anonymous plays
Christ appears to the disciples
(Chester). Anonymous plays
Christ at the house of Simon the
leper (Chester). Anonymous
plays
Christ on the road to Emmaus
(Chester). Anonymous plays
Christmas carol, A. Shay, F.
Christmas mumming, A. Anonymous
plays
Christmas play, The (from Benedikt-
beuern). Anonymous plays
Christmas play of St. George. See
Anonymous plays. A Christmas
mumming
Christmas story, A. Williams, A.
Christophe Colomb. Ghelderode, M.
Christopher Blake. Hart, M.
Christopher Columbus. Hasenclever,
W. and Tucholsky, K.
Christopher Columbus. See
Ghelderode, M. Christophe
Colomb
Christ's appearances to the dis-
ciples (N Town). Anonymous
plays
Christ's ascension (Chester).
Anonymous plays
Christ's burial and resurrection
(Digby). Anonymous plays
Christ's death and burial (York).
Anonymous plays
Christ's ministry (Chester).
Anonymous plays
Christ's passion (Chester).
Anonymous plays
Christ's resurrection (Chester).
Anonymous plays
Chronicle history of Perkin
Warbeck, The. Ford, J.
Chronicle of the Battle of Ichino-
tani. Namiki, S., [et al]
Chronicles of hell. Ghelderode, M.
Chrononhotonthologos. Carey, H.
Chucky's lunch. Owens, R.
Chung-shen ta-shih. See Hu, S.
The greatest event in life
Church fight, The. Gaines-
Shelton, R.
Church street. Robinson, L.
Churl, The. See Plautus, T.
Truculentus
Ciascuno a suo modo. See Piran-

dello, L. Each in his own way
Le cid. Corneille, P.
Cid, The. See Corneille, P. Le
cid
Cigale chez les fourmis, La.
Legouvé, E. and Labiche, E.
Cinder, Tell-It. Williams, M.
Cinderellagame. Rummo, P.
Cinna; or, The mercy of Augustus.
Corneille, P.
Cinque. Melfi, L.
Circle, The. Maugham, W.
Circular staircase, The. See
Rinehart, M. and Hopwood, A.
The bat
Circus story, A. Tardieu, J.
Cistellaria. See Plautus, T.
The casket
Cit turned gentleman, The. See
Molière, J. Le bourgeois
gentilhomme
Cities in Bezique: The owl
answers and A beast story.
Kennedy, A.
Citizen, The. Murphy, A.
Citizen Kane: the shooting script.
Mankiewicz, H. and Welles, O.
La città morta. See Annunzio, G.
d'. The dead city
City, The. Anonymous plays.
City, The. Fitch, C.
City night-cap, The. Davenport,
R.
City madam, The. Massinger, P.
City wives confederacy. Vanbrugh,
J.
Clam made a face, The. Nicol, E.
Clandestine marriage, The. Colman,
G. and Garrick, D.
Clarence. Tarkington, B.
Claudia. Franken, R.
Claws, The. Linares Rivas, M.
Clean kill, A. Gilbert, M.
Clearing in the woods, A.
Laurents, A.
Cleone. Dodsley, R.
Clérambard. Aymé, M.
Climate of Eden, The. Hart, M.
Climbers, The. Fitch, C.
Clive of India. Lipscomb, W. and
Minney, R.
Clod, The. Beach, L.
Close quarters. Somin, W.
Closed door, The. Praga, M.
Cloud 9. Churchill, C.
Clouds, The. Aristophanes
Clutterbuck. Levy, B.

Der einsame weg. See Schnitzler,
A. The lonely way
El capitan and the corporal. Cor-
win, N.
Elche mystery play, The. See
Anonymous plays. The mystery
play of Elche
Elckerlijk. See Anonymous plays.
Everyman
Electra. Euripides
Electra. Giraudoux, J.
Electra. Hofmannsthal, H. von
Electra. Pérez Galdós, B.
Electra. Sophocles
Electra. Theobald, L.
Electre. See Giraudoux, J.
Electra
Electronic nigger, The. Bullins, E.
Elephant man, The. Pomerance, B.
Elfrida. Mason, W.
Elijah. Davidson, R.
Elizabeth the queen. Anderson, M.
Elvira. Mallet, D.
Elvira. See also Calderón de la
Barca, P. No siempre lo peor
es cierto
Embers. Beckett, S.
Emilia Galotti. Lessing, G.
Empedocles on Etna. Arnold, M.
Emperor, The. See Pirandello, L.
Henry IV
Emperor Jones, The. O'Neill, E.
Emperor of Haiti. Hughes, L.
Emperor of the moon, The. Behn,
A.
Emperor's clothes, The. Tabori,
G.
Empire builders, The. Vian, B.
Employee, The. Quiles, E.
Empress of Morocco, The. Settle,
E.
En attendant Gaudreault. See
Simard, A. Waiting for
Gaudreault
En gespräch zwischen zweb
demokrate über politiks.
Miller, D.
En gggarrrde! Daumal, R.
Enchanted, The. Giraudoux, J.
Enchanted castle, The. See
Duffett, T. The mock-tempest
Enchanted island, The. See
Dryden, J. and D'Avenant, W.
The tempest
Enchanted isle, The; or, 'Raising
the wind' on the most approved
principles. Brough, W. and

Brough, R.
Encore. Korr, D.
Encore un peu. See Mercier, S. A
little bit left
End of summer. Behrman, S.
End of the beginning, The. O'Casey,
S.
End of the world, The. Galczyński,
K.
End of the world, The; or, Frag-
ments from a work in progress.
Neilson, K.
Endgame. Beckett, S.
Endimion. See Lyly, J. Endymion
Ends of justice, The. McDaniel, C.
Endymion, The man in the moon.
Lyly, J.
Enemy. Maugham, R.
Enemy, The. Pollock, C.
Enemy, The. See Wincelberg, S.
Kataki
Enemy of society, An. See Ibsen,
H. An enemy of the people
Enemy of the people, An. Ibsen,
H.
L'enfant du mystère. See Pixéré-
court, R. Coelina
Engaged. Gilbert, W. and Sullivan,
A.
Engineer Sergeyev. Rokk, V.
England preserved. Watson-Taylor,
G.
English as it is spoken. See
Bernard, T. L'anglais tel qu'on
le parle
English merchant, The. Colman, G.
Englishman in Paris, The. Foote,
S.
Englishman return'd from Paris,
The. Foote, S.
Enough. Beckett, S.
Enough is as good as a feast.
Wager, W.
Enough stupidity in every wise man.
See Ostrovskii, A. The diary
of a scoundrel
Enquiry into the voyage of the
Santiago, An. MacLennan, D.
Enrico IV. See Pirandello, L.
Henry IV
Enter madame. Varesi, G. and
Byrne, D.
Enter Solly Gold. Kops, B.
Enterlude called Lusty Iuuentus, An.
See Anonymous plays. An enter-
lude called Lusty Juventus
Enterlude called Lusty Juventus, An.

Festival of peace, The. See
  Hauptmann, G. Des friedensfest
Die feuerprobe. See Kleist, H.
  Kaethchen of Heilbronn
Fiddler on the roof. Stein, J.
Il fido amico. See Scala, F. The
  faithful friend
Field god, The. Green, P.
Field Marshal Kutuzov. Solovev, V.
Field of the cloth of gold, The.
  Brough, W.
Fiend of Fleet Street, The. See
  Pitt, G. The string of pearls
Fifteen strings of cash. Anonymous
  plays
Fifteen years of a drunkard's life.
  Jerrold, D.
Fifth of July, The. Wilson, L.
Fighter, The. Eisenstein, M.
La figlia di Jorio. See Annunzio,
  G. d'. The daughter of Jorio
Fill the stage with happy hours.
  Wood, C.
La fille de Madame Angot. See
  Lacocq, A. The daughter of
  Madame Angot
Filumena Marturano. Filippo, E.
El fin de Chipí González. See
  Matto, J. The fate of Chipí
  González
Fin de partie. See Beckett, S.
  Endgame
Final judgment, The. Anonymous
  plays
Financier, The. See Le Sage, A.
  Turcaret
Find me. Wymark, O.
Find your way home. Hopkins, J.
Finders-keepers. Kelly, G.
Fingernails blue as flowers.
  Ribman, R.
Finian's rainbow. Harburg, E.
Finishing touches. Kerr, J.
Fiorello! Weidman, J. and Abbott,
  G.
Fire in the basement. Kohout, P.
Fire in the opera house, The.
  Kaiser, G.
Fire raisers, The. See Frisch, M.
  Biedermann and the firebugs
Fire, water, earth and air. See
  Dibdin, T. Harlequin in his
  element
Firebrand, The. Mayer, E.
Firebugs, The. See Frisch, M.
  Biedermann and the firebugs
Fires of St. John, The. Sudermann,

H.
First and last love. See Payne, J.
  The Spanish husband
First blood. Monkhouse, A.
First communion. Arrabal, F.
First gentleman, The. Ginsbury, N.
First lady. Dayton, K. and Kauf-
  man, G.
First militant minister, The. See
  Caldwell, B. Prayer meeting
First Mrs. Fraser, The. Ervine,
  St. J.
First Monday in October. Lawrence,
  J. and Lee, R.
First part of the reign of King
  Richard the second; or, Thomas
  of Woodstock, The. See Anony-
  mous plays. Woodstock
First part of the return from Par-
  nassus, The. See Anonymous
  plays. The return from Parnas-
  sus
First president, The. Williams, W.
First shepherds' play, The (Wake-
  field). Anonymous plays
First sin, The. Megged, A.
First year, The. Craven, F.
Fisherman and the sea king's
  daughter, The. See Feldshuh, D.
  Fables here and then
Fishermen, The. Houston, D.
Fishermen's child, The. See Herne,
  A. Drifting apart
Five easy payments. Lewis, J.
Five finger exercise. Shaffer, P.
Five fingers on the black hand side.
  Russell, C.
Five posts in a market place. Lands-
  bergis, A.
Five star final. Weitzenkorn, L.
Fixin's: The tragedy of a tenant
  farm woman. Green, P., and
  Green, E.
Flies, The. Sartre, J.
Flight into danger. Hailey, A.
Flight into Egypt, The (Wakefield).
  Anonymous plays
Flight into Egypt, The (York).
  Anonymous plays
Flight of the natives, The. Richard-
  son, W.
Flight to the west. Rice, E.
Flirtation. See Schnitzler, A. Light-
  o'-love
Flite cage. Hadler, W.
Flittermouse. Reely, M.
Floating light bulb, The. Allen, W.

La gabbia. See Fratti, M. The cage

Gabriel. Mason, C.

Galateau. See Gilbert, W. and Sullivan, A. Pygmalion and Galatea

Galenpannan. See Forssell, L. The madcap

Galgamannen; en midvintersaga. See Schildt, R. The gallows man

Galileo. Brecht, B.

Gallant, the bawd, and the fair lady, The. Ruiz, J.

Gallathea. Lyly, J.

Galley slave, The. Campbell, B.

Gallows humour. Richardson, J.

Gallows man, The: a midwinter story. Schildt, R.

Galtra-Loftur. See Sigurjónsson, J. The wish

Gamblers. Gogol, N.

Gambler's fate, The. See Dunlap, W. Thirty years

Game at chess, A. Middleton, T.

Game of folly vs. wisdom, The. Theotokas, G.

Game of love, The. Okonkwo, R.

Game of love, The. See Schnitzler, A. Light-o'-love

Game of love and chance, The. See Marivaux, P. Le jeu de l'amour et du hazard

The Gamecock, The. Livings, H.

Games. Klíma, I.

Gamester, The. Moore, E.

Gamester, The. See Shirley, J. Gamesters

Gamesters. Shirley, J.

Gammer Gurton's nedle. See Stevenson, W. Gammer Gurton's needle

Gammer Gurton's needle. Stevenson, W.

Gap, The. Ionesco, E.

Garage sale. Ringwood, G.

Le garçon et l'aveugle. Anonymous plays

Gardener's dog, The. See Vega Carpio, L. The dog in the manger

La garra. See Linares Rivas, M. The claws

Gas company, The. See Feldshuh, D. Fables here and then

Gas heart, The. Tsara, T.

Gas I. Kaiser, G.

Gas II. Kaiser, G.

Gaslight. See Hamilton, P. Angel street

Gassir the hero. See Feldshuh, D. Fables here and then

Gastone the animal tamer. Morselli, E.

Gauntlet, A. Bjørnson, B.

Gay invalid, The. See Molière, J. Doctor's delight

Gay Lord Quex, The. Pinero, A.

Gem. See Keeffe, B. Gimme shelter

Gemini. Innaurato, A.

Le gendre de M. Poirier. Augier, E. and Sandeau, J.

General, The. Petch, S.

General returns from one place to another, The. O'Hara, F.

Generation. Goodhart, W.

Generations. Pollock, S.

Generous Portugal, The. See Fletcher, J. The island princess

Gengangere. See Ibsen, H. Ghosts

Le gentilhomme Guespin. Donneau de Visé, J.

Gentle craft, The. See Dekker, T. The shoemaker's holiday

Gentle gunman, The. MacDougall, R.

Gentle savage, The. See Brougham, J. Pocahontas

Gentle shepherd, The. Ramsay, A.

Gentleman caller. Bullins, E.

Gentleness and nobility. Heywood, J.

George a Greene, the pinner of Wakefield. Greene, R.

George and Margaret. Savory, G.

George Barnwell. See Lillo, G. The London merchant

George Washington slept here. Kaufman, G. and Hart, M.

Georgie porgie. Birmisa, G.

Der gerettete Alkibiades. See Kaiser, G. Alkibiades saved

Gestern und heute. See Winsloe, C. Children in uniform

Der gestiefelte kater. Tieck, J.

Get out of my hair. Feydeau, G.

Getaway. See Keeffe, B. Gimme shelter

Getting by, and going home. See Taylor, C. Walter

Getting married. Shaw, G.

Getting out. Norman, M.

Das gewissen. See Iffland, A. Conscience

Ghost of Abel, The. Blake, W.
Ghost of Benjamin Sweet, The.
  Gilsdorf, F. and Gibson, P.
Ghost patrol, The. Clarke, W.
Ghost sonata, The. Strindberg,
  A.
Ghosts. Ibsen, H.
Ghosts. San Francisco Mime Troupe
Giant's stair, The. Steele, W.
La giara. See Pirandello, L. The
  jar
Gibson upright, The. Tarkington,
  B. and Wilson, H.
Gideon. Chayefsky, P.
Gift, The. Duncan, R.
Gigi. Loos, A.
Gimme shelter. Keeffe, B.
Gin game, The. Coburn, D.
Ginger Anne. Washburn, D.
Ginberbread lady, The. Simon, N.
Gioconda. Annunzio, D. d'
Giovanni in London; or, The
  libertine reclaimed. Moncrieff,
  W.
Gipsies metamorphosed, The.
  Jonson, B.
Girl from Lorraine, A. See Ander-
  son, M. Joan of Lorraine
Girl from Persia, The. Plautus, T.
Girl from Samous, The. Menander
Girl I left behind me, The.
  Belasco, D. and Fyles, F.
Girl of the golden west, The.
  Belasco, D.
Girl on the Via Flaminia, The.
  Hayes, A.
Girl setting out for trial, A.
  Nü, C.
Girl with the green eyes, The.
  Fitch, C.
Girls' acquiescence, The. See
  Moratín, L. El sí de las niñas
Girls in uniform. See Winsloe, C.
  Children in uniform
Gismond of Salerne. See Wilmot, R.
  Tancred and Gismond
Give all the terrors to the wind.
  Sifton, C. and Sifton, P.
Gladiator, The. Bird, R.
Glamour. Bernard, J.
Glass darkly, A. Gilbert, S.
Glass menagerie, The. Williams, T.
Glass of water, A. See Scribe, A.
  Le verre d'eau
Glaube und heimat. See Schönherr,
  K. Faith and fireside
Glaucus. Boker, G.

Glengarry Glen Ross; a play in two
  acts. Mamet, D.
Glittering gate, The. Dunsany, E.
Gloaming, oh my darling, The.
  Terry, M.
Gloria. Marinković, R.
Le glorieux. Destouches, P.
Glorious morning. MacOwan, N.
Glory of Columbia: Her yeomancy!,
  The. Dunlap, W.
Glove, A. See Björnson, B. A
  gauntlet
Das glück im winkel. See Suder-
  man, H. The vale of content
Glutt. See Schrock, G. Two for
  the silence
Der gnopp. Birmelin, J.
Goal, The. Jones, H.
Goat song. Werfel, F.
God bless our home. See Barry, P.
  The youngest
God Fudō, The. See Tsuuchi, H.;
  Yasuda, A.; and Nakada, M.
  Saint Narukami and the God Fudō
God of Gods, The. Aikins, C.
God of the lightning. Anderson, M.
  and Hickerson, H.
God of vengeance. Asch, S.
Godley Queen Hester. Anonymous
  plays
Gods of the mountain, The. Dunsany,
  E.
God's promises. Bale, J.
Goethe: Ein fragment. McClure, M.
Goetz von Berlichingen. Goethe, J.
Goin' a Buffalo. Bullins, E.
Going to see the elephant. Hensel,
  K.; Johns, P.; Kent, A.; Mere-
  dith, S.; Shaw, E.; and Toffenet-
  ti, L.
Gold. Myrtle, F.
Golden age restored. Jonson, B.
Golden apple, The. Latouche, J.
Golden boy. Odets, C.
Golden bull of boredom, The. Yerby,
  L.
Golden circle, The. Patrick, R.
Golden fleece, The. Gurney, A.
Golden gate, The. Stefánsson, D.
Golden lover, The. Stewart, D.
Golden pippin, The. O'Hara, K.
Golden steed, The. Rainis, J.
Golem, The. Halper, L.
Good. Taylor, C.
Good day. Peluso, E.
Good doctor, The. Simon, N.
Good evening, clown. Afanasjew, J.

Der gruene kakadu. See Schnitzler, A. The green cockatoo

La guarda cuidadosa. See Cervantes Saavedra, M. The vigilant sentinel

Guárdate del agua mansa. See Calderón de la Barca, P. Keep your own secret

Guardian, The. Garrick, D.

Guardian of the tomb, The. Kafka, F.

Guerillas of the Ukrainian Steppes. Korneichuk, A.

La guerre de Troie n'aura pas lieu. See Giraudoux, J. Tiger at the gates

El guerrero ciego. See Rellán, M. The blind warrior

Guillermo Tell tiene los ojos tristes. See Sastre, A. Sad are the eyes of William Tell

Guilty party. Ross, G.

Gullna hlidid. See Stefánsson, D. The golden gate

Gun play, A. Udoff, Y.

Gunpowder, treason and plot. Williamson, H.

Gustavus Vasa, or, The deliverer of his country. Brooke, H.

Der gute mensch von Sezuan. See Brecht, B. The good woman of Setzuan

Guys and dolls. Swerling, J.; Burrows, A. and Loesser, F.

Guzmán el Bueno. Gil y Zárate, A.

Gypsy. Anderson, M.

Gypsy. Laurents, A.

H.M.S. Parliament, or, The lady who loved a government clerk. Fuller, W.

H.M.S. Pinafore; or, The lass that loved a sailor. Gilbert, W. and Sullivan, A.

Hachi no ki. See Seami, M. The dwarf trees

Hadrian VII. Luke, P.

Hai Jui dismissed from office. Wu, C.

Hai Jui pa-kuan. See Wu, C. Hai Jui dismissed from office

Hair. Ragni, G. and Rado, J.

Hairy ape, The. O'Neill, E.

Haiti. Dubois, W.

Hajj; the performance. Breuer, L.

Haku Rakuten. Seami, M.

Half a loaf. See Lonsdale, F. Let them eat cake

Hall of healing. O'Casey, S.

Hallelujah. Lebović, D.

Hamadryads, The. Irwin, W.

Haman's downfall. Sloves, C.

El hambriento. Anonymous plays

Hamlet. Shakespeare, W.

Hamlet and the waitress (a play about the life of the intellectual elite entitled). Gałczyński, K.

Hamlet of Stepney Green, The. Kops, B.

Hamlet, or, Not such a fool as he looks. Hilton, A.

Hamlet; or, The new wing at Elsinore. See "Mr. Punch" [pseud.] A dramatic sequel to Hamlet

Hamlet, Prince of Denmark. Rice, G.

Hamlet revamped; a travesty without a pun. Soule, C.

Hamlet the dainty. Griffin, G.

Hamlet the Dane, a burlesque burletta. Beckington, C.

Hamlet! the ravin' Prince of Denmark!!, or, The Baltic swell!!! and the diving belle!!! Anonymous plays

Hamlet travestie. Poole, J.

Hamlet travestie. Talfourd, F.

Hamp. Wilson, J.

Han Kung Ch'in. See Ma, C. Autumn in the Palace of Han

Hand of Siva, The. Goodman, K. and Hecht, B.

Handcuffs (part three of the Donnellys). Reaney, J.

Hands around. See Schnitzler, A. Round dance

Hands in the mirror. Welch, L.

Hanging of Judas, The (Wakefield). Anonymous plays

Hanjo. See Seami, M. Lady Han

Hannele. Hauptmann, G.

Hannelle's assumption. See Hauptmann, G. Hannele

Hanneles himmelfahrt. See Hauptmann, G. Hannele

Hannibal and Scipio. Nabbes, T.

En hanske. See Bjørnson, B. A gauntlet

Happening in the bungalow, The. Lee, J.

Happiest days of your life. Dighton, J.

Hinkelmann. Toller, E.

Hiob. See Kokoschka, O. Job

Hippolytus. Euripides

Hippolytus. Howe, J.

Hirsh Lekert, or, Heroic years.
Halper, L.

His first step. Oyamo

His widow's husband. Benavente
y Martínez, J.

L'histoire de Tobie et de Sara.
See Claudel, P. Tobias and
Sara

Histoire de Vasco. See Schehadé,
G. Vasco

L'histoire du cirque. See Salacrou, A. A circus story

Historical register for year 1736,
The. Fielding, H.

Histories of Lot and Abraham, The.
See Anonymous plays. Abraham,
Melchisedec and Isaac

History of George Barnwell, The.
See Lillo, G. The London merchant

History of Jacob and Èsau, The.
See Anonymous plays. Jacob and
Esau

History of King Lear, The. Tate,
N.

History of Vasco, The. See
Schehadé, G. Vasco

Hoarse muse. Campbell, P.

Hob; or, The country wake. Dogget,
T.

Hob in the well. See Dogget, T.
Hob

Hoboken blues; or, The black Rip
Van Winkle. Gold, M.

Hobson's choice. Brighouse, H.

Die hochzeit der Sobeide. See
Hofmannsthal, H. von. The
marriage of Sobeide

Di hoffning. Brendle, T.

Hogan's goat. Alfred, W.

Hole in the wall. Kreymborg, A.

Holiday. Barry, P.

Holly and the ivy, The. Browne,
W.

Holy experiment, The. See Hoch-
walder, F. The strong are
lonely

Holy ghostly, The. Shepard, S.

Holy Resurrection, The. See
Anonymous plays. La seinte
Resureccion

Homage of the arts, The. Schiller,
J.

El hombre de mundo. Vega, V.

El hombre del siglo. See Frank, M.
The man of the century

El hombre y la mosca. See Ruibal,
J. The man and the fly

Home. See Maeterlinck, M. Interior;
Sudermann, H. Magda

Home. Storey, D.

Home. Williams, S.

Home at seven. Sherriff, R.

Home free. Alexander, R.

Home of the brave. Laurents, A.

Homecoming, The. Pinter, H.

L'homme et ses fantômes. Lenormand, H.

Honest whore, The. Dekker, T.
and Middleton, T.

Honeymoon, The. Tobin, J.

Honeymoon in Haiti. Kleb, W.

Hongi. Mason, B.

L'honneur de Dieu. See Anouilh, J.
Becket

Honor of God, The. See Anouilh, J.
Becket

Honorable history of Friar Bacon
and Friar Bungay, The. Greene,
R.

Hope deferred. Davies, R.

Hope for a harvest. Treadwell, S.

Hoppla! See Toller, E. Hoppla!
Such is life!

Hoppla! Such is life! Toller, E.

Hoppla, wir leben. See Toller, E.
Hoppla! Such is life!

Horace. Corneille, P.

Horestes. Pikeryng, John

Horizon. Daly, A.

Horse, The. Hay, J.

Horse-shoe Robinson. Tayleure, C.

Horse thief, The. Sachs, H.

Hoss drawin'. Martell, L.

Hostage, The. Behan, B.

Hostages. Akritas, L.

Hot l Baltimore, The. Wilson, L.

Hotel, The. See Hoyt, C. A bunch
of keys

Hotel Universe. Barry, P.

Hotel Universe. San Francisco Mime
Troupe

Hourglass, The. Alexander, R.

Hour-glass, The. Yeats, W.

House, The. Borgen, J.

House by the lake, The. Mills, H.

House in the quiet glen, The.
Coulter, J.

House in the square, A. Morgan, D.

House of Atreus, The (Trilogy). See

Godley Queen Hester
Interlude of impatient poverty,
An. See Anonymous plays.
Impatient poverty
Interlude of John the evangelist,
The. See Anonymous plays.
John the evangelist
Interlude of vice, The. Pikerying,
J.
Interlude of wealth and health, An.
See Anonymous plays. Wealth
and health
Interlude of youth, The. See Ano-
nymous plays. Youth
Intermezzo. See Giraudoux, J. The
enchanted
Intermezzo. Schnitzler, A.
International stud, The. See Fier-
stein, H. Torch song trilogy
Interview. Van Itallie, J.
Interview, The. Donleavy, J.
Intimate relations. Cocteau, J.
Intimate strangers, The. Tarking-
ton, B.
Intrigue at Ah-pah. The Dell' Arte
Players
Intriguing chambermaid, The.
Fielding, H.
Intruder, The. Maeterlinck, M.
L'intruse. See Maeterlinck, M. The
intruder
Invasion. Leonov, L.
Invisible bond, The. Sentongo, N.
L'invitation au chateau. See Anouilh,
J. Ring round the moon
L'invitation au voyage. See Bernard,
J. Glamour
Iolanthe; or, The peer and the peri.
Gilbert, W. and Sullivan, A.
Ion. Euripides
Iphigenia among the Tauri. See
Euripides. Iphigenia in Tauris
Iphigenia at Aulis. Euripides
Iphigenia at Aulis. Rexroth, K.
Iphigenia in Aulis. See Euripides.
Iphigenia at Aulis
Iphigenia in Tauris. Euripides
Iphigenia in Tauris. Goethe, J.
Iphigenia of Tauris. See Goethe, J.
Iphigenia in Tauris
Iphigenie auf Tauris. See Goethe, J.
Iphigenia in Tauris
Irawan rabi. See Anonymous plays.
Irawan's wedding
Irawan's wedding. Anonymous plays
Irene. Johnson, S.
Irene. See Verneuil, L. Affairs of

state
Irene, o el tesoro. Buero Vallejo,
A.
Iris. Pinero, A.
Irish stew. Bradley, J.
Iron chest, The. Colman, G., the
younger
Iron crown, The. Anonymous plays
Iron harp, The. O'Conor, J.
Iron manufacturer, The. Ohnet, G.
Iron master, The. See Ohnet, G.
The iron manufacturer
Irregular verb to love, The. Wil-
liams, H. and Williams, M.
Isaac. Anonymous plays.
Isabella. Southerne, T.
Isak Juntti had many sons. Höijer,
B.
Isak Juntti hade många söner. See
Hoijer, B. Isak Juntti had many
sons
Island, The. Fugard, A.
Island, The. Hodge, M.
Island, The. Kani, J. See Fugard,
A. The island
Island of Barrataria, The. Tyler,
R.
Island of Goats. See Betti, U.
Crime of Goat Island
Island of jewels, The. Planché, J.
Island princess, The; or, The
generous Portugal. Fletcher, J.
It cannot be. See Crowne, J. Sir
Courtly Nice
It happened in Irkutsk. Arbuzov,
A.
It is so (if you think so). See
Pirandello, L. Right you are!
If you think so
It pays to advertise. Megrue, R.
and Hackett, W.
It should happen to a dog. Man-
kowitz, W.
Italian bride, The. Payne, J.
Italian straw hat, An. Labiche, E.
and Michel, M.
Item de resurrectione Domini. See
Anonymous plays. Of the resur-
rection of the Lord (from St.
Gall)
"It's a bird, it's a plane, it's super-
man." Newman, D. and Benton,
R.
It's called the sugar plum. Horo-
vitz, I.
It's time for a change. Berger, A.
Ivan the terrible: the screenplay,

King Stag, The. Gozzi, C.
King Stephen. Keats, J.
King, the greatest Alcalde, The.
Vega Carpio, L.
King Ubu. Jarry, A.
King Victor and King Charles.
Browning, R.
Kingdom of God, The. Martínez
Sierra, G. and Martínez
Sierra, M.
King's daughter. See Lewis, S.
Siwan
King's dilemma, The. Richardson,
W.
King's henchman, The. Millay, E.
King's jewry, The. Glover, H.
King's threshold, The. Yeats, W.
Kirflugèn. See Clausen, S.
The bird of contention
Kiss and tell. Herbert, F.
Kiss in Xanadu, A. Ames, W.
Kiss me Kate. Spewack, B. and
Spewack, S.
Kiss the boys good-bye. Boothe,
C.
Kitchen, The. Wesker, A.
Kjaerlighedens tragedie. See
Heiberg, G. The tragedy of
love
Kjarnorka og kvenkylli. See
Thórdarson, A. Atoms and
madams
Eine kleine nachtmusik. Mozart, W.
See Wheeler, H. A little night
music
Knack, The. Jellicoe, A.
Knacker's ABC, The. See Vian, B.
Knackery for all
Knackery for all. Vian, B.
Knave and queen. Young, C. and
Howard, B.
Knight in four acts. Harrison, J.
Knight of the burning pestle, The.
Beaumont, F. and Fletcher, J.
Knights, The. Aristophanes
Knights, The. Foote, S.
Knives from Syria. Riggs, L.
Knock about, The. See Andreev,
L. He who gets slapped
Knock, knock. Feiffer, J.
Know thyself. Hervieu, P.
Komachi and the hundred nights.
Kwanze, K. K.
Komachi at Sekidera. Seami, M.
Kongsemnerna. See Ibsen, H. The
pretenders
König Nikolo. See Wedekind, F.

Such is life
König Ottokars glück und ende.
Grillparzer, F.
Konkylien. See Krog, H. The
sounding shell
Das konzert. See Bahr, H. The
concert
Die koralle. See Kaiser, G. The
coral
Korczak und die Kinder. See
Sylvanus, E. Dr. Korczak and
the children
Kramer, The. Medoff, M.
Krapp's last tape. Beckett, S.
Kreig, ein Te Deum. See Haupt-
mann, C. War, a Te Deum
Kremlevskie kuranty. See Pogodin,
N. The chimes of the Kremlin
Kremlin chimes. See Pogodin, N.
The chimes of the Kremlin
K2. Meyers, P.
Kuan Han-ch'ing. T'ien, S.
Kurka wodna. See Witkiewicz, S.
The water hen
Kuruwa Bunshō. See Anonymous
plays. Love letter from the
licensed quarter
Die Kurve. See Dorst, T. The
curve
En kvinde er overflodig. See
Sonderby, K. A woman too many
Kynge Johan. See Bale, J. King
John

"L." Atlas, L.
La la noo. Yeats, J.
Laburnum grove. Priestley, J.
Lace on her petticoat. Stuart, A.
La lâche. See Lenormand, H. The
coward
La lacune. See Ionesco, E. The gap
Ladies in waiting. De Anda, P.
Ladies in waiting. Fox, E.
Lady Aoi. See Zenchiku, U. Aoi
no Uye
Lady Audley's secret. Hazlewood,
C.
Lady from Dubuque, The. Albee,
E.
Lady from the sea, The. Ibsen, H.
Lady Han. Seami, A.
Lady in the dark. Hart, M.
Lady Jane Gray. Rowe, N.
Lady Margaret. See Scribe, A.
Les doigts de fée

Raising of Lazarus; Resurrection
and appearance to Mother; The
salutation and conception; The
shepherds' play; Story of the
watch; Three Marys at the tomb;
The trial of Christ; Trial of
Joseph and Mary; The woman
taken in adultery
Na Catita. Segura, M.
Nachstück. See Hildesheimer, W.
Nightpiece
Nagananda. Harsha, son of Hira
Naim. Chilton, N.
Nakamitsu. Seami, M.
Naked. Pirandello, L.
Naked island. Braddon, R.
Nanine. Voltaire, F.
Nannie's night out. O'Casey, S.
Napoleon crossing the Rockies.
MacKaye, P.
Naropa. Van Itallie, J.
Narukami. Danjūrō I
Narukami Fudō Kityama Zakura.
See Tsuuchi, H.; Yasuda, A.;
and Nakada, M. Saint Narukami
and the God Fudō
Nat Turner. Peters, P.
Nathan der weise. See Lessing, G.
Nathan the wise
Nathan Hale. Fitch, C.
Nathan the wise. Lessing, G.
National health, The. Nichols, P.
National velvet. Bagnold, E.
Native son. Wright, R. and Green,
P.
Nativity, The. See Anonymous
plays. The pageant of the shear-
men and tailors (N Town)
Nativity (The Chantilly play), The.
Bourlet, Katherine
Nativity, The (Chester). Anonymous
plays
Nativity, The (Wakefield). See
Anonymous plays. The second
shepherds' play
Nativity, The (York). See Anony-
mous plays. The York nativity
Nativity play, The. See Anonymous
plays. The pageant of the shear-
men and tailors (N Town)
Nativity play (Coventry). See
Anonymous plays. The pageant of
the shearmen and tailors
Natural man. Browne, T.
Natural son, The. Cumberland, R.
Natural son, The. See Kotzebue, A.
Lovers' vows

Nature. Medwall, H.
Nature of the four elements, The.
Anonymous plays
La Nau. See Benet I Jornet, J.
The ship
Naughty Anthony. Belasco, D.
Naval encounter. Goering, R.
Neck or nothing. Garrick, D.
Necklace, The. See Harsha, son
of Hira. Retnavali
Nec-natama. Shiels, J.
Ned Kelly. Stewart, D.
Ned McCobb's daughter. Howard,
S.
Nederlaget. See Grieg, N. The
defeat
Needles and pins. Daly, A.
Les nègres. See Genêt, J. The
blacks: a clown show
Neptune's triumph for the return
of Albion. Jonson, B.
Nero. Anonymous plays
Nest, The. Geraldy, P.
Nest of another, The. See Bena-
vente y Martínez, J. El nido
ajeno
Never come Monday. Knight, E.
Nevis mountain dew. Carter, S.
New anatomies. Wertenbaker, T.
New arrival, The. Roman, M.
New Chautaqua, The. Gaines, F.
New custom. Anonymous plays
New gossoon, The. Shiels, G.
New house, The. Behan, B.
New men and old acres. Taylor,
T.
New morality, The. Chapin, H.
New sin, The. Hastings, B.
New tenant, The. Ionesco, E.
New trick to cheat the divell.
Davenport, R.
New way to pay old debts, A.
Massinger, P.
New wing at Elsinore, The. See
"Mr. Punch" [pseud.] A
dramatic sequel to Hamlet
New year country. See Bolt, C.
Buffalo jump
New Year's eve. Frank, W.
New York idea, The. Mitchell, L.
Newcastle play, The. Anonymous
plays
Newe enterlude of vice conteyning
the history of Horestes with the
cruell rengment of his fathers
death upon his one naturall
mother. See Horestes

News from the new world discovered in the moon. Jonson, B.

News item, The. Olmo, L.

News of the night; or, A trip to Niagara. Bird, R.

Next. McNally, T.

Next door neighbors. Inchbald, E.

Next thing, The. Smith, M.

Next time I'll sing to you. Saunders, J.

Nice people. Crothers, R.

Nice wanton. Anonymous plays

Nicholas Nickleby. Dickens, C. See Edgar, D. The life and adventures of Nicholas Nickleby; a play in two parts

Nick of the woods. Hamblin, L.

El nido ajeno. Benavente y Martínez, J.

Nie-Boska Komedia. See Krasiński, Z. The un-divine comedy

Nie wieder friede. See Toller, E. No more peace!

Niels Ebbesen. Munk, K.

Night. Melfi, L.

Night and war in the Prado Museum. Alberti, R.

Night at an inn, A. Dunsany, E.

Night-cap. Anonymous plays

Night coil. Jones, J.

'night, Mother. Norman, M.

Night must fall. Williams, E.

Night of the iguana, The. Williams, T.

Night of the twentieth, The. Sobol, Y.

Night out, A. Pinter, H.

Night shelter, A. See Gorki, M. [pseud.] The lower depths

Night time stood still, The. See Mitson, R. Beyond the bourn

Night to make the angels weep, A. Terson, P.

Nightmare abbey. Sharp, A.

Nightpiece. Hildesheimer, W.

Night's lodging. See Gorki, M. [pseud.] The lower depths

Nightwalk. Open Theater

Nihilist, The. Monson, W.

Nil carborundum. Livings, H.

Nine. Kopit, A.

Nishikigi. See Seami, M. The brocade tree

No 'count boy, The. Green, P.

No exit. See Sartre, J. Huis clos

No fumadores. See Benavente y Martínez, J. No smoking

No hay mal que por bien no venga (Don Domingo de Don Blas). Ruiz de Alarcón y Mendoza, J.

No more frontier. Jennings, T.

No more ladies. Thomas, A. E.

No more peace! Toller, E.

No mother to guide her. Mortimer, L.

No nos venceremos. Garza, R.

No place to be somebody. Gordone, C.

No quarter. Bermange, B.

No room at the inn. Temple, J.

No siempre lo peor es cierto. Calderón de la Barca, P.

No smoking. Benavente y Martínez, J.

No song no supper. Hoare, P.

No strings attached. Moss, H.

No thoroughfare. Smee, L.

No time for comedy. Behrman, S.

No time for sergeants. Levin, I.

No trifling with love. See Musset, A. de. On ne badine pas avec l'amour

Noah. Obey, A.

Noah. See Anonymous plays. The deluge (Chester)

Noah (Wakefield). Anonymous plays

Noah and his sons. See Anonymous plays. The deluge

Noah's ark. Holt, B.

Noah's ark. See Anonymous plays. The Newcastle play

Noah's deluge. See Anonymous plays. The deluge

Noah's flood. See Anonymous plays. The deluge

Noble souldier, The. Anonymous plays

Noch eppes vom Peter seim Handwerk. Miller, D.

Les noces d'argent. See Geraldy, P. The nest

Noche de guerra en el Museo del Prado. See Alberti, R. Night and war in the Prado Museum

La noche de los asesinos. See Triana, J. The criminals

Noel Coward in two keys. Coward, N.

Noises off. Frayn, M.

None beneath the king. See Rojas Zorrilla, F. Del rey abajo, ninguno

Nonomiya. See Anonymous plays. The shrine in the fields

Queen of camelias, The. See
Dumas, A. fils. La dame aux
camélias
Queen of hearts, The. Pakington,
M.
Queen of Scots. MacKintosh, E.
Queen of Scots, The. Montchrestien,
A.
Queen on tour, The. Abell, K.
Queen's enemies, The. Dunsany, E.
Queen's highland servant, The.
Home, W.
Quem quaeritis, The (Trope).
Anonymous plays
Querolus. Anonymous plays
Quest divine, The. Goold, M.
Quest of the Gorgon, The. Tharp,
N.
Questa sera si recita a soggetto.
See Pirandello, L. Tonight we
improvise
Question of obedience, A. See
Williamson, H. Teresa of
Avila
Questioning the irrevocable.
Schnitzler, A.
Qui Hu tries to seduce his own
wife. Shi, J.
Qui Hu xi-gi. See Shi, J.
Qui Hu tries to seduce his own
wife
Quick nut bread to make your
mouth water, A. Hoffman, W.
Quiet wedding. McCracken, E.

R.U.R. Čapek, K.
Rachel. Grimke, A.
Racket, The. Cormack, B.
Rackey. Culbertson, E.
Radio primer. Corwin, N.
Rafferty's chant. Dewhurst, K.
Raft of the Medusa, The. Kaiser, G.
Rage, The. Reynolds, F.
Rags. Walter, N.
Raigne of King Edward the third,
The. See Anonymous plays.
The reign of King Edward the
third
Railroad women. Ratcliffe, H.
Rain. Colton, J. and Randolph, C.
Rain. Gałczyński, K.
Rain from heaven. Behrman, S.
Rain on the Hsiao-Hsiang. Yang, H.
Rain-killers, The. Hutchinson, A.
Rainmaker, The. Ringwood, G.

Rainmakers, The. Nash, R.
Raisin in the sun, A. Hansberry, L.
Raisin' the devil. Gard, R.
Raising of Lazarus, The. Hilarius
Raising of Lazarus, The (Chester).
Anonymous plays
Raising of Lazarus, The (Wake-
field). Anonymous plays
Raising the devil. Sachs, H.
Raising the wind. Kenney, J.
"Raising the wind" on the most ap-
proved principles. See Brough,
W. and Brough, R. The en-
chanted isle
Rakinyo. Ajibade, S.
Rākshasa's ring. See Vishakadatta.
The signet ring of Rākshasa
Ralph Roister Doister. Udall, N.
Ramah Droog. Cobb, J.
Rama's later history. See
Bhavabhūti. The later story
of Rama
Ranae. See Aristophanes. The
frogs
Ranchos, Dos; or, The purification.
Williams, T.
Ranke viljer. See Weid, G.
2 x 2 = 5
Rasmus Montanus. Holberg, L.
Raspberry picker, The. Hoch-
wälder, F.
Ratnavali. See Harsha, son of Hira.
Retnavali
Rats, The. Hauptmann, G.
Rat's mass, A. Kennedy, A.
Rats of Norway, The. Winter, J.
Die ratten. See Hauptmann, G.
The rats
Rattle of a simple man. Dyer, C.
Ravens, The. See Becque, H. Les
corbeaux
Rawson's Y. See De Mille, H. and
Barnard, C. The main line

La raza pura; or racial, racial.
Sierra, R.
Reactivated man, The. Zahn, C.
Real inspector hound, The. Stop-
pard, T.
Real thing, The. Stoppard, T.
Really, my dear... Morley, C.
Rebel women. Babe, T.
Rebound. Stewart, D.
Rebound, The. See Picard, L.
Les ricochets
Reckoning, The. See Schnitzler, A.
Light-o'-love

Tou Ngo. See Kuan, H. Snow in
midsummer
Touch it light. Storey, R.
Touch of the poet, A. O'Neill, E.
Touch wood. Smith, D. G.
Tour. McNally, T.
Tous contre tous. See Adamov, A.
All against all
Tovarich. Deval, J.
Tower, The. Porter, H.
Tower, The. Weiss, P.
Tower of Babel, The. Goodman, P.
Town of Titipu, The. See Gilbert,
W. and Sullivan, A. The mikado
Towneley play, The. Anonymous
plays
Toy cart, The. See Shudraka. The
little clay cart
Toy shop, The. Dodsley, R.
Toys in the attic. Hellman, L.
Tracers. DiFusco, J.
Trachiniae, The. Sophocles
Trafford Tanzi. Luckham, C.
La tragédie de Carmen; a full-
length musical in one act. Brook,
P., Carrière, J., and Constant,
M.
Tragedy of a tenant farm woman.
See Green, P. and Green, E.
Fixin's: The tragedy of a
tenant farm woman
Tragedy of Antony and Cleopatra,
The. See Shakespeare, W.
Antony and Cleopatra
Tragedy of Hamlet, Prince of Den-
mark, The. See Shakespeare,
W. Hamlet
Tragedy of Jane Shore, The. Rowe,
N.
Tragedy of King Lear, The. See
Shakespeare, W. King Lear
Tragedy of King Richard II, The.
See Shakespeare, W. King
Richard II
Tragedy of King Richard III, The.
See Shakespeare, W. King
Richard III
Tragedy of love, The. Heiberg, C.
Tragedy of Macbeth, The. See
Shakespeare, W. Macbeth
Tragedy of Mr. No-Balance. Musinga,
V.
Tragedy of Mustapha, the son of
Solyman the magnificent. Orrery,
R.
Tragedy of Nero. Anonymous plays
Tragedy of Othello, The. See

Shakespeare, W. Othello, The
Moor of Venice
Tragedy of Pompey the great, The.
Masefield, J.
Tragedy of the Duchess of Malfi.
See Webster, J. The Duchess of
Malfi
Tragedy of tragedies, The; or,
The life and death of Tom Thumb
the great. Fielding, H.
Tragedy or interlude manifesting the
chief promises of God unto man.
A. See Bale, J. God's promises
Tragedy rehearsed, A. See Sheridan,
R. The critic
Tragic end of mythology, The (its
author wielding a terrible pen).
Gałczyński, K.
Tragi-comedy of Calisto and Melibea.
The. See Rojas, F. Celestina
Tragical history of the life and death
of Doctor Faustus, The. See
Marlowe, C. The tragical history
of Doctor Faustus
Tragical history of Doctor Faustus,
The. Marlowe, C.
Tragicomedia de Calixto y Melibea.
See Rojas, F. Celestina
Tragidie of [Gorboduc; or of] Ferrex
and Porrex, The. See Sackville,
T. and Norton, T. Gorboduc
Trail of the torch, The. See
Hervieu, P. La course du flam-
beau
Train to H... Bellido, J.
Traitor, The. Shirley, J.
Traitor, The. Wilde, P.
Trängningen. See Gorling, L.
The sandwiching
Trans-Canada Highway. Tallman, J.
Transcending. Cregan, D.
Transfiguration. Toller, E.
Transformation. See Toller, E.
Transfiguration
Translation of John Snaith, The.
Cooke, B.
Translations. Friel, B.
Trapolin's vagaries. See Tate, N.
A duke and no duke
Trappolin suppos'd a prince.
Cokain, A. See Tate, N. A
duke and no duke
Traum ein leben, Der. Grillparzer,
F.
Traveling dragon teases a phoenix,
The. Anonymous plays
Travels of Heikiki, The. Kates, C.

Wit and science. See Anonymous
plays. The marriage of wit and
science; Redford, J. The play
of wit and science
Wit and wisdom. See Anonymous
plays. The contract of marriage
between wit and wisdom
Wit works woe. Griboĭedov, A.
Witch of Edmonton, The. Ford, J.,
Dekker, T., and Rowley, W.
Witches' mountain, The. Sánchez
Gardel, J.
Witches' sabbath, The. Benavente
y Martínez, J.
Witching hour, The. Thomas, A.
With intent. Williams, H. and
Williams, M.
With malice aforethought. Stranack,
J.
Within an inch of his life. Herne, J.
Within the law. Veiller, B.
Witness for the prosecution.
Christie, A.
Wits, The. D'Avenant, W.
Witty false one, The. See D'Urfey,
T. Madam Fickle
Wives metamorphos'd, The.
See Jevon, T.; Coffey, C.;
Mottley, J. and Cibber, T. The
devil to pay
Wiz, The. Brown, W.
Woe from wit. See Griboĭedov, A.
Wit works woe
Wolf-hunt, The. Verga, G.
Wolf of Mount Zhong. Wang, J.
Die Wölff. See Brust, A. The
wolves
Wolves, The. Brust, A.
Wolves. Robinson, J.
Woman and man. Kabahar, P.
Woman and the walnut tree, The.
Box, S.
Woman is a weathercock. Field, N.
Woman killed with kindness, A.
Heywood, T.
Woman of Andros, The.
Terentius Afer, P.
Woman of no importance, A.
Wilde, O.
Woman of Paris, The. See Becque,
H. La Parisienne
Woman of Samos. See Menander.
The girl from Samos
Woman taken in adultery, The
(Chester). Anonymous plays
Woman taken in adultery, The.
(N town). Anonymous plays

Woman too many, A. Sønderby, K.
Woman's craze for titles. Dancourt,
F.
Woman's revenge. Payne, J.
Woman's work is never done, A.
See Red Ladder Theatre. Strike
while the iron is hot
Women, The. Boothe, C.
Women, beware women. Middleton,
T.
Women celebrating the Thesmophoria,
The. See Aristophanes.
Thesmophoriazusae
Women have their way, The. See
Alvarez Quintero, S. and Alvarez
Quintero, J. The women's town
Women of Trachis, The. See
Sophocles. The Trachiniae
Women's representative, The. Sun,
Y.
Women's town, The. Alvarez Quin-
tero, S. and Alvarez Quintero,
J.
Won at last. MacKaye, S.
Wonder, The. Centlivre, S.
Wonder, The! A woman keeps a
secret. See Centlivre, S. The
wonder
Wonder-working magician, The.
Calderón de la Barca, P.
Wonderful town. Fields, J. and
Chodorov, J.
Wonderful wizard of Oz, The.
Baum, L. See Brown, W. The
Wiz
Wood demon, The. See Chekhov, A.
Uncle Vanya
Woodstock. Anonymous plays
Word to the wise, A. Kelly, H.
Words upon the window-pane, The.
Yeats, W.
Workhouse ward, The. Gregory, I.
World a mask, The. Boker, G.
World and his wife, The. See
Echegaray y Eizaguirre, J. El
gran Galeoto
World and the child, The. Anony-
mous plays
World is not such a bad place...,
The. Afanasjew, J.
World of boredom, The. See
Pailleron, E. Le monde où l'on
s'ennuie
World tipped over, and laying on
its side, The. Feldhaus-Weber,
M.
World we live in, The. See Čapek,